I0139004

ESSAYS

CRITICAL AND HISTORICAL

ESSAYS

CRITICAL AND HISTORICAL

BY

JOHN HENRY CARDINAL NEWMAN

VOLUME II

with an Introduction, Notes and Textual Appendix
by

NICHOLAS SCHOFIELD

GRACEWING

Individual essays first published 1840-1846
Collected in two volumes 1871
Revised editions 1881, 1885

Published in the Birmingham Oratory Millennium Edition
in 2019
by
Gracewing
2 Southern Avenue
Leominster
Herefordshire HR6 0QF

www.gracewing.co.uk

All rights reserved. No part of this publication may be
reproduced, stored in a retrieval system, or transmitted in
any form, or by any means, electronic, mechanical,
photocopying, recording or otherwise, without the written
permission of the publisher.

Editor's Introduction, Editor's Notes and Textual Appendix
© Nicholas Schofield, 2019

The right of Nicholas Schofield to be identified as the
author of the Editor's Introduction, Editor's Notes and
editorial arrangement of the Textual Appendix to this work
has been asserted in accordance with the Copyright,
Designs and Patents Act 1988.

ISBN 978 0 85244 411 5

CONTENTS

ACKNOWLEDGEMENTS

I would like to thank firstly Dr. James Tolhurst, the General Editor of the Millennium Edition, for inviting me to prepare this volume and for allowing me to use some of his notes for his edition of *An Essay on the Development of Christian Doctrine*. A very special note of gratitude must go to Dr. Andrew Nash, who edited the first volume of *Essays Critical and Historical*, not only for his patient support and invaluable advice, but also for his hard work in checking and completing the footnotes and formatting the text for this second volume. Dr. Guy Nicholls, Cong. Orat., and Dr. Nicholas Richardson kindly translated several Latin passages. All mistakes remain my own.

It is a great joy that this edition is published in the year of the canonisation of its author. May St. John Henry Newman intercede for us all!

Nicholas Schofield

EDITOR'S INTRODUCTION

This second volume of Newman's *Essays Critical and Historical* brings together a selection of his writings between the crucially important years of 1840 and 1846. All but one were originally published in the *British Critic*, which Newman edited between 1838 and 1841. The exception is the final essay, a review of John Keble's *Lyra Innocentium* originally published in the *Dublin Review* and one of Newman's first works as a Catholic.

The essays in the two volumes of *Essays Critical and Historical* are published chronologically, with the exception of the ninth and the tenth essays, namely 'Selina, Countess of Huntingdon' (October 1840), which concludes the first volume, and 'Catholicity of the Anglican Church' (January 1840), which begins the second volume. As with the first volume, Newman freely edited these articles for republication in 1871, including in some cases the deleting of whole paragraphs and quotations. The Textual Appendix in this edition provides a full listing of these changes, both major and minor. In many cases Newman's editorial decisions make little difference to the substance of the articles. But this can be bewildering for the reader, since the articles are presented as if they are accurate reprints of the original and are dated as such. Indeed, in the 'Advertisement' Newman stated that he was not 'making alterations, which would destroy its original character and force' but rather wished 'to accompany it with additions calculated to explain why it has ceased to approve itself to his own judgment.' His aim was to 'reduce what was uncatholic in them' and thus seize control of his earlier corpus of writings, so that they could not be misused 'in spite of his later disavowal' of them.[1] Two of the essays have accompanying Notes, added in 1871, which show Newman in dialogue with his younger, Anglican self.

Some of these essays, which originated as reviews of publications that are now largely forgotten, may seem obscure and their republication little more than an antiquarian enterprise. However, they provide valuable insights into the development of Newman's thought, which, through his long life, made such marked changes while, at the same time, displaying an admirable consistency. Further, as the Editor of Volume I of the *Essays Critical and Historical*, Andrew Nash, has argued, Newman's republication of them in 1871 shows him taking advantage of the new Anglican readership which the publication of his *Apologia Pro Vita Sua* in 1864 had gained him: these essays were effectively Appendices to the *Apologia*, illustrating how his Oxford Movement writings had led him – and could now lead others - to the Catholic Church.

X: The Catholicity of the Anglican Church

The first essay in this volume, and the tenth in the collection of *Essays Critical and Historical*, is perhaps the most celebrated. It follows on from the article on 'Selina, Countess of Huntingdon', at the end of the first volume, which contained a marked criticism of the Church of England. Although cracks were appearing in Newman's belief in the *Via Media*, this essay comprised one of his last great defences of the Anglican Church against charges of

---

[1] *Ess.* I, pp. vii-viii

schism and lack of universality. Originally published in the *British Critic* of January 1840 with the title 'Catholicity of the Church'[2], it was a review of Arthur Philip Perceval's *An Apology for the Doctrine of Apostolical Succession, with an Appendix on English Orders* (1839). The author, a graduate of Oriel College, was Rector of East Horsley (Surrey), a royal chaplain and a prolific author, who was a supporter of the Tractarians. His *Vindication of the Authors of the Tracts for the Times* (1841) would defend Newman in the aftermath of *Tract 90*.

The essay was written in the summer of 1839. That spring Newman had felt 'supreme confidence in my controversial *status'*, and felt 'a great and still growing success, in recommending it to others.'[3] However, he began to doubt his position as he studied two heresies of the early Church. His summer reading that year focussed on the Monophysite controversy of the fifth century and the Council of Chalcedon of 451, with a view to continuing his *Library of the Fathers* project and preparing an edition of Fleury's *Church History*. He noted 'the great power of the Pope (as great as he claims now almost), and the marvellous interference of the civil power, as great almost as in our kings.'[4] There was an uncomfortable realisation that the Monophysites themselves followed a sort of *Via Media* between the extremism of Eutyches and the orthodoxy of Chalcedon:

> My stronghold was Antiquity: now here, in the middle of the fifth century, I found, as it seemed to me, Christendom of the sixteenth and the nineteenth centuries reflected. I saw my face in that mirror, and I was a Monophysite. The

[2] *British Critic*, vol. xxvii (January 1840), pp.40-88
[3] *Apologia Pro Vita Sua*, p.192
[4] *LD* VII, p.105 (Newman to F. Rogers, 12 July 1839)

Editor's Introduction

> Church of the *Via Media* was in the position of the Oriental
> Communion [i.e. moderate Monophysites], Rome was
> where she now is; and the Protestants were the Eutychians.[5]

Another blow was received when his friend Robert
Williams alerted him to Nicholas Wiseman's article on
'Tracts for the Times: Anglican Claims of Apostolical
Succession' in the *Dublin Review* that August. This
focussed on another group of heretics, the fourth century
Donatists. Newman told Frederic Rodgers that it was 'the
first real hit from Romanism which has happened to me',
leaving him with 'a stomach-ache.'[6] In the *Apologia*, he
described his reaction:

> my friend, an anxiously religious man, now, as then, very
> dear to me, a Protestant still, pointed out the palmary words
> of St. Augustine, which were contained in one of the
> extracts made in the *Review*, and which had escaped my
> observation. "Securus judicat orbis terrarum." He repeated
> these words again and again, and, when he was gone, they
> kept ringing in my ears. "Securus judicat orbis terrarum;"
> they were words which went beyond the occasion of the
> Donatists: they applied to that of the Monophysites. They
> gave a cogency to the Article, which had escaped me at
> first. They decided ecclesiastical questions on a simpler rule
> than that of Antiquity; nay, St. Augustine was one of the
> prime oracles of Antiquity; here then Antiquity was
> deciding against itself. What a light was hereby thrown
> upon every controversy in the Church! not that, for the
> moment, the multitude may not falter in their judgment,—
> not that, in the Arian hurricane, Sees more than can be
> numbered did not bend before its fury, and fall off from St.
> Athanasius,—not that the crowd of Oriental Bishops did not
> need to be sustained during the contest by the voice and the

---

[5] *Ap.*, 108
[6] *LD* VII, p.154 (Newman to F. Rogers, 22 September 1839)

eye of St. Leo; but that the deliberate judgment, in which the whole Church at length rests and acquiesces, is an infallible prescription and a final sentence against such portions of it as protest and secede. Who can account for the impressions which are made on him? For a mere sentence, the words of St. Augustine, struck me with a power which I never had felt from any words before. To take a familiar instance, they were like the "Turn again Whittington" of the chime; or, to take a more serious one, they were like the "Tolle, lege,—Tolle, lege," of the child, which converted St. Augustine himself. "Securus judicat orbis terrarum!" By those great words of the ancient Father, interpreting and summing up the long and varied course of ecclesiastical history, the theory of the *Via Media* was absolutely pulverized.[7]

The entire quotation from St Augustine was: *Quapropter securus judicat orbis terrarum, bonos non esse qui se dividunt ab orbe terrarum quacumque parte orbis terrarum,* 'the entire [Catholic] world judges with security that they are not good, who separate themselves from the entire world in whatever part of the world.'[8] For Newman, the *orbis terrarum* increasingly became identified with the Roman Catholic Church and the Roman Catholic Church alone, present as it was all around the world and united in its doctrine and discipline. It was equally clear to Newman that the Church of England lacked this Catholicity and was separate from the worldwide church.

But Newman was not yet ready to give up on his *Via Media* and his article on the 'Catholicity of the Church' was designed 'to stop up the leak in our boat.'[9] It continued the polemic found in Keble's 1836 Visitation Sermon at

---

[7] *Ap.,* 116-117
[8] St Augustine, *Contra epistulam Parmenieni,* lib 3, cap 4, para 24
[9] *LD* VII, p.202 (Newman to J. W. Bowden, 5 January 1840)

Editor's Introduction

Winchester (*Primitive Tradition recognized in Holy Scripture*), Manning's *Rule of Faith* and Newman's own *Lectures on the Prophetical Office*.

In the essay Newman declared that 'the question of English Orders is now settled once for all'; that even some Catholic writers conceded the Apostolical Succession in the Church of England 'for argument's sake.' The problem was that though the Orders may be 'good in themselves,...still they may be given and continued *in schism*.'[10] Newman dealt with an important objection:

> on the one hand, that unity is the tenure of divine favour; that communion with our brethren is the means of communion with our Lord and Saviour; that the Church is not only Apostolic, but Catholic; that schism cuts off the fountains of grace; and that estrangement from the Christian world is schism; and, on the other, that in matter of fact our Church is emphatically in a state of estrangement, having intercourse with no other Christian body in any part of the world, excepting her own dependencies and offshoots.[11]

Newman considered both the Catholic and Anglican positions and acknowledged strong points on either side – Catholicity on the one hand and Antiquity or Apostolicity on the other. 'Our strong point,' he wrote, 'is the argument from the past', for 'our teaching is the true, because it is the primitive' and 'Rome has added to the Creed', while the Romanists could claim a strong 'argument from the present' and point out that the Anglicans are 'estranged from the great body of Christians over the world.'[12] The Roman argument had the advantage of being 'far more level to the

---

[10] *Ess.* II, pp.2-3
[11] *Ibid.*, p.4
[12] *Ibid.*, p.6

apprehension of men in general than that which we allege against him.' It is obvious that 'the English Church is separated from the rest of Christendom; it is not evident, except to a very few, that the faith of Rome is an addition to the primitive.'[13]

Newman attacked the theory of development which he would expound six years later. 'Their theory seems to be that the whole faith was present in the minds of the Apostles', maintaining (he supposed) that 'the Apostles were implicit Tridentines': 'Does the Romanist mean, for instance, to tell us that St Paul the Apostle, when he was in perils of robbers or peril by the sea, offered up his addresses to St. Mary, and vowed some memorial to her, if she would be pleased *"deprecari pro illo filium Dei"*?'[14] While admitting that some development took place – the Athanasian Creed, for example, stated and clarified the teaching handed down by the apostles – Newman writes sharply:

> Children grow to men, as the Romanist reminds us; but, in like manner, men grow old and wax feeble, and their limbs drag after them, and their voice falters; shall the decrepitude of the nineteenth century more interfere with the inward life and perfection of the Church than the inexperience and feebleness of the Antenicene era?[15]

Moving on from the subject of Antiquity and assuming that 'our creed is sounder than the Roman', Newman asked whether the Church of England could be considered part of the 'one' Church? The ultra-Protestant theory was simpler, 'if Rome is apostate, she no longer claims on us as a

---

[13] *Ibid.*, p.11
[14] *Ibid.*, pp.12-13
[15] *Ibid.*, pp.44-45

Church', but 'while she is allowed to be a Church, she has claims'. He continued:

> One point is acknowledged, one must be conceded, and one will be maintained, by all Anglo-Catholics;—that the Church is One, is the point of *doctrine*; that we are estranged from the body of the Church, is the point of *fact*; and that we still have the means of grace among us, is our point of *controversy*. These points being set down, there are various ways of reconciling them, such as the following:— 1. That intercommunion is not necessary to unity. 2. That, though it be, the absence of unity does not at once involve a state of schism. 3. That, though it do, yet that the grace of the ordinances is not necessarily suspended in a state of schism. Different minds will resign themselves to one or other of these solutions, or modify them by one another, according to their particular feelings and principles.[16]

The Anglican ecclesiological position is compared to 'a number of colonies sent out from a mother country, or as the tribes or nations which spring from a common parent.' The separate portions need not be united 'except by the tie of descent from one original.'[17] Newman later summarised this argument in the *Apologia*:

> For myself, I held with the Anglican divines, that, in the Primitive Church, there was a very real mutual independence between its separate parts, though, from a dictate of charity, there was in fact a close union between them. I considered that each See and Diocese might be compared to a crystal, and that each was similar to the rest, and that the sum total of them all was only a collection of crystals. The unity of the Church lay, not in its being a polity, but in its being a family, a race, coming down by

---

[16] *Ibid.*, p.17
[17] *Ibid.*, p.18

> apostolical descent from its first founders and bishops. And
> I considered this truth brought out, beyond the possibility of
> dispute, in the Epistles of St Ignatius, in which the Bishop
> is represented as the one supreme authority in the Church,
> that is, in his own place, with no one above him, except as,
> for the sake of ecclesiastical order and expedience,
> arrangements had been made by which one was put over or
> under another.[18]

Thus, 'each diocese is a perfect independent Church, sufficient for itself; and the communion of Christians one with another, and the unity of them all together, lie, not in a mutual understanding, intercourse, and combination, not in what they do in common, but in what they are and what they have in common, in their possession of the Succession, their Episcopal form, their Apostolic faith, and the use of the Sacraments.'[19]

Although this Anglican argument could be supported by extracts from the writings of St Ignatius and St Cyprian, St Augustine held that the principle of unity lay not in the individual bishop but the body of the Church, presided over by the pope. Catholicity was all important. Newman grappled with this problem: 'We are far from intending to disparage the duty of visible active communion; we can understand the great doctors of the Ancient Church raising it ever so high; but Christians now are in a different position from theirs.' The question was this: did the English Church's 'state of estrangement from the great Christian body' constitute 'formal schism, and an utter severance of us from the fountains of divine grace'?[20]

---

[18] *Ap*, 204-205
[19] *Ess.* II, p.20
[20] *Ibid.*, pp.33-34

Newman posed a number of possible answers. He asked how essential a mark of the Church is her oneness; it was indeed considered a sign of the Church's divine origin 'while it exists' but did the divisions of history still make it essential? He tackled the quote from St Augustine that had so disturbed him, *securus judicat orbis terrarum*. It is fascinating to see, in the 1871 edition, a dialogue between the Anglican and Catholic Newman:

> *[Anglican Newman:]* It is hard upon St. Augustine to suppose that his striking and beautiful principle against the Donatists, "*securus judicat orbis terrarum*," was intended as a theological verity equally sacred as an article in the Creed.

> *[Catholic Newman in footnote:]* It is a great practical principle, not a doctrine; and the question is, what array of arguments in a particular case is sufficient to overcome it? For instance, is the argument for Anglicanism of such an overpowering character as to be able, by a *consensus* of opinion, in itself to overcome it?[21]

Submission to the *orbis terrarum* was a presumption rather than a law.

Summing up, Newman wrote:

> As soon as it is granted that active intercourse is not *absolutely necessary* as a note of the Church, an opening is made for adducing *other* circumstances which may serve to be an evidence of that, which such intercourse would evidence, if it existed. We conceive then that, in spite of our being separated from Greece and Rome, shut up in ourselves and our dependencies, and looked coldly on or forgotten by the rest of Christendom, there is sufficient ground for still believing that

---

[21] *Ibid.,* p.40

the English Church is at this time the Catholic Church in England.[22]

He went on to list several grounds. Firstly, 'either *we* are the Catholic Church in England, or there is *no* Catholic Church here'; 'no other bishops claim our sees.'[23] Newman was, of course, writing prior to the restoration of the Catholic Hierarchy in England and Wales (1850) and just before the numbers of Apostolic Vicariates was increased from four to eight (1840). 'If it be a fact that we are estranged from the Continent, it is also a fact that we have possession of the thrones of Cuthbert, Becket, and Wykeham. Is it probable that the noble line of Canterbury should be extinct? Has the blood of martyrs dried up, and the voice of the confessors failed? Have our cathedrals no living spirit in them, and is our hierarchy a form only, and not a power?' Alluding to Wiseman's article, he argued: 'They delight to compare us to the Donatists, but these surely were in a very different position. The Donatists had not possession; their only tenure of existence was hatred and opposition to all the rest of Christendom.'[24]

There was, indeed, an argument from reality. If intercommunion is such an essential mark of the Church, then there is a problem since the Roman Catholics can claim little or no presence not only in England but in Russia and Greece, 'except on that pen-and-paper plan which gives them an indefinite abundance of bishops *in partibus infidelium.*'[25] Moreover, if it was sometimes claimed that the Church of England did not call herself Catholic, St Robert Bellarmine himself stated that 'there is *no* heresy which

[22] *Ibid.,* p.47
[23] *Ibid.,* p.47
[24] *Ibid.,* pp.48-49
[25] *Ibid.,* p.50

does not take a name from some man as its author, and leave the name of Christian to them from whom it departs.'[26] This would apply to Lutherans or Calvinists but not Anglicans.

For Newman, the Church of England clearly exhibited the notes of life:

> Revolutions have come upon it sharply and suddenly, to and fro, hot and cold, as if to try what it was made of. It has been a sort of battle-field on which opposite principles have been tried. No opinion, however extreme any way, but may be found, as the Romanists are not slow to reproach us, among its bishops and divines. Yet what has been its career upon the whole? ... As far as its formularies are concerned, it may be said all along to have grown towards a more perfect Catholicism than that with which it started at the time of its estrangement; every act, every crisis, which marks its course, has been upward.[27]

Newman ended with a call to conversion. Looking at several historical cases – including Meletius of Antioch, Lucifer of Cagliari and those who followed the various anti-popes – to show that 'schism is not necessarily a forfeiture of grace and hope',[28] he writes that 'much as Roman Catholics may denounce us at present as schismatical, they could not resist us, if the Anglican communion had but that one Note of the Church upon it, to which all these instances point, - sanctity':

> Unless our system really has a power in it, making us neglectful of wealth, neglectful of station, neglectful of ease, munificent, austere, reverent, childlike, unless it is able to bring our passions into order, to make us pure, to

---

[26] *Ibid.,* pp.51-52
[27] *Ibid.,* p.55
[28] *Ibid.,* p.69

make us meek, to rule our intellect, to give government of speech, to inspire firmness, to destroy self, we do not deserve to be acknowledged as a Church, and we submit to be ill-treated.[29]

The same argument applied to those on the other side of the Tiber:

When we go into foreign countries, we see superstitions in the Roman Church which shock us; when we read history, we find its spirit of intrigue so rife, so widely spread, that "Jesuitism" has become a by-word; when we look round us at home, we see it associated everywhere with the low democracy, pandering to the spirit of rebellion, the lust of change, the unthankfulness of the irreligious, and the enviousness of the needy...Who can but feel shame when the religion of Ximenes, Borromeo, and Pascal is so overlaid?...We Englishmen like manliness, openness, consistency, truth. Rome will never gain on us till she learns these virtues, and uses them.[30]

In exposing some of the perceived inconsistencies of Roman Catholicism and claiming that the Anglican Communion was not completely cut off from the fountains of grace, Newman convinced himself to stay put for a little longer; he later confessed to Manning, 'for two years it quieted me.'[31] But Newman was on his Anglican deathbed. In later life he admitted that in many of his writings of the time, 'the argument in behalf of Rome is stated with considerable perspicuity and force,' almost to the degree of imprudence.[32]

---

[29] *Ibid.*, p.70

[30] *Ibid.*, pp.71-72

[31] Newman to Manning, 25 October 1843, quoted in Peter C. Erb (ed), *The Correspondence of Henry Edward Manning and William Ewart Gladstone* (2013), p.396

[32] *Ap.*, p.205

Editor's Introduction

Note on Essay X

Reflecting on his arguments three decades later, Newman freely admitted in the 'Note to Essay X' that if they 'did not retain me in the Anglican Church, I do not see what could keep me in it.'

> The truth is, I believe, I was always asking myself what would the Fathers have done, what would those whose works were around my room, whose names were ever meeting my eyes, whose authority was ever influencing my judgment, what would these men have said, how would they have acted in my position? I had made a good case on paper, but what judgment would be passed on it by Athanasius, Basil, Gregory, Hilary, and Ambrose? The more I considered the matter, the more I thought that these Fathers, if they examined the antagonist pleas, would give it against me.[33]

Newman was aware that 'those more than friendly critics of mine' attributed his conversion merely to 'a desire for a firmer ground of religious certitude, and a clearer view of revealed truth, than is furnished in the Church of England.'

In the 'Note on Essay X', Newman briefly examined three topics: Anglican Orders, the unity of ecclesiastical jurisdiction and 'the apparent exceptions to that unity in the history of the early Church.'[34]

As an Anglican, Newman considered the question of Orders 'settled once for all' and accepted Perceval's arguments for apostolic succession. The Catholic Newman viewed Anglican Orders with greater suspicion, though he was cautious in expressing his opinion since the Church was yet to speak authoritatively; *Apostolicae curae* was still a

---

[33] *Ess.* II, p74
[34] *Ibid.,* p.76

quarter of a century in the future.[35] In 1868 Newman had expressed his views in a correspondence with the Jesuit Fr Henry Coleridge, editor of *The Month*. In a letter of 6 February he wrote:

> I cannot *conceive* that they are valid – but I could not *swear* they are not – I should be most uncommonly surprised if they were – It would require the Pope *ex cathedra* to convince me.... It is difficult to prove a negative – but it is not for us to prove the Anglican orders are not valid, but for them to prove that they are.[36]

Coleridge had been preparing an article on the subject and wanted clarification from Newman, especially to counter rumours that he held Anglican orders to be valid. Newman's longer letter of 5 August, which was published in *The Month* that September, is included (with minor changes) at the end of his 'Note on Essay X'.[37] However, he had left his argument unfinished since he felt 'that I was distressing, without convincing, men whom I love and respect, by impugning an article of their belief, which to them is sacred, in proportion as it is vital.' Time had now moved on and in making these remarks 'I am opposing not them but my former self'.[38] This allowed him to speak freely, without fear of causing offence, and to set the record straight once and for all: 'as to Anglican Orders, I certainly think them doubtful and untrustworthy.'[39]

Newman saw the Anglican consecrations of 1559 as profoundly untrustworthy, for they were 'done by men of

---

[35] This Bull of Leo XIII, dated 13 September 1896, declared that Anglican Orders were 'null and void'.

[36] *LD* XXIV, p.29 (Newman to Coleridge, 6 February 1868)

[37] *Ess.* II, pp.109-111

[38] *Ibid.*, pp.76-77

[39] *Ibid.*, p.76

certain positive opinions and intentions, and none of those opinions and views, from first to last, of a Catholic complexion, but on the contrary erroneous and heretical.'[40] Moreover, 'an Apostolical ministry necessarily involves an Apostolical teaching' and yet 'the Anglican Bishops for three centuries have lived and died in heresy'.[41]

It was undeniable that in many cases ordination

> is the one great day of their lives, which cannot come twice, the day on which, in their fresh youth, they freely dedicated themselves and all their powers to the service of their Redeemer,—solemn and joyful at the time, and ever after fragrant in their memories:—it is so; but devotion cannot reverse the past, nor can good faith stand in the stead of what is true.

No 'earnestness of mind and purity of purpose could ever be a substitute for the formal conditions of a sacrament.'[42]

Newman next dealt with the question of ignorant, 'bad ecclesiastics' proposed by the likes of Chillingworth and Macauley: 'if Anglican Orders are untrustworthy because of the chance mistakes in three hundred years, much more so are Catholic, which have run a whole eighteen hundred.' Newman affirmed that the Church is not merely human; 'if a Succession *be* apostolical, then indeed it is protected from errors; but it has to be proved apostolical before such protection can be claimed for it.'[43] There is a fundamental difference in approach: 'Catholics believe their Orders are valid, because they are members of the true Church; and Anglicans believe they belong to the true Church, because their Orders are valid…. Their Succession is indispensable

---

[40] *Ibid.*, p.78
[41] *Ibid.*, pp.78, 81
[42] *Ibid.*, p.84
[43] *Ibid.*, p.85

to their position, as being the point from which they start,' while for Catholics 'our starting-point is not the fact of a faithful transmission of Orders, but the standing fact of the Church, the Visible and One Church, the reproduction and succession of herself age after age. It is the Church herself that vouches for our Orders, while she authenticates herself to be the Church not by our Orders, but by her Notes.'[44]

If 'the Orders depend on the Church, not the Church on the Orders,' then the assumption is that 'there is in fact a Church, that is, a visible body corporate, gifted with supernatural privileges, present and future.' Newman no longer believed, as he proposed in the Essay, that the Church 'is every separate bishopric, every diocesan unit, of which that whole is composed,... each equal to each, each independent of each, each invested with full spiritual powers, *in solidum*, as St Cyprian speaks, none subject to any,... but all free from all except as regards the duty of mutual love, and only called one Church, when taken in the aggregate or in its catholicity.'[45] This now seemed to him a desperate argument and directly contradicted the New Testament, which show that 'the Church of Christ was a *body, visible; one; Catholic,* and *organised*'[46] and 'that all Christians were in that first age bound together in one body, with an actual intercommunion and mutual relations between them,... and that this organized association was "the body of Christ," and that in it, considered as One, dwelt the "One Spirit."'[47] Newman asks himself how he could have maintained the inherently impracticable Anglican theory and confesses that 'though swayed by great names, I

---

[44] *Ibid.*, pp.87-88
[45] *Ibid.*, pp.90-91
[46] *Ibid.*, p.92
[47] *Ibid.*, p.96

never was without misgivings about the difficulties which it involved.'

Newman finally dealt with the nature of the schism 'between England and the Catholic world', which, despite the arguments of his Anglican self, were very different from the schisms of the early Church:

> Year after year, the conscience of our great country more determinately confronts and defies the principles and the practices of the Roman Curia. At the era of Elizabeth, this opposition was founded on passion or policy; in Victoria's time it is an intellectual and moral antipathy. It is as different now from what it was then, as the severe but transient influenza, which is the first step of a consumption, differs from the hectic fever and organic ruin, in which it ends. All things are possible to God; I am not saying that this antagonism between Rome and England must last for ever, because it is so energetic now; but I am stating what it is at this time; and I protest that to compare it to the coolness between Meletius and Athanasius, or the jealousies between Basil and Damasus, or the parties and partizanship which the untoward act of Lucifer created at Antioch, is to do what Catholics are on certain other questions charged with doing,—to pervert history in the interest of controversy.[48]

XI: The Protestant Idea of the Antichrist
The second essay in this volume was originally published as a review of James Henthorn Todd's *Discourses on the Prophecies relating to Antichrist* in the *British Critic* of October 1840.[49] Todd was a Fellow of Trinity College,

---

[48] *Ibid.*, pp.103-104
[49] *British Critic*, vol. xxviii (October 1840), pp.391-440. Newman's review of the Memoir of the Countess of Huntingdon, reprinted in *Essays* I., appeared in the same edition.

Editor's Introduction

Dublin, and the *Discourses* originated as the Donnellan Lectures for 1838 and dealt with the prophet Daniel and St Paul's second letter to the Thessalonians. A second projected volume covering the Book of Revelation was never published.

Todd was a High Churchman who was in contact with Newman and showed much sympathy towards the Tractarians. Shortly before taking over as editor in 1838, Newman invited him to contribute to the *British Critic*:

> Now as far as I know, I really do not think you would disapprove of anything we are likely to say. The point on which, judging at a distance, disapproval on your part was most likely was the Revolution question; but from what I have read or heard you say, I think you are not bigoted to King William. We are not strongly opposed to the Romanists as an *existing system* in these countries, as you can be; though we do not like abusing them. I am not aware that you are especially attached to Luther either – as we are not. We do not praise Cranmer or Jewell: but we keep silent; and I think ever should. We have very high views of the abstract power and position of the Church as a ruling body – but then, considering it to be in captivity, we hold it a Christian duty to obey our Masters, as the Jews obeyed Nebuchadnezzar.[50]

However, Todd does not appear to have made any contributions to the journal. In the meantime, his lectures caused a stir in Ireland. Newman wrote to Bowden in March 1839: 'what a row poor Todd of Dublin has raised.'[51] This is no surprise, for he was offering a fresh perspective on the vexed issue of the Antichrist prophecies.

---

[50] *LD* VI, pp.216-17 (Newman to Todd, 19 March 1838)
[51] *LD* VII, p.4 (Newman to Bowden, 19 March 1839)

Editor's Introduction

The Protestant Reformers of the sixteenth century had identified papal Rome with the Antichrist, and this interpretation was still common in Newman's time. If the Puritan radicals of the mid-seventeenth century had put many off these claims, Thomas Newton (1704-82), Bishop of Bristol and Dean of St Paul's, had done much to return them to respectability in the following century. Moreover, the advent of millenary sects such as the Plymouth Brethren (1830), the Church of Jesus Christ of the Latter Day Saints (1830), the Adventists (1831) and the Catholic Apostolic Church (1832) kept the doctrine of the Second Coming and the End Times in people's minds.

In the autumn of 1816, when Newman 'fell under the influences of a definite Creed', he had 'read Newton on the Prophecies, and in consequence became most firmly convinced that the Pope was the Antichrist predicted by Daniel, St Paul and St John.'[52] He preached on the subject at Christmas 1824-25. He later admitted:

> My imagination was stained by the effects of this doctrine
> up to the year 1843; it had been obliterated from my reason
> and judgment at an earlier date; but the thought remained
> upon me as a sort of false conscience. Hence came that
> conflict of mind, which so many have felt besides myself; -
> leading some men to make a compromise between two
> ideas, so inconsistent with each other, - driving others to
> beat out the one idea or the other from their minds, - and
> ending in my own case, after many years of intellectual
> unrest, in the gradual decay and extinction of one of them, -
> I do not say in its violent death, for why should I not have
> murdered it sooner, if I murdered it at all?[53]

His views on the matter mellowed as the years went by:

---

[52] *Ap.*, p.136
[53] *Ibid.*, p.137

Editor's Introduction

> From the time that I knew Froude[54] I got less and less bitter on the subject. I spoke (successively, but I cannot tell in what order or at what dates) of the Roman Church as being bound up with "the *cause* of Antichrist," as being *one* of the "*many* antichrists" foretold by St. John, as being influenced by "the *spirit* of Antichrist," and as having something "very Antichristian" or "unchristian" about her.[55]

Newman's mature view on the subject is apparent not only in the review of Todd's *Discourses* but in the four sermons he delivered at Advent 1835 which were published as *Tract 83* and later included in *Discussions and Arguments on Various Subjects* (1872). Here he argued that the Antichrist prophecies had not yet been revealed, although in *Prophetical Office* (1837) he was not afraid of identifying Antichristian elements in the Roman Church.

Todd wrote to Newman on 15 April 1839: 'I am afraid you will think my attack on all the common systems of interpretations very daring – and I fear you will not agree with me in my defence of literal interpretations of Kings, days, years and Kingdoms.'[56] When his *Discourses* at last appeared, Newman declared they were 'both bold and seasonable.'[57]

Newman thought highly of Todd's approach. Too often when commentators had tried to link a historical personage or event with a Biblical prophecy, 'they start with a prejudice, they argue as advocates, and they end in a foregone conclusion. Faults such as these cannot be imputed

---

[54] Hurrell Froude (1803-36), Fellow of Oriel College and Newman's close friend. Newman edited his posthumous *Remains* which shocked his contemporaries with Froude's criticism of the Protestant Reformers and sympathy for the pre-Reformation Catholic Church.
[55] *Ap.*, p.153
[56] *LD* VII, p.62 (Todd to Newman, 15 April 1839)
[57] *LD* VII, p.202 (Newman to J. W. Bowden, 5 January 1840)

to Dr Todd.'[58] Although his text had its weaknesses, Newman declared that 'in matters of doctrine we entirely agree with Dr Todd.'[59] Indeed when Newman originally invited Keble to write the review, he told him: 'Whoever takes it, I think ought to treat Todd not only kindly but on the whole cordially and almost as a partisan'. Others were bound to attack him, and if the *British Critic* joined them 'he will be left in the lurch.'[60]

Todd, we are told, had made perhaps 'the first attempt for a long course of years in this part of Christendom to fix a dispassionate attention and a scientific interpretation upon the momentous "Prophecies".'[61] However, he had been influenced by the recent writings of Samuel Maitland, the first English scholar to popularise the 'futurist' school that had been developed by the Jesuit Fr Francisca Ribera in the 1590s. As Newman summarises, this school claimed that 'the prophecies concerning Antichrist are as yet unfulfilled, and that the predicted enemy of the Church is yet to come.'[62]

Many eminent writers had identified Rome as the Antichrist and, on a superficial level, it was an attractive claim for those wearied by religious polemic: 'when the simple principle is once mastered that the Pope is Antichrist, nothing more is necessary in the controversy. It answers to the dogma of the Pope's infallibility in the Roman system... A Church can have no rights if it ceases to be a Church.'[63] For Newman, however, this ultra-Protestant argument was highly dangerous – not only because it

---

[58] *Ess.* II, p.112
[59] *Ibid.,* p.113
[60] *LD* VII, p.323 (Newman to Keble, 8 May 1840)
[61] *Ess.* II, p.112
[62] *Ibid.,* p.113
[63] *Ibid.,* p.132

implied that 'there is nothing to look out for or to fear' but because

> it is impossible to hold certain branches of the Church to be the communion of Antichrist, as it has long been the fashion with Protestants to maintain, without involving our own branch in the charge... It is very well for Sandemanian, Ranter, or Quaker to call Rome the seat of Antichrist. We cannot afford to do so; *nostra res agitur*: we come next.[64]

Indeed, the English Church herself had been accused of apostasy by Puritan authors and thus was 'a partner in a cross which Athanasius and Augustine have borne in their day.'[65]

Newman then traced the origins of the classical Protestant argument to the Albigenses, Waldenses and the spiritual Franciscans and highlighted some of the mistakes made by previous commentators: 'it may readily be granted that some of these writers are not possessed of that seriousness and earnestness of mind which entitles them to our respect.'[66]

There follows an excursus on the personal qualities of Bishop Newton to make the point that 'a man must be almost an Angel, to stand forth to teach us that the great multitude of Christian bishops are children of the devil.'[67] Here we see Newman at his sharpest: the bishop may have been kind and amiable but he 'cast a regretful look back upon his dinner while he was at supper, and anticipated his morning chocolate in his evening muffins.' Newman would even prefer to 'be found with Whitfield and Wesley, than

---

[64] *Ibid.,* p.114-15
[65] *Ibid.,* p.158
[66] *Ibid.,* pp.128-29
[67] *Ibid.,* p.134

Editor's Introduction

with ecclesiastics whose life is literary ease at the best, whose highest flights attain but to Downing Street or the levee.'[68] He contrasts Newton with St Charles Borromeo and St Francis de Sales – how could such holy pastors belong to the seat of Satan?

Newman admitted in the *Apologia* that the ultra-Protestant argument haunted him until 1843. As Vincent Blehl has pointed out, 'it is not as though he still imagined the Pope as Antichrist.' Rather, his imagination was 'stained' by 'images of the Church of Rome as corrupt, wily, idolatrous, worshipping the Virgin and the saints, adding to revelation, e.g. its doctrine of purgatory, in short images that repelled him.'[69] In his review of Todd, he wrote that Rome is not 'bodily God's enemy, but that it has in it Satanical principles.'[70]

Newman turned the argument on its head. If the Church must suffer like its Divine Master and if Christ himself was called 'Beelzebub' by his enemies, so the Church can glory in being called 'Antichrist'; the ultra-Protestant attacks acted in her favour. Newman refers to Baxter's gibe that 'if the Pope was not Antichrist, he had bad luck to be so like him.' 'Not "bad luck",' Newman continued, 'but sheer necessity. Since Antichrist simulates Christ, and bishops are images of Christ, Antichrist is like a bishop, and a bishop is like Antichrist. And what is the Pope but a bishop?'[71] In the final section of the essay, Newman provided what Sheridan Gilley has called 'a curiously literal inversion of Protestant prophecy' in which he saw 'in the medieval Church, not a realization of Antichrist, but an "imperial Church",

---

[68] *Ibid.,* pp.138-40
[69] Vincent Ferrer Blehl, *Pilgrim Journey* (Continuum, 2001), p.261
[70] *Ess.* II, p.150
[71] *Ibid.,* p.173

anticipated in the glorious prophecies concerning Israel of old.'[72]

Newman was clear that the Antichrist was 'a person, yet future'.[73] However, he was careful to read the 'signs of the times' and saw the mark of the Antichrist in the proponents of the French Revolution and their successors in 1830. Indeed, in his *Letter to Faussett* (1838), Newman playfully suggests that if the prophecies of Revelation were interpreted figuratively, so that Babylon is Rome, then 'we may with equal success make it London', which makes 'a *figurative* Rome, as being an Imperial City.'[74]

XII: Milman's View of Christianity

The twelfth essay in *Essays Critical and Historical* was originally published in the *British Critic* of January 1841 as a review of Henry Hart Milman's three volume *History of Christianity, from the Birth of Christ to the Abolition of Paganism in the Roman Empire*.[75] Milman (1791-1868), a son of George III's physician, was Keble's immediate predecessor as Professor of Poetry at Oxford (1821-31). In 1827 he delivered the prestigious Bampton Lectures on 'The character and conduct of the Apostles considered as an evidence of Christianity'. He eventually became Dean of St Paul's and, in addition to the book reviewed here, produced a *History of the Jews* (1829) and a *History of Latin Christianity* (1855). He also wrote the popular Palm Sunday hymn, 'Ride On, Ride On in Majesty!' Milman became a notable critic of Newman, publishing a scathing attack on

---

[72] Sheridan Gilley, *Newman and His Age* (Darton, Longman and Todd, 1990), p.192
[73] *LD* VII, p.34 (Newman to Manning, 28 February 1837)
[74] *VM* II, p.222
[75] *British Critic*, vol. xxix (January 1841), pp.71-114

the *Essay on the Development of Christian Doctrine* in the *Quarterly Review* in 1846.[76]

Newman respected Milman's scholarly achievements - 'of very considerable ability, and bears upon it tokens of much thought and varied research'[77] - but was highly critical of his reductive rationalism, which minimized the supernatural and the miraculous. 'A great battle is coming on,' he wrote to Keble in November 1840, 'of which Milman's new book is a sort of earnest. The whole of our day may be a battle with this spirit.'[78] Earlier that year, he had included Milman's writings in his concerns over 'a great attack upon the Bible':

> those wretched [Owenite] Socialists on the one hand – then Carlile [sic] on the other, a man of first rate ability, I suppose, and quite fascinating as a writer – His book on the Fr Rev is most taking (to me) – I had hope he might have come round right, for it was easy to see he was not a believer, but they say that he has settled the wrong way. *His* view is that Xty has good *in* it, or is good *as far as it goes* – which when applied to Scrip is of course a picking and choosing of its contents. Then again you have Arnold's school, such as it is (I do hope he will be frightened back) giving up the inspiration of the OT or of all Scrip (I do not say Arnold himself does). Then you have Milman clenching his History of the Jews by a history of Xty which they say is worse; and just in the same line. Then you have all your political Economists, who *cannot* accept (it is impossible) Scripture rules about almsgiving, renunciation of wealth, self-denial, etc, etc. And then your Geologists, giving up

---

[76] Henry Hart Milman, *Savonarola, Erasmus and Other Essays* (John Murray, 1870)
[77] *Ess.* II, p.186
[78] *LD* VII, p.434 (Newman to Keble, 6 November 1840)

part of the OT. All these and many more spirits seen uniting
and forming into something shocking.'

Newman even suspected that only the Roman Church had
the strength 'to withstand the league of evil.'[79]

Despite the strength of his disagreement, Newman
seemed reluctant in his criticism of Milman. He told Pusey,
'I do not at all enter into the notion that we are a sort of Jack
the Giant Killer or Knight Errants to attack all nuisances
and offences. It does not fall into our way to attack
M[ilman] – leave it to Faussett. We should be wasting our
strength.'[80] As editor of the *British Critic*, he had originally
asked Henry Wilberforce to consider writing the review,
adding: 'you must treat him very gently and courteously,
and only show up his errors.'[81] Newman admitted that
Milman was certainly 'not a Gibbon, but a clergyman' and
his work could not 'fail to be useful to those who are in
search of facts, and have better principles than his own to
read them by.'[82]

Indeed, several years later, in the aftermath of the
controversy caused by *Tract 90*, Pusey asked Bishop Bagot
why attention had been focussed on Newman's piece when
other works 'against which the gravest charges are brought'
were left untouched. He mentioned Milman as an example:
his 'book explains away many of the miracles of our Lord
in a shocking way, is read, but passes wholly unnoticed'.[83]

In reviewing Milman's work, Newman stressed that
Christian history had an external and an internal aspect; in a

[79] *LD* VII, pp.244-45 (Newman to Mrs Mozley, 25 February 1840)
[80] *LD* VII, p.283 (Newman to Pusey, 29 March 1840). Godfrey Faussett, Lady Margaret Professor of Divinity at Oxford, may have been no friend of the Tractarians but he had also attacked Milman's *History of the Jews*.
[81] *LD* VII, p.363, (Newman to Wilberforce, 19 July 1840)
[82] *Ess.* II, p.187
[83] *LD* VIII, p.126, (Pusey to Bagot, 26 March 1841)

Editor's Introduction

sense, it was sacramental – 'an outward visible sign of an inward spiritual grace' - and 'to attempt to touch the human element without handling also the divine, we may fairly seem unreal, extravagant, and sophistical.' Milman's weakness is that his account of Christianity is 'such as it would appear to a man of the world.'[84]

To illustrate his critique, Newman reflected briefly on the subject of causality.

> If then He is still actively present with His own work, present with nations and with individuals, He must be acting by means of its ordinary system, or by quickening, or as it were, stimulating its powers, or by superseding or interrupting it; in other words, by means of what is called nature, or by miracle; and whereas strictly miraculous interference must be, from the nature of the case, rare, it stands to reason that, unless He has simply retired, and has left the world ordinarily to itself,—content with having originally imposed on it certain general laws, which will for the most part work out the ends which He contemplates,— He is acting through, with, and beneath those physical, social, and moral laws, of which our experience informs us. Now it has ever been a firm article of Christian faith, that His Providence is in fact not general merely, but is, on the contrary, thus particular and personal; and that, as there is a particular Providence, so of necessity that Providence is secretly concurring and co-operating with that system which meets the eye, and which is commonly recognized among men as existing. It is not too much to say that this is the one great rule on which the Divine Dispensations with mankind have been and are conducted, that the visible world is the instrument, yet the veil, of the world invisible,—the veil, yet still partially the symbol and index: so that all that exists or happens visibly, conceals and yet

[84] *Ess.* II, p.188

suggests, and above all subserves, a system of persons, facts, and events beyond itself.[85]

Jan Hendrik Walgrave, John Holloway and Laurence Richardson have all pointed out that 'it is important to bear in mind the central role that Newman gives to divine providence in his philosophy.'[86] It is little surprise, then, that Milman was criticised for ignoring this internal, supernatural dynamic. If Newman thought 'the great characteristic of Revelation is addition, substitution', using the 'existing system' and building upon nature,[87] then Milman had 'been viewing the history of the Church on the side of the world'.

Milman's design, it seemed, was 'of merely stating the *facts* of Christianity, without notice, good or bad, of the *principles* which are their life.'[88] Newman was bold enough to state that, regardless of the author's intention, 'this external contemplation of Christianity necessarily leads a man to write as a Socinian or Unitarian *would* write,' giving 'scandal to his brethren and cause of triumph to the enemy.'[89] The Socinians, let it be remembered, rejected the orthodox understanding of the Trinity, the Divinity of Christ and the Atonement. If Milman focussed on what is externally seen, then he would fall into the same trap of acknowledging Christ's humanity but not his Divinity and to 'make the message of the Gospel to relate mainly to moral improvement, not to forgiveness of sins... Hence, the general *effect* of Mr. Milman's work, we cannot deny,

---

[85] *Ibid.*, p.192
[86] Laurence Richardson, *Newman's Approach to Knowledge* (Gracewing 2007), p.27
[87] *Ess.* II, p.194
[88] *Ibid.*, p.213
[89] *Ibid.*, p.202

though we wish to give as little offence as possible, is heretical'[90] – not only Socinianism but Nestorianism and Sabellianism as well! Indeed, as Stephen Thomas notes:

> Newman's characterisation of one of the most distinguished liberal Anglican historians as "Sabellian" indicates his attitude to a school which was both near, and far, from Tractarianism. Like Newman, the Liberal Anglicans were opposed to the sceptical, static rationalism of the Enlightenment; like Newman they opposed the glib optimism of the "march of mind" mentality, and like Newman they saw that Christian civilisation had come to a crisis. But they offered a middle way, an accommodation with the apparently destructive inroads of the new historical sciences, which would provide a way forward without obscurantism, to avert the collapse of the "house of antiquity."[91]

Despite claiming to write 'as an historian rather than as a religious instructor' and 'professing to keep to fact', Milman managed to produce much 'dogmatic thought and statement'.[92] Newman thus attacked not only his methodology, which could easily be misunderstood and fall into the realm of heresy, but also his conclusions:

> As regards then the settlement of Christian doctrine, Mr. Milman's External Theory seems to us to result or manifest itself in the following canon:—That nothing belongs to the Gospel but what originated in it; and that whatever, professing to belong to it, is found in anterior or collateral systems, may be put out of it as a foreign element. Such a maxim easily follows upon that denial of the supernatural

---

[90] *Ibid.,* p.203
[91] Stephen Thomas, *Newman and Heresy, The Anglican Years* (CUP 1991), pp.163-64
[92] *Ess.* II, pp.214-15

system, which we have above imputed in large measure to
Mr. Milman.[93]

Newman spoke of two theories:

> the advocates of the one imply that Revelation was a single,
> entire, solitary act, or nearly so, introducing a certain
> message; whereas we, who maintain the other, consider that
> Divine teaching has been in fact, what the analogy of nature
> would lead us to expect, "at sundry times and in divers
> manners," various, complex, progressive, and supplemental
> of itself.[94]

Throughout her history, Newman argued, 'the Church has
been a treasure-house, giving forth things old and new,
casting the gold of fresh tributaries into her refiner's fire, or
stamping upon her own, as time required it, a deeper
impress of her Master's image.'[95] It is true 'that great portion
of what is generally received as Christian truth, is in its
rudiments or in its separate parts to be found in heathen
philosophies and religions.' Hence 'the doctrine of the
Divine Word is Platonic' and 'a sacerdotal order is
Egyptian' but 'Mr. Milman argues from it,—"These things
are in heathenism, therefore they are not Christian:" we, on
the contrary, prefer to say, "these things are in Christianity,
therefore they are not heathen."'[96]

Newman's argument would reach its climax, of course,
in his famous *Essay on the Development of Christian
Doctrine* (1845), and it is indeed significant that Newman
chose to include a passage from his Milman review in later
editions of that work.[97] This was sparked off by a sermon

---

[93] *Ibid.*, p.230
[94] *Ibid.*, p.233
[95] *Ibid.*, p.233
[96] *Ibid.*, p.231
[97] Pp.231-34 of *Ess.* II were quoted in pp.280-82 of later editions of *Development.*

preached at the University Church in Oxford in 1879 by
Rev. H. P. Liddon, who stated that the development of
doctrine was 'a confession that the creed of the modern
Roman Church cannot properly be said to be identical with
the Creed of the Apostles ... and even that the fully
developed creed of Rome contains some elements which
have no germinal counterpart in the Creed of the Apostles,
since they have come to it by a process of accretion from
without.'[98] Newman wrote to the Jesuit, Fr Coleridge:

> I had observed Liddon's word 'accretion' which I disallow
> – and was going to cancel the last page or two of my
> Volume, in order to be able to reprint them with the
> inclosed explanatory passage from my Essays, Review of
> Milman. ... PS I see that towards the end of the passage I
> use the word 'accretion', this I must alter in the edition *just*
> coming out.

Newman changed the word 'accretion' to 'enlargement' in
new editions of *Development* and *Essays.*[99]

Newman's review, then, reveals glimpses of his later
thought and stands as a solid critique of the liberalism of
writers such as Milman. He was clear that if Milman's view
of Christianity was indulged, then

> Christianity will melt away in our hands like snow; we shall
> be unbelievers before we at all suspect where we are. With
> a sigh we shall suddenly detect the real state of the case.
> We shall look on Christianity, not as a religion, but as a
> past event which exerted a great influence on the course of
> the world, when it happened, and gave a tone and direction
> to religion, government, philosophy, literature, manners; an
> idea which developed itself in various directions strongly,
> which was indeed from the first materialized into a system

---

[98] *LD* XXIX, p.162, fn
[99] *LD* XXIX, pp.162-63 (Newman to Fr H J Coleridge, 27 July 1879)

or a church, and is still upheld as such by numbers, but by
an error; a great boon to the world, bestowed by the Giver
of all good, as the discovery of printing may be, or the
steam-engine, but as incapable of continuity, except in its
effects, as the shock of an earthquake, or the impulsive
force which commenced the motions of the planets.[100]

XIII: Reformation of the Eleventh Century
The thirteenth essay first appeared as 'Bowden's Life of
Gregory VII – Reformation of the Eleventh Century' in the
British Critic of April 1841, the last edition that Newman
edited before handing over to Thomas Mozley.[101] John
William Bowden (1798-1844) had been a close friend of
Newman's since undergraduate days and was closely
involved in the Oxford Movement. He contributed a number
of articles to the *British Critic*, as can be seen in the short
memoir that Newman included in the 'Note on Essay XI',[102]
but his life of Gregory VII was his major published work,
written 'during his intervals of leisure from official
duties.'[103] He died on 15 September 1844; his widow,
Elizabeth, became a Catholic two years later and built the
church of St Thomas, Fulham, designed by Augustus Welby
Pugin, in memory of her husband. Their son, also called
John, became an Oratorian in London and wrote a
biography of Fr Faber.

Throughout his life Newman was chiefly concerned with
the patristic period but recognised the importance of the
Middle Ages. After all, the Tractarians claimed continuity
not only with the early Church but with the period before

---

[100] *Ess.* II, p.242
[101] *British Critic*, vol. xxix (April 1841), pp.280-331
[102] *Ess.* II, pp.318-19
[103] Bowden, *The Life and Pontificate of Gregory the Seventh*, 2 vols, (Rivingtons)
1840

the Reformation. In his article on the 'Catholicity of the Anglican Church', for example, Newman had defended the *Ecclesia Anglicana*: 'we have the thrones of Cuthbert, Becket and Wykham.'[104] In this he was influenced not only by Bowden but Hurrell Froude, who was, as Newman wrote, 'smitten with the love of the Theocratic Church' which he found in the period.[105]

Newman was convinced, moreover, of the importance of church history. 'Perhaps the greatest of the wants under which our religious literature labours at this day,' he wrote in his review of Milman, 'is that of an ecclesiastical history.'[106] Indeed, 'it is difficult justly to estimate the injury done to our whole view of the Gospel truth by our ignorance of ecclesiastical history. Every department of theology acts upon the rest, and if one is neglected the others suffer.' History also offers a key to understanding 'our scene of trial'; 'the present is a text, and the past its interpretation.'[107] Ignorance of the past and reliance merely on 'visible expediency' can give a distorted impression of reality, rather like 'the clever Oriental who defined the English as a nation who live on the sea, and make penknives.' There was a need for historical facts; 'let us take good care that our arbitrary views do not get ahead of our knowledge.'[108] Bowden was to be thanked for providing a 'narrative of facts; he has drawn out the facts of a momentous and wonderful period of history with great distinctness and perspicuity.'[109]

---

[104] *Ess.* II, p.48
[105] *Ap.,* p.25
[106] *Ess.* II, p.249
[107] *Ibid.,* p.250
[108] *Ibid.,* p.253
[109] *Ibid.,* p.254

Editor's Introduction

Newman saw the medieval struggles between Church and State as a continuation of those between St Athanasius with the Arian and semi-Arian Emperors or St Ambrose with Justin and Valentinian.[110] The period of papal reform under Hildebrand (St Gregory VII) was especially pertinent. One of their major complaints was that the State interfered too much in Church matters. In his 'Remarks on State Interference in Matters Spiritual', originally printed in the *British Critic*, Hurrell Froude argued that

> It seems at first sight something short of reasonable that persons, not necessarily interested in the welfare of the Church, should deliberate for its good; and still less so, that they should be allowed to dictate laws to it, without the consent of those who are necessarily interested; and least reasonable of all, when we add the consideration, that many of the persons so dictating are, as a fact, its avowed enemies, and that their dictates are deeply reprobated by the great body of its avowed members.[111]

Here he was thinking especially of the repeal of the Test and Corporation Acts (1828), Catholic Emancipation (1829) and the Reform Act (1832), which he thought effaced 'in at least one branch of our Civil Legislature that character which, according to our great Authorities, qualified it to be at the same time our Ecclesiastical Legislature and thus to cancel the conditions on which it has been allowed to interfere in matters spiritual.'[112]

Froude did much to introduce the age of Hildebrand and papal reform into the polemic. This was his ideal: the

---

[110] *H.S.*, I, pp.342-374
[111] R. H. Froude, *Remains of the Late Reverend Richard Hurrell Froude, M.A. Felow of Oriel College, Oxford*, edited by J. H. Newman and J. Keble (1838-39), III, p.187
[112] *Ibid.*, p.185

complete ascendancy of the spiritual over the temporal powers. His article for the *British Magazine* on St Thomas Becket, later reprinted in his *Remains*, made even Newman nervous.[113]

Bowden's work, then, was especially opportune and as Newman summarised the work, the reader was given the impression that the reviewer saw in the eleventh century a reflection of his own. The tenth century was a veritable dark age, especially in Rome. Had one lived at the time, 'we should have felt for certain, that if it was possible to retrieve the Church, it must be by some external power; she was helpless and resourceless; and the civil power must interfere, or there was no hope.' The Emperor Henry III, 'though unhappily far from a perfect character, yet deeply felt the shame to which the Immaculate Bride was exposed, and determined with his own right hand to work her deliverance.'[114] He called a Council of his own bishops but realised soon enough that Rome, 'as the centre of the ecclesiastical commonwealth', should be the instrument of reform.[115]

Thus, 'the State reformer struck his foot against the hidden rock, and found to his surprise that, in that apparently disorganized and lifeless frame, which he was attempting to new-make, there was a soul and a power of self-action adequate both to its recovery and to its resistance against foreign interference.'[116] For Bowden and his reviewer

---

[113] *LD* VI, p.317 (Newman to Keble, 13 September 1838) 'the *preface* to the Becket papers might frighten people considerably – on Church and State'.
[114] *Ess.* II, p.261
[115] *Ibid.*, p.262
[116] *Ibid.*, p.265

Editor's Introduction

in spite of the dreadful demoralization of the Church and
popedom in the tenth and eleventh centuries, there was laid
in the temper of the age and the feelings of society a deep
and firm groundwork, if men could be found who had the
heart to appeal to it, for reforming and purifying the Church
by an internal effort, and without recurring to the temporal
power, which seemed at first sight the obvious, or rather the
only resource.[117]

The problem was that imperial proposals for Church reform
'involved and perpetuated the very evils which it was
intended to remove.' The Investiture Controversy stood as a
stark reminder that 'if the Church was under secular
jurisdiction, it was fairly open to secular use.'

When Christians have but a partial confidence in their own
principles, there is a great temptation, when Church matters
go wrong, to give up God's way, and take whatever is
recommended by the expediency of the moment. The
ancient and true methods of proceeding appear quite out of
date and place; the old materials, instruments, centres, and
laws, on which the Church once moved, are apparently
worn out by use; and what remains but to take up whatever
comes to hand? We need not go to past ages for illustrations
of this remark. In all times, weeds and scum, and all that is
worthless, float on the surface, and precious gems lie at the
bottom of the deep; and where there is neither faith to
accept nor penetration to apprehend, what does not obtrude
itself upon the senses, men are very ready to put up with
what they see, in despair of meeting with what may be
more to their purpose.[118]

The exact point of battle was this:

---

[117] *Ibid.*, pp.274-275
[118] *Ibid.*, p.268-69

The State said to the Church, "I am the only power which can reform you; you hold of me, and your dignities and offices are in my gift." The Church said to the State, "She who wields the power even of smiting kings, cannot be a king's creature; and if you attempt to reform her, you will be planting the root of corruption by the same hand which cuts off its branches."[119]

It was this Erastianism that the Oxford Movement was struggling against, and Newman must have thought the Tractarians similar to that 'remnant of holy men, out of sight, scanty perhaps in numbers, but great in moral strength' who saved the Church in the eleventh century?[120]

In the person of Hildebrand, Newman found inspiration as he set about calling the English Church to reform. He noted particularly that pope's enforcement of clerical celibacy and the abasement of the temporal below the spiritual power. He seemed almost to refer of himself when he wrote: 'No wonder a mind of such incessant energy should complain of nothing but weariness and disappointment; and this seems to have been the habitual feeling under which he went to his work.'[121] 'Gregory thought he had failed,' but Newman concluded, 'so it is; often a cause seems to decline as its champion grows in years, and to die in his death; but this is to judge hastily; others are destined to complete what he began. No man is given to see his work through.'[122] It was a theme Newman would return to in his *Parting of Friends* sermon.

Having argued, in 'The Protestant View of Antichrist', that the Pope was not the Antichrist of Prophecy, Newman

---

[119] *Ibid.,* p.275
[120] *Ibid.,* p.270
[121] *Ibid.,* p.298
[122] *Ibid.,* p.317

Editor's Introduction

now demonstrated that 'the great reformation of the Church in the middle ages' was conducted by Providence 'through the instrumentality, partly divine, partly human, of the Papal Monarchy.'[123] Despite his reforms relying upon the aid of the emperor, Hildebrand was seen as a model of anti-Erastianism. It is interesting, though, that, as Paul Misner has noted, 'Newman's historical view of the papacy seems to have stopped, for all practical purposes, on this high plateau of the Gregorian reform and its consolidation under Innocent III.'[124]

Looking back on these Anglican writings as a Catholic, Newman thought no additional remarks were needed, 'except as relates to the subject of the forged Decretals.'[125] This was a much-discussed issue in Anglican/Catholic polemic and, as an appendix, he added an extract from the writings of Fr Henry Ignatius Dudley Ryder, a priest of the Birmingham Oratory (who eventually succeeded Newman as Provost) and nephew by marriage of Cardinal Manning.

In a letter to Bowden, Newman quoted the reaction of Richard Waldo Sibthorp (soon to convert to Rome) to the *Life of Gregory VII*: 'it is one of the most deeply interesting books I have read for some time, and his views respecting the papal office, and its utility in past times, very striking. What a fearful rent did the Reformation make!'[126] Newman's reflections on Hildebrand certainly did nothing to slow down the deathbed of his Anglicanism.

---

[123] *Ibid.*, p.254
[124] Paul Misner, *Papacy and Devlopment: Newman and the Primacy of the Pope* (Brill, 1976), p.35
[125] *Ess.* II, p.320
[126] *LD* VIII, p.65 (Newman to Bowden, 11 March 1841)

Editor's Introduction

XIV. Private Judgment

Newman was unsure about the inclusion of the fourteenth article in *Essays Critical and Historical* since he judged it 'heavy and dull.'[127] Indeed, he had found it hard to write and wondered in June 1841 whether he would ever complete it, 'for I do not see my theory clear.'[128] It originally appeared in the *British Critic* for July 1841.[129] This issue was the first to be edited by Thomas Mozley. Newman's piece was designed to balance a strongly-worded article by Frederick Oakeley on 'Bishop Jewel: His Character, Correspondence and Apologetic Treatises'. Newman advised the new editor to refer 'at a proper place (in a note) to *another* article in the number against joining Rome, which should be mine.'[130]

The title that Newman gave his piece when he republished (and significantly abbreviated) it in *Essays* obscured the fact that it originated as a review of eight publications:

1. *Autobiography of Thomas Platter, a Schoolmaster of the XVIth Century. Translated from the German.* Wertheim. London. 1839

2. *Reasons for becoming a Roman Catholic. Addressed to the Society of Friends.* By F. Lucas, Esq., of the Middle Temple, Barrister at Law. Booker and Dolman. London. 1839.

3. *A Letter to the Hon. and Rev. George Spencer, on his Sermon preached at Manchester.* By the Rev. G. B. Sandford, M.A., Parker. Oxford. 1840.

4. *Geraldine, a Tale of Conscience.* By E. C. A. Vol. iii. Dolman. 1839.

---

[127] *LD* XXV, p.238 (Newman to B. M. Pickering, 1 December 1870)

[128] *LD* VIII, p.202 (Newman to Mozley, 7 June 1841)

[129] *British Critic*, vol. xxx (July 1841), pp.100-34

[130] *LD* VIII, p.151 (Newman to Thomas Mozley, 1 April 1841)

5. *A Few Words in Support of No. 90 of the Tracts for the Times.* Parker. Oxford.

6. *A few more Words in Support of No. 90 of the Tracts for the Times.* By the Rev, W. G. Ward, M.A., Fellow of Baliol College. Parker. Oxford.

7. *Letters 1,2, 3,4,5, to N. Wiseman, D.D.; containing Remarks on his Letter to Mr. Newman,* &c. By the Rev. V. Palmer, M.A. Parker. Oxford.

8. *The Articles treated on in Tract 90 reconsidered and their Interpretation vindicated, in a Letter to the Rev. R. W.Jeff, D.D., Canon of Christ Church.* By the Rev. E. B. Pusey, D. D. Parker. Oxford.

These included three accounts of conversion to Rome (Lucas, Sandford, *Geraldine*) and one sixteenth century Swiss conversion to Protestantism (Platter), to which Newman 'added some of the pamphlets which the Oxford controversy has produced, in the belief that they furnish suitable illustrations of a point which must be introduced rather prominently in the course of our discussion.'[131]

Newman criticised the Protestant tendency to rely on private judgment, since it obviously 'leads different minds in different directions.' What particularly concerned Newman was that private judgment could lead one person to Rome and another to, say, the Society of Friends.

This Protestant view of 'private judgment, all private judgment, and nothing but private judgment' was, in actual fact, 'held by very few persons indeed.' After all

> if a staunch Protestant's daughter turns Roman, and betakes herself to a convent, why does he not exult in the occurrence? Why does he not give a public breakfast, or

---

[131] *British Critic,* p.100

hold a meeting, or erect a memorial, or write a pamphlet in honour of her, and of the great undying principle she has so gloriously vindicated?' People generally 'hold, not the right of private judgment, but the private right of judgment; in other words, their own private right, and no one else's.[132]

Newman was highly suspicious of changes in religion. As a rule, 'considering, in a word, that change is really the characteristic of error, and unalterableness the attribute of truth, of holiness, of Almighty God Himself, we consider that when Private Judgment moves in the direction of innovation, it may well be regarded at first with suspicion and treated with severity.'[133] Conversions were often due to personal or emotional motives rather than rational ones – 'whenever news of a conversion … is brought to us, we say, one and all of us, "No wonder, such a one has lived so long abroad;" or, "he is of such a very imaginative turn;" or, "he is so excitable and odd"…'[134]

It is undeniable, then, if the popular feeling is to be our guide, that, high and mighty as the principle of private judgment is in religious inquirers, as we most fully grant it is, still it bears some similarity to Saul's armour which David rejected, or to edged tools which have a bad trick of chopping at our fingers, when we are but simply and innocently meaning them to make a dash forward at truth.[135]

He went on to look at conversion narratives in Scripture and argued that private judgment was only legitimately used in sanctioning 'not an inquiry about Gospel doctrine, but about the Gospel teacher; not what has God revealed, but

---

[132] *Ess.* II, pp.340-41
[133] *Ibid.,* p338
[134] *Ibid.,* p.339
[135] *Ibid.,* p.341

whom has He commissioned?'[136] Thus, 'the conversions recorded in Scripture are brought about in a very marked way through a *teacher*, and *not* by means of private judgment, so again, if an appeal *is* made to private judgment, this is done in order to settle who the teacher is, and what are his notes or tokens, rather than to substantiate this or that religious opinion or practice.'[137] Private judgment was all about answering the question: 'what and where is the Church?'

The obvious question, then, was which of the rival teachers should be chosen. Just as in Scripture 'very grave outward differences seem to have existed between Christian teachers' – he cites the factions around Paul, Cephas (Peter) and Apollos – then 'is not this, at least in great measure, the state of the Churches of England and Rome? Are they not one in faith, so far forth as they are viewed in their essential apostolical character?' Therefore 'our duty is, remaining where we are, to recognize in our own Church, not an establishment, not a party, not a mere Protestant denomination, but the Holy Church Catholic which the traditions of men have partially obscured.'[138] In a letter to a would-be convert around the time of this review, Newman made the same point: 'It does seem safest to remain where we are, and wait for light, wait for improvement, strive for a reform, be zealous in protestations and teaching in our own sphere.'[139]

The objection might be made that the Church of England had separated itself from the rest of Christendom, but if 'the English glories in what looks so very like schism', 'the

---

[136] *Ibid.,* p.350
[137] *Ibid.,* p.351
[138] *Ibid.,* p.361
[139] *LD* VIII, p.262 (Newman to Miss Holmes, 6 September 1841)

Roman Church practises what looks so very like idolatry.'[140] This apparently schismatic nature of the English Church could be seen in 'an arrogant John Bull way' of viewing Christians in other countries as foreigners rather than 'brethren'.

> When our thoughts turn to the East, instead of recollecting that there are sister Churches there, we leave it to the Russians to take care of the Greeks, and to the French to take care of the Romans, and we content ourselves with erecting a Protestant Church at Jerusalem, or with helping the Jews to rebuild their temple there, or with becoming the august protectors of Nestorians, Monophysites, and all the heretics we can hear of, or with forming a league with the Mussulman against Greeks and Roman together.[141]

This referred to the controversy surrounding the Jerusalem Bishopric, when it was proposed to establish a joint Anglo-Prussian Bishopric in Jerusalem, nominated alternately by these two countries. This was designed to check the influence of the French (Catholic) and Russians (Orthodox) in the Holy City. The new bishop would be ordained in the Anglican rite but would be able to ordain Lutherans who subscribed to both the Thirty-Nine Articles and the Augsburg Confession.

However, the Tractarians were shocked by the proposal, with its underlining political motivations and cooperation with another 'heretical' Church. Newman wrote to Bowden, 'So far from thinking lightly of the Jerusalem matter I said something very strong about it in my Priv. J. article, before most people suspected what was going on.'[142] Newman famously wrote in the *Apologia* that 'it brought me on to the

---

[140] *Ibid.,* p.367
[141] *Ibid.,* pp.365-66
[142] *LD* VIII, pp.294-95 (Newman to Bowden, 12 October 1841)

beginning of the end.'[143] His *Via Media*, for which he had argued so eloquently, appeared to be very fragile.

XV. John Davison, Fellow of Oriel

In October 1841, Newman expressed his desire to review John Davison's *Remains and Occasional Publications* (1840).[144] The article was subsequently written in March 1842, the same week as 'roman cement was laid down in the cloister' at Littlemore,[145] and included in the *British Critic* of April 1842.[146] However Newman was initially unsure about the review's republication in 1871, doubting 'whether it would interest readers'.[147]

Much of the piece, it is true, concerns general comments about the writings of Davison. He had been a Fellow of Oriel and shown sympathy towards the *Tracts for the Times* before his death in 1834; Newman told Bowden he was 'more or less connected with us'.[148] Newman was not a personal friend, belonging to a different generation, though he clearly admired his work. The future cardinal thought Davison an original and deep thinker who was 'fitted to be a doctor of the Church'. Davison's contributions to theology were to be found in his Warburton lectures, *Discourses on Prophecy, in which are considered its Structure, Use, and Inspiration* (1824), and his *An Inquiry into the Origin and Intent of Primitive Sacrifice, and the Scripture Evidence respecting it* (1825). His theology was 'high', at a time when most Anglican theology was protestant or latitudinarian (rationalist). Newman was therefore interested

---

[143] *Ap.*, 136
[144] *LD* VIII, p.280, (Newman to Mozley, 1 October 1841)
[145] *LD* VIII, p.479 (Diary, 7 March 1842).
[146] *British Critic*, vol.xxxi (April 1842), pp.367-401
[147] *LD* XXV, p.238 (Newman to Pickering, 1 December 1870)
[148] *LD* IV, p.54, (Newman to Bowden, 23 September 1833)

in him as part of that continuing presence of more Catholic ideas in the Church of England despite the Reformation. By the time Newman was writing this article, however, he had resigned as Vicar of St. Mary's, following the rejection of *Tract 90* by the Church of England authorities and the university, and had retired to Littlemore to ponder his future. His own work as leader of the Oxford Movement had come to an abrupt end, and we can perhaps see Newman comparing himself with Davison when he says that Davison was the victim of that mysterious law 'that they who seem gifted for the definite purpose of influencing and edifying their brethren, should be allowed to do so much less than might be expected.'[149] The parallel with Newman becomes even more marked when he says that a man who has gone far 'in Catholic opinions' is found acceptable if he 'does but conform himself to the existing state of things, adopt the tone of the world, take his place in the social body, and become an integral member ... and a contented servant, of things that perish.' But if he will not 'do homage to ... wealth as such, or official eminence as such, then he is out of joint with the age'[150] This certainly fits with Newman's feelings about his situation at the time of writing this article.

Newman says that Davison's character was elusive and his style inconsistent, 'unattractive in its general course, yet as happy in its separate portions, as being a sort of type of that economy of reserve which an unseen hand wrapped round him.'[151] He had flashes of brilliance and originality yet had difficulty in expressing himself:

---

[149] *Ess.* II, p.375
[150] *Ibid.*, p.379.
[151] *Ibid.*, p.384

We suppose it then to be undeniable, that there are persons, whose minds are full of thought even to bursting, in whom it is pent up in a strange way, and in whom, when it at last forces itself out in language, it does so with the suddenness, brevity, completeness, and effectiveness (if the comparison be allowed) of a steam-boiler. The more fully formed is the image of truth in the mind, the greater task is it to find door or window for it to escape by; and, when it makes egress, perhaps it comes head-foremost.[152]

He praises the way that Davison was always highly reverent when speaking of religious subjects. His 'habitual and ruling idea' was the 'awful contemplation of the providential dealings of God with man',[153] but this led him to write with embarrassment and constraint, 'analogous to what a subordinate feels every day when told to do a thing in the presence of superiors.'

If we consider how awkward a young teacher or a schoolmaster feels when bid to catechise when his instructor or employer is by, or the anxiety and distrust of self with which a well-conducted child undergoes an examination, we shall have some insight perhaps into the diffidence and fear with which Mr. Davison touches on sacred subjects.[154]

He did not concern himself with dogma but rather with principles. Newman briefly reflects upon the relationship between the two:

Doctrines are the limits or issues of principles, and if the principles be religious, they do legitimately and naturally lead to revealed doctrines, where such revelation is made. It was Mr Davison's unhappiness to live at a time when

---

[152] *Ibid.*, p.381
[153] *Ibid.*, pp.394-395
[154] *Ibid.*, p.397

> Christian doctrine was under a partial eclipse, and hence his principles are far more Catholic, or, we will rather say, positive and defined, than his dogmatic statements. His principles and their definiteness are his own; his doctrines, or rather their indistinctness, is the peculiarity of his age.[155]

So far Newman has been presenting Davison as in some ways a forerunner of what the Oxford Movement was trying to promote in the Church of England – a revival of Catholic principles which had been 'under a partial eclipse' in the preceding century. But Newman is also aware of Davison's limitations and thus of the old 'High and Dry' party within Anglicanism which, while quite Catholic in its theology, nevertheless maintained many of the Protestant antipathies towards the Catholic Church. He is especially critical of Davison's critique of monasticism in a sermon preached at Deptford in 1817. Whereas it was claimed that the monastic life was destructive and useless, Newman showed that it was 'the great fulfilment of both the first and the second commandment of the law', opening schools and hospitals, defending orthodoxy and providing women with many opportunities: 'How great a number of women in this Protestant land spend their lives in doing nothing! how much labour, to use secular language, is lost to the community! what numbers are led to throw themselves and their happiness away on husbands unworthy of them, because, when they would fain not be useless in their day, marriage is the only path open to their ambition!'[156] Newman was, of course, writing his article from the 'monastic seclusion' of Littlemore and throughout his life had a high regard for the monastic ideal, from his reflections as an

---

[155] *Ibid.*, pp.408-409. This discussion is continued in *Dev.*
[156] *Ess.* II, p.416

Editor's Introduction

Anglican in the *Church of the Fathers* to his later Benedictine essays published in *Atlantis* (1858-59). However, what he says here about women is particularly interesting as showing how Newman, whom we often think of in an exclusively male environment, was acutely aware of how women's roles were restricted in Protestant culture, whereas in Catholicism the female religious orders gave a much greater freedom for women beyond the domestic sphere.

Davison's prejudice against the monastic orders meant that he was yet another example of 'a great mind' that was 'unconsciously swayed by deference to the opinions among which he lived, and which, for what we know, could not have been rejected by him, in his particular place and time, without some portion of irreverence, love of paradox, or self-confidence, most foreign to his character.' Yet, Newman stressed that 'it is the trial and mystery of our position in this age and country, that a religious mind is continually set at variance with itself, that its deference to what is without contradicts its suggestions from within, and that it cannot follow what it presages without rebelling against what it has received.'[157] This is exactly what Newman himself had experienced and was continuing to experience in the seclusion of Littlemore. This Essay, therefore, which at first sight seems a piece of slightly irrelevant biography, turns out to be part of Newman's journey towards his conversion to the Catholic Church. Its indirect message, as in so much of what he chose to republish in these *Essays*, was an implicit call to other Catholic-minded Anglicans to resolve the contradictions

---

[157] *Ibid.*, pp.419-420

which he had struggled with, and which those before him like Davison had experienced in their own way.

XVI. John Keble, Fellow of Oriel

The final essay stands apart since it originally appeared in the Catholic journal *The Dublin Review* in June 1846 as 'Lyra Innocentium by the author of the Christian Year'.[158] It is the first published work of Newman following his conversion and, as might be expected, there is an air of sensitivity and self-justification. Despite this, the essay picks up several themes mentioned elsewhere and complements the article on John Davison, a friend and colleague of Keble in the Oriel Senior Common Room.

The Oxford Movement has been described as 'the religious manifestation of a change in sensibility, a new kind of awareness made possible in a large part by the European-wide phenomenon of Romanticism.'[159] Poetry was an important element of its literary output and the verses of Newman, Keble and Isaac Williams reached a wide readership.

Keble's *Lyra Innocentium* was published in 1846 and followed on from his previous volumes of poetry, including the highly influential *Christian Year* (1827). In this new collection of poems, Keble initially aimed to produce 'a sort of *Christian Year* for Teachers and Nurses, and others who are much employed about Children'; however, 'by degrees it has taken a different shape.'[160] Newman noted its uncontroversial, 'equitable' character, although one of the book's aims was to present an apologia for the author's

---

[158] *Dublin Review*, vol. xx (June 1846), pp.434-61
[159] G. B. Tennyson, *Victorian Devotional Poetry: The Tractarian Mode* (Harvard, 1981), p.9
[160] 'Advertisement' in J. Keble, *Lyra Innocentium* (1846)

ongoing loyalty to the Church of England. Part of this
rationale can be found in the opening verses:

> And with no faint nor erring voice
>   May to the wanderer whisper, "Stay;
> God chooses for thee; seal his choice,
>   Nor from thy Mother's shadow stray;
> For sure thy Holy Mother's shade
>   Rests yet upon thine ancient home:
> No voice from Heaven has clearly said
>   'Let us depart;' then fear to roam."[161]

Newman observed that in his new work, Keble 'abstains
almost entirely from any allusion whatever to the existing
state and prospects of the English Church.' This was in
contrast to the *Christian Year* which 'abounds in sentiments
about ecclesiastical matters.'[162] Keble is himself childlike,
living in a dream:

> he leaves bishops and clergy, cathedral chapters and
> ecclesiastical judges, town mobs and country squires, to the
> tender mercies of history, in order to enjoy a blameless
> Donatism, to live in a church of children, to gaze on their
> looks and gestures, to encourage them in good, and to guard
> them from harm and sin.[163]

He is like 'singing-birds' which are 'silent when a storm is
at hand.'[164] Keble obviously found comfort in his poetry,
seeing it as 'a method of relieving the over-burdened mind;
it is a channel through which emotion finds expression, and
that a safe, regulated expression.'[165]

---

[161] *Ibid.*, p.vii
[162] *Ess.* II, pp.427-428
[163] *Ibid.*, p.432
[164] *Ibid.*, p.430
[165] *Ibid.*, p.442

Editor's Introduction

Writing as an Anglican in 'Prospects of the Anglican Church', Essay VII in Volume I of these *Essays*, Newman had said that 'poetry of a religious kind has in modern times in a certain sense taken the place of the deep contemplative spirit of the early Church.'[166] Now, in this final Essay the Catholic Newman wrote that 'poetry is the refuge of those who have not the Catholic Church to flee to and repose upon, for the Church herself is the most sacred and august of poets':

> Her very being is poetry; every psalm, every petition, every collect, every versicle, the cross, the mitre, the thurible, is a fulfilment of some dream of childhood, or aspiration of youth. Such poets as are born under her shadow, she takes into her service; she sets them to write hymns, or to compose chants, or to embellish shrines, or to determine ceremonies, or to marshal processions; nay, she can even make schoolmen of them, as she made St. Thomas, till logic becomes poetical.

This 'poetic' was lost at the Protestant Reformation:

> a ritual dashed upon the ground, trodden on, and broken piece-meal;—prayers, clipped, pieced, torn, shuffled about at pleasure, until the meaning of the composition perished, and offices which had been poetry were no longer even good prose;—antiphons, hymns, benedictions, invocations, shovelled away;—Scripture lessons turned into chapters;—heaviness, feebleness, unwieldiness, where the Catholic rites had had the lightness and airiness of a spirit;—vestments chucked off, lights quenched, jewels stolen, the pomp and circumstances of worship annihilated ...[167]

---

[166] Vol.I, p.290
[167] *Ibid.*, pp.442-444

'The Catholic Church speaks for itself,' argued Newman, 'the Anglican needs external assistance.' However, Keble himself had been the great 'renovator'; he had changed the Church's ethos and 'his happy magic made the Anglican Church seem what the Catholicism was and is.' The beauty and poetry of Christianity had been revived, so that the faithful learned, for instance, 'that what their pastors had spoken of, and churchwardens had used at vestry meetings, as a mere table, was "the dread altar;" and that "holy lamps were blazing;" "perfumed embers quivering bright," with "stoled priests ministering at them," while the "floor was by knees of sinners worn."'[168] For G. B. Tennyson, Newman's review is the 'sublime encomium on the Catholic Church as poetry', 'alive with the themes and images and even the language of Tractarian poetry', and could be seen as 'the final resting-place of Tractarian theory.'[169]

Newman noted the inconsistencies of *Lyra Innocentium* and its author. He praised Keble for his contribution to the English Church but criticised him for not going far enough. He pointed out that the doctrine behind his poems was notably Catholic, speaking of baptismal regeneration, Eucharistic sacrifice, Guardian Angels and reverence for the Blessed Virgin: 'there is but one Church which has firmly, precisely, consistently, continually held and acted upon these doctrines of the *Lyra Innocentium*; and, if holding them to be token of the true Church, one and only one Church is true.'[170] Keble's book, Newman claimed, could ironically result in further conversions to Rome.

Despite this critique, Newman is respectful towards Keble. His name is 'so revered, so loved ... by Oxford men

---

[168] *Ibid.*, pp.444-445
[169] G. B. Tennyson, *op. cit.*, pp.194-196
[170] *Ess.* II, p.448

for thirty years and more'; in his youth he 'caused the eyes of younger men to turn keenly towards him, if he was pointed out to them in public schools or college garden,' and when he was 'removed from his loved University, was still an unseen silent influence moving hearts at his will.'[171] Indeed, at the end of 1845 he had written to Keble: 'To you I owe it, humanly speaking, that I am what and where I am.'[172]

Newman was aware that many had criticised his conversion to Catholicism. The depth of his hurt is revealed not only by his criticism of the Church of England but by a telling paragraph, which ends: 'May they who have spoken or written harshly of recent converts to the Catholic Church, receive at the Great Day more lenient measure than they have in this case given!'[173] Keble avoided such harsh criticism himself but his personal disapproval of Newman's conversion remained the backdrop to the article. In October 1846, Henry Wilberforce wrote to Newman: 'When you congratulate yourself and K[eble] that *he* does not judge those who have gone – I believe I told you that no one *feels* more than he.'[174]

This second volume of *Essays Critical and Historical* thus provides a snapshot of the development of Newman's thought in a crucially important period. He began the 1840s defending the 'Catholicity' of the Church of England, highlighting the perceived inconsistencies of Rome and encouraging would-be converts to remain where they were. However, as we can see in these pages and as had already

---

[171] *Ibid.,* pp.445-446
[172] *LD* XI, p.34, (Newman to Keble, 14 November 1845)
[173] *Ess.* II, p.427
[174] *LD* XI, p.215, (H. Wilberforce to Newman , October 1846)

Editor's Introduction

begun to be revealed in some of the articles in the first volume, he came to see the weaknesses within his own Via Media, the possibility of doctrinal development, the value of a papacy that was not the Antichrist of the Prophecies and the need to counter a liberal view of Christianity. The final essay ends from the safety of the Roman harbour that Newman had eventually reached, hoping that others would follow. Indeed, he prayed 'that that sweet and gracious Lady', whose image had once hung in Keble's rooms, 'will not forget her servant, but will recompense him, in royal wise, seven-fold, bringing him and his at length into the Church of the One Saviour, and into the communion of herself and all Saints whom He has redeemed.'[175]

Nicholas Schofield

---

[175] *Ess.* II, p. 453

A NOTE ON THE TEXT

The first edition of these collected essays was published by Basil Montagu Pickering in 1871. The text used for this Gracewing edition is the sixth edition published by Longmans, Green and Co. in 1885 which was Newman's final revised version (subsequent editions published in his lifetime being reprints of this). Other works by Newman, except the Letters and Diaries, are also cited in the uniform Longmans editions.

Footnotes

The page layout and headings in this Gracewing edition exactly copy the Longmans edition, except for the addition of the Editor's footnotes. Newman's own footnotes are followed by [N] to distinguish them from the Editor's footnotes. Where Newman's footnotes are in square brackets, they are the ones he added to his original texts for the 1871 and 1885 editions. Some of Newman's notes need further explanation, so the [N] is sometimes followed by an Editor's Note. All other footnotes are by the Editor.

Page numbering

It is the practice of Newman scholars to cite his works using the uniform Longmans editions. To facilitate this in the present volume the page numbers of the Longmans edition are placed in square brackets at the appropriate places in the margins of the text. All references in the Editor's Introduction and the Textual Appendix are to these page numbers.

ESSAYS CRITICAL AND HISTORICAL

VOLUME II

ESSAY X

CATHOLICITY OF THE ANGLICAN CHURCH

IN his recent work on the Apostolic Succession and the English Orders, Mr. Perceval[1] has done us a service which was very much needed, and had never been attempted. Many living writers have treated of the Apostolical Succession as well as he; but no one but he has had the opportunity, and been at the pains, of exhibiting to the general reader the evidence of the *fact* of the Succession in the English Church.[2] We are referring to the elaborate Appendix to his Volume, in which he has brought together a great number of documents and tables illustrative of some of the more important points in the history of the spiritual descent of our existing bishops and clergy from the Apostles. He begins by enumerating the chief objections which the Roman Catholics have urged against our Succession, as passing through Archbishop Parker[3] and his

---

[1] *Mr. Perceval*: Arthur Philip Perceval (1799-1853) Educated at Oriel College, Oxford (BA 1820, BCL 1824) and elected Fellow of All Souls (1821), he worked as Rector of East Horsley, Surrey (1824-26) and royal chaplain (1826-50). A supporter of the Oxford Movement, he wrote Tracts 23, 35 and 36. In 1839 Perceval produced *An Apology for the Doctrine of Apostolical Succession, with an Appendix on English Orders* and two years later defended Newman and *Tract 90* in his *Vindication of the Authors of Tracts for the Times*. However, in later years he distanced himself from the Tractarians.

[2] *Succession in the English Church*: Newman omits a lengthy passage found in the original *British Critic* article summarising Perceval's book. See Textual Appendix.

[3] *Archbishop Parker*: Matthew Parker (1504-75), Archbishop of Canterbury from 1559 until his death. He was appointed to succeed Cardinal Pole shortly after Elizabeth's accession, and considerable controversy surrounded his consecration – Catholic controversialists even alleged the ceremony was performed informally at the Nag's Head Tavern in Lambeth. Given the dismissal of fourteen of the Marian

3

colleagues, and he lays before us some chief portions of the evidence in its favour, presenting us with the records of Parker's consecration as contained in the registers at Lambeth and in the library of Corpus Christi College, Cambridge, and with the offices for consecration and ordination, according to the Antenicene, Eastern, Ancient Western, Coptic, and Queen Elizabeth's Ritual. Next, he has printed a list of between 400 and 500 English consecrations, from Cranmer[4] and his consecrators, inclusive, down to the present time, containing name, see, date of consecration, and names of consecrators in the case of each bishop. After this we have the respective Episcopal descents of Parker and Pole[5] traced back, by way of contrast, for four steps; by which it appears that the proof from existing records of the transmission of the apostolical commission to Pole, is far less complete than what is producible on the side of Parker. Mr. Perceval next traces up the Episcopal descent of the present Archbishop of Canterbury[6] for four antecedent steps, all the consecrations being in this case known, and finds, to use his own words, that "in transmitting the apostolical commission to the present Archbishop of Canterbury there were, in the first step, four bishops concerned; in the second, twelve; in the third, twenty-seven; in the fourth, about fifty; nearly enough to fill all the English dioceses

[2]

---

bishops, it was difficult finding bishops who were qualified and willing to consecrate Parker, and the Edwardian Ordinal was used despite it having been repealed by Mary I.

[4] *Cranmer*: Thomas Cranmer (1489-1556), Archbishop of Canterbury 1533-55. One of the chief architects of the English Reformation, he was burned at the stake in Oxford under Mary I on 21 March 1556.

[5] *Pole*: Reginald Pole (1500-58), Archbishop of Canterbury (1556-58), created a Cardinal by Paul III in 1537.

[6] *the present Archbishop of Canterbury*: William Howley (Archbishop 1828-48).

twice over; so that, not a single consecration here and there, but all the consecrations in England for successive generations, must be supposed to have failed, before the objection can be worthy of consideration, that the failure of the due consecration of any one single bishop in a line would destroy the whole theory."—P. 218.

Other tables are added; among which not the least interesting is one containing the consecrations of the non-jurors, the last bishop of whom died as lately as 1805.[7]

1.

We do trust and believe that the question of English Orders is now settled once for all. If, indeed, members of our Church again forget the great privilege therein involved, as they have forgotten it in no slight measure more than once, then indeed the whole controversy will have to be run [3] through again, as lately, at a miserable waste of time, labour, and peace. The world will become ignorant of the grounds on which we claim the privilege; and will require fresh discussion upon its nature, its probability, its evidence, and its place in the Anglican system. We hope better things of our Church than to anticipate such an event; and at all events the controversy is at an end for the present. And so our opponents seem to consider; for they evince a disposition to concede to us the Succession "for argument's sake;" or in other words they find that it is not *safe* or *tenable* in argument to deny it, since what they call "for argument's sake" really means "for their own sake." But

---

[7] *the non-jurors* . . . : The original non-jurors were Anglican clergy (including nine bishops) who refused to take the Oath of Allegiance to William III and Mary II in 1689. The result was a schism, continued by the secret consecration of non-juring bishops, the last of whom, Charles Boothe, died in Ireland in 1805.

though we have gained this point, it does not follow that we have driven the enemy from the field and put an end to the war. There is another important and difficult post which the Roman party have not yet surrendered, and from which we must dislodge them. Mr. Perceval does scarcely more than refer to it, nor does it properly fall in his way. That our Orders are good in themselves is indisputable; but still they may be given and continued *in schism*; our Church may be a true but a schismatical branch of the Catholic body, though ever so legitimately descended from the Apostles. She may at present have a bar upon her ordinances, Sacraments as well as Orders, which deprives them of grace, as a son may be really a son yet disinherited, or a man in a fainting fit or in derangement is still a man, yet unable to use his functions. This is a ground which Roman writers have very commonly taken up, and with considerable advantage. Our writers, on the other hand, have not discussed it with the exactness and fulness which it requires at the hands of those who profess to defer to the opinions of the Fathers. We are

[4]   not unmindful of what our learned champions have done long ago; but every age has its own character, its own mode of stating things, its own exigencies; and cannot use, or at least cannot be content with, the controversial efforts of a former time.

The objection which we have in mind, concisely stated, is this: on the one hand, that unity is the tenure of divine favour; that communion with our brethren is the means of communion with our Lord and Saviour; that the Church is not only Apostolic, but Catholic; that schism cuts off the fountains of grace; and that estrangement from the Christian world is schism; and, on the other, that in matter of fact our

Church is emphatically in a state of estrangement, having intercourse with no other Christian body in any part of the world, excepting her own dependencies and offshoots. This is the point, which deserves, as we think, to be attentively considered; we make no pretences and have no hopes of doing justice to it in the pages of a Review; yet it is something to direct attention to it, and so much we propose to do in the pages which follow.

2.

Now the first step towards duly answering the objection is to enter into it and master it; and the best way of effecting this is to put it before our minds as strongly as we can. With this view, then, we shall first of all endeavour to make a strong statement of our opponents' case, and then bring forward what means we have for overthrowing it. And perhaps we shall best begin by setting down the pleadings on the one side and the other in the form of dialogue, which shall be conducted favourably to the Church of Rome, so as to bring matters to an issue. We are promising a great deal, but, our intentions being good, we have a sort of claim upon [5] the kind feeling of all upholders of the Catholicity of the English Church.

The *Roman Catholic* then begins thus:—There is but One true Church, and its characteristic, both in Scripture and in the Fathers, is, that it should be in many countries, or rather all over the earth. Thus it differs from what it was during the Dispensation of the Law; then it was one in one country; under the Gospel it is one in many countries.

Anglo-Catholic.—I grant; and that it is schism to separate from it, and that schism is a state of sin.

7

Rom.—The flock of Christ is one, not two flocks; though in many countries, is still but one flock, as sheep moving in a body over a plain. If there be two flocks claiming to be the true flock, it cannot be both of them. If it is the one, it is not the other; if the other, it is not the one. It cannot be both the Church of Rome and the Church of England; if the English Church is true, the Roman is a pretence; and the English is a pretence, if the Roman is true.

Angl.—This does not follow: a flock of sheep that straggles is still one flock. One part may be on one side of the hedge and yet the other on the other.

Rom.—A flock of sheep may spread widely and yet be one; but they would cease to be one if they formed into parties shunning and worrying each other. It is said "a house divided against itself cannot stand;"[8] if both you and we are the Catholic Church, the Church is falling or has even fallen.

Angl.—We do not differ from each other in all things; we agree together in fundamentals, and where you agree with us, there we do not act hostilely towards you.

[6]   *Rom.*—On the contrary, you, as a body, oppose and denounce us, as a body, in all possible ways; and we too oppose and denounce you. Let us look at facts, and not speak by book. And you are small, we are large; therefore we, not you, are the Church.

Angl.—If we two cannot be at peace, the worse for you; for your teaching is corrupt, and ours is pure.

---

[8] *"a house divided against . . .* : Matthew 12:25

Rom.—No, we preach the whole gospel, and you halve it.[9]

Angl.—Our teaching is the true, because it is the primitive; yours is not true, because it is novel.

Rom.—Our teaching is the true, for it is everywhere the same; yours has no warrant, for it is but local and private.

Angl.—We go by Antiquity; that is, by the Apostles. Ancient consent is our standard of faith.

Rom.—We go by Catholicity. Universal consent is our standard of faith.

Angl.—You are cut off from the old Fathers.

Rom.—And you are cut off from the present living Church.

Here each disputant has a strong point; our strong point is the argument from the past, that of the Romanists is the argument from the present. It is a fact, however it is to be explained, that Rome has added to the Creed; and it is a fact, however it be justified, that we are estranged from the great body of Christians over the world; and each of these facts is at first sight a grave difficulty in the respective systems to which they belong.

The difficulty in the Roman view is as great as can well be conceived. The state of the case is this:—Scripture declares that there is one faith, that it is once for all delivered to the saints, that it is a deposit and is to be jealously guarded and transmitted. It gives in various places the particular articles of this faith, corresponding pretty

---

[9] The Catholic Newman editing this Anglican essay makes the imaginary dialogue shorter and blunter; in the original version, for example, the Roman Catholic says here: 'How do you determine that you are pure and we corrupt?'. See Textual Appendix for the dialogue that appeared in the *British Critic*, in which we are given access to the internal debates that were beginning to dominate Newman's mind at this time.

[7] nearly when put together to the articles of the Apostles' Creed. This Creed we find in substance in all the early churches, used at baptism as the substance of the revealed message brought to us in the Gospel, the privilege of every Christian and the foundation of the Church; and declared by the Fathers, who speak of it, in various ages and countries, to be sacred and unalterable, level to the most unlearned, sufficient for the most profound, the framework of faith, admitting indeed of development and enucleation,[10] but ever intended to preserve the outline and the proportions with which it was originally given. Moreover, when controversies arose, such as the Arian, this rule was prominently insisted on, not only "keep to what you have been taught," but "keep to what has been ever taught, keep to the old and first paths." Further, this Creed did remain thus inviolate till the time of the Deutero-Nicene Council, A.D. 787,[11] when, for the first time, a General Council, or what is called so, made an article of faith, in addition to not in development of, the Creed;[12] and it did so under the

---

[10] *enucleation*: literally, extracting the nucleus; hence, unfolding, explanation.

[11] *Deutero-Nicene Council, AD 787*: The Second Council of Nicaea (the seventh Ecumenical Council) met in 787 to deal with the iconoclastic crisis and issued a declaration concerning the veneration of sacred images. Some Eastern Churches honour the memory of this Council each year in the 'Sunday of the Triumph of Orthodoxy' and the 'Sunday of the Fathers of the Seventh Ecumenical Council.'

[12] [It is surely a paradox to say that the simple words of the Seventh General Council in 787, "Credentes in unum Deum, in Trinitate collaudatum, honorabiles ejus imagines salutamus; Qui sic non habent, anathema sint," or the Tridentine words, "Imagines Christi in templis habendas, eisque debitum honorem et venerationem impertiendam," are sufficient to constitute an extrinsic addition to the Creed, and are not a mere carrying out in worship, of faith in our crucified Lord, and in the communion of saints.] [N]

"*Credentes in unum* . . . : "We believe in one God, praised in Trinity, whose honourable images we salute; let anyone who does not hold this be condemned." Decree of the 2nd Council of Nicæa, 787.

following significant circumstances; first, this said General Council was the first of the Councils which rested the proof of its decree on grounds short of Scripture; the first that violated the doctrine of adherence to the practice or received opinion of Antiquity; the first which was held in a divided state of the Church, as the events before it and after it show; held with protests both from east and west; and enforced not without something like rebellion at first sight on the part of the Pope against the Imperial Power. Such is the history of the departure itself from the primitive theory [8] concerning the Creed; such was the first step. Now what has it issued in? in an assemblage of doctrines, which, as was observed above, whether right or wrong, have scarcely closer connection with the doctrines whether of the primitive Creed or the primitive Church than the doctrines of the Gospel have with those of the Law. In Antiquity, the main aspect in the economy of redemption comprises Christ, the Son of God, the Author and Dispenser of all grace and pardon, the Church His living representative, the sacraments her instruments, bishops her rulers, their collective decisions her voice, and Scripture her standard of truth. In the Roman schools,[13] we find St. Mary and the

---

"Imagines Christi . . . : "The images of Christ, of the Virgin Mother of God, and of the other saints are to be placed and retained especially in the churches, and that due honour and veneration is to be given them." Council of Trent, 25th Session, December 1563.

[13] [Of these heads of accusation, the only one which will be allowed by Catholics is that "the Pope is the ruler and teacher of the Church;" but this cannot be said to be a mere mediæval or modern doctrine; it seems to have been claimed as true and apostolic from the first in the Roman Church itself; *vide* the history of Popes Victor, Stephen, and Dionysius.] [N]

Victor: Pope St. Victor I (189-198). He excommunicated Polycrates, Bishop of Ephesus, who refused to support him over the date of Easter. Cf. Eusebius, Book 7, chapter 5. See below p.[102].

Stephen: Pope St. Stephen I (reigned 254-7). He over-ruled of Cyprian of Carthage on the rebaptism of heretics; cf. Letter to Cyprian ML 3.1154-1178 (AD

Saints the prominent objects of regard and dispensers of mercy, purgatory or else indulgences the means of obtaining it, the Pope the ruler and teacher of the Church, and miracles the warrant of doctrine. As to the doctrines of Christ's merits and eternal life and death, these are points not denied (God forbid!) but taken for granted, and passed by in order to make way for others of more present, pressing, and lively interest. That a certain change, then, in objective and external religion has come over the Latin, nay, and in a measure the Greek, Church, we consider to be a plain historical fact; a change indeed not so great as is common Protestantism, for that involves a radical change of inward temper and principle as well, as indeed its adherents are sometimes not slow to remind us, but a change sufficiently startling to recall to our minds, with very unpleasant sensations, the words of the Apostle, about preaching any other Gospel besides that which has been received.[14]

[9]

So much on the difficulty on the side of Rome; now let us consider the difficulty on our side: it is this. The Church was intended to be one kingdom or polity in all lands: this is its mark or note. Now there *is* a body mainly answering to this description, the communion of Rome, lineally descended from the ancient Church, and in possession of her territory. If there be a Church now, in nature and office

---

255/6) . Cf. 'On the resistance of Cyprian and Firmilian to the Church of Rome, in the question of baptism by heretics.' *Dev.* p. 26.; he also censured Marcian, the Novatianist Bishop of Arles and rehabilitated two repentant Spanish bishops. See below p.[102]

Dionysius: Pope Dionysius I (reigned 259-268). He held a Synod in Rome in 260 to correct the teaching of Bishop Dionysius of Alexandria and sent letters and money to persecuted churches in the East.

[14] *the words of the Apostle* . . . : cf. Galatians 1:9.

like the ancient Church, and like her image in prophecy, the Roman communion, it will be urged, and nothing but the Roman, is it. If there be Notes of the Church now, such as are given in prophecy and were fulfilled in Antiquity, she has them. If schism is separation from the body of Christians, we are schismatical. If schism now be what schism was formerly, we are excommunicated from the grace of the Gospel.

3.

This being the state of the case on both sides, divines of our Church are forced, as if from necessity, to make light of separation from Christendom, or to maintain that the few may be right and the many wrong; and divines of the Church of Rome are forced, by a like necessity, to make light of the judgment of Antiquity, or to maintain that Revelation is progressive, and that Christians now know more than the Fathers. Thus Archbishop Laud[15] says to Fisher, "As for the number and worth of men, they are no necessary concluders for truth. *Not number*; for who would be judged by the many? the time was when the Arians were too many for the orthodox."[16]—P. 302. His antagonist, on the other hand, says, "We acknowledge all due respect to the Fathers, and as much (to speak modestly) as any of our adversaries' party. But they must pardon us, if we prefer the [10] general interpretation of the present Church, *before the result of any man's particular fancy.*"—*Stillingfleet's*

---

[15] *Archbishop Laud*: William Laud (1573-1645), Archbishop of Canterbury from 1633 known for his High Church views. He was executed in 1645.
[16] *Archbishop Laud says to Fisher . . . :* The quotation is taken from *A relation of the conference between William Laud, Archbishop of Canterbury, and Mr Fisher the Jesuit* (1639). This concerned a public debate staged in 1622 between Laud and John Fisher (*vere* John Percy, 1569-1641), a Jesuit priest then in captivity.

Grounds, i. v. § 19.[17] On the one hand, Anglo-Catholics say, "Even though we were in schism, as we are not, such separation would not be disadvantageous, when faith is in danger;" and Roman Catholics say, "Even though we had innovated, as we have not, such innovation is not in error, when the Church is the author of it." Such is the difficulty on either side of the controversy. There seems to be but the alternative of saying, on the one hand, that the Church Catholic can go wrong; on the other, that the faith of ages may be remodelled. It is a difficulty meeting every inquirer, which he must fairly look in the face and be content to begin with. And it is felt to be a difficulty by the two parties in the controversy; by the Anglo-Catholic, as shown in the anxious endeavour of our divines, till the course of events made it hopeless, to fraternize with the Protestants of the Continent, which, considering the men who have evinced it, is quite unaccountable till we come to see what their sore point in the discussion was their separation from Christendom; and by Roman Catholics, as is abundantly evidenced by their shufflings and shiftings to and fro on the question, whether they do or do not keep to Antiquity. On this subject it is plainly impossible to get an intelligible answer from them; whether they have added to the articles of faith or not, go by the Fathers or not, keep to the ancient creed or not,—what they hold, what they do not hold, what is the true sense of their decrees, what their practical interpreters, and what the limits of interpretation.

---

[17] *Stillingfleet's Grounds – A Rational Account of the Grounds of Protestant Religion:* (1664) by Edward Stillingfleet (1635-99), a prominent Anglican theologian who became bishop of Worcester in 1689.

But now, as to the respective views themselves, Roman and Anglican, the maintainer of the former has this advantage, that the fact which he alleges against us, want of Catholicity, is far more level to the apprehension of men in general than that which we allege against him, want of primitiveness in doctrine, while the logical force of his fact is such as plausibly to throw discredit upon our contrary fact. It is very obvious to the whole world that the English Church is separated from the rest of Christendom; it is not evident, except to a very few, that the faith of Rome is an addition to the primitive. Again, suspicion is thrown on the allegation that it is an addition, by the very fact, unquestionable as it is, that far the greater part of Christendom denies that allegation. Our argument then has to sustain the disadvantage both of the certainty in fact, and the apparent cogency in reasoning, of their argument. And while the argument of the Romanists is thus practically efficient, it has a simplicity in its form which is very plausible. It provides for the special difficulty which we urge against their religious system, before we bring it; whereas ours does not similarly account for and dispose of the difficulty which they bring against our system. Roman Catholics urge against us that we are separated from Christendom; now the fact of our keeping to the primitive faith had no tendency whatever to bring about their deflection from it, that is, to explain how it comes to pass that we are practically estranged from the great Christian body. On the other hand, when we in turn urge against them that they have added to the faith, they are not unwilling in a certain sense to grant it; they account for it by referring it to a cause recognized in their system,—to the power which they maintain is possessed by the great Christian body in

[11]

matters of faith, of developing the faith. Their alleged fact, that they are the Church Catholic, serves to account for our alleged fact, that they believe more than the ancients. We bring little against them which is not at once solved on the supposition of their assumption being true; they bring a charge against us which remains just where it was, though our assumption be ever so much granted. It is still a difficulty how the great body of Christians should have gone wrong, even granting our assumption that they have; it is no difficulty that the great body should have added to the faith, when we grant their assumption that they have the power.[18]

[12]

Yet, in spite of all this, they are in a difficulty, even in this portion of their theory, when it is narrowly considered,—not to go to other portions, which do not here come into notice. Allowing the Church Catholic ever so much power over the faith, allowing that it may add what it will, provided it does not contradict what has been determined in former times, yet let us come to the plain question, Does the Church, according to Romanists, know more now than the Apostles knew? Their theory seems to be that the whole faith was present in the minds of the Apostles, nay, of all saints at all times, but in great measure as a matter of mere temper, feeling, and unconscious opinion, that is, implicitly, not in the way of exact statements and in an intellectual form. All men certainly hold a number of truths, and act on them, without knowing it; when a question is asked about them, then they are

---

[18] ["I am very far more sure that England is in schism than that the Roman additions to the Primitive Creed may not be developments."—May 4, 1843. *Vid.* Apologia, 1841-1845.] [N]

obliged to reflect what their opinion has ever been, and they bring before themselves and assent to doctrines which before were but latent within them. We have all heard of men changing to so-called Unitarianism, and confessing on a review of themselves that they had been Unitarians all along without knowing it, till some accident tore the bandage off their eyes. In like manner, the Roman Catholics, we suppose, would maintain that the Apostles were implicit Tridentines; that the Church held in the first age what she holds now; only that heresy, by raising questions, has led to her throwing her faith into dogmatic shape, and has served to precipitate truths which before were held in solution. Now this is all very well in the abstract, but let us return to the point, as to what the Apostles held and did, and what they did not. Does the Romanist mean, for instance, to tell us that St. Paul the Apostle, when he was in perils of robbers or peril by the sea, offered up his addresses to St. Mary, and vowed some memorial to her, if she would be pleased "deprecari pro illo filium Dei"?[19] Does he mean to say that the same Apostle, during that period of his life when as yet he was not "perfect" or had "attained,"[20] was accustomed to pray that

[13]

---

[19] [No; he need not so mean. "It is sometimes asked, 'Why do not the sacred writers mention our Lady's greatness?' I answer, she was or may have been alive when the Apostles and the Evangelists wrote; there was just one book of Scripture, the Apocalypse, certainly, written after her death, and that book does (so to say) canonize and crown her ... If invocation of her were necessary to salvation, there would be grave reasons for doubting of the salvation of St. Chrysostom, St. Athanasius, or of the primitive martyrs; nay, I should like to know whether St. Augustine in all his voluminous writings, invokes her once."—Letter to Dr. Pusey. Invocations are matters of practice, usage, and discipline, not simply of dogma.] [N]

"deprecari pro illo filium Dei": "intercede for him to the Son of God"

[20] *"perfect" or had "attained"*: "Not as though I had already attained, either were already perfect: but I follow after, if that I may apprehend that for which also I am apprehended of Christ Jesus." Philippians 3:12.

the merits of St. John the Baptist should be imputed to him? Did he or did he not hold that St. Peter could give indulgences to shorten the prospective sufferings of the Corinthians in purgatory? We do not deny that St. Paul certainly does bring out his thoughts only in answer to express questions asked, and according to the occasion; or that St. John has written a Gospel, on the one hand later, on the other more dogmatic, than his fellow-Evangelists, in consequence of the rise of heresy. We do not at all mean to affirm that the sacred writers said out at one time all they had to say. There are many things we can imagine them doing and holding, which yet, in matter of fact, we believe they did not do, or did not hold. We can imagine them administering extreme unction or wearing copes. Again, there are many things which they could neither hold nor do, merely from the circumstances of the times or the moment. They could not determine whether General Councils might or might not be held without the consent of princes, or determine the authority of the Vulgate before it was written, or enjoin infant baptism before Christians had children, or decide upon the value of heretical baptism before they were heretics, and before those heretics were baptized. But still there are limits to these concessions; we cannot imagine an Apostle saying and doing what Romanists say and do; can they imagine it themselves? Do they themselves, for instance, think that St. Paul was in the habit of saying what Bellarmine[21] and others say,—"Laus Deo *Virginique*

[14]

---

[21] *Bellarmine*: St Robert Bellarmine (1542-1621), Jesuit, Cardinal and Doctor of the Church; a leading theologian of the Catholic Reformation, known especially for his apologetical works defending Catholicism against Protestant critics.

Matri"?[22] Would they not pronounce a professed Epistle of St. Paul's which contained these words spurious on this one ground?

It may be objected that this argument proves too much for our purpose, since our doctrines also, as those of the Trinity and Incarnation, are developments; so that it may in turn be asked of us, did the Apostles hold the Athanasian doctrine,[23] or, on the other hand, do we know more than they? But we avow they *did* hold the Athanasian doctrine; they did hold those developments which afterwards were incorporated in the Church system. There is no paradox in maintaining of any individual in the Apostles' lifetime that [15] he held them; for heresies arose while they were on earth, quite sufficient to lead to their holding and transmitting to the Church views as explicit and formal as those which were afterwards recognized and adopted in Councils and fixed in creeds; not to say that a mystery naturally leads the mind of itself, without external stimulus, to trace it to its ultimate points. There is nothing strange then in maintaining that the Apostles held just what the after centuries held; it is natural that they should do so. On the other hand, there being nothing in the Apostles' day to elicit the worship of St. Mary or knowledge of purgatory, which did not also exist in the age immediately after them,—that age not having these portions of Christian truth, (as Romanists allege,) because there was nothing to elicit them,—it would be very strange to maintain that the Apostles had what the age immediately after them had not. If the argument of the

---

[22] *Laus Deo* Virginique Matri: 'Praise be to God *and to his Virgin Mother*', a Latin prayer often found at the end of Catholic published works.
[23] *the Athanasian doctrine*: the teaching of St. Athanasius (c.296-373), Doctor of the Church; the great champion of the divinity of Christ against Arianism.

absence of an external cause avails to account for the ignorance of the early Church, it is a reason for a similar ignorance on the part of the Apostles; on the other hand, if the Apostles did teach the doctrines of purgatory or the worship of the Saints, as Rome teaches them, it is incredible that they should not have transmitted them to the generations immediately following.[24] As it is, the early Church not knowing, and the later knowing them, it is difficult to say which it is most congruous for such a system to maintain, that the Apostles did not know them, or that they did.

[16]

To this must be added the exceeding and almost incredible boldness of saying that popes and bishops, nay, private Christians, know now, what Apostles did not know then; as if we are to St. Paul and St. John as they are to Moses. The feeling of this difficulty has led some Roman writers to the theory of a *disciplina arcani*[25] in the Church, as if this would serve to extricate them from it.

4.

However, our object here is not to expose the difficulty which occurs in the Roman theory of the Church, but to solve that which is urged against our own. We said above

---

[24] [The age following the Apostles did hold, in various parts of Christendom, one doctrine in particular about the Blessed Virgin, which, because of its proximity to the Apostles, and of its reception in such various parts, must reasonably be referred to their teaching,—which has been taught continuously from that time to this,—and which contains in it all that Catholics hold concerning her intrinsic gifts and powers, viz., that "she is the Second Eve." This dogma required no heresy for its development.—Vid. Letter to Dr. Pusey.] [N]

[25] disciplina arcani: 'discipline of the secret', a seventeenth century term referring to the custom practised by the early Christians of keeping a detailed knowledge of the sacred mysteries from the pagans and even from catechumens until they had fully received the sacraments of initiation.

that we considered the English difficulty had not been sufficiently met, and we promised some remarks upon it, to which all that has hitherto been said is but introductory.

The difficulty is this: the Church being "one body," how can we, estranged as we are from every part of it except our own dependencies, unrecognized and without intercommunion, maintain our right to be considered part of that body? This is the objection: and in discussing it we are of course to put out of question the circumstance that our creed is sounder than the Roman. For we are not stating the grounds on which we keep aloof from Rome, but have to meet an incidental difficulty which that keeping aloof involves. If indeed we considered that the Pope was Antichrist, and had denied the foundation of the faith, then indeed our keeping aloof would justify itself. If Rome is apostate, she has no longer claims on us as a Church; but while she is allowed to be a Church, she has claims. In this point of view it is, that the ultra-Protestant theory, which [17] ignores or denies the Scripture promises made to the Church, becomes thereby much simpler than our own. It denies the Church of Rome to be a Church, and so gets rid of the question why we are estranged from it; and this is why the theory that Rome is the city of Antichrist was so popular at the time of the Reformation. It made short work with a number of questions, which else would have been perplexing. It would be a similar simplification of the Roman theory, if Rome gave up the Fathers. But while Rome, though not deferring to the Fathers, recognizes them, and England, while not deferring to the larger body of the Church, recognizes it, both Rome and England have a point to clear up. We are now to clear up our own difficulty; and we repeat, it avails nothing towards doing so, to say that our faith is more ancient than the faith of Rome. Still the communion of Rome more nearly answers to the Church of the prophecies than ours.

One point is acknowledged, one must be conceded, and one will be maintained, by all Anglo-Catholics;—that the Church is One, is the point of *doctrine*; that we are estranged from the body of the Church, is the point of *fact*; and that we still have the means of grace among us, is our point of *controversy*. These points being set down, there are various ways of reconciling them, such as the following:— 1. That intercommunion is not necessary to unity. 2. That, though it be, the absence of unity does not at once involve a state of schism. 3. That, though it do, yet that the grace of the ordinances is not necessarily suspended in a state of schism. Different minds will resign themselves to one or other of these solutions, or modify them by one another, according to their particular feelings and principles. What [18] we are going to say on the subject will bear on them all, in a measure embrace them all, and therefore in turn is exposed to be modified by all, and may be adapted to any of them; but is intended, instead of following any one of them exclusively, rather as a statement of the general view maintained by our divines, whatever be the more correct analysis of it.

The Anglican view, then, of the Church has ever been this, that its separate portions need not be united together, for their essential completeness, except by the tie of descent from one original. They are like a number of colonies sent out from a mother country, or as the tribes or nations which spring from a common parent. Jerusalem was the mother Church; they all come from her; they are Churches in that they come from her; but they are not bound to any union together in order to be Churches, any more than branches of an extended family, or colonies of a mother country, need have a common table or common purse, in order to have the blood and name of their ancestor. The Apostolical Succession is necessary in order to their possessing claim of descent; but that being secured, each branch is bound to conform to the country, and form alliance with the institutions, in which it finds itself, quite irrespectively of all the rest. Each Church is independent of all the rest, except indeed so far as the civil power unites any number of them together. They are in consequence, as Churches, under the supremacy of the state or monarch whom they obey in temporals, and may be used by him as one of the functions of his government, as his ministers of public instruction. Further, it is a natural, though of course not necessary, consequence of this view of the Church, to confine spiritual power to the sacramental or quasi-sacramental privileges. Ordination is the bishop's prerogative; but everything else [19] save ordination comes from the king. The whole jurisdiction is his; his are all the spiritual courts; his the right of excommunication; his the control of revenues; his the organization of dioceses; his the appointment of bishops. It is another extreme consequence of this theory, that our own Church was not allowed to recognize her own daughters in Scotland and America; nor was accounted as one Church with the Irish, till the Act of Union[26] in the beginning of this century, determined by the authority of Parliament, that the established Irish Church was the Church of England in

---

[26] *Act of Union*: or more accurately Acts of Union: the Union with Ireland Act and Act of Union (Ireland) were both passed in 1800 but came into effect the following year.

Ireland. It was this same extreme view upon which Cranmer acted, upon the accession of Edward the Sixth,[27] and which is expressed in the commission which he took out for his archbishopric. "Whereas," says the king, "all authority of jurisdiction, and indeed jurisdiction altogether, that which is called ecclesiastical as well as secular, emanated from the first from the royal power as from a supreme head, and the source and spring of all magistracies within our kingdom, etc.: We decree that thou shouldst *take our stead* in the manner and form below mentioned, and shouldst be licensed to ordain whomsoever within thy diocese of Canterbury thou shalt find fitting in character and learning, etc., etc." Sometimes indeed this document has been supposed to claim to the king the power of Ordination; so extravagant an assumption has of course no connection with the theory under review; for the words need only be taken to mean, what has been usually held among us after Cranmer's time,—that the Church, though really possessed of powers, is precluded from exercising them without the leave of the State, and has no jurisdiction independent of it. Lord Thurlow,[28] however, took a view of our Church's theory still

[20] more extreme than this imputed to Cranmer, when he maintained, as it is reported, against Horsley,[29] that the Scotch Bishops were not Bishops, except by a play upon words, because they had no seats in the House of Lords.

---

[27] *Edward the Sixth*: Edward VI (1537-53), only surviving son of Henry VIII and his third wife, Jane Seymour; King of England and Ireland, 1547-53.
[28] *Thurlow*: Edward Thurlow, First Baron Thurlow (1731-1806), lawyer and Lord Chancellor of Great Britain (1778-92).
[29] *Horsley*: Samuel Horsley (1733-1806), appointed (at Lord Thurlow's recommendation) to the bishopric of St David's in 1788. He was later translated to Rochester (1793) and St Asaph (1802).

These extravagances serve to illustrate the English theory, even if it were only by way of contrast. But they also show what it will admit, without infringing its notion of what a Church consists in. If indeed the Church is essentially one and one only organized body in every age and country, then such an absorption of a branch of it into a nation is nothing else but a formal state of schism. If, on the other hand, her essence consists in her descent from the Apostles, such an absorption, or such a suspension of intercommunion with other branches, as is consequent upon it, may be expedient or inexpedient, allowable or culpable, but does not touch the life of the Church, or compromise the tenure of its privileges. Each diocese is a perfect independent Church, sufficient for itself; and the communion of Christians one with another, and the unity of them all together, lie, not in a mutual understanding, intercourse, and combination, not in what they do in common, but in what they are and what they have in common, in their possession of the Succession, their Episcopal form, their Apostolic faith, and the use of the Sacraments. Accordingly Stillingfleet says: "We have not separated from the whole Christian world in anything wherein the whole Christian world is agreed; but to disagree from the particular Churches of the Christian world in such things wherein those Churches differ among themselves, is not to separate from the Christian world, but to disagree in some things from such particular Churches ... There can be no separation from the true Catholic Church but in such things wherein it is Catholic; now it is not Catholic in anything, but what properly relates to its being a constitution."—*Grounds*, ii. 4, § 2.

[21]

25

In this extract it is implied that mutual intercourse is but an *accident* of the Church, not of its essence. The same view is strongly maintained by Barrow[30] in his Discourse on the Unity of the Church. Prefacing it with a motto from Augustine,[31] "Non habet charitatem Dei, qui ecclesiæ non diligit unitatem,"[32] he proceeds to determine in what this unity consists; viz., first, in unity of faith; next, in mutual charity and goodwill; thirdly, in the gift of one and the same Spirit; fourthly, in the mystical body of Christ; fifthly, in the mutual intercourse of individual Christians, in mutual peace and love, in common works of piety and devotion, common prayer, Eucharist, conferences, and common defence of the truth; sixthly, in agreement of all bishops in faith and good offices; seventhly, in sameness of order and government; eighthly, in matters of prudential discipline. Then he adds:

"All these kinds of unity do plainly agree to the universal Church of Christ; but the question is, whether the Church is also necessarily, by the design and appointment of God, to be in way of external policy under one singular government or jurisdiction of any kind; so as a kingdom or commonwealth are united under the command of one monarch or one senate? That the Church is *capable* of such

---

[30] *Barrow*: Isaac Barrow (1630-77) was Master of Trinity College, Cambridge (1673-77), a leading mathematician (his students included Isaac Newton) and a theologian ('Arminian' in sympathy). His works were published posthumously, including volumes of sermons, *Exposition of the Creed*, *A Treatise of the Pope's Supremacy* and the *Discourse on the Unity of the Church*. Barrow is not to be confused with his uncle, also Isaac Barrow (1613-80), Bishop of Sodor and Man and St Asaph.

[31] *St Augustine*: (354-430), Bishop of Hippo and Doctor of the Church; celebrated for his many writings which have been highly influential in shaping Catholic theological thought.

[32] *"non habet charitatem Dei, qui ecclesiae non diligit unitatem"*: "He does not have the love of God, who does not love the unity of the Church."

an union, is not the controversy; that it is *possible* it should be so united, (supposing it may happen that all Christians may be reduced to one *nation* or one *civil* regiment, or that several nations *spontaneously* may confederate and combine themselves into one ecclesiastical commonwealth, administered by the same spiritual rulers and judges according to the same laws,) I do not question; that when in a manner all Christendom did consist of subjects to the Roman Empire, the Church then did arrive near such an unity, I do not at present contest; but that such an union of all Christians is *necessary*, or that it was ever *instituted by Christ*, I cannot grant; and for my refusal of that opinion, I shall assign divers reasons."—P. 449, ed. 1836.

[22]

These reasons are, first, that Scripture nowhere insists on a political union, on "one monarch, or one senate, or one sanhedrim, which is a pregnant sign that none such was then instituted;" next, that the Apostles took no pains to establish any such polity; thirdly, that the Fathers "do make the unity of the Church to consist only in these virtues of faith, charity, peace, not in this political union;" fourthly, that it could not be without a sovereign authority, which is nowhere established by Christ or His Apostles; fifthly, that the primitive state of the Church did not well comport with such an unity;" sixthly, that the autonomy or liberty of the Churches long continued in practice inviolate;" seventhly, that such a political unity is unevangelical; eighthly, inconvenient; ninthly, needless; tenthly, not expedient for the design of Christianity; eleventhly, not necessary to the idea of unity.

In the course of his remarks he lays down the following principle, which other writers have improved upon, and which does admit of such improvement: "The case of bishops was like that of princes, each of whom hath a free superintendence in his own territory, but for to uphold justice and peace in the world, or between adjacent nations, the intercourse of several princes is needful. The peace of the Church was preserved by communion of all parts together, not by the subjection of the rest to one part." This is a statement which writers like Dodwell[33] and Hickes[34] have illustrated with especial pains and fulness. They teach, agreeably with what has above been called the Anglican theory, that the Church is complete in one bishopric; that a number of bishoprics are but reiterations of one, and add nothing to the perfection of the system. As there is one Bishop invisible in heaven, so there is but one bishop on earth; and the multitude of bishops are not acknowledged in the Gospel system *as* many, or as if (viewed *as* representatives of the Bishop invisible) they were *capable* of mutual relations one with another, but as being one and all shadows and organs of one and the same divine reality. If so, they are neither capable of direct communion one with another as bishops, nor of schism one from another, since their only communion as bishops is with Him whom they represent, and they have communion with each other in and through Him; and while they have communion with Him, they have communion one with another, though they never

[23]

---

[33] *Dodwell*: Henry Dodwell (1641-1711), Dublin-born non-juring clergyman and theologian, who was much concerned in fighting against the Erastianism of his time. His theological works included *Dissertationes Cyprianicae* (1682) and *A vindication of the deprived bishops, asserting their spiritual rights against a lay-deprivation* (1692), which argued from St Cyprian that the new bishops were essentially schismatical.

[34] *Hickes*: George Hickes (1642-1715), nonjuring bishop, antiquary and theologian. *Of the Christian Priesthood* and *Of the Dignity of the Episcopal Order*, both published in 1707, were reprinted in the *Library of Anglo-Catholic Theology* (1847).

saw, never acted with each other. It is true they can act with each other in Synods, but then they form a sort of board of presbyters, and are our Lord's Council, as Ignatius[35] views them. Considered as bishops, each is the ultimate centre of unity and independent channel of grace; they are all equal; and schism consists in separating from them, or setting up against them in their particular place. Introducing one Church into the heart of another, or erecting altar against altar, is schism, in the ecclesiastical sense of the word, and forfeits the gifts of the Gospel: for it strikes at the principle of unity and touches the life of the Church.

Such is the essence of unity, and the essence of schism; but an organized union of Churches, though proper and fitting, does not enter into the formal notion of a Church; [24] and the fact of dissensions between Churches, though a breach of the law of love, as little avails to unchurch them, as lukewarmness, or corruption of doctrine, or ambition, or covetousness. Intercommunion is a duty as other duties, but is not the tenure or instrument of the communion between the unseen world and this; and much more is the confederacy of sees and churches—the metropolitan, patriarchal, and papal systems—mere matter of expedience, or of natural duty from long custom, or of propriety from gratitude and reverence, or of necessity from voluntary oaths and engagements, or of ecclesiastical force from the canons of Councils, but not necessary in order to the conveyance of grace, or for fulfilment of the ceremonial law, as it may be called, of Unity. Bishop is superior to

---

[35] *Ignatius*: St. Ignatius of Antioch (35-108), Father of the Church, was St Peter's successor at Antioch and wrote seven epistles to various Christian communities as he was being taken to Rome to be thrown to the wild beasts. These epistles contain much teaching on the episcopate. See 'The Theology of St.Ignatius', *Ess.* I, p.222ff.

bishop only in rank, not in real power; and the Bishop of
Rome, the head of the Catholic world, is not the centre of
unity, except as having a primacy of order. Accordingly,
even granting for argument's sake that the English Church
violated a duty in the sixteenth century, in releasing itself
from the Roman Supremacy, still it did not thereby commit
that special sin which cuts off from it the fountains of grace,
and is called schism. It was essentially complete without
Rome, and naturally independent of it; it had in the course
of years, whether by usurpation or not, come under the
supremacy of Rome, and now, whether by rebellion or not,
it is free from it; and as it did not enter into the Church
Invisible by joining Rome, so it was not cast out of it by
breaking from Rome. These were accidents in its history,
involving, indeed, sin in individuals, but not affecting the
Church as a Church.

This view of the subject throws light upon the Oath of
[25]   Supremacy,[36] which declares that "no foreign prelate hath or
ought to have any jurisdiction, power, pre-eminence, or
authority within this realm." In other words, there is nothing
in the Apostolic system which gives authority to the Pope
over the Catholic Church, more than to any other bishop. It
is altogether an ecclesiastical arrangement; not a point *de
fide*, but of expedience, custom, or piety, which cannot be
claimed as if the Pope *ought* to have it, any more than, on
the other hand, the king could claim the Supremacy by
divine right, the claim of both the one and the other resting,

---

[36] *Oath of Supremacy*: Initially introduced by the 1534 Act of Supremacy and
reintroduced by Elizabeth I in 1559, it recognised the monarch as Supreme Head
or (from 1559) Governor of the Church of England and had to be taken by all
those appointed to public or ecclesiastical office.

not on duty or revelation, but on specific engagement. We find ourselves as a Church under the king now, and we obey him; we were under the Pope formerly, and we obeyed him. "Ought" does not in any degree come into the question.

5.

Dodwell has illustrated this subject at great length in his Discourse concerning the one Altar and one Priesthood; and in his treatise *De Episcopo Unitatis principio*, which is the seventh of his Cyprianic Dissertations.[37] In the former of these he is led to comment on the language of St. Ignatius, as in the latter on that of St. Cyprian;[38] both Fathers strongly confirming the view of unity which we have been drawing out, viz., that the Episcopal is the only divine jurisdiction. He begins the former treatise by referring to the constitution of the Jewish Church, and observes that the Apostolical Fathers consider Christianity to be in point of worship and Church government, what it is in other respects also, nothing else than a mystical Judaism; that as baptism took the place of circumcision, so has the Bishop taken the place of the High Priest, and the Christian altar the place of the Jewish. Hence St. Clement of Rome[39] deduces from the [26] budding of Aaron's rod the sacredness of the episcopal office under the Gospel, and from the subordination of the Temple hierarchy infers the necessity of the Orders of the Christian ministry. He next shows that among the Jews the altar had ever been the symbol and centre of unity, and a setting up a rival altar the essential mark of schism. This

---

[37] *Cyprianic Dissertations*: Henry Dodwell's *Dissertationes Cyprianicae* of 1682.

[38] *St Cyprian*: St Cyprian (d. 258) was bishop of Carthage, a leading opponent of the Novatian heresy and a martyr under the Emperor Valerian.

[39] *St Clement of Rome*: St Clement I (d. 97) was the third bishop of Rome after St Peter and the author of a letter to the Corinthians. He is honoured as a martyr.

doctrine was first insisted on in their controversy with the Samaritans, and is sanctioned by our Lord in His discourse with the woman at the well.[40] It was brought out into system by the Hellenistic Jews, who, on the ground of such commands as that made to Moses, to "make all things according to the fashion showed him in the Mount," held that the provisions of the Mosaic ritual were adumbrations of things unseen, and felt that there was some deep mystical sense under the letter; and, not having the true key which the Gospel afterwards supplied, made a conjectural interpretation, which at least serves to illustrate the true one;—"They designed their visible altar," he observes, "as a means of communicating with that which was mystical and invisible. They also allowed a mystical invisible priesthood of the Logos, with whom they were to communicate by maintaining a communication with their visible priesthood."—P. 190. "Accordingly He must be the invisible or spiritual Hierophanta[41] and Priest, performing invisibly all that was visibly transacted by the High Priest in their visible ministry. He was to assist in the invisible ideal altar, and to offer up mystical sacrifices, as the High Priest did visible ones on the visible altar. The title of Ἀρχιερεύς[42] is accordingly given to the Λογος,"[43] by Philo;[44] "and the High Priest in going into the Holy of Holies personated the

---

[40] *his discourse with the woman at the well*: cf. John 4:5-42

[41] *Hierophanta*: Greek ἱεροφάντης, interpreter of sacred mysteries.

[42] Ἀρχιερεύς: archiereus or high priest

[43] Λογος: Logos, Word

[44] *Philo*: Philo of Alexandria (20 BC – 50 AD), who tried to harmonize Greek and Jewish philosophy and whose writings on the Logos influenced early Christian writers.

entrance of the Logos into heaven, according to the reasoning of the author to the Hebrews."[45]—Pp. 204, 205.

Dodwell then goes on to show that bishops have taken [27] the place of the High Priest in a similar but still higher office than was ascribed by the Hellenists to the latter, as if in fulfilment of our Lord's words, that not Sichem only and Jerusalem, but that every city everywhere should have a temple and an altar, a priest and a sacrifice of its own[46]. St. Clement's implied testimony in behalf of the continuance of the Jewish ritual in a spiritual form under the Gospel, has already been mentioned. Dodwell argues the same, at length, from the book of Revelations and St. Ignatius's Epistles. In the inspired Apostle's prophecy, the Almighty is described with seven Spirits around His throne;[47] and, in like manner, our Lord is represented with seven stars and seven candlesticks, or seven churches[48] with their bishops, who are the messengers between Christ and His people, as the Spirits are between God and the world. But again, the bishop in his turn was attended, according to the ancient rule, by seven deacons, to signify that he was not only the messenger, but the representative or type of our Lord, or that he was to the Church on earth what God was to the Church in Heaven. That the deacons answer to the Angels or Spirits is plain from such passages as Heb. i. 14, where the latter are called "ministering" or diaconic "Spirits;" or again, from Zech. iii. 9, iv. 10, where they are called "the *eyes* of the Lord which *run to and fro* through the whole earth," words which exactly describe both the title and

---

[45] *according to the Letter to the Hebrews*: Cf. Hebrews 9

[46] *our Lord's words . . .* : Cf. John 4:5ff

[47] *seven Spirits around His throne*: Cf. Revelation 1: 4; 4: 5

[48] *seven stars and seven candlesticks, or seven churches*: Cf. Revelation 1: 20

office of deacons in the early Church. Since then the deacons represent the Angels, it follows that, in like manner, the bishop to whom they minister represents Christ. And in order to preserve this mystical meaning, great stress was laid in primitive times on the number of the deacons being neither more nor less than seven. Seven were [28] appointed by the Apostles at their first institution;[49] seven, according to tradition, was the number appointed by St. Mark at Alexandria; seven were in use at Rome not only in the pontificate of Cornelius,[50] but even as late as the age of Sozomen.[51] And the council of Neocæsarea[52] made it a universal rule, whatever was the size of each Church.

This will enable us to understand the high language in which bishops are spoken of in St. Ignatius's Epistles. As soon as we comprehend that there is a correspondence between the celestial and ecclesiastical hierarchy, words, which at first sight seem extravagant, have their legitimate and sufficient meaning; and still more so when it is considered that the especial sin he is warning his brethren against is schism, for if the bishop be Christ's representative, the effect of separating from the bishop is thus simply shown to be a separating from Christ. For instance, he says, "Jesus Christ, our inseparable life, is the mind of the Father; like as the bishops, appointed through

---

[49] ... *at their first institution*: Cf. Acts 6:5

[50] *Cornelius*: St Cornelius, Pope 251-53. His election was contested by Novatian, who declared himself anti-pope. The two disagreed over the *lapsi*, Christians who had apostasised during times of persecution and now wished to return to full communion with the Church. Unlike Novatian, St Cornelius favoured their readmission and in this he was supported by St Cyprian.

[51] *Sozomen*: Salminius Hermias Sozomenus (c.400-c.450), Palestinian-born historian and author of the *Historia Ecclesiastica*.

[52] *council of Neocaesarea*: (315) produced fifteen disciplinary canons later adopted at Chalcedon (451).

all coasts of the earth, are according to the mind of Jesus Christ."—*Eph.* 3. "A man is not misleading this his visible bishop, but is trifling with the Bishop Invisible; and so the question is not with flesh, but with God, who seeth the secrets."—*Magn.* 3. "Likewise let all men give heed to the deacons, as to Jesus Christ, as also to the bishop as to the Son of the Father, and to the presbyters as to a council of God, and as a company of Apostles; without these the name of church is not."—*Trall.* 3. In this last passage, according to Dodwell, presbyters are added as typifying the Apostolic College, and completing the hierarchy; agreeably to St. John's vision of the heavenly Presence above, where before the throne were "seven lamps of fire burning, which are the seven spirits of God,"[53] and "round about the throne four and twenty elders sitting,"[54] emblematical of the College of Apostles, (doubled, as St. Clement of Alexandria[55] says, to show the interest which Gentiles as well as Jews had in them,) and of the presbyterate, because they have the sacerdotal symbol of "vials full of odour, which are the prayers of saints."[56] Such is the substance of this work of Dodwell's, which has surely much solid and cogent matter, even if it has something of fancifulness or refinement in parts; his object in it being to urge upon Dissenters the necessity of conformity, without his being forced to carry on the argument to conclusions favourable to the Church of Rome, and this, by the maintenance of the simple principle

[29]

---

[53] *"seven lamps of fire burning, which are the seven spirits of God"*: Revelation 1: 4, 4: 5

[54] *"round about the throne four and twenty elders sitting"*: Revelation 4:4

[55] *St Clement of Alexandria*: (c.150-c.215), Church Father in the Alexandrian School and teacher of Origen.

[56] *"vials full of odour, which are the prayers of the saints"*: Revelation 5:8

that Bishops everywhere, and not the Pope, are the elementary centres of unity.

In his Cyprianic Dissertations he discusses the subject more immediately in relation to the Romanists. It is well known that St Cyprian has written a treatise on the Unity of the Church, besides various Epistles on the same subject, with a view of meeting an error of his day, that, in the case of the lapsed, the communion of martyrs was efficacious and saving, even though the bishop refused to reconcile them to the Church. He insists in consequence, in the work in question, on there being but one Church; on the Catholic Church; on the instrumentality of Cornelius, the then Bishop of Rome, in uniting men with the Church; on St. Peter as the principle of unity, and on similar topics. Now the question between us and the Romanists is, whether *the* Church spoken of, in which is salvation, is the particular and local Church everywhere, (or, again, the abstract Church of which the local is its realization under the bishop,) or whether it is the literal and actual extended communion of all Christians everywhere viewed as one body under the supremacy of the Pope. Dodwell maintains [30] the former side of the alternative—that the whole Church is (if the expression may be allowed) crystallized out of a number of independent organic and complete units. Schism then, in its formal sense, is not the separation of Church from Church, which when separated from each other are still perfect, but laceration of the organic structure of the particular or local Church itself. In proof of this view he urges St. Cyprian's remarkable words, "Episcopatus unus est, cujus à singulis *in solidum* pars tenetur"—*De Unit.* "The episcopate is one which each bishop shares *in fulness*," or "so shares as to have a full interest in it." Again, his definition of a Church is, "a people united to a priest, and a flock adhering to its pastor."—*Ep*. 69. Accordingly, as this illustrious Father proceeds, "the Bishop is in the Church and the Church in the Bishop; and whoever are not with the Bishop are not in the Church;" where "the Bishop" cannot mean the Pope, and therefore "the Church" means the Church under the Bishop; that is, the local or integral Church. Again, elsewhere he uses the word "Bishops" in the plural. "Let those only remain outside the Church, who have receded from the Church. Let those only be apart from the Bishops, who have rebelled against the Bishops."—*Ep*. 43. And elsewhere he says, that "heresies and schisms have ever had their rise in disobedience to the priest of God, and neglect of the *one priest in the Church at the time*, the one judge at the time, in the place of Christ."—*Ep*. 59. So much may be argued from the passages themselves; but what decides the matter is, that in these and similar letters Rome does not come into the controversy, the matters spoken of relating to Africa.

This relation to Africa also decides his meaning when he speaks of the see of St. Peter, Cathedra Petri, and claims [31] authority for it. In one place he so speaks with reference to Cornelius, Bishop of Rome, whom he supports in preference to Novatian,[57] as filling "the place of Peter, and the rank of the sacerdotal see."—*Ep*. 40. But elsewhere he uses the same language writing to his own people in

---

[57] *Novatian*: (200-58), theologian and anti-pope (251-58) who took a more rigorist approach than Cornelius towards those who had lapsed from the faith under persecution.

condemnation of Felicissimus, the African schismatic:[58] "God is one, and Christ is one, and the Church one, and the see one, founded by the Lord's voice upon Peter." This plainly shows that he considers St. Peter's authority not as bound up in the see of Rome only, but as extending to all bishops. He does not speak of him merely as the local Bishop of Rome, but as the type of all bishops, and as if ruling in every see all over Christendom. And every Bishop is St. Peter's successor: and to separate from St. Peter does not mean separation from Rome, but from the local see wherever a man finds himself; though it was natural, of course, since that Apostle had a more intimate connexion with Rome than with other places, that, when St. Cyprian speaks of Rome, he should especially be led to mention St. Peter. But the best proof that by St. Peter's see Cyprian did not mean simply to designate Rome, or by St. Peter's authority the Papal power, is contained in the history of his own controversy with Pope Stephen[59] on the subject of heretical baptism. Had he so accounted him to be the one Bishop in the Church, as the Roman interpretation of these passages requires, he never would have spoken of Stephen's "obstinatio," or, as he did, in his translation of Firmilian's letter,[60] of his "audacia et insolentia."[61] But if by the

---

[58] *Felicissimus, the African schismatic*: a deacon of Carthage who briefly led a schism, sometimes interpreted as a presbyteral reaction to the episcopate of St Cyprian.

[59] *Pope Stephen*: St Stephen I (Pope, 254-57), who is chiefly remembered for his disagreements with St Cyprian, especially over the validity of baptism administered by heretics (Stephen argued that it was and that reconciled heretics needed absolution rather than re-baptism).

[60] *Firmilian's letter*: Firmilian (d. c.269), Bishop of Caesarea, who wrote a strong-worded letter to St Cyprian, supporting his arguments in favour of rebaptising heretics. St Cyprian translated the letter and it is preserved in his Epistles, 74.

"supremacy of Peter" it is not meant to designate the power of the Pope, it remains that it must designate that of the Bishop.

And here we may be content to end our description of what may be specially called the Anglican theory of ecclesiastical unity, viz., that each Church is naturally [32] independent of every other; each bishop an autocratic channel of grace, and ultimate centre of unity; and that unions of see with see are only matters of ecclesiastical arrangement; further, that no jurisdiction but the episcopal is of divine right; and further still, as some have carried it, that all jurisdiction belongs by right to the temporal sovereign, as the supreme governor of the Church in each state, the sole authority in every spiritual act beyond ministry of the word and sacraments, and the *sine qua non* sanction and permissive author even of that ministry.

6.

But now comes this difficulty; that, distinct and satisfactory as the above theory appears to be, being consistent in itself, and founded on the doctrine of St. Ignatius and St. Cyprian, it would certainly seem as if St. Augustine did not hold it, or rather held a doctrine more nearly approaching to the Roman, as though the principle of unity lay, *not* in each individual bishop, but in the body of the Church, or, if in any one bishop, in the Pope; and as though the union of Church with Church were *not* a mere accident, but of the essence of ecclesiastical unity—not for the sake of convenience or piety, but as a sacramental form; and as though schism were separation from this one whole

[61] *"audacia et insolentia"*: "audacity and insolence", in criticism of Pope Stephen's letter

body, and from this or that bishop only as far as he was the organ or representative of all bishops, that is, of the Bishop of Rome.

Now that it is so strong a duty for the whole Church to be in active communion together, that it can hardly be made too strong, and can hardly be exaggerated before the actual event of separation, we do not doubt. So strong we feel the duty to be, that, while it would be shocking and wrong to contemplate a state of extensive and lasting disunion before it happened, it also would be right to consider the consequences of it, did it happen, to be greater than we could master,—so vast as to be vague. It would not be wholesome or pious, it would perhaps mark a bold and a cold heart, even to think to set about determining, before the event, whether or not the friendly intercourse of branch with branch was or was not of the essence of Church unity. We trust, then, nothing we have said above will be taken to countenance the miserable notion that Church may stand aloof from Church without sin; sin somewhere or other; and, in the deplorable controversy which is our main subject, without sin in Rome, sin in us, or sin in both. The simple question is, whether the sin goes so far as to violate the primary notion, the essence of the Church; whether all that remains when this intercommunion is broken, the communion of succession, doctrine, temper, warfare, and the like, go for nothing; whether they may not be enough, in the sight of a merciful Master, to allow of His continuing that secret intercourse in heart and spirit, of Christians so divided, both with each other and with the dead, through and in Him, which is the true communion of saints, and the substantial unity of the Church. We are far from intending

[33]

to disparage the duty of visible active communion; we can understand the great doctors of the Ancient Church raising it ever so high; but Christians now are in a different position from theirs, a position which those doctors could not without a fault have realized to themselves; and it comes upon us,—not as a cold-hearted or curious speculation, or the inquiry of those who would fain go to the very verge of safety, and who bend the stick with no fear except that of actually breaking it,—to ask whether or not that state of [34] estrangement from the great Christian body,—in which we find ourselves, not into which we brought ourselves,— which we are kept in, first by our duty to our own particular Church, next by the terms of communion which Rome enforces on all who would be at peace with her—whether this state is or is not formal schism, and an utter severance of us from the fountains of divine grace? We are forced to do, what the opposers of the profligate Arians[62] or the fanatical Donatists[63] had no need to do—to investigate the essence of the Church, and the elementary idea of unity, in order to ascertain what our duty is, in certain painful circumstances in which we find ourselves.

We are neither, then, for disallowing the duty of what Barrow calls, somewhat invidiously, "political union"

---

[62] *Arians*, followers of the widespread heresy named after an Alexandrian priest, Arius (256-336), that denied the Son's consubstantiality with the Father.

[63] *Donatists*: Followers of Donatus Magnus (d. c.355) who denied the validity of sacraments celebrated by bishops and priests who had been 'traditores' durng the persecution of Diocletian, i.e. they had handed over copies of the Scriptures, sacred vessels or the names of fellow Christians. Donatus insisted that, even though they had subsequently returned to the Church, they had to be re-baptised and, if priests, re-ordained. He therefore opposed the consecration of Cæcilian as Bishop of Carthage in 311, on the grounds that he had been a *traditor* or at least had been consecrated by one. The Pope and the wider church did not accept Donatus's position, and the Donatists became a schismatic sect. St. Augustine was their chief opponent and especially criticised their violent supporters, the 'circumcelliones', who terrorised Catholics.

among Churches, for which, "brotherly," we think, would be a better word;[64] nor can we complain of the holy Fathers in their more happy state for speaking strongly of its importance—nay, so strongly as at first sight to smite ourselves. We will thank them for their severity, knowing that we deserve stripes, and will smile under their unintentional blows, not taking our chastisers to mean more than they surely need, not resenting their chastisement pettishly, not rising against their authority, but gaining a lesson from them, and meekly thanking them for it. Sweet are the wounds of a friend;[65]—it is better to listen to honest words though harsh, than to be offended at them on the one hand, or to explain them away on the other. We experience this every day in common matters; our truest friends often [35] little sympathise with us, nay, hurt us, but they give good advice, and if we are wise, we follow it: let us look at St. Augustine as one of such free-spoken guides, not less valuable because he could not foresee or enter into the miserable condition in which we find ourselves.

It is certain, then, that Augustine does explain St. Cyprian differently from Dodwell. The famous passage in St. Cyprian's De Unitate, "Tear the ray from the sun's substance, unity will not admit this division of light; break the branch from the tree, it will not bud when broken; cut off the channel from the spring, the channel will dry up," which Dodwell applies only to the episcopal and diocesan unit, Augustine unhesitatingly interprets of the body of the

---

[64] [Is not "visible" a better word still? and is not the proposition maintained in the text simply this, "The unity of the Church is an invisible unity?" But if this is allowed, will it be possible long to deny the proposition, "The Church is invisible"?] [N]

[65] *Sweet are the wounds of a friend*: Proverbs 27: 6

universal Church, "Ecclesia universa toto terrarum orbe diffusa."[66]—*contr. Cresconium Donat.* ii. 33. And it seems to be a fixed notion with him, that the universal Church is right in a quarrel with a particular Church, that the universal Church is that which is diffused through all countries, and that "diffused," an expressive word, includes the idea of active communion, as being analogous to life or blood in the animal body. He says that the great difficulty of the Donatists began "posteaquam ipsis rebus experti sunt *cum Cæciliano permanere communionem orbis terrarum*, et *ad eum* à transmarinis Ecclesiis *communicatorias litteras mitti,* non ad illum quem sibi scelerate ordinaverant."[67]—*Ibid. Ep.* 43, 19, *ad Glorium.* And he lays down this as a general principle, "The whole does ever, by the best of rights, take precedence of the parts."—*De Bapt. contr. Donat.* ii. 14. And in like manner, he elsewhere says, "Securus judicat orbis terrarum."[68]—*Contr. Epist. Parmen.* iii. 24.

Now let us for a moment grant this in the general, without going on to the consideration of the limitations by which the concession is to be guarded. Let us grant it, and what is the inference from it? why, this, which is never to be lost sight of in the controversy, to which it will be profitable here to draw attention, and which Gallican[69] divines have

[36]

---

[66] *"Ecclesia universa toto terrarum orbe diffusa"*: "The universal Church is that which is diffused through all the world."

[67] *"posteaquam ipsis rebus experti sunt* cum Caeciliano permanere communionem orbis terrarum, *et ad eum a transmarinis Ecclesiis* communicatores litteras mitti, *non ad illum quem sibi scelerate ordinaverant."*: "after they had found out by actual experience that the communion [or 'union'] of the world remained with Caecilian, and that communicatory letters were being sent to him by the Churches overseas, not to the person whom they had wrongly ordained for themselves."

[68] *"securus judicat orbis terrarum"*: "the whole world [of the Church] judges justly"

[69] *Gallican*: the term describes a view held by many French churchmen that papal authority was subject to General Councils and that the Crown had authority over many aspects of the French Church, including episcopal appointments.

not been slow in urging, that *Catholicity*, and not the *Pope*, is the essence of the Church. This argument, whatever embarrassment it may give to us, is at least fatal to the Ultramontanes,[70] and, if it galls us, as being separate from Christendom, at the same time it releases us from the special difficulty which we have with Rome. This, it is conceived, is practically no small advantage, and may be proved so as time goes on; for, after all, Rome has but a party in the Roman Catholic Church, though it has the active party; and much as the Church has been identified with that party in times past, and is still identified, yet it is something to find that what the English Church wants of perfect Catholicity, supposing it to want anything, may be supplied without going all the way to Rome.

The point in question has been drawn out with great care by Launoy[71] (*vid.* especially *Epistles*, v. 1, vii. 13), in the latter of which he attacks the doctrine of Bellarmine and Canisius,[72] who, he contends, have introduced a new definition of the Church unknown to former times. Bellarmine defines it to be "a congregation of men bound by common profession and sacraments, under legitimate pastors, especially the Pope:" "cœtus hominum ejusdem Christianæ fidei professione et eorundem sacramentorum communione colligatus, sub regimine legitimorum pastorum

---

[70] *Ultramontanes*: Catholics 'beyond the mountains' [i.e. the Alps] who emphasised the Pope's authority as opposed to that of local bishops. Originally a defence against encroachments by national governments on local churches, it developed into a theology of the centralisation of all authority within the Church and a cult of the pope's personality and was to reach its zenith in the campaign for an extreme definition of Papal Infallibility. It is significant that the Anglican Newman was aware that this was a 'party' within the Catholic Church and that he did not amend this passage in the 1878 edition. His *Letter to the Duke of Norfolk* (1875) had explained the true scope of the Vatican Council's definition.
[71] *Launoy*: Jean de Launoy (1603-78), a French historian tending towards Jansenist and Gallican views.
[72] Canisius: St Peter Canisius (1521-97), a Dutch Jesuit theologian and Doctor of the Church.

et præcipue unius Christi in terris Vicarii Romani Pontificis." In opposition to this view, Launoy contends that its simple definition is "cœtus" or "congregatio fidelium," the supremacy of the Pope not being of its essence; a view, let it be observed, between that of our divines who consider [37] each particular diocese to be the normal Church and the Bishop its essence, and of the Ultramontane which makes the extended Church one unit, and the Pope its essential principle. He observes that in Scripture the main idea of a Church is a united congregation; for instance, "all this *assembly* shall know that the Lord saveth not with sword and spear,"—universa Ecclesia.—1 Sam. xvii. 47. "O sing unto the Lord a new song; let the *congregation of saints* praise Him,"—Ecclesia sanctorum, or cœtus fidelium.—Ps. cxlix. 1. "If a man know not how to rule his own house, how shall he take care of the *Church* of God," or the multitude under his rule.—1 Tim. iii. 5. And that this definition is acknowledged by the Fathers, Launoy shows at length. For instance, by Justin,[73] "men many in number, are called by one name (the Church), as if they were one thing."—*Tryph*. 42. Clement of Alexander defines the Church "the congregation of the elect."—*Strom* 6. The same intercommunion is implied by Irenæus[74] when he speaks of the Church as "cherishing the faith all over the earth, as in one house, as though she had one soul, one heart, and preaching it most concordantly, as though she had one

---

[73] *Justin*: St Justin Martyr (c.100-165), a Palestinian convert to Christianity who wrote two *Apologies* and the *Dialogue with the Jew Trypho*. He was martyred in Rome in 165.
[74] *Irenæus*: St Irenæus (c.130-200), a disciple of St Polycarp and bishop of Lyons, was the first significant western theologian.

mouth."—*Hær.* xi. 31. Isidore of Pelusium[75] defines the Church to be "a collection of the holy brought together on a right faith, and the best rules for living."—ii. 246. Cyril of Alexandria[76] describes "the city of God" to be "as though a certain territory and region of men sanctified and enriched *by unity* in God through the Spirit."—In Mic. v. § 49. And Theodoret,[77] "the company of those who believe."—In 1 Tim. iii. fin. 657. Gregory the Great[78] says that "the Holy Church *consists* in the *unity* of believers, as our body is united by the framework of its limbs."—In Job. xix. § 43. At the same time, however expressions such as these tell against the Pope as a visible head of the Church, still they surely must in fairness be taken also to show that, in the opinion of those who use them, *perfect* church communion consists, not simply in union with a common invisible Head, but in visible communion with each other,—that, sufficient as the Episcopate may be for the essence, or τὸ ζῆν of a particular Church, yet for the εὖ ζῆν, or health, it should be united in bonds of active intercourse with all its fellow-branches.

[38]

The same conclusion would result still more strongly, if, instead of quoting passages from the Fathers which speak of the Church, we adduced such as speak of branches which

---

[75] *Isidore of Pelusium*: St Isidore of Pelusium (d. c.450) was an Egyptian ascetic and abbot who produced some two thousand extant letters.

[76] *Cyril of Alexandria*: St Cyril of Alexandria (c.376-444) spent much of his life fighting the Nestorian heresy. He was Patriarch of Alexandria and presided over the Council of Ephesus (431).

[77] *Theodoret*: Theodoret (c.393-c.457) was a theologian and bishop of Cyrrhus (Syria), critical of Cyril of Alexandria's condemnation of Nestorianism.

[78] *Gregory the Great*: St Gregory (c.540-606) was a Roman monk who worked as a diplomat in Constantinople before becoming pope (590). He is a Doctor of the Church and known as the 'Apostle of the English', since he sent St Augustine to Kent in 597.

are estranged from it. But we need not say more on the point, except to remark, by the way, what is not a little curious, that our 19th Article, on the face of its wording, prefers the Gallican, to what we have above called the Anglican definition of unity, speaking of the Church as "cœtus fidelium, in quo verbum Dei purum prædicatur, et sacramenta quoad ea quæ necessario exiguntur juxta Christi institutum recte administrantur."[79] If these words are to be strictly construed by the light of such passages as Launoy brings from a multitude of antecedent writers against Bellarmine, our Reformers held but *one* Church in the world, and entertained the idea of intercommunion, reciprocity, and mutual understanding, in short, political union, as the *perfection* of ecclesiastical unity.

7.

It will be asked then, admitting as much as this, how do we escape from the conclusion which would seem to follow, and which St. Austin especially, as the spokesman of other Fathers, seems to urge upon us, that the English Church is [39] cut off from the Catholic body, a ray from the sun, a branch from the tree, a channel from the fountain? I answer,—by such considerations and facts as the following, which will be seen to be tenable without any breach of respect and piety towards those holy men, to whom both Roman Catholics and ourselves appeal.

---

[79] "cœtus fidelium, in quo verbum Dei purum praedicatur, et sacramenta quoad ea quae necessario exiguntur juxta Christi institutum recte administrantur": from the nineteenth of the Thirty Nine Articles, defining the Church to be "a congregation of faithful men, in which the pure Word of God is preached, and the Sacraments be duly ministered according to Christ's ordinance, in all those things that of necessity are requisite to the same."

Now, first, the one Church was in the days of the Fathers, in matter of fact, in a state of perfect intercommunion; it is not then at all wonderful, rather it could not be otherwise, especially as such a state was a fulfilment of Divine prophecy, that they should appeal to that fact as a mark of its divine origin. It was a mark of the true Church; the only question is, whether it was an indispensable mark of truth, an essential condition, the absence of which was fatal. While it existed it was a divine witness; but it might possibly admit of being lost, and then the Church and the truth which the Church taught, would be so far obscured. While the Jewish Temple remained, that Temple was a proof of God's faithfulness to the Jews; its demolition was a trial, "they saw not their tokens;"[80] but Israel was a holy people notwithstanding. And in the same way we may be part of the Church, even granting, for argument's sake, that *as far as this particular note is concerned*, we have it not in the degree in which the Roman Church has it. There are various notes of truth of various cogency; the only question is, what is the *essential* note? because intercommunion is an important one, it does not therefore follow that it is a *sine quâ non*, or that the essence of the Church does not rather lie in the possession of Apostolic Succession. Before the notes were impaired, the question of comparison between them would not arise. Till then, one might seem as strong as another.

[40]   Again, the circumstance that a particular note was wanting in a particular country, this would of course be an

---

[80] *"they saw not their tokens"*: Cf. Job 21:29ff: 'Have ye not asked them that go by the way? and do ye not know their tokens, That the wicked is reserved to the day of destruction? they shall be brought forth to the day of wrath.'

especially strong presumption against that country; and the Fathers, as was natural, treated what was mainly an antecedent probability as if it rose to the fulness of a principle; and because it was to be expected that the great body of the Church would always be in the right, they laid it down as a general truth that it would and must always be so. Nothing surely is more likely than that the unanimous opinion of ninety-nine men in a matter in which they can judge should be more correct than the contrary opinion of the hundredth. Might not we say, ninety-nine witnesses are sure to be right, without deciding, that in every particular instance the minority must for certain be in the wrong? We have such maxims as, "cuique credendum in arte suâ;"[81] yet no one would take such maxims as rigorous regulations which admitted of no exception. All moral propositions are but general; nor is it any paradox to urge this consideration in ecclesiastical matters. It is hard upon the Fathers to convert their presages and vaticinations[82] into unchangeable truths, as if earthly things might not in turn be their subject-matter as well as heavenly. It is hard upon St. Augustine to suppose that his striking and beautiful principle against the Donatists, "securus judicat orbis terrarum," was intended as a theological verity equally sacred as an article in the Creed.

[83]So many instances may be produced in illustration of this remark as to make selection difficult. For example, it is a great principle of the Fathers, recognized by the Church of Rome, to prefer what is old to what is novel; yet, as they   [41]

---

[81] *"cuique credendum in arte sua"*: "everyone is to be believed in his own art"

[82] *vaticinations*: predictions

[83] [It is a great practical principle, not a doctrine; and the question is, what array of arguments in a particular case is sufficient to overcome it? For instance, is the argument for Anglicanism of such an overpowering character as to be able, by a *consensus* of opinion, in itself to overcome it?] [N]

themselves maintain, the Church has power of altering or renovating in matters of discipline. They have dropped the practice of infant communion, they have prohibited the cup to the laity, they have enforced celibacy on the clergy; they will not, we conceive, deny that in these points they have never thought the apostolic age their necessary rule. Now might we not bring against them the great maxims of the Fathers about "standing on the old ways," with equal cogency, to say the least, as they urge us with St. Austin's maxim about authority of the "orbis terrarum"? Might we not insist on the "antiquitati inhærendum,"[84] "nihil innovandum nisi quod traditum est,"[85] τά ἀρχαία κρατείτω,[86] and the like, as at once condemning them out of their own mouths? and how will they show themselves consistent except by such distinctions and explanations as we feel it equitable to adopt in the case of their charge against us? Or, again, how does the decision of Vincent of Lerins,[87] "Quid si novella aliqua contagio, non jam portiunculam tantum, sed *totam* pariter Ecclesiam commaculare conetur? tunc item providebit ut *antiquitati* inhæreat,"[88]—how does it stand with the "securus judicat" of Augustine, if we are bent on pressing the letter rather than the drift of the Fathers? Or

---

[84] *"antiquitati inhaerendum"*: *"*one must adhere to antiquity [or 'tradition']"

[85] *"nihil innovandum nisi quod traditum est"*: "there must be no innovation, except for what has been handed down"

[86] τά ἀρχαία κρατείτω: let the things which are ancient prevail

[87] *Vincent of Lerins*: St Vincent of Lérins (d. c.445) was a Gaulish monk who wrote the *Commonitorium* and is best known for his teaching on doctrinal development.

[88] *"Quid si novella aliqua contagio, non jam portiunculam tantum, sed* totam *pariter Ecclesiam commaculare conetur? Tunc item providebit ut* antiquitati *inhæreat"*: "What if some new form of corruption should try to pollute not merely a small part, but the whole Church equally? Then likewise he will ensure that he should adhere to antiquity."

again, how shall we account for Lactantius's[89] "That is the true Catholic Church *in quâ est confessio et pœnitentia*,"[90] or Jerome's[91] "ecclesia ibi est, ubi *fides est*,"[92] unless we understand them, not as strict definitions, but as great and general truths, useful for the occasion, elicited by the presence of the Novatian or Arian heresy? Or again, the words above quoted from Augustine, in which he says that the part must yield to the whole, run thus: "Et *concilia posteriora prioribus* apud posteros *præponuntur*, et universum partibus semper jure optimo præponitur."[93] Is the Church of Rome willing to stand by both clauses, and, while the English Convocation yields to a General Council, to supersede the Council of Trent[94] by a Council yet to come? Or, if the former clause need limitation, why not the latter?

[42]

Or again, it is well known what jealousy and dislike were felt, in the early Church, of dialectics, rhetoric, and the kindred sciences. Aristotle[95] was looked upon as the teacher of all that was unfit for a Christian to hold, "That miserable

---

[89] *Lactantius*: Lucius Caecilius Firmianus Lactantius (c.240-c.320) was a Christian writer and adviser to the Emperor Constantine.

[90] in quâ est confessio et pœnitentia: 'in which there is confession and penance', Lactantius, *Divinae Institutiones* IV: *De vera sapientia at religione*, 30, 13.

[91] *St Jerome*: (c.341-420) lived in both Rome and Palestine, for many years living the eremitical life, and is best remembered for his translation of the Bible from Hebrew and Greek into Latin (Vulgate) and for his Scriptural commentaries and homilies.

[92] *"ecclesia ibi est, ubi* fides est": or more accurately, "Ecclesia ibi est ubi fides vera est" – "the Church is where there is true faith" (see St Jerome, *Breviarium in Psalmos*, Ps 83, PL 26: 1223).

[93] *"Et* concilia posteriora prioribus ... optimo præponitur."*: "For later Councils are preferred among later generations to those of earlier date; and the whole is always, with good reason, looked upon as superior to the parts." Augustine, *De Baptismo Contra Donatistas*, XIV.

[94] *Council of Trent*: General Council of the Church held between 1545 and 1563 in response to the Protestant Reformation.

[95] *Aristotle*: (384-322 BC), influential philosopher who was the pupil of Plato and tutor of Alexander the Great.

Aristotle!" says Tertullian,[96] "who invented dialects, the art of building up and pulling down."—*De Præscr.* 7. Nazianzen[97] speaks of "the artifice of Aristotle's art as among the plagues of Egypt."—*Orat.* 26. Jerome says, that "the dialecticians, whose master is Aristotle, pass whole days and nights in asking and answering questions, giving or accepting a thesis, stating, proving, concluding."—*In Tit.* iii. 9. Faustinus,[98] the Luciferian, calls Aristotle the Bishop of the Arians; and Damascene[99] says that the Monophysites[100] made him a thirteenth Apostle. All parts of the Church unite in condemning him and his art; we have a *consensus veterum* on the subject, and the general feeling is summed up by Ambrose[101] in the beautiful apothegm, "Non in dialecticâ complacuit Deo salvum facere populum

---

[96] *Tertullian*: Quintus Septimius Florens Tertullianus (c.160-c.225) of Carthage, a layman, was an important early Latin theologian who helped develop a theological terminology in that language. Best known for his *Apology*, Tertullian was never recognised as a saint since he later became a Montanist.

[97] *Nazianzen:* St Gregory Nazianzen (329-389), born in Cappadocia and friend of St Basil, was much concerned with attacking the Arian heresy. In 381 he became Bishop of Constantinople, although he had to retire to his native Nazianzus due to mounting opposition.

[98] *Faustinus*: (fl. 389) A priest in Rome, follower of Bishop Lucifer of Cagliari and author of *De Fide contra Arianos*, ML 11.37-80. The Luciferians, in Newman's words, regarded the Church as 'the devil's harlot and the synagogue of Satan', *Dev.* p. 254.

[99] *Damascene*: St John Damascene (c.657-749) was born in Damascus (Syria) and became a monk in the monastery of St Sabbas, near Jerusalem. He wrote many theological works and hymns and is considered the last Eastern Father of the Church.

[100] *Monophysites*: heretics who believed that Christ had one nature; they were condemned at the Council of Chalcedon (451).

[101] *Ambrose:* St Ambrose (c.340-397) was born in Trier and became Governor of Liguria and Aemilia, with a residence in Milan. In 374 he was chosen to be the city's bishop, much to his surprise: not only was he a layman, but he was a catechumen preparing for baptism. He proved to be an outstanding bishop, unafraid to challenge the actions of the emperor and uncompromising in his struggle against Arianism. His converts included St Augustine, and his teachings have led him to be numbered as one of the Latin Doctors of the Church.

suum."[102] Now, philosophical and undeniable as the statement is, would it not be altogether preposterous to take it as a necessary truth in the letter, instead of a truth relative to the thing spoken of, heresy; to deny that reasoning is of any use in theology, forbid the study of dialectics, and bring up an array of Fathers against Aristotle in defence of such a proceeding? Would it be wise or satisfactory, upon this basis, to denounce the dialectical labours of these very Fathers in theology, and (what is more to the purpose) the works of the Schoolmen, and to cherish and make much of St. Ambrose's dictum, as supplying a safe rule and guide in [43] matters of faith, to the sacrifice of creeds, to the triumph of infidels, and the utter dissolution of the Church? Not less unreasonable surely is it to make a saying of St. Augustine the turning-point of our religion, and to dispense with all other truths in order that we may maintain this in the letter.[103]

But here another instance occurs, which it would be superfluous to add, except that it carries us out from these disputes about syllables into a wider and more generous line of thought. When we object to the Romanists that their Church has changed in the course of years, they not unfrequently acknowledge it, and are philosophical on the subject. They say that all systems have their development; that nothing begins as it ends; that nothing can come into the world *omnibus numeris*,[104] that the seed becomes a tree,

---

[102] *"Non in dialectica complacuit Deo salvum facere populum suum"*: 'It did not please God to save His people through dialectic.' Newman later used this as the epigraph of his *An Essay in Aid of a Grammar of Assent* (1870).

[103] [My first feeling about this saying, I have described *Apol.*, p. 117, ed. 2, thus:— "A mere sentence struck me with a power, which I never had felt from any words before." My second thoughts are given above in the text. My third thoughts came back to my first. In some matters, second thoughts are not the best.] [N]

[104] omnibus numeris: lit. 'with all its numbers', i.e. exactly, fully formed

and the child a man. And they urge, moreover, that the full-grown fulfilment, to superficial observers, necessarily seems different from what it was in its rudiments, just as a friend, not seen for many years, is strange to us at first sight, till, by degrees, we catch the old looks, or the well-remembered tones, or the smile or the remark, which assure us that, with whatever changes of age or circumstance, he is the same man. And so upon the present Church of Rome, its advocates grant that time has brought changes; that many things have been introduced which once were not; that the internal principles of the Church may have developed [44] disproportionably compared with what they once were. The relation of people to bishop, or of bishop to pope, or of pope to council, is not what it was; but so a child's face changes into a man's; the features are variously enlarged,—what was prominent, retires,—what was not a feature, becomes the ruling expression of the countenance,—yet the face is the same, and the child is the man. They will grant perhaps that the papacy is a development; but why, they ask, should not this be intended? why should it not be intended that, saving the Church and her faith, her internal constitution should determine in a monarchy, as the Mosaic polity might be intended in the counsels of Divine Wisdom to end in a dynasty of kings? And how groundless and peevish it is, they say, on such grounds to find fault with the Roman Catholic Church, as if it had departed from Antiquity and forfeited its trust! We think there is a great deal of force in this view; it does seem to reconcile one to much that otherwise it is difficult to comprehend in the history of religion; only we would propose to carry it out a little further. Why should it not be the intention of Divine

Providence, as on the one hand, still to recognize His Church when contracted into a monarchy, so also not to forsake her when relaxed and dissolved again into a number of aristocratic fragments?[105] why may not the impieties of the sixteenth century have been overruled by His sovereign arm as well as the ambition and superstition of the eighth or the eleventh? Children grow to men, as the Romanist reminds us; but, in like manner, men grow old and wax feeble, and their limbs drag after them, and their voice falters; shall the decrepitude of the nineteenth century more interfere with the inward life and perfection of the Church than the inexperience and feebleness of the Antenicene era? Shall Dionysius[106] be called the forerunner of Arius, yet in truth be a great saint? shall Cyprian live in the Church as a glorious martyr, though he erred in his controversy about baptism? and shall the names of Andrewes[107] or Butler[108] be erased from the catalogue, because they were in less intimate union than was abstractedly desirable with Christians of the south, or were prisoners in an Erastian[109] court? It is surely unfair to carry on the development of the Church only just to the point which serves our purpose, and

[45]

---

[105] ["Why not?" because, in fact, it is *not* so dissolved; doubtless, *were* it so dissolved, were the Pope, as indistinct a power as he was in the first centuries, and the Bishops as practically independent, the Church would still be the Church.] [N]

[106] *Dionysius*: Dionysius of Alexandria (c.190-264), 'the Great', Bishop; when the Emperor Decius began persecuting the church, Dionysius escaped into the Libyan desert with two of his followers, returning when the persecution ended.

[107] *Andrewes*: Lancelot Andrewes (1555-1626), Anglican Divine and Dean of Westminster (1601-1605), Bishop of Chichester (1605-1609), Bishop of Ely (1609-1619) and Bishop of Winchester (1619-1626).

[108] *Butler*: Joseph Butler (1692-1752), theologian, Bishop of Bristol (1738-1750) and Durham (1750-1752) and a critic of Hobbes, Locke and the Deists..

[109] *Erastian*: relating to the doctrine that the Church should be subject to the State, derived from the writings of Thomas Erastus (1524-83), Swiss protestant theologian.

to be indulgent towards tyranny within it, while we make no allowance for insubordination.

Now against this view of course will be brought to bear St. Austin's doctrine, already discussed, that the general Church's judgment is final against particular branches. Here then we come to the point from which we seem to have digressed; for, granting he says so, still we wish to urge this, viz., that just as he says the Church's judgment is above its branches, so does he elsewhere insist on its being above the decision of the Pope. He makes it final both against individual branches *and* against the Pope; and, as his decision against the Pope is not reckoned by Romanists fatal to their theory of development, neither need his decision against individual branches be considered as fatal to our theory of development. Here again we will avail ourselves of the labours of the learned Launoy, though Augustine's judgment on the subject is too well known to need assistance from any controversial writer. For instance, he speaks in the following manner of Pope Stephen's controversy with Cyprian about heretical baptism: "The [46] obscurity of this question caused in the early ages of the Church, before the schism of Donatus,[110] such controversy and fluctuation, as far as peace would allow, in great men and endowed with great charity, that for a long while there was uncertainty in the decrees of councils in distinct places, until by a plenary council of the whole world the most sound view was confirmed to the removal of all doubt."— *De Bapt.* i. 9. In his letter to Glorius and others, having said

---

[110] *Donatus*: (d. c. 355), founder of the Donatist heresy. He worked for a time at Casae Nigrae, in what is now Algeria, and was consecrated as Bishop of Carthage in 313.

that Melchiades,[111] the Pope of the day, had in council condemned Donatus, Augustine proceeds to say: "Let us suppose that those bishops who gave sentence at Rome, were not fair judges; *there still remained* a plenary council of the Universal Church, in *which the cause might be argued against those very judges*, in order that if they had been convicted of wrong judgment, *their sentence might be reversed*."—*Ep*. 43, 19. And he thus speaks against Petilian[112]: "Whatever Marcellinus was, or Marcellus, or Silvester, or Melchiades" (these were Popes),[113] "or Mensurius,[114] or Cæcilian,[115] and others, to whom in their defence they object what they please, *this does nothing to prejudice the Catholic Church diffused over the whole world*; we in no measure are victorious in their innocence, in no measure are found guilty in their iniquity."—*De Unic. Bapt*. 30. It is a plain matter of fact, then, that, as far as the constitution of the Church is concerned, the division between Rome and England does not make so great a difference between this age and the age of St. Cyprian, as

---

[111] *Melchiades*: otherwise known as Pope St Miltiades (311-14). During his Pontificate, Constantine granted toleration to the Church in the so-called Edict of Milan (313).

[112] *Petilian*: or Petilianus, an influential fifth century Donatist, mostly known to us through the writings of St Augustine.

[113] *Marcellinus*: Pope 296-304, accused of apostasy by the Donatists since, during the Diocletian persecution, he handed over the Scriptures to the authorities and allegedly offered incense to the gods. Several prominent members of the presbyterate are said to have also participated in this act, including the future popes *Marcellus I* (Pope 306-308), *Silvester I* (Pope 314-335) and *Melchiades or Miltiades* (Pope 311-314). The alleged apostasy was much debated in the Donatist controversy. All four popes are venerated as saints.

[114] *Mensurius*: Mensurius, Bishop of Carthage (fourth century), accused by the Donatists of handing over the Scriptures, though this seems not to have happened.

[115] *Cæcilian*: Cæcilian or Cæcilianus, (4th century) Bishop of Carthage; he opposed the Donatists, and their opposition to him caused great controversy. He was supported by the Emperor Constantine and by the Council of Arles (341).

the Papal monarchy makes between the age of Hildebrand[116] and the age of St. Augustine.[117]

[47]   On the whole then, it being considered that the dicta of the Fathers upon the temporal state of the Church are not to be taken as first principles, and that from the happy circumstances of their times the Fathers may have been led to lay an extreme stress upon the necessity of intercommunion as a condition of Churchmanship, and that the Church may possibly be intended to bear a different appearance in different ages, and to wear her bridal ornaments and the signs of her rank, some at one time, some at another, and in consequence that branches estranged from the rest of the body, may, nevertheless be part of the body, let us proceed to show that what *may possibly* be, is *probably*, as regards the English Church. As soon as it is granted that active intercourse is not *absolutely necessary* as a note of the Church, an opening is made for adducing *other* circumstances which may serve to be an evidence of that, which such intercourse would evidence, if it existed. We conceive then that, in spite of our being separated from Greece and Rome, shut up in ourselves and our dependencies, and looked coldly on or forgotten by the rest of Christendom, there is sufficient ground for still believing that the English Church is at this time the Catholic Church in England.

---

[116] *Hildebrand*: St Gregory VII (c.1021-85), originally called Hildebrand, who as bishop of Rome promoted ecclesiastical reform and stressed papal prerogatives over lay rulers. See Essay XIII below.

[117] [If so, then, the division between Jerusalem and Samaria does not make so great a difference between the age of Jeroboam and that of Joshua, as the Israelitish monarchy makes between the age of Solomon and the age of Samuel.] [N]

8.

Let it be considered then, first, that either *we* are the Catholic Church in England, or there is *no* Catholic Church here. There has been a Church here from the first, consisting of many sees; those sees remain, they are filled; the Church exists still; it may be schismatical, or heretical, but here it is. If it be in heresy or in schism, then, as Romanists say, it certainly is not a true branch; but then, if so, there is no other that *is* true. If so, England is lost to the Catholic world; no other bishops claim our sees. As far as the argument from visibility goes, if it be a fact that we are [48] estranged from the Continent, it is also a fact that we have possession of the thrones of Cuthbert,[118] Becket,[119] and Wykeham[120]. Is it probable that the noble line of Canterbury should be extinct? has the blood of martyrs dried up, and the voice of the confessors failed? Have our cathedrals no living spirit in them, and is our hierarchy a form only, and not a power? Is it usual with Holy Church to retire where once she has stationed herself? shall she suddenly leave a haunt frequented and illustrated by her presence through 1300 years? Shall Cranmer, if so be single-handed, destroy the work of ages? So great, so monstrous an improbability, gives some weight of evidence on the other side that we are what our ancestors were. The Romanists urge against us as a providential badge that we dare not openly take the name of Catholic; and may we not retort that they too have not

---

[118] *Cuthbert*: St Cuthbert (c.634-87), monk, hermit and bishop of Lindisfarne. He was one of the most popular English saints up until the Reformation, his shrine being found at Durham Cathedral.
[119] *Becket*: St Thomas of Canterbury (c.1119-70), Archbishop of Canterbury from 1162, famously murdered in his cathedral as a result of his on-going struggle with Henry II over the liberty of the Church.
[120] *Wykeham*: William of Wykeham (c.1320-1404), Bishop of Winchester from 1368 and Chancellor of England. He founded Winchester College and New College, Oxford.

dared openly to fill our sees, and that the hand of Providence is seen in the fact? They have given us possession; we have it in the open face of day without rival interference from them; and the matter is reduced to a question of opposite probabilities, whether we shall suppose active communion dispensable, or shall proceed utterly to extinguish the candlesticks of an old and famous Christian country, dear to Christendom. Well were it if they would look back upon the past, and show us some little love "for the Fathers' sake." Would that both parties would look back on that ancient time which they both claim as theirs, and would love each other in it! Would that our Fathers could plead somewhat for us in the affections of our opponents, and bring them to relent from the cruel purpose with which they follow after us to destroy us!

[49] They delight to compare us to the Donatists, but these surely were in a very different position. The Donatists had not possession; their only tenure of existence was hatred and opposition to all the rest of Christendom. They were *forced* to call the Catholic Church the "scortum diaboli,"[121] in order to justify their continuing a rival succession against her in their country. They could not acknowledge her abroad, without betraying the cause of Donatus at home. It was a decisive argument against the Donatists, to say that the Church was prophesied of as Catholic, diffused over various countries, and therefore could not be a Church, which was all but shut up in Africa. Their very principle of separation obliged them to deny that the Church elsewhere was the true Church; for, if true, why had they made a

---

[121] *"scortum diabolic"*: "whore of the devil"

distinct and second succession in Africa? If the general Church was true, its African branch was true, and they were setting up a second Church without reason. It was a great inconsistency to say that the general Church was true and sound, yet not to join that branch of it which had been from the first among themselves. This was the great absurdity of a Donatist bishop, famous in those times, of the name of Tichonius.[122] He gave up his point, and yet did not give up his Church. If altar cannot lawfully be erected against altar, Augustine and his rival bishop at Hippo could not both be free from schism; yet Tichonius seemed to affirm it. On the other hand, though we hold, as we do, that altar cannot be lawfully erected against altar, yet our bishops and those of France, ours and the German, ours and the Roman, may still both be free from schism. Nor would this view of the subject be affected, even were the Roman Catholics ill-advised enough at this time of day to fill our sees; for it would be absurd to suppose that at the end of three centuries they could claim what they had so long ago abandoned. [50] However, by the time they recover the sees of England, we on the other hand, perchance, shall have succeeded in regaining the name of Catholic.

Here another thought is suggested to us. We have been saying that, unless the English be a Catholic branch, the Catholic Church is defrauded of the "orbis terrarum." This leads us to observe how much more real the fulfilment of the prophecies is on our interpretation than on the Roman. Insisting, as they do, on intercommunion as an essential mark of the Church, they are obliged to make its Catholicity in no small degree a mere fiction of law. Surely it is but a

---

[122] *Tichonius*: fourth century African Donatist writer who was quoted by St Augustine and wrote works on Biblical interpretation and the Book of Revelation.

legal fiction to say that there is a Church in England, if the Roman communion be it, compared with the full and adequate truth of the proposition, supposing it be possible, in spite of the difference of faith and discipline between England and Rome, to call them one and the same Church, extending into the two countries. And this applies still more strongly to the case of the Greek Church; for in what sense can the Church of Rome be said to extend through the vast spaces of Russia, except on that pen-and-paper plan which gives them an indefinite abundance of bishops in *partibus infidelium*? If then intercommunion be a Note of the Church, reality is one also; and unless Roman divines are content to create a territory for themselves by merely mapping it, and to appropriate it by compasses, they must relax their ideas, high and primitive though they be, of the necessary intercommunion and mutual brotherly affection of the various portions of the present Catholic Church.

But to return to our own. It is made an objection to us that we are not, and that we dare not call ourselves, Catholic; as if the common sense of mankind and our own conscience thereby gave judgment against us. Certainly the title has been principally cherished by us with a sort of *disciplina arcani*, not claimed indeed, but not abandoned; and so far of course it has not served us as a Note of the Church. We should have thought, however, that our Church's being so often called Popish and Papistical by the world would have saved it from this reproach at the hands of the Romanists; for what do the speakers mean, and what can the Romanists wish to understand by "Popish," but just the very same thing as Catholic by another name? However, admitting the charge, which is hard as coming from them,

[51]

still on the other hand it must be borne in mind as a very striking contrary fact, that if we do not possess the title Catholic, at least we have never borne the name of mortal man. Heretical and schismatical bodies are formed upon a certain doctrine, or begin in a certain leader. We have none such. What exact parallel is there to our position in former times? The Donatists formed a large Church and spread through Africa, yet they were called from Donatus; if they are our prototypes, why are we not called Cranmerites or Jewellists?[123] The Monophysites got possession of whole districts, and might seem, if any men, identified with the local Churches in those districts, yet they are named from Eutyches,[124] from Severus,[125] from Jacob,[126] from Gaianus,[127] and from Theodosius[128]; not to mention their more common title of Acephali,[129] which implies that at least a great portion of them had lost the Succession altogether. If then our present forfeiture of the title Catholic be against us, our freedom from human title is for us, and is a Note of the true Church. Surely a note, even in Bellarmine's judgment; who thus speaks, even when he is explaining the force of the

[123] *Cranmerites or Jewellists?*: Newman is referring to two of the founding fathers of the Church of England: Thomas Cranmer (see note on page [2]) and John Jewel (1522-71), Bishop of Salisbury from 1559 and notable controversialist, who defended the Elizabethan Settlement in works such as *Apologia Pro Ecclesia Anglicana* (1562).

[124] *Eutyches*: (c.380-c.456), a priest of Constantinople who taught the Monophysite doctrine that there was only one nature in Christ; he was condemned at the Council of Chalcedon (451).

[125] *Severus*: Severus of Antioch (c.465-538), Patriarch of Antioch and important Monophysite leader.

[126] *Jacob*: Jacob Baradæus (d.578), Monophysite Bishop of Edessa

[127] Gaianas: Gaianas or Gainas (6th century) served as Patriarch of Alexandria (536–537) in opposition to Theodosis. He was later exiled to Sardinia.

[128] *Theodosius*: Theodosius (d.567), Patriarch of Alexandria from 543 but exiled by Justinian I in 536 because of his heretical views.

[129] *Acephali*: literally meaning 'without head', a name given to Donatists and other heretical groups.

word Catholic: "Heretical sects," he says, are "branches or parts cut off from the tree of the Church." "There is *no* heresy," he continues, "which does not take a name from some man as its author, and leave the name of Christian to them from whom it departs." And then he instances this remark from Justin Martyr, who says, "They (sectaries) are distinguished by surnames, called after individuals, according as each was the author of any new doctrine, some Marcionists,[130] others Valentinians,[131] others Basilidians,[132] others Saturninians,[133] others by other names from the first inventor of their respective doctrine."—*In Tryph.* 35. "When men are called Phrygians,[134] or Marcionites, etc.," says Lactantius, "they cease to be Christians; for they have lost Christ's name, and put on human and foreign titles."— *Inst.* iv. 30. "Never has people," says Athanasius,[135] "received name from their bishops, but from the Lord in whom they have believed; even from the blessed Apostles, our teachers, we have not received titles, but from Christ we are and are called Christians."—*Orat.* 2. *contr. Arian.* "Wherever you shall hear," says Jerome, "those who are called Christians, named not from the Lord Jesus Christ, but from any one else, as Marcionites, Valentinians, etc., know that it is not Christ's Church, but the synagogue of Antichrist."—*In Lucif. fin.* All this is almost prophetically

[52]

---

[130] *Marcionists*: a 2nd century Gnostic sect, founded by Marcion (fl.14-155).

[131] *Valentinians*: a 2nd century Gnostic sect, founded by Valentinus (c.100-c.160).

[132] *Basilidians*: a 2nd century Gnostic sect, founded by Basilides of Alexandria (fl. 117-138), who is mentioned sixteen times in St Irenaeus' *Adversus Hæreses*.

[133] *Saturninans*: a 2nd century Gnostic sect, founded by Saturninus of Antioch.

[134] *Phrygians*: a name sometimes given to followers of the Montanist heresy, since Montanus had been a Phrygian priest.

[135] *Athanasius*: St Athanasius (296-373), Bishop and Doctor of the Church; he was the great champion of orthodoxy against Arianism and one of the saints most admired by Newman.

fatal to Lutherans,[136] Calvinists,[137] Socinians,[138] and Wesleyans;[139] but for us it is a note of our Churchmanship, on Bellarmine's own admission, that we are proof against it. However, if Romanists among us still taunt us with our present loss of the name Catholic, as far as the world's witness goes, then we take leave to remind them that if we have let slip "Catholic," at least we have kept "Church," which in this country they have not; and thus we have a popular witness in our favour as well as they. It is a common reproach of theirs against us, that if we were to take St. Cyril's test, and ask in the street for the "Catholic" place of worship, no one would dream of directing us to any but their's. Now it has been retorted, truly and happily, that in like manner, if they ask for the "Church," they will be directed to none other than our's. We go to church, and they to chapel. They possess Catholic meetings, conciliabula Apostolorum, a contradiction in terms.

[53]

9.

While we are on the subject, we will notice another Note of the Church, which Bellarmine does not distinctly mention, but is equal to any, *life*. The Church is emphatically a living body, and there can be no greater proof of a particular communion being part of the Church than the appearance in it of a continued and abiding energy, nor a more melancholy symptom of its being a corpse than torpidity. We say an energy continued and abiding, for accident will cause the activity of a moment, and an

---

[136] *Lutherans*: Protestants who follow the teachings of Martin Luther (1483-1546).

[137] *Calvinists*: Protestants who follow the teachings of John Calvin (1509-1564).

[138] *Socinians*: theological movement that rejected orthodox beliefs in the Trinity and the divinity of Christ, named after Lelio Sozzini (1525-1562).

[139] *Wesleyans*: followers of John Wesley (1703-1791).

external principle give the semblance of self-motion. On the other hand, even a living body may for a while be asleep. And here we have an illustration of what we just now urged about the varying cogency of the Notes of the Church according to times and circumstances. No one can deny that at times the Roman Church itself, restless as it is at most times, has been in a state of sleep or disease, so great as to resemble death; the words of Baronius,[140] speaking of the tenth century, are well known: "Dormiebat tunc planè alto, ut apparet, sopore Christus in navi, cum hisce flantibus validis ventis, navis ipsa fluctibus operiretur. Una illa reliqua consolatio piis, quia, etsi Dominus dormivit, in eadem tamen navi dormivit."[141] It concerns then, those, who [54] deny that we are the true Church because we have not at present this special note, intercommunion with other Christians, to show cause why the Roman Church in the tenth century should be so accounted, with profligates, or,

---

[140] *Baronius*: Cesare Baronius (1538-1607) was an Oratorian priest and Cardinal who (at the insistence of St Philip Neri) wrote the *Annales Ecclesiastici* (1588-1607), in response to the Protestant *Magdeburg Centuries*. He is rightly called 'The Father of Modern Church History'.

[141] *"Dormiebat tunc ... navi dormivit."*: "At that time Christ was certainly sleeping, as it appears, in deep slumber on the ship, when, as these strong winds were blowing, the ship itself was being covered by the waves. That is the only remaining consolation for the faithful, that even if our Lord slept, at least he slept in the same ship."

Ann. A.D. 912, n. 14, vol. 15, p. 571. Just before he had said:—"Quæ tunc facies sanctæ Ecclesiæ Romanæ! quam fœdissima, cùm Romæ dominarentur potentissimæ æquè ac sordidissimæ meretrices! quarum arbitrio mutarentur sedes, darentur Episcopi, et, quod auditu horrendum et infandum est, intruderentur in sedem Petri earum amasii pseudo-pontifices, qui non sint nisi ad consignanda tantum tempora in catalogo Romanorum Pontificum scripti." [N] "What was then the appearance of the holy Roman Church! How utterly disgraceful, when at Rome the most powerful and at the same time most sordid courtesans had control! At whose will positions were changed, Bishoprics bestowed, and what is horrific to hear and unspeakable, there were admitted to the seat of Peter pseudo-pontiffs who were their lovers, whose names are only recorded in the list of pontiffs in order to mark the dates."

rather, the profligate mothers of profligate sons, for her supreme rulers. And still, notwithstanding, life *is* a Note of the Church; she alone revives even if she declines; heretical and schismatical bodies cannot keep life; they gradually become cold, stiff and insensible. They may do some energetic work at first from excitement and remaining warmth, as the Arians converted the Goths, though even this seems, as the history shows us, to have been an accident, for which they can claim no praise; or as the Nestorians spread in the East, from circumstances which need not here be noticed. But wait awhile, and "see the end of these men." "I myself," says the Psalmist, "have seen the ungodly in great power, and flourishing like a green-bay tree. I went by, and lo, he was gone; I sought him, but his place could nowhere be found."[142] Heresies and schisms, whatever be their promise at first, and whatever be their struggles, yet gradually and surely tend not to be. Utter dissolution is the scope to which their principles are directed from the first, and towards which for the most part they steadily and continually move. Or, if the principle of destruction in them be not so living as to hurry them forward in their career, then they remain inert and motionless, where they first are found, kept together in one by external circumstances, and going to pieces as soon as air is let in upon them.

Now if there ever were a Church on whom the experiment has been tried whether it had life in it or not, the English is that one. For three centuries it has endured all vicissitudes of fortune. It has endured in trouble and prosperity, under seduction and under oppression. It has been practised upon by theorists, browbeaten by sophists, [55]

---

[142] *"I myself ... "*: Psalm 37: 35-36

intimidated by princes, betrayed by false sons, laid waste by tyranny, corrupted by wealth, torn by schism, and persecuted by fanaticism. Revolutions have come upon it sharply and suddenly, to and fro, hot and cold, as if to try what it was made of. It has been a sort of battle-field on which opposite principles have been tried. No opinion, however extreme any way, but may be found, as the Romanists are not slow to reproach us, among its bishops and divines. Yet what has been its career upon the whole? Which way has it been moving through three hundred years? Where does it find itself at the end? Lutherans have tended to Rationalism; Calvinists have become Socinians; but what has it become? As far as its formularies are concerned, it may be said all along to have grown towards a more perfect Catholicism than that with which it started at the time of its estrangement; every act, every crisis, which marks its course, has been upward. It never was in so miserable case as in the reigns of Edward and Elizabeth[143]. At the end of Elizabeth's there was a conspicuous revival of the true doctrine. Advancements were made in the Canons of 1603. How much was done under Charles the First,[144] need not be said; and done permanently, so as to remain to this day, in spite of the storm which immediately arose, sweeping off the chief agents in the work, and for a time levelling the Church to the ground. More was done than even yet appears, as a philosophical writer has lately

[56]

---

[143] *Elizabeth*: Elizabeth I (1533-1603), daughter of Henry VIII and Anne Boleyn, Queen of England and Ireland, 1558-1603.

[144] *Charles the First*: Charles I (1600-49), second son of James VI of Scotland and Anne of Denmark, King of England, Scotland and Ireland 1625-49.

remarked, in the Convocation of 1661.[145] One juncture there was of a later date (1688) which seemed to threaten a relapse; yet it was the only crisis in which no ecclesiastical act took place. The temper, however, of the Church certainly did go back; a secular and semi-sceptical spirit came in. Now then was the time when the Church lay open to injury; yet, by a wonderful providence, the Convocation being, during this period, suspended, there was no means of making permanent impressions on its character; and thus civil tyranny was its protection against itself. That very Convocation too expired in an act of zeal and faith. In our own times, temporal defences have been removed which the most strenuous political partisans of the Church considered essential to its well-being, and the loss of which they deplored as the first steps towards its ruin. To their surprise these well-intentioned men have beheld what they thought a mere establishment, dependent on man to create and destroy, rise up and walk with a life of its own, such as it had before they and their constitution came into being.

How many learned divines have we had, even our enemies being judges? and in proportion to their learning, so on the whole has been their approximation towards the full ancient truth. Or take again those whom by a natural instinct "all the people count as prophets," and will it not be found that either altogether, or in those works which are most popular, those writers are ruled by primitive and Catholic principles? No man, for instance, was an abler writer in the last century than Warburton,[146] or more famous

---

[145] *Convocation of 1661*: synodal meeting that approved the revised Book of Common Prayer following the Restoration of Charles II.
[146] *Warburton*: William Warburton (1698-1779), theologian and (from 1760) bishop of Gloucester, whose works included *The Alliance between Church and*

in his day; yet the glare is over, and now Bishops Wilson[147] and Horne,[148] men of far inferior powers, but of Catholic temper and principles, fill the doctor's chair in the eyes of the many. What a Note of the Church is the mere production of a man like Butler, a pregnant fact much to be meditated on! and how strange it is, if it be as it seems to be, that the real influence of his work is only just now beginning! and who can prophesy in what it will end? Thus our divines grow with centuries, expanding after their death in the minds of their readers into more and more exact Catholicism, as years rolled on. Nay, even our errors and heterodoxies turn to good: Wesleyanism in itself tends to heresy, if it was not heretical in the outset; but, so far as it has been in the Church, it has been overruled to rouse and stimulate us, when we were asleep. Moreover, look at the internal state of the Church at this moment; much that is melancholy is there, strife, division, error. But still on the whole, enlarge on the evils as you will, there is *life* there, perceptible, visible life;[149] rude indeed, undisciplined, perhaps self-willed, but life; and not the life of death, not

[57]

State (1736) and *The Divine Legation of Moses* (1737-41), which was aimed against the Deists.

[147] *Wilson*: Thomas Wilson (1663-1755) served as Bishop of Sodor and Mann from 1697 and was remembered for his personal piety, pastoral zeal and concern for ecclesiastical reform. He supported the publication of the first work in Manx, *The Principles and Duties of Christianity* (the so-called 'Manx Catechism'). Wilson was much admired by the Tractarians. Keble wrote his biography and edited his works; the bishop was quoted ten times in the Tracts for the Times and Newman provided the 'Preface' to a reprint of his *Sacra Privata* (1839), writing that 'the English soil indeed had its own witnesses and teachers at the time; but none at once so exalted in station and so saintly in character, so active and so tried in his lifetime, and so influential in his works' (p.i-ii).

[148] *Horne*: George, Bishop of Norwich (1730-1792), High Church but also sympathetic to Wesley. He wrote *Commentary on the Psalms*, 1771.

[149] [*Vid. supr.* Note, vol. i., pp. 379, 380.] [N]

that heretical restlessness, which, as we have observed, only runs out the quicker for its activity, and hastens to be no more, but, as we may humbly trust, a heavenly principle after all, which is struggling towards development, and gives presage of truth and holiness to come. Look across the Atlantic to the daughter Churches of England in the States; shall one that is barren bear a child in her old age? yet "the barren hath borne seven."[150] Schismatic branches put out their leaves at once in an expiring effort; our Church has waited three centuries, and then blossoms, like Aaron's rod, budding and blooming and yielding fruit, while the rest are dry. And lastly look at the present position of the Church at home; there too we shall find a note of the true city of God, the Holy Jerusalem. She is in warfare with the world, as the [58] Church Militant should be; she is rebuking the world; she is hated, she is pillaged by the world. And, as if it were providentially intended to show this resemblance between her and the sister branches, what place she has here, that they have there; the same enemies encompassing both them and her, and the same trials and exploits lying in prospect. She has a common cause with them, as far as they are faithful, if not a common speech and language; and is together with them in warfare, if not in peace.

Much might be said on this subject. At all times, since Christianity came into the world, an open contest has been going on between religion and irreligion, and the true Church, of course, has ever been on the religious side. This then is a sure test in every age, *where* the Christian should stand. There may have been corruptions or errors, and great difficulties of judgment about details; but in spite of them

---

[150] [*Vid. ibid.*, pp. 381-383.] [N] *"the barren hath borne seven"*: 1 Samuel 2: 5

all, he would feel no hesitation, did he live in the eleventh century, that Hildebrand was the champion of heaven, not the Cæsar; in the twelfth, Becket,[151] not Henry.[152] Now applying this simple criterion to the public parties of this day, it is very plain that the English Church is at present on God's side, and therefore so far God's Church;—we are sorry to be obliged to add, that there is as little doubt on which side English Romanism is. It must be a very galling thought to serious minds who profess it, to feel that they are standing with the enemies of God, co-operating with the haters of truth and haters of the light, and thereby prejudicing religious minds even against those verities which Rome continues to hold.[153]

[59]   As for the English Church, surely she has notes enough, "the signs of an Apostle in all patience, and signs and wonders and mighty deeds;" she has the note of possession, the note of freedom from party titles; the note of life, a tough life and a vigorous; she has ancient descent, unbroken continuance, agreement in doctrine with the ancient Church. Those of Bellarmine's Notes, which she certainly has not, are intercommunion with Christendom, the glory of miracles, and the prophetical light; but the question is, whether she has not enough of divinity about her to satisfy her sister Churches on their own principles, that she is one body with them.

---

[151] *Becket*: St Thomas Becket (1118-70), Lord Chancellor and (from 1162) Archbishop of Canterbury. As Archbishop he came into conflict with Henry II over state interference in the Church and, after returning from a six year exile on the continent, was murdered in his own Cathedral in 1170.

[152] *Henry*: Henry II (1133-1189), King of England from 1154.

[153] It cannot be said that this reproach now applies to English Catholicism: witness the years 1850-1, and 1860-70. [N]

10.

But we do not mean to leave the subject here. It has been observed above, that Augustine's maxim about submission to the *orbis terrarum*, as a sign of Churchmanship, is a presumption rather than a law, not a criterion but a general evidence; this will be confirmed by referring to transactions which took place in the Church shortly before his own day. We shall find instances in point in the history of Arianism, which serve to fix our sense upon his words.

1. Let us take the case of the Semi-Arians. These religionists had separated off from the Arians on the death of Constantius,[154] who had managed to keep together a very miscellaneous party, and they formed a communion of their own under the name of Macedonians. After a little while, they determined on abjuring their heresy and professing the creed of Nicæa;[155] and for this purpose they sent deputies to Pope Liberius,[156] who received their adhesion, and reconciled them. On the return of the deputies, a portion of the body seceded again, refused to accept the word Homoüsion,[157] though they seemed to have accepted the doctrine implied in it. As to the divinity of the Holy Spirit, [60] some of the seceders positively denied the doctrine, others doubted. Against these latter, then, who were merely in

---

[154] *Constantius*: The Emperor Constantius II (317-361), a supporter of Arianism.

[155] *Nicæa*: Nicæa, General Council held in 325 defining the Catholic belief in the divinity of Christ against Arian errors.

[156] *Pope Liberius*: Pope 352-366 and the first bishop of Rome not to be honoured as a saint. A weak leader, he endured exile, and much pressure was put on him by the Emperor Constantius to support Arianism. As a result, Liberius famously condemned St Athanasius and signed a doctrinal statement that could be given an Arian interpretation. Critics of the Papacy often accused Liberius of heresy.

[157] *Homoüsion*: 'of one substance' or 'consubstantial' with the Father, the term used by opponents of the Arians at Nicaea in stressing Christ's Divinity. Arians suggested a different term, *homoiousion*, 'of similar substance', implying that the Son was lower than the Father and that there was a time when He was not.

perplexity and suspense, there could be no real complaint on the part of the Church, except so far as they were in a state of separation. The seceding body were in possession of sees, at least to the number of thirty-four. Now one would have thought that a strong case might be made out in favour of any Catholic, who had kept aloof from them. They came of the Arians, had attempted to rival them in court favour, had separated from them of necessity, not of choice, had betaken themselves to Liberius in order to escape the persecution they had met at their hands, had cooled in their Catholicity as soon as they got reinstated in their sees, and a portion at least had retraced their steps and formed a separate connection. Their conduct had been of so marked a character that they gained from St. Athanasius the title of Tropici or Turn-abouts. Yet how did the Fathers treat them? had they rejected them in a mass from the first as schismatics? far from it; in spite of their separation from the general body, they took them one by one, rested their opinion of them solely on their personal faith, and were ready to honour and to communicate with those, whom, in spite of whatever perplexities of belief, they considered to be orthodox at bottom. Athanasius, Basil,[158] Gregory Nazianzen, and Hilary,[159] all take this view of the Semi-Arians. Of these, it may suffice to dwell upon the instance of St. Basil. He was baptized, probably between the ages of twenty and thirty, by a bishop who, for twenty years, had sided with the Arian party, and who soon afterwards signed

---

[158] *Basil*: St Basil the Great (330-79), Bishop of Caesarea and Doctor of the Church.
[159] *Hilary*: St Hilary (c315-368) was a Christian convert who, as Bishop of Poitiers, was a leading defender of the Church against the Arian heresy, which caused him to be exiled to Phrygia by the Arian emperor Constantius.

the prevaricating symbol of Ariminum.[160] Shortly after, he made the friendship of Eusebius of Samosata,[161] who eventually indeed conformed to the Church, and lost his life from Arian violence, but at the time in question was found among the Semi-Arians, and was accounted an Arian by Damasus,[162] Bishop of Rome, up to the year before St. Basil's[163] death. Next, while he was a reader, he attended the Council of Constantinople[164] held at the end of the reign of Constantius, as the assistant of a celebrated Semi-Arian bishop, his namesake, Basil of Ancyra.[165] And about the same time he became intimate with Eustathius,[166] afterwards Bishop of Sebaste, a man far less sound in faith than the Eusebius above mentioned, and from whom, in the course of years, he was obliged to separate. At an earlier day he

[61]

---

[160] *symbol of Arminum*: the Council of Arminum (modern day Rimini) was called by the Arian Emperor Constantius in 359. The Arian bishops drew up a creed or symbol which was later condemned by Pope Liberius.

[161] *Eusebius of Samosata*: St Eusebius of Samosata (d. c. 380) was an associate of SS Basil and Gregory Nazianzen, much involved in the Arian controversy, for which he was banished to Thrace. He is venerated as a martyr since he died after being attacked by an Arian woman.

[162] *Damasus, Bishop of Rome*: St Damasus (c.304-384) was probably born in Rome and eventually became Pope in 366. He proved to be a strong leader, promoting devotion to the martyrs and their relics, strengthening the administration of the Church and summoning synods and councils to counter heresy.

[163] *St Basil*: St Basil (c.330-379) was born into a saintly family in Caesarea, Cappadocia (Turkey); his brother was St Gregory of Nyssa, also a notable theologian. For some years St Basil lived in a monastic community before becoming Bishop of Caesarea in 370. He was a keen defender of the reality of the Incarnation against attacks from Arian heretics. St Basil also gave his name to a Liturgy and a set of monastic rules which are still used in the East.

[164] *Council of Constantinople*: referring not to the General Council of 381 but the Arian Council called by Constantius in 359.

[165] *Basil of Ancyra*: St Basil of Ancyra (d. 362), originally from Galatia, was a defender of orthodoxy against Arianism and suffered martyrdom under Julian the Apostate.

[166] *Eustathius, afterwards Bishop of Sebaste*: Eustathius of Sebaste (c.300-c.377) was a pupil of Arius who lived an extremely ascetic life and became bishop of Sebaste. Despite signing the Nicene Creed during a visit to Rome, he seems to have been a semi-Arian at the time of his death.

had also taken part in the Council held by the Semi-Arian party at Lampsacus. Silvanus of Tarsus[167] was another Semi-Arian whom he visited at the same time. Now, though there could be no doubt about the estrangement of these men from the great Christian body, yet, as Basil tells us himself, he was attracted by the purity and strictness of their lives, and was persuaded, though in one instance wrongly, of the soundness of their faith.

Their conspicuous seriousness of life indeed is especially insisted on by contemporaries and others, and though not an infallible sign of their communion with the invisible Church, as the event proved, yet was considered a note sufficient to outweigh many adverse suspicions.

"No small portion of the people followed them," says Sozomen, "in Constantinople, Bithynia, Thrace, the Hellespont, and the neighbouring districts; for their lives, to which the multitude especially attends, were irreproachable; their address was grave, and their mode of living approaching to the monastic; their speech cultivated, and their moral qualities attractive. Such, they say, was Marathonius at that time; who, having made a large fortune as paymaster of the pretorian soldiers, gave up the army, and took the charge of a hospital of sick and poor."—*Hist.* iv. 27.

[62]   "May you be granted," says Nazianzen to them, "the reward of your manner of life, to confess the Spirit perfectly, and to preach with us, yea, before us, whatever is fitting. I dare to speak some great thing in your behalf, even the saying of the Apostle. So do I embrace you, and so much I reverence that decent dress of yours, and that complexion of continence, and those sacred assemblies,

---

[167] *Silvanus of Tarsus*: Silvanus (d. c.376) was a semi-Arian bishop who participated in the Councils of Sirmium, Ancrya and Seleucia and was on friendly terms with several orthodox leaders. When St Cyril was exiled from Jerusalem in 358, Silvanus received him at Tarsus.

and that grave virginity and purity, and your psalmody through the night, and your love of the poor, and of the brethren, and of strangers, that I am ready even to be anathema from Christ, and to suffer somewhat as condemned, so that ye might stand with us, and that we might glorify the Trinity in common."—*Orat.* 41, p. 737.

2. The history of Meletius, Bishop of Antioch, [168] at the same date, is still more in point, and will bear dwelling on somewhat at length. Summed up in a few words it is this:— he was the friend of St. Basil; he presided at the second General Council; his funeral sermon was preached by St. Gregory Nyssen[169]; he is spoken of as a saint by St. Chrysostom,[170] and has a place in the Roman calendar; yet, on the other hand, he was not acknowledged by the Pope of his day; he was denied *litteræ formatæ*;[171] he was not in communion with Alexandria; he refused to communicate with Athanasius, and he is severely spoken of by Jerome. Let us review both sides of this contrariety.

Meletius had been of the Semi-Arian party, but had after a time, with as much boldness as sincerity, avowed the orthodox doctrine. However, as was not unnatural, the

---

[168] *Meletius, Bishop of Antioch*: St. Meletius (357-381), Bishop of Antioch. Although personally orthodox, he initially subscribed to an ambiguous formula which aimed to comprehend both the Nicene and Arian doctrines. He was exiled several times under Arian emperors but was also held in suspicion by the orthodox party. The church in Antioch was split between his followers and those of Paulinus who strongly supported Nicene orthodoxy, the 'Meletian schism'. He presided over the opening of the First Council of Constantinople and after his death was considered a saint.

[169] *Gregory Nyssen*: St Gregory of Nyssa (c.335-395), the youngest of the Cappadocian Fathers and, from 372, Bishop of Nyssa. He took a leading role in the Second Council of Constantinople (381).

[170] *St. Chrysostom*: St. John Chrysostom, (c.349-407), Archbishop of Constantinople, Doctor of the Church; known for his 'golden-mouthed' eloquence in his many sermons and other writings and for his contribution to the Liturgy which bears his name.

[171] litteræ formatæ: communicatory letters which vouched for his genuineness as a bishop

Catholics, suspecting him, consecrated another bishop in his see, who was acknowledged by Rome, by all the West, and Alexandria. The East supported the claims of Meletius, and St. Basil interested himself at Rome and Alexandria in his behalf, but in vain. To Peter, the successor of Athanasius,[172] he writes in a tone of serious disappointment at the failure of his attempt.

"Dorotheus," he says, "related to us on his return the conversations he had had in the presence of the most reverend Bishop Damasus" [of Rome] "with your excellency; and he pained us by saying that our most gracious brothers and fellows Meletius and Eusebius" [of Samosata] "were numbered among the Arian heretics. Yet the battle which the Arians wage against them is by itself no slight proof of their orthodoxy to candid judges."—*Ep.* 266.

As to Athanasius himself, who seems to have been well inclined to Meletius, it happened, when he came to Antioch, that Meletius, for reasons unknown, refused to communicate with him.—(*Vid. Basil, Epp.* 89, 258.) Nor did Athanasius take any steps towards acknowledging Meletius, though he is said to have wished to do so.

But *audi alteram partem*;[173] thus separate from his brethren of the West and South was Meletius; yet even in his lifetime he had the affections of Christendom with him, and on his death the debt of reverence is paid him by three great Fathers, Nazianzen, Nyssen, and Chrysostom.

As to his own day, Theodoret relates a curious account which we extract, not for its own sake, so much as to show

---

[172] *Peter, the successor of Athanasius*: Peter (d. 311), Patriarch of Alexandria, venerated by the Orthodox as a saint.
[173] *audi alteram partem*: 'hear the other side too'

how little his schismatical position affected his reputation even in his lifetime.

"[The Emperor] Theodosius," he says, "thought he saw in a dream the divine Meletius, Bishop of Antioch, arraying him in a royal robe, and beautifying his head in a like crown. When the bishops were come together," [to the council of Constantinople] "being 150 in number, he forbade any to tell him which was the great Meletius; for he wished to single him out from the memory of his dream. When the whole multitude of bishops had entered into the palace, passing by all the rest, he ran up to the great Meletius, and as an affectionate son, enjoying the sight of his father after a long time, he embraced and kissed him, eyes, lips, breast, and head, and the hand which crowned him." —*Hist.* v 6, 7.

And after his death, Gregory Nazianzen says of him in verse, which we must be content to render in humble prose—"-Of whom" the bishops in the Council "there was one man, the president, most religious, simple, straightforward, full of God, of calm aspect, blending boldness with modesty in the eyes of beholders, a field cultivated by the Spirit."—*De Vit. sua*, p. 24. He adds with reference to his death, which took place while he was attending the General Council, "After many exhortations to peace, he departed to the company of Angels, and with a divine attendance and the outpouring of the city."—*Carm.* Pp. 24, 25. Gregory Nyssen's funeral sermon, which begins by calling him a new Apostle, who has increased the number of Apostles, proceeds:—

[64]

"We have lost our head, and together with our head have disappeared our precious senses. No longer have we an eye, to gaze on things heavenly; nor ear, hearing the divine voice, nor that tongue, the pure consecrated organ of truth. Where is the sweet sereneness of the eyes? where the bright smile upon the lips? Where the ready hand, which moved its fingers in accordance with the blessing of his mouth? I pity thee, O Church; to thee I speak, O Antioch: who shall tell the children that they are made orphans? who shall take the news to the bride that she is a widow? Alas, for what they sent out and what they receive back! They sent forward an ark, and they receive back a bier. An ark, my brethren, was that man of God, an ark, containing in itself the divine mysteries; there the golden pot of the divine manna, of the heavenly food. In it were the tables of the Covenant, inscribed on tables of the heart by the Spirit of the living God, not with ink."

Whatever is thought of such passages as these, so far is clear, that want of intercommunion with Rome, Italy, France, Spain, Africa, and Egypt, was thought no disadvantage to his memory. The saint's body was taken to Antioch, where a vast multitude met it, and was buried near his illustrious predecessor, St. Babylas,[174] by the Orontes. The anniversary day seems to have been kept from the first, and the sermon of St. Chrysostom, which remains, was delivered by him on its fifth return.

[65] "It is the way," he says, "with those who love, to cherish the very names of the objects beloved, and to kindle at the very sound; which is your feeling as regards this blessed saint. For from the time you first received him into this city, every one of you was wont to call his child after his name, thinking thus to introduce the saint into his own house; and mothers, passing over fathers, grandfathers, and forefathers, gave the name of the blessed Meletius to the children they had borne. Nor was it towards his name only that you felt thus affectionately, but towards his person too. What you did as to his name, that you

---

[174] *St Babylas*: Patriarch of Antioch who died in prison during the Decian persecution (253). St John Chrysostom preached a sermon on the saint.

were frequent in, as regards his likeness. On the stones of rings, on cups, on jugs, on the walls of their chambers, many there were who had engraved his sacred likeness."

Epiphanius,[175] who was of the Roman party, and acknowledged Meletius's rival in his see, uses the same language in his lifetime. "His life is serious," he says, "his conduct kind; he is entirely loved by the people, on account of his life, which all concur in extolling." We are told that, on occasion of his banishment for conforming to the Nicene doctrine, the governor of Antioch, who was conveying him out of the city, was imprudent enough to pass through the market-place, and the people greeted him with a shower of stones. His prisoner threw his cloak round him, and so saved his life. Such was Meletius. It is remarkable how distinct and consistent is the picture which all accounts give us of this holy and most amiable man; whose meekness, gentleness, sweetness of temper, and generosity of feeling, seem to have been notes of his churchmanship, which outweighed his separation from Rome and Alexandria, and prove that saints may be matured in a state which Romanists of this day would fain call schism.

3. Lucifer, Bishop of Cagliari[176] in Sardinia, and the main author of Meletius's unsatisfactory position, affords another instance to our purpose. His noble efforts and his sufferings in the cause of orthodoxy against the Arians are well known. When Julian[177] put an end to their ascendancy,

[66]

---

[175] *Epiphanius*: St Epiphanius of Salamis (c.315-403) was a prominent opponent of Arianism and was known as 'the oracle of Palestine'. In 367 he became bishop of Salamis.

[176] *Lucifer, Bishop of Cagliari*: or Lucifer Calaritanus (d. 370/371), a Sardinian bishop known for his staunch opposition to Arianism. He was subsequently exile to Palestine, Syria and Egypt.

[177] *Julian*: Julian the Apostate (330-363), Roman Emperor.

Athanasius, Eusebius of Vercellæ,[178] Lucifer, and Hilary, seemed the four remaining beacons of the Church, "rari in gurgite,"[179] to whom her fortunes were committed. Yet in a very short time Lucifer had quarrelled with his brethren, and thrown himself out of communion with the whole of Christendom, on a ground not unlike that of the Donatists. The Bishops of the whole Catholic Church, with a few exceptions, had been seduced during the preceding two years, by Arian address, into signing the ambiguous formulary of Ariminum. Athanasius and the rest decided that, on submitting to the creed of Nicæa, they might be acknowledged in their sees. But Lucifer, refusing to hold any intercourse with bishops who had thus betrayed their trust, or with those who had intercourse with them, shut himself out from the whole Catholic world, and confined the Church of God to Sardinia. He died in this estrangement. Yet, in spite of the history of his latter years, he seems, after his death, to have been reverenced as a saint both in Sardinia and some parts of Italy. In the Church of Vercellæ he is named in an invocatory hymn with Eusebius, bishop of that city, and Dionysius of Milan;[180] and in the middle of the seventeenth century the disputes seem to have run so high concerning him, that the Pope of the day published a decree, in which he forbids "all and every, for the future, from daring to treat publicly, dispute, or

---

[178] *Eusebius of Vercellæ*: St Eusebius (c.283-371) served as bishop of Vercelli from 340 and was a defender of orthodoxy against Arianism. Although dying naturally, he has been venerated as a martyr as a result of his sufferings and exile.

[179] *"rari in gurgite"*: the full quotation, taken from the *Aeneid* (I, 118), is *rari nantes in gurgite vasto*, rare survivors in the immense sea.

[180] *Dionysius of Milan*: St Dionysius (d. c.359) became bishop of Milan in 351 but died in exile in Cappadocia as a result of his opposition to Arianism.

controvert about the sanctity, worship, and veneration of Lucifer, or write or print for it or against it, till it shall be otherwise ordered by his Holiness or the Holy See."—*Vit. ed. Ven.*

But perhaps the strongest fact is St. Jerome's language about him, in his tract, written after Lucifer's death, against his followers; he calls him Beatus, a title which, while [67] explained away by some as a mere appendage to his episcopal office, has been the main cause of others maintaining, against the concurrent testimony of history, that he was either reconciled before his death, or never seriously opposed himself to the Catholic body. What makes Jerome's evidence the more valuable, is the circumstance that he felt the full difficulty of Lucifer's position, as having become the author of a real and serious schism; and yet, far from deciding that the mere fact of his personal estrangement decided against him, he thinks it worth while to mention and deny certain minor charges against him, such as vain-glory and resentment, charges which it would be superfluous to notice, were he by his estrangement notoriously put out of grace and beyond hope.

"I am come," he says, "to a most difficult point, in which, against my own will and design, I am compelled to judge of the blessed Lucifer, somewhat otherwise than is accordant with his merits and my own kind feeling towards him. But what can I do? Truth unlocks my mouth, and a conscious heart forces into words an unwilling tongue. In that crisis of the Church, amid that fury of the wolves, he withdrew his few sheep, and abandoned the rest of his flock, good shepherd as he was himself, yet leaving much prey to the beasts. I pass over the charge which certain censorious speakers maintain to be true, viz., as that he acted thus from desire of notoriety and posthumous repute; or again, from the resentment which he felt towards Eusebius, on account of the misunderstanding at Antioch. I believe no such thing of such a man. One thing I will firmly maintain about him even now, that he differs from us in words, not in things, if he receives those who had obtained baptism from the Arians."—*In Lucif.* 20.

[68]

Now what do all these instances show but this, that in troubled times of the Church much allowance ought to be made on all hands for jealousies, misunderstandings, estrangements between the parts of the Church; and that it is a very serious matter for any individual to pronounce what perhaps the whole Church alone can undertake, that this or that part of itself is in formal and fatal schism. Nor are we aware, taking Romanists on their own principles, that their Church has ever given such a sentence against ours.

4. Again, the Church of Rome has, in ancient and modern times, canonized persons who have lived and died in communion with an anti-Pope, on the plea of involuntary ignorance. Some instances occur in the fourteenth century;[181] but let us confine ourselves to one which Pope Gregory mentions, and which, by the way in which the doctrine of purgatory is introduced, shows incidentally, what we have had above to insist upon in another connexion, the unprimitive character of the Roman creed. Paschasius,[182] a Roman deacon, took part with the anti-Pope Laurence[183]

---

[181] Vide also Perrone, Prælect. Theol. t. i. pp. 263, 264 [p. 316.] [N]

[182] *Paschasius*: St Paschasius (d. c.512), a Roman deacon venerated as a saint despite supporting the antipope Laurence.

[183] *anti-Pope Laurence*: antipope on two occasions (498-99 and 501-6) as a result of a contested election with St Symmachus. He agreed to stand on in 499, becoming bishop of Nuceri but was encouraged by his supporters (especially the leader of the senate, Festus) to return in 501. He was finally expelled from Rome in 506 and spent his remaining years living a life of asceticism on a farm belonging to Festus.

against Pope Symmachus[184] in the end of the fifth century; he died in schism, so to name it, yet he is on the list of saints in the Roman catalogue. Gregory speaks thus of him in his Dialogues:—

"When I was yet quite a youth, and still had on my lay habit, I have heard from old and competent persons, that Paschasius, deacon of the Apostolic See, whose most orthodox and perspicuous treatises on the Holy Ghost are still extant among us, was a man of singular sanctity, especially devoted to alms deeds, a cherisher of the poor, and a neglecter of self. However, in the dispute which took place from the kindling of zeal of the faithful between Symmachus and Laurence, he chose Laurence for Pontiff, and, *when he was worsted afterwards by the unanimity of all*, yet *he persisted in his own opinion even to the day of his death*, in loving and preferring him who, by the judgment of the bishops, the Church had refused as her president. He then dying in the time of Symmachus, bishop of the Apostolic See, a possessed person touched his dalmatic, as it lay on the bier, and immediately was cured. After a long time Germanus, bishop of Capua,[185] was ordered by the physicians for his health to bathe in the hot wells at Angolos, who, on entering the said wells, saw the aforesaid deacon Paschasius, standing obediently in the heat. Exceedingly frightened at the sight, he asked what such a man was there doing. He made answer, 'For this sole cause I am placed here, because I sided with Laurence against Symmachus. But I pray thee, entreat the Lord for me, and thou wilt hereby know that thou art heard, if returning hither thou findest me not.' Therefore that man of the Lord, Germanus, devoted himself to prayer, and on returning after a few days, found the said Paschasius plainly gone from that place. For since he had sinned not from fault of wickedness but of

[69]

---

[184] *Pope Symmachus*: pope (498-514), who did much to defend orthodoxy and embellish the city of Rome, despite having to deal with the schism caused by the antipope Laurence.

[185] *Germanus, bishop of Capua*: (d. c. 545) a friend of St Benedict, who had a vision of the bishop's soul being carried to heaven at his death.

ignorance, he could be purged from sin after death. We must believe, however, that it was through the largeness of his alms deeds that he obtained this power of thus meriting pardon, then when he could no longer work. *Peter.*—How is it that *in these last times so many things dawn upon us about souls, which before lay hid*; so that, by open revelations and disclosures, the world to come seems entering in and opening upon us? "—*Dial.* iv. 40.

Let Roman Catholics be consistent. If they accept part of this alleged disclosure, let them take all. If such supernatural appearances prove the doctrine of purgatory, at least they also prove that schism is not necessarily a forfeiture of grace and hope.

11.

But enough of an *argumentum ad hominem*, which certainly is not the highest line of controversy. Looking at this instance in itself, as well as at the foregoing, which the Arian history furnishes, we seem to see this clearly: that, much as Roman Catholics may denounce us at present as schismatical, they could not resist us, if the Anglican communion had but that one Note of the Church upon it, to which all these instances point,—sanctity. The Church of his day could not resist Meletius; his enemies were fairly [70] overcome by him, by his meekness and holiness, which melted the most jealous of them. He had the suffrages of all Christian people with him in life and death, and when the schism was happily ended at a late period, he was acknowledged as a saint by the whole Church. And so as regards ourselves; in vain would a few controversialists taunt us in that case with the disorders of the sixteenth century, or attempt to prove our alienation from the commonwealth of Israel. The hearts of their own people would be with us; we should have an argument more intelligible than any which the schools could furnish, could we appeal to this living evidence of truth, in our bishops, our chapters, our clergy, our divines, our laity, causing men to glorify our Father which is in heaven. We should not be unwilling to place the matter on this issue. We are almost content to say to Romanists, Account us not yet as a branch of the Catholic Church, though we be a branch, till we are like a branch, so that when we do become like a branch, then you consent to acknowledge us. Unless our system really has a power in it, making us neglectful of wealth, neglectful of station, neglectful of ease, munificent, austere, reverent, childlike, unless it is able to bring our passions into order, to make us pure, to make us meek, to rule our intellect, to give government of speech, to inspire firmness, to destroy self, we do not deserve to be acknowledged as a Church, and we submit to be ill-treated.

And, on the other hand, we put the matter on the same issue as regards themselves. Without here speaking upon points of faith, without pressing on them what we account corruption in doctrine and cruelty in enforcing it,—we urge against them simply the lack of what in other respects we desiderate in ourselves. Till we see in them as a Church more straightforwardness, truth, and openness, more of [71] severe obedience to God's least commandments, more scrupulousness about means, less of a political, scheming, grasping spirit, less of intrigue, less that looks hollow and superficial, less accommodation to the tastes of the vulgar, less subserviency to the vices of the rich, less humouring of men's morbid and wayward imaginations, less indulgence of their low and carnal superstitions, less intimacy with the revolutionary spirit of the day, we will keep aloof from them as we do. In perplexed times such as these, when the landmarks of truth are torn up or buried, here is a sure guide providentially given us, which we cannot be wrong in following, "By their fruits ye shall know them."[186] When we go into foreign countries, we see superstitions in the Roman Church which shock us; when we read history, we find its spirit of intrigue so rife, so widely spread, that "jesuitism" has become a by-word; when we look round us at home, we see it associated everywhere with the low democracy, pandering to the spirit of rebellion, the lust of change, the unthankfulness of the irreligious, and the enviousness of the needy. We see its grave theologians connecting their names with men who are convicted by the common sense of mankind of something very like perjury, and its leaders in alliance with a political party notorious in the *orbis terrarum* as a sort of standard in every place for liberalism and infidelity. We see it attempting to gain converts among us, by unreal representations of its doctrines, plausible statements, bold assertions, appeals to the weaknesses of human nature, to our fancies, our eccentricities, our fears, our frivolities, our false philosophies. We see its agents smiling and nodding and ducking to attract attention, as gipsies make up to truant boys, holding out tales for the nursery, and pretty pictures, and gold gingerbread, and physic concealed in jam, and sugar-plums for good children.

[72]

---

[186] *"By their fruits ye shall know them"*: Mt 7:16

Who can but feel shame when the religion of Ximenes,[187] Borromeo,[188] and Pascal[189] is so overlaid? Who can but feel sorrow when its devout and earnest defenders so mistake its genius and our capabilities? We Englishmen like manliness, openness, consistency, truth. Rome will never gain on us till she learns these virtues, and uses them; then she may gain us, but it will be by ceasing to be what we now mean by Rome, by having a right, not to "have dominion over our faith,"[190] but to gain and possess our affections in the bonds of the Gospel. Till she ceases to be what she practically is, a union is impossible between her and England; but if she does reform, (and who shall presume to say that so large a part of Christendom never can?) then it will be our Church's duty at once to join in communion with the Continental Churches, whatever politicians at home may say to it, and whatever steps the civil power may take in consequence. And though we shall not live to see that day, at least we are bound to pray for it; we are bound to pray for our brethren that they and we may be led together into the pure light of the Gospel, and be one as once we were; that Ephraim may no longer envy Judah, or Judah vex Ephraim; that "all who profess and call themselves Christians may be led into the way of truth, and hold the faith in unity of spirit, in the bond of peace, and in righteousness of life;"[191] "that all who do

---

[187] *Ximenes*: Francisco Jiménez de Cisneros (1436-1517), Spanish Franciscan, Cardinal, religious reformer and statesman. His involvement with the Spanish Inquisition made him a favourite subject of anti-Catholic polemicists.

[188] *Borromeo*: St Charles Borromeo (1538–1584), nephew of Pius IV and, as Archbishop of Milan, one of the leading proponents of the Catholic Reformation..

[189] *Pascal*: Blaise Pascal (1623-1662), French mathematician, physicist and theologian. He was influenced by the Jansenist movement and among his religious works are *Les Provinciales* and *Pensées*.

[190] *"have dominion over our faith"*: 2 Cor 1:24

[191] *"all who profess and call themselves Christians may be led into the way of truth, and hold the faith in unity of spirit, in the bond of peace, and in*

confess" God's "holy name, may agree in the truth of His Holy Word, and live in unity and godly love."[192] It was most touching news to be told, as we were lately, that Christians on the Continent were praying together for the spiritual well-being of England.[193] We are their debtors thereby. May
[73] the prayer return abundantly into their own bosom, and while they care for our souls may their own be prospered! May they gain light while they aim at unity, and grow in faith while they manifest their love! We too have our duties to them; not of reviling, not of slandering, not of hating, though political interests require it; but the duty of loving brethren still more abundantly in spirit, whose faces, for our sins and their sins, we are not allowed to see in the flesh.

January, 1840.

---

righteousness of life": from the Book of Common Prayer (Prayer for All Sorts and Conditions of Men).

[192] *"that all who do confess ... holy name, may agree in the truth of His Holy Word, and live in unity and godly love."*: taken from the Order of Holy Communion in the Book of Common Prayer.

[193] *It was most touching news to be told, as we were lately, that Christians on the Continent were praying together for the spiritual well-being of England*: In 1838 the converts Ambrose Phillipps and George Spencer (youngest son of Earl Spencer) had set up the 'Association of Universal Prayer for the Conversion of England'. Initially approved by the Archbishop of Paris, it found many adherents on the continent. In January 1840 Spencer visited Newman at Oriel: 'So glad in my heart was I to see him, when he came to my rooms with Mr. Palmer of Magdalen, that I could have laughed for joy; I think I did laugh; but I was very rude to him, I would not meet him at dinner, and that, (though I did not say so,) because I considered him "in loco apostatæ" from the Anglican Church, and I hereby beg his pardon for it.' (*Ap.*, p.124).

NOTE ON ESSAY X.

IF the arguments used in the foregoing Essay did not retain me in the Anglican Church, I do not see what could keep me in it; yet the time came, when I wrote to Mr. Keble,[1] "I seem to myself almost to have shot my last arrow [against Rome], in the article on English Catholicity."—*Apolog. Ed.* 2, p. 134.

The truth is, I believe, I was always asking myself what would the Fathers have done, what would those whose works were around my room, whose names were ever meeting my eyes, whose authority was ever influencing my judgment, what would these men have said, how would they have acted in my position? I had made a good case on paper, but what judgment would be passed on it by Athanasius, Basil, Gregory, Hilary, and Ambrose? The more I considered the matter, the more I thought that these Fathers, if they examined the antagonist pleas, would give it against me.

I expressed this feeling in my Essay on the Development of Christian Doctrine. "Did St. Athanasius, or St. Ambrose, come suddenly to life, it cannot be doubted," I said ironically, "what communion they would mistake for their own. All surely will agree that these Fathers, with whatever differences of opinion, whatever protests, if we will, would find themselves more at home with such men as St.

---

[1] *when I wrote to Mr Keble*: 26th October 1840, *LD* 7 p. 418.

[75] Bernard,[2] or St. Ignatius Loyola,[3] or with the lonely priest in his lodgings, or the holy sisterhood of Charity, or the unlettered crowd before the altar, than with the rulers or members of any other religious community. And may we not add, that were the two Saints, who once sojourned in exile or on embassage at Treves, to come more northward still, and to travel until they reached another fair city, seated among groves, green meadows, and calm streams, the holy brothers would turn from many a high aisle and solemn cloister which they found there, and ask the way to some small chapel, where mass was said, in the populous alley or the forlorn suburb? And, on the other hand, can any one who has but heard his name, and cursorily read his history, doubt for one instant, how the people of England, in turn, 'we, our princes, our priests, and our prophets,' Lords and Commons, Universities, Ecclesiastical Courts, marts of commerce, great towns, country parishes, would deal with Athanasius,—Athanasius, who spent his long years in fighting against kings for a theological term?"—P. 138.

I recommend this passage to the consideration of those more than friendly critics of mine, who, in their perplexity to find a motive sufficient for my becoming a Catholic, attribute the step in me personally (without any warrant, I think, from anything that I have said or written) to a desire for a firmer ground of religious certitude, and a clearer view of revealed truth, than is furnished in the Church of [76] England.[4] I should also venture respectfully to offer the

---

[2] *St Bernard*: St Bernard of Clairvaux (1090- 1153), Abbot and Doctor of the Church; founder of the Cistercian Order, a reform of the Benedictines.
[3] *St Ignatius Loyola*: St Ignatius Loyola (1491-1556), founder of the Society of Jesus.
[4] Mr. Hutton, in his recently published most interesting Essays, speaking of converts, wonders "what is the charm which has power to retain them, *after experience* of Rome's coarse splendours and of her vigilant and oppressive rule." I suppose he is contemplating in Rome what I had in mind in 1850 when I spoke of

same passage to the notice of an eminent statesman and brilliant writer,[5] who has lately gone out of his way to observe that "the secession of Dr. Newman" is an "extraordinary event," which, "has been 'apologized for,' but has never been explained;" except that I doubted whether a genuine politician could possibly enter into any motives of action, not political, and was not likely, even in the province of physics, to demand reasons of state or party interests in explanation of a chimpanzee being delivered of a human baby, or a Caucasian man developing into an Archangel. But to our immediate subject:—

The foregoing Essay calls on me for a reconsideration of its contents in three respects: as regards, first, the validity of Anglican Orders; secondly, the unity of ecclesiastical jurisdiction; thirdly, the apparent exceptions to that unity in the history of the early Church. And first as to Anglican Orders.

1.

As to the Anglican Orders, I certainly do think them doubtful and untrustworthy; and that, independent of any question arising out of Parker's consecration, into which I will not enter. Granting, for argument's sake, that that consecration was in all respects what its defenders say it

---

her aspect as "peremptory, stern, resolute, overbearing, and relentless;" but this is what I felt, as I then expressly said, *before* "experience" of her "rule," and an impression which did not deter me from becoming a Catholic, or rather helped me to become one, can have no power to affect me unfavourably now, when I have been a Catholic so long. [N]

    what I had in mind in 1850: Cf. *Diff* I, 387, where Newman writes 'The Church then, as now, might be called peremptory and stern, resolute, overbearing and relentless…'

[5] *an eminent statesman and brilliant writer*: In 1870, Benjamin Disraeli wrote in the 'General Preface' to *The Works of Benjamin Disraeli, Earl of Beaconsfield* (vol. 1, pp.xxiv-xxv): 'Little more than a year after the publication of *Coningsby*, the secession of Dr Newman dealt a blow to the Church of England under which it still reels. That extraordinary event has been "apologized for," but has never been explained. It was a mistake and a misfortune.'

was, still I feel a large difficulty in accepting the Anglican Succession and Commission of Ministry, arising out of the historical aspect of the Anglican Church and of its prelates, an aspect which suggests a grave suspicion of the validity of their acts from first to last. I had occasion to make some remarks on this subject several years ago;[6] but I left them unfinished, as feeling that I was distressing, without convincing, men whom I love and respect, by impugning an [77] article of their belief, which to them is sacred, in proportion as it is vital. Now, however, when time has passed, and I am opposing not them but my former self, I may be allowed, *pace charissimorum virorum*,[7] to explain myself, and leave my explanation on record, as regards some points to which exception was then taken. And, in so doing, I do but profess to be setting down a view of the subject which is very clear to my own mind, and which, as I think, ought to be clear to them: but of course I am not laying down the law on a point on which the Church has not directly and distinctly spoken, nor implying that I am not open to arguments on the other side, if such are forthcoming, which I do not anticipate.

First of all, I will attempt to set right what I thought I had set right at the time. A mis-statement was made some time ago in *Notes and Queries*,[8] to the effect that I had expressed "doubts about Machyn's Diary."[9] In spite of my immediate denial of it in that publication, it has been

---

[6] *some remarks on this subject several years ago*: This refers to the letter from Newman to Fr Coleridge of 5 August 1868, which is included at the end of this 'Note' (in a slightly adapted form), pp.[109-11].

[7] *pace charissimorum virorum*: 'with due deference to men of the greatest charity' or possibly 'to men who are dearest to me'.

[8] Notes and Queries: a scholarly journal on historical and literary subjects, first published in 1849. The reference to Newman's alleged doubts about Parker's consecration appeared in the issue of 21st November 1868, p.493.

[9] *Machyn's Diary*: the chronicle kept by Henry Machyn (c.1496-1563), a London merchant, between 1550 and his death, presumably from plague, in 1563. It includes details of Parker's consecration.

repeated in a recent learned work on Anglican Orders. Let me then again declare here that I know nothing whatever about Machyn, and that I have never even mentioned his name in anything I have ever written, and that I have no doubts whatever, because I have no opinion at all, favourable or unfavourable, about him or his Diary. Indeed, it is plain that, since, in the letter in which I was supposed to have spoken on the subject, I had dismissed altogether what I called the "antiquarian" question concerning the consecrations of 1559, as one which I felt to be dreary and interminable, I should have been simply inconsistent, had I introduced Machyn or his Diary into it, and should, in point of logic, have muddled my argument.

That argument, which I maintain now as then, is as follows:—That the consecrations of 1559 were not only [78] facts, they were acts; that those acts were not done and over once for all, but were only the first of a series of acts done in a long course of years; that these acts too, all of them, were done by men of certain positive opinions and intentions, and none of those opinions and views, from first to last, of a Catholic complexion, but on the contrary erroneous and heretical. And I questioned whether men of those opinions could by means of a mere rite or formulary, however correct in itself, start and continue in a religious communion, such as the Anglican, a ministerial succession which could be depended on as inviolate. I do not see what guarantee is producible for the faithful observance of a sacred rite, in form, matter, and intention, through so long a period in the hands of such administrators. And again, the existing state of the Anglican body, so ignorant of fundamental truth, so overrun with diversified error, would be but a sorry outcome of Apostolical ordinances and graces. "By their fruits shall ye know them." Revelation involves in its very idea a teaching and a hearing of Divine Truth. What clear and steady light of truth is there in the Church of England? What candlestick, upright and firm, on which it has been set? This seems to me what Leslie[10] calls "a short and easy method;" it is drawn out from one of the Notes of the Church. When we look at the Anglican communion, not in the books, in the imagination, or in the affections of its champions, but as it is in fact, its claims to speak in Christ's Name are refuted by its very condition. An Apostolical ministry necessarily involves an Apostolical teaching.

[79]   This practical argument was met at the time by two objections: first, that it was far-fetched, and next, that in a Catholic it was suicidal. I do not see that it is either, and I proceed to say why.

1. As to its being far-fetched or unreasonable; if so, it is strange that it should have lately approved itself to a writer placed in very different circumstances, who has used it, not indeed against Anglican Orders, for he firmly upholds them, but against Swedish;—I mean, Dr. Littledale.[11] This learned and zealous man, in his late lecture at Oxford, decides that a certain uncatholic act, which he specifies, of the Swedish ecclesiastical Establishment, done at a particular time and place, has so bad a look, as to suffice, independent of all investigation into documents of past history, at once to unchurch it,—which is to go much further in the use of my argument than I should think it right to go myself.

---

[10] *Leslie*: Henry Leslie (1580-1661), Church of Ireland clergyman and Bishop of Down and Connor, whose works included *Treatise on the Authority of the Church* (1637).

[11] *Dr Littledale*: Richard Frederick Littledale (1833-90), a prominent Anglo-Irish ritualist and controversialist, whose works included the popular *Plain Reasons for not joining the Church of Rome* (1880), sparking off replies from Catholic writers such as the Oratorian Fr H. I. D. Ryder.

"Sweden," he says, "*professes* to have retained an Apostolical Succession; I am satisfied from historical evidence that she has nothing of the kind; *but* the late chaplain to the Swedish embassy in London has been good enough to supply me with *an important disproof of his own Orders*. During a long illness, from which he was suffering some time ago, he entrusted the entire charge of his flock to a Danish pastor, until such time as his own successor was at length sent from Sweden. *His official position* must have made *the sanction of the authorities*, both in Church and State, necessary for a delegation of his duties; so that the *act* cannot be classed with that of an obscure Yorkshire incumbent, the other day, who invited an Anabaptist minister to fill his pulpit. And thus we gather that the quasi-Episcopal Church of Sweden treats Presbyterian ministers on terms of perfect equality."—P. 8.

Here then a writer, whose bias is towards the Church of England, distinctly lays down the principle, that a lax [80] ecclesiastical practice, ascertained by even one formal instance, apart from documentary evidence, or ritual observance, is sufficient in itself to constitute it an important disproof of the claim advanced by a nation to the possession of an Apostolical Succession in its clergy. I speak here only of the principle involved in Dr. Littledale's argument, which is the same as my own principle; though, for myself, I do not say more than that Anglican ordinations are doubtful, whereas he considers the Swedish to be simply null. Nor again should I venture to assert that one instance of irregularity, such as that which he adduces, is sufficient to carry on either me or (much less) him to our respective conclusions. To what indeed does his "disproof" of Swedish orders come but to this: that the Swedish authorities think that Presbyterianism, as a religion, has in its doctrines and ordinances what is called "the root of the matter," and that the Episcopal form is nothing more than what I have called above (vol. i. p. 365) "the extra twopence"? Do the highest living authorities in the Anglican Church, Queen or Archbishop, think very differently from this? would they not, if they dared, do just what the late Swedish chaplain did, and think it a large wisdom and a true charity to do so?

So much on the reasonableness of my argument. I conceive there is nothing evasive in refusing to decide the question of Orders by the mere letter of an Ordination Service, to the neglect of more elementary and broader questions; nothing far-fetched, in taking into account the opinions and practices of its successive administrators, unless Anglicans may act towards the Swedes as Catholics may not act towards Anglicans. Such is the common sense of the matter; and that it is the Catholic sense, too, a few words will show.

It will be made clear in three propositions:—First, the [81] Anglican Bishops for three centuries have lived and died in heresy; (I am not questioning their good faith and invincible ignorance, which is an irrelevant point;) next, it is far from certain, it is at the utmost only probable, that Orders conferred by heretics are valid; lastly, in conferring the sacraments, the safer side, not merely the more probable, must ever be taken. And, as to the proof of these three points,—as regards the first of them, I ask, how many Anglican Bishops have believed in transubstantiation, or in the necessity of sacramental penance? yet to deny these dogmas is to be a heretic. Secondly, as to Orders conferred by heretics, there is, I grant, a strong case for their validity, but then there is also a strong case against it (*vid.*

Bingham,[12] Antiq. iv. 7); so that at most heretical ordination is not certainly, but only probably valid. As to the third point, this, viz., that in conferring sacraments not merely the more probable but the safer side must be taken, and that they must be practically considered invalid, when they are not certainly valid, this is the ordinary doctrine of the Church. "Opinio probabilis," says St. Alfonso Liguori, "est illa, quæ gravi aliquo innititur fundamento, apto ad hominis prudentis assensum inclinandum. In Sacramentorum collatione *non potest minister uti opinione probabili*, aut probabiliori, de Sacramenti valore, sed tutiores sequendæ sunt, aut moraliter certæ."[13] Pope Benedict XIV.[14] supplies us with an illustration of this principle, even as regards a detail of the rite itself. In his time an answer was given from Rome, in the case of a candidate for the priesthood, who, in

[82]

---

[12] *Bingham*: Joseph Bingham (1668-1726), clergyman and author, whose magnum opus was the *Origines Ecclesiasticae, or Antiquities of the Christian Church* (10 volumes, 1708-22).

[13] The principle of the "tutior" opinion applies also to the rule of three bishops for a consecration, about which Hallier says: "An consecratio episcopi omnino nulla, irrita, et invalida sit, vel solum illegitima, quæ à paucioribus tribus episcopis peracta fuerit: Caietanus, Bellarminus, Vasquez, et alii affirmantem partem sequuntur (nisi ecclesiæ dispensatio acciderit); negantem vero Paludanus ... Sylvester . . et alii ... Difficilis utique hæc controversia est, in quâ tamen posterior longe probabilior et fortioribus innixa mihi videtur argumentis, ... tamen prior communis est, et hocce tempore magis recepta."—De S. Ordin. t. 2, pp. 299, 308. [N] *"An consecration ... magis recepta*: "As to whether the consecration of a bishop is altogether null, ineffective and invalid, or only unlawful, if it is performed by fewer than three bishops: Caietan, Bellarmine, Vasquez, and others follow the side of affirmation (unless a dispensation of the Church has occurred), but Paludanus ... Sylvester ... and others take the side of denying this. This controversy is certainly difficult, in which, however, the latter opinion seems to me far more probable, and reliant on stronger arguments, but the former is common, and more generally accepted at this time."

"Opinio probabilis ... moraliter certae.": "A probable opinion is that which rests on some weighty foundation, fit to move the assent of a man of good sense. In the conferring of the Sacraments the minister cannot use the probable, or more probable opinion, about the validity of the Sacrament, but the safer ones should be followed, or those which are morally certain."

[14] *Benedict XIV*: Pope 1740-58, who prior to his election wrote an important treatise on the canonisation of saints, *De servorum Dei beatificatione et beatorum canonizatione* (1734-38).

the course of his ordination, had received the imposition of hands, but accidentally neglected to receive from the Bishop the Paten and Chalice. It was to the effect that he was bound to be ordained over again *sub conditione*.[15]

What Anglican candidate for the priesthood has ever touched physically or even morally Paten or Chalice in his ordination, from Archbishop Parker to Archbishop Tait?[16] In

---

[15] Benedict says, Syn. Diœc. VIII., 10: "Quidam sacerdotio initiandus, etsi omnes consuetas manuum impositiones ab Episcopo accepisset, ad Episcopum tamen, solita patenæ cum hostiâ et calicis cum vino instrumenta porrigentem, ad alia tunc temporis distractus, non accessit. Re postea detectâ, quid facto opus esset, dubitatum, atque a S. Congregatione petitum est." After giving his own opinion, "Nihil esse iterandum, sed cautè supplendum, quod per errorem prætermissum," he states the decision of the Sacred Congregation, "Sacra Congregatio totam Ordinationem sub conditione iterandam rescripsit." And Scavini Theol. Mor. t. 3, p. 278, referring to the passage in Benedict, says of the "libri traditio" as well as the "manuum impositio" in the ordination of a deacon: "Probabile est libri traditionem esse de essentiâ ... quare pro praxi concludimus, utramque esse adhibendam, cùm agatur de Sacramentis; et, si quidpiam ex istis fuerit omissam, sub conditione ordinationem iterandam esse."

It is true that Father Perrone in 1863, on his asking as to the necessity of the "*physicus tactus*" (as Father Ephrem before him in 1661) received for answer as Ephrem did, that to insist on it was a scruple (Gury de Ord.); but we are here concerned, not with the mere physical "tactus," but the moral "traditio instrumentorum." [N]

Scavini Theol. Mor.: *Theologia Moralis Universa ad mentem S. Alphonsi*, Pietro Scavini, 3 vols., Mediolani, 1880.

Father Perrone: Giovanni Perrone (1794-1876), Jesuit Professor of Dogmatic Theology at the Roman College (now the Gregorian), 1824-30, 1834-1848. He oversaw Newman's *Theses on Development* in 1847 and defended him in 1867 over the accusation that he was preparing Oratory School boys for Oxford. He was the author of *Praelectiones Theologicae* which went into 34 editions.

the necessity of the "physicus tactus": The debate about the *matter* of the Sacrament of Orders, as to whether it was the acceptance of paten and chalice *and* the imposition of hands was settled by Pius XII. He declared that it was uniquely the imposition of hands, and that the giving of the paten and chalice was not of the essence, *Sacramentum Ordinis*, 1947, *DS* 3860. In reply to a question, the Sacred Congregation of Rites said that a *moral* contact of the hands was sufficiently valid, but that "a physical contact was altogether to be preferred." *AAS* 40 (1948) p.7. 94-1876.

Father Ephrem: identity unknown.

Gury de Ord.: Jean-Pierre Gury (1801-1866) French Jesuit, his book *Casus Conscientiae* was published in 1862.

[16] *Archbishop Tait*: Archibald Campbell Tait (1811-82), then Archbishop of Canterbury (1868-82). As a Fellow at Balliol, Tait had had little sympathy with the

truth, the Catholic rite, whether it differs from itself or not in different ages, still in every age, age after age, is itself, and nothing but itself. It is a concrete whole, one and indivisible, and acts *per modum unius*;[17] and, having been established by the Church, and being in present use and possession, it cannot be cut up into bits, be docked and twisted, or split into essentials and non-essentials, genus and [83] species, matter and form, at the heretical will of a Cranmer, or a Ridley,[18] or turned into a fancy ordinal by a royal commission of divines, without a sacrilege perilous to its vitality. Though the delivery of the sacred vessels was not primitive, it was part of the existing rite, three centuries ago, as it is now, and could not, and cannot be omitted, without prejudice to the ecclesiastical *status* of those who are ordained without it.

Whether indeed, as time goes on, the Pope, in the plenitude of his power, could, with the aid of his theologians, obtain that clearer light, which the Church has not at present, on the whole question of ordination, for which St. Leo IX.[19] so earnestly prayed, and thereby determine what at present is enveloped in such doubtfulness, viz., the validity of heretical ordination, and, what is still more improbable than the abstract proposition, the validity of Anglican Orders in particular, is a subject on which I do not enter. As the matter stands, all we see is a hierarchical body, whose opinions through three hundred

---

Oxford Movement and, in response to Newman's *Tract 90*, drafted the protest of 'the Four Tutors'.

[17] per modum unius: as one

[18] *Ridley*: Nicholas Ridley (c.1500-55) served as bishop of Rochester (1547-50) and bishop of London (1550-53) and was burnt for heresy at Oxford in 1555, along with Thomas Cranmer and Hugh Latimer.

[19] *St Leo IX*: Pope 1048-54, a close associate of Hildebrand (later St Gregory VII) and key proponent of Church reform. He died shortly after a brief period of captivity by the Normans.

years compromise their acts, who do not themselves believe that they have the gifts which their zealous adherents ascribe to them, who in their hearts deny those sacramental formulas which their country's law obliges them to use, who conscientiously shudder at assuming real episcopal or sacerdotal power, who resolve "Receive the Holy Ghost" into a prayer, "Whose sins ye remit are remitted" into a license to preach, and "This is My Body, this is My Blood" into an allegory.

And then, supposing if ever, these great difficulties were overcome, after all would follow the cardinal question, which Benedict XIV. opens, as I have shown, about the sufficiency of their rite itself.

[84] Anyhow, as things now stand, it is clear no Anglican Bishop or Priest can by Catholics be recognized to be such. If indeed earnestness of mind and purity of purpose could ever be a substitute for the formal conditions of a sacrament, which Apostles have instituted and the Church maintains, certainly in that case one might imagine it to be so accepted in many an Anglican ordination. I do believe that, in the case of many men, it is the one great day of their lives, which cannot come twice, the day on which, in their fresh youth, they freely dedicated themselves and all their powers to the service of their Redeemer,—solemn and joyful at the time, and ever after fragrant in their memories:—it is so; but devotion cannot reverse the past, nor can good faith stand in the stead of what is true; and it is because I feel this, and in no temper of party, that I refuse to entertain an imagination which is neither probable in fact, nor Catholic in spirit. If we do not even receive the baptism of Anglicans, how can we receive their ordinations?

2. But now, secondly, comes the question, whether the argument, used above against Anglican, may not be retorted

on Catholic ordinations;—for it may be objected that, however Catholics may claim to themselves the tradition of doctrine and rite, they do not profess to be secure against bad ecclesiastics any more than Protestants; that there have been times of ignorance, violence, unscrupulousness, in the history of the Catholic Church; and that, if Anglican Orders are untrustworthy because of the chance mistakes in three hundred years, much more so are Catholic, which have run a whole eighteen hundred. In short, that I have but used against the Anglican ministry the old notorious argument of Chillingworth[20] and Macaulay,[21] an argument, which is of a sceptical character in them, and, in a Catholic, suicidal also.   [85]

Now I do not well know what is meant by calling such an argument sceptical. It seems to me a very fair argument. Scepticism is the refusal to be satisfied with reasons which ought to satisfy. To be sceptical is to be unreasonable. But what is there unreasonable, what extravagant in idea, or inconsistent with experience, in recognizing the chance of important mistakes, here or there, in a given succession of acts? I do certainly think it most probable, that an intricate series of ordinations through three hundred years, and much more through eighteen hundred, will have flaws in it. Who does not think so? It will have them to a certainty, and is in itself untrustworthy. By "untrustworthy in itself," I mean, humanly speaking; for if indeed there be any special

---

[20] *Chillingworth*: William Chillingworth (1602-44), godson of William Laud and Fellow of Trinity College, Oxford, best known for his *The Religion of Protestants a Safe Way to Salvation* (1637), published as part of a controversy between Edward Knott (a Jesuit) and Dr Potter (Provost of The Queen's College, Oxford). As a young man Chillingworth had briefly converted to Catholicism and spent a year at the English College, Douay. His writings also include *The Apostolic Institution of Episcopacy demonstrated* (1644).

[21] *Macaulay*: Thomas Babington Macaulay, 1st Baron Macaulay (1800-59), historian and Whig politician. He attacked the theory of Apostolic Succession in his *Gladstone on Church and State* (1839). Picking up from Chillingworth, he argued the unlikelihood of a valid succession over 1800 years.

protection promised to it, beyond nature, to secure it against errors and accidents, that of course is another matter; and the simple question is, whether this or that particular Succession has such a promise, or in other words, whether this or that Succession is or is not apostolical. It is usual for Anglicans to say, as we say, that they have "the Apostolical Succession;" but that is begging the question; if a Succession *be* apostolical, then indeed it is protected from errors; but it has to be proved apostolical before such protection can be claimed for it; that is, we and they, both of us, must give reasons in our own case respectively for this our critical assumption of our *being* apostolical. We, Catholics, do produce our reasons,—that is, we produce what are commonly called "the Notes of the Church,"—by virtue of those reasons, we consider we belong to that Apostolical Church, in which were at the beginning stored the promises; and therefore our Succession has the apostolic promise of protection and is preserved from accidents, or is apostolic; on the other hand, Anglicans must give reasons on their part for maintaining that they too belong to the Apostolic Church, and that their Succession is Apostolic. There is then nothing unfair in Macaulay's argument, viewed in itself; it is fair to both of us; nor is it suicidal in the hands of a Catholic to use it against Anglicans, if, at the same time, he gives reasons why it cannot by opponents be used against himself. Let us look, then, at the objection more closely.

[86]

Lord Macaulay's remarks on the "Apostolic Succession," as contained in one of his Reviews, written with the force and brilliancy for which he is so well known, are far too extended to admit of insertion here; but I will quote a few words of his argument from its beginning and ending. He begins by laying down, first, that, whether an

Anglican clergyman "be a priest by succession from the Apostles depends on the question, whether, during that long period, some thousands of events took place, any one of which may, without any gross impropriety, be supposed not to have taken place;" and next "that there is not a tittle of evidence for any one of these events." Then after various vivid illustrations of his argument, he ends by a reference to Chillingworth's "very remarkable words," as he calls them. "That of ten thousand probables no one should be false, that of ten thousand requisites, whereof any one may fail, not one should be wanting, this to me is extremely improbable, and even cousin-german to impossible."

I cannot deny, certainly, that Catholics, as well as the high Anglican school, do believe in the Apostolic Succession of ministry, continued through eighteen hundred years; nor that they both believe it to be necessary to an Apostolical ministry; nor that they act upon their belief. But, as I have said, though so far the two parties agree, still they differ materially in their respective positions, relatively [87] towards that Succession, and differ in consequence in their exposure respectively to the force of the objection on which I have been dwelling. The difference of position between the two may be expressed in the following antithesis:— Catholics believe their Orders are valid, because they are members of the true Church; and Anglicans believe they belong to the true Church, because their Orders are valid. And this is why Macaulay's objection tells against Anglicans, and does not tell against Catholics.

In other words, our Apostolical descent is to us a theological inference, and not primarily a doctrine of faith; theirs with them is a first principle in controversy, and a patent matter of fact, the credentials of their mission. That they can claim to have God's ministers among them, depends directly and solely upon the validity of their Orders; and to prove their validity, they are bound to trace their Succession through a hundred intermediate steps till at length they reach the Apostles; till they do this their claim is in abeyance. If it is improbable that the Succession has no flaws in it, they have to bear the brunt of the improbability; if it is presumable that a special Providence precludes such flaws, or compensates for them, they cannot take the benefit of that presumption to themselves; for to do so would be claiming to belong to the true Church, to which that high Providence is promised, and this they cannot do without arguing in a circle, first proving that they are of the true Church because they have valid Orders, and then that their Orders are valid because they are of the true Church.

Thus the Apostolical Succession is to Anglican divines a *sine quâ non*, not "necessitate præcepti" sed "necessitate medii." Their Succession is indispensable to their position, as being the point from which they start; and therefore it [88] must be unimpeachable, or else, they do not belong to the Church; and to prove it is unimpeachable by introducing the special Providence of God over His Church, would be like proving the authority of Scripture by those miracles of which Scripture alone is the record. It must be unimpeachable before, and without taking that special Providence into account, and this, I have said above, it cannot be. We, on our side, on the contrary, are not in such a dilemma as this. Our starting-point is not the fact of a faithful transmission of Orders, but the standing fact of the Church, the Visible and One Church, the reproduction and succession of herself age after age. It is the Church herself that vouches for our Orders, while she authenticates herself to be the Church not by our Orders, but by her Notes. It is the great Note of an ever-enduring *cœtus fidelium*, with a fixed organization, a unity of jurisdiction, a political greatness, a continuity of existence in all places and times, a suitableness to all classes, ranks, and callings, an ever-energizing life, an untiring, ever-evolving history, which is her evidence that she is the creation of God, and the representative and home of Christianity. She is not based upon her Orders; she is not the subject of her instruments; they are not necessary for her idea. We could even afford, for argument's sake, to concede to Lord Macaulay the uncertainty of our Succession. If Providence had so willed, she might have had her ministers without any lineal descent from the Apostles at all. Her mere nomination might have superseded any rite of Ordination; there might have been no indelible character in her ministers; she might have commissioned them, used them, and recalled them at her pleasure. She might have been like a civil state, in which there is a continuation of office, but not a propagation of [89] official life. The occupant of the See of St. Peter, himself made such by mere election, might have made bishops and unmade them. Her Divine Founder has chosen a better way, better because He has chosen it. A transmission of ministerial power ever has been, and ever shall be; and He who has so ordained, will carry out His ordinance, preserve it from infraction or make good any damage to it, because it is His ordinance, but still that ordinance is not simply of the essence of the Church; it is not more than an inseparable accident and a necessary instrument. Nor is the Apostolic descent of her priests the direct warrant of their power in the eyes of the faithful; their warrant is her immediate, present, living authority; it is the word of the Church which marks them out as the ministers of God, not any historical or antiquarian research, or genealogical table; and while she is most cautious and jealous that they should be ordained aright, yet it is sufficient in proof of their ordination that they belong to her.

Thus it would appear, that to Catholics the certainty of Apostolical Orders is not a point of prime necessity, yet they possess it; and for Anglicans it is absolutely indispensable, yet they have it not.

On such grounds as these it is, that I consider the line of argument, which I have adopted against Anglican Orders, is neither open to the charge of scepticism, nor suicidal in the hands of a Catholic.

2.

My second point does not require so many words. I have been urging that there is no security for the transmission of the Apostolical Ministry, except as continued in that Church which has the promises. We must first be sure that we are in that Church, and then we shall inherit the Church's security about her Orders. If we are in the Church, in that case we know well that He, who overrules everything for her good, will have taken full account of the infirmity of her human instruments, and have prevented or remedied, in His own way, any faults which may have occurred in past centuries in the administration of His own ordinance, and will prevent or remedy them still. Thus the Orders depend on the Church, not the Church on the Orders.

This argument presupposes that there is in fact a Church, that is, a visible body corporate, gifted with supernatural privileges, present and future; and if there be not, then the Apostolical Succession has no meaning or object, and vanishes out of theology with the Church itself of which it is a function. But I am assuming that there is a Church, for the high school of Anglicans, against whom these remarks are directed, upholds the existence of a visible Church as firmly as Catholics, and the only question between the two

[90]

parties is, what and where the Church is; in what it consists; and on this point it is that they differ. This Church, this spiritually endowed body, this minister of the sacraments, teacher of Gospel truth, possessor of that power of binding and loosing, commonly called the power of the keys, is this Divine creation coincident, as Catholics hold, with the whole extended body of Christians everywhere, so as to be in its essence one and only one organized association,—or, on the other hand, as insisted on in the above Essay, is every separate bishopric, every diocesan unit, of which that whole is composed, properly and primarily the Church which has the promises, each of them being, like a crystallization, only a repetition of the rest, each of them in point of privileges as much the perfect Church as all together, each equal to each, [91] each independent of each, each invested with full spiritual powers, *in solidum*, as St. Cyprian speaks, none subject to any, none bound to union with other by any law of its being or condition of its prerogatives, but all free from all except as regards the duty of mutual love, and only called one Church, when taken in the aggregate or in its catholicity, though really multiform, by a conversational misnomer, or figure of speech, or abstraction of the mind, as when all men, viewed as one, are called "man"? In taking in my Essay this view of the Church, I followed in the main, not only Dodwell and Hickes, whom I cited, but such high authorities as Pearson, Barrow, Stillingfleet, and Bingham.

Now it is very intelligible to deny that there is any divinely established, divinely commissioned, Church at all; but to hold that the one Church is realized and perfected in each of a thousand independent corporate units, co-ordinate, bound by no necessary intercommunion, adjusted into no divine organized whole, is a tenet, not merely unknown to Scripture, but so plainly impossible to carry out practically, as to make it clear that it never would have been devised, except by men, who conscientiously believing in a visible Church and also conscientiously opposed to Rome, had nothing left for them, whether they would or would not, but to entrench themselves in the paradox, that the Church was one indeed, and the Church was Catholic indeed, but that the one Church was not the Catholic, and the Catholic Church was not the one.

1. First, as to the scriptural view of the subject. That the writers of the New Testament speak of many local Christian bodies, called churches, is indisputable; but the question is, whether these various local bodies, so-called, were, or were not, brought together by divine command into a higher unity than any local association, and into a union rendered imperative by the special privileges attached to its observance; whether by the word "Church" was not properly and really denoted, not any local body, but one and only one large association extending as widely as the Christian name, including in it all merely local bodies, having one organization, a necessary intercommunion, fixed mutual relations between its portions, and supernatural powers and gifts lodged primarily in it, the association itself, and thence communicated, by aggregation and incorporation, to each subdivision and each individual member of it. This latter view is the teaching of Scripture.

That is, in the lifetime of the Apostles, according to the Scripture record, the Church of the promises, the Church of Christ, was a *body*, (1) *visible*; (2) *one*; (3) *Catholic*, and (4) *organized*.

1. That it is *visible*, is allowed on all hands, for even the churches or congregations of Independents or Unitarians are visible; the word "Ecclesia" means an assembly of men, and if men are visible, their assembling must be visible also.

[92]

Note on Essay X

2. Next it is *one*: true though it be that St. Paul, St. Luke, and St. John, when engaged on historical fact speak of many "churches," the style of Scripture changes when it speaks of the great Christian gifts doctrinally. In presence of these gospel prerogatives there is but one body with many members. Our Lord builds, upon the rock of Peter and of Peter's faith, not churches, but "My Church;"[22] St. Paul speaks of the "House of God, the Church of the Living God" in which St. Timothy is called to be a ruler, and not of "churches;" of the Church "being the pillar and ground of the truth."[23] Again he speaks, as of "One God and Father of [93] all, one Lord, one Spirit, one faith, one hope, one baptism,"[24] so also of but "one body;" and again our Lord as "the Head of the body, the Church,"[25] not of the churches.

3. This one Church, as it necessarily follows, is *Catholic*, because it embraces all Christians at once in one extended whole, its catholicity being coincident with its unity. This is a subject on which St. Paul delights to expatiate. Where has he a word of dioceses or bishoprics, each a complete whole, each independent of the rest, each with the power of the keys, each a facsimile of each? On the contrary, he declares "we are *all* baptized by one Spirit into *one* body,"[26] the Spirit who is one, being the pledge of the body's unity, and the one body being the condition of the Spirit's presence. Both Jews and Gentiles "are fellow-heirs, and of the same body;"[27] are "framed together and grow into a holy

---

[22] *"My Church"*: Matthew 16:18
[23] *"House of God, the Church of the Living God"* ... *"being the pillar and ground of the truth"*: 1 Timothy 3:15
[24] *"One God and Father of all, one Lord, one Spirit, one faith, one hope, one baptism"*: Cf. Ephesians 4:5-6
[25] *"the Head of the body, the Church"*: Colossians 1:18
[26] *"we are all baptized by one Spirit into one body"*: 1 Corinthians 12:13
[27] *"are fellow-heirs, and of the same body"*: Ephesians 3:6

111

Note on Essay X

temple,"[28] "a habitation of God through the Spirit." "There is neither Jew nor Greek, ye are *all one* in Christ Jesus."[29] "To the peace of God ye are called in *one* body."[30] We, *being many*, are *one body* in Christ." "The body is one and hath many members; ye are the body of Christ and members in particular."[31] Is it not clear then that according to St. Paul, the whole Church comes first, and its portions or individual members come second, that its portions are not wholes, that they are accidents, but the one whole body is no accident, no conglomerate, but the object of Apostolic zeal, and the direct and primary recipient of divine grace?

4. Once more, this visible, one, and whole or Catholic body, is, as indeed the word "body" implies, an *organization*, with many members converging and concurring into one ecclesiastical corporation or power. I mean, this the Church was, in matter of fact, in the days of the Apostles. Even Apostles, though each of them had a universal jurisdiction, had not the power to break up the one Church into fragments, and each of them to make a communion of his own in it. "Who is Paul, who is Apollos," says the Apostle, "but ministers"?[32] "Ye are *God's* husbandry, ye are God's building, ye are the temple of God."[33] In like manner St. Luke tells us that those who were baptized "continued steadfastly in the Apostles' doctrine and *fellowship*;"[34] and St. Paul that the many members of the

[94]

---

[28] *"framed together and grow into a holy temple"*: Ephesians 2:21
[29] *"There is neither Jew nor Greek, ye are* all one *in Christ Jesus"*: Galatians 3:28-29
[30] *"To the peace of God ye are called in* one *body."* Colossians 3:15
[31] *"The body is one and hath many members; ye are the body of Christ and members in particular"*: 1 Corinthians 12:12
[32] *"Who is Paul, who is Apollos ... but ministers?"*: 1 Corinthians 3:5
[33] *"Ye are* God's *husbandry, ye are God's building, ye are the temple of God."*: Cf. 1 Corinthians 3:9,17
[34] *"continued steadfastly in the Apostles' doctrine and* fellowship*"*: Acts 2:42

body have not the same office, nor are all equally honourable,—implying in all he writes a formed ecclesiastical polity. On this point I cannot do better than make an extract from one of the early *Tracts for the Times*, which runs as follows:

"Some time ago I drew up[35] the Scripture proof of the doctrine of the Visible Church, which I will here transcribe. I am not arguing for this or that form of polity, nor for the Apostolical Succession, but simply for the duties of order, union, and ecclesiastical obedience. I limit myself to these points, as being persuaded that, when they are granted, the others will eventually follow.

"I. That there was a Visible Church in the Apostles' day.
"1. General texts. Matt. xvi. 18, xviii. 17; 1 Tim. iii. 15; Acts passim, etc.
"2. Organization of the Church.
"(1) Diversity of ranks. 1 Cor. xii; Eph. iv. 4-12; Rom. xii. 4-8; 1 Peter iv. 10, 11.
"(2) Governors. Matt. xxviii. 19; Mark xvi. 15, 16; John xx. 22, 23; Luke xxii. 19, 20; Gal. ii. 9, etc.
"(3) Gifts. Luke xii. 42, 43; John xx. 22, 23; Matt. xviii. 18.
"(4) Order. Acts viii. 5, 6, 12, 14, 15, 17; ix. 27; xi. 2-4, 22, 23; xv. 2, 4, 6, 25; xvi. 4; xviii. 22; xxi. 17-19. Comp. Gal. i. 1-12; 1 Cor. xiv. 40; 1 Thess. v. 14.   [95]
"(5) Ordination. Acts vi. 6; 1 Tim. iv. 14, v. 22; 2 Tim. i. 6; Titus i. 5; Acts xiii. 3; cf. Gal. i. 1-12.
"(6) Ecclesiastical obedience. 1 Thess. v. 12, 13; Heb. xiii. 17; 1 Tim. v. 17.

---

[35] *"Some time ago I drew up..."*: taken from *Tract 11* 'The Visible Church (In Letters to a Friend)' (1840). This Tract was written by Newman.

"(7) Rules and discipline. Matt. xxviii. 19; Matt. xviii. 17; 1 Cor. v. 4-7; Gal. v. 12, etc.; 1 Cor. xvi. 1, 2; 1 Cor. xi. 2, 16, etc.

"(8) Unity. Rom. xvi. 17; 1 Cor. i. 10; iii. 3; xiv. 26; Col. ii. 5; 1 Thess. v. 14; 2 Thess. iii. 6.

"II. That the Visible Church, thus instituted by the Apostles, was intended to continue.

"1. Why should it not? The *onus probandi* lies with those who deny this position. If the doctrines and precepts already cited be obsolete at this day, why should not the following texts? *e.g.*, 1 Peter ii. 13; or *e.g.*, Matt. vii. 14; John iii. 3.

"2. Is it likely so elaborate a system should be framed, yet with no purpose of its continuing?

"3. The objects to be obtained by it are as necessary now as then. (1) Preservation of the faith. (2) Purity of doctrine. (3) Edification of Christians. (4) Unity of operation. *Vid.* Epistles to Tim. and Tit. passim.

"4. If system were necessary in a time of miracles, much more is it now.

"5. 2 Tim. ii. 2. Matt. xxviii. 20, etc."

So far the Tract. If then the New Testament is to be our guide in matters ecclesiastical, one thing at least is certain. We may doubt whether Bishops are of obligation, whether there is an Apostolical Succession, whether presbyters are [96] priests, whether St. Stephen and his six associates were the first deacons, whether the Sacraments are seven or two; but of one thing we cannot doubt, that all Christians were in that first age bound together in one body, with an actual intercommunion and mutual relations between them, with ranks and offices, and with a central authority; and that this organized association was "the body of Christ," and that in it, considered as One, dwelt the "One Spirit." This external unity is a duty prior in order and idea to Episcopacy; in it, and not in Episcopacy, lies the transmission and warrant of Divine privilege. It is emphatically a "Sacramentum Unitatis,"[36] and is presupposed, typified, required by the Sacraments properly so-called; and divines who substitute a diocese for the *orbis terrarum* as the first rudiment of the Church, must in consistency be prepared to answer those who, going a little farther, substitute a congregation for a diocese; for Episcopalians are only one species of Independents, with far less to say for themselves from Scripture.

2. Secondly, this theory is as impracticable, as an ecclesiastical system, as it is unknown to Scripture. Not only has it never worked, but it never has been fairly attempted, or even imagined, at least for any length of time or on a large scale. Regarded in its probable results and actual tendencies, it is a sure and easy way of not effecting those very ends which ecclesiastical arrangements are intended to subserve. The first idea of the Gospel is Revelation,—that is, right faith, certain knowledge, truth and light; the first precept of the New Law is charity,—that is, mutual goodwill, brotherly love, peace: now if our Lord had intended to promote, not these merciful ends, but ignorance, confusion, unbelief, discord, strife, enmity, mutual alienation, could He have provided a better way, than that of ordaining by express command, and sanctioning by supernatural privilege, a thousand or two local Episcopates, all over the earth, each sovereign, each independent of the rest? Of course it might be His will to [97]

---

[36] *"Sacramentum Unitatis"*: "Sacrament of Unity". This phrase is used by St Cyprian in his *De ecclesiae unitate*, 4 and 6.

manifest His overruling might amid human pride, passion, and selfishness, and to work by miracle; nor again do I deny that history tells us of great abuses and disorders in religious matters, arising out of despotic power, and the indignant re-action of the oppressed. Certainly there is no form of polity which is safe from the inroads of human infirmity and sin; but at the same time there are some forms which can withstand or prevent these evils better than others;—the present British Constitution, for instance, is more conducive to peace, internal and external, than was the Heptarchy,[37] nor should we be so happy in temporal respects as we are, were each of our cities a sovereign state, as some are just now scheming to bring about in France;—but if there be any polity, ecclesiastical or civil, which has proved itself above others a working system, strong, coherent, enduring, and full of resource, surely it is the world-wide ecclesiastical power which alone, among forms of Christianity, has ever preserved and carried on that Unity in Catholicity which we see initiated in Scripture. Natural gifts and virtues, statesmanlike principles, sagacious policy, have found large room for their development in that organization which inspired Apostles commenced; it alone, as Protestant writers have confessed, has carried civilization and Christianity across the gulf which separates the old world from the modern; and, while it is only a matter of opinion whether it has on any important subject added to the faith once delivered, it has beyond all question, and in matter of fact, answered the ends of its institution, in preserving to us every page of inspired Scripture, every doctrine of the

[98]

---

[37] *Heptarchy*: the collective name given to the seven kingdoms of Anglo-Saxon England (East Anglia, Essex, Kent, Mercia, Northumbria, Sussex, Wessex). It was a misleading concept for there were many smaller groupings and sub-kingdoms which did not fit into the Heptarchy, such as Hwicce (which included parts of Gloucestershire, Warwickshire, Worcestershire and elsewhere).

primitive Church, a host of immemorial rites and traditions, and the voluminous writings of the Ancient Fathers. This has been the result of ecclesiastical unity.

On the other hand, as to the Anglican theory, how is it even to be put upon the course? how is it to start? how are we to find for it life and strength enough even to allow of its attempting and breaking down? It has an initial difficulty before it comes into the region of fact: its necessary church unit is diocesan; what is diocesan is local; what is local must have boundaries; boundaries do not come by nature, but by positive enactment; who is to draw them? Suppose two neighbouring Bishops draw lines intersecting each other, who is to enforce a settlement between them? suppose each of them thinks that the two dioceses naturally form but one diocese, then we have altar set up against altar. And further, who is to map out a whole province? Is it not very plain that the civil power must come in from the first, either as guiding or compelling an arrangement? Thus, from the first, episcopal autonomy is close upon erastianism.

But there may be Councils held, laws passed, oaths taken, and a central authority created;—of course; but that authority is after all human and conventional; how is it a match for that episcopal *magisterium* which on the hypothesis is divine? Each Bishop has the power of the keys; each can bind and loose; each can excommunicate all his brethren. Each can proclaim and defend a heresy. What then can keep them in the unity of the faith, but to suppose each of them alike infallible? Yet must a theory, which protests against one infallibility, fall back upon a thousand? Would Christianity, as regards truth and peace, faith and charity, fare worse, would it not fare better, without any [99] Church at all, than with a thousand Churches, scattered through the world, all supreme and independent?

If it be asked of me how, with my present views of the inherent impracticability of the Anglican theory of Church polity, I could ever have held it myself, I answer that, though swayed by great names, I never was without misgivings about the difficulties which it involved; and that as early as 1837, in my Volume in defence of Anglicanism as contrasted with "Romanism and popular Protestantism," I expressed my sense of these difficulties. I said much on the subject in my Introductory Chapter. Among other things, "The proof of reality in a doctrine," I said, "is its holding together when actually attempted ... Not till Christianity was tried, could the coherence of its parts be ascertained. Now the class of doctrines in question as yet labours under the same difficulty. Indeed, they are in one sense as entirely new as Christianity when first preached. The *Via Media*, viewed as an integral system, has scarcely had existence, except on paper ... Bystanders accuse us of tendering no proof to show that our view is not self-contradictory, and, if set in motion, would not fall to pieces, or start off in different directions at once ... It still remains to be tried whether what is called Anglo-Catholicism, the religion of Andrewes, Laud, Hammond,[38] Butler, and Wilson,[39] is capable of being professed, acted on, and maintained on a large sphere of action, and through a sufficient period, or whether it be a mere modification or transition-state either of Romanism or of popular Protestantism, according as we view it."—Pp. 19-22.

This, I said, in honesty, though it was in a measure an unravelling of the work which I was then completing, and in

---

[38] *Hammond*: Henry Hammond (1605-1660), theologian with Royalist and High Church sympathies.

[39] *Wilson*: Thomas Wilson (1663-1755), Anglican Divine and Bishop oif Sodor and Man (1697-1755). His works were edited by John Keble for the *Library of Anglo-Catholic Theology* (1847-1863).

consequence, when published, a cause of deep offence to the late Mr. Rose,[40] nay, of an estrangement from me, for some months, of a friend whom I so much valued and respected. But he had forgiven me by February 1838, and, when he left England for good in October of that year, in the kindness of his heart, he would not go away without bidding me farewell; and he wrote to me a friendly letter, wishing me all success in the *British Critic*, which I was then undertaking, I on my part dedicating to him, with his leave, and with all my heart, my fourth volume of Parochial Sermons. [100]

3.

The doctrine of the unity of ecclesiastical jurisdiction, which I have been dwelling upon from Scripture and from the reason of the case, might also be copiously illustrated from the Fathers; but this is not denied in the Essay which has given rise to these remarks. Rather, the witness of the Fathers in its favour is granted, by the very fact that it does no more than bring forward, as if exceptions to the rule, certain passages from their writings, or facts in their history, which admit or perhaps teach a contrary doctrine, and thereby suggest that the unity of jurisdiction was not always insisted on in fact, and that a local Church, as the Anglican, may withdraw from the Catholic jurisdiction without necessarily and at once forfeiting its claim to Catholic communion. On these exceptional passages I shall now say a few words.

The argument in the Essay is of the following kind: There are strong passages in the Fathers against schism and

---

[40] *a cause of deep offence to Mr Rose*: Rev. Hugh James Rose (17995-1838) was a theologian, second Principal of King's College, London and founder of the *British Magazine*, which brought him into contact with Newman and other Tractarians. He died on 22 December 1838 while in Florence and was buried in the Protestant Cemetery near Fiesole.

[101] separatism certainly, but then there is no rule but has exceptions; and these strong passages only embody general truths, proverbial sayings, aspects, types, symbols of Catholic doctrine, principles applicable to particular subjects, times, and places, and are sometimes in their letter even contradictory to each other, showing that they carry with them an antecedent or presumptive force and nothing more. Thus our Lord sometimes says, "Follow Me,"[41] at another "Count the cost;"[42] and "He that is not with Me, is against Me,"[43] yet also, "He that is not against us, is for us."[44] And He says, "Blessed are the poor;"[45] "Woe unto you rich;"[46] yet no one would deny that such enunciations do need a careful handling, and may be grievously misapplied. Therefore, in like manner, though St. Augustine, after St. Cyprian, says, "Break the branch from the tree, it will not bud," or "The universal Church is in its judgments secure of truth," it does not thence follow for certain that the Church of England may not be a living Church amid its supreme isolation, or is *ipso facto* condemned because it has the whole East and West absolutely against it and its doctrines. So much as to the doctrines of the Fathers; next, as to facts in their history. It is certain, that Eusebius of Samosata is a saint in the Roman calendar, though for years and almost till his death he was in the ranks of the Semi-Arians; Meletius, a saint also, died out of communion with Rome; Lucifer died in schism, yet is called "Beatus" by Jerome, and up to the seventeenth century was honoured as a saint in Sardinia and parts of Italy; and Paschasius to the last adhered to the

---

[41] *"Follow Me"*: e.g. Matthew 4:19
[42] *"Count the cost"*: Luke 14:28
[43] *"He that is not with Me, is against Me"*: Matthew 12:30, Lk 11:23
[44] *"He that is not against us, is for us"*: Mark 9:40, Luke 9:50
[45] *"Blessed are the poor"*: Matthew 5:3
[46] *"Woe unto you rich"*: Luke 6:24

anti-Pope Laurence against Pope Symmachus, yet he too is in the Roman calendar. If these men are saints, in spite of their separation from Rome, why may not England, though accidentally in a state of protest, enjoy, as those primitive saints enjoyed, the communion and the blessings of the Catholic Church? Such is the argument, and now I shall give my answer to it.

1. And first as to the examples adduced:—I begin by drawing attention to what I conceive to be an erroneous [102] assumption in an earlier Essay, which this is the proper place to set right. I said in my remarks upon Mr. Palmer (*supr.*, vol. i., pp. 164-5). "If division is not *ipso facto* formal schism, length of time cannot make it such. If thirty-five years do not deprive a separated branch of its Catholicity, neither does a hundred." This is what I have said above; but now I venture to suggest, that the truth is just the contrary to this statement, while the distinction, which it denies to exist, is just that which forms the critical contrast between those instances of ecclesiastical differences which occur in ancient times, and the utter alienation which exists at this time between England and Rome. In the early centuries there were frequent quarrels among Christians: Pope Victor[47] declared the Asian Bishops excommunicate, by reason of their Quartodeciman[48] observance of the Easter Festival; Stephen[49] threatened the Easterns, on the question of heretical baptism, and Firmilian

---

[47] *Pope Victor*: See above p.[9].

[48] *Quartodeciman observance*: The practice, followed by a number of churches in the early Christian centuries, of celebrating Easter on the eve of the14[th] day of Nisan, mentioned in Leviticus 23:5 as the start of the Passover, thus following the Jewish calendar. After much controversy, the practice of celebrating Easter on a Sunday was universally adopted. Cf. Eusebius, Book 7, chapter 5.

[49] *Stephen*: See above p.[9]. Cf. his *Letter to Cyprian*, ML 3.1154-1178 (AD 255/6).

of Cæsarea[50] retorted in sharp words; Acacius of Constantinople,[51] as favouring the Monophysite party, drew on him the anathema of Pope Felix; first the African bishops, and then the ex-archate of Ravenna and the churches of Istria refused the decrees of the fifth Ecumenical Council.[52] Such acts implied separation, and sometimes those separations were long; but it is difficult to treat any of them as perfected schisms. They were the threatenings and beginnings of schism; they tended to schism, as disorders of the body, not in themselves fatal, yet, if neglected, may terminate in death. Estrangements, in early times, were often but "amantium iræ;" and there was sooner or later an "amoris integratio."[53]

[103]   Such were the instances of schismatical proceedings in early times, the like of which I have adduced above in my Essay; but very different surely from these is the chasm which has long yawned between England and the Catholic world. This separation is surely no lover's quarrel; arising today, spent and over tomorrow. Each of the contending parties has broken off from the other now for long centuries; each has for centuries continued on in its own territory supreme, and thus grown into its own shape; each has formally turned its back upon the other, or has recognized it only to affront it; each has framed decrees and passed laws against the faith and the claims of the other. The whole of

---

[50] *Firmilian of Cæsarea*: (died c. 269) Bishop of Caesarea Mazaca; he denied the validity of Baptism which had been administered by heretics. Cf. 'On the resistance of Cyprian and Firmilian to the Church of Rome, in the question of baptism by heretics.' *Dev*, p. 26.

[51] *Acacius of Constantinople*: He succeeded Gennadius in 471. Pope Felix III (483-492) who had appointed him (cf. *Dev*, p. 164) also condemned and deposed him.

[52] *the decrees* . . . : against Theodore of Mopsuestia, Theodoret of Cyr and Ibas, bishop of Edessa, in the 2nd Council of Constantinople 553. Cf. *Dev*, p 286.

[53] *"amantium irae"* . . . *"amoris integratio"*: "hatreds of lovers" . . . "renewal of love", Terence, *Andria*, 555.

England, with its multitude of sects, tolerant for the most part of each other, protests against Rome: its Court, its legislators, its judicial bench, its public press, its literature and science, its populace, forcibly repudiate, view with intense jealousy, any advance, in any quarter, even of a hair's breadth, towards the Roman Church. Its Bishops at home and from abroad, once in a way assembled in a Pan-Anglican Synod, cannot part in peace with mutual good wishes, without a parting fling at the Holy See. All this animosity against Catholicism is conscious, deliberate, and hearty, the coagulate of bitter experiences and of festering resentments. Year after year, the conscience of our great country more determinately confronts and defies the principles and the practices of the Roman Curia. At the era of Elizabeth, this opposition was founded on passion or policy; in Victoria's[54] time it is an intellectual and moral antipathy. It is as different now from what it was then, as the severe but transient influenza, which is the first step of a consumption, differs from the hectic fever and organic ruin, in which it ends. All things are possible to God; I am not saying that this antagonism between Rome and England must last for ever, because it is so energetic now; but I am stating what it is at this time; and I protest that to compare it [104] to the coolness between Meletius and Athanasius, or the jealousies between Basil and Damasus, or the parties and partizanship which the untoward act of Lucifer created at Antioch, is to do what Catholics are on certain other questions charged with doing,—to pervert history in the interest of controversy. Say that Luther and Leo[55] quarrelled

---

[54] *Victoria*: Victoria (1819-1901), Queen of Great Britain and Ireland from 1837.
[55] *Leo*: Leo X (1475-1521); Pope from 1513.

Note on Essay X

no worse than Paul and Barnabas,[56] and then you will be consistent in maintaining that Rome does not wish the Church of England dead and buried, and England does not fear and detest the See of Rome.

I had occasion to insist upon the principle, on which these remarks are grounded, in Lectures published in 1850, *apropos* of the Gorham decision, and I will extract a portion of what I then said in answer to two writers of name, now both deceased, Archdeacon Hare[57] and Dr. Neale.[58]

"I have spoken of the tests," I said, "which the last twenty years have furnished, of the real character of the Establishment; for I must not be supposed to be inquiring whether the Establishment has been unchurched during that period, but whether it has been proved to be no Church already. The want of congeniality which now exists between the sentiments and ways, the moral life of the Anglican communion, and the principles, doctrines, traditions of Catholicism,—of this I speak in order to prove something done and over long ago, in order to show that the movement of 1833 was from the first engaged in propagating an unreality. The eloquent writer just quoted, in ridicule of the protest made by twelve very distinguished men, against the Queen's recent decision concerning the sacrament of baptism, contrasts 'logical dreams' and 'obscure and perplexing questions of dogmatic theology' [105] with 'the promise' in the Establishment of a large family 'of daughters, spread round the earth, shining and brightening every year.' Now I grant that it has a narrow and technical

---

[56] *Paul and Barnabus*: In Acts 15 Paul and Barnabas have a fierce disagreement and go their separate ways.
[57] *Archdeacon Hare*: Julius Hare (1795-1855), Archdeacon of Lewes (Sussex). His brother was the writer Augustus Hare (1792-1834)
[58] *Dr Neale*: John Mason Neale (1818-1866), Anglican priest and writer, best known today for his hymns and carols.

124

appearance to rest the Catholicity of a religious body on particular words, or deeds, or measures, resulting from the temper of a particular age, accidentally elicited, and accomplished in minutes or in days. I allow it, and feel it; that a particular vote of Parliament, endured or tacitly accepted by bishops and clergy, or by the metropolitans, or a particular appointment, or a particular omission, or a particular statement of doctrine, should at once change the spiritual character of the whole body, and *ipso facto* cut it off from the centre of unity and the source of grace, is almost incredible. In spite of such acts, surely the Anglican Church might be today what it was yesterday, with an internal power and a supernatural virtue, provided it had not already forfeited them, and would go about its work as of old time. It would be today pretty much what it was yesterday, though in the course of the night it had allowed an Anglo-Prussian see to be set up in Jerusalem, and subscribed to a disavowal of the Athanasian creed.

"This is the common sense of the matter, to which the mind recurs with satisfaction, after zeal and ingenuity have done their utmost to prove the contrary. Of course I am not saying that individual acts do not tend towards, and a succession of acts does not issue in, the most serious spiritual consequences; but it is so difficult to determine the worth of each ecclesiastical act, and what its position is relatively to acts and events before and after it, that I have no intention here of urging any argument deduced from such acts. A generation may not be long enough for the completion of an act of schism or heresy. Judgments admit of repeal or reversal; enactments are liable to flaws and informalities; laws require promulgation; documents admit of explanation; words must be interpreted either by context or by circumstances; majorities may be analyzed; [106]

responsibilities may be shifted. I admit the remark of another writer in the present controversy, though I do not accept his conclusion. 'The Church's motion,' he says, 'is not that of a machine, to be calculated with accuracy, and predicted beforehand,—where one serious injury will disturb all regularity, and finally put a stop to action. It is that of a living body, whose motions will be irregular, incapable of being exactly arranged and foretold, and where it is nearly impossible to say how much health may co-exist with how much disease.' And he speaks of the line of reasoning which he is opposing as being 'too logical to be real.' 'Men,' he observes, 'do not, in the practical affairs of life, act on such clear, sharp, definite theories. Such reasoning can never be the cause of any one leaving the Church of England. But it looks well on paper, and therefore may perhaps be put forward as a theoretical argument by those who, from some other feeling, or fancy, or prejudice, or honest conviction, think fit to leave us.'

"Truly said, except in the imputation conveyed in the concluding words. I will grant that it is by life without us, by life within us, by the work of grace in our communion and in ourselves, that we are all of us accustomed practically to judge whether that communion be Catholic or not; not by this or that formal act, or historical event. I will grant it, though of course it requires some teaching, and some discernment, and some prayer, to understand what spiritual life is, and what is the working of grace. However, at any rate, let the proposition pass; I will allow it at least for argument's sake; for I am not here going to look out, in the last twenty years, for dates when, and ways in which, the Establishment fell from Catholic unity, and lost its divine privileges. No; the question before us is nothing narrow or technical; it has no cut and dried premises, and

[107]

peremptory conclusions; it is not whether this or that statute or canon at the time of the Reformation, this or that ''further and further encroachment' of the State, this or that 'Act of William IV.,'[59] constituted the Establishment's formal separation from the Church; not whether the Queen's recent decision binds it to heresy; but, whether these acts and abundant others are not, one and all, evidences, in one out of a hundred heads of evidence, that whatever were the acts which constituted, or the moment which completed the schism, or rather the utter disorganization, of the National Church, cut off and disorganized it is."—*Difficulties of Anglicanism, Lect. 2.*

2. On the principles, then, enforced in this extract I consider such passages in ecclesiastical history, as are adduced in my foregoing Essay, to be merely instances of inchoate schism, proceedings and arrangements which were reversed before they issued in a formal state of schism. For this reason they cannot fairly be taken to constitute precedents and pleas for the present and past position of the Anglican communion. Schism indeed, abstractedly speaking, is separation from the *orbis terrarum*, but a schism cannot be completed in a day or a year. The abstract proposition requires various corrections when viewed in the medium of the concrete, corrections and supplements varying with each case to which it is applied. And thus I am brought to notice, or I rather have anticipated, what I have to say on the second point questioned in my Essay, viz., the argumentative value of the strong dicta of the Fathers which I there employ myself in explaining and modifying. I am willing to modify them still. I admit without any difficulty, [108]

---

[59] *William IV*: William IV (1765-1837), King of Great Britain and Ireland from 1830.

as the Essay maintains, that such dicta are not to be taken in the bare letter, but are general truths, which do not at once and definitively apply to the particular cases which seem to fall under them, but are of the nature of antecedent probabilities and presumptions against each particular case as it comes. I should be as little disposed to decide against England in 1560 as against Antioch in 362, that it was at once summarily excluded from the Catholic Church because of St. Jerome's famous words to Pope Damasus:[60] "Ego nullum primum nisi Christum sequens, Beatitudini tuæ, id Cathedræ Petri, communione consocior. Non novi Vitalem, Meletium respuo, ignoro Paulinum. Quicunque tecum non colligit, spargit, hoc est, qui Christi non est, Antichristi est."[61] I should be dealing violently with a great truth, if I so used them. Nor again, because "Life is a note of the true Church," should I therefore at once unchurch the Rome of John XII.[62] and Boniface VII.,[63] or include the Nestorians of the middle ages within the pale of Catholicism. The sun is the source and centre of light, but clouds may darken the day, and the moon illuminates the night.

---

[60] *St Jerome's famous words to Pope Damasus*: in AD 374-379. ML 22. 355.

[61] *"Ego nullum primum* . . . : "I who follow no primate except Christ am united in communion to your blessedness, that is, to the chair of Peter. I know nothing of Vitalis, of Meletius or Paulinus. Whoever does not gather with you, scatters: that is, whoever is not of Christ is of Antichrist." *ML* 22. 355. Jerome is referring to the three claimants to the See of Antioch and asking Pope Damasus which of them he should support: *Vitalis*, an Arian, *Meletius*, who was orthodox but who had been ordained by an Arian bishop, or *Paulinus*, who was orthodox and whom the Pope supported. Jerome ultimately supported Paulinus who later ordained him a priest and whom he accompanied to the Council of Constantinople in 381. Newman has silently omitted some sentences in this passage, but they do not affect the meaning.

[62] *John XII*: Pope (955-964), elected at the age of eighteen and notorious for his debauched life, although he was not afraid to assert papal authority and promote monastic reform.

[63] *Boniface VII*: Antipope 974, 984-985, who was not afraid to have his opponents murdered: first Count Sicco (974) and then John XIV (984). Though classified by modern historians as an antipope, he was included in most official lists of popes and the next pope to assume that name was 'Boniface VIII'.

Note on Essay X

On the other hand, I use the admission I have made, as in the case of the just-mentioned medieval Popes, on the Catholic side of the controversy. Vincent's famous dictum, "*Quod semper, quod ubique,*" etc., admits of exceptions, and must not be pushed to an extremity against our theology, as if doctrines did not admit of development. And again, as to "*securus judicat orbis terrarum,*" while no Catholic would contend that this aphorism precludes or supersedes the appeal to Antiquity, at the same time it avails at least for as much as this, which is all that is needed, viz., in proof that other tests of revealed truth exist, besides [109] Antiquity; and those other tests may sometimes be more easy of application. The general reception, for instance, of the definition of an Ecumenical Council may avail to determine for us what the records of Antiquity now extant leave doubtful, or only imperfectly testify.

———————

I think it well to append the letter referred to at p. 77. I have now somewhat altered the words in which mention is made of Mr. Knox.[64]

THE ORATORY, BIRMINGHAM,
August 5th, 1868.

MY DEAR FATHER COLERIDGE,[65]

You ask me what I precisely mean, in my *Apologia*, Appendix, p. 26, by saying, *apropos* of Anglican Orders, that

---

[64] *Mr. Knox*: Alexander Knox, (1757–1831), Church of Ireland lay theologian. Newman refers to him in 'Prospects of the Anglican Church', *Ess.* I, p.269, as one of the precursors of the Oxford Movement. His *Remains* were published in 1834.
[65] *Father Coleridge*: Henry James Coleridge (1833-1893), a disciple of Newman, convert and Jesuit.

"Antiquarian arguments are altogether unequal to the urgency of visible facts."[66] I will try to explain:—

I. The inquiry into Anglican Orders has ever been to me of the class which I must call dreary; for it is dreary surely to have to grope into the minute intricate passages and obscure corners of past occurrences, in order to ascertain whether this man was ever consecrated, whether that man used a valid form, whether a certain sacramental intention came up to the mark, whether the report or register of an ecclesiastical act can be cleared of suspicion. On giving myself to consider the question, I never have been able to arrive at anything higher than a probable conclusion, which is most unsatisfactory except to antiquarians, who delight in researches into the past for their own sake.

II. Now, on the other hand, what do I mean by "visible facts"? I mean such definite facts as throw a broad antecedent light upon what may be presumed, in a case in which sufficient evidence is not forthcoming. For instance—

[110]   1. The Apostolical Succession, its necessity, and its grace, is not an Anglican tradition, though it is a tradition found in the Anglican Church. By contrast, our Lord's divinity *is* an Anglican tradition—every one, high and low, holds it. It is not only in Prayer Book and Catechism, but in the mouths of all professors of Anglicanism. Not to believe it, is to be no Anglican; and any persons in authority, for three hundred years, who were suspected to doubt or explain it away, were marked men, as Dr. Colenso is now marked. And they have been so few that they could be counted. Not such is the Apostolic Succession; and, considering the Church is the *columna et firmamentum veritatis*,[67] and is ever bound to stir up the gift that is in her, there is surely a strong presumption that the Anglican body has not, what it does not profess to have. I wonder how many of its bishops and deans hold the doctrine at this time; some who do not, occur to the mind at

---

[66] *"Antiquarian arguments are altogether unequal to the urgency of visible facts"*: *Apo.*, p.341.

[67] columna et firmamentum veritatis: 'pillar and ground of the truth', I Tim 3:15.

once. One knows what was the case thirty or forty years ago by the famous saying of Blomfield, Bishop of London.[68]

2. Where there is a true Succession, there is a true Eucharist, if there is not a true Eucharist, there is no true Succession. Now what is the presumption here? I think it is Mr. Alexander Knox who says or suggests that, if so great a gift *be* given, it must have a rite. I add, if it has a rite, it must have a *custos*[69] of the rite. Who is the *custos* of the Anglican Eucharist? The Anglican clergy? Could I, without distressing or offending an Anglican, describe what sort of *custodes* they have been, and are, to their Eucharist? "O bone custos," in the words of the poet, "cui commendavi Filium Meum!"[70] Is it not charitable towards the bulk of the Anglican clergy to hope, to believe, that so great a treasure has not been given to their keeping? And would our Lord leave Himself for centuries in such hands? Inasmuch, then, as "the sacrament of the Body and Blood of Christ" in the Anglican communion is without protective ritual[71] and jealous guardianship, there seems to me a strong presumption that neither the real gift, nor its appointed guardians, are to be found in that communion.

3. Previous baptism is the condition of the valid administration of the other sacraments. When I was in the Anglican Church I saw enough of the lax administration of baptism, even among High Churchmen, though they did not of course intend it, to fill me with great uneasiness. Of course there are definite persons whom one might point out, whose baptisms are sure to be valid. But my [111]

---

[68] *Blomfield, Bishop of London*: Charles James Blomfield (1786–1857), Anglican divine and classical scholar; he was appointed Bishop of London in 1828.

[69] custos: guardian

[70] *"O bone custos," in the words of the poet, "cui commendavi Filium Meum!"*: The full quotation is "O bone custos, salve, columen vero familiæ, cui commendavi Filium Meum!", "Oh good guardian, welcome pillar of the family, to whom I entrusted my son!" *Phormio*, Terence, lines 65-58. Demipho is speaking to his aged servant Geta who was entrusted with looking after his son Antipho while he has been away but has in fact been facilitating Antipho's marriage to a girl of whom Demipho does not approve. Geta is thus an example of an unreliable guardian. Newman later adapted the *Phormio* for performance by boys of the Oratory School.

[71] *without protective ritual*: The Book of Common Prayer had rubrics which specifically forbade the worship of Christ present in the Sacrament.

131

argument has nothing to do with present baptisms. Bishops were baptized, not lately, but as children. The present bishops were consecrated by other bishops, they again by others. What I have seen in the Anglican Church makes it very difficult for me to deny that every now and then a bishop was a consecrator who had never been baptized. Some bishops have been brought up in the north as Presbyterians, others as Dissenters, others as Low Churchmen, others have been baptized in the careless perfunctory way once so common; there is then much reason to believe that some consecrators were not bishops, for the simple reason that, formally speaking, they were not Christians. But at least there is a great presumption that where evidently our Lord has not provided a rigid rule of baptism, He has not provided a valid ordination.

By the light of such presumptions as these, I interpret the doubtful issues of the antiquarian argument, and feel deeply that, if Anglican Orders are unsafe with reference to the actual evidence producible for their validity, much more unsafe are they when considered in their surroundings.

Most sincerely yours,

(Signed) JOHN H. NEWMAN.

112

XI

THE PROTESTANT IDEA OF ANTICHRIST

THE Discourses which Dr. Todd[1] has recently given to the world, are, perhaps, the first attempt for a long course of years in this part of Christendom to fix a dispassionate attention and a scientific interpretation upon the momentous "Prophecies relating to Antichrist in the writings of Daniel and St. Paul." When men set out by resolving that a certain ecclesiastical power, or foreign enemy, or political principle, or historical personage, must and shall be the scope of the inspired announcement, which is too often done, they are not, of course, sure to be wrong in their conclusion, but they are pretty sure to be unfair in their proofs. Candour, judgment, critical acumen, exactness in reasoning, adherence to principles, whether of interpretation or of theology, these and similar qualities are not to be expected of such expositors; they start with a prejudice, they argue as advocates, and they end in a foregone conclusion.

---

[1] *Dr. Todd*: James Henthorn Todd (1805-69), born in Dublin on 23 April 1805, the son of a surgeon; Todd studied at Trinity College, Dublin (BA 1825; BD 1837, DD 1840). He was elected a Fellow in 1831 and ordained a priest the following year. For the Donnellan lectures of 1838 and 1839 Todd studied the Biblical prophecies relating to the Antichrist, published in 1840 as *Prophecies relating to Antichrist in the writings of Daniel and St Paul*. Todd showed a balanced approach, arguing that the Pope was not the Antichrist and that the Catholic Church held the essential truths of Christian Revelation. Todd went on to become Regius Professor of Hebrew at the University of Dublin (1849) and Librarian of Trinity College (1852), sorting and expanding the collection and making a significant contribution to the study of Irish history and literature.

Faults such as these cannot be imputed to Dr. Todd; he is methodical, careful, and accurate in his investigations, and clear and unaffected in his manner of presenting them before his readers.

[113] Far from imposing a meaning upon Scripture, in order to make it tally with events in the history of the day, if he has a fault, it rather lies in his proving too little from it; that is, in his being rather bent on disproving what others advance than in establishing, according to the sense of the Catholic Church, anything positive and substantial instead. An adversary would impute to his discussions some deficiency of poetry, by which we mean a deficiency of that subtlety of thought and sensitiveness of feeling which is the best preparative for entering into those superhuman announcements and descriptions upon which he has written. We have pleasure in believing that in matters of doctrine we entirely agree with Dr. Todd; and, judging from what Dr. Arnold has published, we are sorrowfully conscious that we do not agree with Dr. Arnold;[2] still, as regards the principles of prophetical interpretation, we think that there is a deeper philosophy in Dr. Arnold's two Sermons lately published[3] than in the Discourses before us. This, however, we avow merely because by our profession we are critics, and, in giving an opinion on the subject, are performing a task

[2] *Dr. Arnold*: Thomas Arnold (1795-1842), Anglican divine, liberal scripture scholar; he later became an influential reforming Headmaster of Rugby School.
[3] *Dr Arnold's two Sermons lately published*: Thomas Arnold's *Two Sermons on the Interpretation of Prophecy, Preached in the Chapel of Rugby School. With Notes* (1839). In a letter to Jemima dated 25 February 1840, Newman expressed fear of 'a great attack on the Bible' from several directions, including 'Arnold's school, such as it is (I do hope he will be frightened back) giving up the inspiration of the Old Testament or of all Scripture (I do not say that Arnold himself does)' (*LD* VII, pp.244-5).

which may even be expected of us. Having given it, we may with a safe conscience proceed to the consideration of the main position on which Dr. Todd has employed himself, which we cannot but consider to be most true and most important, and to entitle him to the gratitude of all churchmen.

That position is this, that the prophecies concerning Antichrist are as yet unfulfilled, and that the predicted enemy of the Church is yet to come. No one can deny the importance of such a view of the subject, if it be true. If dreadful scenes still await the Church, if they have been foretold, and foretold that Christians may be prepared for them, no calamity can be greater than a belief that they have already been fulfilled, and that there is nothing to look out for or to fear; no device of Satan can be more crafty than to [114] make us think that they are not to come, that they have come to pass already,—nay, that they have been fulfilled in a branch of the Church herself, that Church which was ordained by her Divine Author ever to be one, all over the earth, and to live in internal peace, not in mutual revilings and accusations, in strife and hatred.

But there is another reason why Dr. Todd's work is seasonable and important. We consider that it is impossible to hold certain branches of the Church to be the communion of Antichrist, as it has long been the fashion with Protestants to maintain, without involving our own branch in the charge; if any part of the Church be anti-Christian, it will be found that all the Church is so, our own branch inclusive. We are much disposed to question whether any tests can be given to prove that the Roman communion is the Synagogue of Satan, which will not, in the judgment of the many, implicate the Church of England. This is a most serious consideration, in proportion as we believe it to hold good. In such case it will not be from any special leaning towards Romanism that we shall be eager to prove that Rome is not the seat of the Enemy of God; it will arise simply from prudential motives, if we have no other. As to Rome, we owe her of late years nothing at all, except indeed, according to the Scripture rule, love for hatred. Nothing that we can say will soften one whit that obdurate temper, or touch that secular political spirit, which at present is dominant among her children. Therefore we take up Dr. Todd's position, if we must give our reason, from nothing more or less than the mere instinct of self-preservation. It is very well for Sandemanian,[4] Ranter,[5] or Quaker[6] to call Rome the seat of Antichrist. We cannot

[115] afford to do so; *nostra res agitur:*[7] we come next. Members of our Church are entreated to consider this carefully. In thus assaulting Rome, they are using an argument which is with equal certainty, if not with equal fulness, available against their own religious position; an argument which, if they use it consistently, must drive them forward into some still more simple system of religion, nay, on and on they know not whither, till "*tota* jacet Babylon."[8] If, indeed, it be

---

[4] *Sandemanian*: originally the Glasites, a Protestant sect founded by the Scottish Presbyterian minister, John Glas, around 1730, and spread by his son-in-law, Robert Sandeman.

[5] *Ranter*: a radical sect existing in Cromwellian England, with pantheistic and amoral beliefs. The real nature of Ranterism is difficult to discover since the main documentary evidence comes from their opponents.

[6] *Quaker*: member of the Religious Society of Friends, nicknamed 'Quakers' in ridicule of their founder, George Fox (1624–91) having said that he had come to make people 'tremble at the word of the Lord'.

[7] nostra res agitur: it is our business

[8] "tota *jacet Babylon.*": The distich, framed at the time of the Reformation by one of the extreme Protestant party, was this:

"Tota jacet Babylon, destruxit tecta Lutherus,

a truth that the Bishop of Rome is Antichrist, let us of
course boldly follow it out; but surely, considering the
uncertain arguments on which prophetical interpretations
must rest, and that clear evidence on which the Articles of
the Creed and the principles of Christian ethics are received,
it is necessarily no slight argument against a certain
interpretation, that it is found legitimately to lead to the
denial whether of Christian doctrine or of Christian duty. If
we cannot consistently hold that the Pope is Antichrist,
without holding that the principle of establishments, the
Christian ministry, and the most sacred Catholic doctrines,
are fruits of Antichrist, surely the lengths we must run are a
reductio ad absurdum[9] of the position with which we start.
If we must deny either that Christian Rome is Babylon, or
affirm that Socinus[10] was right, it is not difficult to see
which proposition must give way.

And another serious question is this, whether we ought
not to be very sure before we assert that a branch of Christ's
Church, not merely has evil extensively prevailing within it,
but is actually the kingdom of evil, the kingdom of God's
enemy; considering that, if it be not the kingdom of [116]
darkness, it is the Church, the dwelling-place of the Most
High. The question really lies, be it observed, between those
two alternatives, *either* the Church of Rome is the house of
God *or* the house of Satan; there is no middle ground

Calvinus muros, et fundamenta Socinus," [N]
"Lofty Babylon lies prostrate, Luther destroyed the roof, Calvin the walls and
Socinus the foundations." This was inscribed on the tomb of Socinus by his
followers.
[9] *reductio ad absurdum*: reduction to absurdity, a type of logical argument first
seen in the writings of Aristotle.
[10] *Socinus*: Fausto Socinus or Sozzini (1539-1604), an Italian theologian who gave
his name to Socianism and was a prominent member of the anti-Trinitarian 'Polish
Brethren'.

between them. Now, surely our Lord's strong language about the consequences of speaking against the Gracious Presence which inhabits the Church, or of ascribing the works of the Spirit to Beelzebub, is enough to make us very cautious of forming a judgment against particular branches of the Church, unless we are very certain what we are saying. If we are not "treading upon the adder,"[11] we are "kicking against the pricks."[12]

These are some principal reasons which lead us to feel thankful to Dr. Todd for the careful and learned work which he has presented to the Christian public; and with the hope of strengthening the Scripture argument to which he has for the most part confined himself, we shall here employ ourselves on some collateral thoughts upon the subject, chiefly of an antecedent nature, whether in answer to like antecedent objections, or the expansion of considerations which we have already suggested.

1.

That Scripture contains intimations of the coming of a special enemy of Christ and His Church, of great power, craft, and wickedness, is undeniable. He is described by St. Paul and Daniel, in the prophecies which Mr. Todd undertakes to elucidate, as "the man of sin,"[13] "the lawless one,"[14] "the son of perdition,"[15] "a king of fierce

---

[11] *"treading upon the adder"*: Psalm 91: 13

[12] *"kicking against the pricks"*: Cf. Acts 9:5, 22: 8b and 26:14 (e.g. 'I am Jesus whom thou persecutest: it is hard for thee to kick against the pricks'). The 'prick' is the sharp rod used to till the soil which beasts of burden would futilely kick at out of irritation.

[13] *"the man of sin"*: 2 Thessalonians 2:3

[14] *"the lawless one"*: 2 Thessalonians 2:8

[15] *"the son of perdition"*: 2 Thessalonians 2:3 (also John 17:2, referring to Judas)

countenance, and of look more stout than his fellows;"[16] as "having eyes,"[17] and "a mouth speaking very great things," and "understanding dark sentences;"[18] as a liar and [117] hypocrite, and of a seared conscience; as "doing according to his will;"[19] as "opposing, exalting, and magnifying himself above every god,"[20] and "all that is called God, or that is worshipped;"[21] as "speaking marvellous things against the God of gods;"[22] as "sitting as God in the temple of God," and "showing himself that he is God;"[23] "with all power, and signs, and lying wonders, and with all deceivableness of unrighteousness;"[24] as coming "when the transgressors are come to the full,"[25] with or after an "apostasy," and that "from the faith," in a mystery of iniquity which even in the Apostles' day "did already work;" as "prospering till the indignation be accomplished,"[26] till "the Lord consume him with the spirit of His mouth, and destroy with the brightness of His coming."[27] Such is the prophecy, as Dr. Todd delineates it; the question is, whether, as he maintains, its fulfilment is yet to come, or whether it has taken place in the person of

---

[16] *"a king of fierce countenance, and of look more stout than his fellows"*: Daniel 7:20, 8:23

[17] *"having eyes", "a mouth speaking very great things"*: Daniel 7:8, 20

[18] *"understanding dark sentences"*: Daniel 8:23

[19] *"doing according to his will"*: Daniel 11:3

[20] *"opposing, exalting, and magnifying himself above every god"*: Daniel 11:36

[21] *"all that is called God, or is worshipped"*: 2 Thessalonians 2:4

[22] *"speaking marvellous things against the God of gods"*: Daniel 11:36

[23] *"sitting as God in the temple of God," and "showing himself that he is God"*: 2 Thessalonians 2:4

[24] *"with all power, and signs, and lying wonders, and with all deceivableness of unrighteousness"*: 2 Thessalonians 2:10

[25] *"when the transgressors are come to the full"*: Daniel 8:23

[26] *"prospering till the indignation be accomplished"*: Daniel 11:36

[27] *"the Lord consume him with the spirit of His mouth, and destroy with the brightness of His coming"*: 2 Thessalonians 2:8

the Bishop of Rome, as Protestants have very commonly supposed.

Now, one of the first questions which it is natural to ask on entering upon the subject is, whereas the Pope is said to be Antichrist, sometimes from the fourth, sometimes from the seventh century, when was he first detected and denounced, and by whom? In other words, what is the history of that interpretation of prophecy on which Protestants rely? On this point Dr. Todd supplies us with much information, from which it appears that the belief that the Pope was Antichrist was the conclusion gradually formed and matured out of the belief that the Church of Rome was Babylon, by three heretical bodies, between the eleventh and sixteenth centuries, in consequence of their being submitted to persecution for their opinions:

[118]

"In the middle of the eleventh century, numerous emigrants from Thrace and the East had established themselves in the north of Italy, and especially in the neighbourhood of Milan; and some, despising a fixed habitation, or unable to obtain one, itinerated throughout various parts of France and Germany. The doctrines of these sects exhibit various shades of extravagance and error, and appear to have had a close affinity with the Oriental Manichees[28] or Paulicians,[29] from whom they are historically descended. They are accused of holding that the material world was the work of an evil being, and not of the Supreme Deity; that the Incarnation and Crucifixion of the Lord were therefore visions, or at least so far unreal events as to be disconnected with matter; that abstinence from flesh and wine was necessary to salvation; that marriage was

---

[28] *Manichees*: Manichaeism was a dualist religion founded by Manes (c.216-274) in Persia. It saw the whole cosmos as involved in a struggle between equally powerful principles or deities of good (spirit) and evil (matter).

[29] *Paulicians*: a sect flourishing in Armenia between the seventh and ninth centuries, which seems to have held dualist and adoptionist doctrines.

a carnal state, and inconsistent with Christian perfection. They are said also to have rejected the authority of the Old Testament, as the work of the evil principle; and to have condemned the temporal possessions and rank of the clergy, on the ground that the true Church of Christ should imitate to the letter the poverty of the first Apostles; they despised all external religion, ridiculed the office and powers of the priesthood, the efficacy of the Sacraments, and especially the use of baptism."—Pp. 28-30.

These were the Albigenses,[30] the first of the three independent families of heresy above mentioned.

The second protesting sect which those times produced was, according to Dr. Todd, of a much purer and more respectable character. It originated at the end of the twelfth century, in the celebrated Peter Waldo;[31] was free from the Manichæan errors of the Albigenses and the Paulicians; and, though its members held, at least ultimately, the unlawfulness of oaths, the necessity of poverty, and the inefficacy of the sacraments, yet the innocency of their lives, and their seasonable vehemence against the superstitions of the day, procured them acceptance in almost every part of Europe. Pursuing the line of research which the learned Mr. Maitland[32] has opened, Dr. Todd has brought together a mass of information on this subject, and

[30] *Albigenses*: 12th/13th century branch of the Cathars, akin to Manicheess, and condemned by the Fourth Lateran Council in 1215.

[31] *Peter Waldo*: (c.1140-c.1218), a French merchant who gave his name to the Waldensians and emphasised poverty and universal priesthood in his teaching. He was excommunicated in 1184 and his doctrines were condemned by successive church councils.

[32] *Mr Maitland*: Samuel Roffey Maitland (1792-1866), clergyman and Fellow of the Royal Society, who brought to Protestant England the 'futurist' interpretation of the Antichrist prophecies. His works included *Facts and Documents illustrative of the History, Doctrine, and Rites of the ancient Albigenses and Waldenses* (1832).

[119]   the notes which stand at the end of his Lectures, form one of the most interesting parts of his work. It would appear from these that the Albigenses founded their opposition to the Church on a Manichæan principle, viz., that, as there was an evil deity, and he the author of the visible world, so was he author also of the visible Church, which in consequence was "the devil's basilica and synagogue of Satan," and, in the language of the Apocalypse, "the mother of fornications."[33] This they maintained; though, as denying our Lord's Incarnation, condemning holy matrimony, and prohibiting meats, they themselves came nearest of all religious parties, then existing, to that prophetic description, which they are at this day supposed by their protest to have fastened upon Rome. The Waldenses,[34] on the other hand, far from participating in these grave errors, seem at first to have differed in no article of faith from the received orthodoxy of the thirteenth century; nay, they were in the habit of disputing against the Albigenses, and that "acutissimè,"[35] even after their own separation from the Church. Moreover, far from wishing to separate, they in the first instance attempted to take a place in the Church, such as the Mendicant Friars soon afterwards occupied under the leading of St. Francis[36] and St. Dominic,[37] and applied to the Pope with a view of obtaining his sanction to their rules,

---

[33] *"the mother of fornications"*: Revelation 17:5

[34] *Waldenses*: a heretical movement which originated in the late twelfth century and is named after Peter Waldoo. It was characterised by a belief in the universal priesthood, voluntary poverty and the reading of Scripture in the vernacular. It was soon condemned by the Church.

[35] *acutissimè*: most sharply

[36] *St Francis*: (c.1182-1226), the son of a wealthy merchant in Assisi who embraced poverty and founded the Order of Friars Minor (Franciscans).

[37] *St Dominic*: (c.1170-1221), who founded the Order of Preachers (Dominicans) to uproot the Albigensian heresy.

and of being permitted to found a religious order. Failing in this, they seceded, and proceeded to denounce the Church of Rome, not on the Manichæan principle, nor exactly on the Protestant, though on one which Protestants have often taken, viz., that the Church or its clergy lost their spiritual powers from the period of their consenting to receive temporal endowments. But, as to any opposition to the Church simply founded on the prophecies in the Apocalypse, of this, Dr. Todd contends, and with great force of argument, there is no trace among them, till after [120] the rise of the last of the three families of heresy aforesaid, to which that opposition really belonged, and of which an account shall now be given in our author's words:

"The third class of heretics, amongst whom a similar doctrine prevailed, arose in the bosom of the Church of Rome itself. The great popularity of the sects, to whose history I have alluded, afforded a lesson which was not lost upon the court of Rome; and accordingly, in the beginning of the thirteenth century, the papal sanction was given to the proposal of certain zealous individuals for the establishment of the mendicant orders, upon principles which embraced everything that was attractive to the multitude in the discipline of the heretics, while pains were taken to retain their votaries in strict obedience to the papal authority. These orders acknowledged the great principle, so vehemently contended for by the Vaudois[38] and other reputed heretics, that voluntary poverty was the primary virtue of the Christian religion, the necessary condition of Christian perfection, and the true mode of imitating our Lord and His disciples; and thus a door was opened by which the diseased and dissatisfied spirits, who would otherwise perhaps have joined the ranks of the heretical revolutionists, were afforded a field for the exercise of their zeal and devotion, and at the same time retained in the communion of the Roman Church.

---

[38] *Vaudois*: another name for the Waldensians

"But although the stream of heresy was thus apparently turned into a less dangerous channel, and made subservient to the ambitious projects of the see of Rome, yet the evil broke out afresh in a new and unexpected form. The Franciscan order, especially, soon split into factions which reproduced all the most fatal errors of the heretics, and set the papal power at defiance. The rule of poverty admitted of laxer or of severer interpretation, and furnished the first great subject of internal division among the brethren of St. Francis. The fanatical opinion also, that the life of St. Francis was an exact imitation of the life of our Lord, and that in him were fulfilled many prophecies, especially in the Apocalypse, soon led to serious evils. The *spiritual* Franciscans, as they were called, who maintained the absolute illegality of all possessions, under any pretence or fiction whatsoever, were also distinguished for an affectation of prophetical powers, and for peculiar interpretations of the book of Revelation. They insisted [121] that St. Francis was the Angel whom the Apostle had seen in vision flying in the midst of heaven, having the everlasting Gospel to preach to them that dwell on the earth; and that the mendicant friars of his order were destined, like the Apostles of our Lord, to introduce a new dispensation which should regenerate the Church and the world.

"The court of Rome, as was naturally to have been expected, opposed these extreme opinions, and supported the modified interpretation of the Franciscan rule; and hence, notwithstanding many efforts to appease the storm, the spiritual Franciscans soon attacked the papal chair itself. At the close of the thirteenth century, indeed, an effort was made to re-unite them to the Roman Church, by erecting them into a separate order, under the name of Celestine-Eremites,[39] but the evil was too deeply rooted to admit

---

[39] *Celestine-Eremites*: A group of 'poor hermits' attached to the 'Spiritual Franciscans' who were brought into the Church by Pope Celestine V (1294), hence their name. These should not be confused with the Celestine Benedictines, founded by the same pope in 1254 (before his election).

of so easy a cure, and soon ended in their total separation from the order, and from the Church. The Fratricelli, which was one of the names assumed by the new separatists, denied the right of the Sovereign Pontiff himself to interpret or to dispense with the letter of their rule; they maintained that they themselves were the true Church of Christ, that the bishops and priests of the Roman communion were no longer true bishops or priests; that the Church of Rome was the synagogue of Satan, the beast or harlot of the Apocalypse. They asserted that the Gospel preached by Christ and His Apostles was an imperfect and temporary dispensation, like that of Moses; that St. Francis was the inspired founder of a new and more glorious Gospel, which was to be preached in all the world by the mendicant friars of his order, and which was destined to endure for ever."—Pp. 31-34.

In maintaining these views concerning the Roman communion, the spiritual Franciscans were much indebted to the writings of the Abbot Joachim,[40] the celebrated founder of the Florensian order at the close of the twelfth century, the warm supporter of the Popedom, and the friend of Popes Lucian, Urban, and Clement,[41] and eventually a canonized saint. This is not the place to enter into the discussion of a system of prophetical interpretation, to which much attention has been lately drawn. Its effect upon the Franciscan party will be seen by enumerating some out of the twenty heretical tenets charged upon Olivi, or Peter John,[42] the most remarkable of their writers, according to Dr. Todd, who flourished towards the end of the thirteenth

[122]

[40] *Abbot Joachim*: (c.1132-1202), Cistercian abbot of Fiore and mystic.
[41] *Popes Lucian, Urban and Clement*: namely Lucius III (1181-85), Urban III (1185-87) and Clement III (1187-91). Despite their friendship with Abbot Joachim, his ideas (as developed by his followers) were later condemned by the Church.
[42] *Olivi, or Peter John*: Peter John Olivi (1248-98) was a Franciscan theologian whose controversial teachings on poverty were highly influential with the 'Spiritual Franciscans.'

century. Olivi taught, according to Eymericus,[43] that "the rule of the Minor Friars, put forth by St. Francis, is truly and properly that Evangelical rule which Christ observed in His own person, enjoined on the Apostles, and caused to be written in His Gospels; that, as the Synagogue was propagated from twelve Patriarchs, and the Church of the Gentiles from twelve Apostles, so the last Church of the remnant of Jews and Gentiles is to be propagated by means of twelve Evangelical men; whence St. Francis had twelve sons and associates, through whom and in whom was founded and begun the Evangelical order; that the angel Francis will perceive himself to prosper not so much in the carnal Church of the Latins, as in the Greeks, Saracens, Tartars, and, at length, the Jews; that that Church, which we call the universal Church Catholic militant, is a carnal Church, Babylon, the great harlot corrupting herself and all the nations subjected to her with foul carnalities and Simoniacal[44] lusts, and earthly glory of this world; that the Roman Church is that woman, the great harlot, spoken of in the Apocalypse, which once was in the state of paganism, and afterwards in the faith of Christ, which now in many ways has committed fornication with this world."

This is a specimen of the doctrine of the spiritual Franciscans, and, considering how much more it is to the purpose of our ultra-Protestant brethren than that of either Albigenses or Waldenses, we do wonder that Bishop Newton[45] does not include them among the witnesses,

---

[43] *Eymericus*: Nicholas Eymericis (c.1320-99) was a Dominican who acted as Inquisitor General and produced the *Directorium Inquisitorium*.

[44] *Simoniacal*: Simony is the sin of obtaining church appointments for money.

[45] *Bishop Newton*: Thomas Newton (1704-82), noted as a Biblical scholar, Bishop of Bristol (1761-82) and Dean of St Paul's (1768-82). He wrote *Dissertations on*

"Protestants before even the name came into use," who he conceives have been raised up against the Church of Rome. [123] "Our Saviour," he says, "sent forth His disciples two and two, and it has been observed, that the principal reformers have usually appeared in pairs, as the Waldenses and Albigenses, John Huss[46] and Jerome of Prague,[47] Luther[48] and Calvin,[49] Cranmer[50] and Ridley.[51]" Why should not Peter John Olivi pair with the Abbot Joachim? Yet, ungrateful towards those who were the first inventors and propagators of the view adopted by himself, he presently puts forward these Waldenses and Albigenses again, sects which controverted with each other, one orthodox, the other heretical, the one akin to the Begging Friars, the other of the stock of the Manichees, as "the true witnesses, and, as I may say, the Protestants of that age."

Surely it is not without reason that Dr. Todd asks, "Are these the expositors from whom the Church of Christ is to receive the true interpretation of the Prophecies?" and "whose *bare assertion* that their enemies are the Antichrist is to be received as itself the fulfilment of prophecy, and a proof that 'the time of the end' is arrived?"—P. 34. "These sects," he observes elsewhere, "were for the most part corrupt in doctrine, or ignorant and superstitious in their

---

the Prophecies, which have been remarkably fulfilled, and are at this time fulfilling in the world (1754) and also produced an annotated edition of John Milton's *Paradise Lost* (1749).

[46] *John Huss*: Jan Huss (1369-1415), Czech theologian and reformer who inspired the Hussite movement and was burned at the stake during the Council of Constance, despite the Emperor Sigismund's promise of safe conduct.

[47] *Jerome of Prague*: Jerome of Prague (1379-1416), a follower of Huss also burned during the Council of Constance.

[48] *Luther*: Martin Luther (1483-1546), German reformer.

[49] *Calvin*: John Calvin (1509-1564, French reformer.

[50] *Cranmer*: See note on p.[1].

[51] *Ridley*: See note on p.[83].

practice; and ... their denunciations of the Roman Church as the Babylon of Prophecy were the offspring of a spirit very different indeed from that in which we should seek for the true interpretation of a book, of which it is written, 'Blessed is he that readeth, and they that hear the words of this prophecy, and *keep those things that are written therein.*'"[52]—P. 497.

2.

"Our Protestant forefathers," then, as these unhappy misbelievers have, we believe, with a boldness which we hardly know whether to applaud or to reprobate, sometimes been called, do not themselves shed much lustre upon the doctrine which they originated. However, it is obvious that the more modern witnesses to it are of a much more respectable cast; and its maintainers will not be slow probably in urging this circumstance upon our attention, as a set-off against the disreputable nature of its origin. The Protestant world, it may be said, contains in it multitudes of that high character and intellectual calibre, so learned, so acute, so profound, and so honest, that nothing can stand against the testimony which they bear to the truth of the views of Prophecy which the Albigenses or the Franciscans began. This, then, is the next point to which our attention is naturally called; and here, though we are far of course from presuming to speak disrespectfully of the qualities of mind which Protestant expositors have possessed (to do which would be the extreme of arrogance and ignorance), yet so far is quite clear, that this is a case which has put their learning, acuteness, and other endowments, sorely to task;

[124]

---

[52] *'Blessed is he ...* are written therein.': Revelation 1:3

for a very little examination of the matter will show that they have made some most considerable slips in their treatment of it.

This is a most important circumstance in an inquiry in which so much blind reliance must inevitably be placed by students upon their teacher. There is no department of theology in which ordinary men are more at the mercy of an author than that of prophetical interpretation. Creeds are restraints upon divines, and safeguards to readers, in point of doctrine; moral sense in questions of duty; the text of Scripture itself in direct exposition and comment; the existing form and establishment of religion in matters of discipline and polity; but who shall warrant, and who shall verify, discussions which embrace on the one hand the wide [125] range of history, and necessarily plunge on the other into the subtleties of allegory and poetry, which profess to connect and adjust a field so fertile in facts with a page so recondite in character, and that upon no principles, perhaps, but such as approve themselves to the judgment of the individual interpreter? What a temptation is there under such circumstances for unconscious practising upon the inspired text, or unconscious management of the historical materials? The relative importance of events, their aspect and meaning, the probability of their having occurred, the value of the particular testimony produced, the force of words, the arrangement of dates, these are but a few out of the many matters, in which, from the nature of the case, the personal judgment of the reader is almost excluded, and the dictum of the teacher must be received as law. When then we actually meet with grave and obvious instances of misrepresentation in the statements of certain writers upon Prophecy, and these same repeated from writer to writer, strong suspicion is thrown at once over all such interpretations, which, for what we know, are not better founded than those of which we happen to be able so plainly to discern the unfairness and fallaciousness. These writers are discovered to have taken points for granted, which they had better have examined for themselves, and which turn out to be mistakes, and that in matters of a very sacred character, and involving conclusions most awful towards a great part of the Christian world. Now Mr. Maitland, who is one of the few persons who have undertaken to sift the facts on which the ultra-Protestant interpreters of the Prophecies rely, has at once brought to light so many strange mistakes in their statements as to [126] make a candid reader very suspicious, or, rather, utterly incredulous, of all allegations made on the mere authority of these writers.

What can be thought of the zealous Mr. McNeile,[53] for instance, who has been taught by Bishop Hurd[54] to select for a motto to a sermon, which he publishes under the name of "Antichrist," a passage from St. Bernard,[55] as if in reprobation of the Papacy, to the effect that "that beast of the Apocalypse, to whom is given a mouth speaking blasphemies, occupies the chair of Peter, as a lion ready for the prey"? whereas it turns out that St. Bernard is not speaking of the Pope, but of the Antipope; is defending the Pope against the Antipope Peter Leo, on whose name he is

---

[53] *Mr McNeile*: Hugh Boyd McNeile (1795-1879) was an Anglican clergyman of Calvinist sympathies. Highly critical of the Oxford Movement and an opponent of Catholic Emancipation, he was a prominent member of the Protestant Association.
[54] *Bishop Hurd*: Richard Hurd (1720-1808), a theologian who served as bishop of Lichfield and Coventry (1774-81) and Worcester (1781-1808).
[55] *St. Bernard*: See note on p.[74].

playing when he compares him to a lion, and whose conduct he denotes by the word *occupat*, which does not mean "*occupies*," but "*seizes*," or "*usurps*."

A second instance occurs in the colour put upon the words of Abbot Joachim by Bishops Hurd and Newton, Mr. McNeile and Mr. Irving,[56] to which Dr. Todd refers in his notes, and Mr. Burgh[57] also in his excellent sermon on Antichrist. These four writers either distinctly state or imply that the Abbot Joachim interpreted of the Pope the passage in 2 Thess. ii., and even the text about the beast in the Apocalypse, whereas he does but say that "Antichrist is born in Rome, and will be elevated to the Apostolic See;" and that, as his system of prophecy proves him to mean, by a *usurpation*, to the *overthrow* of the Pope, whose dignity he specifies, because it was the highest which any one could aim at.

Another misstatement which might be mentioned, not so violent, but quite as real, is the common assertion that Pope Gregory the Great[58] asserted that whoever claimed to be Universal Bishop was Antichrist; a statement which, even when corrected so as to be true in the] letter, conveys a very [127] incorrect opinion of his meaning to an unlearned reader. St. Gregory says, that "whosoever adopts or desires the title of Universal Priest is the *forerunner* of Antichrist;" by which he does not mean to assert that Antichrist will be a

---

[56] *Mr Irving*: Edward Irving (1792-1834), a Scottish clergyman whose works included *Babylon and Infidelity foredoomed: A Discourse on the Prophecies of Daniel and the Acopalypse which relate to these latter times, and until the Second Advent* (1826). Eventually excommunicated by the Church of Scotland for his heterodox views, he founded the Catholic Apostolic Church.

[57] *Mr Burgh*: William Burgh of Trinity College, Dublin, author of *Lectures on the Second Advent of Our Lord Jesus Christ* (1835) and *Antichrist: A discourse with an appendix containing an answer to the sermon of the Rev. H. McNeile bearing same title* (1839).

[58] *Pope St. Gregory the Great*: See note on p.[37].

Universal Bishop, that is, the Pope, as Protestants suppose, but that the affectation of supremacy is the presage of some vast evils near to come, even of the reign of the expected Antichrist. The ancients, ever looking out as they were for the end of all things, and knowing that the coming of Antichrist was to be its immediate sign, as the Apostle had determined, were led to discern in every serious evil which happened to the Church tokens of the coming woe, and called them "forerunners of Antichrist;" as we might speak of "crimes which call down judgment," or "are evidence of divine wrath." Instead of speaking of "*crying* sins," they spoke of "forerunners of Antichrist." Thus Tertullian,[59] St. Dionysius,[60] and St. Cyprian,[61] consider the heathen persecution as the token of Antichrist. St. Cyril of Jerusalem,[62] and St. Athanasius[63], call the Arian disturbances "the forerunner of Antichrist;" as do also St. Gregory Nazianzen[64] and St. Hilary.[65] St. Leo[66] in one place calls Nestorius[67] and Eutyches[68] "forerunners of Antichrist;" in another, persons who resist what the Church has once

[59] *Tertullian*: See note on p.[42].
[60] *St. Dionysius*: Probably St. Dionysius of Alexandria (d.264); among his writings was a critique of the Book of Revelation against Millennialist interpretations.
[61] *St. Cyprian*: See note on p.[25].
[62] *St. Cyril of Jerusalem*: (c.313-386), Bishop and Doctor of the Church.
[63] *St. Athanasius*: See note on p.[52].
[64] *St. Gregory Nazianzen*: See note on p.[42].
[65] *St. Hilary*: St Hilary of Poitiers (c.310-c.367), Bishop and Doctor of the Church, champion of orthodoxy the Arians by whom be was persecuted.
[66] *St. Leo*: Pope Leo I (c.400-461), the first Pope to be called 'the Great'; his *Tome* proved decisive at the Council of Chalcedon (451) against Monophysitism (vividly described by Newman in his *Essay on the Development of Christian Doctrine*, p.307ff.).
[67] *Nestorius*: (386-451), Archbishop of Constantinople; he rejected the doctrine of the hypostatic union of the divine and human natures of Christ and denied the title *theotokos* (God-bearer, Mother of God) to the Virgin Mary. His teachings were condemned at the Council of Ephesus.
[68] *Eutyches*: See note on p.[51].

settled, or who oppose the see of St. Peter. Anastasius speaks of the "ten horns" of the Monophysite heresy as such. And at a later period, Theodorus Studites,[69] writing against the Iconoclasts, considers their proceedings "the apostasy which must first come, the invasion of Antichrist." Pope Gregory then meant doubtless, in the words in question, to denounce a great evil; but is in no respect a witness for the Protestant doctrine concerning Antichrist, unless indeed we are willing to say that by St. Athanasius   [128] Arius was considered to be Antichrist, or by St. Leo Eutyches.

Again, to take another instance: Bishop Newton states that the Pope *"is styled* and *pleased* to be styled our Lord God the Pope."—*Dissert*. 22. Now the state of the case, as Mr. Maitland has elicited it, seems at greatest disadvantage to be this: that the words occurred in a gloss of a canonist named Zenzelius,[70] in one, or more than one, edition of the Decretals,[71] and occurred in the course of an argument, the object of which was to prove that the Pope's words were to be obeyed, *because, as all law, civil inclusive*, they were the decision *of God*;—that in other editions they did not occur;—and that there is reason to believe that they were erased from that in which they did occur; while it is certain that from ancient times the title Deus has been applied to all bishops, after the pattern of the text quoted by our Lord, "I

---

[69] *Theodorus Studites*: St. Theodore of Studium (759-826), monk; he defended the use of images against Iconoclasm.

[70] *Zenzelius*: more correctly Zenzelinus (d.1347), a professor at Montpelier and canonist, who produced the *Viginti Extravagantes*, twenty decrees of John XXII with a gloss (or commentary). Protestant writers claim that it included the statement that it was heresy to deny the power of 'Our Lord God the Pope.' This phrase does not appear in early editions, where it reads '*Dominum nostrum Papam*' (the '*Deum*' may have been added by mistake or deliberately in the early modern period).

[71] *Decretals*: the letters of Popes giving decisions on matters of Church law.

said ye are Gods."[72] Now we repeat what we have said before, our object is not to defend the Roman Catholics, who must look about them for themselves, but to inquire how *facts* lie. After such a result of the inquiry in this particular case, what are we to think of a writer like Mr. Edgar,[73] who (in his Varieties of Popery, p. 131, ed. 2), says—

"A fourth variety, on this subject, makes the Pope *superior* to God. Equality with the Almighty, it might have been expected, would have satiated the ambition of the pontiff, and satisfied the sycophancy of his minions. But this was not the giddiest step in the scale of blasphemy. The superiority of the Pope over the Creator *has been boldly and unblushingly maintained* by pontiffs, theologians, canonists, and councils."

3.

Now it may readily be granted that some of these writers

[129] are not possessed of that seriousness and earnestness of mind which entitles them to our respect; but when we consider the character of others, of Mr. McNeile for instance, or Mr. Irving, or others who might be named, it is quite plain that evidences of no common, or rather very uncommon, candour, impartiality, and calmness may fairly be required, before we venture to resign ourselves to an interpreter of prophecy, who, from his particular creed or other cause, is under any special temptation (unconsciously) to distort facts, and to wrest or explain away the Scripture text. If men so eminent, so religious, as some of those who

---

[72] *"I said ye are Gods."*: John 10.34, quoting Psalm 82:6.
[73] *Mr Edgar*: Samuel Edgar DD, author of *Varieties of Popery* (1831, 2nd ed.1838).

might be named, have not come out of this temptation unscathed, who can hope to overcome it? none surely but those rare specimens of evangelical sanctity which are scattered through the heavens, like stars, each in his turn; none but saints and doctors and confessors, men of sound judgment and well-digested learning, whose sufferings in the cause of truth prove their sincerity, and whose mortified lives are the warrant for their illumination. All of us indeed may edify each other, as in doctrine and precept, so in interpretation of prophecy; viz., by transmitting what we have received from the Church, or by illustrating what is on the surface of Scripture, or by refuting extravagances. But we are speaking of *new* or *further* interpretations, whether of the sacred text or of the world's history: and, not at all denying that there is room for these, not at all denying that the new may surpass the old, not denying their desirableness, yet we repeat that no ordinary man can undertake to enunciate them, no man can command our assent, unless he has some portions of that spirit which inspired the prophecy itself. And if this be true generally, what an uncommon man must he be, who is to be our guide in unchurching the greater part of Christendom?

No one can be at a loss to detect a number of feelings [130] and principles which may be present to prejudice sensible and amiable men, or even men of deep intellects, to whom no one would impute that carnal political spirit, or that bitter fanaticism, or that scoffing tone of mind, each of which has in its turn been the fruitful source of interpretations of the Apocalypse. To go no further, even a dutiful temper will lead a writer to say what others of his own party, school, or sect have said before him. He takes for granted their statements, which he has heard from his youth, and repeats them. He has not thrown his mind upon this subject; he has not examined it for himself; hence it does not occur to him to doubt what he has been taught. Endowments, too, have been provided for the inculcation of a particular view of Prophecy; and a writer may be exercising his thoughts *under* them, and thereby be led to say out what he had hitherto but passively held, and would never otherwise have put into words, though he might profess to hold it. The Warburton Lectures,[74] it is well known, were founded as the words run, "to prove the truth of Revealed Religion in general, and of the Christian in particular, from the completion of the prophecies in the Old and New Testament, which relate to the Christian Church, *especially to the apostasy of Papal Rome*." It is only surprising that such a foundation has not done more in behalf of its object. In matter of fact, after three lecturers had passed in succession, a fourth could not be found, and for some time there was a suspension of the lecture. Mr. Davison[75] has but one discourse on the subject, and an able and respected writer, whose Lectures have just appeared, does not bestow upon us even one.[76]

[131]   Again, venerated writers have been stirred up to speak of the bishops of Rome as Antichrist, from the fierce persecuting spirit which these bishops have so often evidenced. Men, who are smarting under injuries inflicted, will naturally view their tormentor in the least favourable

---

[74] *Warburton Lectures*: or Warburtonian Lectures, normally held in the chapel of Lincoln's Inn Fields in London between 1768 and 1931.

[75] *John Davison*: See Essay XV below for Newman's article on this Oriel don.

[76] [Archdeacon Lyall.] [N] William Rowe Lyall (1788-1857), high church Anglican divine; his Warbuton lectures had just been published as *Propædia Prophetica* (1840).

light. It was persecution which led the Waldenses to call Rome the Apocalyptic Babylon; and it has been persecution, or the fear of it, which has led much better and more learned men of modern times to call the Pope Antichrist. Moreover, it should be carefully borne in mind, that Protestants will ever feel a strong temptation to this view, by the ease with which it disposes of the plausible and apparently cogent proofs with which Rome fights her battles. No one can deny that the Roman theory is in the abstract most exceedingly specious and persuasive; nor can it be refuted without considerable labour and learning, and an appeal to principles which are not felt to be axioms by ordinary minds, and are deficient in practical persuasiveness. The problem then which lies before the Protestant controversialist is, to find some popular answer to popular and intelligible pretensions, and the position that Papal Rome is Babylon is the "wherefore" to the "why,"—a brief, clear, strong, and simple refutation of them. If once we assume that the Pope is Antichrist, then all the apparent evidences in favour of Rome only become the more convincing evidences of the truth of the assumption with which we start. Antichrist doubtless is to deceive many; he is to bring with him a plausible doctrine; he is to be very *like* the truth. In consequence, universality, antiquity, claim to miraculous power, sanctity, all the Notes of the Church, become but symptomatic of its being the Synagogue of Satan. Is it far spreading?—The reign of Antichrist was to be over the earth. Is it ancient?—The mystery doth already work, from the Apostles' time downwards. Does it profess the power of doing miracles?—Antichrist is to come with "lying wonders." Is it in appearance holy?—Antichrist is to be Satan transformed into an Angel of light. Has it all these

[132]

157

and much more of cumulative evidence in favour of its divine origin? It is a mystery of iniquity. Excellently speaks Mr. McNeile, as quoted by Mr. Burgh:

"It is *extremely difficult*, without giving rise to misapprehension or misconstruction, to contend against the chamelion shifting of its hypocritical professions. It professes truth, while it circulates falsehood. It professes faith, while it cultivates sight. It professes spiritual worship, while it practises gross idolatry. It professes charity, while it is based on intolerance. It professes purity, while it encourages sin. With an oily tongue it professes Christ, while in the depth of an unsanctified heart it is Antichrist."—*Antichr.*, p. 340.

Again, the Protestant polemic is harassed with questions about the duty of "hearing the Church," about preserving unity, about the patriarchal authority, episcopal grace, long and unbroken tradition, and the weight of synodal decisions. We do not say the claims of Rome on these various grounds may not be separately and satisfactorily met, but that such answers in detail must be abstruse, circuitous, and ineffective; on the contrary, when the simple principle is once mastered that the Pope is Antichrist, nothing more is necessary in the controversy. It answers to the dogma of the Pope's infallibility in the Roman system. A bold, forcible, decisive argument is taken, intelligible to the meanest capacity; it is a tactic which puts an end to skirmishing, manœuvring and desultory warfare. A Church can have no rights which has ceased to be a Church. Thus surely it was that Luther made progress, not by appeals to the Fathers, not by reasonings on the nature of the case, not by elaborate deductions from Scripture, but by positions venturous, striking, stamped with originality, and suited even to the

[133]

ignorant,—that we are justified by the sole instrumentality of faith, that our best works are sins, that assurance is possession, and, among these, that the Pope is Antichrist. The advantage of this mode of warfare is pointed out with much *naïveté*, and not less truth, by a controversialist, whose words we quote from a periodical, in which we find them.

"There are two modes of viewing Popery," he observes, "1st. As a gigantic system of evil *foretold* in Scripture, essentially satanic in its origin, distinguished by a variety of errors, and called the 'Apostasy of the latter times;' 2ndly. As a *Church infected by various errors*, but not the apostasy foretold, its errors being, however, demonstrable from Scripture. On these two modes of viewing Popery, there are grounded two different methods of attacking it. In the first case *it is attacked bodily*, if I may so speak. It is identified as a system, from its corporate characteristics, with the apostasy, or Babylon of the Scriptures, and all its errors and corruptions are brought forward as illustrations of this truth, and as strong confirmatory reasons, on account of which we should obey the mandate issued by God Himself, namely, 'Come out of her, my people.' In the second case, instead of attacking the system of Popery, or rather, I should say perhaps, the Popish Church, the assailant exposes the errors which it holds, and the *contest becomes one simply about doctrines*, maintained too, as I have shown elsewhere, by the Protestant advocate, *under circumstances very disadvantageous to the cause of truth*."

This writer certainly puts the advantage of calling Christian Rome Babylon in a clear point of view.

4.

But more may be said on this subject; we just now hinted that mere honesty, and impartiality, and talent, are not

[134]

enough for an interpreter of these awful prophecies, but qualities are needed for him more akin to those possessed by the inspired writers themselves. Daniel, St. Paul, and St. John, the three prophets of the last days, are also saints. We do not see what good could come to theology from the expositions of the Manichees or the Fratricelli of the middle ages; no, nor in later times from attendants on Walpole[77] or Pelham,[78] or frequenters of the back-stairs at St. James's.[79] Mere decency of life is not a candle bright enough to read withal holy Apostles or the "man greatly beloved;"[80] and much more when the matter taken in hand is no less than that of unchurching the greater part of Christendom. A man must be almost an Angel, to stand forth to teach us that the great multitude of Christian bishops are children of the devil. And if he is not an Angel, then he has to show that he himself is not of the family of him who is emphatically, we are told, the "accuser of the brethren."[81] Who, indeed, but the like of ascetic Daniel, much-suffering Paul, and contemplative John, will suffice to establish the paradox that Carlo Borromeo[82] sucked the breast of Babylon, and that Pascal[83] died in her arms? Now, let a candid Protestant decide: is he prepared to match Warburton, Newton, or Hurd, against, we will not say these saints of Scripture, but

---

[77] *Walpole*: Sir Robert Walpole (1676-1745), politician often regarded as the first British Prime Minister (1721-42). He was later created Earl of Orford.

[78] *Pelham*: Henry Pelham (1696-1754), Whig politician and Prime Minister (1743-54)

[79] *St James's*: referring to the Court of the British Sovereign, officially based at St James's Palace.

[80] *"man greatly beloved"*: Daniel 10:11 (referring to the prophet himself)

[81] *"accuser of the brethren"*: Revelation 12:10

[82] *Carlo Borromeo*: See note on p.[72]. Newman returns to Borromeo later in the article.

[83] *Pascal*: See note on p.[72].

even against the saints of degenerate Rome? Is he prepared to sit in judgment on such men as have been named, with nothing better than Newton for our saint, doctor, bishop, and confessor? What is there to command respect in Newton's life and character, what to command confidence in his intellectual or moral illumination?

Now we are going to commit what may seem an invidious act, to appeal to the private life of a respectable and amiable man.[84] His Dissertations on the Prophecies, however, are the main source, we suppose, of that anti-Roman opinion on the subject of Antichrist, now afloat among us, as far as men have an opinion; and if we venture to speak hardly against him, it is only to prevent his being believed, when he speaks hardly of his betters. His work, on its first appearance, went through six large editions in the course of thirty years, and was translated into German and Danish. Its influence has undoubtedly been great: let us then see what its author was worth; and this we are enabled to do from the circumstance of his having also bequeathed to the world an Autobiography, never to be forgotten. It was written with a winning gentleness and calmness; but some extracts will soon decide for us whether he had much of insight into the spiritual world. Surely an author who charged the greater part of Christendom with satanical error, has no right to complain of being convicted out of his own mouth of a secular spirit.

[135]

---

[84] *to appeal to the private life of a respectable and amiable man ...* : Newman now concentrates on the life of Thomas Newton (1704-82), scholar; Bishop of Bristol 1761-82. His *Dissertations on the Prophecies which have remarkably been Fulfilled, and at this time are Fulfilling in the World* were published in 1754.

"In the first year of the king's reign,"[85] he says, "there was a remarkable mortality among the great bishops: Hoadly, of Winchester,[86] who died April 17; Sherlock, of London,[87] who died July 18; and Gilbert, of York,[88] who died August 9, all in the year 1761. Dr. Newton" [this is the writer himself] "had the honour of being in some measure known to the Earl of Bute,[89] having baptized one or two of his children, and having sometimes met him at Leicester House, when as chaplain he had been in attendance upon the Princess of Wales. *He had also presented to him the three volumes of his Dissertations on the Prophecies, having obtained the favour of his lordship to present them to the Prince of Wales.* Upon the death of Bishop Sherlock, Lord Bute told a noble lord, a particular friend of Dr. Newton's, *that he would certainly be the new bishop*, and would be obliged to no minister for his promotion: it was entirely the doing of the king himself[90] and the Princess of Wales[91] ... He" [the Duke of

---

[85] *"In the first year of the king's reign"*: 1761, the year of George III's coronation. The extract that follows is taken from *The Lives of Dr Edward Pocock, the Celebrated Orientalist by Dr Twells, of Dr Zachary Pearce, Bishop of Rochester, and of Dr Thomas Newton, Bishop of Bristol, by Themselves, and of the Rev. Philip Skelton by Mr Burdy* (London, 1810, 2 volumes).

[86] *Hoadly, of Winchester*: Benjamin Hoadly (1676-1761), low church Anglican divine, successively bishop of Bangor, Hereford, Salisbury and Winchester, while living almost entirely in London and devoting himself to Whig politics; he initiated the Bangorian controversy in which he took the Erastian view of the rights of the state over the church and denied that the church should have any government of its own.

[87] *Sherlock, of London*: Thomas Sherlock (1678-1761), successively bishops of Salisbury, Bangor and London; opponent of Hoadly in the Bangorian controversy.

[88] *Gilbert, of York*: John Gilbert (1693-1761), successively bishop of Llanduff, Salisbury and York.

[89] *the Earl of Bute*: John Stuart, Marquis of Bute, who was tutor to the future George III and briefly served as Prime Minister (1762-63) at the beginning of that King's reign.

[90] *the King himself*: the new king, George III (1738-1820) who had succeeded his father in 1760.

[91] *the Princess of Wales*: Princess Augusta, widow of Frederick, Prince of Wales, who had died in 1751.

Newcastle[92]] "had been so long used to shuffle and cut the cards, that he well knew how to pack them in such a manner as to have the *honours*" [for instance, the see of London] "dealt to his particular friends; and on the day when they were all appointed to kiss the king's hand,[93] Drummond for York,[94] Hayter for London,[95] Thomas for Salisbury,[96] Yonge for Norwich,[97] and Green for Lincoln,[98] Newton, who was to succeed Yonge in the bishopric of Bristol and residentiariship[99] of St. Paul's, had no notice sent him from the office as the rest had; so much less regard was paid to the king's nomination than to the minister's. He was in some doubt whether he ought to go to court; but being persuaded to go, he met the Duke of Newcastle upon the great stairs, and asked him whether he was in the right, whether he was come for any good purpose. Aye, aye, said the duke, you are right, *go on and prosper*; and the same was confirmed to him above stairs by Mr. Jenkinson,[100] who was then Lord Bute's secretary ... The Bishop of Bristol" [himself] "*was no great gainer by preferment*; for he was *obliged* to give up the prebend[101] of Westminster, the [136]

---

[92] *Duke of Newcastle*: Thomas Pelham-Hobbes (1693-1768), on two occasions Whig Prime Minister (1754-56, 1757-62) and brother of another Prime Minister, Henry Pelham (see above). The Pelhams were a notable political dynasty in Georgian England.

[93] *kiss the king's hand*: the ritual by which a bishop or other government appointee expressed his loyalty to the sovereign on being appointed.

[94] *Drummond for York*: Robert Hay Drummond (1711-1776), successively bishop of St. Asaph, Salisbury and York.

[95] *Hayter for London*: Thomas Hayter, (1702-62), scholar; bishop of Norwich, supporter of the Pelhams.

[96] *Thomas for Salisbury*: This is incorrect. John Thomas (1696-1781) was bishop of Salisbury from 1757 to 1761 in which year he became bishop of Winchester, succeeding Hoadly.

[97] *Yonge for Norwich*: Philip Yonge (1709-83), previously bishop of Bristol; described as 'notoriously idle'.

[98] *Green for Lincoln*: John Green (1706-79), divine and academic; he wrote against the Methodists.

[99] *residentiariship*: more correctly residentiaryship, the office of a (canon) residentiary, i.e. an ecclesiastic who is bound to official residence (*OED*).

[100] *Mr Jenkinson*: Charles Jenkinson (1727-1808), Under-Secretary to Lord Bute and later created Earl of Liverpool. His son Robert served as Prime Minister (1812-27).

[101] *prebend*: the office of a prebendary, a canon of a cathedral

precentorship[102] of York, the lectureship[103] of St. George's Hanover Square,[104] and the *genteel office* of sub-almoner;[105] but, however, he was *rather better pleased* with *his little bishopric* and the residentiarship of St. Paul's, than he would have been with the large and extensive and *laborious* diocese of Lincoln, for which his friend was in all respects much better qualified. *St. Paul's had always been the object of his wish*, and he used to say that if he could get into Amen Corner,[106] *he should arrive at the end of his prayers*. 'Hoc erat in votis,' but 'Dii melius fecere.'"[107]—*Life*, pp. 112-115.

Or take another anecdote of an earlier date:

"When he waited upon the archbishop" [Gilbert, of York,] "at Kew,[108] his grace further informed him that among other things the king had said, that, though he had no reason to *find fault* with the length of Dr. Newton's sermons, yet, as he would now preach oftener before him, he must desire that he would be *particularly short*, especially on the great festivals, for he was an old man, and

---

[102] *precentorship*: the office of a precentor, a minor canon who administers the musical life of a cathedral.

[103] *lectureship*: not the modern university post, but the position of paid preacher in a church.

[104] *St. George's Hanover Square*: the church of a parish formed in the early eighteenth century in the fashionable West End of London with a congregation of the wealthy and aristocratic.

[105] *sub-almoner*: deputy to the distributor of alms, i.e. money or gifts for the poor. By the eighteenth century, many of these ecclesiastical posts had become sinecures, providing a comfortable income but having no duties.

[106] *Amen Corner*: a street near St. Paul's Cathedral

[107] *'Hoc erat in votis,' but 'Dii melius fecere.'*: From Horace's *Satire* VI, lines 1-4: 'Hoc erat in votis, modus agri non ita magnus, / Hortus ubi, etc tecto vicinus jugis aquæ fons, / Et paulum sylvæ super his soret, auctius atque / Dii melius fecere' – 'This was ever among the warmest of my wishes: a parcel of ground not too extensive, in which was a garden, and a fountain, with a perennial stream, adjoining to my house, and a little woodland into the bargain. The gods have done liberally'.

[108] *Kew*: Kew Palace, situated in what are now the Royal Botanical Gardens (near Richmond), was a favourite residence of Frederick, Prince of Wales and his son George III. It was here that Queen Charlotte died in 1818.

if the sermon was long he was in danger of falling asleep and catching cold, and it would fatigue him too much, especially on those days when he was afterwards to come down into the chapel to receive the Sacrament. The doctor" [himself] "had before *taken care* in his sermons at court to come within the compass of twenty minutes, but after this, especially on the great festivals, he never exceeded fifteen, so that the king sometimes said to the clerk of the closet,[109] *a short good sermon*. But Archbishop Gilbert's favours did not stop here. The *Archbishop of York is not a very good patron*, but he gave him one of the *most valuable pieces of preferment* in the church of York, the precentorship which he held till he was promoted to a bishopric, etc., etc."—Pp. 104, 105.

In a like spirit, he tells us of the mastership of the [137] Charter House,[110] that Bishop Benson[111] and Dr. Jortin[112] used to say that there was a certain time of their lives, when *of all preferments they wished for it the most*.—P. 32. Speaking of his own residence in Lord Carpenter's[113] family, he says that, "Here he" (that is himself) "*stuck* some time *without any promotion* ... he waited often upon the bishop," of Durham, "and sat with him an hour or two in the evening,

---

[109] *the clerk of the closet*: the clergyman in charge of the Sovereign's household chaplains, usually a bishop.

[110] *the Charter House*: Originally a Carthusian monastery, the London Charterhouse was destroyed at the Reformation and its monks martyred at Tyburn. The surviving monastic buildings were enlarged and eventually became a Public School of the same name. The 'mastership' was the post of Headmaster of this expensive and exclusive school and therefore a prestigious and well-paid ecclesiastical appointment.

[111] *Bishop Benson*: Martin Benson (1689–1752), appointed bishop of Gloucester in 1734. A friend of the Irish philosopher and bishop, George Berkeley, the poet Alexander Pope wrote of them: 'Manners with candour are to Benson given,/To Berkeley every virtue under heaven'.

[112] *Dr Jortin*: John Jortin (1798-1770), church historian and, in his later years, Archdeacon of London. His works include the five volume *Remarks on Ecclesiastical History* (1751-73).

[113] *Lord Carpenter*: Newton acted as tutor to George Carpenter (1723-62), son of George, second Baron Carpenter of Killaghy (1702-49), in whose house he lived. The younger George went on to become the first Earl of Tyrconnell.

and often dined with him on a Sunday;" and he adds that, though the bishop continued in his see about twenty years, "*yet* in all that time he *bestowed no preferment* upon this young man, of whose company he seemed so desirous," p. 41; he says that "Mrs. Devenish,[114] *like a true friend*, took every opportunity of commending him to" the Prince and Princess of Wales, "and leaving a good impression of his character, which long after was of *great service to him*, and may be said to be the groundwork *of his best preferment*," and that she also "first introduced him to the acquaintance of Lord Bath,"[115] two introductions which "he ever esteemed as two of the most fortunate circumstances, *the most happy incidents in all his life*."—P. 45. He tells us, moreover, that the rectory of St. Mary-le-Bow, to which he was afterwards preferred through the interest of Lord Bath, though he was forty years old before he obtained any living, "was likewise esteemed a *fortunate living*, the two former rectors, Dr. Lisle[116] and Dr. Blandford,[117] having been made bishops," pp. 72, 73; that "the bishopric, *which of all others*" Dr. Pearce[118]

---

[114] *Mrs Devenish*: Anne Deanes Devenish, daughter of Joseph Devenish of Buckham, Dorset. Her first husband was the playwright, Nicholas Rowe, and Newton helped her prepare a posthumous edition of his works.

[115] *Lord Bath*: William Pulteney (1684-1764), Whig politician, created first Earl of Bath in 1742.

[116] *Dr Lisle*: Samuel Lisle (1683-1749), bishop of St Asaph (1744-48) and Norwich (1748-49). In his youth, he worked as Chaplain to the Levant Company and the inscriptions he collected were printed in the Edmund Chishull's *Antiquitates Asiaticae* (1728).

[117] *Dr Blandford*: [sic] surely Samuel Bradford (1652-1731), sometime Rector of St Mary-le-Bow who acted as bishop of Carlisle (1718-23) and Rochester (1723-31), as well as the first Dean of the revived Order of the Bath.

[118] *Dr Pearce*: Zachary Pearce (1690-1774), one of Newton's patrons, who was offered the See of Bangor in 1748 and, having refused it twice, reluctantly accepted it when the Lord Chancellor asked him 'if Clergymen of learning and merit will not accept of Bishopricks, how can the Ministers of State be blamed, if they are forced to fill them with others less deserving?' (Pearce, *A commentary,*

"*most desired* was Peterborough, but *Providence saw fit to dispose of matters otherwise, and sent him further to a better* bishopric,—to Bangor."—P. 79.

Moreover, as if to give us some further insight into his character, he informs us that "as long as Dr. Trebeck[119] lived, Dr. Newton continued to board with his family, from his *old principle* of avoiding as much as possible the *trouble* of housekeeping; but the breaking up of the family naturally engaged him to *think seriously again of matrimony*; for he found the study of sacred and classic authors ill agreed with accounts of butchers' and bakers' bills, and by daily experience he was convinced more and more that it was not good for man to live alone without an help meet for him." "And *especially*," he continues, "*when he had some prospect of a bishopric*, fresh *difficulties* and *troubles* opened to his view; there would be a better table and public days to be kept; and he plainly foresaw that he must either fall a prey to servants or must look out for some clever sensible woman to be his wife, who had some knowledge and experience of the world, who was a prudent manager, who could do the honours of his table in a becoming manner, who had no more taste and love of pleasure than a reasonable woman should have, who would be happier in staying with her husband at home than in perpetually gadding abroad, would be careful and tender of his health, and in short be a friend and companion of all hours."—Pp. 110, 111. He was at this time fifty-seven, and "it was happy

[138]

---

with notes, on the four evangelists, 1777 vol. 1, p.xxiii). Pearce was later translated to Rochester in 1756.
[119] *Dr Trebeck*: after the death of his mother, Newton's father (John Newton) married the sister of Dr Andrew Trebeck (1681-1759), first rector of St George's, Hanover Square. Trebeck made the young Newton his curate, providing him with speedy access to fashionable society.

for him," he adds, "that such a woman was in his eye," one whom "he had known from a little child in a white frock, and had observed her through all the parts of her life." [120]

Assuredly there is nothing high in all this; of Newton's kindness of heart and amiableness we have no doubt at all; but a man so idolatrous of comfort, so liquorish[121] of preferment,[122] whose most fervent aspiration apparently was that he might ride in a carriage and sleep on down, whose keenest sorrow that he could not get a second appointment [139] without relinquishing the first, who cast a regretful look back upon his dinner while he was at supper, and anticipated his morning chocolate in his evening muffins, who will say that this is the man, not merely to unchurch, but to smite, to ban, to wither the whole of Christendom for many centuries, and the greater part of it even in his own day, if not, as we shall presently show to be the case, indirectly his own branch also. Nay, he does not spare even the Church of the Nicene era, for while he maintains that the monks *"revived and promoted the worship of demons,"* and either out of credulity or for worse reasons recommended it to the people with all the pomp and power of their eloquence in their homilies and orations, he refers to *"some of the most celebrated fathers,"* St. Basil,[123] St. Ephrem,[124] St.

[120] *"such a woman was in his eye ... "*: In 1747 Newton married Jane Trebeck (c.1716-54), eldest daughter of Dr Trebeck.
[121] *liquorish*: literally, fond of alcohol; it is also an archaic form of *lickerish*, meaning lecherous. Newman uses the word to mean 'greedy', while perhaps retaining overtones of the word's literal meanings.
[122] *preferment*: promotion (within the church)
[123] *St. Basil*: the Great (329-379), Bishop of Caesarea, Doctor of the Church; known for his writings against Arianism and Apollinarianism and also for his care for the poor.
[124] *St. Ephrem*: (c.306-373), deacon, Doctor of the Church; known especially for his many hymns which are rich in theology.

Gregory Nazianzen,[125] St. Gregory Nyssen,[126] and St. Chrysostom,[127] as being "full of this sort of superstition;" and, he adds, "all these were monks, and most of them bishops too; the monks, these were the principal promoters of the worship of the dead in former times;—and who are the great patrons and advocates of the same worship now? Are not *their legitimate successors and descendants*, the monks, and priests, and bishops of the Church of Rome?"— *Dissert.* 23. Now, if this be so, if Chrysostom, Basil, and the rest, were but monks and bishops, one is tempted to ask what was Thomas Newton? Not a monk certainly, but a bishop, and such a bishop as felt thankful that his diocese did not give him much trouble, and thereby resigned himself to the loss of more eminent dignities. Is this the man to sit in judgment on Chrysostom? is he the man to be trusted rather than Chrysostom? To which of the two do the souls of men owe the more? which was the more zealous preacher? which resisted luxury and mammon more boldly? which was more like St. John the Baptist in a royal court? Let us know then where we are to find ourselves if we are to [140] interpret prophecy on this rule; will it be pleasant to have exchanged St Chrysostom for Newton, or St Basil for Warburton? Is this good company to live and die in? Who would not rather be found even with Whitfield[128] and Wesley,[129] than with ecclesiastics whose life is literary ease

---

[125] *St. Gregory Nazianzen*: See note on p.[42].

[126] *St. Gregory Nyssen*: See note on p.[62].

[127] *St. Chrysostom*: See note on p.[62].

[128] *Whitfield*: George Whitefield (1714-70), a promoter of the 'Great Awakening' in Britain and the American colonies. His contemporaries reported that when preaching in the open air his voice could carry for five miles.

[129] *Wesley*: John Wesley (1703-91), the founder of Methodism.

at the best, whose highest flights attain but to Downing Street or the levee?[130]

5.

We are engaged in a very invidious task; but still, since we have begun it, we wish to go through with it by submitting to the reader some notice of certain persons whom Newton's theory cuts off from the hope of salvation. And first let us consider the life and character of that limb of Antichrist, as Newton must think him, Carlo Borromeo, Archbishop of Milan, Cardinal of the Roman Church, and nephew to Pope Pius IV. For this purpose we make use of the valuable work of Mr. Palmer.[131] It seems that, when he came to reside at Milan, he voluntarily resigned benefices and estates to the value of 80,000 crowns per annum, reserving only an income of 20,000 crowns. The principality of Oria, which had become his property by the death of his brother, he sold for 40,000 crowns, which he commanded his almoners to distribute among the poor and the hospitals. When the list which the almoners showed him for the distribution amounted, by mistake, to 2,000 crowns more, Carlo said the mistake was too much to the advantage of the poor to be corrected, and the whole was accordingly distributed. When his brother died, he also caused all the rich furniture and jewels of the family to be sold, and gave

---

[130] *levee*: a reception held by a monarch or other great person, attended by those who hoped to curry favour, win influence or obtain promotion; so called because it was held as the monarch was getting up in the morning.

[131] *Mr. Palmer*: William Palmer (1803-85), High Church Anglican divine, whose *Treatise on the Church of Christ* (1838) Newman had enthusiastically reviewed in the *British Critic* (republished in *Essays Critical and Historical*, Vol.I, pp.180ff.) The 'valuable work' Newman is quoting from here is Palmer's *A Compendious Ecclesiastical History from the Earliest Period to the Present Time* (1840).

the price, which amounted to 30,000 crowns, to the poor. Several other cases of charity, on an equally large scale, might be added. His chief almoner was ordered to distribute [141] among the poor of Milan, of whom he kept an exact list, 200 crowns every month; Carlo would never permit any beggar to be dismissed without some alms, whatever he was. He was exceedingly hospitable and liberal in entertaining princes, prelates, and strangers of all ranks, but always without luxury; and he endeavoured as much as possible to conceal his own abstemiousness. His religious foundations, his repairs of churches, of the dwellings of the clergy, and of the seminaries of learning, not only at Milan but at Bologna, Rome, and many other places, were on the most magnificent scale of liberality.

He found his diocese in extreme disorder. The great truths of salvation were little known or understood; and religious practices were profaned by the grossest abuses, and disfigured by superstitions. The sacraments were neglected; the clergy seem scarcely to have known how to administer them, and were slothful, ignorant, and depraved. The monasteries too were in a scandalous condition. Carlo instituted seminaries for the instruction of the clergy; appointed a number of vicars, or rural deans, who exercised a vigilant superintendence over every part of his diocese; and held many provincial and diocesan synods, in which the most excellent and judicious regulations were made and enforced with inflexible firmness. In the course of his proceedings he frequently encountered the most violent opposition from those who were unwilling to be corrected. The order of monks called Humiliati were particularly irritated by his labours for their reform, and excited against him one of their members, who actually fired a musket at the archbishop, as he was one evening at prayers. Carlo calmly finished his prayers, though the ball had struck his vestment, and then, with truly Christian charity, forgave the assassin, and even solicited his pardon. But justice took its course, and the order was suppressed by the Pope.

[142]

Carlo divided the revenue of his see into three parts; one of which was appropriated to his household, another to the poor, and a third to the repairs of churches: and it was his custom to lay before the Provincial Councils the accounts of his revenues to the last farthing, saying that he was no more than an administrator or steward. He employed no clergy of his own kin in the government of his diocese; nor did he make over to them any of the benefices which had been conferred on him.

"It was one of his greatest pleasures," continues Mr. Palmer, "to converse with and catechise the poor; and he would often visit them in the wildest and most mountainous parts of his diocese. On one occasion while he was engaged in his visitation, the Bishop of Ferrara, coming to meet him, found him lying under a fit of ague on a coarse bed, and in a very poor cottage. Borromeo, observing his surprise, remarked, 'that he was treated very well, and much better than he deserved.' During the dreadful ravages of a pestilence, this excellent man encouraged his clergy to administer the consolations of religion to the sick and dying, and he was himself assiduous in the performance of this dangerous duty." On this occasion he sold all his furniture to procure medicine and nourishment for the unhappy sufferers. He was careful not to lose a moment of his time; even at table he listened to some pious book, or dictated letters or instructions. He was remarkable for sincerity; it appeared in all his words and actions; and his promises were inviolable. He delighted in prayer, to which he gave a large part of his time; and he never said any prayer or performed any religious office with precipitation, whatever business of [143] importance might be on his hands, or however he might be pressed for time. In giving audience and in the greatest hurry of business his countenance, his modesty, and all his words, showed that he was full of the recollection of God. "His spirit of prayer and the love of God which filled his heart gave to him remarkably the power of exciting and encouraging others to religion. A short address, even a single word or action, sometimes produced the most powerful effects in animating his clergy to repentance and to virtue.

"This great and good man died in 1584, in the forty-seventh year of his age; with the same piety and sanctity which adorned his short but admirable life."—*Church History*, pp. 226-229.

Or what would Bishop Newton say to that other great saint whose life Mr. Palmer sketches, St. Francis de Sales?[132]

"He was much respected by Beza[133] and the rest of the Reformed in Switzerland; and the excellence of his own character, and the piety and meekness which he always evinced, probably did more for his cause than any other arguments by which it was sustained. The plague at one time raged violently in the place where he resided, but this did not deter him from assisting the sick in their last moments by day and night; and he was wonderfully preserved in the pestilence, which carried off several of the clergy who aided him. In 1599 he became coadjutor of the Bishop of

---

[132] *St. Francis de Sales*: (1567-1622) Bishop of Geneva, Doctor of the Church; author of the widely popular *An Introduction to the Devout Life* (1609).

[133] *Beza*: Theodore Beza (1519-1605), French reformer and disciple of Calvin.

Annecy, with the right of succession to that see; and soon after he was obliged to go to France, where he was received by all ranks and classes with the utmost distinction. He preached before the king, who endeavoured to detain him in France by promises of a large pension and of the first vacant bishopric: but Francis de Sales declined all these offers, and, returning to the poor bishopric of Annecy, was soon after, on the death of his predecessor, consecrated its pastor in 1602. He now laid down a plan of life, to which he ever after rigorously adhered. He resolved to wear no expensive clothing; to have no paintings except of a devotional character in his house; to possess no splendid furniture; to use no coach or carriage, but make his visitations on foot. His family was to consist of two priests, one to act as his chaplain, the other to superintend his servants and temporalities; his table to be plain and frugal. He resolved to be present at all religious and devotional meetings and festivals in the churches; to distribute abundant alms; to visit the sick and poor in prison; to rise every day at four, meditate for an hour, read private service, then prayers with his family, then to read the Scriptures, celebrate the holy eucharist, and afterwards apply to business till dinner. He then gave an hour to conversation, and the remainder of the afternoon to business and prayer. After supper he read a pious book to his family for an hour, then prayed with them, and retired to his private devotions and to rest. Such was the general mode of life of this excellent man.

[144]

"Immediately after he became bishop he applied himself to preaching and to all the other duties of his station. He was very cautious in conferring holy orders, ordaining but few clergy, and only after a most rigid examination of their qualifications. He was also exceedingly diligent in promoting the instruction of the ignorant by catechising on Sundays and holy days; and his personal labours in this respect had a very great influence in persuading the clergy of his diocese to follow so good an example. He still continued to delight in preaching in small villages and to the poorest people, whom he regarded as the special objects of his care."—*Ibid.*, p. 230.

The disinterested spirit which he had early manifested always continued. When he was solicited by Henry IV., king of France,[134] to accept an abbey of large income, he refused it, saying, "that he dreaded riches as much as others desired them; and that the less he had of them the less he should have to answer for." The same prince offered to name him for the dignity of cardinal at the next promotion; but he replied that, though he did not despise the proffered dignity he was persuaded that great titles did not suit him, and might raise new obstacles to his salvation. His conscientious firmness was also remarkable. On one occasion the parliament of Chambery,[135] in Savoy, seized his [145] temporalities for refusing, at its desire, to publish an ecclesiastical censure which he thought uncalled-for by the circumstances of the case. When he heard of the seizure of his possessions, he said that he thanked God for teaching him by it, "that a bishop is altogether spiritual." He did not desist from preaching, or apply to the sovereign for redress; but behaved in so kind and friendly a manner to those who had insulted him most grossly, that at length the parliament became ashamed of its proceedings, and restored his temporalities. In 1619, while he was in Paris, he preached a course of Lent Sermons, which, aided by his conferences, the example of his holy life, and the sweetness of his discourse, most powerfully moved, not only the devout, but even libertines and atheists. He was entreated, for the sake

---

[134] *Henry IV, King of France*: (1553-1610), King from 1589.

[135] *parliament, of Chambery*: one of the French regional assemblies that existed up until the Revolution, acting as a final court of appeal. The *parlement* of Chambery was established in 1536.

of his health, not to preach twice in the day. He replied, with a smile, "that it cost him much less to preach a sermon than to find an excuse for himself when invited to perform that office. God had appointed him to be a pastor and a preacher, and ought not every one to follow his profession?" "On one occasion," says Mr. Palmer, "seeing a vicious and scandalous priest thrown into prison, he fell at his feet, and with tears conjured him to have compassion on him his pastor, on religion which he scandalized, and on his own soul. The man was so deeply impressed with his conduct, that he was entirely converted, and became a virtuous man from that moment."

6.

Here the reader may be tempted to exclaim, "All this is unfair and a fallacy. It is a fallacy to contrast Newton with Chrysostom or Borromeo; it is to take a bad specimen of a [146] good system and a good specimen of a bad one. How does it prove that the Protestant system is bad or the Roman good, because holy men have been not *of,* but *in,* the latter, and sycophants or worldlings *in,* though not *of,* the former?" Now such an objection is founded on a misapprehension of the state of the case; and to show this will carry us on to a further remark to which we wish to direct attention. The truth is, that when people so freely call Rome Babylon and the Pope Antichrist, they know not what they are saying and whither they are going. They think to make exceptions; they think to confine their imputation of corruption and apostasy within bounds; they think, on the one hand, to except Bernard[136] or Fenelon,[137] and to keep clear of their own

---

[136] *Bernard*: See note on p.[74].

Church on the other. On the latter point something more presently; here we do but observe in answer to that wish to make exceptions, which the objection, as we have stated it, involves, that it is directly in opposition to the plain letter of Scripture. If the bishop of Rome be "the man of sin, the son of perdition, the lawless one,"[138] what are those who receive and submit to him? Hear the Apostle's description of them: "They received not the love of the truth, that they might be saved; and for this cause God shall send them *strong delusion* that they should believe a lie, *that they all might be damned* who believed not in the truth, but had pleasure in unrighteousness."[139] But it may be said that if Papists *have* the love of the truth, they are *not* involved in the ruin of Antichrist;—rather surely we ought to say, since Papists *may* have the love of the truth, therefore the Pope is not Antichrist. Followers of Antichrist are in the above text described as utterly lost; which Papists, it seems, need not be. However, let us suppose this text of doubtful cogency; what will be said of the following?—"He opened his mouth [147] to blaspheme His name and His tabernacle, and them that dwell in heaven; and power was given him over all kindreds and tongues and nations, and *all* that dwell upon the earth shall worship him, *whose names are not written in the book of life*."[140] Now who could be said to worship the Pope, if Borromeo and Fenelon did not; Fenelon who implicitly resigned his private judgment to him; Borromeo, a Pope's nephew, who was especially employed by him in the composition of the Catechism of Trent? However, it may be

---

[137] *Fenelon*: François Fénelon (1651–1715), influential writer and Archbishop of Cambrai.
[138] *"the man of sin, the son of perdition, the lawless one"*: 2 Thessalonians 2:3
[139] *"They received not the love of the truth..."*: 2 Thessalonians 2:10-12
[140] *"He opened his mouth to blaspheme His name..."*: Revelation 13:6-8

said, captiously as we think, that, though all whose names are *not* written *do* worship him, still (if so be) some whose names *are* written may worship him also. Must then the screw be driven tighter still?—then listen. "If *any man* worship the beast, and his image, and *receive his mark* in his forehead, or in his hand,"[141] (and we are told shortly before that "he caused *all*, both small and great, rich and poor, free and bond, to receive a mark in their right hand or in their foreheads,") the same *shall drink of the wine of the wrath of God*, which is poured out without mixture into the cup of His indignation; and he shall be tormented with fire and brimstone in the presence of the holy angels, and in the presence of the Lamb, and the smoke of their torment ascendeth up for ever and ever, and they have no rest day nor night who worship the beast and his image, and whosoever receiveth the mark of his name."[142]

We entreat indulgence of serious minds for quoting such very awful words in a composition of this kind; but it is most necessary to bring before all thinking men the real state of the case, and respectfully and anxiously to warn them what they are doing, when they so confidently and solemnly pronounce Christian Rome to be Babylon. Do [148] they know what they say? do they really resign themselves *in faith*, as they profess to do, to the sovereign word of God as they interpret it? Do they *in faith* make over the millions upon millions now and in former times who have been in subjection to the Roman See to utter and hopeless perdition? Do they in very truth look upon them as the direct and open enemies of God, and children of Satan?

---

[141] *"If any man worship the beast... "*: Revelation 14:9-11
[142] *"he caused all, both small and great... "*: Revelation 13:16

Then surely they ought to show this much more in acts, in the fruits of such faith, than even the most zealous of them have adopted; then is mere exclusion of Romanists from political power a very poor and miserable way of separating themselves from the kingdom of Satan. If even heresy stops the channels of sacramental grace, if there are degrees of moral corruption which bid fair to destroy the being of a Church and annul even the most canonical Succession, if we are to shun and abhor those in whom the prince of this world works, what ought to be our acts and our feelings towards the embodied idea of rebellion and pride, towards him who is pure evil, who is to be *revealed* as the son of perdition, and who is destined from the beginning for divine wasting and destruction? How any thoughtful person can hold, though we know there are very thoughtful persons who do, that any one can be in communion with Antichrist without partaking of his plagues, or that to receive Orders from him is not an act of communion with him in those who receive those Orders, or that they who transmitted to us our Orders from Rome could give the Orders without the plagues;—or again, how men can conceive that the English Church can recognize the Orders of a Roman priest on his coming over to it, and yet hold that he gained them from Babylon,—or how men, thinking that the Pope is the Beast of the Apocalypse, can endure the sight of any of his [149] servants, can join in distributing the Bible with them, or can sit with them in the same Council or Parliament, or can do business with them, buy and sell, trade and traffic, or can gaze upon and admire the architecture of churches built by Antichrist, or make much of his pictures,—or how they can

179

read any book of his servants, Pascal's "Thoughts"[143] or Kempis's[144] "Imitation of Christ,"—or works of theology, as those of the Benedictines, Tillemont,[145] or Fleury,[146]—or even school books, Delphin classics,[147] or Gradus ad Parnassum,[148]—or how they can go abroad into Roman Catholic countries without necessity, prying into their churches and gazing on their processions;—all this is to us inexplicable. "What fellowship," as the Apostle asks, "hath righteousness with unrighteousness? and what communion hath light with darkness? and what concord hath Christ with Belial, or what part hath he that believeth with an infidel? and what agreement hath the Temple of God with idols?"[149] Or in the words of another Apostle, to which Dr. Todd refers, p. 321, "doth a fountain send forth at the same place sweet water and bitter? Can the fig-tree bear olive-berries?

---

[143] *Pascal's "Thoughts"*: The *Pensées*, an unfinished work defending Christianity, was published posthumously in 1669.

[144] *Kempis*: Thomas à Kempis (c.1380-1471), born in Kempen (Germany) and a member of the Canons Regular of the Congregation of Windesheim in Zwolle (Holland). He is best remembered for *The Imitation of Christ*, one of the classics of Christian spirituality.

[145] *Tillemont*: Louis-Sébastien Le Nain de Tillemont (1637-98), a French priest and historian connected to Port Royal, who wrote *Mémoires pour servir à l'histoire ecclésiastique des six premiers siècles* and the *Histoire des empereurs et autres princes qui ont régné pendant les six premiers siècles de l'Église* (1693-1712).

[146] *Fleury*: Claude Fleury (1640-1723, Paris), French priest and historian, who wrote the influential *Histoire ecclésiastique* (1691). Newman prepared a translation of part of this in 1842, including his second 'Essay on Miracles' as the preface.

[147] *Delphin classics*: an edition of the Latin classics edited by Pierre-Daniel Huet and dedicated to the Dauphin, the son of Louis XIV (hence the name 'Delphin').

[148] *Gradus ad Parnassum*: a popular thesaurus used in relation to classical poetry and compiled by Fr Paul Aler, SJ (1686). The title was also used by the composer Johann Fux for his famous textbook on counterpoint (1725).

[149] *"What fellowship hath righteousness with unrigtheousness?..."*: 2 Corinthians 6:14-16a

either a vine figs?"[150] What then is there in Antichrist that we can admire or take interest in?

This surely is a principle which comes home to us, and approves itself both to our feelings and judgments. If Englishmen, as is certain, do not start with abhorrence from the members of the Church of Rome, surely this is a clear proof that they do not really account Rome to be Babylon, though they may seem to affirm it. We are surely fighting with a shadow; there is no difficulty here; those who denounce Rome and its bishops do not mean what they say. They do not mean to say that this Pope and that Pope are utterly and hopelessly lost beyond the power of repentance: they do not mean that to hold communion with him is to be involved in his plagues. They may say so in their closets; they do not say so, in proportion as they come into contact with those whom they denounce. They keep their ground, as far as their insular position has hold upon them; but they do give way, just so far as they cease to be islanders. This then, after all, is what thoughtful persons mean when they call Rome the seat of Antichrist,—nothing more than that it has the *spirit* of Antichrist in it; not that it is bodily God's enemy, but that it has in it Satanical *principles*. And then perhaps in process of time they go on to the further doctrine, that these same bad *principles* are *also*, though not of course in the same degree, in Protestant countries and Protestant systems of doctrine. But all this is to give up the point in dispute, for either the Popes come up to the full stature of Antichrist, or we must look for Antichrist elsewhere. This is what Dr. Todd has remarked in his Discourses:—

[150]

---

[150] *"doth a fountain send forth..."*: James 3:11-12

"The advocates of the opinion," he says, "that the corruptions of popery have been foretold in these prophecies, are reduced to this dilemma; they must either evade and soften down the obvious declarations of Scripture by misrepresenting the real characters of the prediction; or else they must deny the possibility of salvation in the Church of Rome,—they must be prepared to assert that every one who has lived and died in that communion is utterly and irretrievably perished for ever."—P. 323.

7.

So much on the calumny itself; but it may be objected that the mere fact that the Continental Churches should be called, and called so extensively, by such fearful or such shocking names, is a proof that they in some degree merit it. Even a heathen said, "Cæsar's wife must not be suspected;"[151] and, in like manner, there is at first sight surely a slur cast on the sanctity of a communion which has, in matter of fact, been designated by titles which are almost too odious to mention. Honour is almost part of chastity; and shall the immaculate Bride of the Lamb be called sorceress, harlot, mother of abominations, habitation of devils, and her chief ruler be considered the man of sin, the enemy of God, and the son of perdition? The Church of Rome is thus circumstanced, therefore she is not the true Church.

We consider this to be an argument eminently successful with the imagination, and yet a few sentences of Scripture and facts of history will serve, if we mistake not, to destroy

[151] *"Cæsar's wife must not be suspected;"*: Julius Caesar said this about his wife Pompeia whom he divorced even though he had no evidence against her; when challenged why he had divorced her, he replied "I thought my wife ought not even to be under suspicion." (Plutarch, *Life of Julius Caesar*, 10, 9.)

its force.—For, first of all, our Saviour was called a deceiver, a man gluttonous and a wine-bibber, a blasphemer, a Samaritan, a demoniac. He was crucified, and that between thieves; has "the offence of the cross"[152] ceased? are we better than He?

But further, it is a very impressive and touching fact, that He Himself has told us that His Church should have to bear the same reproach with Him:—"If they have called the Master of the house Beelzebub, *how much more* shall they call them of the household?"[153]

Antichrist, then, is almost foretold to be the title which His representatives and servants should bear. The imputation of it may almost be called one of the Notes of the Church. We say deliberately, that "Antichrist," "Babylon," "Mother of Harlots," "Beast," these titles given to the Church by the world, are as much a note of her being Christ's Church as her real inward sanctity is. Rome must not monopolize these titles; Rome has them not alone; we share them with Rome; it is our privilege to share them; Anglo-Catholics inherit them from the Roman family, from their common Lord and Saviour. Rome must not appropriate them; the early Church had them. We take it as [152] a clear mark that we are the Church, and Rome the Church, and both the same Church, because in these titles we are joint-heirs of the Church of St Cornelius[154] and St. Augustine.[155] Heretics have generally taken high ground, considered themselves saints, called the Church by foul and frightful names; it is their very wont to speak, not against

---

[152] *"the offence of the cross"*: Galatians 5:11
[153] *"If they have called the Master of the house Beelzebub, how much more shall they call them of the household?"*: Matthew 10:25
[154] *St. Cornelius*: See note on p.[28].
[155] *St. Augustine*: See note on p.[21].

the Son of Man, for He is away, but against those who represent Him during His absence. The Montanists[156] called Catholics "the natural men," the Novatians[157] called them "the Apostates," the Donatists[158] called them "traitors" and "sinners," called St. Peter's chair the seat of pestilence, washed the very pavement which Catholics had trodden, and maintained that the whole Church had perished except the fragment in connexion with themselves; the Luciferians[159] called the Church "the devil's harlot," and "the synagogue of Satan." This is a sample of the language which has ever been applied to the fold of Christ by those who are cast out of it. Dr. Todd has shown us that the Albigenses, gross Manichees as they were, disbelievers in the Incarnation, deriders of Baptism, and enemies of all external religion, still conceived themselves in a position to call the Roman Church "the mother of fornications, and the basilica of the devil, and the synagogue of Satan, and the den of thieves, and the Apocalyptic harlot;" while the Waldenses called it "the Church of the malignants," and "Babylon." There is then nothing to surprise us in the language which Protestants have used, whether against us or against the Roman Catholics; they do but know and take their own place, and act conformably to their function in the history of Christianity.

---

[156] *Montanists*: followers of Montanus (2nd century), a Phrygian priest who founded a sect based on charismatic prophecy, thus superseding the Church. They practised a strict moralism and regarded the rest of the Church as corrupt.
[157] *Novatians*: a third century heresy who adopted a rigorism similar to the Donatists, denying absolution for certain sins (such as murder and adultery).
[158] *Donatists*: See note on p.[34].
[159] *Luciferians*: followers of Lucifer of Cagliari, a small sect of the fourth century.

We are tempted to add one remarkable illustration in point, in addition to the above furnished to us by Dr. Todd, from a treatise now in course of publication,[160] which from circumstances has attracted some attention. A work indeed of such talent and such range as "Ancient Christianity" of course deserves attention on its own ground from persons interested in its subject,—that is, *will* deserve it when it is completed. At present it is only in an inchoate state, and if we attempted at this moment to master the author's argument, we might find on his finishing it in subsequent numbers, that it as little resembled our conceptions of it, as any complete copy of a work resembles its first rough draught. We have in consequence felt it right to be patient, and to wait and see where he ends, a resolution in which we are confirmed by finding it adopted by others beside ourselves, and persons too not agreeing with us in theological views. The particular point for which we now refer to him, is his avowal, as Dr. Todd quotes him, that the state of the Church of the fourth century is the fulfilment of the prophecy in 1 Tim. iv., concerning "the apostasy of some from the faith,"[161] in "forbidding to marry, and commanding to abstain from meats."[162] Dr. Todd's remarks on this passage, which form the subject of his sixth lecture, are very valuable. He observes, (after Mede[163] so far,) that the prophecy is a continuation of the train of thought begun

---

[160] *a treatise now in course of publication*: Todd's *Six Discourses on the Prophecies relating to Antichrist in the Apocalypse of St. John, preached before the University of Dublin, at the Donnellan Lecture*, eventually published in 1846.

[161] *"the apostasy of some from the faith"*: Cf. 1 Timothy 4:1, 'in the latter time some shall depart from the faith.'

[162] *"forbidding to marry, and commanding to abstain from meats"*: 1 Timothy 4:4

[163] *Mede*: Joseph Mede (1586-1639), a Fellow of Christ's College, Cambridge, who wrote widely on the prophecies of Daniel and Revelation (see his *Clavis Apocalyptica* of 1627).

at the conclusion of the foregoing chapter. The Apostle had said, "great is the mystery of godliness,"[164] and, after describing it, he adds, "*but* the Spirit speaketh expressly that some shall apostatize from the faith,"[165] this faith once for all delivered,—"the great mystery of godliness." If this be so, it will follow that the falling away or apostasy to come is a *denial of the Incarnation*; a conclusion which is singularly confirmed by St. John's words, "Every spirit that confesseth

[154] not that Jesus Christ is come in the flesh is not of God, and *this* is *that spirit of Antichrist*, whereof ye have heard that it *shall* come, and even now already is it in the world;"[166] or, as St. Paul speaks, "the mystery of iniquity doth already work;"[167]—a pointed contrast being intended by the Apostle between the mystery of truth and the mystery of error. St. Peter confirms this view by prophesying, as the great evil which lies before the Church, "false teachers" who shall "privily bring in damnable heresies, even *denying the Lord that bought them.*"[168] Then as to the two specified points which mark the Apostasy,—of forbidding marriage and meats,—every one who can read his Greek Testament must know quite well, that the word rendered "meats" has as little to do with *flesh* specially, (which is what the Roman Church or the Nicene Church has in view when it enjoins fasting,) as the word sweetmeat in English has. "It denotes *food*," says Dr. Todd, whether animal or vegetable; in short,

---

[164] *"great is the mystery of godliness"*: 1 Timothy 3:16
[165] *"but the Spirit speaketh expressly that some shall apostatize from the faith"*: 1 Timothy 4:1
[166] *"every spirit that confesseth not that Jesus Christ is come ... "*: 1 John 4:3
[167] *"the mystery of iniquity doth already work"*: 2 Thessalonians 2:7
[168] *"privily bring in damnable heresies, even* denying the Lord that bought them *"*: 2 Peter 2:1

whatsoever is employed for the aliment and sustenance of man."—P. 309. But, independently of this, it is very wonderful how any one can see in this passage a condemnation of fasting, who professes to hold, with the English Church, its religious use, or can make it a peculiar badge either of the Roman or of the Primitive. Well may Mr. Maitland say,—as Dr. Todd quotes him,—

"I feel quite at a loss how to express my astonishment, that any expositor should have been hardy enough to carry on the interpretation, by applying this part of the prophecy to the fasts of the Church of Rome. Strange indeed it will be, if the predicted mark of apostasy should turn out to be a practice commanded in the word of God, recognized as a religious duty by every Christian communion, and placed first and foremost in her list of 'good works' by the purest Protestant Church in the world. (See the Homily 'Of Good Works, and first of Fasting.') To say that *this*, which the Church of England enjoins on her members as a 'good work,' whose commendation is both in the law and in the [155] Gospel," changes its character so far as to become a badge of apostasy, when excessively or superstitiously performed, is a shift which it would not be worth while to answer, if the reply were not so close at hand. Has the Church of Rome ever commanded such excessive abstinence as had been practised by voluntary superstition long before that Church was distinguished as the apostasy, or, in fact, distinguished at all from the rest of the Catholic Church? And has the Greek Church never been excessive or superstitious on this point?"—P. 341.

On the other hand, it is a very observable fact that such an unnatural or rather murderous abstinence, as is spoken of in this text of the Apostle, did exist among the Albigenses. Our author says,—

"The most remarkable instance, perhaps, of voluntary suicide recommended, under the name of religion, by a sect pretending to

Christianity was the *endura* or fasting to death, practised among the Albigenses of Thoulouse, in the thirteenth and fourteenth centuries. It seems that these heretics recommended the *endura* to such persons as were received into the communion of their sect during their last illness, or what was supposed to be so; and that these unhappy dupes of a miserable superstition were taught to believe, that by submitting to be thus starved to death, their everlasting happiness was secured. Abundant proofs of the existence of this cruel and monstrous practice among these heretics, will be found in the Book of Sentences of the Inquisition[169] ... The well-known superstitions of the natives of India exhibit numerous instances of self-immolation performed from a religious motive, and widely spread, nay popular, for centuries, among an intelligent, and not in other respects an uncivilised, people."—Pp. 309, 310.

In like manner, the Manichees and Gnostics commanded abstinence from certain kinds of food, not for a moral end, but on the ground of their being unlawful or unfit for use, or, contrariwise to St. Paul, as if *not* "every creature of God was good."[170] Dr. Todd also quotes St. Augustine, who says of the Tatianists,[171] that "they condemn marriage, and hold it all one with fornication and other impurity; and do not receive into their number man or woman living in a married state. Nor do they eat flesh, but abominate it altogether."— P. 31. As to this other characteristic of the Apostasy, that it shall forbid marriage, Dr. Todd observes, in behalf of the

[156]

---

[169] *the Book of Sentences of the Inquisition*: the *Liber sententiarum* by Bernard Gui (1261-1331), Dominican friar and Bishop pf Lodève, a leading inquisitor active in the Languedoc region against the Cathars.

[170] *"every creature of God was good"*: Genesis 9:3

[171] *Tatianists*: followers of Tatian, a 2nd century Christian teacher who held the beliefs of the Encratites, a Gnostic sect; he was also a follower of the Gnostic Valentinus.

Church of Rome, what will apply still more strongly to the Nicene Church, that the words in the inspired text

"imply, in their natural and obvious signification, an absolute prohibition of marriage, on some such principles as those which led to the prohibition of it in the ancient Gnostic and Manichæan sects; or else, perhaps, on the licentious principles which are not without their advocates in our own times ... Without attempting, therefore, in the least to defend or to excuse this part of the discipline and doctrine of the Roman Church,—for I believe it indefensible,—I trust I may be permitted to express my doubts, whether the injunction or recommendation to celibacy to certain classes of persons in that communion, can in fairness and candour be represented as equivalent to a general prohibition of the holy ordinance of matrimony, or a denial of its divine institution. I am persuaded that the prophecy before us is intended to predict a much more fatal error than that of Romanism; an error more destructive to morality and to society; an error, which, if we are to seek for its antitype in modern times, would seem to be represented rather by what we have seen was always the result of infidel domination, both in our own country,—during the temporary overthrow of our religion and monarchy,—and in still later times, in France, where the marriage contract was capable of being legally dissolved at any time by the mutual consent of the parties; and that infidel opinions of a similar tendency are not without their victims in our own nation, at the present day, none need be told who are acquainted with what is now commonly maintained on this subject by the enemies of our faith and institutions. We have not indeed, as yet, seen men go to the length of *prohibiting* the ordinance of the Church, or the public recognition of the civil contract; but we have seen in our own times a legal sanction given to a mode of entering upon this contract, wherein neither the blessing of the Almighty is besought, nor the Church admitted as a witness. How far this may be considered as a step to a more anti-Christian state of things, it

189

[157] would ill become me to predict; at present it can only be appealed to as one amongst many still more unequivocal indications of the tendency of a certain class of opinions, now widely spread amongst us, and an earnest of what may fairly be expected from a national recognition of infidelity, and an overthrow of the Christian Church.

"But the subject is one upon which it would be manifestly impossible to enter here; and I shall therefore only say that I believe the prophecy to have foretold an infidel prohibition of the ordinance of marriage, rather than a superstitious preference for a life of celibacy, and that a state of things is hereafter to be revealed, far, far exceeding in impiety and immorality any example of superstition, hypocrisy, or mistaken devotion that has ever been tolerated in the darkest period or region of the Church."—Pp. 333-339.

But now to return to the imputation upon Ancient Christianity cast by the author to whom we have referred in connexion with this text, an imputation which, in the case of writers of his cast of opinions, we do really consider, as we have said, to be one of the Notes of the Church in every age.—Dr. Todd thus records and comments on it:—

"This writer abandons as untenable the interpretation which supposes this prophecy to have been fulfilled in the Roman Church, on the ground that, in the sense in which the Apostle's words have been applied to that communion, they are equally applicable to the Church Catholic, Eastern and Western, of the Nicene age. He says, "but here again we are met by that Protestant habit of thinking, which has, in so many instances, impelled the anxious opponents of the Papacy to attribute specifically to the Romish Church what in truth belongs to it only in common with the Eastern and with the Nicene Church ... Protestant commentators, in referring to this prediction, have been wont to call it a striking prediction of Popery. But why Popery? as well say of Spanish Catholicism, or of Irish Catholicism ... In our eagerness ... to attach this brand to Papacy we have too much forgotten that Rome only inherited and shared the more ancient *Apostasy*." ... The author of Ancient Christianity ... not only admits, but broadly asserts, ... that the Nicene Church was apostate ... 'Popery will live and triumph so long as those corruptions continue to be called Popish, which, in fact, were much more ancient. In the present instance, I appeal to serious and candid minds, competently informed in Church history, and ask, whether the *brand of Apostasy* be not herein fixed by the Apostolic hand upon ... *the Nicene Church*?'"—*Todd*, pp. 516-518.

[158]

8.

Here then we have ancient and modern dissentients from the Primitive Church, Donatists, Luciferians, and the author of "Ancient Christianity," not satisfied with dissenting, but accusing her of apostasy. One should not wish the English Church to be other than a partner in a cross which Athanasius and Augustine have borne in their day and down to these times. And now let us see whether, for well-nigh three centuries, the Reformed Anglo-Catholic communion has not also in fact borne it. The writings of Puritan and other authors will afford us abundant materials on this subject, of which the following may serve as a specimen, which are extracted from the works which first come to hand.

For instance, these dissentients from us are in the habit of calling our Church Babylon, and Antichrist, especially on the ground of our Church's *union with the State*; a more outrageous reason cannot well be conceived, of course; but we must beg our readers to bear with what is monstrous for the sake of the various lessons, which the survey brings with it. "The kingdom of Christ," says the celebrated Robert Browne,[172] founder of the Brownists, as quoted by Mr. Hanbury,[173] in his late elaborate collection of "Historical Memorials relating to the Independents,"—"The kingdom of Christ is His office of government, whereby He useth the obedience of His people to keep His laws and commandments to their salvation and welfare. *The kingdom of Antichrist is his government confirmed by the civil magistrate*, whereby he abuseth the obedience of his people to keep his evil laws and customs to their own damnation."—P. 21. Barrowe,[174] taking "a little view of the ecclesiastical government and ordinances of" the Church of England, says, "Great hath been their craft and manifold their devices to cover their *anti-Christian* practices, and to uphold this their ruinous and tyrannous kingdom. I had need express my meaning to be of their false ecclesiastical regiment, *the Kingdom of the Beast*; lest they be my interpreters, and draw me with danger and treason."—P. 45. Again, to take a recent instance—"What I denounce as *anti-Christian*," says the late Mr. Walker, of Dublin,[175] "is not this or that corruption in the Establishment, nor is it the

[159]

---

[172] *Robert Browne*: (d. 1633) an English clergyman and one of the first separatists from the Church of England. Imprisoned over thirty times, he is sometimes called the 'Father of the Pilgrims' since many of those who travelled to America on the *Mayflower* were 'Brownists'.

[173] *Mr Hanbury*: Benjamin Hanbury (1778-1864), nonconformist historian and first treasurer of the Congregational Union of England and Wales. His magnum opus was *Historical Memorials Relating to the Independents ... from their Rise to the Restoration* (1839–44).

[174] *Barrowe*: Peter Barrowe or Baro (1534-99), a French Huguenot who sought refuge in Elizabethan England and became a well-known religious controversialist.

[175] *the late Mr Walker, of Dublin*: John Walker (1767-1833), a former Fellow of Trinity College, Dublin, who founded a separatist sect known as the 'Walkerites'. Working for many years in London, he died in Dublin in October 1833 and two volumes of his *Essays and Correspondence* were published in 1838.

religious establishment of England and Ireland, etc., etc. *It is the generic thing of a religious establishment*, under the name of Christian, under whatever modifications and specific differences, the thing *per se* cannot but be anti-Christian; and when such a thing is put forward as Christianity, Christians are called to discern in it the man of sin usurping the prerogative of God."—*Works*, vol. 1., p. 341. Again, he says that "One of the distinguishing characters of the Christian religion is, that it cannot possibly be made a political establishment—cannot be made a national institution." "When the Church of Christ," he continues, "espoused as a pure virgin unto Him, becomes a *common harlot*, committing fornication with the kings of the earth, she ceases to be the Church of Christ."—*Ibid.*, p. 339. Again, "Multitudes in anti-Christian Europe burn with zeal for the *false Christ*, whom they have set up *in their union of Church and State*, while they scorn and detest the only true Christ, the Christ of God, and manifest this by their contemptuous rejection of the word that testifies of Him."—vol. ii., p. 93. And to the same purport is the [160] following avowal of Wesley's, as it occurs in a pamphlet from which we shall further quote below: "From the time that Church and State, the kingdom of Christ and of the world, were so strangely and unnaturally blended together, *Christianity and heathenism were so thoroughly incorporated with each other* that they will hardly ever be divided till Christ comes to reign on the earth. So that instead of fancying that the glory of the New Jesusalem covered the earth at that period, we have the terrible proof that it was then, *and has ever since been*, covered with *the smoke of the bottomless pit*."

Another ground taken against us is the circumstance of our considering the Church as an *hierarchy*, a religious, spiritual, or divine, and not a human society. For instance, Bishop Hall, in his answer to Robinson,[176] tells us that the latter had cast "upon her honourable name blasphemous imputations of *apostasy, anti-Christianism, whoredom, and rebellion*;" and Robinson thus defends himself: "The *mystery of iniquity* did advance itself by degrees, and, as the rise was, so must the fall be. That *man of sin* and *lawless man* must languish and die away of a consumption ... You have renounced many false doctrines in Popery, and in their places embraced the truth. But what if this truth be taught under the same *hateful prelacy*, in the same devised office of the ministry, and confused communion of the profane multitude? If Antichrist held not many truths, wherewith should he countenance so many forgeries? Or how mould his work to a '*mystery of iniquity*' which in Rome is more gross and palpable, but in England is *spun with a finer thread, and so more hardly to be discovered*? I desire to

[161] know of you whether the office of archbishops, bishops, and the rest of that rank, were not parts of that accursed hierarchy in Queen Mary's days, and members of 'the man of sin'? All the Reformed Churches in the world renounce the prelacy of England as part of that pseudo-clergy and anti-Christian hierarchy derived from Rome."—Pp. 186-

---

[176] *Bishop Hall, in his answer to Robinson*: Joseph Hall (1574-1656) was bishop of Exeter from 1627 and a religious controversialist. Newman here refers to his *A Common Apology against the Brownists* of 1610, responding to a pamphlet by the leading congregationalist John Robinson (1576-1625), *An Answer to a Censorious Epistle* (1610). Hall was a Calvinist but was eirenical in his approach to other Christians. *The Olde Religion* (1628) argued that Catholics could indeed be saved.

193. And Burton[177] speaks in like manner of the bishops of his day: "Beware of all those factors for Antichrist, whose practice is to divide kings from their subjects and subjects from their kings, that so, between both, they may fairly erect *Antichrist's throne* again ... Herein have we cause to comfort ourselves and to bless the name of our God, who hath raised up faithful ministers of His word, who chose rather to lose all they had than to submit to the commands of *usurping anti-Christian mushrooms*."—P. 555. And no less a man than Milton[178] says, "Mark, readers, the crafty scope of these prelates; they endeavour to impress deeply into weak and superstitious fancies the awful notion of a 'Mother;' that thereby they might cheat them into a blind and implicit obedience to whatsoever they shall decree or think fit. And if we come to ask a reason of aught from our 'Dear Mother,' she is invisible, under the lock and key of the Prelates, *her spiritual adulterers*. They only are the internuncios, or the go-betweens of this time-devised mummery. Whatsoever they say, she says must be a deadly sin of disobedience not to believe. So that we, who by God's special grace have shaken off the servitude of a great male tyrant, our pretended father, the Pope, should now, if we be not betimes aware of these wily teachers, sink under the slavery of a female notion; the cloudy conception of a demi-island 'Mother;' and, while we think to be obedient sons, shall make ourselves rather *the bastards, or the*

---

[177] *Burton*: Henry Burton (c.1578-c.1647), Independent minister and anti-Catholic controversialist. His works included *The Seven Vials* (1628), a commentary on the Book of Revelation, which predicted the imminent destruction of the papal Babylon. He also attacked Bishop Hall's *The Olde Religion*, which he thought might encourage conversions to Catholicism.

[178] *Milton*: John Milton (1608-74), best known as a poet but also a polemicist who attacked Catholicism and episcopacy, as can be seen in his five antiprelatical tracts.

centaurs, of their spiritual fornications."—*Hanb.*, p. 187.
[162] How precisely the fanatic spirit of the Donatist Circumcellionists![179]

The Apostolical succession and priesthood is another ground on which these modern heretics call us Antichrist. "Our prelates," says Burton, "have no other claim for their hierarchy than the Popes have and do make; which all our divines, since the Reformation, till but yesterday, have disclaimed, and our prelates cannot otherwise *but by making themselves the very limbs of the Pope*, and so our Church a *member of that synagogue* of Rome."—P. 553. In like manner, Mr. Walker: "It is now many years since I have renounced with abhorrence the title of 'Reverend,' and the whole clerical character connected with it. *That character*, under whatever name or modification, is one of the ungodly fictions *of the man of sin*, and one of the main pillars of *Antichrist's kingdom*."—Vol. ii., p. 354. Again: "Stare not, when I assert that the distinction between clergy and laity is essentially *anti-Christian*, and indeed one of the main pillars supporting the edifice of *the man of sin* ... The blasphemous titles assumed by the Pope of Rome go little beyond the profane arrogance of our English bishops in styling themselves 'Successors of the Apostles in the government of the Church ... From the prime ministers of *Antichrist* all the inferior orders of clergy received their ordination, their appointment, and their sacred function ... 'This do in remembrance of Me,' saith the Lord. 'No, no!'

---

[179] *Donatist Circumcellionists*: The Circumcellionists sprang from the heresy of Donatism in fourth century northern Africa. Their name comes from *circum* ('around') and *cella* ('cell') since they were itinerant missionaries, roving about from house to house. Prizing martyrdom as a central virtue, they made random attacks with the hope that their would-be victim would fight back and kill them.

say the clergy, 'presume not to do it, unless ye have among you one of the clerical caste, to consecrate the elements, and administer them to you.'"—Vol. ii., p. 520.

Another ground taken by these writers is that of our *rites and liturgical services*. "Your temples," says Robinson, "especially your Cathedrals and Mother Churches, stand still in their proud majesty, possessed by archbishops and lord bishops, *like the Flamens and Arch-flamens[180] amongst the Gentiles*, from whom they were derived, and furnished with all manner of pompous and superstitious monuments, as carved and painted images, massing copes and surplices, chanting and organ music, and *many other glorious ornaments of the Romish harlot*, by which her majesty is commended to and admired by the vulgar; *so far are you* in these respects from being gone, or fled, yea or crept either, out of *Babylon*."—P. 197. "If a man," says the same writer, "should set the Church of England before his eyes, as it differeth but from the Reformed Churches, it would be no very beautiful bird; yea, what could it in that colour afford but Egyptian bondage, *Babylonish confusion*, carnal pomp, and a company of *Jewish*, *Heathenish* and *Popish* ceremonies?"—P. 205. "Shall we think that the services of *Antichrist*," says Bastwick,[181] "only taken out of the *language of the Beast* and put into English, and in French, or any other tongue, is acceptable unto God? And, that our services, the whole Prayer-book, is taken out of the Mass-book and other Popish pamphlets, I myself, being in Italy,

[163]

---

[180] *Flamens and Arch-flamens*: pagan priests in ancient Rome

[181] *Bastwick*: John Bastwick (c.1595-1654), religious controversialist who wrote *Elenchus religionis papisticae* ('A refutation of the religion of the papists', 1624) and the anti-episcopal *Letanie of Dr. John Bastwicke* (1637). Together with Henry Burton (see above) and William Pyrnne, he was pilloried and had his ears cut off at Westminster Palace Yard for 'seditious libel'.

compared them together. And for our Litany, if I do not forget myself, it is translated, word for word, out of the Litany to our Lady, as they call it: Lady being turned into Lord, as in the Lady's Psalter, Lord and God are turned into Lady."—P. 575. "*These blasphemous wretches*," says Barrowe, "not to darken only, but to reproach the truth yet further, proceed and give out 'that the heavenly order and ordinances which Christ hath appointed in His Testament,' the government of His Church, which they call discipline, 'are but accidental, and no essential work of the Established Church.' ... Thus is *Antichrist* extolled, and openeth his mouth against God and all His ordinances."—P. 45. And in like manner, Mr. Walker, in answer to Archbishop Whately's Tract on the Sabbath[182], "The Church,' he (the Archbishop) tells us, 'has full power to sanctify any day that may be thought most fitting.' Power to sanctify! the *assumption of the man of sin can scarcely be carried higher* than this. Here he appears indeed *as God sitting in the Temple of God*."—*Works*, vol. ii., p. 144.

[164]

Again, the *mixture of good and bad men* in our Church, and her injunctions to unity, are made a fresh proof of her kindred with Antichrist. "For your graces," says Robinson, "we despise them not, nor any good thing amongst you; no more than you do such graces and good things as are to be found in the Church of Rome, from which you separate notwithstanding. We have, by God's mercy, the pure and right use of the good gifts and graces of God in Christ's

---

[182] *Archbishop Whately's Tract on the Sabbath*: Richard Whately (1787-1863), initially a mentor of Newman when they were both Fellows of Oriel, though they later became estranged, produced his *Thoughts on the Sabbath* in 1832. He later became Archbishop of Dublin.

ordinance, which you want. Neither the Lord's people nor the holy vessels could make Babylon Sion; though both one and the other were captive for a time."—P. 201. Robinson, in a passage above cited, observes, that we have still the prelacy, the ministry, and the *"confused communion of the profane multitude,"* which are badges of Antichrist. And Mr. Walker observes to a friend, "You quote Eph. iv. 3 as warranting your tender apprehensions, lest you should disturb the tranquillity of that ungodly confederacy in which you are engaged, by the introduction of Scriptural truth. The 'unity of the Spirit' indeed! let me freely tell you, that I view the unity of the Spirit which you are endeavouring thus to keep, as no other than *the unity of the Spirit of Antichrist.*"—P. 374.

Much might be said in addition on the subject of faith and works, baptism, and other doctrines, by way of showing   [165] how fully our Church is practically involved in the charge of Antichristianism by those who adopt Luther's view of the "articulus stantis vel cadentis ecclesiæ."[183] "Dissenters," says a clever pamphlet from one of themselves, "whether justly or not, believe that baptismal regeneration, the exclusive validity of the Orders conferred by bishops, the consequent exclusive right of the clergy 'to be quite sure that they have the body of Christ, to give to the people,' the conversion of the Christian ministry into a priesthood, with the inevitable association of some mysterious nature connected with their services ... they believe that *that from which they naturally spring, really is contained and taught*

---

[183] *Luther's view of the "articulus stantis vel cadentis ecclesiae"*: "the article by which the Church stands or falls", referring to justification by faith alone. The phrase was commonly attributed to Luther but seems to have originated at a later date.

in the offices and canons of the Church; and if not, they know that the things themselves are extensively assumed and circulated as if they were there; and that, even when denied in the pulpit, the belief of them is fostered by the fact, that the uniform phraseology of the Book of Common Prayer is, apparently at least, founded upon them. They consider that pernicious and perilous errors lurk in the language and are supported by the use of the Confirmation Service and the form of Absolution, both public and private; and they think that very much that is awfully deceptive is engendered or aggravated by the manner in which the Lord's Supper is dispensed to the dying, and the Burial Service read over the dead."[184]

9.

Our object in making the foregoing selections has been mainly this, to show that the charge on the part of its enemies of being Antichrist, or verging on Antichrist, is one [166] of those notes or characteristics which go to ascertain the true Church; next, that in consequence, much as there is to condemn in the Roman communion, yet, if that communion is not proved on other grounds to be the Babylon of prophecy, the mere fact that it is so called, however startling at first sight, affords no presumption that it is so; and lastly, and what most concerns members of our own body, that we should be cautious of calling Rome by the name of Babylon, inasmuch as we are certain of being so called

---

[184] What? And who says it?—P. 64. [N] *What? And who says it? An exposition of the statement that the established church "destroys more souls than it saves"*, Thomas Chalmers (1780-1847), Church of Scotland and Free Church of Scotland minister.

ourselves if ours is the true Church[185], and that, in matter of
fact, we have ever been so called,—more so, since we
became separate from Rome, than before,—and that down
to this day. If any of us think to gain for ourselves some
relief from the odious imputation, by casting it boldly upon
Rome, he quite mistakes both our position and the feelings
of our opponents. They will take what we give, and use it
against ourselves. Let us be quite sure of the truth of the
sacred and heathen proverbs in this case, one of which says,
that stones cast into the air fall back upon the caster's head;
and the other, that curses, like young chickens, always come
home to roost. Newton tells us in one place, that "The seeds
of popery, sown even in the Apostles' day, were idolatry,
strife, and division, adulterating God's word, making 'a
gain of godliness, and teaching for filthy lucre's sake,'"
(Oh, Dr. Newton!) "a vain observance of festivals, a vain
distinction of meats, a neglecting of the body, and traditions
and commandments of men." How ill would the "plurima
pietas,"[186] which suggested such an enumeration to this mild
logician, have fared in the rude unmannerly hands of Henry
Ainsworth,[187] who, in his "Arrow against *Idolatry*," reckons   [167]
among its relics existing among *us*, our "Diocesan,
Provincial, and National Churches," our "Liturgies" and
"organs," our holy days with their eves, our hierarchy, our
"Churches, baptized bells, hallowed fonts, and holy
churchyards," or, as he appropriately calls them, "high
places," our "lands, livings, tithes, offerings, garments,

---

[185] [It is undeniable that the Anglican Church has retained large portions of the
Catholic doctrine and ritual; so far forth as it has done so, of course it will be
called anti-Christian by those who call Rome pure Antichrist.] [N]
[186] *plurima pietas*: 'very great piety', Virgil, *Aeneid*, Book II, line 429.
[187] *Henry Ainsworth*: (1569-1622), separatist writer of works such as *An Arrow
Against Idolatrie* (1610).

signs, gestures, ceremonies, courts, canons, customs, and many more abominations wherewith have been enriched *the merchants of the whore* and all that sail with ships in her sea." These and others, (he proceeds to say,) are "very Gilluhim,[188] the loathsome *idols* and excrements of the *Queen of Sodom* and the filthiness of her fornication" with which "she defileth the consciences of men."[189] We desiderate in Newton's Treatise an answer to these railings; and we think no English divine does us a service who so vaguely delineates Antichrist that at a little distance his picture looks not very unlike ourselves. He should be precise enough *not* to include England *while* he includes Rome; and this task, whatever be the grievous errors of Rome, we hold to be impossible. All the great and broad *principles* on which she may be considered Babylon, may be retorted on us. Does the essence of Antichrist lie in interposing media between the soul and its God? we interpose baptism;—In imposing a creed? we have articles for the clergy and creeds for all men;—In paying reverence to things of time and place? we honour the consecrated elements, take off our hats in churches, and observe days and seasons;—In forms and ceremonies? we have a service book;—In ministers of religion? we have bishops, priests, and deacons;—In claiming an *imperium in imperio*?[190] such was the convocation, such are elective chapters;—In the high state of prelacy? our bishops have palaces, and sit among princes;—In supporting religion by temporal

[168]

---

[188] *Gilluhim*: Hebrew 'giluliym', idols.
[189] Hanbury's Memorials, p. 238. [N]
[190] imperium in imperio: 'an empire within an empire', i.e. the church having its authority within the state

sanctions? we are established;—In the mixture of good and bad? we are national;—In discipline of the body? we fast. England does not differ then from Rome in *principles*, but in questions of *fact*, of *degree*, of *practice*; and whereas Antichrist differs from Christ, as darkness from light, if one of the two Churches is Antichrist, the other must be also.

Nay, let not even the Kirk[191] be too sure that she has succeeded in ridding herself of the same frightful imputation. So far as she still retains upon her the shadow of a Church, so far does she, in the eyes of those who have cast off all churchmanship, bear tokens of the enemy of truth. A Church, as such, as Mr. Walker confesses in his own case, is what Protestants really mean by Antichrist. We have a strange paper before us, which has been widely circulated, and is written by a late Fellow of a College in the University of Oxford,[192] which, after deciding that the first Beast is the Papacy, the seven horns the seven sacraments, war with the beast the Protestant league, the mouth speaking great things, the Council of Trent, goes on to say, that the second Beast is the Queen's supremacy, the two horns like a lamb, are the two Universities, Oxford and Cambridge, the image to the first Beast, the book of Common Prayer, the name of the second Beast the supreme head of the Church, and ends by warning the Kirk that the Queen's High Commissioner in the General Assembly "sits there, as in the Temple of God, showing himself that he is God," (that is, supreme head of the Church in its ecclesiastical capacity,) and by asking "If the Church of England be an *idolatrous* Church, as was

---

[191] *the Kirk*: the Church of Scotland which is Presbyterian in structure, unlike the Church of England, but is also the religion established by the state.
[192] *a strange paper* ... : This has not proved identifiable; perhaps the 'paper' was a letter or an address to the Kirk which though 'widely circulated' was not published.

[169] universally held by all Presbyterians in the reign of the Stewarts, identifying as they did, Prelacy with Popery throughout, upon what principle does the Evangelical portion in particular of the Church of Scotland now seek a closer union with the Church of England, when the latter Church has notoriously become more superstitious than ever, with her crosses, and candlesticks, and altars, and faldstools, and though last, not least, with her priestly robes and royal dalmatics?" Let it be observed that this writer, as well as Ainsworth and the rest, accuses us of *idolatry*, the one point in which we might seem at first sight specifically to *differ* from Rome; but it is a remarkable circumstance that, real as this difference is, as *we* should contend, *Idolatry is not mentioned in Scripture as a mark of Antichrist*; just the reverse. "Neither shall he regard the God of his fathers," says the prophecy, "nor regard *any* god, for he shall magnify himself *above all*; but in his estate he shall honour the god of forces."[193] "Who opposeth and exalteth himself *above* all that is *called god* or that is *worshipped*."[194] "He opened his mouth in blasphemy against God, to blaspheme His name, and *His tabernacle, and them that dwell in heaven*."[195]

10.

Enough has been said to show the deficiency of theological *principle*, on which the attack upon Rome has commonly been conducted among us. Writers of our

---

[193] *"Neither shall he regard the God of his fathers... "*: Daniel 11:37-38
[194] *"Who opposeth and exalteth himself above all that is called god or that is worshipped"*: 2 Thessalonians 2:4
[195] *"He opened his mouth in blasphemy against God... "*: Revelation 13:6

Church who call her Babylon, ought to have laid down definitely what they considered the essence of Antichrist, and have shown that our own was clear of it. They ought, before attacking the foundations of Rome, to have shown that we ourselves had not built upon them. Instead of this, in their eagerness to strike a blow at Rome, they have done no little to overturn all visible, all established religion in the world, and to involve the Primitive Church, our own, the Kirk—nay, all sects and denominations whatever,—in one common ruin. And now we will make a suggestion towards remedying their deficiency, that is, towards analysing the *principle* on which alone Rome can logically be called the seat of Antichrist: whether such principle, when stated, will be satisfactory to ourselves, and available in our warfare with our Roman Catholic brethren, is another matter. [170]

Now, whatever has been said above to make it probable that the calumny of being Antichrist is in fact one of the Notes of the true Church, yet nothing has been suggested to *account for the phenomenon* that the Church, or what is like the Church, should be exposed to so strange an imputation. It is satisfactory indeed to be told that, if we *are* called Beelzebub, we are but fulfilling our Master's pattern; but still the question remains *how* men come to call us so? We conceive upon the following principle.

We observe then that the essence of the doctrine that there is "One only Catholic and Apostolic Church" lies in this;—that there is on earth a representative of our absent Lord, or a something divinely interposed between the soul and God, or a visible body with invisible privileges. All its subordinate characteristics flow from this description. Does it impose a creed, or impose rites and ceremonies, or change ordinances, or remit and retain sins, or rebuke and punish, or accept offerings, or send out ministers, or invest its ministers with authority, or accept of reverence or devotion in their persons?—all this is because it is Christ's visible presence. It stands for Christ. Can it convey the power of the Spirit? does grace attend its acts? can it touch, or bathe, or seal, or lay on hands? can it use material things for spiritual purposes? are its temples holy?—all this comes of its being (so far) what Christ was on earth. Is it a ruler, prophet, priest, intercessor, teacher?—it has titles such as these in its measure, as being the representative and instrument of the Almighty Lord who is unseen. Does it claim a palace and a throne, an altar and a doctor's chair, the gold, frankincense and myrrh of the rich and wise, an universal empire and a never-ending succession?—all this is so, because it is what Christ is. All the offices, names, honours, powers which it claims depend upon the determination of the simple question—Has Christ, or has He not, left a representative behind Him?

[171]

Now if He has, then all is easy and intelligible; this is what churchmen maintain; they welcome the news; and they recognize in the Church's acts but the fulfilment of the high trust committed to her. But let us suppose for a moment the other side of the alternative to be true;—supposing Christ has left no representative behind Him. Well, then, here is an Association which professes to take His place without warrant. It comes forward instead of Christ and for Him; it speaks for Him, it developes His words; it suspends His appointments, it grants dispensations in matters of positive duty; it professes to minister grace, it absolves from sin;—and all this of its own authority. Is it not forthwith, according to the very force of the word, "Antichrist"? He who speaks for Christ must either be His true ambassador or Antichrist; and nothing but Antichrist can he be, if appointed ambassador there is none. Let his acts be the same in both cases, according as he has authority or not, so is he most holy or most guilty. It is not the *acts* that make the difference, it is the *authority* for those acts. The very same acts are Christ's acts or Antichrist's, according to the doer: they are Christ's, if Christ does them; they are Antichrist's, if Christ does them not. There is no medium [172] between a Vice-Christ and Antichrist.

It is no accident then or strange occurrence that the Church should have been called Antichrist. She must be called so in consistency by those who separate from her. Such an imputation is the necessary result of disbelief in her commission. Her acts are known in all the world; there is no mistaking them. Difference of opinion about them will be shown not in disputing against what is mere matter of history and public notoriety, but in viewing them in a different light, and referring it to a distinct origin. Convince the Presbyterian or Wesleyan that the Church has spiritual powers, and he will find no great difficulty in her general conduct: she does not act up to her commission. If the Church be from Christ, even her least acceptable words or deeds *ex cathedrâ* may be taken on faith: if she be not, even her best are presumptuous, and call for a protest. She is an honoured servant in one case; an usurper and tyrant in another. There is on the whole then but one issue in the controversy about the Church, and that a very plain and simple one. Its children and its enemies both understand that the Church professes to act for God, but the one party says *rightfully*, the other *wrongfully*. This then is the point on which the controversy turns, and before which all other questions sink in importance. All may easily be arranged when this one question is settled. Neglect it, and we shall be arguing without understanding where we are; master this one principle, and you may change your whole position in a day: the Church will be henceforth faithful for arrogant, diligent for officious, charitable for political, firm for violent, holy for blasphemous, Christ for Antichrist. If we [173] believe she has a commission, we shall be Catholics, and call her holy: if we make our inward light, or our reason, or our feelings, our guide, and set up Antichrist within us, then, with Gnostics, Montanists, Novatians, Manichees, Donatists, Paulicians, Albigenses, Calvinists, and Brownists, we shall, in mere self-defence and mere consistency, call her Babylon, Sodom, sorceress, harlot, Jezebel, Beelzebub, and Antichrist. A sacerdotal order is historically the essence of the Church; if not divinely appointed, it is doctrinally the essence of Antichrist.

And thus we answer a gibe, we believe of Baxter's,[196] which at first sight is not without its force. He said that "If the Pope was not Antichrist, he had bad luck to be so like him." Not "bad luck;" but sheer necessity. Since Antichrist simulates Christ, and bishops are images of Christ, Antichrist is like a bishop, and a bishop is like Antichrist. And what is the Pope but a bishop? his peculiarity lying, not in his assuming to be *omnibus numeris* a bishop, but in his disfranchising all bishops but himself; not in his titles nor in his professed gifts, which are episcopal, but in his denying these to other bishops, and absorbing the episcopate into himself.

---

[196] *Baxter*: Richard Baxter (1615-91), Puritan divine; theologian and controversialist.

The only question then is this, "Has Christ, or has He not, appointed a body representative of Him on earth during His absence?" If He has, the Pope is not Antichrist;—if He has not, every bishop in England, Bishop Newton, Bishop Warburton, Bishop Hurd, is Antichrist; every priest is Antichrist, Mr. McNeile, Dr. Jortin, and Dr. Faussett[197] inclusive. We hold most firmly that He has, or of course we could not belong to the Church of England; this, however, is not the place to prove it *in extenso*.[198] We have done all that falls within the scope of Dr. Todd's lectures, if we have shown that members of the English Church are not quite the persons to venture to speak of "that woman Jezebel," meaning thereby the Holy Church Catholic, sojourning in Rome; however, before concluding, we may be allowed to make one or two suggestions in behalf of our side of the main principle itself, which is in dispute, viz., that Christ has left behind Him a representative society.

[174]

11.

Now, that He has condescended so to do, is so clearly declared in the sacred volume, especially when its announcements are viewed in the light of historical facts, that we could almost say that the argument did but require to be fairly brought out, in order to the conviction of any serious and unbiassed mind. Not even the proof of our Lord's divinity is plainer than that of the Church's commission. Not even the promises to David or to Solomon more evidently belong to Christ, than those to Israel, or

---

[197] *Dr Faussett*: Godfrey Faussett (c.1781-1853) held the Lady Margaret Chair in Divinity at Oxford and was a critic of Newman and the other Tractarians. His 1838 sermon 'The Revival of Popery' led Newman to respond with his 'Letter to Faussett'.

[198] *in extensor*: at full length, extensively

Jerusalem, or Sion, belong to the Church. Not even Daniel's prophecies are more exact to the letter, than those which invest the Church with powers which Protestants consider Babylonish. Nay, holy Daniel himself is in no small measure employed on this very subject. He it is who announces a fifth kingdom, like "a stone cut out without hands,"[199] which "broke in pieces and consumed" all former kingdoms, but was itself to "stand for ever," and to become "a great mountain," and to "fill the whole earth." He it is also who prophesies, that "the Saints of the Most High shall take the kingdom and possess the kingdom for ever."[200] He "saw in the night visions, and behold one like to the Son of Man came with the clouds of heaven, and came to the Ancient of Days, and there was given Him dominion and glory and a kingdom, that all people, nations, and languages should serve Him."[201] Such too is Isaiah's prophecy, "Out of Zion shall go forth the law, and the word of the law from [175] Jerusalem, and He shall judge among the nations and rebuke many people."[202] Now Christ Himself was to depart from the earth: He could not then in His own person be intended in these great prophecies; if He acted, it *must* be by delegacy. Let us then for a moment suppose that the Church *has* been really His vicar and representative. Supposing her so to be, He has as truly and literally judged among the nations, and rebuked many people, reigned in righteousness, promoted

---

[199] *"a stone cut out without hands"*: Daniel 2:45

[200] *"the Saints of the Most High shall take the kingdom and possess the kingdom for ever"*: Daniel 7:18

[201] *"saw in the night visions, and behold one like to the Son of Man came with the clouds of heaven, and came to the Ancient of Days..."*: Daniel 7:13-14

[202] *"Out of Zion shall go forth the law, and the word of the law from Jerusalem, and He shall judge among the nations and rebuke many people"*: Isaiah 2:3-4

peace, taught the nations, repressed the wicked, as the sovereign of England keeps the peace, administers justice, punishes offences, and performs other regal offices by his courts of law, magistrates, army, police, and other functionaries. All works indeed in which man has part are marked with imperfection; divine promises and counsels are but fulfilled on the whole and in due measure in this sinful world. It is easy to point out ten thousand instances in which the functionaries of the Church have failed of their duty to their Lord and Master, when, according to His own announcement, the "wicked servant" has said "in his heart, my Lord delayeth His coming,"[203] and has begun "to beat the man-servants and the maidens, and to eat and drink, and be drunken;" still it is impossible surely to read the history of the Church, up to the last four or five hundred years, with an unprejudiced mind, without perceiving that whatever were the faults of her servants, and the corruptions of her children, she has on the whole been the one element of civilization, light, moral improvement, peace, and purity in the world. In the darkest times, with exceptions too brief or local to bear insisting on, she has been far the superior, in [176] those respects in which she was designed to be superior, of those earthly powers among whom she has moved. In the darkest times, and when the conduct of her organs was least defensible, and her professed aims and principles most extreme, she will be found, when contrasted with other powers, to be fighting the cause of truth and right against sin,—to be a witness for God, or defending the poor, or purifying or reforming her own servants and ministers, or promoting peace, and maintaining the holy faith committed

---

[203] *"in his heart, my Lord delayeth His coming"*: Luke 12:45

to her. This she was till she quarrelled with herself, and divided into parts; what she has been since, what she is now, a future age must decide; we can only trust in faith that she is what she ever has been, and was promised ever to be,—one amid her divisions, and holy amid her corruptions.

But returning to the thought of former and happier times, what, we ask, are her acts as then displayed, so lordly and high, so maternal, so loving yet so firm, so calm yet so keen, so gentle yet so vigorous, so full of the serpent's wisdom yet of the dove's innocence; what is all this but a literal accomplishment of the sure word of prophecy concerning the reign of Christ upon earth? The writings of the Fathers, as they have come down to us, form an historical comment upon the inspired pages of Isaiah, supplying numberless instances of the execution of that high mission, whereby the spiritual Israel was set forth in the world, as the elect of God, created as an instrument of righteousness to set forth his Maker's glory, to teach truth and righteousness, "to relieve the oppressed, to judge the fatherless, to plead for the widow,"[204] to feed the hungry, to shield the imperilled, to raise the fallen, to repress the tyrannical, to reconcile enemies, and largely to dispense benefits to and fro. Even what is visibly exhibited in the page of history is an abundant and a most wonderful accomplishment of the prophetic word. We find, for instance, St. Ambrose[205] journeying across the Alps in the winter to protect Justina[206] from the usurper Maximus; we

[177]

---

[204] *"to relieve the oppressed, to judge the fatherless, to plead for the widow,"*: Isaiah 1:17
[205] *St. Ambrose*: See note on p.[42].
[206] *Justina*: (c.340-c.391) second wife of the Emperor Valentinian I. Despite having received the assistance of St Ambrose, she supported the Arian heresy.

read of the bishops throughout France interceding with the latter for members of their flock or for others, who had taken part against him; while Flavian, Bishop of Antioch,[207] on that city having grievously insulted the emperor, betakes himself in his old age to Constantinople, presents himself before his offended sovereign, and gains his pardon. St. Basil founds an hospital for lepers in his diocese in Cappadocia, and his example is followed throughout the neighbouring country. He writes to Valerian to offer his mediation between Valerian and certain Cæsareans;[208] to Elias, the imperial collector, to gain longer time for his people's contribution; to Callisthenes, to persuade him to deal mildly with certain slaves; to the Count of the private purse, for a diminution of the tribute of iron exacted of the people of Taurus, and of mares exacted of another place; to two parties going to law, offering himself as arbitrator, in order to save them expense; to a civil officer, to save the country people from the oaths usual on paying taxes; to Duke Andronicus, to soften his feelings towards Domitian; to a commissioner of taxes, to relieve the hospitals from imposts; and to Modestus, to relieve Helladius from a civil employment.

"Certain Circumcellianists and Donatist clergy," says St. Austin to Apringius, "have confessed horrible enormities of theirs against my brethren and priests, that they waylaid and murdered one, carried off from his home another, pulled out his eye, cut off his finger, and mutilated him. Finding that they would fall under your axe, I write in haste to your nobility, by way of deprecating, for the mercy of Christ, any strict retaliation. Though the law's punishment cannot lie in the very same acts in which the

[178]

---

[207] *Flavian, Bishop of Antioch*: Patriarch between 381 and 404.
[208] *Cæsareans*: inhabitants of Cæsarea, St. Basil's home town.

offenders showed their fury, yet I fear lest they, at least the murderers, should meet with sentence at your hands. That they may not, a Christian petitions the judge, a bishop admonishes the Christian. You bear not the sword in vain; but it is one thing when a province is the party injured, another when the Church. Fear with us the rigorous judgment of God our Father, and be a pattern of the clemency of your mother. For when you act, the Church acts, for whom you act, whose son you are in acting. They with the sword of guilt drew blood of Christians; you from their blood hold back even the sword of justice for Christ's sake. They robbed the Church's minister of his time for living; do you prolong to her enemies their time for repenting."

Or, to take another department of their high duties, St. Ambrose suspends the Emperor Theodosius from communion for a passionate massacre of the inhabitants of Thessalonica; St. Athanasius excommunicated a military chief of Libya, for immoral conduct, forbidding him throughout Christendom fire, water, and shelter at the hands of the faithful; St. Basil interdicts a certain refractory person from the Church services; and Synesius[209] abandons to the divine anger Andronicus, president of Libya, a cruel tyrant, who had invented instruments of torture to extort money from the people.

Or, let us view a third aspect of the episcopal character.

"I lived," said Theodoret[210] when accused of heresy, "in a monastery up to the time of my episcopate, and received that charge against my will. Five-and-twenty years have I lived bishop, nor have ever been appealed against by any, nor any have

[209] Synesius: (c.373-c.414), Bishop of Ptolemais in Lybia.
[210] Theodoret: (c.393-c.460), Bishop of Cyrrhus; he tried to stop Nestorius from being condemned but eventually took part in the Council of Chalcedon's anathematising of his teaching.

I accused. Not an obol, not a cloke have I received from any. Not one loaf or one egg has domestic of mine ever received. Except the rags that cover me, nought have I endured to take. *Public porticos have I erected out of my ecclesiastical revenue. Two bridges have I built of largest size; I have taken the charge of public baths.* Finding the city wanting in supply from the river that runs near it, *I made the aqueduct*, and have filled with water this deficient city. To change the subject, eight villages of Marcionites[211] and their neighbourhoods I have led with their good will into the truth; another full of Eunomians,[212] another of Arians, I have brought to the light of divine knowledge. By God's grace not one tare of heresy remains among us. And all this not without peril; *often have I shed my blood*, often have I been stoned by them, and brought even to the very gates of hell. But I am become a fool in glorying, yet I speak of necessity, not of will. This the thrice-blessed Paul was forced to do once, to stop the mouth of accusers."

[179]

These are but specimens of a varied and widely extended phenomenon which rose up, like a plant out of the ground, from the very beginnings of the Gospel, wherever and whenever, and just so far as the iron hand of persecution relaxed its hold upon the infant religion. Shall we say it is a usurpation of His power from whom all authority comes? or a delegated exercise of it? Is there a kingdom of Christ upon earth or not? This is the simple question, on which all turns. And that there is, would be probable enough, merely considering it is said in Scripture that Christ shall reign, though He is gone away; that there *shall* be a kingdom, while the Church *has* in fact fulfilled the objects proposed by it. But the case is far stronger than this; a power short of

---

[211] *Marcionites*: See note on p.[52].
[212] *Eunomians*: a 4th century sect of extreme Arian beliefs, associated with Eunomius (d.c.393).

Christ is expressly addressed in the Prophets, and dominion promised it; a viceroy and vicar is named by them as ruling for Him. "Arise, shine, for thy light is come," says the inspired oracle, "and the glory of the Lord is risen upon thee. And the Gentiles shall come to thy light and kings to the brightness of thy rising. [213] The mountain of the Lord's house shall be established in the top of the mountains, and *all nations* shall flow into it."[214] "A king shall reign in righteousness, and *princes* shall rule in judgment, and a man shall be as a *hiding place* from the wind, and a covert from the tempest, as *rivers of water* in a dry place, as the *shadow of a great rock* in a weary land. The *liberal* deviseth liberal things, and by liberal things shall he stand."[215] "Though the Lord give you the bread of adversity, and the water of affliction, *yet shall not thy teachers be removed into a corner any more*, but thine eyes shall see thy teachers."[216] "The spirit that is upon thee, and my words which I have put in thy mouth, *shall not depart out of thy mouth*, nor out of the mouth of thy seed, nor out of the mouth of thy seed's seed, henceforth and for ever."[217] "Ye shall be named the priests of the Lord; men shall call you the ministers of our God. Ye shall eat the riches of the Gentiles, and in their glory shall you boast yourselves.[218] I will make thy officers *peace*, and thine exactors *righteousness*. Violence shall no more be heard in thy land, wasting nor destruction within thy borders; for thou shalt call thy walls Salvation and thy

[180]

---

[213] *"Arise, shine, for thy light is come and the glory of the Lord ... : Isaiah 60:1,3*
[214] *"The mountain of the Lord's house shall be established ... : Isaiah 2:2*
[215] *"A king shall reign in righteousness, ... : Isaiah 32:1-2,8*
[216] *"Though the Lord give you the bread of adversity, ... : Isaiah 30:20*
[217] *"The spirit that is upon thee, ... : Isaiah 59:21*
[218] *"Ye shall be named the priests of the Lord ... : Isaiah 61:6*

gates Praise."[219] "Behold, I have graven thee upon the palms of my hands: thy walls are continually before me."[220] "No *weapon that is formed against thee shall prosper*, and every tongue that shall rise against thee in judgment thou shalt condemn." [221]

12.

One more remark shall we make, and that shall be the last. What is the real place of the Church of the middle ages in the divine scheme need not be discussed here. If we have been defending it, this has been from no love, let our readers be assured, of the Roman party among us at this day. That party, as exhibited by its acts, is a low-minded, double-dealing, worldly-minded set, and the less we have to do with it the better. Nothing but a clear command from above could make a member of our Church recognise it in any way. We are not speaking against the Church of Rome: it is a sister Church; we are not speaking against individual [181] members of it; far from it: it is our delight to think that God has many saints among them, it ought to be our prayer that among us may be as great saints as have been among them. But what we protest against and shrink from is, that secular and political spirit which in this day has developed itself among them into a party, and at least in this country is that party's motive-principle and characteristic manifestation. We have no sympathy at all with men who are afraid to own the doctrines of their religion, who try to hoodwink the incautious and ignorant, who ungenerously cast off their and our ancestors, the Church's great champions in former times, who take part in political intrigue, who play the

---

[219] *"I will make thy officers peace* ... : Isaiah 60:17-18
[220] *"Behold, I have graven thee upon the palms of my hands* ... : Isaiah 49:16
[221] *"No* weapon that is formed against thee shall prosper, ... : Isaiah 54:17

sycophant to great men, who flatter the base passions of the multitude, who join with those who are further from them to attack those who are nearer to them, who imitate the low ways of the popular religion, who have music parties in their chapels, and festivals aboard steamers, and harangue at public meetings. Such was not Borromeo, such was not Pascal; such was not Beckett,[222] Innocent,[223] Anselm,[224] Bernard, Hildebrand,[225] or the first Gregory; such were not the men of holy and humble heart, whom Rome commemorates in her services. With such we wish to be "better strangers," the longer we live; and not a word of what we have said, or are about to say, against the notion of Rome being apostate, is spoken for the sake of the like of them. Dismissing them then with this protest, we proceed to our proposed remark.

We take it then for granted, as being beyond doubt, that one main reason why Protestants are suspicious both of the Fathers of the early Church, and of the more orthodox of our writers, is the dread that the doctrine and system which these divines teach is *denounced in prophecy* as the element of Antichrist, and savours of the predicted apostasy. When pressed with arguments from Scripture or reason, they cannot perhaps answer them, but they see, as they consider, the *end* to which the Catholic system tends. They judge that the teaching recommended to them is of Antichrist, because

[182]

---

[222] *Beckett*: See note on p.[48].

[223] *Innocent*: Pope Innocent III (1160-1216), reformer, especially of canon law; he presided over the Fourth Lateran Council and encouraged St. Francis of Assisi.

[224] *Anselm*: St. Anselm (c.1033-1109), Archbishop of Canterbury; author of influential theological and philosophical works, including *Cur Deus Homo* and the *Proslogion* in which he formulated the 'ontological' argument for the existence of God.

[225] *Hildebrand*: See note on p.[46]. Hildebrand is the subject of Essay XIII.

it has before now resulted in Popery; and, under the impression that Popery is Antichrist, they say to themselves that somewhere or other there must be a fallacy in the reasoning, for that the fruit is the proof of the tree. Their dread of what is really Apostolical doctrine mainly, nay often solely, rests upon a religious apprehension that the *prophecies* have denounced it. To persons in this state of mind we propose the following question: If we must go by prophecy, *which set of prophecies* is more exactly fulfilled in the Church of the middle ages, those of Isaiah which speak of the evangelical kingdom, or those of St. Paul and St. John which speak of the anti-Christian corruption? If the history of Christian Rome corresponds to the denouncements of the Apocalypse, does it not more closely and literally correspond to the promises of Isaiah? If there is a chance of our taking part with Antichrist, taking into account the Apocalypse, is there not a greater chance of our "speaking against the Holy Ghost,"[226] considering the book of Isaiah?

To take a broad view of the subject, two traits of Antichrist, we suppose, will be particularly fixed upon as attaching to the see of Rome, pride and luxury, the one seen in its extravagant temporal power, the other in its splendour. For instance, St. Paul speaks of Antichrist as "exalting himself above all that is called God, or that is worshipped," sitting "as God in the temple of God, showing himself that he is God."[227] Again, the beast is said to have *seven heads* and *ten crowned horns*; and the dragon gives him *power*.[228]   [183]

---

[226] *"speaking against the Holy Ghost"*: Mark 3:28-30
[227] *"exalting himself above all ..."* : 2 Thessalonians 2:4
[228] *the beast is said to have ... given him* power: Cf. Revelation 13:1-2

And Babylon is called "that *great* city,"[229] and she has power over other cities, and over kings, because she is said to have "made all nations drink of the wine of" her "wrath,"[230] and "the kings of the earth had committed fornication with her."[231] And the Beast "opened his mouth in blasphemy,"[232] and the woman was on a scarlet-coloured beast "full of names of blasphemy."[233] All this, it is urged, is fulfilled in the Medieval Church's proclaiming herself (as the early Church did before her) to be Christ's vicar, in her assumption of power over kings, and her claim to define and maintain the faith, and to confer spiritual gifts. Now, as to the mode in which her functionaries did this, their motives, their characters, their individual knowledge of the faith, with all this we are not here concerned; but as to the ultimate facts in which the action of the whole system resulted, surely they far more literally correspond to the inspired prophecy of Isaiah than to that of St. John. "The sons of the strangers shall build up thy walls, and their *kings shall minister to thee*. The nation and kingdom that will not *serve* thee shall perish; yea, those nations shall be utterly wasted. The sons of them that afflicted thee shall come *bending* unto thee; and all they that despised thee *shall bow themselves down at the soles of thy feet*."[234] "Kings shall be thy nursing fathers, and their queens thy nursing mothers; they shall *bow down to thee with their face towards the*

---

[229] *"that* great *city"*: Revelation 18:21
[230] *"made all the nations drink ... "* : Revelation 14:8
[231] *"the kings of the earth ... "* : Revelation 18:3
[232] *"opened his mouth in blasphemy"*: Revelation 13:6
[233] *"full of the names of blasphemy"*: Revelation 17:3
[234] *"The sons of the strangers shall build up thy walls, ... "*: Isaiah 60:10, 12, 14

earth, and lick up the dust of thy feet."[235] "Fear not, thou worm Jacob, and ye men of Israel. Behold I will make thee a *new thrashing instrument having teeth*; and thou shalt *thrash the mountains*, and beat them small, and make the hills as chaff. Thou shalt fan them, and *the wind shall carry them away*, and the whirlwind shall scatter them."[236] Surely [184] if the correspondence, whatever it is, of the prophecies of Antichrist with the history of the Medieval Church should frighten us from that Church, much more should that of the prophecies concerning Christ's kingdom with her history draw us to her.

The other point commonly insisted on is the Medieval Church's wealth and splendour, the rich embellishment of her temples, the jewelled dress of her ministers, the offerings, shrines, pageants, and processions, which were part of her religious service. All these are supposed to be denoted by "the purple and scarlet colour, and gold, and precious stones, and pearls,"[237] with which the sorceress in the Apocalypse is arrayed; where mention is also made of the merchandize of gold and silver, precious stones, and of pearls and fine linen, and purple, and silk, and scarlet, and all thyine wood, and all manner of vessels of ivory, and precious wood, and brass, and iron, and marble, and cinnamon, and odours, and ointment, and frankincense, and wine, and oil, and fine flour, and wheat, and beasts, and horses, and chariots, and slaves, and souls of men, and the voice of harpers and musicians, and of pipers and trumpeters."[238] All such magnificence would of course, in

---

[235] *"Kings shall be thy nursing fathers, ... "*: Isaiah 49:23

[236] *"Fear not, thou worm Jacob ... "*: Isaiah 41:14-16

[237] *"the purple and scarlet, colour and gold, and precious stones and pearls"*: Revelation 17:4

[238] *"the merchandize of gold and silver, ... "*: Revelation 18:12-13, 22

itself, as little prove that the Church is Antichrist, as that any king's court is Antichrist, where it is also found. But, whatever cogency be assigned to the correspondence, still let a candid mind decide whether it can be made to tell more strongly against the Church, than the following account of the evangelical kingdom tells in her behalf. "I will lay thy stones with fair colours, and thy foundations with *sapphires*, and I will make thy windows of *agates*, and thy gates of *carbuncles*, and all thy borders of *precious stones*."[239] "The

[185] multitude of camels shall cover thee, the dromedaries of Midian and Ephah: all they from Sheba shall come; they shall bring *gold and incense*, and they shall show forth the praises of the Lord. The glory of Lebanon shall come unto thee, the fir-tree, the pine-tree, and the box together, to *beautify the place of My sanctuary*. For *brass* I will bring *gold*, and for iron I will bring silver, and for wood, brass, and for stones, iron."[240] Passages such as these, at least show that precious stones are no peculiar mark of Antichrist; which is sufficiently clear even from a later chapter of the Apocalypse, in which jasper, sapphires, and other jewels are mentioned among the treasures of the New Jerusalem.

On this ground then we would rest the matter with all serious students of Scripture. If they listen to the deep mysteries of St. John, they are inconsistent surely in being deaf to the uplifted voice of Isaiah; and in saying this, we must not be supposed to be conceding that the words of St. John in the Apocalypse, or of St. Paul in his Epistles, have met yet with their due solution in the Church's history. How wide they fall short of it, has been shown in one instance

---

[239] *"I will lay thy stones with fair colours, ... "*: Isaiah 54:11
[240] *"The multitude of camels shall cover thee ... "*: Isaiah 60:6,13,17

from St. Paul, in the course of our remarks; and in Dr. Todd's volume the reader will find similar instances, in the case of the other passages, whether in that Apostle or in Daniel, which relate to Antichrist, but which cannot by any sober mind be applied to the ecclesiastical events or persons of the past ages of Christianity.

October, 1840.

ESSAY XII

MILMAN'S VIEW OF CHRISTIANITY

THE "History of Christianity" which Mr. Milman[1] has lately given to the world, is a work of very considerable ability, and bears upon it tokens of much thought and varied research. No one could doubt that such would be the character of any publication of the author's, and the expectation raised by his name has been increased by the length of time during which reports have been current of his having a work on Christianity in hand. It consists of three ample volumes, but even these are but an instalment of the whole design to which he has devoted himself. "If he should be blessed with life and leisure," says his Preface, "the author cannot but look forward to the continuation of this history with increasing interest, as it approaches the period of the re-creation of European society under the influence of Christianity."—P. 10. It is notorious that the English Church is destitute of an Ecclesiastical History; Gibbon[2] is almost our sole authority for subjects as near the heart of a Christian as any can well be. We do not indeed mean to say that Mr. Milman will supply this want; rather we conceive

---

[1] *Mr. Milman*: See Editor's Introduction, p.xxxi.
[2] *Gibbon*: Edward Gibbon (1737-94), historian, author of *The History of the Decline and Fall of the Roman Empire* (6 vols.). Newman admired him as a writer, despite his scoffing attitude towards Christianity.

him to hold that it is a want which ought not to be supplied. Our impression at least is,—we do not mean to state it as more than an impression,—that he considers Church histories, as such, to be nothing better than "tolerabiles [187] ineptiæ."[3] His present volumes are rather the substitute than the supply of this desideratum in our ecclesiastical literature, and are meant to supersede the history of the Church by the history of Christianity. But we acknowledge even this as a boon; without agreeing to Mr. Milman's historical views or doctrinal opinions, as what we shall presently say will show, we consider it to be impossible even for a Gibbon to write an uninstructive history of the Evangelical Dispensation; and much less can Mr. Milman, who is not a Gibbon, but a clergyman, fail to be useful to those who are in search of facts, and have better principles than his own to read them by. We frankly confess that he has not pleased us; nor, on the other hand, will he please any clear-headed, long-sighted adherents of that philosophy which he has allowed himself just to taste,—except, indeed, as far as, in the present state of things they will thankfully accept whatever is conceded to them, and welcome it as a precedent and pattern for fresh innovations.

1.

However, we shall be very unjust to Mr. Milman, unless we try carefully to place ourselves in the position which he has chosen for contemplating and delineating the Christian religion. Unless we succeed in this, we shall cruelly misunderstand him, as if he held certain opinions, when he does but state the premisses which practically involve them.

---

[3] *"tolerabiles ineptiæ."*: bearable absurdities

It is obvious that the whole system of Revelation may be viewed in various, nay antagonist aspects. He who regards our Lord as man, does not in consequence deny that He is more than man; and they who with Mr. Milman love to regard the whole Christian history as much as possible as a thing of earth, may be wise or unwise, reverent or irreverent, in so doing, may be attempting what is practicable or impracticable, may eventually be led on to commit themselves to positive errors about it, and may accordingly be wantonly trifling with serious matters, but cannot without unfairness be charged with an *ipso facto* denial of its heavenly character. The Christian history is "an outward visible sign of an inward spiritual grace:"[4] whether the sign can be satisfactorily treated separate from the thing signified is another matter; but it seems to be Mr. Milman's intention so to treat it, and he must be judged by that intention, not by any other which we choose to impute to him. Christianity has an external aspect and an internal; it is human without, divine within. To attempt to touch the human element without handling also the divine, we may fairly deem unreal, extravagant, and sophistical; we may feel the two to be one integral whole, differing merely in aspect, not in fact: we may consider that a writer has not mastered his own idea who resolves to take liberties with the body, and yet not insult the animating soul. So we do; but all this is another matter; such a person does not *mean* any harm; nor does the writer who determines, as far as he can, to view the Christian as a secular fact, to the exclusion of all theological truth. He gives a representation of it, such as it would appear to a man of the world. This, at least, is

[188]

---

[4] *"an outward visible sign of an inward spiritual grace:"*: the classic definition of a sacrament

our *primâ facie* view of Mr. Milman's book, and to draw it out shall be our first step,—in doing which we shall have an opportunity, without unkindness to the author, of convicting him of what seems to us a want of clearness and definiteness of conception in his original design.

And first he shall state his object for himself, as it is set before us in his Preface:

"As the Jewish annals might be considered in relation to the [189] general history of man, to the rank which the nation bore among the various families of the human race, and the influence which it exercised on the civilization of mankind: so Christianity may be viewed *either in a strictly religious, or rather in a temporal, social, and political light*. In the former case, the writer will dwell almost exclusively on the religious doctrines, and will bear continual reference to the new relation established between man and the Supreme Being: the predominant character will be that of the theologian. In the latter, *although he may not altogether decline* the examination of the religious doctrines, their development, and their variations, his leading object will be to trace the *effect* of Christianity on the individual and social happiness of man, its influence on the polity, the laws and institutions, the opinions, the manners, even on the arts and the literature of the Christian world: he will write *rather as an historian than as a religious instructor*. Though, in fact, a candid and dispassionate survey of the connexion of Christianity with the temporal happiness, and with the intellectual and social advancement of mankind, even to the religious inquirer, cannot but be of high importance and interest; while with the general mass, at least of the reading and intellectual part of the community, nothing tends so powerfully to the strengthening or weakening of religious impression and sentiment, nothing acts so extensively, even though perhaps indirectly, on the formation of religious opinions, and on the speculative or practical belief or rejection of Christianity, as the notions we entertain of its influence on the history of man, and its relation to human happiness and social improvement."—Pp. v. vi.

In another place he tells us that the course of his history

"will endeavour to trace all the *modifications* of Christianity, by which it accommodated itself to the spirit of successive ages; and by this apparently almost skilful, but in fact necessary, condescension to the predominant state of moral culture, of which itself formed a constituent element, maintained its uninterrupted dominion. It is the author's object, *the difficulty of which he himself fully appreciates*, to portray the genius of the Christianity of each successive age, in connexion with that of the age itself; *entirely to discard all polemic views*; to mark the origin and [190]   progress of all the subordinate diversities of belief; their origin in the circumstances of the place and time at which they appeared; their progress from their adaptation to the prevailing state of opinion or sentiment: rather than to confute error or to establish truth; in short, to exhibit the reciprocal influence of civilization on Christianity, of Christianity on civilization. To the accomplishment of such a scheme he is well aware that besides the usual high qualifications of a faithful historian, is requisite, in an especial manner, the union of true philosophy with perfect charity, if indeed they are not one and the same. This *calm, impartial, and dispassionate tone* he will constantly endeavour, he dares scarcely hope, with such warnings on every side of involuntary prejudice and unconscious prepossession, uniformly to maintain. In the honesty of his purpose he will seek his excuse for all imperfection or deficiency in the execution of his scheme."—P. 47.[5]

These extracts, setting forth the intellectual idea under which the author writes, contain matter more than sufficient

---

[5] Newman originally included a longer section of Milman's text; see the Textual Appendix.

for the limits within which we wish our remarks upon him to be confined.

2.

Now let us see how much we are disposed to grant to Mr. Milman, and where we part company with him: in doing which we must be allowed to begin somewhat *ab ovo*,[6] and for a while to exchange a critical for a didactic tone. We maintain then, as we have already said, that Christianity, nor Christianity only, but all God's dealings with His creatures, have two aspects, one external, one internal. What one of the earliest Fathers says of its highest ordinance, is true of it altogether, and of all other divine dispensations: they are twofold, "having one part heavenly, and one part earthly."[7] This is the law of Providence here below; it works beneath a veil, and what is visible in its course does but shadow out at most, and sometimes obscures and disguises what is invisible. The world in which we are placed has its own system of laws and [191] principles, which, as far as our knowledge of it goes, is, when once set in motion, sufficient to account for itself,—as complete and independent as if there was nothing beyond it. Ordinarily speaking, nothing happens, nothing goes on in the world, but may be satisfactorily traced to some other event or fact in it, or has a sufficient result in other events or facts in it, without the necessity of our following it into a higher system of things in order to explain its existence, or

---

[6] ab ovo: from the beginning (literally 'from the egg')

[7] *one of the earliest fathers ... "having one part heavenly, and one part earthly.":* St.Irenæus (c.130-c.202), Bishop of Lyon, *Adversus Hæreses*, 4,31,5: "For as the bread, which is produced from the earth, when it receives the invocation of God, is no longer common bread, but the Eucharist, *consisting of two realities, earthly and heavenly*; so also our bodies, when they receive the Eucharist, are no longer corruptible, having the hope of the resurrection to eternity."

to give it a meaning. We will not stop to dwell on exceptions to this general statement, or on the narrowness of our knowledge of things: but what is every day said and acted on proves that this is at least the impression made upon most minds by the course of things in which we find ourselves. The sun rises and sets on a law; the tides ebb and flow upon a law; the earth is covered with verdure or buried in the ocean, it grows old and it grows young again, by the operation of fixed laws. Life, whether vegetable or animal, is subjected to a similar external and general rule. Men grow to maturity, then decay, and die. Moreover, they form into society, and society has its principles. Nations move forward by laws which act as a kind of destiny over them, and which are as vigorous now as a thousand years ago. And these laws of the social and political world run into the physical, making all that is seen one and one only system; a horse stumbles, and an oppressed people is rid of their tyrant; a volcano changes populous cities into a dull lake; a gorge has of old time opened, and the river rolls on, bearing on its bosom the destined site of some great mart,[8] which else had never been. We cannot set limits either to the extent or to the minuteness of this wonderful web of causes [192] and effects, in which all we see is involved. It reaches to the skies; it penetrates into our very thoughts, habits, and will.

Such is confessedly the world in which our Almighty Creator has placed us. If then He is still actively present with His own work, present with nations and with individuals, He must be acting by means of its ordinary system, or by quickening, or as it were, stimulating its powers, or by superseding or interrupting it; in other words,

---

[8] *mart*: market, centre of trade

by means of what is called nature, or by miracle; and whereas strictly miraculous interference must be, from the nature of the case, rare, it stands to reason that, unless He has simply retired, and has left the world ordinarily to itself,—content with having originally imposed on it certain general laws, which will for the most part work out the ends which He contemplates,—He is acting through, with, and beneath those physical, social, and moral laws, of which our experience informs us. Now it has ever been a firm article of Christian faith, that His Providence is in fact not general merely, but is, on the contrary, thus particular and personal; and that, as there is a particular Providence, so of necessity that Providence is secretly concurring and co-operating with that system which meets the eye, and which is commonly recognized among men as existing. It is not too much to say that this is the one great rule on which the Divine Dispensations with mankind have been and are conducted, that the visible world is the instrument, yet the veil, of the world invisible,—the veil, yet still partially the symbol and index: so that all that exists or happens visibly, conceals and yet suggests, and above all subserves, a system of persons, facts, and events beyond itself.

Thus the course of things has a natural termination as well as a natural origin: it tends towards final causes while it springs from physical; it is ever issuing from things which we see round about us; it is ever passing on into what is matter of faith, not of sight. What is called and seems to be cause and effect, is rather an order of sequence, and does not preclude, nay, perhaps implies, the presence of unseen spiritual agency as its real author. This is the animating principle both of the Church's ritual and of Scripture interpretation; in the latter it is the basis of the theory of the

[193]

231

double sense; in the former it makes ceremonies and observances to be signs, seals, means, and pledges of supernatural grace. It is the mystical principle in the one, it is the sacramental in the other. All that is seen,—the world, the Bible, the Church, the civil polity, and man himself,—are types, and, in their degree and place, representatives and organs of an unseen world, truer and higher than themselves. The only difference between them is, that some things bear their supernatural character upon their surface, are historically creations of the supernatural system, or are perceptibly instrumental, or obviously symbolical: while others rather seem to be complete in themselves, or run counter to the unseen system which they really subserve, and thereby make demands upon our faith.

This may be illustrated from the creation of man. The Creator "formed man of the dust of the ground, *and* breathed into his nostrils the breath of life, and man became a living soul."[9] He first formed a material tabernacle, and then endued it with an unseen life. Now some philosophers, somewhat after the manner of the ancient Gnostics whom Mr. Milman mentions (vol. ii., p. 113), have speculated on the probability of man's being originally of some brute nature, some vast misshapen lizard of the primeval period, which at length by the force of nature, from whatever secret causes, was exalted into a rational being, and gradually shaped its proportions and refined its properties by the influence of the rational principle which got possession of it. Such a theory is of course irreconcilable with the letter of the sacred text, to say no more;[10] but it bears an analogy, and

[194]

---

[9] *"formed man out of the dust ... "*: Genesis 2:7

[10] *some philosophers ... to say no more*: a reference to pre-Darwinian theories of evolution. Newman's statement here that such a theory is 'irreconcilable with the

at least supplies an illustration, to many facts and events which take place in this world. When Providence would make a Revelation, He does not begin anew, but uses the existing system; He does not visibly send an Angel, but He commissions or inspires one of our own fellows. When He would bless us, He makes a man His priest. When He would consecrate or quicken us, He takes the elements of this world as the means of real but unseen spiritual influences. When He would set up a divine polity, He takes a polity which already is, or one in course of forming. Nor does He interfere with its natural growth, development, or dependence on things visible. He does not shut it up in a desert, and there supply it with institutions unlike those which might naturally come to it from the contact and intercourse of the external world. He does but modify, quicken, or direct the powers of nature or the laws of society. Or if He works miracles, still it is without superseding the ordinary course of things. He multiplies the flocks or the descendants of Jacob, or in due season He may work signal or public miracles for their deliverance from Egypt; but still the operation of ordinary causes, the influence of political arrangements, and what is called the march of events, are seen in such providences as truly, and

---

letter of the sacred text' is carefully worded and should not be taken as a fundamentalist attitude towards Scripture and evolution. Writing to an Anglican correspondent in 1868 about Darwin's theory, Newman said: 'It does not seem to me to follow that creation is denied because the Creator, millions of years ago, gave laws to matter. He first created matter and then he created laws for it—laws which should *construct* it into its present wonderful beauty, and accurate adjustment and harmony of parts *gradually*. ... Mr Darwin's theory *need* not then to be atheistical, be it true or not; it may simply be suggesting a larger idea of Divine Prescience and Skill.' (*Letters and Diaries*, Vol.XXIV, p.77) In a private paper on the inspiration of Scripture he wrote that he was willing to 'go the whole hog with Darwin' (Newman, *The Philosophical Notebook*, ed. Edward J. Sillem, 1970, p.158).

can be pointed out as convincingly, as if an Angel and a pillar of a cloud were not with them.

Thus the great characteristic of Revelation is addition, substitution. Things look the same as before, though not[11] an invisible power has taken hold upon them. This power does not unclothe the creature, but clothes it. Men dream everywhere: it gives visions. Men journey everywhere: it sends "the Angels of God to meet them."[12] Men may elsewhere be hospitable to their brethren: now they entertain Angels. Men carry on a work; but it is a blessing from some ancestor that is breathing on and through it unseen. A nation migrates and seizes on a country; but all along its proceedings are hallowed by prophecy, and promise, and providence beforehand, and used for religious ends afterwards. Israel was as much a political power, as man is an animal. The rites and ceremonies enjoined upon the people might be found elsewhere, but were not less divine notwithstanding. Circumcision was also practised in Egypt, frequent ablutions may be the custom of the East, the veil of Moses may have been the symbol of other rulers (if so be) before him,—though the fact has to be proved; a Holy of Holies, an altar, a sacrifice, a sacerdotal caste, *in* these points the Mosaic law resembled, yet *as to* these it differed from, the nations round about. The Israelitish polity had a beginning, a middle, and an end, like other things of time and place; its captivities were the natural consequences, its monarchy was the natural expedient, of a state of political weakness. Its territory was a battle-ground, and its power was the alternate ally, of the rival empires of Egypt and

[195]

---

[11] *not*: presumably a mistake for 'now'
[12] *"the angels of God to meet them"*: Cf. Genesis 32:1: 'And Jacob went on his way, and the angels of God met him.'

234

Assyria. Heathen travellers may have surveyed the Holy Land, and have thought it but a narrow slip of Syria. So it was; what then? till the comparative anatomist can be said by his science to disprove the rationality and responsibility of man, the politician or geographer of this world does nothing, by dissertations in his own particular line of [196] thought, towards quenching the secret light of Israel, or dispossessing its angelic guardians of the height of Sion or of the sepulchres of the prophets. Its history is twofold, worldly to the world, and heavenly to the heirs of heaven.

What is true of Judaism is true of Christianity. The kingdom of Christ, though not of this world, yet is in the world, and has a visible, material, social shape. It consists of men, and it has developed according to the laws under which combinations of men develop. It has an external aspect similar to all other kingdoms. We may generalize and include it as one among the various kinds of polity, as one among the empires, which have been upon the earth. It is called the fifth kingdom; and as being numbered with the previous four which were earthly, it is thereby, in fact, compared with them. We may write its history, and make it look as like those which were before or contemporary with it, as a man is like a monkey. Now we come at length to Mr. Milman: this is what he has been doing. He has been viewing the history of the Church on the side of the world. Its rise from nothing, the gradual aggrandizement of its bishops, the consolidation of its polity and government, its relation to powers of the earth, its intercourse with foreign philosophies and religions, its conflict with external and internal enemies, the mutual action for good or for evil which has been carried on between it and foreign systems, political and intellectual, its large extension, its growth and resolution into a monarchy, its temporal greatness, its gradual divisions and decay, and the natural causes which operated throughout,—these are the subjects in which he delights, to which he has dedicated himself,—that is, as far as they can be detached from their directly religious bearing; and unless readers understand this, they will think that what is but *a contemplation of what is outside*, is intended by him for *a denial of what is inside*. Whether such denial has in any measure resulted, even in Mr. Milman's own mind, from such contemplation, is a farther question, afterwards to be considered; but, anyhow, it is to be feared that too many persons will unfairly run away from his book with the notion that to ignore the Almighty in ecclesiastical history is really to deny Him.

[197]

3.

Some specimens of Mr. Milman's peculiarity will serve further to explain what we mean. The following, for instance, are some of his observations on the *resemblance* between the Magianism[13] of the East and Judaism after its return from captivity there:

"The earliest books of the Old Testament fully recognize the ministration of Angels, but in Babylonia this simpler creed grew up into a regular hierarchy, in which the degrees of rank and subordination were arranged with almost heraldic precision. The seven great archangels[14] of Jewish tradition *correspond* with the Amschaspands[15] of the Zendavesta;[16] and in strict mutual analogy,

---

[13] *Magianism*: the religion of the Magi of ancient Persia

[14] *Seven great archangels*: In the apocryphal Book of Enoch, these are named as Michael, Raphael, Gabriel, Uriel, Saraqael, Raguel and Remiel.

[15] *Amschaspands*: in Zoroastrianism, the seven great spirits who assist Ahura Mazda, the creator of the universe

both systems arrayed against each other a separate host of spiritual beings with distinct powers and functions. Each nation, each individual had in one case his Ferver[17], in the other his guardian angel, and was exposed to the hostile Dev[18] or Dæmon ... The great impersonated *Principle of Evil* appears to have assumed much of the *antagonist power of darkness*. The name itself of Satan, which in the older poetical book of Job is assigned to a spirit of *different* attributes, one of the celestial ministers who assemble before the throne of the Almighty, ... *became appropriated* to the prince of the malignant spirits,—the head and representative of the spiritual world, which ruled over physical as well as moral evil."—Pp. 70-72.

Our object in quoting this passage is neither to deny the similarity between the two theologies, nor to inquire how [198] this came to pass, but to give an instance of Mr. Milman's peculiar *manner*, and the facility with which he may be taken, not unnaturally, but still over-hastily, to be saying what he does not say, that the Jewish theology is worth no more than the Magian. He as little says it as, in asserting that man is an animal, he would be denying that he is rational.

And in like manner when he calls the Magnificat "Jewish," he need not mean more than to be an "historian rather than a religious instructor;" we take him to be merely stating what he considers a *fact*, whatever comes of it, whatever theory is to be built upon it, what explanation is to be given of it, viz., that the language which the Blessed Mary uses, is such as the Scribes and Pharisees, Judas the Zealot, or Caiaphas the High Priest might use also; in spite

---

[16] *Zendavasta*: The Avesta is the collection Zoroastrian hymns; the Zend is the commentary on them.
[17] *Ferver*: in Zoroastrianism, the soul
[18] *Dev*: in Zorosatrinism, a devil

of this, he may consider the spirit and meaning in each party to be quite different. "It is *curious*," he says, "to observe how completely and exclusively consistent every expression appears with the state of belief at that period; *all is purely Jewish*, and accordant with the prevalent expectation of the National Messiah."—Vol. i., p. 102.

Again, when he says that the Baptist "*partook* of the ascetic character of the more solitary of the Essenes,[19] all of whom retired from the tumult and licence of the city," vol. i., p. 141, no one can reasonably suppose that he means to be more than an historical relator, keeping clear of religious principles and doctrinal theories, and stating facts, external facts.

In like manner he parallels Christian asceticism to Oriental; whatever theory he does or may proceed to erect upon this fact of a correspondence between the two, still, as far as the profession of his Preface goes, he is not bound to
[199]   consider it at all in a "strictly religious" but "rather in a temporal, social, and political light." A supernatural *cause* for it may exist in Christianity, a divine authority; but this does not conflict with the fact that the Christian athlete[20] may externally resemble the heathen; unless indeed, which no one will maintain, the parallel fact of the heathen or Jewish ceremonial ablutions be an argument against the divine appointment of evangelical baptism. He says,—

"On the cold table-lands of Thibet, in the forests of India, among the busy population of China, on the burning shores of Siam, in Egypt and in Palestine, in Christianised Europe, in

---

[19] *Essenes*: Jewish sect of a quasi-monastic nature, associated with the Dead Sea Scrolls. Many modern scholars would agree about the likely influence of the Essenes on St. John the Baptist.

[20] *athlete*: not in the modern sense; an ascetic, one who disciplines his body for a spiritual purpose

Mahommetanised Asia, the worshipper of the Lama,[21] the Faquir,[22] the Bonze, the Talapoin,[23] the Essene, the therapeutist,[24] the monk, and the dervish,[25] have withdrawn from the society of man, in order to abstract the pure mind from the dominion of foul and corrupting matter. *Under each system*, the perfection of human nature was estrangement from the influence of the senses, those senses which were enslaved to the material elements of the world; an approximation to the essence of the Deity, by a total secession from the affairs, the interests, the passions, the thoughts, the common being and nature of man. The practical operation of this elementary principle of Eastern religion has deeply influenced the whole history of man. But it had made no progress in Europe till after the introduction of Christianity."—Vol. ii., pp. 86, 87.

Again he says, speaking of the time of Christ's coming,

"Man, as *history and experience teach*, is essentially a religious being; there are certain faculties and modes of thinking and feeling apparently inseparable from his mental organization, which lead him irresistibly to seek some communication with another and a higher world. But at the present juncture the ancient religions were effete; they belonged to a totally different state of civilization; though they retained the strong hold of habit and interest on different classes of society, yet the general mind was advanced beyond them; they could not supply the religious necessities of the age. Thus, the world, peaceably united under one temporal monarchy might be compared to a vast body without a soul: the *throne of the human mind appeared vacant*; among the rival competitors for its dominion, none advanced more than claims local, or limited to a certain class."—Vol. i., p. 8.

[200]

---

[21] *Lama*: Tibetan Buddhist priest or teacher

[22] *Faquir*: a Moslem ascetic

[23] *the Bonze, the Talapoin*: Buddhist priests or teachers

[24] *therapeutist*: healer (not in the modern medical sense)

[25] *dervish*: a Sufi ascetic holy man

These instances will be sufficient of Mr. Milman's manner. We proceed next to observe that, as if in order that there may be no mistake, he often gives his readers intimation, more or less express, of the external view he is taking of his subject; as a few out of the many instances, which might be quoted in point, will show.

Thus he says of the Jews, that "to the loose manner in which religious belief hung on the greater part of the subjects of the Roman empire, their recluse and uncompromising attachment to the faith of their ancestors *offered the most singular contrast.*"—Vol. i., p. 345; and that "the Jews stood alone, *according to the language and opinion of the Roman world*, as a nation of religious fanatics".—*Ibid.* Again, "so long as" the Christians "made no visible impression upon society, their *unsocial and self-secluding disposition* would be treated with contempt and pity rather than with animosity."—Vol. ii., p. 144. Words like these bear on their very face the writer's intention merely to describe how Christians *appeared* to the heathen.

Still more expressly he speaks of "One who *appeared* to the mass of mankind in His own age as a peasant of Palestine," vol. i., p. 35: he says that the establishment of the Mosaic Law was "accompanied, *according to the universal belief*, with the most terrific demonstrations of Almighty power," *ibid.*, p. 168; and he makes the solemn announcement, "in the stable of the inn or caravansera[26] was born the CHILD ... who has been for centuries *considered* the object of adoration as the divine Mediator between God and man by the most civilized and enlightened nations of the earth."—*Ibid.*, p. 108.

[201]

---

[26] *caravansera*: usually, *caravanserai*, an inn giving accommodation to travellers

Speaking of the Greeks who came to Christ at the feast, he says, "*to their surprise* ... the somewhat ambiguous language of Jesus dwells at first on His approaching fate, etc."—P. 306. Speaking of our Lord's injunction to secrecy on occasion of His miraculous cures, he says, that this was so frequent "that one evangelist *considers* that the cautious and unresisting demeanour of Jesus, thus avoiding all unnecessary offence or irritation, exemplified that characteristic of the Messiah so beautifully described by Isaiah, 'He shall neither strive, etc.'"[27]—P. 224. That *one* evangelist *considered* a prophecy *exemplified*, is quite consistent, of course, with a belief that at the same time *inspiration pronounced* it to be *fulfilled*. Mr. Milman need not mean more than to state an external fact.

In the same spirit he calls our Saviour's miracles "preternatural," not "supernatural works."—*Vid.* vol. i., pp. 283, 389. The latter word would *assume* the point in debate between the world and the Church, their divinity, whereas he is taking up an impartial or philosophical position between the two. He speaks of Christ as a man "who as *far as he* [Pilate] *could discover*, was a harmless, peaceful, and benevolent enthusiast."—P. 346. And, in describing the attempt of the Nazarenes to cast our Lord down the brow of their hill, he cautiously says, in the same historical tone, "they *found* that the intended victim of their wrath had disappeared."—*Ibid.*, p. 188. And in another passage where he is led to compare Budhism with Christianity, he expressly "deprecates misconstruction." "The characteristic of the Budhist religion," he says, "which in one respect may be considered (*I deprecate misconstruction*) the Christianity

---

[27] *"He shall neither strive"*: Matthew 12:19, referring to Isaiah 42:3

[202] of the remoter East, seems an union of political with religious reformation." And then he even takes the trouble to mention *where* Christianity, in his opinion, parts company with Budhism, as well as *what* it shares with it. "Its end," he observes, "is to substitute purer morality for the wild and multifarious idolatry into which Brahminism had degenerated, and to break down the distinction of castes. *But* Budhism appears to be essentially monastic; *and* how different the superstitious regard for life in the Budhist from the enlightened humanity of Christianity!"—P. 98. Thus Christianity certainly is superior to Budhism.

4.

We have said nothing to imply that we approve of the *judgment* which has determined Mr. Milman to this mode of writing. Still less can we speak well of it, considering it has led him to that *apparent* suppression of doctrinal truth which we are now to notice. For the fact is undeniable, little as Mr. Milman may be aware of it, that this external contemplation of Christianity necessarily leads a man to write as a Socinian or Unitarian *would* write, whether he will or not. Mr. Milman has not been able to avoid this dreadful disadvantage, and thus, however heartily he may hate the opinions of such men himself, he has unintentionally both given scandal to his brethren and cause of triumph to the enemy. A very few words will account for this. The great doctrines which the Socinian denies are our Lord's divinity and atonement; now these are not external facts;—what he confesses are His humanity and crucifixion; these *are* external facts. Mr. Milman then is bound by his theory to dwell on the latter, to slur over the former. Nay,

[203] further still, the forgiveness of sins is not an external fact;

but moral improvement is; consequently he will make the message of the Gospel to relate mainly to moral improvement, not to forgiveness of sins. Again, those who maintain most earnestly the divinity of Christ as a matter of doctrine, must yet admit that what is *"manifested"* in Him, is not, cannot be, more than a certain attribute or attributes of the divinity, as, for instance, especially love. Accordingly, Mr. Milman, speaking mainly of what is externally seen, will be led to speak almost in a Sabellian[28] fashion, as if denying, because not stating, the specific indwelling which Scripture records, and the Church teaches. Hence the general *effect* of Mr. Milman's work, we cannot deny, though we wish to give as little offence as possible, is heretical.

On these considerations, for instance, we account for the following passages:—he says that the "structure of the new faith" is "a temple to which all nations in the highest degree of civilization may *bring* their offerings *of pure hearts, virtuous dispositions, universal charity,*" and that "our natural emotion on beholding it," is "the recognition of the Divine goodness in the promulgation of this beneficent code of religion, and adoration of that Being in whom *that Divine goodness* is thus embodied and made *comprehensible to the faculties of man*. In the language of the Apostle, God is in Christ *reconciling* the world unto Himself."[29]—Vol. i., p. 51.

We all know it to be an essential and most practical doctrine that the Person of Christ is Divine, and that *into*

---

[28] *Sabellian*: Someone who holds the views of Sabellius, a third century heretic who taught that that the Son and the Holy Spirit were not divine Persons but different manifestations or 'masks' of God the Father, thus denying the Incarnation.

[29] *God is in Christ* reconciling *the world to himself*. Cf. 2 Corinthians 5:19

His Divine Personality He has taken human nature; or, in other words, the Agent, Speaker, Sufferer, Sacrifice, Intercessor, Judge, is God, though God in our flesh; not man with a presence of Divinity. The latter doctrine is Sabellianism, Nestorianism, and Socinianism.

[204]   Yet it is adopted to the letter by Mr. Milman, who, admitting nothing but what is of this world when he contemplates Christ's person, is *obliged* to see in it by his very theory nothing more than a man. Thus, he says, that "Jesus declared" "that the Son of God ... had descended from heaven," and was "present *in His Person*."—Vol. i. p. 173.

Again, what could be more lax and unsatisfactory than such discrimination as the following between the Gospel and the religions of the East, but for the salvo that Mr. Milman's very object and only object is to show how like Christianity is to heathenism?

"The incarnation of the Deity, or the union of *some part of* the Divine Essence with a material or human body, is by no means an uncommon religious notion, more particularly in the East. Yet in the doctrine as subsequently developed by Christianity, there seems the same important difference which characterizes the whole system of the ancient and modern religions. It is in the former a mythological impersonation of the power, in Christ it is the *goodness* of the Deity, which *associating* itself with a human form assumes the character of a representative of the human race; in whose person is exhibited a pure model of human perfection, and whose triumph over evil is by the slow and gradual progress of *enlightening* the mind and *softening and purifying the heart*."—Vol. i., p. 97.

The concluding words of this extract should be well observed; the victory of the Cross and the free pardon of sin are not mentioned among Christ's "triumphs." The author adds presently that the sole design of the "Christian scheme is to work a moral change, *to establish a new relation between man and the Almighty creator*, and to bring to light the great secret of the immortality of man." It is said that the exception proves the rule; now it so happens that the vague words put into italics are the nearest approach which we have observed in Mr. Milman's volumes to the doctrine of forgiveness of sins, let alone that of the atonement. We are far from pronouncing for certain that there is nothing more definite to be found in them, but we are sure that we are faithful to the general *tone* of his work in thus speaking.

[205]

Again, he speaks of the more opulent Romans being "tempted to make themselves acquainted with a religion, the *moral influence* of which was so manifestly favourable to the happiness of mankind, and which offered so *noble a solution* of the *great problem of human philosophy*, the immortality of the soul."—Vol. ii., p. 156. Surely this account of the great problem awkwardly fits in with the real and deep cry of human nature embodied in the jailor's words, "What shall I do to be saved?"[30]

Again, he speaks of Christ as one "whose *moral doctrines*, if adopted throughout the world, would destroy more than half the misery, by destroying all the *vice* and *mutual hostility* of men," vol. i., p. 108; where the last phrase is perhaps intended as an explanation of Christ "having made *peace*."[31]

Elsewhere he dwells upon the beauty of the picture presented to us in Christ's removing bodily afflictions; and on the other hand, "gently instilling into the minds of the

---

[30] *"What shall I do to be saved?"*: Acts 16:30

[31] *"having made peace"*: Colossians 1:20

people those pure, and humane, and gentle principles of *moral goodness* to which the wisdom of ages has been able to add nothing;" and God's condescending "to show this image and reflection of His own inconceivable nature for the benefit of" men, "to restore them to, and prepare them for, a higher and eternal state of existence."—Pp. 197, 198. He is, it seems, precluded by his position from expressing definitely the idea conveyed in the proclamation, "Repent ye,"[32] and in the announcement, "Thy sins be forgiven thee."[33]

[206] In another place he expressly sets himself to interpret the last-mentioned words. When the woman that was a sinner washed our Saviour's feet with her tears, He said, "Thy sins be forgiven thee;" Mr. Milman paraphrases, "the reply of Jesus *intimates* that His religion was intended to *reform* and *purify* the worst."—P. 233. That is, Christ's reply *hints* less than it *expresses*.

Again, speaking of what he considers the growing illumination of society, he says:—

"Even if (though I conceive it impossible) the imagination should entirely wither from the human soul, and a severer faith enter into an exclusive alliance with pure reason, Christianity would still have its moral perfection, its *rational promise of immortality*, its approximation to the one pure, spiritual, incomprehensible Deity, to satisfy that reason, and to infuse those *sentiments of dependence*, of *gratitude*, of *love to God*, without which human society must fall to ruin, and the human mind, in humiliating desperation, suspend all its noble activity, and care not to put forth its sublime and eternal energies."—Vol. i., p. 132.

---

[32] *"Repent ye"*: Matthew 3:2
[33] *"Thy sins be forgiven thee."*: e.g. Matthew 9:5

Again, he speaks of baptism as being a mark of the convert's "initiation into the new faith," while "a secret internal transmutation was to take place by divine agency in his heart, which was to communicate a new principle of *moral life*."—Vol. i., p. 172. Still no mention of the forgiveness of sins.

Again, he tells us that the object of the Temptation was "to withdraw" Christ "from the purely religious end of His being upon earth, to transform Him from the author of a *moral revolution* to be slowly wrought by the introduction of new *principles of virtue*, and new rules for *individual and social happiness* ... who was to offer to man the gift of *eternal life*, and *elevate his nature* to a previous fitness for that exalted destiny."—Vol. i., p. 156.

5.

Now it is very far from our intention indeed to say that [207] the solemn topics of atonement, and forgiveness, and of our Lord's divine nature, are to be introduced upon all occasions, and especially in an historical work such as Mr. Milman's. He is, as he truly says, "an historian rather than a religious instructor." But still, when he is engaged in *specifying expressly* what the revealed doctrine consists in, and what the object of Christ's coming was, we consider it to be a very unhappy view of historical composition, which precludes him from mentioning what all members of the Church hold to be fundamental in that doctrine, and primary in that object.

Yet, singular to say, Mr. Milman makes this mode of writing a subject of especial self-congratulation; and this is a phenomenon which deserves dwelling on. It is impossible then to mistake the satisfaction which he feels in adopting the external view of Christianity, and the sort of contempt, we are sorry to say it, in which he holds theological science; yet we really do not see what the merit is, which he seems to claim for his historical method. Not that we cannot conceive many reasons for contemplating sacred things as they show themselves externally; but there is a broad intelligible difference between throwing one's mind into the feelings of a certain state of society, or into the views of certain persons, for an occasion or purpose, and habitually taking their feelings or views as one's own, and making what is not the true position for surveying them the centre of our own thoughts about them. Men may take this external view of sacred things by way of putting themselves into the place of unbelievers, and entering into their difficulties, and so assisting them in finding the truth. Such is the case with Paley and other writers on External Evidence.[34] Again, there [208] is certainly a silent and soothing pleasure in viewing great things in the littleness and feebleness in which they appear to the world, from the secret feeling of their real power and majesty, and an exulting anticipation of their ultimate and just triumph. Such is the pleasure excited by the recognitions or discoveries of Greek tragedy, which, as being generally foreseen from the beginning, feed the imagination. Moreover, a mean exterior cast over what we admire and revere acts as a veil of mystery heightening our feeling of its greatness. And again, the very keenness and fulness of our feelings may often act, in leading us in very

---

[34] *Paley and other writers on External Evidence*: William Paley (1743-1805) was a clergyman and influential philosopher, best known for his *Natural Theology* (1802) and the teleological argument for the existence of God. Here Newman is referring to his *View of the Evidences of Christianity* (1794). Newman in fact had reservations about the effectiveness and validity of this 'evidences' approach, cf. *University Sermons*, Sermon 10, pp.197-8.

despair or from deep awe to use simple and homely words concerning what is more constraining with us, and more affecting, than anything else in the world. None of these considerations, however, will serve to explain Mr. Milman's course of proceeding. Neither as a conscientious exercise of mind, nor except very partially in the way of evidence, nor from any poetical pleasure, nor to gratify the love of mystery, nor in admiration, nor from a principle of reserve, does he display the earthly side of the Gospel; but, strange to say, from a notion of its being philosophical to do so. It is quite undeniable, and quite as astonishing, that he thinks there is something high and admirable in the state of mind which can thus look down upon a Divine Dispensation. He imagines that it argues a large, liberal, enlightened understanding, to be able to generalize religions, and, without denying the divinity of Christianity, to resolve it into its family likeness to all others. He thinks it a sign of an acute and practised intellect to pare down its supernatural facts as closely as possible, and to leave its principal miracles, the multiplying bread, the raising Lazarus, or the Resurrection, standing alone like the pillars of Tadmor[35] in the wilderness. He evidently considers that it is an advance [209] in knowledge to disguise Scripture facts and persons under secular names. He thinks that it is so much gain if he can call Abraham an Emir or a Sheik; that it is a victory to be able to connect Church doctrine with Magianism, or Platonism, or Judaism, or Essenism, or Orientalism; and to liken holy Basil or Bernard to Faquir, Bonze, Talapoin, and

---

[35] *pillars of Tadmor*: Tadmor, or ancient Palmyra (Syria), was located in the midst of the desert and constituted an important stop for those travelling in caravans. It was famous for its 'Great Colonnade' linking the Temple of Bel with the West Gate and built in the second and third centuries BC. Its remains can still be seen.

Dervish. This is what meets us on the very surface of his book, and it is, we must speak frankly, no promising trait. What, for instance, should we say to a comparative anatomist, who not only exercised his science in his own line and for its own ends, but should profess to write an account of man, and then should talk much of man's animality and materiality, of his relation to the beasts of the field, of the processes of nutrition, digestion, disease, and dissolution, and should boast of his having steered clear of all mention of the soul, should waive the question of the moral sense, should deprecate the inquiry into a future life, leave the debate upon responsibility to the schools, and all this with the air of one who was no common man, but was breathing the pure, elevated, and serene atmosphere of philosophy? Yet such as this in the eyes of all serious men will be an author who speaks of any inquiry into the doctrines of Christianity as a sort of condescension, and looks upon its outward and secular aspect as its glory. We cannot exempt Mr. Milman from the force of this comparison.

For instance, he speaks in the first extract above given, as not being able "*altogether*" to "*decline* the examination of the religious doctrines, their development, and their variations," though "his leading object" is to trace the effect of Christianity on the individual and social happiness of [210] man, its influence on the polity, laws, and institutions, the opinions, the manners ... the arts and literature of the Christian world." He implies that his survey is to be "*candid* and *dispassionate*," and says that though mainly relating to what is temporal, intellectual, and social, it will be of high importance and interest "*even* to the religious inquirer," and will be of a nature to act upon "the general mass at least of the reading and intelligent part of the community," in forming their religious opinions, and in their "speculative or practical belief" of Christianity. He goes on to congratulate himself that, as regards the sceptical and infidel writers of Germany, for so we understand him, he "shall not be accused of that *narrow jealousy*, and, in his opinion, *unworthy and timid suspicion*, with which the writers of that country are proscribed by many."—P. viii. He compliments them on "their profound research and *philosophical* tone of thought." He celebrates St. Thomas the Apostle as "remarkable for his *coolness* and *reflecting temper* of mind."—P. 226. As to the points at present in controversy in our Church, including, let it be observed, baptismal regeneration and other doctrines not less important, "though of course," he says, "I cannot be, yet I have written as if, *in total ignorance* of the existence of such discussions."—P. ix. This ought to mean, we suppose,—I have my definite opinion, but I will not controvert; but it sounds very like,—I hold a great and a calm view, and all others are partizans and zealots. He continues: "*I have delivered* without fear and without partiality what *I* have conscientiously believed to be the truth. *I* write for the general readers *rather than for the members of my own profession*;"—and now let us attend to the reason of this great resolve: "*as* I cannot understand why such subjects of universal interest should be *secluded*, as the *peculiar* objects of study to *one* class or order alone." [211] In other words,—My own profession cannot be brought to take an external view of Christianity; but I write for the world, which does.

He further tells us that—

"As Christian History, surveyed in a *wise and candid spirit*, cannot but be a useful school for the promotion of Christian faith;

so no study can tend more directly to, or more imperatively enforce on all *unprejudiced* and *dispassionate* minds, *mutual forbearance, enlightened toleration,* and the greatest even of Christian virtues, Christian Charity."—P. xi.

In the second of the extracts with which we commenced, he repeats his hope of attaining a *"calm, impartial,* and *dispassionate* tone;" that is, the calmness and dispassionateness, we suppose, which can bring a man comfortably through an assimilation of the later Jewish prophets to Zoroaster, and Christianity to Buddhism. Moreover, he tells us, that "his disposition inclines" to labour even more, "to show the good *as well* as the evil of each phasis[36] of Christianity."—Vol. i. p. 49.

We have further light what Mr. Milman means by "calmness and dispassionateness" by the tone in which he speaks of any show of zealous feeling in others. He *contrasts* it with his own state of mind. For instance, in one place he disavows, though he excuses, the *"isolation* of the history of Christ in a kind of *sacred seclusion,"* though, he proceeds, it "has *no doubt* a beneficial effect on the *piety* of the Christian, which delights in contemplating the Saviour *undisturbed and uncontaminated* by less holy associations."—Vol. i., p. 52. Now is not this unreal? Mr. Milman surely *himself* is contemplating, not *"the* Saviour," but *his* Saviour; and the question with the Christian is, not what *effect* it has upon his piety—as if he cherished reverent thoughts of Christ from a mere calculation of the benefit such reverence will do to his own mind—but "How can I, independently of a call of duty, forget, or speak as if I forgot, *who* and *what* He is?" Mr. Milman's language

[212]

---

[36] *phasis*: stage, phase

certainly implies that calmness and dispassionateness and an absence of prejudice are shown in being able to hear and to repeat, without wincing, as regards our great Benefactor, the profane things which infidels and scorners say of Him. We know he cannot mean this; yet his language implies it, and in consequence we cannot wonder at his exciting a clamour. Presently he speaks of a departure "from the evangelical simplicity in the relation of facts," such as he has adopted, offending "the reverential feelings of *the reader*;" why not of the writer?

However, we should be unfair unless we added that there are occasions when he can respond personally to the calls of reverence made upon him by the subject on which he is employed. For instance, of the last scenes of our Lord's life, he writes, with imposing effect, "As we approach the *appalling* close, *we tremble* lest the *colder process of explanation* should deaden the *solemn* and *harrowing* impression of the scene, or weaken the contrast between the wild and tumultuous uproar of the triumphant enemies and executioners of the Son of Man with the *deep and unutterable misery* of the few faithful adherents who still followed His footsteps."—Vol. i., p. 359.

6.

Our object hitherto has been, to the best of our ability, to analyze the view, with which Mr. Milman apparently starts, of his position and office, freely to censure it, but at the same time to vindicate him from any sinister intentions in assuming it. That view involves, as we have incidentally [213] shown, a great error in judgment; it necessarily lays the author open to misrepresentation, as if he held or countenanced what he disapproves; and it could not avoid paining many excellent persons, whom so kindly-tempered a man as Mr. Milman would be very unwilling to perplex or alarm. We should have said thus much, had Mr. Milman adhered ever so rigidly, were that possible, to what seems to us his original design of merely stating the *facts* of Christianity, without notice, good or bad, of the *principles* which are their life. But such an adherence was impossible; as in fact he confesses when he speaks of "not altogether declining" theological subjects. He does make a *theory* of the facts which he records, and such a theory as unhappily implies that they belong mainly to that external system of things of which he writes, and must be directly referred to visible causes and measured by intelligible principles. His mode of writing does not merely pass over, but actually denies the existence and presence among us of that higher and invisible system of which we have spoken above. Not content with claiming for the historical facts of Christianity a place in the course of this world, which they have, he disallows that supernatural world, in which they have a place also. As anatomists might treat man simply according to their science and become materialists, as physical experimentalists might teach pantheism or atheism, as political economists might make wealth the measure of all things and deny the social uses of religion, as the professors of any science may deny the existence of any world of thought but their own, and refer all facts which meet them to it, so Mr. Milman, viewing Christianity as an external political fact, has gone very far indeed towards viewing it as nothing more; denying in one or two places, in so many words, the great truth, which we have been employed above in drawing out, that it is in two worlds at once, and that the same occurrences, persons, and actions seem to be natural

[214]

consequences of what is seen, and yet really have as natural a place in a system which is not seen. The effects of this denial upon Mr. Milman's history are now to be shown. We have candidly said where we think he is open to unfair misrepresentation; we shall as candidly say where we think he has given just cause of offence and dissatisfaction to all Churchmen.

Just one word, however, first on the author's evident inconsistency, unavoidable as it is under his circumstances, in professing to keep to fact, and yet insinuating a theory. He promised us in his Preface a political and social history—he disclaimed theology. Presently he deprecated polemics. Had we not otherwise been sure of the line he was taking, that protestation alone would have been equivalent, in our judgment, to a declaration of war. As liberals are the bitterest persecutors, so denouncers of controversy are sure to proceed upon the most startling, irritating, blistering methods which the practice of their age furnishes. We never knew of any one of them who set about charming and lulling the spirit of bigotry without joining "Conjuro te, scelestissima," to "good Mrs. Margaret Merrilies."[37] Further evidence how matters stood would have been afforded us, had we fallen upon his concluding pages, in which he tells us that a "clergyman who in a credulous or enthusiastic age dares to be rationally pious, is a *phenomenon of moral courage*."—Vol. iii., p. 535. These signs of conflict, before and after, have abundant accomplishment in the body of his work. It is quite impossible in the few pages which we are devoting to it (in which we think it best to confine ourselves

---

[37] *"Conjuro te, scelestissima," to "good Mrs. Margaret Merrilies."*: "I adjure you, O most infamous". In Walter Scott's *Guy Mannering* (1815), a schoolmaster addresses the gypsy, Meg Merrilies, with these words.

[215]   to one subject), to give an idea of the range and variety of
dogmatic thought and statement in which he has allowed
himself. To take a few instances which come first to
hand:—he tells us, for instance, that the millennium is a
"fable of Jewish dotage"—vol. i., p. 79, note; that "among
the vulgar there is a passionate attachment to religious
tyranny"—p. 292; that "a kind of latent Judaism has
constantly lurked within the bosom of the Church"—p. 456;
that "the sacerdotal and the sectarian spirit had an equal
tendency to disparage the 'perfection of piety' and
'sublimity of virtue'"—p. 457; that "sacerdotal domination
is altogether alien to genuine Christianity;" yet that "an
hostility to every kind of priesthood," is a sign of a
"vitiated" mind—pp. 10, 11, note; that "the sole difference"
in a church from a synagogue was, "that God was
worshipped in it through the mediation of the crucified
Jesus of Nazareth"—vol. ii., p. 2; that Christianity is
"grounded on the abrogation of all local claims to peculiar
sanctity"—vol. i., p. 319; that the Almighty's "pure and
essential spirituality" does not under the Gospel "attach
itself to, or exhibit itself under, any form"—p. 22; that "God
is power in the old religion, love under the new"—*ibid.*; that
"Christian morality" is, "strictly speaking, no law," but "the
establishment of certain principles"—p. 206; that St. Paul
"could scarcely be entirely dead to or ignorant" of the
"elevating associations" of Athens—vol. ii., p. 16; that the
age when Christ came was in an "advanced state of
intellectual culture"—vol. i., pp. 8, 36, and "enlightened"—
p. 41; and that, because of its "reasoning spirit"—p. 37,
Christianity has "accommodated itself to the spirit of
successive ages"—p. 47; that it "will advance with the
advancement of human nature," and that "intellectual

culture is that advancement"—p. 50; and that "the development of a rational and intellectual religion" is "perhaps not yet complete, certainly not general"—p. 49. [216]

These are some of the enunciations of doctrine, true or false, peremptorily advanced by Mr. Milman, and yet he tells us that he writes "as an historian rather than as a religious instructor"—he only does "not decline" theological subjects, writes "as if in total ignorance of the existence" of pending controversies, and "entirely discards all polemic views." Such is Mr. Milman's mode of keeping the peace; and he observes, we suppose, partly with reference to it, that "he himself fully appreciates the *difficulty*" of his undertaking.—P. 47. All this is so very strange, that we can only suppose that he considers it to be among the rights of philosophy to profess opinions without incurring their responsibilities, to have a sort of *lasciar passare*,[38] which enables it to introduce bag and baggage free of examination; or that it lives on some high cliff, or some remote watch-tower, and is able thence to contemplate with the poet the sea of human opinion, "alterius spectare laborem;"[39] and in a pure ethereal region to discern Christianity abstracted from all religion, and to gauge it without molestation by principles simply incommensurable with its own. But now to the business in hand.

7.

We will begin with citing a passage at the end of his volumes, in which he describes and condemns the peculiar religious sentiments of the Middle Age, sentiments which

---

[38] *lasciar passare:* allow to pass (Italian)
[39] *"alterius spectare laborem"*: "to watch the labour of another", Lucretius, *De Rerum Natura*, Bk 2, line 2.

are in fact based upon the very principles which we have above advocated as primitive and true. In doing this, we are fair to Mr. Milman, for it is beautifully written.

[217]   "The Christian of these days lived in a supernatural world, or in a world under the constant and felt and discernible interference of supernatural power. God was not only present, but asserting His presence at every instant, not merely on signal occasions and for important purposes, but on the most insignificant acts and persons. The course of nature was beheld, not as one great uniform and majestic miracle, but a succession of small, insulated, sometimes trivial, sometimes contradictory interpositions, often utterly inconsistent with the moral and Christian attributes of God. The divine power and goodness were not spreading abroad like a genial and equable sunlight, enlightening, cheering, vivifying, but breaking out in partial and visible flashes of influence; each incident was a special miracle, the ordinary emotion of the heart was divine inspiration. Each individual had not merely his portion in the common diffusion of religious and moral knowledge or feeling, but looked for his peculiar and especial share in the divine blessing. His dreams came direct from heaven; a new system of Christian omens succeeded the old; witchcraft merely invoked Beelzebub or Satan instead of Hecate;[40] hallowed places only changed their tutelary nymph or genius for a saint or martyr ... God had been brought down, or had condescended to mingle himself with the affairs of men. But where should that faith, which could not but receive these high and consolatory and reasonable truths, set limits to the agency of this beneficent power? How should it discriminate between that which in its apparent discrepancy with the laws of nature (and of those laws how little was known!) was miraculous, and that which, to more accurate observation, was only strange or wonderful, or perhaps the result of ordinary but dimly-seen causes? How still more in the mysterious world of the human mind, of which the laws are

---

[40] *Hecate*: the goddess of magic and ghosts in Greek mythology

258

still, we will not say in their primitive, but, in comparison with those of external nature, in profound obscurity? If the understanding of man was too much dazzled to see clearly even material objects; if just awakening from a deep trance, it beheld everything floating before it in a mist of wonder, how much more was the mind disqualified to judge of its own emotions, of the origin, suggestion, and powers of those thoughts and emotions which still perplex and baffle our deepest metaphysics."—Vol. iii., pp. 532-534.

No one can deny that this is a very eloquent and striking passage, and, to complete our admissions, we must candidly add that it is a view of the medieval religion in which a [218] number of persons, not friends of Mr. Milman, will concur, and which others again, with greater reason, will consider partly true, and partly false:—now let us see what comes of it, as Mr. Milman uses it.

For instance, two kinds of miracles are recorded in Scripture, public and sensible[41], and private;—those which many saw, and which had for their object something material; and those which one person or no one saw, or which belonged to the world of spirits. Our Saviour's cures, which were subjected to the scrutiny of the senses, are instances of the former class; the Annunciation and Transfiguration, of the latter. The former form part of the evidences, the latter of the matter or mode of Revelation. The former are facts of this world, and have their place in the political course of things, as fully as facts which are not miraculous; the latter have no such place, but belong solely to the spiritual system. Now Mr. Milman inclines, to say the least, to deny the reality of the latter. Speaking of "the more imaginative incidents of the early Evangelic History" (by

---

[41] *sensible*: i.e. accessible to the senses of sight, sound etc.

which he especially means "the angelic appearances, the revelations of the Deity addressed to the senses of man," in the first chapters of St. Matthew and St. Luke), he observes that "these passages in general are not the vital and essential truths of Christianity, but the *vehicle* by which these truths were communicated, a *kind of language* by which opinions were conveyed, and sentiments infused, and the general belief in Christianity implanted, confirmed, and strengthened."—Vol. i., p. 130. He continues:

"Whether then these were actual appearances, or *impressions* produced on the mind of those who witnessed them, is *of slight importance*. In either case they are real historical facts; they partake of poetry in their form, and, in a certain sense, in their groundwork; but they are imaginative, not fictitious; true as relating that which appeared to the minds of the relators exactly as it did appear ... The incidents were so ordered that they should thus live in the thoughts of men ... Could, it may be inquired, a purely rational or metaphysical creed have survived for any length of time during such stages of human civilization?"

[219]

That is, he considers, that when St. Luke says, "In the sixth month the Angel Gabriel was *sent* from God to a Virgin," etc., first, that there are reasons *for* the Blessed Virgin's having an *impression* that there was an Angel Gabriel, and that he was sent to her; and, secondly, that there are reasons *against* the occurrence being a real fact external to her mind. That she should think she saw an Angel, is important, he observes, because a religion with such poetical incidents is more influential and long-lived than one that has them not. Well, then, if so, why should not the incidents have really been vouchsafed? has Almighty God no Angels? why should He not have done what He is said to have done, since there is so good a reason for His doing it? Mr. Milman proceeds to give us the reason on the other side, "the purely rational and metaphysical" reason; viz., that according to a certain class of writers, (followers of Hume and Bentham[42] we suppose,) "these incidents, being *irreconcilable with our actual experience*, and rendered suspicious by a multitude of later fictions, which are rejected in the mass by most Protestant Christians, cannot accord with the *more subtle and fastidious intelligence* of the present times. Some writers go so far as to assert that it is *impossible* that an inquiring and reasoning age should receive these supernatural facts as historical verities."—P. 130. And for the sake of these persons Mr. Milman proposes an intermediate view, as a sort of irenicon or peace-offering, to reconcile the faith of eighteen centuries and the infidelity of the nineteenth; on the one hand suggesting that St. Mary's *imagination* may have been deceived, or that her *"reminiscences"* were dim and indistinct, and, on the other, defending her *veracity* and that of her contemporaries. The circumstances recorded "are too slight," he says, "and wanting in particularity, to give the idea of *invention*; they seem like a few scattered fragments preserved from oral tradition."—P. 132. On the whole, then, it seems that Mr. Milman inclines to think that God will never do anything which to philosophers is difficult to receive, and that the Blessed Virgin is more likely to have been mistaken than unbelievers to be irrational.

[220]

---

[42] *followers of Hume and Bentham* David Hume (1711-1776) was an economist and historian, author of *Treatise on Human Nature* (1739-40). "Mere reason is insufficient to convince us of the veracity of religion." (Newman *US* p.251). Jeremy Bentham (1748- 1832) was an economist, lawyer and Utilitarian, "Mr Bentham would answer, that the knowledge which carries virtue along with it, is the knowledge how to take care of number one." *DA* p.262. Newman would say 'Rationalism is the exercise of reason instead of faith in matters of faith.' *Dev.* p. 191.

Again, he thus glances at the true explanation of the Angel's appearance to Zacharias:—

"Almost the most important [function of the officiating course] was the watching and supplying with incense the great brazen altar, which stood within the building of the temple, in the first or Holy Place. Into this, at the sound of a small bell, which gave notice to the worshippers at a distance, the ministering priest entered alone; and in the sacred chamber, *into which the light of day never penetrated*, but where the *dim fires* of the altar, and the chandeliers which were never extinguished, gave a *solemn and uncertain light, still more bedimmed by the clouds of smoke* arising from the newly fed altar of incense, *no doubt* (!), in the *pious* mind, the sense of the more immediate presence of the Deity, only separated by the veil, which divided the Holy Place from the Holy of Holies, would constantly have awakened *the most profound* emotions ... *In the vision* of Zachariah, he had beheld an Angel standing on the right side of the altar," etc.—Vol. i., pp. 90, 91.

Again, of the miracle attendant on our Lord's Baptism, Mr. Milman says, "Neander[43] represents it as a symbolic vision."—P. 151. And he refers to the passages of the Fathers, not happily, as we think, to show that the [221] "explanation of voices from heaven, as a mental perception, not as real articulate sounds, but as inward impressions, is by no means modern, or what passes under the unpopular name of Rationalism." Possibly not; but let us for argument's sake grant it; yet what do we gain by such a view of the subject? this,—we tend to rid ourselves of the unseen world, of the belief that the things which we see have relations to, and are parts of, a system of things which

---

[43] *Neander*: Johann Neander (1789-1850), German protestant historian and theologian.

ordinarily does not disclose itself to us. This does not seem to be any great achievement.[44]

Again, when Mr. Milman comes to our Lord's Temptation, after an announcement, with much circumstance but obvious drift, that "on the interpretation of no incident in the Gospels do those who insist on the literal acceptation of the Evangelists' language, and those who consider that even in the New Testament much allowance is to be made for the essentially allegoric character of oriental narrative, depart so far asunder," he adds, in a note, "this is one of those points which will be differently understood according to the turn and cast of mind of different individuals. I would therefore *deprecate* the making either interpretation an article of faith, or deciding with dogmatic certainty on so *perplexing* a passage."—P. 153. Afterwards he says, that whether we believe Christ tempted by Satan, or by the High Priest, or by His own feelings, "the *moral purport* of the scene remains the same, the intimation that the strongest and most lively *impressions* were made upon the mind of Jesus to withdraw Him," etc.—P. 156. Here is a writer admitting, without "perplexity," the great invisible miracle that the Son of God took on Him a human soul and body, yet finding a difficulty in receiving literally the narrative of His being tempted in that body and soul by the [222]

---

[44] Mr. Milman says of the pool of Bethesda, that it "was *supposed* to possess remarkable properties for healing diseases. At certain periods there was a strong commotion in the waters, which probably bubbled up from some chemical cause connected with their medicinal effects. *Popular belief*, or *rather perhaps popular language*, attributed this agitation of the surface to the descent of an Angel."— Vol. i., p. 215. On the other hand, the Evangelist says expressly, "an Angel *went down* at a certain season into the pool." Mr. Milman adds in a note, that "the verse relating to the Angel is rejected as spurious by many critics, and is wanting in some manuscripts." *That* is a fair argument against it: if the verse cannot be supported on external evidence, let it be rejected; but let it not be kept, and explained away on a theory. [N]

Evil One in person, and "*deprecating*" the necessity of doing so.

The principles, which the above extracts have been illustrating, make it impossible for Mr. Milman to believe in the reality of demoniacal possession. All the phenomena which demoniacs exhibit can be referred to the laws of pathology; *therefore* they cannot *also* have relation to an unseen state of things, and be caused by evil spirits. He says,

"I have no scruple in avowing my opinion on the subject of the demoniacs to be that of Joseph Mede,[45] Lardner,[46] Dr. Mead,[47] Paley, and all the learned modern writers. It was a kind of insanity, not unlikely to be prevalent among a people peculiarly subject to the leprosy and other cutaneous[48] diseases; and nothing was more probable than that lunacy should take the turn and speak the language of the prevailing *superstition* of the times. As the belief in witchcraft made people fancy themselves witches, so the belief in possession made men of distempered minds fancy themselves possessed."—Vol. i. p. 234, note.

None of us can go a little way with a theory; when it once possesses us, we are no longer our own masters. It makes us speak its words, and do violence to our own nature. Would it be believed that Mr. Milman's zeal against the reality of possessions as a preternatural phenomenon, [223] actually carries him on here to the denial of external and

---

[45] *Joseph Mede*: (1586-1639) biblical scholar.

[46] *Lardner*: Nathaniel Lardner (1684-1768), nonconformist minister who wrote *The Credibility of the Gospel History; or the Principal Facts of the New Testament confirmed by Passages of Ancient Authors, who were contemporary with our Saviour or his Apostles, or lived near their time* (Part 1, 1727; Part 2, 1733-55). (1727-1757).

[47] *Dr. Mead*: Richard Mead (c,1673-1754), doctor, author *Medica Sacra, A Commentary on the Most Remarkable Diseases Mentioned in the Holy Scriptures*.

[48] *cutaneous*: of the skin

visible fact, which is the very basis on which he has rested his opinion that they were not preternatural? It is obvious that the miracle of the swine[49] interferes with his theory; accordingly he hints at an explanation, which seriously compromises the outward historical fact attendant upon the miracle; that is, first he denies demoniacal possession, *because* the recorded phenomena of its visitation *upon man* do not necessarily involve its reality; next he denies the recorded phenomena of its visitation *on the swine*, which do involve its reality, *because* there is no such thing as demoniacal possession. How too does this hold with what he assures us elsewhere, that his doubts about invisible or private miracles would not entrench upon sensible or public ones? He told us, that such doubting, "of *course*, does not apply to *facts* which must have been either historical events or direct fictions," such as the Resurrection of Jesus.—Vol. i., p.131. And he promised that he would "*strictly maintain* this important distinction" between them and "the more imaginative incidents of the history." Now for the performance of his engagement.

"The moral difficulty of this transaction has always appeared to me greater than that of reconciling it with the more rational view of demoniacism. Both are much diminished, if not entirely removed, by the theory of Kuinoël,[50] who attributes to the *lunatics* the *whole* of the conversation with Jesus, and supposes that *their* driving the herd of swine down the precipice was the *last* paroxysm in which their insanity exhausted itself."—P. 238, note.

Would it be a much greater violence to the history than this, to say, with some unbelievers, that our Lord was taken

---

[49] *miracle of the swine*: Cf. Mark 5:11 and parallels.
[50] *Kuinoël: Christian* Kühnöl (1768-1841), German Protestant theologian, author of *Commentarius in Libros Novi Testamenti Histcoricos.*

down from the Cross alive, and showed Himself again without a Resurrection? For after all, as Mr. Milman said just now, would not "the *moral purport* of the scene remain [224] the same?" What limits are we to put to this denial of historical truth? Where is theory to stop, if it is once allowed?

Again, we read in the Acts a narrative of an *evil spirit* answering, "Jesus, I know,"[51] etc., but Mr. Milman paraphrases it to the effect that the possessed party "had probably before been *strongly impressed* with the teaching of Paul, and the religion which he preached; and *irritated* by the interference of persons whom he might know to be hostile to the Christian party, *assaulted them with great violence*," etc.—vol. ii., p. 28; that is, what Scripture calls an evil spirit, he calls a Christian convert. How long will this interpretation stand? How many will receive it? Will Mr. Milman himself this time next year?

8.

Now let us proceed to some further, though hardly more violent practisings, upon the Christian documents and facts, which these volumes exhibit. The following is curious as a *reductio ad absurdum* of Mr. Milman's *beau ideal* of the Christian temper. He observes that James and John, who "received the remarkable name of Boanerges, the Sons of Thunder[52] ... do not appear remarkable among their brethren either for energy or vehemence:" and he adds, that accordingly "it is not easy to trace" its "exact force;" and that "the peculiar *gentleness* of" St. John "both in character and in the style of his writings, *would lead us to doubt* the

---

[51] *"Jesus, I know,"* etc: Acts 19:15
[52] *Boanerges, the Sons of Thunder*: Cf. Mark 3:17

correctness of the interpretation generally assigned to the appellation."—Vol. i., p. 225. Strange to say, his only idea of St. John's, as of our Lord's character, as seen in Scripture, is *gentleness*; and then, strong in this most gratuitous assumption, he finds a *difficulty* in the received interpretation of a plain passage.

In the same way, in another place, he "would *reject*, as the offspring of a *more angry and controversial age*, the story of St. John's "flying in fear and indignation from a bath polluted by the presence of the heretic Cerinthus."[53]— Vol. ii., p. 62. Did not our author recollect certain "angry and controversial" words ascribed to St. John in Scripture? "If there come any unto you and bring not this doctrine, *receive him not into your house, neither bid him Godspeed*."[54] [225]

Striking too is the contrast between the clear, keen, majestic, and awful language of the Evangelists and Mr. Milman's circuitous, inadequate, and (we must add) feeble version of it. St. Luke says of Herod, "immediately the Angel of the Lord *smote* him, *because* he gave not God the glory;"[55] Mr. Milman explains away both the fact and the reason. "In [the] terrific and repulsive circumstances" of his death, he says, "the Christians *could not but behold* the hand of their protecting God,"—vol. i., p. 410; whereas the

---

[53] *a bath polluted by the presence of the heretic Cerinthus*: Cerinthus was a first century heretic of the Gnostic-Ebionite school, who believed that Jesus only became 'the Christ' at the moment of his baptism in the Jordan. St John may have written his first two Epistles as a response to his heretical teachings. According to St Irenæus, the Apostle once fled the baths when he realised that Cerinthus was also there (*Adv. Hær.*, III.3.4).
[54] *"If there come any unto you and bring not this doctrine, receive him not into your house, neither bid him Godspeed"*: 2 John 1:10
[55] *"immediately the Angel of the Lord smote him, because he gave not God his glory"*: Acts 12:23

remarkable thing is that it is not represented in Scripture as an interposition in behalf of the Church at all.

Again, "Whosoever sinneth against the Holy Ghost, it shall not be forgiven him, neither in this world, nor in the world to come,"[56] is turned into "an offence which argued such total obtuseness of moral perception, such utter incapacity of feeling or comprehending the beauty either of the conduct or the doctrine of Jesus, as *to leave no hope that they would ever be reclaimed* from their rancorous hostility to His religion, or be *qualified* for admission into the pale and to the benefits of the new faith."—Vol. i., p. 235. Forgiveness of sins, the one subject of our Lord's announcement in this passage, is literally obliterated from it by Mr. Milman;—whence this strange aversion to mention sin and the forgiveness of sin?

[226]

Again: of the passage which speaks of "the unclean spirit going out of a man,"[57] etc., he observes that Christ "reverts *in language of more than usual energy*," (that is, *not* "gentle" language, we presume,) "to the *incapacity* of the age and nation to discern the real and intrinsic superiority of His religion."—P. 236.

In our Lord's slowly granting the request of the Syrophœnician, who wished for the crumbs that were the dog's portion, with the words, "O woman, *great is thy faith*,"[58] Mr. Milman discerns but a *condescension* to the prejudices of the Jews and His Apostles, by which "Jesus was enabled to display His own benevolence without awakening, or confirming if already awakened, the quick suspicion of His followers."—P. 253.

---

[56] *"Whosoever sinneth against the Holy Ghost ... ":* Luke 12:10; Matthew 12:32

[57] *"the unclean spirit going out of a man,":* e.g. Matthew 12:43

[58] *"O woman, great is thy faith":* Matthew 15:28

In the same spirit he elsewhere observes that the Apostles, "with *cautious deference to Jewish feeling*, were forbidded to proceed beyond the borders of the Holy Land."[59]—P. 238. The words, "Ye are of your father the devil," (words which Mr. Milman apparently feels to be inconsistent with what he considers our Lord's "gentleness,") become "the spirit of evil, in whose darkest and most bloody temper they were ready to act, was *rather* the parent of men with dispositions so diabolic."—P. 268.

The discourse in the Synagogue of Capernaum, after the miracle of the loaves, related by St. John, ch. vi., is explained to mean merely "the *improvement* of the moral and spiritual condition of man, described under the *strong but not unusual* figure of nourishment administered to the soul."—P. 243. How can an earnest mind, contemplating our Lord's most mysterious words, thus satisfy itself? Further, Mr. Milman tells us that in the rite of the Lord's Supper there really are "*allusions* to the breaking of His body and for the pouring forth of His blood."—P. 329.

He says respecting the incident in John xii., that what "the unbelieving part of the multitude heard only as an accidental burst of thunder, to others ... *seemed* an *audible*, a *distinct*,—or, according to those who adhere to the strict letter,—the"—(it avails not to delay, out with it!)—"the *articulate* voice of an Angel."—P. 306. Yes, the real articulate voice; how painful to our "subtle and fastidious intelligence"! [227]

As to the power of binding and loosing, promised first to St. Peter, then to all the Apostles, then afterwards bestowed, the subject is too formidable, we suppose, to approach *siccis*

---

[59] *"Ye are of your father the devil"*: John 8:44

oculis.[60] Mr. Milman thus hurries by: "the Apostle" St. Peter, "is commended in language so strong *that* the *pre-eminence* of Peter over the rest of the Twelve has been mainly supported by the words of Jesus *employed* on this occasion."—P. 256. What? do these memorable words, in substance thrice uttered, only account for a certain interpretation of them? do they determine but a relative question? do they decide nothing at all positive about *all* the Apostles?

It is quite perplexing what satisfaction a man of Mr. Milman's religious character can have in explaining away the supernatural accompaniments of our Lord's last conflict; and yet he certainly does seem to think it even more philosophical to make the Resurrection an isolated miracle. "This spake he," says the Evangelist, of Caiaphas, "not of himself, but being high priest that year, he *prophesied*:"[61] "his language," says Mr. Milman, "was afterwards *treasured* in the memory of the Christians *as inadvertently* prophetic."—P. 286. He says that Pilate's wife's dream was in "her morning slumbers, when visions *were supposed* to be more than ordinarily true."—P. 355. The impenitent thief is "infected" with a "fanatical Judaism;" his companion is "of *milder* disposition;" and "*inclines* to believe in Jesus," who, "*speaking in the current language*, promises him an immediate reward."—P. 361. As to the resurrection of "many *bodies* of the saints that slept," Mr. Milman is of opinion that the earthquake opened the tombs and *exposed* the dead to public view. He adds, "To *the awestruck and*

[228]

---

[60] *siccis oculis*: 'dry eyes', a reference to one of Horace's *Odes* (1: 3): *qui siccis oculis monstra natantia qui vidit mare turgidum* – 'He who sees with his own dry eyes the monster swimming, sees a wave-tossed sea'.
[61] *"This spake he not of himself, but being high priest that year, he prophesied"*: John 11:51

depressed minds of the followers of Jesus, *no doubt*, were confined those visionary appearances of the *spirits* of their deceased brethren, which are *obscurely intimated* in the *rapid* narratives of the Evangelists."—P. 365. What antecedent objection does the "intelligence" of this age find to the resurrection of the bodies of these saints which will not apply also to the resurrection at the last day? They must rise some time; why should they not have risen then? because, Mr. Milman seems to answer, there is no system going on in the world now, except the visible, political, temporal system which our eyes and ears experience. Again: to the minds of the women he says "*highly excited* and *bewildered* with astonishment, with terror, and with grief, appeared *what is described* by the Evangelist as a 'vision of angels.'[62] One or more beings in human form seated in the *shadowy twilight* within the sepulchre."—P. 378.

One circumstance, however, we cheerfully acknowledge,—that Mr. Milman does not, with some writers of latter times, in violence to our Lord's words, explain away the guilt, or what he calls "the extraordinary conduct," of Judas. He candidly says, "Much ingenuity has been displayed by some recent writers in attempting to palliate, or rather account for, this extraordinary conduct of Judas; but the language in which Jesus spoke of the crime *appears to confirm* the common opinion of its enormity."— P. 326. As to his remorse, he considers that there were quite circumstances enough to "drive him to desperation, *little short of insanity*."—P. 329. This, we suppose, is to show

---

[62] *'vision of angels'*: Luke 24:23

that he need not have a verdict of *felo de se*[63] recorded against him.

[229]

9.

We have now seen how Mr. Milman's theory operates upon the facts and documents of Christianity; now let us observe what it does for its fundamental and essential doctrines, which, even without taking it into account, have, as we have already seen, fared very hardly from his mere negative method of historical composition. In doing this, however, we do not make Mr. Milman responsible for our account of his views. Principles have a life and power independent of their authors, and make their way in spite of them;—this at least is our philosophy. Mr. Milman may in his own instance limit or modify what nevertheless has its mission, and, whether he like it or not, will be sure to tell its tale to an end, before it has done. By others, then, it must be viewed, not shackled, and as it were muzzled, according to any careful directions which this or that writer may deliver, but in itself. We are sure that Mr. Milman does not see the tendency of the line of thought of which both his present and a former work[64] give such anxious evidence; and therefore, while we need not, we clearly could not, if we tried, delineate the principles which are contained in them, as they are held by himself personally;—he would be sure to say we were unfair. The very inconsistency which, in a former place, we pointed out, between the design and the execution of his work, is an intelligible warning to us what a false position we should be taking up, if we were to attempt to draw out for ourselves his doctrinal notion of Christianity. We disclaim such an intention altogether. No

---

[63] felo de se: suicide
[64] *a former work*: Milman's *History of the Jews* (1829)

writer likes to accept his opinions in the wording of an opponent. We shall use Mr. Milman's volumes, therefore, only in illustration of those momentous principles, which he has adopted indeed, but which are outside of him, and will not be his slaves.

As regards then the settlement of Christian doctrine, Mr. [230] Milman's External Theory seems to us to result or manifest itself in the following canon:—That nothing belongs to the Gospel but what originated in it; and that whatever, professing to belong to it, is found in anterior or collateral systems, may be put out of it as a foreign element. Such a maxim easily follows upon that denial of the supernatural system, which we have above imputed in large measure to Mr. Milman. They who consider with him that there was, for instance, no spiritual agency in what is called demoniacal possession, on the ground that the facts of the case may be satisfactorily referred to physical causes, are bound, or at least are easily persuaded, to deny for the same reason any doctrine to come from Christ, which they can trace to the schools of men. Such persons cannot enter into the possibility of a visible and an invisible course of things going on at once, whether co-extensive or not, acting on each other more or less, and sometimes even to the cognizance of our senses. Were the electric fluid ascertained to be adequate to the phenomena of life, they would think it bad philosophy to believe in the presence of a soul; and, sooner than believe that Angels now minister to us unseen, they deny that they were ever seen in their ministrations. No wonder then that in like manner as regards the articles of the Creed, they deny that what is historically human can be doctrinally divine, confuse the outward process with the secret providence, and argue as if instruments in nature preclude the operations of grace. When they once arrive at a cause or source in the secular course of things, it is enough; and thus, while Angels melt into impressions, Catholic truths are resolved into the dogmas of Plato or Zoroaster.

[231]   A theory does not prove itself; it makes itself probable so far as it falls in with our preconceived notions, as it accounts for the phenomena it treats of, as it is internally consistent, and as it excels or excludes rival theories. We should leave Mr. Milman's undisturbed, and proceed at once, as we proposed, merely to give instances of its operation, except that it might seem to be allowing to that theory, as it were, possession of the field, when, in truth, there is another far more Catholic philosophy upon which the facts of the case, as Mr. Milman states them, may be solved. Now, the phenomenon, admitted on all hands, is this:[65]—that great portion of what is generally received as Christian truth, is in its rudiments or in its separate parts to be found in heathen philosophies and religions. For instance, the doctrine of a Trinity is found both in the East and in the West; so is the ceremony of washing; so is the rite of sacrifice. The doctrine of the Divine Word is Platonic; the doctrine of the Incarnation is Indian; of a divine kingdom is Judaic; of Angels and demons is Magian; the connexion of sin with the body is Gnostic; celibacy is known to Bonze and Talapoin; a sacerdotal order is Egyptian; the idea of a new birth is Chinese and Eleusinian[66]; belief in sacramental virtue is Pythagorean;[67]

---

[65] *Now the phenomenon admitted on all hands ...* : Newman quoted the whole of the paragraphs from this point to the end of section 9, p.[234], in his 1878 edition of *An Essay on the Development of Christian Doctrine*, pp.380-382.

[66] *Eleusinian*: the mystery cult of Demeter and Persephone, celebrated at Eleusis in Greece

and honours to the dead are a polytheism. Such is the general nature of the fact before us; Mr. Milman argues from it,—"These things are in heathenism, therefore they are not Christian:" we, on the contrary, prefer to say, "these things are in Christianity, therefore they are not heathen." That is, we prefer to say, and we think that Scripture bears us out in saying, that from the beginning the Moral Governor of the world has scattered the seeds of truth far and wide over its extent; that these have variously taken root, and grown up as in the wilderness, wild plants indeed but living; and hence that, as the inferior animals have tokens of an immaterial principle in them, yet have not [232] souls, so the philosophies and religions of men have their life in certain true ideas, though they are not directly divine. What man is amid the brute creation, such is the Church among the schools of the world; and as Adam gave names to the animals about him, so has the Church from the first looked round upon the earth, noting and visiting the doctrines she found there. She began in Chaldea, and then sojourned among the Canaanites, and went down into Egypt, and thence passed into Arabia, till she rested in her own land. Next she encountered the merchants of Tyre, and the wisdom of the East country, and the luxury of Sheba. Then she was carried away to Babylon, and wandered to the schools of Greece. And wherever she went, in trouble or in triumph, still she was a living spirit, the mind and voice of the Most High; "sitting in the midst of the doctors, both hearing them and asking them questions;"[68] claiming to

---

[67] *Pythagorean*: the cult founded on the teaching of the philosopher and mathematician Pythagoras in the 6th century BC. It eventually became a mystery cult.
[68] *"sitting in the midst of the doctors ... "*: Luke 2:46

herself what they said rightly, correcting their errors, supplying their defects, completing their beginnings, expanding their surmises, and thus gradually by means of them enlarging the range and refining the sense of her own teaching. So far then from her creed being of doubtful credit because it resembles foreign theologies, we even hold that one special way in which Providence has imparted divine knowledge to us has been by enabling her to draw and collect it together out of the world, and, in this sense, as in others, to suck the milk of the Gentiles and to suck the breast of kings.[69]

How far in fact this process has gone, is a question of history; and we believe it has before now been grossly exaggerated and misrepresented by those who, like Mr. Milman, have thought that its existence told against [233] Catholic doctrine; but so little antecedent difficulty have we in the matter, that we could readily grant, unless it were a question of fact not of theory, that Balaam[70] was an Eastern sage, or a Sibyl[71] was inspired, or Solomon learnt of the sons of Mahol,[72] or Moses was a scholar of the Egyptian hierophants[73]. We are not distressed to be told that the doctrine of the angelic host came from Babylon, while we

---

[69] *suck the milk of the Gentiles and to suck the breast of kings*: Cf. Is 60:16

[70] *Balaam*: the non-Israelite prophet who, after an incident in which his donkey is miraculously given the power of speech, pronounces various blessings on Israel (cf. Numbers 22ff.) but who later entices the Israelites into evil behaviour (cf. Numbers 31:16); in the New Testament he is seen as evil (cf. 2 Peter:15, Jude 1:11, Revelation 2:14).

[71] *a Sibyl*: Sibyls were pagan priestesses who spoke oracles in the religion of ancient Greece, In Virgil's fourth *Eclogue* the Cumæan Sibyl prophesies a future saviour, intended by Virgil to refer to Augustus Cæsar but interpreted by some Christian writers as a reference to Christ which is presumably what Newman is implying here.

[72] *the sons of Mahol*: Cf. 1 Kings 4:31: "For he [Solomon] was wiser than all men, than Ethan the Ezrahite, and Heman and Chalcol, and Darda, the sons of Mahol."

[73] *hierophants*: priests

know that they did sing at the Nativity; nor that the vision of a Mediator is in Philo,[74] if in very deed He died for us on Calvary. Nor are we afraid to allow, that, even after His coming, the Church has been a treasure-house, giving forth things old and new, casting the gold of fresh tributaries into her refiner's fire, or stamping upon her own, as time required it, a deeper impress of her Master's image.

The distinction between these two theories is broad and obvious. The advocates of the one imply that Revelation was a single, entire, solitary act, or nearly so, introducing a certain message; whereas we, who maintain the other, consider that Divine teaching has been in fact, what the analogy of nature would lead us to expect, "at sundry times and in divers manners,"[75] various, complex, progressive, and supplemental of itself. We consider the Christian doctrine, when analyzed, to appear, like the human frame, "fearfully and wonderfully made;"[76] but they think it some one tenet or certain principles given out at one time in their fulness, without gradual enlargement before Christ's coming or elucidation afterwards. They cast off all that they also find in Pharisee or heathen; we conceive that the Church, like Aaron's rod, devours the serpents of the magicians.[77] They are ever hunting for a fabulous primitive simplicity; we repose in Catholic fulness. They seek what never has been found; we accept and use what even they acknowledge to be a substance. They are driven to maintain, on their part, that the Church's doctrine was never pure; we say that it never [234]

---

[74] *the vision of a Mediator is in Philo*: Philo of Alexandria (c.20 BC – c.50 AD), Hellenistic Jewish philosopher; he taught that the world was created through a mediator, the Logos.

[75] *"at sundry times and in divers manners,"*: Hebrews 1:1

[76] *"fearfully and wonderfully made;"*: Psalm 139:14

[77] *like Aaron's rod ...*: Cf. Exodus 7:12

can be corrupt. We consider that a divine promise keeps the Church Catholic from doctrinal corruption; but on what promise, or on what encouragement, they are seeking for their visionary purity does not appear.

10.

Which of these theories is the true, this is not the place for discussing; our business here, to which we now address ourselves, is to trace out some of the applications of the one on which Mr. Milman proceeds, as his volumes enable us to do, and to inquire *how much* will be left of Christianity at the end of the process. He states then, that in her first ages the Church separately *encountered* Judaism, Orientalism, and Paganism, and again, that her system *resembles* all three. From the encounter, he would argue the *probability* of their influencing her; from the resemblance the *fact*. He says:

"As a universal religion aspiring to the complete moral conquest of the world, Christianity had to encounter three antagonists, Judaism, Paganism, and Orientalism. It is our design successively to exhibit the conflict with these opposing forces, its final triumph, *not without detriment to its own native purity and its divine simplicity*, from the interworking of the yet unsubdued elements of the former systems into the Christian mind; until each, at successive periods, and in different parts of the world, formed a *modification* of Christianity equally removed from its unmingled and unsullied original; the Judæo-Christianity of Palestine, of which the Ebionites[78] appear to have been the last representatives; the Platonic Christianity of Alexandria, as, at least at this early period, the new religion could coalesce only

---

[78] *Ebionites:* a Jewish-Christian sect which insisted that the Jewish law must still be observed and who may have denied the divinity of Christ

with the sublime and more philosophical principles of Paganism; and, lastly, the Gnostic Christianity of the East."—Vol. i., p. 413.

In like manner he speaks elsewhere of an "*inveterate* [235] Judaism," which "has perpetually revived in the Christian Church in days of excitement."—P. 148. "The Grecian philosophy," he says, "and, at a later period, influences still more adverse to that of Judaism, *mingled* with the prevailing Christianity. A kind of latent Judaism has, however, constantly *lurked* within the bosom of the Church."—P. 456. Again, "Asiatic influences have *worked* more completely *into the body and essence* of Christianity than any other foreign elements."—Vol. ii., p. 82. Such, we say, is the theory; now to apply it.

To begin with the hierarchy of Angels, to which we have already referred. Speaking of Simon Magus's[79] doctrine on that subject, Mr. Milman says:

"This peopling of the universe with a regular descending succession of beings was *common to the whole East*, perhaps in great part to the West. The later Jewish doctrines of angels and devils *approached nearly to it*; it *lurked* in Platonism, and assumed a higher form in the Eastern cosmogonies."—Vol. ii., p. 101.

And more strongly in an earlier passage:

"It is generally admitted that the Jewish notions about the angels, one great subject of dispute in their synagogues, and what may be called their demonology, received a *strong foreign tinge* during their residence in Babylonia ... In apparent allusion to or coincidence with this system, the visions of Daniel *represent* Michael, the titular angel or intelligence of the Jewish people, in

---

[79] *Simon Magus*: the magician who became a Christian but later tried to buy the gift of the Holy Spirit from Peter, cf. Acts 14-24. In later writers he was seen as the founder of a Gnostic sect.

opposition to the four angels of the great monarchies; and *even* our Saviour *seems to condescend to the popular language* when He represents the parental care of the Almighty over children under the significant and beautiful image, 'for in heaven,'" etc.— Vol. i., p. 70.

[236]

It seems, then, the angelic hierarchy is not a doctrine of divine truth, because it was taught in the Zendavesta; and further, what is still more observable, even our Lord's teaching it does not make it so. This illustrates forcibly the view given above of Mr. Milman's canon for ascertaining what is matter of Revelation. Our Lord cannot say a thing in earnest, which heathen sages taught or surmised before Him.

Next, Mr. Milman tells us that "the Jew *concurred* with the worshipper of Ormusd[80] in expecting a *final restoration of all things* through the agency of a Divine Intelligence."— Vol. i., p. 77. The words of St. Peter might come into the reader's mind, about the time of refreshing, when "He shall send Jesus Christ, whom the heavens must receive until the *times of restitution of all things*;"[81] but Mr. Milman overturns the authority of the whole passage, observing that it seems "as if even yet Peter himself was not *disencumbered of that Jewish notion* of an immediate re-appearance of Christ."—Vol. i., p. 391. "The disciple is not better than his Lord;"[82] if not Christ's, much less are St. Peter's words, though spoken after a miracle, matter of Divine Revelation, provided they betray any resemblance to a doctrine of Zoroaster.

---

[80] *Ormusd*: In Zoroastrianism, Ormusd is Ahura Mazda, the creator of Gayomart, challenged by Angra Mainyu.

[81] *"He shall send Jesus Christ, whom the heavens must receive until the times of restitution of all things"*: Acts 3:20.

[82] *"The disciple is not better than his Lord"*: Matthew 10:24

Speaking of the Resurrection, he says, "It appears ... in its more perfect development, soon after the return from the captivity. As early as the revolt of the Maccabees, it was so deeply rooted in the public mind, that we find a solemn ceremony performed for the dead ... In the Zoroastrian religion, a resurrection holds a *place no less prominent* than in the later Jewish belief."—Vol. i., p. 75. In spite of this, Mr. Milman of course insists, though we see not with what consistency, on the doctrine of the Resurrection as proper to Christianity; however, soon after the above passages, speaking of the "Oriental colouring" which the Jews adopted, he says, "even the doctrine of the Resurrection was singularly harmonized with their exclusive nationality. At least the *first Resurrection* was to be their separate portion; it was to summon them, if not all, at least the more righteous, from Paradise, from the abode of departed spirits; and under their triumphant king they were to enjoy a *thousand years* of glory and bliss upon the recreated and renovated earth."—P. 78. Is not this "colouring," as Mr. Milman calls it, very like St. John's language in the Apocalypse? Is that language to fare as the words of our Lord and St. Peter? or is it, on the other hand, to be considered as Eastern tradition which is appropriated and guaranteed by St. John?

[237]

But there are instances in which Mr. Milman recoils from his own theory. For example, he tells us, that "the practice of the external washing of the body, as emblematic of the inward purification of the soul, is *almost universal.* The sacred Ganges cleanses all moral pollution from the Indian; among the Greeks and Romans, even the murderer might, it was supposed, *wash the blood clean from his hands* ... The perpetual similitude and connexion between the uncleanness of the body and of the soul, which run through the Mosaic law ... must *have familiarized the mind* with the mysterious effects attributed to such a rite."—P. 142. True; but then why might not Orientalism in like manner "familiarize" the mind with the *religious observance* of celibacy, instead of throwing discredit on its divine authority?

Again, concerning the doctrine of a Mediator, Mr. Milman says:

"*Wherever* any approximation had been made to the sublime truth of the one great First Cause, either awful religious reverence or philosophic abstraction had removed the primal deity entirely beyond the sphere of human sense, and supposed that the intercourse of the Divinity with man, the moral government, and [238] even the original creation, had been carried on by the intermediate agency, either in Oriental language of an emanation, or in the Platonic, of the wisdom, reason, or intelligence of the one Supreme. This Being was more or less distinctly impersonated according to the more popular or more philosophic, the more material or more abstract notions of the age or people. This was the doctrine from the Ganges, or even the shores of the Yellow Sea to the Ilissus;[83] it was the fundamental principle of the Indian religion and Indian philosophy; it was the basis of Zoroastrianism, it was pure Platonism, it was the Platonic Judaism of the Alexandrian school. Many fine passages might be quoted from Philo, on the impossibility that the first self-existing Being should become cognizable to the sense of man."—Vol. i., pp. 72, 73.

Now, here again, as before, the principle which Mr. Milman elsewhere applies, is too much for him: and since he will not admit that this universal belief is from tradition or secret suggestion, (as we would maintain,) and of course

---

[83] *the Ilissus*: a river in Athens

dare not take the alternative, which in consistency he ought to take, of denying that what is found outside of Christianity is part of Christianity, he is obliged to have recourse to the following expedient by way of accounting for the fact: "From this remarkable uniformity of conception and coincidence of language," he says, "has sometimes been assumed a common tradition, generally disseminated throughout the race of man. I should be *content* with receiving it as the *general acquiescence of the human mind* in the necessity of some mediation between the pure spiritual nature of the Deity and the intellectual and moral being of man."—P. 74. "Content," means "too happy, thus to turn my back upon my own theory;" however, supposing others are not content? all minds have not equal piety; they are carried away by reason; they are run off with by a principle; what is to hinder a writer less religious-minded than Mr. Milman, proceeding to infer concerning the doctrine of mediation what he himself does infer concerning the angelic host? Is not mediation proved to be an Orientalism? and may not the "moral effect" of its idea be the same on the vulgar, even though the "refined intelligence" of the educated, who do not need it, should decline it? And again, if the universality of the doctrine of mediation is to be accounted for on an instinct, why may not the doctrine of celibacy also? [239]

In like manner all the divine and regal titles of Christ had been anticipated in one quarter or another; why are they not to be rejected as Oriental, Jewish, or Alexandrian? Mr. Milman tells us—

"Each region, each rank, each sect, the Babylonian, the Egyptian, the Palestinian, the Samaritan, the Pharisee, the lawyer, the zealot, arrayed the Messiah in those attributes which suited his own temperament. Of that which was more methodically taught in the synagogue of the adjacent school, the populace caught up whatever made the deeper impression. The enthusiasm took an active or contemplative, an ambitious or a religious, an earthly or a heavenly tone, according to the education, habits, or station of the believer; and to different men the Messiah was man or angel, or more than angel; he was king, conqueror, or moral reformer; a more victorious Joshua, a more magnificent Herod, a wider-ruling Cæsar, a wiser Moses, a holier Abraham; an angel, the angel of the Covenant, the Metatron,[84] the Mediator between God and man; Michael, the great tutelar archangel of the nation, who appears by some to have been identified with the mysterious Being who led them forth from Egypt; he was the word of God; an emanation from the Deity, himself partaking of the Divine nature."—Vol. i., pp. 82, 83.

Or, to take another passage:

"*In all the systems* a binary, in most a triple, modification of the Deity was admitted. The Logos, the divine word or reason, might differ in the various schemes, in its relation to the parental divinity, and to the universe; but it had this distinctive and ineffaceable character, that it was the mediator, the connecting link between the unseen and unapproachable world and that of man. This Platonism, if it may be so called, was universal. It had gradually absorbed all the more intellectual class; it hovered over, [240] as it were, and gathered under its wings all the religions of the world. *It had already modified Judaism*; it had allied itself with the Syrian and Mithraic[85] worship of the Sun, the visible Mediator, the emblem of the word; it was part of the general Nature worship; it was attempting to renew Paganism, and was the recognized and leading tenet in the higher mysteries."—Vol. ii., p. 427-8.

---

[84] *Metatron*: a supernatural figure in non-Biblical Jewish rabbinical literature
[85] *Mithraic*: referring to the mystery cult of Mithras, a Persian deity, whose worship spread to the Roman empire in the 1st to 3rd centuries AD

Where then are we to stop? What will be left to us of Christianity, if we assume that nothing is of its essence which is found elsewhere? Will even its precepts remain? "If we were to glean," says Mr. Milman, "from the later Jewish writings, from the beautiful aphorisms of other Oriental nations, which we cannot fairly trace to Christian sources, and from the Platonic and Stoic[86] philosophy, their more striking precepts, we might find perhaps a counterpart to *almost all* the moral sayings of Jesus. But the same truth is of different importance as an unconnected aphorism, and as the groundwork of a complete system."—Vol. i., p. 207. Most true; but we suspect the same distinction will be found to hold concerning some other Catholic doctrines and observances, which Mr. Milman would reject as Oriental or Judaic. It will hold too, in a remarkable manner, of a doctrine, which, as we have shown above, Mr. Milman so strangely passes over, but which surely is the practical basis of the whole Revelation, the forgiveness of sins.

However, there *are* two doctrines, which Mr. Milman seems to admit as especially proper to Christianity, which therefore ought to be especially considered of the essence of the Revelation; we suspect, however, that, characteristic as they are, they are not of that liberal and enlarged sort, which will please the "fastidious intelligence" of this age. The two to which we allude, are the principle of dogmatism, and the doctrine of ecclesiastical liberty. This is remarkable.

As to the former of the two, the principle of maintaining [241] the faith, Mr. Milman says, speaking of the times of Athanasius:

---

[86] *Stoic*: Stoicisim was a philosophy founded by Zeno of Citium (c.334-262 BC); it had strong ethical teaching, emphasising reason and self-control.

"How singular an illustration of the *change* already wrought in the mind of man by the introduction of Christianity ... This controversy related to a *purely speculative tenet*. The disputants of either party ... appear to have dwelt little, if at all, on the *practical effects* of conflicting opinions. In morals, in manners, in habits, in usages, in Church government, in religious ceremonial, there was no distinction between the parties which divided Christendom ... The Arians and Athanasians *first* divided the world on a pure question of *faith* ... Religion was become the *one dominant passion* of the whole Christian world; and everything allied to it, or rather, in this case, which seemed to concern its very essence, *could no longer be agitated with tranquillity or debated with indifference*."—Vol. ii., pp. 423-432.

The other principle was that of ecclesiastical liberty:

"It is curious," observes Mr. Milman, "to observe *this new element* of freedom, however at present working in a concealed, irregular, and perhaps still guarded manner, mingling itself up with, and partially upheaving, the general prostration of the human mind. The Christian, or in some respects it might be more justly said, the hierarchical principle, *was entering into the constitution of human society*, as an antagonist power to that of the civil sovereign."—Vol. iii., p. 34.

11.

Instances, however, such as these, deserving as they are of notice, scarcely do more than illustrate the rule to which they are exceptions. We repeat, then, in perfect sincerity and much anxiety, our inquiry,—What tenet of Christianity will escape proscription, if the principle is once admitted, that a sufficient account is given of an opinion, and a sufficient ground for making light of it, as soon as it is historically [242] referred to some human origin? What will be our Christianity? What shall we have to believe? What will be

286

left to us? Will more remain than a *caput mortuum*,[87] with no claim on our profession or devotion? Will the Gospel be a substance? Will Revelation have done more than introduce a *quality* into our moral life world, not anything that can be contemplated by itself, obeyed and perpetuated? This we do verily believe to be the end of the speculations, of which Mr. Milman's volumes at least serve as an illustration. If we indulge them, Christianity will melt away in our hands like snow; we shall be unbelievers before we at all suspect where we are. With a sigh we shall suddenly detect the real state of the case. We shall look on Christianity, not as a religion, but as a past event which exerted a great influence on the course of the world, when it happened, and gave a tone and direction to religion, government, philosophy, literature, manners; an idea which developed itself in various directions strongly, which was indeed from the first materialized into a system or a church, and is still upheld as such by numbers, but by an error; a great boon to the world, bestowed by the Giver of all good, as the discovery of printing may be, or the steam-engine, but as incapable of continuity, except in its effects, as the shock of an earthquake, or the impulsive force which commenced the motions of the planets.

It is impossible that a thoughtful man like Mr. Milman should not feel this difficulty even as a matter of logical consistency, not to speak of it as a deep practical question. Accordingly he has attempted, though, as we think, most arbitrarily and unsuccessfully, to set bounds to his own principle, and to shut the door on innovation, when he has let in as much of it as suited his taste. Some incidental

---

[87] *caput mortuum*: literally, 'dead head', i.e. something left-over that is worthless

[243]   symptoms of his anxiety have appeared in the course of passages lately quoted; but it is elsewhere embodied in protests, cautions, and attempts at explanation. Early in his work he begins by a protest;—after speaking of the successive changes which have taken place in the form of Christianity, he proceeds:

> "While, however, Christianity necessarily submitted to all these modifications, *I strongly protest* against the opinion, that the *origin* of the religion can be attributed, according to a theory adopted by many foreign writers, to the gradual and spontaneous development of the human mind. Christ is as much beyond His own age, as His own age is beyond the darkest barbarism."—Vol. i., p. 50.

Doubtless, no principle of Mr. Milman's book is inconsistent with the proof of our Lord's divine mission concisely stated by him in the last sentence; but proof in behalf of His *mission* does not tend to determine His *doctrine*. The question is, whether Mr. Milman has not taken up a position which puts him out of reach of all means of ascertaining or proving what Christ came to tell the world? For instance, he himself seems to be contented to retreat back as far as the doctrine of the immortality of the soul, and there to take his stand. Now this is confessedly not a *new* doctrine, first proposed by Christianity; let us see then whether he can so state his case in its favour, as not at the same time to suggest proof in behalf of other doctrines which he rejects. He thus defends it from the objection in question:

> "Henceforward that great truth begins to *assume a new character*, and to obtain an *influence* over the political and social, as well as over the individual, happiness of man, *unknown in the former ages of the world*. It is no longer a feeble and uncertain

instinct, nor a remote speculative opinion, obscured by the more pressing necessities and cares of the present life, but the universal predominant sentiment, constantly present to the thoughts, enwoven with the usages, and pervading the whole moral being of man. The dim and scattered rays, either of traditionary belief, of [244] intuitive feeling, or of philosophic reasoning, were brought as it were to a focus, condensed and poured with an immeasurably stronger, an expanding, an all-permeating light upon the human soul. Whatever its origin, whether in human nature, or the aspirations of high-thoughted individuals, propagated through their followers, or in former revelation, it received such an impulse, and was so deeply and universally moulded up with the popular mind in all orders, that from this period may be dated the true era of its dominion. If by no means new in its elementary principle, it was new in the degree and the extent to which it began to operate in the affairs of men."—Vol. i., pp. 371, 372.

A very good argument indeed, as we should say, in favour of the doctrine of the soul's immortality as a part of the special Gospel message. Yet, strange to say, hardly has Mr. Milman uttered it, but he is obliged in a note to make the following most remarkable, though indirect, confession, that the rationalizing principles which he has adopted do not necessarily secure even to this doctrine a place in the idea of Christianity; and that, in the judgment, not of any mere paradoxical minds, but of one of the most profound thinkers, as fame goes, of his age. Mr. Milman says:

"The most remarkable evidence of the extent to which German speculation has *wandered away* from the first principles of Christianity, is this, that one of the most religious writers, the one who has endeavoured with the most earnest sincerity to reconnect religious belief with the philosophy of the times, *has actually represented Christianity without, or almost without, the immortality of the soul*; and this the ardent and eloquent translator of Plato! Copious and full on the moral regeneration effected by Christ in this world, with the loftiest sentiments of the emancipation of the human soul from the bondage of sin by the Gospel, *Schleiermacher*[88] *is silent, or almost silent, on the redemption from death.* He beholds Christ distinctly as bringing life, only vaguely and remotely, as bringing immortality to light."—Vol. i., p. 372, note.

[245]
Christianity did not even bring the immortality of the soul to light; where then, after all, and what is Christianity?

However, Mr. Milman's expedient for limiting his own principles is, as we have seen, this,—to assert that a broad line must be drawn between the starting and the continuance of the religion, Divine Providence watching over it for its purity in the first age in a way in which it did not in the second; and then, as if by way of makeup to the second and following ages for this implied charge of corruption against them, to console them with the concession that perhaps their *corruptions* tended to the *permanence* of Christianity. But the champions of the ages in question, with all due acknowledgments for the compliment, will not allow him thus delicately to tiptoe over the difficulty. His words are these:

"On a *wide* and *comprehensive* survey of the whole history of Christianity, and considering it as left altogether to its own native force and impulse, it is difficult to estimate how far the admission, even the predominance, of these foreign elements, by which it was enabled to maintain its hold on different ages and races, may not have *contributed both to its original success and its final permanence.* If it lost in purity, it gained in power, perhaps in permanence. *No doubt* in its first contest with Orientalism, were

---

[88] *Schleiermacher*: Friedrich Schleiermacher (1768-1834), German philosopher and theologian, early proponent of liberal theology and scriptural interpretation.

sown those seeds which grew up at a later period into Monasticism; it rejected the tenets, but admitted the more insidious principle of Gnosticism; yet there can be little doubt that in the dark ages the monastic spirit was among the *great conservative and influential elements of* Christianity."—Vol. ii., pp. 94, 95.

We neither thank Mr. Milman for granting to us that the monastic spirit has been "conservative," nor will we grant to him in turn that "no doubt" it sprang from the "insidious principle of Gnosticism."

It will be observed that throughout the foregoing remarks on Mr. Milman's volumes, we have been granting generally the existence of a resemblance between Christianity and certain doctrines and practices scattered to and fro in the heathen philosophies and religions. Our purpose was to show that the genuineness of the Catholic creed, ethics, and ritual was unaffected by this fact; their being an existing Catholic theory on which the fact could stand without detriment to Catholicism, as well as a popular and liberalistic theory according to which the fact would throw discredit upon it. But the professed fact itself needs careful looking after, for it has been before now, and is continually, shamefully misstated. We had intended in this place to have added some words upon it, but our limits forbid. [246]

There is another question which obviously arises out of the fact under consideration, viz., as to its effect upon the *authority* of Revealed Religion. It may be objected, that originality is necessary, if not for truth of doctrine, at least for evidence of divinity; and, though there is nothing very profound in the remark, it ought to be answered; and we mention it, that we may be seen not to have forgotten it.

12.

And now, in bringing our remarks on this able work to an end, we must confess the mixed feeling with which we have made them. We have felt it to be an imperative duty to take that view of Mr. Milman's volumes which first presents itself to a Churchman. It is also their prominent aspect, and such as is likely to arrest the attention of the general reader, as well as of those whose habit of mind it is to associate the visible world with the invisible. The second aspect in which we should regard them, is as being a serviceable collection, or commonplace-book, of the worst which can be said by a candid enemy against the theory of Catholicism. The third remark we make upon them, and we make it with great sincerity and much pleasure, only wishing it could come first instead of third, is in their praise as a work of unusual learning and thought, containing a large mass of information, valuable to the students of ecclesiastical history. The author's method has its good side as well as its bad. He treats Catholic persons, proceedings, and events, in a large and tolerant spirit. His sketches of the great bishops of the fourth century are particularly interesting, though defaced, of course, by the peculiarities of his religious theory. With the same drawback, we can express great satisfaction in many of his discussions on particular points, of which we especially notice the chapters called "Christianity and Orientalism," and "Christianity and the Fine Arts."

It is indeed most painful, independently of all personal feelings which a scholar and poet so early distinguished as Mr. Milman must excite in the minds of his brethren, that a work so elaborate and so important should be composed upon principles which are calculated to turn all kindly

[247]

feeling into mere antipathy and disgust. Indeed there is so much to shock people, that there is comparatively little to injure. To one set of persons only is he likely to do much mischief, those who just at this moment are so ready to use his main principle for the demolition of Catholic views, without seeing that it applies to the New Testament History and teaching just as well. He will assist such persons in carrying out their principle. We observe that a publication, prominent in this warfare, cautions its readers against Mr. Milman's most *dangerous* and *insidious* work. We beg to join this publication and all other similar ones in its sage and seasonable warning. Let all who carp at the Fathers and [248] deny Tradition, who argue against sacramental influence, who refer celibacy to Gnosticism, and episcopal power to Judaism, who declaim against mysticism, and scoff at the miracles of the Church while at the same time they uphold what is called orthodox Protestantism, steadily abstain from Mr. Milman's volumes. On their controversial principles his reasonings and conclusions are irresistible.

January, 1841.

XIII

REFORMATION OF THE ELEVENTH CENTURY

PERHAPS the greatest of the wants under which our religious literature labours at this day is that of an ecclesiastical history. It is inconvenient enough to have no good commentary on Scripture, and so little of systematic theology; but the Creed tells us the principal points of doctrine, and Scripture is to the pious mind, in some sense, its own interpreter. But the providences of God towards His Church during eighteen centuries, though contained in outline in prophecy, are consigned to no formula or document, clear enough to convey its own meaning, and minute enough to impress its peculiarities upon the private Christian. Not even the wildest advocate for the right of Private Judgment ever professed to apprehend past facts, as he might think he discovered revealed doctrines, without the assistance of books or teachers. Rather such an one will commonly be found to depreciate, instead of pretending to, historical knowledge: he will apply the Caliph Omar's[1] argument to the events of 1800 years, and say that except for the first and three last centuries they are not to be studied at all, as being little or nothing better than the times

---

[1] *Caliph Omar*: (634-644) first Commander of the Faithful who introduced the Arabian calendar and defeated the Persians, cf. Gibbon, Chapter 50.

of predicted evil. He shuts up God's dealings with His Church under a formula, and is contented with symbols which neither he nor any one else can put into plain English. [250]

It is difficult justly to estimate the injury done to our whole view of Gospel truth by our ignorance of ecclesiastical history. Every department of theology acts upon the rest, and if one is neglected the others suffer. Our view of doctrine affects our view of history, and our view of history our view of doctrine; and our view of doctrine the sense we put upon Scripture: and our interpretation of Scripture our ethics, and our ethics our interpretation of Scripture. And, moreover, the history of the past ends in the present; and the present is our scene of trial; and to behave ourselves towards its various phenomena duly and religiously, we must understand them; and to understand them, we must have recourse to those past events which led to them. Thus the present is a text, and the past its interpretation. To a child there is no difference between one fact and another in the religious world. He does not understand their mutual relations or their respective bearings. He has, when an infant in arms, learned to classify and dispose of objects of sense; he knows that the church spire is not so near him as his nose or his hand, and that leaves are parts of the tree, and not of the sky or the earth, with which they are conterminous. But he cannot learn without the assistance of others the meaning of moral facts; and, as things are, he commonly grows up and lives and dies as ignorant of those of an ecclesiastical character as he was when he first had the faculty of thought. "What is the difference between a Methodist and a Roman Catholic?" and "Why are we not all Quakers?" are the questions which

[251]   a thoughtful child of five years old may ask; and it is not at all clear whether he is likely to have taken any real steps towards the solution of them by the time he is fifty. This of course is witnessed in the case of political and social facts quite as much as in ecclesiastical. What a different meaning, for instance, has the so-called "Catholic Relief Bill,"[2] or the Reform Bill,[3] to men of twenty and of thirty! How differently has the character of the Duke of Wellington[4] come out to the present generation since the publication of his dispatches![5] How differently appear our present relations with Russia to those who know and those who are ignorant of the history of the last century! Men enter into life, and take what they find there, and put their own interpretation upon it, if their imaginations are not pre-occupied with the one true historical comment. This is why there is such difficulty in rousing the public mind to understand the importance of certain measures, proposed or resisted: to the public they are facts without meaning. What virtue is there in a name to those who are dead to it? Why should not Brutus stir a spirit as soon as Cæsar?[6] It is the association

---

[2] *Catholic Relief Bill*: often referred to as Catholic Emancipation, passed by Parliament in 1829. It repealed the Test Act of 1673 and allowed Catholics in sit in Parliament. It caused great controversy, being supported by the Prime Minister, the Duke of Wellington, and Daniel O'Connell, the Irish leader political leader, but opposed by many, including the King himself.

[3] *Reform Bill*: First Reform Act 1832 to enfranchise the upper-middle classes, which increased the number of voters from 500,000 to 1 million.

[4] *Duke of Wellington*: Arthur Wellesley (1769-1852), 1st Duke of Wellington, victor of Waterloo and Prime Minister.

[5] *How differently has the character of the Duke of Wellington ...* : The Duke's private secretary, Colonel John Gurwood, edited the eight volume *Dispatches of Field Marshal the Duke of Wellington* between 1834 and 1839, later reissued in a revised edition in 1844.

[6] *Why should not Brutus stir a spirit as soon as Caesar?*: Cf. 'Brutus will start a spirit as soon as Caesar', William Shakespeare, *Julius Caesar* Act 1, Scene 2, 146.

which is everything; but to those who know not the true history of that to which the name belongs, there are no associations with it, or wrong ones.

The case is the same as regards words written or spoken. Take an orator and he shall make a speech, or an author and he shall write a pamphlet, or a preacher and he shall deliver a sermon; and then let it be considered how differently the speech, or the pamphlet, or the sermon, in each case seems to persons who know him well and those who do not. Very different for better and for worse; let him be a man of pomp and parade, or of smoothness and artifice, and strangers will be taken in, and admire the very words, turns of speech and gestures, which make those who know him well only cry out, "How like so-and-so!" On the other hand, the deep feeling and reality of another sort of man go clean over the heads of those who do not know him, while friends are pierced by every word. Let the very same speech or sentiment come from two persons, and it has quite a different meaning, according to the speaker, and takes a different form in our minds. We always judge of what meets us by what we know already. There is no such thing in nature as a naked text without note or comment. [252]

It is a curious fact, that these remarks even apply to the case of personal appearance, as is sometimes proved by the test of portraits. Let a likeness, taken twenty years ago, be put before two persons, now for the first time, one of whom knew the subject of it at the time, and the other did not, and the former will think it like him as he is now, and the latter will deny the likeness. We colour our ocular vision with the hues of the imagination: as reason is said to deceive our eyes in the phenomenon of the horizontal moon,[7] so memory is a gloss upon them here. Our friend has grown fat, or his temples are higher, or his face is broader, or lines have come to view along his cheek, or across his forehead, and yet in certain cases we shall be heard to say, that such a one has not altered at all since the day we first knew him. To us his youth is stamped upon his maturity, and he lives in our eye, as well as in our mind, as when we first gave him our affection. We are surprised on going into the world to hear him called a middle-aged man.

In such a case, to be sure, we have an instance of an abuse of the important instrument which has been above insisted on. But we adduce it to prove the extent of the influence which the knowledge of the past has on the present;—that it may become excessive and out of place, that we may become mere antiquarians and pedants, that we [253] may bury ourselves in the illusions of history, when we should be contemplating things as they are before us, is very certain: but the danger at this day rather is, lest, from total ignorance of history, we should be obliged to determine every action and every principle by the only test which will practically be left us, the test of visible expediency. And late ecclesiastical occurrences[8] supply some melancholy instances in point. This will be the certain consequence of treating history as an old almanac, whatever persons of some station in the Church may say to the contrary.

---

[7] *the phenomenon of the horizontal moon*: the illusion of the moon looking larger on the horizon than when it is in the sky. Aristotle thought, correctly, that it was due to the atmosphere.

[8] *late ecclesiastical occurrences*: probably a reference to the controversy caused by the publication of Newman's *Tract 90*.

And, again, it must be recollected that men will form their theories and write books on religious subjects, whether or not they have the facts, which alone can enable them to do so justly. To assign causes, to draw out relations, is natural to man; and he will do it on a theory, rather than not at all. A number of answers can be given to the question, What is the Church? We are far from saying that in so complicated a question *only* one, or perhaps that any *one*, is right and true; but whatever is right, whatever wrong, surely we must go to history for the information. If we are content merely to look round us to catch up certain peculiarities which meet our eye, listen to what is said in parliament or the newspapers, or in some fashionable chapel, and then proceed to form our theory, we shall probably approach about as near the truth as the clever Oriental who defined the English as a nation who live on the sea, and make penknives. This is a remark which applies in a measure even to writers of a deeper tone of thought: we are just now becoming rich in treatises on ecclesiastical politics and doctrine: let us take good care that our arbitrary views do not get ahead of our knowledge.

We have now given some of the reasons why we are especially obliged to Mr. Bowden[9] for the life of Hildebrand,[10] known in history as Pope Gregory VII., which he has lately given to the world. No one can write without opinions: we are far from saying that Mr. Bowden has not his own, and that of a very decided character; but what we

[254]

---

[9] *Mr Bowden*: See the Editor's Introduction, p.xxxiii.
[10] *Hildebrand*: Gregory VII's name before his election as pope in 1073. See note on p.[46].

principally thank him for is his narrative of facts; he has drawn out the facts of a momentous and wonderful period of history with great distinctness and perspicuity, and we are sure that no one will rise from the perusal of his volumes without respectful feelings towards their author for the information and instruction he has provided. We do not intend to make this article a panegyric on Mr. Bowden; but to convey to the reader by means of it some account of his subjects. Yet, before proceeding to business, it is but justice to him to say, that he has given us at once a very learned and very well-arranged history. To have read the original sources diligently and to report them accurately is one great praise; but a far more difficult task is the combination and adjustment of materials. To bring out the course of events so that a reader may go away with a definite impression upon his mind of what has passed through it, is a very difficult art. We are not perhaps quite satisfied with Mr. Bowden's style; but we eulogize his composition. He is a very neat and skilful artist, a clear and forcible narrator; makes a great many points, and every one of them tells.

2.[11]

But now let us proceed to his work itself. It is the history of the commencement of that great reformation of the Church in the middle ages, which Providence conducted through the instrumentality, partly divine, partly human, of [255] the Papal Monarchy. It is usual to call the times in which it occurred the dark ages; but, properly speaking, that title applies to the centuries which preceded it. No exaggeration

---

[11] *2.:* incorrectly numbered either by Newman or the original printer; this should be §1.

is possible of the demoralized state into which the Christian world, and especially the Church of Rome, had fallen in the years that followed the extinction of the Carlovingian line (A.D. 887).[12] The tenth century is even known among Protestants *par excellence* as the sæculum obscurum,[13] and Baronius expresses its portentous corruption in the vivid remark that Christ was as if asleep in the vessel of the Church. "The infamies prevalent among the clergy of the time," says Mr. Bowden, "as denounced by Damiani[14] and others, are to be alluded to, not detailed."—Vol. i., p. 144. When Hildebrand was appointed to the monastery of St. Paul at Rome,[15] he found the offices of devotion systematically neglected, the house of prayer defiled by the sheep and cattle who found their way in and out through its broken doors, and the monks, contrary to all monastic rule, attended in their refectory by women. The excuse for these irregularities was the destitution to which the holy house was reduced by the predatory bands of Campagna;[16] but when the monastic bodies were rich, as was the case in Germany, matters were worse instead of better. Unworthy brethren of the conventual orders, Mr. Bowden tells us, incessantly beset the ears of princes and great people, who

---

[12] *AD 887*: The Carolingian line ended with the deposition of Charlemagne's great-grandson, Charles the Fat (839-888), as Holy Roman Emperor.

[13] *saeculum obscurum*: The tenth century was known as 'the dark age', a term coined by the Catholic historian Caesar Baronius (1538-1607, like Newman, an Oratorian and Cardinal) in his twelve volume *Annales ecclesiastici* (1588-1607).

[14] *Damiani*: St Peter Damian or Petrus Damiani (1007-72), a reforming Benedictine Abbot who was created Cardinal Bishop of Ostia in 1057 and a close associate of Gregory VII. Dante placed the saint in a lofty position in the *Paradiso* and he was declared a Doctor of the Church by Leo XII in 1828.

[15] *monastery of St Paul at Rome*: St Paul outside the Walls, one of the four major basilicas in Rome, founded by Constantine over the tomb of the apostle.

[16] *predatory bands of Campagna*: The area around Rome, the Campagna, was for centuries characterised by warring nobles and groups of bandits.

had the presentation to abbeys and benefices, offering sums so large in purchase that secular competitors were excluded. The world wondered, says an historian of the times, himself a monk, from what springs such rivers of wealth could flow; and understood not how the riches of Crœsus[17] or Tantalus[18] could be amassed by men who had taken on them the scandal of the Cross and the profession of poverty. Adelbert, Archbishop of Bremen,[19] though himself a man of pure life and austere practice in an age of general dissoluteness, conceived a plan, by means of the imperial influence which he enjoyed, of making Hamburg the seat of his power, and establishing a sort of papacy in the North. With this purpose in view, he was tempted to grasp at every method of increasing his revenues, and disgraced his rule by a wide-spread system of corruption and plunder. Associating himself with a profligate favourite of the Emperor, he despoiled without shame the lands and revenues of the less powerful religious communities, and put up to sale every office, civil or ecclesiastical, which fell to his disposal. On an archbishop in France, who had contrived to bribe to silence the principal evidences against him of simony, at length being brought to confess his guilt and being deposed, no less than forty-five bishops and twenty-seven other dignitaries or governors of churches

[256]

---

[17] *Croesus*: King of Lydia (560-547 BC), whose wealth has become proverbial. He is thought to have produced the first gold coins. Croesus was eventually captured by the Persians.

[18] *Tantalus*: in Greek mythology the son of Zeus and ruler of a city variously called 'Tantalis', 'Tantalus' or 'Sipylus'. He is also sometimes called 'King of Phrygia' and is best known for sacrificing his son, Pelops, and serving him to the gods at a banquet. His great wealth was attributed, by the Greek historian Strabo, to the mines in this area.

[19] *Adelbert, Archbishop of Bremen*: (c.1000-72), Archbishop of Hamburg-Bremen from c.1043.

came forward to confess the criminal mode by which they had obtained their benefices, and retired from stations which they had no valid right to retain. In Lombardy, the Archbishop Guido[20] in the eleventh century was said to have invariably demanded a price for the favour of admission into holy orders; his clergy were in their own way as deeply involved in the guilt of simony as himself, till their very flocks learned to treat them with open manifestations of contempt, reviled them in the house of God itself, and hooted them along the streets. In the times of St. Romauld,[21] who died in 1027, the practice of emperors selling bishoprics, bishops their preferments, and laymen their benefices, was so recognized and ordinary, that when the saint had spoken even to religious persons of simony as a sin, he seemed to them to inculcate over-strained and fanciful notions.

Even two centuries earlier than this,[22] when, as appears on the face of the facts, the corruption was not so general, a [257] Council of Paris had complained that many of the clergy were so occupied in the pursuit of gain and other worldly avocations that they suffered many infants to die without baptism. A Council of Aix-la-Chapelle[23] of the same date prohibits extortion and intemperance in bishops, and protests against their non-residence. A Synod of Pavia[24] a

---

[20] *Archbishop Guido*: Guido da Velate, Archbishop of Milan 1045-71, a notable opponent of ecclesiastical reform, especially the *pataria* (a reformist movement led by Anselm of Lucca and Arialdo).

[21] *St Romauld*: [sic] St Romuald (c.951-1027), founder of the Camaldolese Benedictines who combined the eremitical and cenobitical lives.

[22] This paragraph is an addition to the original article; see the Textual Appendix.

[23] *Council of Paris ... Aix-la-Chapelle*: These local church councils met in 829 and 836 respectively, having been called by Louis the Pious.

[24] *Synod of Pavia*: met in 850.

little later prohibits the clergy the practice of sumptuous banquets and the use of dogs and hawks. Hincmar[25] judged it expedient to issue a decree against the pawning by the clergy of the vestments and the communion plate. In 829, the prelates assembled in council at Paris found it necessary to urge Louis the Debonair[26] to use all his influence in extirpating simony, "this heresy so detestable, this pest so hateful to God," from the Church. The Synod of Meaux, in 845, renewed the warning. And Leo IV.,[27] in or about 847, denounced it in an epistle to the Bishops of Britanny as a crime condemned by many Councils. The nobles secured the ordination of their younger sons or relatives for the sole purpose of qualifying them for the acceptance of lucrative benefices; giving them, while they did so, the same military training and secular habits with the rest of the family. Others procured admission to the priesthood for dependants whom they intended to retain in subordinate stations in their household. "Such," says Agobard, Archbishop of Lyons,[28] "is the disgrace of our times, that there is scarcely one to be found who aspires to any degree of honour or temporal distinction who has not his domestic priest; and this, not that he may obey him, but that he may command his obedience alike in things lawful and things unlawful; in things human and things divine; so that these chaplains are

---

[25] *Hincmar*: (806-82), Archbishop of Reims (from 845), confidante of Charles the Bald and a prolific writer.

[26] *Louis the Debonair*: or 'the Pious' or 'the Fair' (778-840). The son of Charlemagne, with whom he was co-Emperor, he was King of Aquitaine (from 781) and King of the Franks (from 814).

[27] *Leo IV*: Pope 847-855, who not only defended papal rights and restored ecclesiastical discipline but defeated the Muslim fleets outside Ostia (849) and built new defensive walls on the right bank of the Tiber (creating the 'Leonine City').

[28] *Agobard, Archbishop of Lyons*: (c.775-840), the author of a number of treatises.

constantly to be found serving the tables, mixing the strained wine, leading out the dogs, managing the ladies' [258] horses, or looking after the lands."

Mr. Bowden shall inform us of a scene which took place during the minority of the Emperor Henry the Fourth:[29]

"At the commencement of vespers before the king and court at Goslar,[30] at the solemn season of Christmas, 1062, a dispute arose between the servants of the Bishop of Hildesheim and those of the Abbot of Fulda, with regard to the position of the seats of their respective masters. The abbot, by ancient usage, was entitled to sit next to the metropolitan; but the bishop, indignant that any should take this place, within his own diocese, in preference to himself, had commanded his domestics to place the chairs accordingly. The dispute soon led to blows, and but for the interference of Otho of Bavaria,[31] would have terminated in bloodshed. This noble asserted the rights of the abbot, and the bishop was consequently foiled. He looked forward however to a renewal of the contest under more favourable auspices; and at the feast of Pentecost following, previously to the entrance of the king and prelates into the Church, he secreted behind the high altar Count Ecbert[32] and some well-armed soldiers. As the contending prelates proceeded to their seats, the affray between the servants began again; when the count suddenly springing from his ambush, rushed with his followers upon the astonished men of Fulda, and

---

[29] *Emperor Henry the Fourth*: (1050-1106), King of the Romans from 1056 and Holy Roman Emperor from 1086.

[30] *Goslar*: a town in Lower Saxony with an important imperial residence frequently used in the eleventh century. The disputes over precedence at Christmas 1062 and Pentecost 1063, described in Bowden's text, took place at the Collegiate Church of St Simon and St Jude.

[31] *Otho of Bavaria*: 1020-83. Otho or Otto of Nordheim was Duke of Bavaria from 1061, although he was deprived of the title nine years later and went on to become a leader in the Saxon Revolt against Henry IV.

[32] *Count Ecbert*: d.1067, Count of Brunswick and later to become Margrave of Meissen (1066). He was the nephew of Pope St Leo IX.

drove them with blows and menaces from the church. But they too had made preparations for a violent struggle, and had friends and arms at hand. In a body they rushed once more into the sacred building, and engaging their enemies with swords in the midst of the choir, confusedly mingled with the choristers. Fiercely was the combat waged: 'throughout the church,' says Lambert of Aschaffenburgh,[33] 'resounded, instead of hymns and spiritual songs, the shouts of the combatants and the screams of the dying; ill-omened victims were slaughtered upon the altar of God; while through the building ran rivers of blood, poured forth, not by the legal religion of other days, but by the mutual cruelty of enemies.' The Bishop of Hildesheim, rushing to a pulpit or some other conspicuous position, exhorted his followers, according to the same writer, as with the sound of a trumpet, to persevere in the fray, and encouraged them by his authority, and by the promise of absolution, to disregard the sanctity of the place. The young [259] monarch called in vain on his subjects to reverence his royal dignity; all ears were deaf to his vociferated commands and entreaties; and, at length, urged by those around him to consult his own safety, he escaped with difficulty from the thickening tumult, and made his way to his palace. The men of Fulda by the efforts of Count Ecbert, were at length repulsed, and the doors of the church closed against them; upon which, ranging themselves before the building, they prepared to assault their enemies again, as soon as they should issue from it; and there remained until the approach of night induced them to retire."—Vol. i., pp. 235-237.

Miserable as are the above specimens of those truly "dark ages," yet they are decency itself compared with the atrocities which in the same era disgraced the see of Rome. At the close of the ninth century, Stephen VI. dragged the

---

[33] *Lambert of Aschaffenburgh*: (c.1024-88), more commonly known as Lambert of Hersfeld, was a chronicler and author of the celebrated *Annals*. He supported Hildebrand and often showed himself to be critical of Henry IV.

body of an obnoxious predecessor from the grave,[34] and, after subjecting it to a mock trial, cut off its head and three fingers, and threw it into the Tiber. He himself was subsequently deposed, and strangled in prison. In the years that followed, the power of electing to the popedom fell into the hands of the intriguing and licentious Theodora, and her equally unprincipled daughters, Theodora and Marozia.[35] These women, members of a patrician family, by their arts and beauty, obtained an unbounded influence over the aristocratic tyrants of the city. One of the Theodoras advanced a lover, and Marozia a son, to the popedom. The grandson of the latter, Octavian, succeeding to her power, as well as to the civil government of the city, elevated himself, on the death of the then Pope, to the apostolic chair, at the age of eighteen, under the title of John XII. (A.D. 956.)[36] His

---

[34] *Stephen VI dragged the body of an obnoxious predecessor from the grave*: Shortly after his election as pope, Stephen VI (896-97) ordered the body of his predecessor, Pope Formosus (891-896), to be dug up and submitted to a mock trial (often referred to as the 'cadaver synod'). The corpse was dressed in pontificals, placed on a throne and accused of perjury and corruption. His body was thrown into the Tiber and his acts declared null and void: even though it was Formosus who had consecrated the future Stephen VI as bishop of Anagni.

[35] *the intriguing and licentious Theodora…her equally unprincipled daughters, Theodora and Marozia*: Newman is relying on the unreliable *Anecdota* of Procopius of Caesarea. Theodora the daughter of Acacius, a bear-feeder at the Hippodrome, became a courtesan and dancer before her marriage to Justinian, whom he proclaimed Empress in 527. She proved herself an able and courageous consort, although a Monophysite. She died in 548. Her daughter, Theodora was born in 515 and married Flavius Pompeus, Roman consul, in 517. Marozia was the step-daughter of Theophylact and his wife Theodora. She also was a dancer and successively married Alberic I, Guido of Tuscany and Hugo, King of Italy. She was supposedly responsible for the imprisonment and death of John X in 929 and the election of John XI, the illegitimate son of herself and Sergius III, according to Procopius. She was eventually imprisoned by her own son, Alberic II and died in 928.

[36] *John XII*: Formerly called Octavian, John was the illegitimate son of the ruler of Rome, Alberic II of Spoleto, and elected as pope in 955, despite his young age and life of debauchery. He died in 964, allegedly after suffering a stroke while in bed with a married woman.

career was in keeping with such a commencement. "The Lateran palace," says Mr. Bowden, "was disgraced by becoming a receptacle for courtezans: and decent females were terrified from pilgrimages to the threshold of the Apostles by the reports which were spread abroad of the [260] lawless impurity and violence of their representative and successor."—Vol. i., p. 83. At length he was carried off by a rapid illness, or by the consequences of a blow received in the prosecution of his intrigues. Boniface VII. (A.D. 974),[37] in the space of a few weeks after his elevation, plundered the treasury and basilica of St. Peter of all he could conveniently carry off, and fled to Constantinople. John XVIII. (A.D. 1003)[38] expressed his readiness, for a sum of money from the Emperor Basil,[39] to recognize the right of the Greek Patriarch to the title of ecumenical or universal bishop, and the consequent degradation of his own see; and was only prevented by the general indignation excited by the report of his intention. Benedict IX. (A.D. 1033)[40] was consecrated Pope, according to some authorities, at the age of ten or twelve years, and became notorious for adulteries and murders. At length he resolved on marrying his first cousin; and, when her father would not assent except on the condition of his resigning the popedom, he sold it for a large sum, and consecrated the purchaser as his successor. Such are a few of the most prominent features of the

---

[37] *Boniface VII*: Anti-pope on two occasions (974; 984-985), Boniface had to flee Rome after murdering his rival, Benedict VI, in July 974 but managed take loot from the papal treasury with him.

[38] *John XVIII*: Pope 1003-09, a puppet of the powerful Crescentii family.

[39] *Emperor Basil*: Basil II (c.958-1025), Byzantine Emperor from 976, nicknamed 'the Bulgar Slayer'.

[40] *Benedict IX*: Pope uniquely on three occasions between 1032 and 1048.

ecclesiastical history of these dreadful times, when, in the words of St. Bruno,[41] "the world lay in wickedness, holiness had disappeared, justice had perished, and truth had been buried; Simon Magus[42] lording it over the Church, whose bishops and priests were given to luxury and fornication."

2.

Had we lived in such deplorable times as have been above described,[43] when Satan seemed to have been let loose at the end of his thousand years, and had we been blessed with any portion of divine light to understand, and of love to desire better things, we might have asked whether it was [261] conceivable that the Church should ever recover itself from the abyss into which it was sunk. Where was the motive principle—where the fulcrum, by which it was to be righted? What was left but for matters to become worse and worse, till the last ray of truth and righteousness died away, and the last saint was gathered in, and the end of all things came, and the Judge with it? One thing we should have felt for certain, that if it was possible to retrieve the Church, it must be by some external power; she was helpless and resourceless; and the civil power must interfere, or there was no hope. So thought the young and zealous emperor, Henry III. (A.D. 1039),[44] who, though unhappily far from a perfect character, yet deeply felt the shame to which the

---

[41] *St Bruno*: (c.1035-1101) a German theologian who founded the strict Carthusian Order, based at the Grande Chartreuse. Eventually summoned to Rome by Pope Urban II (a former pupil), he was able to establish monasteries in Italy.

[42] *Simon Magus*: See above p.[235].

[43] Newman here omits a lengthy passage from the original essay dealing with the Carolingian Church. See the Textual Appendix.

[44] *Henry III*: (1017-1056), crowned Holy Roman Emperor in 1046, nicknamed 'the Black' or 'the Pious'.

Immaculate Bride[45] was exposed, and determined with his own right hand to work her deliverance. In one respect, indeed, he was plainly unequal for so high a mission, had he had other credentials of it; he who was not possessed of the grace of personal purity, could not hope to remove the more flagrant scandals with which the clergy of the day were laden; but this good thing had he, that, with all his ecclesiastical prerogatives and possessions, he had in no single instance incurred the guilt of simony; he had the most awful impression and the most acute feelings of its heinousness; and thus, if he could not animadvert upon one of the two chief sins of the day, he might aspire to be a censor of the other. And so much is undeniable, that, though he cannot be considered as regularly called to the work, and though a movement had already begun, as we shall presently see, in the Church itself, which, humanly speaking, would have effected it without him, yet in matter of fact, this well-meaning prince did begin that reformation [262] which ended in the purification and monarchical estate of the Church. He held a Council of his bishops in 1047; in it he passed a decree that "Whosoever should make any office or station in the Church a subject of purchase or sale, should suffer deprivation and be visited with excommunication;" at the same time, with regard to his own future conduct, he solemnly pledged himself as follows:—"As God has freely of His mere mercy bestowed upon me the crown of the empire, so will I give freely and without price all things that pertain unto His religion." This was his first act; but he was aware that the work of reform, to be thoroughly executed,

---

[45] *Immaculate Bride*: i.e. the Church.

must proceed from Rome, as the centre of the ecclesiastical commonwealth, and he determined, upon those imperial precedents and feudal principles which Charlemagne[46] had introduced, himself to appoint a Pope, who should be the instrument of his general reformation.

The reigning Pope at this time was Gregory VI.,[47] and he introduces us to so curious a history that we shall devote some sentences to it. Gregory was the identical personage who had bought the papal office of the profligate Benedict IX. for a large sum, and was consecrated by him, and yet he was far from a bad sort of man after all. As to his traffic in holy things, he seems to have viewed it in the light of the worthy persons in our own days, whose advertisements concerning the sale or purchase of advowsons or presentations[48] figure in the newspapers; and he really does seem to have committed his act of simony with the very best intentions, which he did in fact carry out, so far as his bargain was made good to him. He had been known in the world as John Gratianus; and at the time of his promotion was arch-priest of Rome. "He was considered," says Mr. Bowden, "in those bad times more than ordinarily religious; [263] he had lived free from the gross vices by which the clergy were too generally disgraced." He is described as "idiota et miræ simplicitatis,"[49] and, what perhaps is included in this

---

[46] *Charlemagne*: (742-814), King of the Franks and of the Lombards; crowned as Holy Roman Emperor by Pope Leo III in St. Peter's, Rome, on Christmas Day 800.

[47] *Gregory VI*: Pope (1045-46). A friend of Hildebrand and with reformist tendencies, he was deposed by Henry III of Germany because of his alleged simony in obtaining the papacy after the abdication of his godson, Benedict IX. Gregory died in exile soon afterwards.

[48] *advowsons or presentations*: rights to appoint clergy to benefices

[49] *"idiota et mirae simplicitatis"*: ignorant and of wonderful openness

account of him, he was unlettered. He could not be quite said to have come into actual possession of his purchase; for Benedict, his predecessor, who sold it to him, being disappointed in his intended bride, returned to Rome after an absence of three months, and resumed his pontifical station, while the party of his intended father-in-law had had sufficient influence to create a Pope of their own, John, Bishop of Sabina, who paid a high price for his elevation, and took the title of Sylvester III.[50] And thus there were three self-styled Popes at once in the Holy City, Benedict performing his sacred functions at the Lateran, Gregory at St. Peter's, and Sylvester at Santa Maria Maggiore. Gregory, however, after a time, seemed to preponderate over his antagonists; he maintained a body of troops, and with these he suppressed the suburban robbers who molested the pilgrims. Expelling them from the sacred limits of St. Peter's, he carried his arms further, till he had cleared the neighbouring towns and roads of these marauders. On an outcry being raised at the unclerical character of such performances, brilliant as they were, he associated with him Lorenzo, Archbishop of Amalfi,[51] who was an exile at Rome, as his coadjutor, and, while the latter undertook the direct duties of the papal office and government, he devoted himself to that police department in which he seemed so much to excel.

---

[50] *Sylvester III*: Pope (1045). His pontificate followed Benedict IX's first deposition and ended when Benedict managed a triumphal return. He was accused of obtaining the papal office through simony.

[51] *Lorenzo, Archbishop of Amalfi*: a monk at Monte Cassino and learned scholar, who acted as bishop of his home town between 1030 and his banishment in 1039. He spent the rest of his life in Rome, where he taught the future Gregory VII.

This was the point of time at which the Imperial Reformer made his visitation of the Church and See of the Apostles. He came into Italy in the autumn of 1046, and held a Council at Sutri, a town about thirty miles to the north of Rome. Gregory was allowed to preside; and, when under his auspices the abdication of Benedict had been recorded, and Sylvester had been stripped of his sacerdotal rank and shut up in a monastery for life, Gregory's own turn came, and, as there was no one competent to judge the highest ecclesiastical authority upon earth, as he was admitted really to be, the following device was taken to get rid of him: [264]

"His (Henry's) bishops, the cases of Gregory's rivals having been disposed of, requested the pontiff to state, for their information, the circumstances of his own election to the Papal office; and, when they had thus drawn from him an admission of the unholy traffic by which that transaction had been accomplished, they brought before him the impropriety of his conduct in a manner so glaring, that the confounded Pontiff at length exclaimed, 'I call God to witness that, in doing what I did, I hoped to obtain the forgiveness of my sins and the grace of God. But now that I see the snare into which the enemy has entrapped me, tell me what I must do?' The bishops having thus obtained their point, replied, 'Judge thyself—condemn thyself with thine own mouth; better will it be for thee to live, like the holy Peter, poor in this world and to be blest in another, than like the magician Simon, whose example misled thee, to shine in riches here, and to receive hereafter the sentence of condemnation.' And the penitent Gregory, in obedience to the suggestion spoke as follows: 'I, Gregory, bishop, servant of the servants of God, pronounce that, on account of the shameful trafficking, the heretical simony, which took place at my election, I am deprived of the Roman See. Do you agree,' he concluded, 'to this?' 'We acquiesce,' was the reply, 'in your decision;' and the ex-Pope at once divested himself of the insignia of pontifical authority."— Vol. i., p. 119.

[265]

The new Pope whom the Emperor gave to the Church instead of Gregory VI., Clement II.,[52] a man of excellent character, died within the year. Damasus II.[53] also, who was his second nomination, died in three or four weeks after his formal assumption of his pontifical duties. Bruno, Bishop of Toul, was his third choice; he was a relation of Henry's, mild and unambitious in character, fervent in his devotion, courteous and popular in his manners, and possessed, if not of commanding talents, of considerable energy and activity of mind. He was far from desiring his elevation; when the proposal was first made to him, he requested three days to consider of it; at the end of which he made a confession of his faults before the assembled Council, with the hope of gaining their permission to decline it. But they overruled his objections, and he found himself compelled on the spot to assume the style and honours of a pontiff (A.D. 1049). Such was the person, and such the manner of his promotion, who is now known as St. Leo, the ninth of that name.[54]

---

[52] *Clement II*: Pope (1046-47), successor of Gregory VI and formerly bishop of Bamberg (where he was later buried), who took steps to counter simony and reduce the power of the Roman families.

[53] *Damasus II*: Pope (1048), successor of Clement II, but died at Palestrina after only twenty-three days, probably of malaria.

[54] *St Leo, the ninth of that name*: (1049-54), originally Bruno, Bishop of Toul; he pressed ahead with the work of reform and held synods not only in Italy but across the alps at Rheims and Mainz. He worked closely with Hildebrand but his pontificate ended in apparent failure, after he failed in a military defeat against the Normans in southern Italy and was briefly held hostage at Benevento.

3.

And now we are arrived at the moment when the State reformer struck his foot against the hidden rock, and found to his surprise that, in that apparently disorganized and lifeless frame, which he was attempting to new-make, there was a soul and a power of self-action adequate both to its recovery and to its resistance against foreign interference. He had chosen a Pope, but "quis custodiat ipsos custodes"?[55] What was to keep fast that Pope in that very view of the relation of the State to the Church, that plausible Erastianism,[56] as it has since been called, which he adopted himself? What is to secure the Pope from the influences of some Hildebrand at his elbow, who, a young man himself, shall rehearse, in the person of his superior, that part which he is one day to play in his own, as Gregory VII.? Such was the very fact; Hildebrand was with Leo, and thus commences the ecclesiastical career of that wonderful man, to whose history Mr. Bowden has devoted his reading. [266] Hildebrand was at this time from thirty to forty years of age, having been born between 1010 and 1020; his birthplace, as it is supposed, Soana, in Tuscany; his father a carpenter. He had been soon removed from home to the care of an uncle, the Abbot of St. Mary's on the Aventine, who is supposed to be the same with that Lorenzo, Archbishop of Amalfi, whom Gregory VI. had made his coadjutor, and whose assertion of ecclesiastical power had previously led to his banishment from his own diocese by Guaimar, prince of the

---

[55] *"quis custodiat ipsos custodies"?*: 'who will guard the guards themselves' or 'who watches the watchmen?' From Juvenal's *Satires* VI, 347-48.

[56] *Erastianism*: See note on p.[45].

city.[57] Such a man was a happy master for the champion of the Church; and under his auspices Hildebrand had rapidly acquired a knowledge of the seven liberal sciences, while he exhibited from his earliest years the rudiments of that devotional temperament, which in after-life so strikingly characterized him. He was, says one of his annalists, a monk from his boyhood; his life, from its very commencement, was one of abstinence, mortification, and self-command.

Arrived at man's estate, he had undertaken a journey across the Alps, and resided for some time in the celebrated monastery of Cluni[58] in Burgundy, the strictness of which formed an acceptable contrast, in the eyes of the austere youth, with the laxity of manners which prevailed at Rome. The Abbot Odilo,[59] himself an eminent saint, was equally pleased with Hildebrand, applying to him prophetically the words, used by the Angel of the commissioned Reformer who went before the first Advent,[60] "He shall be great in the sight of the Lord." On his return to Rome, disgusted with the prevalent corruptions, Hildebrand would have quitted the city again and for good, but was fixed in a resolution to stay after an occurrence not unlike, in character and termination (if we may compare together such opposite [267] fortunes as those of a Pope and a Lord Mayor), the "turn-

---

[57] *Guaimar*: Guaimar III (c.983-1027), Prince of Salerno and Duke of Amalfi.

[58] *the celebrated monastery of Cluni*: The Abbey of Cluny (France) was founded in 910 and became one of Europe's great Benedictine abbeys and a centre of reform. The abbey closed in 1793, as a result of the French Revolution.

[59] *the Abbot Odilo*: (d.1049) One of three Abbots of Cluny who have been canonised as saints, St. Odilo was a keen reformer through his foundation of monasteries and his friendship with popes, bishops and rulers.

[60] *the Angel of the commissioned Reformer who went before the first Advent*: St. Gabriel, who told Zacharias that John the Baptist would be 'great in the sight of the Lord' (Luke 1:15).

again" passage in the history of Whittington.[61] He afterwards served under the unfortunate Gregory VI. On Gregory's downfall, Hildebrand was carried by Henry across the Alps with Gregory himself; and thus he was at hand, when Leo, on his appointment to the papacy, invited his assistance. Such was Hildebrand, and such his previous history; and now what advice will he give to the mild and unassuming Bruno? Mr. Bowden shall tell us.

"Bruno knew and respected his zeal and ability, and, as he happened to be at Worms during the session of the Council, the newly-chosen pontiff sent for him, and requested him to be the companion of his intended journey to Rome. 'I cannot,' said Hildebrand, 'accompany you;' and, when pressed to declare the reason of this, probably unexpected, refusal, he said, 'Because you go to occupy the government of the Roman Church, not in virtue of a regular and canonical institution to it, but as appointed to it by secular and kingly power.' This led to a discussion, in which Bruno, gentle and candid by nature, and already, perhaps, inclined in his heart to favour the principles which Hildebrand now advocated before him, permitted himself to be convinced that the legitimate electors of the See of St. Peter were the Roman clergy and the people; and he prepared to shape his course accordingly. Returning to Toul, to make the necessary preparations, and to take a farewell of his diocese, he set out thence in a style very different from that which had usually been adopted by the nominees of Teutonic sovereigns in their inaugural journeys to the papal city. Instead of the rich pontifical attire which they were wont, from the day of their nomination, to

---

[61] *the "turn-again" passage in the history of the Whittington*: the popular rags-to-riches folk tale, first found in written form in the seventeenth century: Dick Whittington finally leaves his harsh pauper's life in London with his cat, but as he reaches Holloway (still the site of the 'Whittington Stone') he fancies the Bow bells ring out 'Turn again, Whittington, Lord Mayor of London.' The story was based around a real life fifteenth century Lord Mayor.

assume, he clothed himself in the simple habit of a pilgrim, thus publicly testifying to the world that, notwithstanding the act of the German Henry and his Council, he considered that his real election was yet to come. Leaving Toul on the third day from the festival of Christmas, he halted on his way, at the monastery of Cluni, and from hence, if not from Toul itself, was accompanied by Hildebrand, in his unostentatious progress to the papal city. At that city, barefooted, and clad in the humble guise which he had thus assumed, Bruno arrived in the early part of February, 1049; [268] and as he found the clergy and people assembled, and uttering hymns of thanksgiving and shouts of joy in honour of his arrival, he at once addressed them, and having announced to them the mode of his election in Germany, entreating them fully and freely to declare their sentiments on the subject. Their election, he said, was of paramount authority to every other; and if what had been done beyond the Alps did not meet with their general approval, he was ready to return—a pilgrim as he had come—and to shake off the burden of a responsibility, which he had only upon compulsion undertaken. His discourse was responded to by an unanimous shout of approval; and Bruno, installed without delay in his office, assumed thenceforward the name of Leo IX."—Pp. 137-139.

It seems, then, there is a hidden power in the Church struggling with Henry in the person of his own nominees, and that, as regards the very point through which the system of Charlemagne introduced corruption into it. The State appointment to the Church offices, which was the result of the Carlovingian changes, implied the secular character of offices held by virtue of such an appointment; and that presumed secular character led to their being treated as secular, that is, to simony in obtaining them, and to a worldly use of them. Henry's reform then was conducted on a principle which involved and perpetuated the very evils which it was intended to remove; if the Church was under secular jurisdiction, it was fairly open to secular use. This feeling it was, the perception of this axiomatic truth, which the Church's instinct, or divine sense, seemed to be travailing with and bringing into effect at the era before us; and now let us, under Mr. Bowden's guidance, inquire into the history of the momentous doctrines, which it eventually succeeded in establishing.

When Christians have but a partial confidence in their own principles, there is a great temptation, when Church matters go wrong, to give up God's way, and take whatever [269] is recommended by the expediency of the moment. The ancient and true methods of proceeding appear quite out of date and place; the old materials, instruments, centres, and laws, on which the Church once moved, are apparently worn out by use; and what remains but to take up whatever comes to hand? We need not go to past ages for illustrations of this remark. In all times, weeds and scum, and all that is worthless, float on the surface, and precious gems lie at the bottom of the deep; and where there is neither faith to accept nor penetration to apprehend, what does not obtrude itself upon the senses, men are very ready to put up with what they see, in despair of meeting with what may be more to their purpose. Thus in Hildebrand's age, it might be plausibly argued that ecclesiastical affairs had, in the changes of society, devolved to the civil power; that the State was their natural administrator; that it had the means, and none but it, of reforming the Church. It might be urged that the old high spirit, beautiful as it had been, was no more; that there was no place within the Church on which a reformer could place himself, who desired to operate upon it; that whether he attempted pastors or flock, regulars or seculars, the ground would give way under him. The necessity of the case then formed the vindication of the Emperor's conduct, were there no other plea in its behalf; and yet in matter of fact, out of that hopeless chaos rose, and upon it found a seat, the broadest and most sovereign rule which the Christian world has seen.

In truth, taking the corruptions of that day at the worst, they were principally on the surface of the Church. Scandals are petulant and press into view, and they are exaggerated from the shock they communicate to beholders. Friends [270] exaggerate through indignation, foes through malevolence. In the worst of times there is always a remnant of holy men, out of sight, scanty perhaps in numbers, but great in moral strength, and there is always even in the multitude an acknowledgment of truths which they do not themselves practise. Among all men, educated and unlettered, there is a tacit recognition of certain principles as the cardinal points of society, which very rarely come distinctly into view, and of which the mind is the less conscious because of their being intimately near to it. Such there were in Hildebrand's day, and the secret of his success lay in his having the genius or the faith to appeal to them. We should rather say the faith; for this is remarkably the case, and is exemplified in our own day; that what is commonly admired as commanding talent is far more rightly to be regarded as a firm realizing grasp of some great principle, and that power of developing it in all directions, and that nerve to abide faithful to it, which is involved in such a true apprehension.

The fundamental notion of the Hildebrandine period was the ecumenical power of the Pope, which had been matured by a variety of circumstances, and remained in the European mind even in the most scandalous and trying times. Mr. Bowden has struck off some of these operative causes with great power. In the first place, Rome was the only apostolical see in the West, and thereby had a natural claim to the homage of those sees which were less distinguished. This pre-eminence was heightened by her inflexible orthodoxy amid the doctrinal controversies in which the Eastern sees had successively erred, and by the office of arbitrator and referee, which she held, amid their rivalries and quarrels. Further, when the descent of the barbarians had over-whelmed or exterminated the nations and churches [271] of the Empire, Christian Rome became the instrument of the conversion of the heathen population, and the patriarchal centre of the new world which it created. And when the seat of temporal power had been removed to Constantinople, or re-founded in France or Germany, the Roman See came into a position of independence and sovereignty which could not be the lot of Churches living under the immediate shadow of the imperial throne. It became the rival of the eastern Cæsars and the viceroy of the western. Moreover, in the age of feudalism, when monarchy was the only form of civil polity, there would be at once a tendency in the ecclesiastical state to imitate it, and an expediency in doing so in order to meet and counteract its aggressions. And, amid national changes and the rise and fall of dynasties, it was natural for struggling leaders to seek support from a settled power like Rome, and to recognize that power by asking for its exercise. And it must be considered too that power has always a tendency to increase itself and that, independently, as it would seem, of the wishes or efforts of its possessors.

To these historical causes, doctrinal sanctions, true or pretended, lent their aid. From the first, indeed, prerogatives were attached to the Church of Rome which belonged to no other but her; but these were extravagantly increased by certain well-known forgeries, of which Mr. Bowden gives us an interesting account. The chief of these were the pretended Decretals, a variety of letters, decrees, and other documents, purporting to be the work of bishops of Rome from the very earliest times. This celebrated forgery made its appearance between the years 830 and 850, and what is remarkable did not proceed from Rome, but from the North, [272] from Mentz, being, as would appear, the work of a deacon of that city of the name of Benedict. Under all circumstances it is natural for the weaker portion of the community to desire the means of appeal from the arbitrary will of their rulers, and that to a power safe from the local influences of those against whom they themselves desire protection; and this operated in an especial way in disposing the German bishops towards Rome, passing over their own metropolitans, at a time when the civil power was in the hands of tyrants but partially reclaimed from barbarism. The Churches then of Germany naturally looked to Rome for protection against their secular governors; and the forgery in question was the expression of their previous wishes, as well as the formal basis in justification of them in time to come. The spurious series, says Mr. Bowden, is throughout consistent with itself, and is occupied throughout in asserting the Church's independence from every species of secular dominion or jurisdiction; and "the bishop of the holy and universal Church" is declared to be the Pope. To him all cases of importance are to be referred; he is the head and cardinal point of all Churches, and by him they are all to be governed.[62] Such was the combination of circumstances under which the supremacy of the Pope over other bishops had been established, both in fact and in public opinion; and in this connexion we are led to quote the following just and important remark of our author:

73] "The pontiffs," he says, "did not so much claim new privileges for themselves as deprive their episcopal brethren of privileges originally common to the hierarchy. Even the title by which these autocratical prelates, in the plentitude of their power, delighted to style themselves, 'Summus Sacerdos,'[63] 'Pontifex Maximus,'[64] 'Vicarius Christi,'[65] 'Papa'[66] itself, had, nearer to the primitive times, been the honourable appellations of every bishop; as 'Sedes Apostolica'[67] had been the designation of every bishop's throne. The ascription of these titles therefore to the Pope only gave to the terms a new force, because that ascription became exclusive; because, that is, the bishops in general were stripped of honours to which their claims were as well founded as those of their Roman brother; who became, by the change, not so strictly universal, as sole, bishop. The degradation of the collective hierarchy, as involved in such a relative exaltation of one of its members, was

---

[62] [Mr. Bowden says that, before the appearance of the forgery, "the theory of papal supremacy already existed in its great, but yet unconnected, elements," though the forgery of course consolidated it; and that "the immediate effect of it was rather to make and consolidate relations already existing between the different orders in the Christian hierarchy than to introduce new ones."]—Vol. i., pp. 52, 56. *Vid.* Note on this Essay, *infra.* [N]

[63] *'Summus Sacerdos,'*: High Priest

[64] *'Pontifex Maximus,'*: Supreme Pontiff

[65] *'Vicarius Christi,'*: Vicar of Christ

[66] *'Papa,'*: Pope (meaning 'father')

[67] *'Sedes Apostolica'*: Apostolic See

seen and resisted by one not likely to entertain unreasonable or exaggerated views of the dangers to be expected from Roman aggrandizement, the truly great and good Pope Gregory I.[68] 'I beseech your Holiness,' said this pontiff to the Patriarch of Alexandria,[69] who had addressed him, contrary to his previously expressed desire, by the title of Papa Universalis, 'to do so no more; for that is taken from you which is bestowed, in an unreasonable degree, upon another ... I do not reckon that to be honour, in which I see their due honour taken from my brethren; for my honour is the honour of the Universal Church, the solid strength of my brethren: I then am truly honoured when the proper share of honour is assigned to each and to all. But if your Holiness styles me "Universal Pope," you renounce that dignity for yourself which you ascribe universally to me. But let this be done no more ... My predecessors have endeavoured, by cherishing the honour of all members of the priesthood throughout the world, to preserve their own in the sight of the Almighty.'

"And even at a much more mature stage of the growth of papal pretensions, in the eleventh century itself, we find the pontiff Leo IX., in an epistle to the Grecian Patriarch, Michael Cerularius,[70] repeating the assertion, made by Gregory in the above epistle, that his predecessor and namesake, Leo the Great,[71] to whom the title of Ecumenical Patriarch had been offered by the Council of Chalcedon,[72] had repudiated the proud appellation, by the ascription of which to one prelate an affront would be offered to the equal dignity of all."—Vol. i., pp. 64-66.

---

[68] *Gregory I*: See note on p.[37].

[69] *Patriarch of Alexandria*: Eulogius, Patriarch 580-608.

[70] *Michael Cerularius*: Patriarch of Constaninople (1043-1058). The Latins excommunicated the Easterns and Michael issued anathemas on 21 June 1054 which started the schism.

[71] *Leo the Great*: See note on p.[127].

[72] *Council of Chalcedon*: 451

The causes we have been enumerating had effected the [274] introduction of papal supremacy, even before the dark times to which the Hildebrandine period succeeded; and it is observable that, even amid the moral and political degradation of the Roman See in the ninth and tenth centuries, the theory still maintained its hold upon the public mind. We find Dietrich, Archbishop of Treves[73] in 969, soliciting and obtaining from John XIII.[74] for himself and his successors that precedence among the archbishops of Germany, which the office of legate was considered to confer. Stephen of Hungary,[75] a secular prince, at the end of the tenth century, with a view of strengthening his authority over his half-converted subjects, had obtained from Sylvester II.[76] the permission to combine his regal title with that of Apostolic Legate. Gregory V.,[77] the immediate predecessor of Sylvester, when he excommunicated the son of Hugh Capet[78] for an illegal marriage, excommunicated also the Archbishop of Treves,[79] who had solemnized it, and the other bishops who had countenanced it with their presence; and on that prince defying the sentence, had put

---

[73] *Dietrich, Archbishop of Treves*: 965-977

[74] *John XIII*: (930-972), Pope from 965.

[75] *Stephen of Hungary*: (975-1038). He obtained a royal crown from the Pope in 1001 and was canonised in 1083.

[76] *Sylvester II*: (c.946-1003), originally Gerbert of Aurillac, Pope from 999. This first French pope also made an important contribution to science, reintroducing to the west the use of the abacus and armillary sphere and promoting the decimal numeral system. Such interests led to later accusations that he was a sorcerer.

[77] *Gregory V*: Pope (996-99) who excommunicated Robert II of France when he continued to live with his cousin Bertha, even after the marriage was declared invalid.

[78] *Hugh Capet*: (c.936-996), King of the Franks (987-996) and founder of the Capetian line of kings. The son mentioned here is Robert II (972-1031), excommunicated for his marriage to his cousin Bertha of Burgundy.

[79] *Archbishop of Treves*: (Trier) Ludolf (Archbishop 994-1008).

his kingdom under an interdict, with such effect that he was deserted by his whole court and household, and even the two domestics who remained with him, avoiding his touch as infected, threw every plate and vessel out of which he had eaten and drunk into the fire. And, to take another specimen of prerogative, John XV.[80] about the same date, had begun the practice of canonization, acting, as he expressed it, "by the authority of the blessed Peter, prince of Apostles," from whom he claimed to be the one visible head of the community of the faithful, the "bishop of the holy Roman Catholic and Apostolic Church." It cannot be denied then, that in spite of the dreadful demoralization of the Church and popedom in the tenth and eleventh centuries, there was laid in the temper of the age and the feelings of society a deep and firm groundwork, if men could be found who had the heart to appeal to it, for reforming and purifying the Church by an internal effort, and without recurring to the temporal power, which seemed at first sight the obvious, or rather the only resource.

[275]

Here then was the point of battle between the Church and the State. The State said to the Church, "I am the only power which can reform you; you hold of me, and your dignities and offices are in my gift." The Church said to the State, "She who wields the power even of smiting kings, cannot be a king's creature; and if you attempt to reform her, you will be planting the root of corruption by the same hand which cuts off its branches."

---

[80] *John XV*: Pope 985-996.

4.

The struggle between the parties began from the commencement of Hildebrand's political history. Before his intimacy with Leo IX., he had, as we have seen, been connected with the unfortunate Gregory VI.; yet, even he, guilty as he was of a crime to which Hildebrand so earnestly opposed himself from first to last, committed it with the object of asserting, against the aristocracy, the dormant right of the Roman clergy and people to elect their own bishops. After this time Hildebrand seems to have been the chief spring in ecclesiastical movements in the papal city, for a space of twenty-four years, till the time of his own elevation. During that period he served the Popes Leo IX., Victor II.,[81] Stephen IX.,[82] Nicholas II.,[83] and Alexander II.,[84]—all of them virtuous or even austere persons,— steadily developing and realizing by successive acts the purification of the Church and the theory of her independence and sovereignty. For the interesting history of [276] this period, we must refer to Mr. Bowden's second book, on which our limits will not allow us to enter, but from which, as a specimen of its contents, we will extract two or three

---

[81] *Victor II*: Pope (1055-57) who held a synod at Florence soon after his election condemning simony, clerical concubinage and alienation of church property.

[82] *Stephen IX*: Pope (1057-58) who remained Abbot of Monte Cassino and created the reformist St Peter Damian a cardinal. He denounced clerical marriage and pushed forward the independence of the Church from lay interference.

[83] *Nicholas II*: Pope (1058-61) who organised a synod at the Lateran in 1059 which legislated against lay investiture.

[84] *Alexander II*: Pope (1061-73) who promoted clerical celibacy and the common life and confirmed decrees against simony; he also defended the Jews against forcible conversion. As part of his reformist strategy, he supported William of Normandy's invasion of England (1066) after he promised to reform the English Church.

passages from the history of two saints, Leo, whom we have already introduced to the reader, and Peter Damiani.

The pontificate of Leo IX. supplies an illustration of that mixture of catholic truth with wild romance, which pervades the history of the times. In his own person he was a model of that reform which he had in view for the whole Church. His "hours of sleep," says Mr. Bowden, "were systematically abridged by his devotions: when at Rome, it was his wont, thrice in the week, to walk barefoot at midnight from the palace of the Lateran to the church of St. Peter (from one extremity, that is, of Rome to the other) accompanied by two or three only of his clergy, for the purposes of praise and prayer: a spectacle which might well strike those with astonishment, who were accustomed to the scenes of infamy and riot, by which the palace in question, and the papal city in general, had been disgraced under the licentious pontiffs of the preceding age."—Vol. i., p. 152. Yet this pure and holy man is next presented to us as leading a military expedition against the Normans, which he seems to have thought to be as little out of character with his pontifical office, as a rector of a parish among ourselves in being a magistrate and reading the riot act, or a clergyman serving the office of proctor in our Universities. It was now about fifty years since the Normans had first become known to the inhabitants of Calabria and Apulia, whither they had at first come as pilgrims, then done battle as champions of the faith, then served as mercenaries, and at length spread devastation as marauders. The pagan, to [277] whom they had opposed themselves, was the Saracen, who from time to time made descents upon the coast, though his power was on the decline; and Mr. Bowden gives the following account of the first collision between young faith and degenerate misbelief:

"In or about the year 1002, a petty flotilla appeared before Salerno, and a body of Saracens, landing under the walls of the place, demanded, with the customary menaces, a pecuniary contribution. Guaimar III., Prince of Salerno, and his timid subjects, felt that they had no course to adopt but submission; and their surprise was great, when about forty pilgrims from a distant land, who happened to be at the moment within their walls, requested of the prince arms, horses, and permission to chastise these insolent marauders. The request was readily complied with: the pilgrim warriors, accoutred in haste, galloped eagerly forth through the gates of Salerno; the Saracens, confounded and dismayed, fled tumultuously from the onset of this unexpected foe; and esteemed themselves happy when their retreating barks bore them out of reach of the swords of the victorious Normans.

"The delighted Guaimar would willingly have been prodigal in his bounty towards his gallant deliverers; but he experienced a second surprise when the costly presents, which he laid before them, were firmly, though courteously, rejected. 'For the love of God, and of the Christian faith,' said the chivalrous pilgrims, 'we have done what we have done; and we may neither accept of wages for such service, nor delay our return to our homes.'"— Vol. i., pp. 156, 157.

"They departed accordingly," adds Mr. Bowden, "but not unaccompanied. Guaimar sent with them, to their native land, envoys laden with presents, such as might best tempt the countrymen of these hardy and disinterested warriors to enlist in his service. Specimens of southern fruits, superb vestments, golden bits, and magnificent horse-trappings, attracted and dazzled the eyes of the population of Normandy, and produced on the enterprising youth of the province their natural effect." This was the commencement of their connexion with southern Italy; but it was not for ever of so edifying a character. They returned in the capacity of soldiers in the pay of its petty princes, and, with the duties, they practised the vices and excesses of their profession. They were a people of warm religious feelings; but a young nation has the waywardness and uncertainty of children, and every now and then these soldiers of fortune, turning to plunder, were tempted to rifle, for the sake of gain, the holy shrines in which, on their first appearance, they had come to worship. Tidings of their sacrilegious acts reached the ears of Leo. "And when," Mr. Bowden tells us, "he saw that the insulters of the Church were also the ruthless oppressors of their fellow-creatures, when he beheld the southern gates of Rome daily thronged by the wretched inhabitants of Apulia, who, destitute, blinded, and horribly mutilated, were seeking a refuge from further tyranny behind the sheltering walls of the papal city, the pitying pontiff yielded himself entirely to the impulses of his benevolent nature," and led an army in person against the Normans. With that object he crossed the Alps and gained of the Emperor 500 Germans, most of them volunteers; then returning, he raised the banner of St. Peter in Italy, and a motley company from Apulia, Campania, and Ancona flocked around it. It is not known whether Hildebrand sanctioned this measure. Benno[85] "his embittered adversary," as Mr. Bowden calls him, charges him with doing so; but "the statement," he continues, "appears to be unsupported by other contemporaneous

---

[85] *Benno*: Bishop of Meisssen, 1010-1106.

authority; and the work of Benno is filled with so many palpable calumnies against Hildebrand, that nothing in the nature of an accusation can be worthy of credit which rests upon his evidence alone." It is undeniable, however, that Hildebrand, when Pope, himself entertained a somewhat similar project. On the other hand, Hildebrand's intimate [279] friend, and the principal organ of his party, Peter Damiani, has left on record his protest against the assumption, on the part of the successor of St. Peter, of that earthly sword, which our Lord Himself denied to the Apostle. Anyhow, it was unprecedented in that age, considering Leo was Pope, and the enemy a Christian people; though bishops were in the habit of accompanying their retainers to the field, and Pope John X.,[86] somewhat more than a century before, had engaged Mahomedans in battle.

"It was on the 18th of June, 1053, that Leo's troops confronted those of the enemy near the town of Civitella. The Normans, when aware of his intentions, had made all preparations in their power to ward off the coming blow. William Ironarm[87] was no more; but his brothers, Humphrey and Robert,[88]—the latter of whom, subsequently surnamed Guiscard, had recently arrived in Apulia with a considerable reinforcement to the Norman forces,— succeeded to the command of his intrepid warriors; and Richard, Count of Aversa, the chief of a smaller, but independent, Norman colony in Italy, brought all the force he could muster to the defence of the common cause. But the Normans were dispirited:

---

[86] *John X:* (d.929), Pope 914-928. His coalition of Italian rulers decisively defeated the Saracens at Garigliano in August 915.

[87] *William Ironarm:* a Norman adventurer (d.1046) and Count of Apulia who gained his nickname by killing the Emir of Syracuse while fighting the Saracens in Sicily.

[88] *his brothers, Humphrey and Robert:* Humphrey (d.1057) and his half-brother Robert Guiscard (d.1085), both Counts of Apulia.

rumour had magnified among them the scale of the papal preparations, and they were awed by the sacred character of him in whom, even while he was their enemy, they recognized their spiritual parent. The heralds, therefore, who approached Leo while he was yet within the walls of Civitella, assumed an humble tone; they deprecated his hostility, and informed him that the Norman princes, though they declined to abandon possessions which they had won, were ready to hold their conquests thenceforth by his grant, and do suit and service for them to him, as to their lord paramount. But the tall, bulky Germans, by whom the pontiff was surrounded, smiled in scorn when they beheld the diminutive though active forms of their adversaries; and Leo, inspired by their confidence, as well as by his conviction of the goodness of his cause, rejected the overtures of the Norman leaders, and demanded the total abandonment of the lands which they had recently usurped from St. Peter. This the Normans declined to concede, and therefore, feeling that no other alternative lay before them, they gave the signal for battle, before

[280]   Leo had issued from the gates of Civitella. The result of the action which now took place, falsified alike the confident anticipations of the one party and the desponding auguries of the other. The impetuous charge of the Norman chivalry at once unmanned the timid Italians who composed the bulk of Leo's army, and who fled in every possible direction. Werner and his German band[89] met the shock with the calm courage of their country; but the Normans, unresisted elsewhere, turned their flanks, and hemmed them in on every side; until this gallant troop, contending valiantly to the last, covered with their corpses the ground which they had occupied. But for their resistance,—so sudden was the flight, so rapid the dispersion of Leo's army,—the business of the day might seem rather to deserve the name of a slaughter than of a battle.

---

[89] *Werner and his German band*: 700 Swabian knights under the command of Werner von Maden and Albert von Winterthur.

"The conquering chiefs pushed on without delay, through the streets of Civitella, into the presence of Leo. But they no sooner beheld the venerable pontiff, than, exchanging the fierceness of the warrior for the subdued tone of the penitent, they fell at his feet, and in abasement and tears besought the absolution and the blessing of their vanquished enemy. Moved by this conduct, and induced by the exigency of his position, Leo revoked the sentence of anathema which he had pronounced against them; and they then escorted him with all reverence and honour to the city of Benevento. There the humbled pontiff remained nine months, during which time, at the request of his captors, he consented to grant them, in the name of St. Peter, the investiture of all their conquests, made or to be made, in Apulia, Calabria, and Sicily; which they were thenceforward to hold as fiefs of the Holy See."—Vol. i., pp. 162-165.

By this turn of events, Leo's defeat and captivity involved more favourable results than could have been reaped from the most brilliant victory. The Pope acquired a claim on the services of the Normans, as of vassals; and, moreover, recognition of his power to confer the investiture, as lord paramount, of extensive domains, over which they had held no previous sway. What was more to the immediate purpose of the war, the presence of the mild old man succeeded in subduing the fierceness and cruelty with which the proceedings of the Normans had hitherto been attended; an effect, moreover, which would be naturally [281] promoted by their admission, in consequence of the compact, into the circle of recognized sovereigns and the responsibilities of legitimate power. However, Leo did not at the time find all this consolation in the issue of his military exploits. He considered the failure of his arms to be a sign of the divine displeasure that he had taken them up.

He gave himself over to acts of penance. Though his health was declining, a carpet on the bare earth was his ordinary couch, a stone his pillow, and a hair shirt his garment. "Under such austerities," says Mr. Bowden, "aided as they were in their effect by the sorrows and anxieties of his mind, his constitution gradually sank; and when he at length left Benevento, and returned, in March, 1054, to the papal city, it was only to breathe his last there on the 19th of the following April, after having committed to his beloved friend Hildebrand the provisional government of the Roman Church, until a new pontiff should be appointed to the Apostolic See."—Vol. i., pp. 166, 167.

St. Peter Damiani, Bishop of Ostia, who has already been incidentally mentioned, is another personage of this period, whom the course of the history brings before us, and to whom, we think, that Mr. Bowden, as regards one passage of his life, is hardly fair, though he treats him always with that respect and honour which is his due. He speaks of him "as a man of sincere and deep devotion, of extraordinary talents, and of a monastic austerity; of too ardent a temperament to be uniformly judicious in his proceedings;" while "his faith was of a description which led him to receive, without question, a host of legends of the most absurd description." "But," he continues, "there shone forth in him a singleness and purity of character, which, in [282] connexion with his abilities, procured him the universal respect and admiration of his contemporaries." He had devoted himself to a monastic life, and he resisted his elevation to the episcopate with all his might. "He feared," says Mr. Bowden, "to be drawn from the unremitting austerities of his retirement; and it was not until he was threatened by Stephen and his Council with excommunication, that he consented to change the life of seclusion and self-denial which he lived for the activity and notoriety of a more responsible situation."—Vol. i., pp. 189, 190.

After a time, he was sent to Milan, as legate, to set right the disorders existing in those parts which the Milanese clergy attempted to shield from reform under colour of the dignity and independence of the Church over which St. Ambrose[90] had presided. Another point on which reform was demanded was their assertion that they had a right to marry, by virtue of a privilege granted them by the same Saint. In this business he was associated with Anselm da Badagio, Bishop of Lucca, afterwards Pope Alexander II.

"Making their appearance in the long-disturbed city, these envoys found the archbishop and his clergy, however hostile in secret to their coming, prepared to acknowledge their authority, and to receive them with every outward mark and sign of deference. But the populace, moved perhaps by the secret instigations of their pastors, soon showed, disposed as they might be themselves to ridicule or revile these careless guides, that they were keenly jealous of the assumed independence of their native Church, and viewed with suspicion any papal interference with the proceedings of its governors. In tumultuous throngs they filled the streets, and entered the building in which the legates had convened the clerical body of the place ... The discontent at length broke out in open tumult ... The clergy, eager to augment the fray, rang the alarm-bell in the various churches of the city; the

---

[90] *St. Ambrose*: (c.340-397), Bishop of Milan, Doctor of the Church; champion of orthodoxy against Arianism and staunch defender of the Church against imperial pressure. Ambrose's preaching influenced St. Augustine, and on his conversion he baptised him.

confusion increased, and even the life of Damiani was apparently in danger. But that bold and high-spirited man was equal to the crisis; ascending a pulpit, he showed himself prepared to address the tumultuous multitude. His dauntless bearing awed them to silence, and he was heard with attention, while with dignity, and all the eloquence which distinguished him, he set forth the claims which the mother Church of Rome possessed on the dutiful obedience of her daughter, the Church of Milan. He cited instances in which St. Ambrose himself had appealed to the protection of the Roman prelate, and acknowledged his pre-eminence. 'Search,' he concluded, 'your own records, and if ye find not there that what we say is the truth, expose our falsehood. But if ye find us true, resist not the truth, resist not undutifully the voice of your mother; but from her, from whom ye first drew in the milk of apostolic faith, receive with gratitude the more solid food of heavenly doctrine.'

"This appeal, and the legate's fearless demeanour, produced a sudden turn in the feelings of his hearers ... and the clergy offered no further opposition to the legatine authority. On Peter's demand, their whole body, with the archbishop at their head, agreed to pledge themselves with a solemn vow against simony and clerical marriage; ... and Peter, thus successful in his mission, pronounced in his official character the reconciliation of Milan to the Apostolic See."—Vol. i., pp. 208-210.

Shortly after this, Damiani resolved on resigning his bishopric and retiring back to his beloved cloister, from which he had been with such difficulty separated. Here it is that we think Mr. Bowden is rather hard upon him, unless, as is certainly possible, he has reasons which do not appear in his work. He calls him "singular-minded," and he speaks of "his morbid craving after ascetic retirement." Now surely there is nothing strange in his desiring quiet, and as to whether he ought to have indulged that desire, that is a question which no one could determine but himself. Supposing he found himself falling back in self-control and divine love, would not that be a reason for doubt and deliberation what it was his duty to do? Gibbon speaks ironically of unwilling monks torn out of their retreats and seated on bishops' thrones,[91] but no one could know but [284] themselves how great a blessing the cloister was, and what a great sacrifice to relinquish it. The ten thousand trivial accidents of the day in a secular life which exert a troublous influence upon the soul, dimming its fair surface with many a spot of dust and damp, these give place to a divine stillness, which, to those who can bear it, is the nearest approach to heaven. A sharp word, or a light remark, or a tone, or an expression of countenance, or a report, or an unwelcome face, or an association, ruffles the mind, and keeps it from fixing itself upon its true good. "One day," says Pope St. Gregory I., "when I was oppressed with the excessive trouble of secular affairs, I sought a retired place, friendly to grief, where whatever displeased me of my engagements might show itself openly, and all that was accustomed to inflict pain might be seen at one view." There he was surprised by "his most dear son Peter the deacon," whom he had made his intimate from the time that the latter was a young man. He opens his grief to Peter in words which are so much to our purpose, that with the reader's indulgence we will digress to quote them. "My sad mind," he says, "labouring under the soreness of its engagements, remembers how it went with me formerly in my monastery, how all perishable things were beneath it,

---

[91] *Gibbons speaks ironically of unwilling monks torn out of their retreats...* : Cf. *Decline and Fall*, chapter 37.

how it was superior to all that was transitory; that it was wont to think of nought but things of heaven; that, though still in the body, it went out beyond the very prison of the flesh in contemplation; that it even loved death, which is nearly to all a punishment, as the entrance of life and a reward of its labour. But now, in consequence of the pastoral charge, it undergoes the occupation of secular men, and for that fair beauty of its quiet, is dishonoured with the dust of earthly work. And after dissipating itself on outward things to serve the many, even when it seeks what is inward, it comes home indeed, but is no more equal to itself."—*Dial.* i. 1.

[285]

Such would be the bitter experience of a mind like Damiani's; and it depends on a number of minute circumstances, whether it was not as much his duty to decline the pastoral charge, as Gregory's to retain it. Mr. Bowden allows, too, that "from his retirement he continued to watch with an attentive eye the fortunes of the Church; by his epistles he still interfered with her concerns and influenced her destiny, nor was he backward, when called on, to devote himself on special occasions to active service in her cause." And we find in the after-history, of his going, in his extreme age, as Alexander's legate, to the young King Henry, and preventing him from the scandalous step of divorcing an innocent wife, against whom he had no charge except that he did not like her. Mr. Bowden notices, however, that his retirement, at a time when the Church had such need of his services in his episcopate, was never forgiven by Hildebrand; and he adds his own suspicion that some personal feelings towards Hildebrand influenced him in retiring from his post.

5.

But it is time to return to Hildebrand himself, in whom all the interest of his times centres.[92] A decree of a Lateran Council had been passed under Nicholas II., in 1059, vesting the election of Pope in the College of Cardinals; with the concurrence and ratification of the Emperor; a decree which opened the way to a still greater innovation, upon the first vacancy in the Holy See. The imperial court resisted the appointment of Alexander, who was the choice of the sacred College, and named an antipope, Cadalous;[93]   [286] but the contest was terminated in favour of the papalists in 1067, at a Council held in Mantua, in which the Emperor gave up Cadalous and acknowledged Alexander II. Six years afterwards Alexander died. Hildebrand had already on a former occasion been put forward for the papal chair, but he had resisted the proposal, it is said, "with many tears and supplications;" now, however, the following scene took place:

"Alexander II. had no sooner breathed his last, than his archdeacon, in concert with the other leading ecclesiastics of the city, directed that the three following days should be devoted to fasting, to deeds of charity, and to prayer; after which the proper authorities were to proceed, in the hope of the divine blessing upon their counsels, to the election of a successor. But long before the period thus prescribed had elapsed, that election was decided.

"On the day following that of Alexander's decease, the dignified clergy of the Roman Church stood, with the archdeacon, round the bier of the departed pontiff, in the patriarchal church of

---

[92] Newman omits here a passage regarding the Empress Agnes; see the Textual Appendix.

[93] *Cadalous*: Peter Cadalous (d.1072), Bishop of Parma and antipope 'Honorius II' (1061-64).

the Lateran. The funeral rites were in progress, and Hildebrand, it is probable, was taking a part in the celebration of these solemn ceremonies. But suddenly, from the body of the building, which had been filled to overflowing by the lower clergy and people, burst forth the cry of 'Hildebrand.' A thousand voices instantly swelled the sound 'Hildebrand shall be Pope.' 'St. Peter chooses our Archdeacon Hildebrand.' These, and cries like these, rang wildly along the church; the ceremonies were interrupted, and the officiating clergy paused in suspense. The subject of this tumult, recovering from a momentary stupor, rushed into a pulpit, and thence, while his gestures implored silence, attempted to address the agitated assembly."

The attempt was vain; the uproar continued, and it was not until the cardinal presbyter, Hugo Candidus,[94] coming forward, declared Hildebrand to be the unanimous choice of the cardinals, that the multitude suffered their cries to subside.

[287] "Then the joyous cries of the populace arose anew. The cardinal, bishops, and clergy approached the object of their choice to lead him towards the apostolic throne. 'We choose,' they cried to the people, 'for our pastor and pontiff, a devout man; a man skilled in interpreting the Scriptures; a distinguished lover of equity and justice; a man firm in adversity, and temperate in prosperity; a man, according to the saying of the Apostle, of good behaviour, blameless, modest, sober, chaste, given to hospitality, and one that ruleth well in his own house.[95] A man from his childhood generously brought up in the bosom of this mother Church, and for the merit of his life already raised to the archidiaconal dignity. We choose, namely, our archdeacon Hildebrand, to be Pope and successor to the Apostle, and to bear

---

[94] *Hugo Candidus*: a monk of Remiremont and cardinal (c.1020-90), who opposed Gregory VII and was excommunicated several times by him.
[95] *according to the saying of the Apostle* ... : Cf. 1 Timothy 3-4

henceforward and for ever the name of Gregory.' The Pope elect, upon this, was forthwith invested by eager hands with the scarlet vestment and tiara[96] of pontifical dignity, and placed, notwithstanding his gestures of reluctance, and even his tears, upon the throne of the Apostle. The cardinals approached him with obeisance, and the people, with shouts yet louder and more joyous than before, repeated the designation of their new pontiff, and tumultuously testified their approbation."—Vol. i., pp. 314-317.

Considering the unparalleled character, or, as we may say, the madness of the plans to which Hildebrand was pledged, and which his spirit within him told him he must attempt at all risks, it is not wonderful at all that he should both have shrunk from the pontificate beforehand, and have been overcome with the burden when it was first put upon him. Power or wealth is pleasant to us when unattended with conditions; but did they involve the necessity of losing limbs, or resigning friends, or risking popularity or good name, they would lose much of their attraction and many of their aspirants. Now Hildebrand was thus circumstanced: while he was a subordinate, he might promote the plans of others, even though short of the best and largest; but when "a dispensation of the Gospel"[97] was committed to him, "necessity was laid on him"[98] to go through all and leave nothing undone. Mr. Bowden tells us, that his election, at [288] the moment unquestionably unexpected by himself, seems to have overwhelmed for a while even his intrepid spirit. In letters written from his couch, he speaks of it in terms of

---

[96] *tiara*: traditional crown of the popes. By the fourteenth century it had three tiers ('Triple Crown'). The last papal coronation was in 1963.

[97] *"a dispensation of the Gospel"*: 1 Corinthians 9:17

[98] *"necessity was laid on him"*: Cf. *ibid.* 9:16

terror, using the language of the Psalms, "I am come into deep waters where the floods overflow me,"[99] imploring the intercessions of his friends in his behalf, and expressing a hope that their prayers, though they had not sufficed to prevent his being called to that post of danger, might nevertheless avail to defend him when placed there.

He wrote a letter shortly after his elevation to Lanfranc,[100] to whom he unbosomed himself more entirely than to others, and from this Mr. Bowden gives us some extracts. "The greater," he says, "the peril in which we are placed, the greater our need of the prayers of all good men. For we, if we would escape the sentence of the Divine wrath, must arise against many, and must incense them against our own soul. And thy prudence will alike see, how fearful it must be for us to abstain from opposing such persons, and how difficult for us to oppose them." Such were his feelings, and that they were replete with faith and conscientiousness there can be no doubt, or that he viewed the course which lay before him with awe. Well he might: we shall confine ourselves to two of the projects which he conceived and carried out,—the chief but not the only acts of his pontificate, and amply sufficient in themselves to exemplify the force of will and fortitude of spirit, which has made his name so memorable in Church history. The first was no less than the obliging the clergy either to separate from their wives or resign their preferments. The second

---

[99] *"I am come into deep waters where the floods overflow me"*: Psalm 69:2

[100] *Lanfranc*: (1005-89) Born in Pavia, he entered the monastery at Bec and was appointed Archbishop of Canterbury in 1070. Working closely with William the Conqueror, he did much to reform and 'Normanise' the English Church.

was the abasement of the temporal below the spiritual power. And first of his enforcement of clerical celibacy:—

6.

We have already noticed that simony and licentiousness were the two crying sins of the clergy; nor did their practice of taking wives at all diminish the latter. Rather it led to it; for, since they knew that in marrying they were transgressing their duty, they were easily led on, from the recklessness which follows upon the wilful violation of conscience in any matter, from a first sin to a second. The prohibitory rule was one of long standing, and Mr. Bowden, waving the discussion of its abstract propriety, has drawn up a succinct account of it from the time of Pope Nicholas I.[101] (A.D. 858), to the date of Hildebrand, a period of two hundred years. Direct condemnations of the practice are found in Nicholas's reply to the Bulgarians, 860; in the Synod of Worms, 868; in Leo VII.'s[102] epistle to the Gauls and Germans, 938; in the decrees of Augsburg, 952; and in Benedict VIII.'s[103] speech, and the decrees passed at Pavia, about 1020. Hincmar of Rheims in 845, Chrodegang, bishop of Metz,[104] in 750, Councils at Mentz and Metz in 888, and at Nantes at the end of the same century, had confirmed the rule with additional circumstances of strictness. And the

---

[101] *Nicholas I*: Pope (858-867), called 'the Great' for his strong leadership and consolidation of papal authority. He wrote a series of responses to questions posed by King Boris of Bulgaria as he considered conversion and joining the Roman Church (*Responsa Nicolai ad consulta Bulgarorum*).

[102] *Leo VII*: Pope (936-939), with a keen interest in monastic reform.

[103] *Benedict VIII*: Pope (1012-24). The Synod of Pavia (1022) passed strong canons prohibiting clerical marriage.

[104] *Chrodegang, Bishop of Metz*: (d.766), author of an influential Rule for the common life of clergy.

association in the case of the clergy between marriage and concubinage, nay, of general laxity of morals, was unhappily so deeply seated, that neither did it occur to the reformers to question their necessary connexion; nor, had they done so, could they have overcome the popular feeling on the subject. Under the circumstances, as Mr. Bowden observes, "the battle which they undertook against their less strict contemporaries, was unquestionably that of purity against impurity, that of holiness against corruption. Seizing the means in their power, they set themselves to achieve, and did achieve, a most important reformation; and we may [290] not think lightly, either of their principles or of their labours, because that reformation was imperfect."

We have already stated what Gregory's proceeding was, and it was carried into effect under circumstances as shocking, as the resolve was ruthless. With a single and severe determination, putting before him the honour of Christ, and the welfare of the Church, like Ezra, the great reformer of Judah,[105] he "said to his father and to his mother, I have not seen him; neither did he acknowledge his brethren, nor knew his own children."[106] Ezra learned, to his deep dismay, that his people had taken to themselves wives of the heathen; "so that the holy seed had mingled themselves with the people of those lands, yea, the hand of the princes and rulers had been chief in this trespass."[107] Upon this he tells us, that he rent his garments and mantle, and plucked off the hair of his head and of his beard, and sat

---

[105] *Ezra, the great reformer of Judah*: A descendant of Seraiah the High Priest, Ezra led a group of exiles back to Jerusalem, where they found many Jews had married Gentiles. Ezra taught the Law and tried to purify the Jews.

[106] *"I have not seen him ... "*: Deuteronomy 33:9

[107] *"so that the holy seed ... "*: Ezra 9:2

down astonished. So he sat till the evening sacrifice; when he rose from his heaviness, deliberately rent his garment and mantle, fell on his knees, spread out his hands towards heaven, and confessed the sin of his people, and interceded for their forgiveness. One thing only could be done, and Shechaniah, the son of Jehiel, exhorted him to it: to make the people "put away all the wives, and such as were born of them," and added, "Arise, for this matter belongeth unto *thee*; we also will be with thee; be of good courage, and do it."[108] Such a voice seemed to sound in Gregory's ears; and, in the strength of a pure conscience, he bade those of his brethren, who against their conscience had taken wives, to make the only reparation which could be made by them for their sin.

But it was not so easy to accomplish as to command; he had, as might be supposed, an opposition to encounter, to which no nerve but his could have been equal.

"Vehement was the indignation of the German clergy, when [291] first the intelligence of this obnoxious enactment reached their ears, and when they found that the great moral power, which the papacy had within the last few years attained, was to be wielded in enforcing, as realities, those principles of austere reformation, which, when promulged as they had been by Gregory's predecessors, a few years before, had probably seemed like theoretical notions, based upon views unsuited to the state of things actually existing in the world. The Pope, the clergy exclaimed aloud, was a heretic, and his decree that of a madman. The execution of it was a childish, an impossible notion. Human nature being what it was, the rigour of his laws, the attempt to make men live like angels, would only plunge the clergy, by a

---

[108] *"put away all the wives ... "*: Ezra 10:3

necessary reaction, into habits more dissolute than ever. And the letter of holy Scripture, the plain teaching as well of our Lord Himself, as of His inspired Apostle, was directly at variance with this wild, this extravagant enactment. But they defied him to proceed to such an extremity as to enforce its general adoption; and protested that, sooner than resign their domestic enjoyments, they would relinquish the priesthood; and, when he had expelled them, for no other reason than that they were men, he might seek where he could for angels, to minister in the churches in their stead.

"And long, and violently, did this tumult rage. Several bishops, among whom was Otho,[109] of Constance, openly put themselves at the head of the clergy opposed to Gregory's authority. And prelates, who, taking a different course, attempted to promulgate the papal edict in their respective dioceses, were assailed by the refractory members of their churches with insolence and outrage. But Gregory, ever watchful of their proceedings, prevented their zeal from flagging by repeated messages of warning, exhortation, and encouragement. And most especially was he urgent with Siegfried,[110] to assume, on the occasion, the determined tone which became him, as primate of Germany, and to enforce the observance of the mandates of the Church, with the full weight of his authority."—Vol. ii., pp. 20-22.

Siegfried was a most unworthy successor of St. Boniface. He had at an earlier date committed himself to an attempt to introduce a tithe payment among the Thuringians, which he prosecuted at all seasons, with a pertinacity not at all inferior to that of the worthy

[292]

---

[109] *Otho*: Otto, Bishop of Constance (1071-1086). He retained his See through military force, despite being excommunicated.
[110] *Siegfried*: Abbot of Fulda (1058-60) and Archbishop of Mainz (1060-84).

Trapbois,[111] for his miserable piece of gold. With the hope of effecting this through the royal power, he had even consented to advocate the project of the royal divorce, and summoned a Council for that purpose in his metropolitan city; when Damiani appeared as the Pope's legate and stopped the infamous proceeding, as was mentioned above. The year following he was summoned by Alexander II. to Rome, to defend himself against a charge of simoniacal practices. Roused to a momentary remorse by the remonstrance of the Pope, he expressed a wish to resign his station, and retire to a life of penitence and seclusion. This proposal, however, was strenuously resisted by Alexander and others; and he returned to Germany, to lose his serious thoughts, and to relapse into his former secularity. At the present crisis, he gave his clergy six months to deliberate on Gregory's injunction, and then summoned a Council, in which he put before them the alternative of renouncing either their wives or those offices which they had accepted on the condition of celibacy. The clergy, after hearing his address, quitted the place of assembly, as if for the purpose of private deliberation, and then resolved at once to set out for home, without his leave. Siegfried, however, pacified them, and persuaded them to return, and then temporized with them; but it all ended in his bringing forward, before a mixed assembly of clergy and laity, the old question of his pretensions to the Thuringian tithes, which had already been settled by treaty in favour of the Thuringians. A tumult ensued; the Council was broken up in confusion, the

---

[111] *the worthy Trapbois*: Trapbois was a character in Sir Walter Scott's *The Fortunes of Nigel* (1822). A lodging-house keeper at Whitefriars, near London's Fleet Street, he was 'a noted usurer' and known as 'Golden Trapbois'.

archbishop with difficulty escaped with his life, and betaking himself to Heiligenstadt, he continued there during the remainder of the year, repeating, but in vain, on every festival, his summons to the disturbers of the Council to do penance for the crime, under pain of excommunication.

[293]

Such were Gregory's proceedings, and such his success with the high prelacy; but he had a new and formidable and, we must add, unjustifiable weapon in his arsenal, which he now brought into the contest. The measure which he was enforcing was founded on four Canons lately passed at Rome in Council, the fourth of which was to the effect that the laity should refuse the ministrations both of simoniacal and of married or licentious clergy. This Canon seemed to oppose the advice of Nicholas I. to the newly converted Bulgarians, who, on asking whether they should receive and honour married priests, had received for answer, that such priests might be in themselves fit subjects for censure, but it was not for them as laymen to pronounce a censure which lay with their bishops only. Gregory, however, seems to have understood that the aversion to a married priesthood, which he felt himself, was shared largely by the multitude, especially as they saw marriage commonly associated with general laxity of life. Another feeling which he had on his side was of a far less defensible character—the opposition to authority, and especially ecclesiastical authority, which is so congenial to human nature. He urged then this canon upon the Germans, and the consequences were dreadful:

"By the last of the four canons above quoted, the laity were thrown into the position,—if not of judges of the priesthood,—at least of punishers of its irregularities. And such invitation, thus made, was of course readily and generally attended to. The occasion seemed,—to the selfish, the irreverent, and the profane,—to legalize the gratification of all the bad feelings with which persons of those dispositions must ever regard the Church and her ministry; and priests, whose disobedience to the papal authority furnished any excuse for such conduct, were openly beaten, abused, and insulted by their rebellious flocks. Some were [294] forced to fly with the loss of all that they possessed, some were deprived of limbs, and some, it is even said, put to death in lingering torments. And to lengths even more horrible than these did the popular violence, thus unhappily, thus criminally sanctioned, proceed. Too many were delighted to find what they could consider a religious excuse for neglecting religion itself, for depriving their children of the inestimable gift conferred in the holy sacrament of baptism, or for making the solemn mysteries of the Church subjects for the most degrading mockery, or of the most atrocious profanation. Deeply is it to be regretted that a pontiff who desired, from the bottom of his heart, the purification of the Church; whose whole life had been devoted to that high and holy cause ... should have evoked, in furtherance of his views, a spirit of so odious a character, as was that which showed itself in these dreadful transactions. But such had been the line marked out for him by those who had gone before him."—Vol. ii., pp. 25-27.

In France the promulgation of Gregory's Canons was received by the clergy with a burst of indignation yet more vehement, if possible, than that which had followed them in Germany. A Council of Paris denounced them, and the only member of the assembly who ventured to defend them was seized, beaten, spit upon, and tumultuously dragged to prison. When the Archbishop of Rouen endeavoured to enforce them upon his clergy, he was pelted with stones and fled for his life. Mr. Bowden tells us that the system of clerical marriage had been so completely established in

Normandy, that churches had become property heritable by the sons, and even by the daughters, of their possessors. This fact shows how the two canonical offences of clerical marriage and simony ran together. Indeed it seems that the French king, breaking a promise he had made to Gregory, was practising a simoniacal traffic in bishops and abbeys without remorse or shame; while the holders of dignities [295] thus obtained were not likely to be more scrupulous, in their turn, in their nomination to such inferior benefices and offices as thus fell under their control. In Spain, again, the papal legate was assailed by the clergy with menaces and outrages, when he attempted to enforce the observance of celibacy upon them. When the ill-treated prelates complained to Gregory, they got some such consolation as the following: "Shall it not shame us," he asks, "while every soldier of the world daily hazards his life for his sovereign, if we, priests of the Lord, shrink from the battle of our King, who made all things out of nothing, who scrupled not to lay down His life for us, and who has promised us eternal rewards." In Hungary, twenty years later, the rule had not made greater way than this, that a council under Ladislaus[112] prohibited second marriages among the clergy, but allowed to married presbyters a time of indulgence, "on account of the bond of peace and the unity of the Holy Ghost, until the paternal authority of the Apostolic See should have been consulted on the subject." England, ruled at this time by the Conqueror, Gregory did not attempt; with that judgment and discrimination which he united to vigour, he waited for the influence of the precedent which he was introducing

---

[112] *a council under Ladislaus*: This met under St Ladislaus, King of Hungary, at Szabolcs on 21 May 1091.

elsewhere. Yet even a few years after this the Council of Winchester[113] enacted that no married persons should be admitted into Orders, though it passed a decree that parish priests who had wives already might retain them; which showed what already was the silent and indirect effect of Gregory's energetic proceedings in the empire. Eventually, the Anglican Church gave its adhesion to the principle of clerical celibacy even more completely than the Church of France.

But at the time Gregory seemed to have success in no quarter, and not the least vexatious opposition was offered [296] him in his own city. Guibert,[114] who in the time of Alexander had been the Imperial Chancellor of Italy, and the supporter of the intruder Cadalous, was at this time Archbishop of Ravenna, having been appointed by the mediation of the Empress Agnes,[115] just at the close of Alexander's life. Alexander himself had seen through the insincerity of his professed repentance, and was reluctant to consecrate him; but Hildebrand, it is said, trusted him and pleaded for him. Upon this, Alexander, with a prescient spirit, said, "I indeed am about to be dissolved; the time of my departure is at hand; but thou shalt feel his bitterness." The prophecy was not long in finding its fulfilment, and he eventually became Anti-Pope in Gregory's later years. "He put himself at the

---

[113] *Council of Winchester*: Church Councils were held at Winchester in 1070, 1072 and 1076 under the guidance of Lanfranc. Newman here refers to the last of these.

[114] *Guibert*: c.1025-1100. Originally from Parma, Guibert acted as imperial chancellor for Italy (1058-63) and Archbishop of Ravenna (from 1072). However, he was excommunicated for his attempts to depose Pope Gregory. In 1080 Henry IV had him elected as the antipope 'Clement III'.

[115] *Empress Agnes*: Agnes of Poitou (c.1025-77), wife of Henry III and mother of Henry IV; after the death of her husband, she had been regent of the Holy Roman Empire during Henry's minority.

head of that party in Rome," says Mr. Bowden, "who were either alarmed by Gregory's rigour, or conceived themselves aggrieved by his measures of reform; attaching to himself the relatives and friends of the married clergy, as well as those many members of the sacerdotal body who had resigned their benefices in preference to adopting a life of celibacy." And there were other classes in Rome whose enormities were confronted by the reforming pontiff. To the Church of St. Peter belonged more than sixty officers of the class called 'Mansionarii.' They were married laymen, many of dissolute habits; and it was their custom,—such had been the disgraceful laxity of the times,—mitred and dressed in sacerdotal vestments, to keep constant watch at all the altars of the church, excepting only the high altar itself, to proffer, as priests, their services to the simple laity, who came from distant parts of Italy, and to receive their oblations. Relieving each other, they occupied the church day and night, and, as though not content with one [297] description of sacrilege, they disgraced the holy place during the hours of darkness by robberies and licentiousness of the most infamous kind. Nor was it without great difficulty that Gregory, even in his own city, could put an end to this portentous abuse, and replace at the altars these impious laymen by priests canonically ordained. Mr. Bowden adds that "the cardinals themselves were wont, in the same church, to disgrace their office by celebrating the Holy Eucharist at irregular hours for the sake of gain; and Gregory's interference, to put a stop to this abuse by wholesome regulations, is described as having excited against him much odium among certain classes of his flock."— Vol. ii., pp. 42, 43.

Gregory was at this time about sixty years of age, and, tried by cares and by a life of rigid mortification from his boyhood, he gave way in health, and it was thought that he was dying. He recovered however; a circumstance, he says himself, "rather for sorrow than for joy. For our soul was tending towards, and with all desire panting for, that country where He, who observes our labour and our sorrow, prepares for the weary refreshment and repose. But we were yet reserved to our accustomed toils, our infinite anxieties; reserved to suffer, as it were, each hour the pangs of travail, while we feel ourselves unable to save, by any steersmanship, the Church which seems almost foundering before our eyes."

Well might Gregory say that he was reserved for something, for he had not yet reached his celebrated struggle with Henry, which Fox the martyrologist,[116] if no one else, has made familiar to Protestant ears, and which is the last and longest passage of his history which we propose to trace.

7. [298]

In 1074 he had waged his battle with the clergy; that was enough for one year; but in the very next spring he opened his assault upon the Emperor. No wonder a mind of such incessant energy should complain of nothing but weariness and disappointment; and this seems to have been the habitual feeling under which he went to his work. "Often," he says, at this point of time, "have I implored the Lord, either to remove me from this present life, or to benefit, through me, our common Mother; and yet has He not

---

[116] *Fox the martyrologist*: John Foxe (1516-1587), author of the widely-read *Acts and Monuments of matters happening in the* Church (1563).

hitherto removed me from tribulation, nor, as I had hoped, made my life profitable to her in whose chains He has bound me. Vast is the grief, wide-spreading the affliction, which encompasses me. Contemplating east, south, north, I perceive scarcely any bishops lawfully admitted to their office, and leading lives conformable to their sacred character. Nor do I find among the secular princes any who prefer God's honour to their own, or righteousness to gain. Those nations among whom I dwell, the Romans, Lombards, and Normans, I conceive, as I often declare to them, to be in some sense worse than Jews or Pagans. And turning inwards, I find myself so laden with the burden of my own doings, that no hope of salvation remains to me but in the sole mercy of Christ. Did I not trust to attain to a better life and to do service to Holy Church, I would on no account remain in Rome; in which city it has been by compulsion, God is my witness, that I have dwelt these twenty years. Whence it comes to pass, that, between this grief daily renewed in me, and the hope which, alas, is too long deferred, I live as it were in death, shaken by a thousand storms. And I await His coming who has bound me with His chains, led me back again to Rome against my [299] will, and girt me round with countless difficulties." Such were the feelings under which he got ready for his greatest exploit.

It is hardly to our purpose to go into the Pope's quarrel with the Emperor in its early stages; it turned principally on Henry's profligate life, his simoniacal appointments, and his cruelties and perfidies towards his subjects. Besides this, the Pope claimed the right of investiture, feeling that from its very form it was undeniably an ecclesiastical, not a secular act; and that, when exercised by laymen, it was necessarily connected with simony, and involved the principle that the Church was the creature of the State. We will but say that Alexander II., at a Council held about two months before his death, had excommunicated five of Henry's profligate favourites, and had even, as some say, sent a message to Henry himself, to appear before the chair of St. Peter and defend himself against the charge of simony and other offences. On Gregory's accession, the new Pope made friendly overtures to him, and the young king, being in great difficulties with his subjects, accepted them with much profession of humility and repentance.

"Smitten in some degree, through God's mercy, with compunction," he said, "and returning to ourselves, we confess our past transgressions, and throw ourselves on your paternal indulgence, hoping in the Lord to obtain the boon of absolution from your apostolical authority. Criminal we have been, and unhappy, partly through the alluring instincts of youth, partly through the licence of unbridled power, partly through the seductive guidance of others. We have not only invaded the property of churches, but have sold to persons infected with the gall of simony the churches themselves; but now, unable without your authority to reform the abuses of the churches, we implore [300] alike your counsel and your aid, in this as in all things. Your command is, in all things, of authority." Subsequently to this, Henry's mother, sent by Gregory, undertook a journey to him with the papal legate; he complied with their demands, made open confession of his simony and other offences, assisted them in degrading the simoniacal bishops, and received absolution at their hands. But, shortly afterwards, his fortunes taking a favourable turn, he was released from the necessity of keeping terms with the Pope; and, recalling the excommunicated nobles to his court, he provided himself with counsellors whose personal feelings would encourage him in courses directly opposed to the wishes and the principles of Gregory. His tone and conduct, in consequence, underwent an entire change. He appointed bishops to the churches of Fermo and Spoleto without consulting Gregory, and, in spite of his promise, to that of Milan; and the preponderance which he thus gave to the anti-papal party in northern Italy, was extended by Guibert of Ravenna into the south by a correspondence with Robert Guiscard, who happened at this time to be under papal ban. On the other hand, the Saxons, who, having been cruelly oppressed by Henry, had risen in arms and been reduced, appealed to Gregory for protection for their bishops, whom Henry had perfidiously seized, deposed, plundered, and imprisoned; and Gregory, answering to their appeal, took the strong step of not only demanding the liberation of the bishops, but, as Alexander is said to have done before him, of summoning Henry himself to appear before the apostolic tribunal, to clear himself of the charges which had been brought against him.

"All things are double, one against another."[117] Every
[301] power, every form of government, every influence strong as it may be, has its natural complement or match, by which it is prevented from doing all things at its will. In constitutional governments men appeal to the law; in absolute monarchies they rise; in military despotisms they

---

[117] *All things are double, one against another*: Ecclesiasticus 42:24

assassinate. James the Second is opposed by legal forms;[118] Louis of France by jaqueries;[119] Paul of Russia is strangled.[120] The only remedy for a reforming Pope was to carry him off and lodge him safe in durance. Guibert of Ravenna has the reputation of being concocter of a plot, with the privity of Henry and Robert Guiscard, which developed itself as follows:—Cencius[121] was the instrument of it, a bold and profligate man, a member of the powerful family which was in possession of the castle of St. Angelo,[122] and which had been the main support of the anti-pope Cadalous in his struggle with Alexander.

"The night of Christmas Eve, 1075, was gloomy and tempestuous; the torrents of rain, according to Paul of Bernreid,[123] were such, as to present a lively image of the general deluge; and although Gregory, according to custom, celebrated the Holy Eucharist at midnight, in the church of Sta. Maria Maggiore, the building instead of being as usual thronged with worshippers, was comparatively silent and deserted; few venturing to leave their homes in weather so inclement.

"Gregory and his clergy had partaken of the holy elements, and were engaged in distributing them to the laity, when, on a sudden, Cencius and his confederates burst in arms into the

[118] *James the Second is opposed by legal* forms: a reference to the revolution of 1688 that deposed James II, in which a coup d'état and foreign invasion were given parliamentary approval.
[119] *Louis of France by jaqueries*: presumably a reference to Louis XVI (1754-93) who was executed during the French Revolution (21 January 1793). The original 'jacquerie' occurred in 1358 but has since been used as a term for any popular uprising.
[120] *Paul of Russia is strangled*: Emperor Paul I (1754-1801) was attacked by a group of dismissed officers on 23 March 1801. When he refused to sign his abdication, he was strangled to death.
[121] *Cencius*: Cencio I Frangipane, a Roman consul.
[122] *castle of St Angelo*: Castel Sant'Angelo in Rome
[123] *Paul of Bernreid*: (d.1131), priest of the Order of Canons Regular; author of the *Vita Gregorii VII*.

church. Interrupting the holy ceremonial, they seized the pontiff at the altar; one of the ruffians aimed a blow with a sword at his head, inflicting a serious wound on his forehead; and the rest then dragged him, amid insults and blows, from the precincts of the sanctuary. He preserved a perfect composure, lifting up his eyes to heaven, but neither struggling nor speaking, while these abandoned wretches thus vented on him their fury. They stripped him of his pallium and chasuble, and then binding him, still clad in his alb and stole, behind a ruffian on horseback, they hurried him to one of the towers, already mentioned, of Cencius; where preparations had been made for bearing him at once beyond the

[302] walls of Rome. But the latter part of this project the conspirators were not able to succeed in accomplishing ... And the first glimpse of dawn showed to the conspirators within it their enemies, provided with ladders, catapults, and every species of engine then used in assaults, and preparing for an immediate and vigorous attack. The sister of Cencius, abandoned as her brother, reviled the illustrious prisoner in the most violent terms; while one of her partizans, drawing a sword, threatened to strike off, on the instant, his head. But the scene was now to change. A lance, or dart, from without, pierced this wretch's throat, and laid him breathless on the ground ... The attack was, therefore, carried on with redoubled fury. The walls of the tower soon gave way before their exertions, and Gregory, borne in triumph from amid the ruins to the church from which he had been torn, there concluded the holy service in which he had been interrupted, amid the enthusiastic rejoicings of the people. Cencius, pursued by the execrations of his countrymen, with difficulty escaped from their fury, and fled with his principal confederates to Germany."—Vol. ii., pp. 81-85.

This attempt then failed—but, meanwhile, the measures of Gregory proceeded. About the same time that Cencius was playing his part in Rome, the Pope's legates appeared before Henry with his summons to appear, warning him at the same time, that, did he not, a sentence of excommunication would issue against him. Henry dismissed them with ridicule and insult; and since force had failed against their master, he resolved to attack him with his own weapons, and summoned in haste a Council of the German Church at Worms for Septuagesima Sunday,[124] January 24, with the view of obtaining from it the condemnation and deposition of Gregory. It was attended by a numerous assemblage of bishops and abbots; and when the session was opened, Hugo Candidus, who played a conspicuous part in Gregory's election, and who had vacillated from side to side several times, stood forward as his accuser. He laid before the Council a variety of forged letters, purporting to come from different archbishops and [303] bishops, and from the cardinals, senate, and people of Rome, filled with complaints of Gregory's conduct, and with entreaties for his deprivation, and the appointment of a successor. Then, as though in explanation of these epistles, Hugo read a document (which seems to have been subsequently the foundation of Benno's work) professing to give an account of Gregory's life, and filled with the most unfounded and incredible calumnies. It insisted on the lowness of his origin, and described his whole life, before and after his election, which was stated to have been simoniacal, as a tissue of crimes, among which enumerated murder, necromancy, the profanation of the Holy Eucharist, and the worship of the devil. In consequence, after two days' consultation, without

---

[124] *Septuagesima Sunday*: the ninth Sunday before Easter

proposing even that Gregory should be heard in his defence, the Council decreed, by its own local act, that he was no longer Pope, and presented to each bishop the following formula for subscription: "I, N., bishop of the city of N., abjure from this hour all subjection and obedience to Hildebrand, and will never more account or style him Pope." All the bishops present seemed to have signed. Messengers were forthwith despatched into Lombardy with the news; the Lombard bishops met forthwith in council at Piacenza, and not only subscribed, but bound themselves by a solemn oath upon the Gospels, to the act of Worms. Roland, a priest of the Church of Parma,[125] was charged with the perilous duty of bearing a copy of the acts of both Councils to Rome, where he arrived in the second week in Lent, just when the Council was assembled to which Henry had been summoned. Much as we have quoted from Mr. Bowden, we must here, as elsewhere, be allowed to prefer his vivid description to any words we could put together ourselves:

[304]

"The Council being assembled, and the echoes of the solemn strain, 'Veni Creator Spiritus,'[126] having scarcely died away amid the holy aisles of the Lateran, Roland suddenly stepped forward before the pontiff and his prelates (p. 95) ... Addressing his speech to Gregory, 'The king,' he said, 'and the united bishops, as well of Germany as of Italy, transmit thee this command,—Descend without delay from the throne of St. Peter, and abandon the usurped government of the Roman Church, for to such honours should none aspire, unsanctioned by their general choice, and by the approval of the Emperor.' And then, ere the assembled

---

[125] *Roland, a priest of the Church of Parma*: Bishop of Treviso (c.1076-90)
[126] *Veni Creator Spiritus*: 'Come Creator Spirit', the hymn written in the ninth century by Rabanus Maurus for the Office of Pentecost.

prelates and clergy had recovered their astonishment, the audacious envoy looked round upon them, and thus addressed them collectively: 'To you, brethren, it is commanded, that you do, at the feast of Pentecost, present yourselves before the king, my master, to receive a Pope and a father from his hands. The pretended pastor before you is detected to be a ravening wolf.'

"'Seize him!' cried John, Bishop of Oporto, a prelate of holy and exalted character, who could no longer contain his indignation. The prefect of the city rushed forward, attended by the guards and attendants of the Council. Swords were brandished, even in that holy place; and the blood of Roland would, on the moment, have expiated his temerity, had not Gregory himself forced his way into the crowd, and restrained, though with difficulty, the fury of his adherents. Having at length succeeded in obtaining comparative tranquillity, the pontiff received from the prisoner the documents which he had been commissioned to deliver; and then, imploring the continued silence of the assembly, he proceeded to read aloud, with his usual composure, the acts of the Councils of Worms and Piacenza, and the following imperial epistle:—

"'Henry, not by usurpation, but by the holy ordinance of God, king, to Hildebrand, no longer the Pope, but the false monk.

"'A greeting like this hast thou for thy confusion deserved; thou who hast left no Order of the Church untouched, but hast brought upon each confusion, not honour,—cursing, not blessing. To speak but of a few of thy most distinguished deeds,—the rulers of the holy Church, the archbishops, bishops, and presbyters, thou hast not only not feared, seeing that they are the Lord's anointed, to touch; but, as though they were servants who know not what their Lord doeth, thou hast trampled them under thy feet. Thou hast obtained favour with the vulgar by their humiliation; and hast thought that they know nothing, and that thou alone knowest all things. Yet, this knowledge of thine thou hast used for the purpose, not of edification, but of destruction, insomuch that we [305] believe the blessed Gregory, whose name thou hast assumed, to have spoken prophetically of thee, when he said, "By the abundance of subjects, the mind of him who is set over them is puffed up, for he supposes that he excels all in knowledge, when he finds that he excels all in power."[127]""—Vol. ii., pp. 95-99.

We wish we had room to continue this exciting scene, which ends in a majestic address of Gregory to the Council, and the enthusiastic acclamations of the prelates assembled in answer to it.

The next day, in the presence of 110 prelates and of the Empress Agnes, whose sense of duty overcame the affections of a mother, he pronounced sentence in form upon the German and Lombard bishops, and above all upon Henry, whom he declared excommunicated from the Church and suspended from the exercise of his imperial power.

8.

In these transactions, we see on both sides what we must account a confusion of the rights of Church and State,—the Emperor in council deposing the Pope, and the Pope deposing the Emperor. Mr. Bowden has some just remarks on the subject, and traces it to the feudalism of the day, which acknowledged but one standard of rank in the community, and forced all powers and offices to measure themselves by it. As in Russia, it is said, that men are only recognized as soldiers, and the clergy take rank as colonels or captains, so in the eleventh century Gregory was forced to place himself in direct relation to the Emperor, and take precedence either above him or beneath him, and with this

---

[127] *"By the abundance of subjects, the mind ... "*: Gregory the Great, *Regula Pastoralis*, Book II, Chapter 6.

alternative he put himself above him, as the nearest approximation to the truth. And in like manner, the Emperor, not the present Henry only, but his father before [306] him, and Conrad his grandfather, not to say the Carlovingians,[128] had placed themselves above the Church, because they were supreme in temporals, and had treated the Pope as one of their subjects, just as a naturalist of this day in despair ranks a whale among the mammalia.[129]

On the present occasion, Mr. Bowden considers it a cause of thankfulness that Gregory, with all the incidental defects of his theological system, was in the chair of St. Peter. He considers that the success of the Imperialists would have been the immediate triumph of simony, licentiousness, and the other crying evils of the time, and would have tended to make that triumph perpetual. On the other hand, Gregory was not only engaged in vindicating what he considered his divine authority, but also an ecclesiastical principle essential to the independence and well-being of the Church. The real question was, whether the Church was or was not a creature of the State? Whether she had or had not temporal rights was an excrescence upon the main question; and she needed a champion, such as, through God's providence, she found, who scorned either to be swayed by menaces, or to be bribed by the promise of a temporary peace, into the compromise of her essential principles.

---

[128] *the Carlovingians*: the dynasty descended from Charles Martel (c.688-741).

[129] *ranks a whale among the mammalia*: Whales are in fact mammals, rather than fish, so the naturalist does not despair in so ranking them, but Newman evidently did not understand the reasons for this classification.

Thus the contest opened; Gregory had on his side many of the leading nobles of Germany, the Saxons, to a certain extent the Swabians, the great mass of the regular and a considerable portion of the secular clergy. And Henry was supported by the Rhenish provinces, by the large towns, as Worms, now rising into some degree of commercial opulence, by a certain number of the nobility, who had felt or feared the papal censures, and the vast body of anti-[307] reforming clergy. It was a moment of extreme excitement, when each of the contending parties had defied his antagonist, and waited to see how the defiance was received by Christendom at large, with whom eventually lay the decision.

As to Henry himself, however, he seems to have thought he had done everything when he had secured the synodal acts of Worms and Piacenza, as if they were to work their effect as a matter of course; he was astounded therefore at the intelligence that the old man, whom he was resisting, far from crouching, had vigorously smitten him in turn with the ban of the Church. For a moment the unfortunate prince seemed overpowered with agitation; then he treated the subject with apparent indifference; then he gave orders that Gregory himself should be publicly excommunicated in turn. He committed this office to Pibo, Bishop of Toul;[130] but Pibo, together with another bishop, set off in the night and left the king to go to the cathedral by himself, where the Bishop of the place (Utrecht)[131] pronounced the sentence. The next thing he heard was, that the German prelates, who

---

[130] *Pibo, Bishop of Toul*: or Poppo, Bishop of Toul 1070–1107.
[131] *the Bishop of the place (Utrecht)*: William, Bishop of Utrecht 1054-76 and a loyal supporter of the Emperor.

had been denounced by Gregory together with himself, were crossing the Alps to make their peace with him; next, the secular princes, who had the charge of the Saxon nobles and bishops, whom Henry had faithlessly seized, having been already shocked at Henry's proceedings in the Council of Worms, on hearing the papal sentence against him, let go their prisoners and sent them off to Saxony. On their arrival there, the Saxons rose in arms, appeared before the strongholds, which the king, in violation of his promise, had rebuilt in their country, took them by assault or capitulation, and then proceeded to resume the lands which had been seized by the royal favourites.

An event occurred which increased the dismay: William, [308] Bishop of Utrecht, who has been mentioned above as excommunicating Gregory in the cathedral, repeated the sentence several times the same Easter, calling the Pope a perjurer, an adulterer, and a false apostle. A month had not passed before he was seized with a violent illness, which carried him off in a few days. In his last moments he cried out that he had forfeited life both here and hereafter, and forbade his friends to pray for him after death, as one destined to perdition. These facts were exaggerated; in addition, stories were circulated that, as he breathed his last sigh, his cathedral and his sovereign's palace were struck with lightning. Other deaths too in the king's party about the same time were interpreted in the light of William's.

Henry appointed a diet at Worms for Whitsuntide; not one of his chief nobles attended: he postponed it to St. Peter's Day at Mentz; even then but a few obeyed the summons. Udo, the venerated Archbishop of Treves,[132] had gone to Rome and received absolution. On his return he refused to hold any intercourse with the Archbishops of Mentz and Cologne. Henry he would only approach for the purpose of counselling; he would not sit at table with him or join in prayer. The more religious members of the king's household withdrew themselves, and withstood Henry's most urgent entreaties to return.

Henry next led a force against the Saxons, and was repelled with loss. At Gregory's suggestion his principal nobles held a solemn Diet of the empire at Worms in the autumn; it was very numerously attended; even Siegfried of Mentz obtained papal absolution and attended; the Patriarch of Aquileia and Bishop of Padua appeared as legates from [309] the Holy See. Henry sent the humblest messages to the Diet in vain: at last they consented to treat with him on these conditions: first, that his continuing to reign should be referred to the Pope; next, that until he could procure reconciliation, he should live as a private individual, neither entering church nor exercising any royal functions; thirdly, that he should renounce the society of all excommunicate persons; and lastly, that, if at the end of a year his own excommunication was not reversed, his right to empire should be lost for ever. A Council was appointed for the beginning of January, to meet at Augsburgh, over which Gregory himself was to preside, and then Henry was to be reconciled. Henry wished to come to Italy, but Gregory forbade him. His anxiety for a release from the anathema

---

[132] *Udo, the venerated Archbishop of Treves*: Udo von Nellenburg, Archbishop of Treves (Trier), 1066-78. He died at the Siege of Tübingen while serving the Emperor.

inflicted on him increased; he could not bear the suspense. Regardless therefore of Gregory's prohibition, of the season, which was unusually severe, and of the difficulty of crossing the Alps in the winter, he set out to find the Pope in Italy. Mr. Bowden shall set him forward on his journey:

"The winter which closed the year 1076 was a season of unusual severity; the Rhine being frozen over from Martinmas[133] almost to the beginning of April, 1077. The difficulties, therefore, of a journey across the Alps, at the time of Henry's expedition, must, under any circumstances, have been great; and the auspices under which the unfortunate monarch set forth were such as to render the undertaking in his case peculiarly arduous. Deprived of his friends and of his resources, it was not in his power to make any proper provision for the journey. Nor could he venture to prosecute his way along any of the more direct tracts which led from his German dominions into Italy; as Rudolf,[134] Welf,[135] and Berthold,[136] who wished to retain him in Germany, sedulously watched the mountain passes of Swabia, Bavaria, and Carinthia. But Henry felt too strongly the danger of furnishing his enemies with any new pretext for setting him aside, to think of giving up the attempt, desperate as it might be, to procure a timely absolution.

"A few days, therefore, before the Christmas which closed the year 1076, the king put himself in motion from Spires. His wife and infant child accompanied his steps, and, whatever meaner followers may have formed his escort, it appears that only one person of gentle blood—and he not distinguished by rank or possessions—attended the fallen sovereign ... He set forward,

[310]

---

[133] *Martinmas*: St. Martin's Day, 11th November.

[134] *Rudolf*: Rudolf of Rheinfelden (c.1025-80), Duke of Swabia.

[135] *Welf*: Welf I, (c.1030/40-1101), Duke of Bavaria; he had originally been a supporter of Henry IV, to whom he owed his appointment as Duke, but changed sides.

[136] *Berthold*: Berthold I (c.1060-90), Rudolf's eldest son.

however, and taking his way through Burgundy, halted to observe the festival of Christmas at Besançon. And thence, passing the Jura, he proceeded to Vevay on the shore of the lake of Geneva ... Even the valleys of the Alps, when Henry began to wind his way among them, were white with snow and slippery with ice. Peasants of the country, whose services he had hired, went before him, and cleared, as best they might, a precipitous and rugged road for the advance of the royal party. As the travellers ascended towards the higher regions of the pass, the difficulties of this process increased, of course, with every step. Happily, however, no serious accident occurred: and after long toils, the monarch and his little train found themselves on the summit of a ridge, a descent from which would lead them into Italy. But this descent appeared in prospect more formidable than anything which they had previously accomplished. The whole of the precipitous mountain slope formed one sheet of ice, on which no foot, it seemed, could for a moment maintain its position. The descent, however, was necessarily attempted. Henry and the men of the party crawled carefully down on their hands and knees, placing their feet on whatever points of support they could find; and he whose footing unfortunately failed him rolled far away into the snowy depths below; from which it was often a matter of great difficulty to extricate him. The queen, her child, and her female attendants, were, by the experienced peasants, lowered down the slope enveloped in skins of cattle; and the whole party reached at length the bottom in safety; though of their horses—which were either drawn down the descent with their legs tied together, or lowered on some rude kinds of machines constructed for the purpose—many died, and many more were rendered unfit for further service."—Vol. ii., pp. 161-164.

Thus it was that Henry and the imperial family at last reached the plains of Lombardy.

9.

In Italy the report was at once spread abroad that he had [311] come to take vengeance on the Pope. People recollected or had been told of Henry III.'s visitation of the Papal See thirty years before, when a Council was held at Sutri, and Gregory, the sixth of that name, was made to abdicate. Accordingly, nobles, prelates, and warriors thronged to greet him, and his crowded and brilliant court formed a strange contrast to the neglect, or rather aversion, which he had had to encounter on the other side of the Alps. But Henry was not so dazzled with the scenes, which now surrounded him, as to forget those which he had left. He asked where the Pope was, and finding he was at Canossa, a fortress of the Appennines, belonging to the Countess Matilda,[137] (whither Gregory had taken refuge on the rumour of Henry's having come at the head of a formidable force,) he betook himself thither.

Matilda goes by the name of the Great Countess. She inherited Tuscany from her mother, and was the enthusiastic friend and servant of Gregory; to him and to his principles her energies, her influence, and her treasures were dedicated. Her talents and learning were as remarkable as her rank and her devotion. Amid the various occupations which her extensive territories occasioned, she found time and opportunity to become the encourager, and, in some degree, the restorer, of ancient literature. She was acquainted with the more recent languages spoken in France and Germany, as well as in her own country. She was active and energetic in the enforcement of justice and the

---

[137] *Matilda*: (1046-1115) Countess of Tuscany and great supporter of Gregory VII.

maintenance of her authority; nor was she unequal to the task of eliciting the military resources of her territory, and bringing well-disciplined armies into the field. She was munificently charitable to the poor; systematically kind and hospitable to the exile and to the stranger; and the foundress or benefactress of a great number of churches and conventual institutions. Throughout her eventful life she never suffered secular matters to interfere with the frequency or regularity of her exercises of devotion; and in adversity, of which she was allotted her share, she found her consolation in the society of holy men and the perusal of Holy Scripture. "Such," says Mr. Bowden, "was the Great Countess; such was she, who, too proud or too humble to recapitulate the roll of her titles, was wont to subscribe herself,—'Matilda, by the grace of God what I am;'" and at the present moment she was especially fitted to undertake the mediation between Gregory and Henry, being a relative of Henry as well as the host of Gregory.

[312]

"Towards Canossa, then, Henry bent his steps, accompanied by his recently formed train of Italian followers. His faithful German adherents, who had, in the preceding month, set out to cross the Alps by different paths, had encountered on the journey a variety of difficulties and sufferings. Dietrich, Bishop of Verdun,[138] was captured by Adelbert, Count of Calw,[139] and plundered of the sums which he had, with much trouble, collected to meet the expenses of his journey. Rupert of Bamberg,[140] being

---

[138] *Dietrich, bishop of Verdun*: a supporter of the Emperor and of the anti-Pope Clement III. Cf. Chronicle of Hugh of Flavigny ML 154 21-404.

[139] *Adelbert, Count of Calw*: c.1030-99; Calw is a town in the south west of Germany.

[140] *Rupert of Bamberg*: bishop (1075-1102), was a supporter of Henry IV and a member of the pseudo-synod of Brixen, for which he was excommunicated by Benedict XII, as Bamberg since 1020 was under the dependence of the Holy See.

seized by Welf while traversing the Bavarian territory, was kept in strict ward from Christmas until the feast of St. Bartholomew[141] in the following year. But the rest of Henry's excommunicated supporters, having surmounted the dangers of their journey, and made good their way into Italy, appeared before Canossa, while the king himself was yet on his way, and humbly presented themselves before the Pope as supplicants for his absolution. 'From those,' said Gregory, 'who rightly acknowledge and bewail their sin, forgiveness cannot be withheld. The petitioners must, however,' he continued, 'submit to the cauterizing process which is needful for the healing of their wounds, that they may not, by too lightly obtaining absolution, be led too lightly to regard the sin which they have committed by disobedience to apostolical authority.' Prelates and lay-nobles alike professed their readiness to undergo whatever penance their spiritual father might think proper to impose; and the former were, by his directions, confined [313] in separate cells with scanty supplies of food, while to the latter penances were assigned of a severity proportioned to the age and strength of each individual. And when he had thus tried them for several days, Gregory summoned them again before him, and after mildly rebuking them for their past conduct, and admonishing them against such demeanour in future, declared them severally absolved, warning them at the same time, anxiously and repeatedly, against holding any communion with their imperial master until he also should have given satisfaction to the Apostolic See; till that should happen they were to be permitted to hold colloquy with him only for the purpose of inducing him, by their persuasions, to abandon the error of his ways.

"At length the principal offender appeared in person before Canossa, and pitched his camp without the walls of the fortress."—Vol. ii., pp. 167, 168.

---

[141] *the feast of St. Bartholomew*: 24th August

The humiliation to which Gregory put the king himself has always been severely animadverted upon, and has done his character much harm with posterity; but Mr. Bowden bids us recollect that severer penances were not at all uncommon at that time, and that it is very unfair to measure them by the standard of drawing-room propriety, and the judgment of an age of kid gloves and Naples soap.[142] It was a most uncomfortable thing to be kept shivering in the cold from morning to night, and likely to cause rheumatism, of which we have no intention at all of speaking lightly; but Henry III., the king's father, would habitually, before presenting himself in royal robes upon his throne, submit in private to a self-imposed scourging. The magnificent and luxurious Boniface of Tuscany,[143] Matilda's father, submitted on one occasion to a similar discipline before the Altar of St. Mary's at Pomposa, at the suggestion, if not at the hands, of his spiritual adviser, as a penance for some simoniacal transactions; and Godfrey of Lorraine,[144] Matilda's stepfather, in remorse for the burning of the cathedral of Verdun in the course of his warlike operations,

[314] not only contributed largely to its rebuilding, but caused himself to be scourged in public, and as publicly took part in the work of building, in the capacity of a common labourer. In the following century took place the well-known scourging of Henry II.,[145] by the monks of

---

[142] *the judgment of an age of kid gloves and Naples soap*: a typically Newmanian aphorism

[143] *Boniface of Tuscany*: Boniface III, Margrave of Tuscany or of Canossa, 985-1052.

[144] *Godfrey of Lorraine*: Godfrey III, Duke of Lorraine, 997-1069.

[145] *well-known scourging*: Henry II underwent penance for his part in the martyrdom of St Thomas Becket at Canterbury on 12 July 1174. After walking barefoot to the cathedral, he was whipped by the monks.

Canterbury, at the shrine of St. Thomas. Such facts as these must be recollected when we read the following extraordinary scene:

"It was on the morning of the 25th of January, 1077, while the frost reigned in all its intensity, and the ground was white with snow, that the dejected Henry, barefooted, and clad in the usual garb of penance, a garment of white linen, ascended alone to the rocky fortress of Canossa, and entered its outer gate. The place was surrounded by three walls, within the two outer of which the imperial penitent was led, while the portals of the third or inner wall of the fortress were still closed against him. Here he stood, a miserable spectacle, exposed to cold and hunger throughout the day, vainly hoping, with each succeeding hour, that Gregory would consider the penance sufficient, and his fault atoned for. The evening, however, came, and he retired, humbled and dispirited, to return to his station with the returning light.

"On a second day, and on a third, the unhappy prince was still seen standing, starved and miserable, in the court of Canossa, from the morning until the evening. All in the castle, except the Pope, bewailed his condition, and with tears implored his forgiveness; it was said, even in Gregory's presence, that his conduct was more like wanton tyranny than apostolic severity. But the austere pontiff continued obstinately deaf to all entreaties. At length Henry's patience failed him, and, taking refuge in the adjacent chapel dedicated to St. Nicholas,[146] he there besought, with tears, the intercession of the aged abbot of Cluni; Matilda, who was present, seconded the king's entreaty, but the abbot, turning to her, replied, 'It is thou alone who canst undertake this business.' And Henry, upon the word, fell upon his knees before his kinswoman, and besought her, in the most impassioned manner, once more to exert her potent intercession. She promised to use her utmost endeavours, and returned into the castle; and

---

[146] *St Nicholas*: (270-342), Bishop of Myra and popular miracle-working saint.

Gregory, feeling that he had now sufficiently vindicated his authority, relaxed at length his rigour, suffering the unfortunate king, still barefooted, and in his linen garment, to be brought into his presence, on the fourth day of his penance.

"The scene, as the suppliant king approached the pontiff, must have been singularly striking. The youthful and vigorous Henry, of lofty stature and commanding features, thus humbling himself before the small, insignificant, and now probably withered, figure of Gregory VII., must have afforded a striking type of that abasement of physical before moral power,—of the sword before the crosier,—which the great struggle then in progress was fated to accomplish."—Vol. ii., pp. 174-176.

10.

Having brought our narrative to this critical point, we must break it off abruptly. What followed upon this, what an immediate triumph to the Pope, what subsequent reverses, what eventual success to his principles after his day; how Henry lapsed again, and how Gregory was at length forced to abandon Rome and died an exile at Salerno,—for these and a multitude of interesting details we must refer the reader to the work itself of which we are availing ourselves. As also for the account of the wonderfully large range of action which Gregory's labours embraced, and the multitude of Churches and States with which he held negotiation, among which were Constantinople, Hippo, Spain, England, Denmark, Russia, and Hungary. On two occasions also we find him directing the attention of the Church to the project of a crusade to the Holy Land, which was taken up in the next generation. But all this we must omit; and shall end our protracted yet incomplete narrative with Mr. Bowden's account of Gregory's death:

"He moved, shortly after his final departure from Rome, to Salerno, where, under the efficient protection of Robert Guiscard, he was enabled to repose in security, and where, while he still kept a watchful eye upon the troublous scenes of the world around him, he sought a solace for its sorrows in assiduous devotion, and in continual meditation on the word of God. As early as in January, 1085, he perceived symptoms of the exhaustion of his powers; the natural consequence of years, and of the arduous and unremitting labours and anxieties in which he had been so long engaged. During the succeeding months his debility increased, and in May it became evident to all around him that from the sick bed, on which he was laid, he was doomed never to rise again. Aware of his approaching end, he summoned around him the cardinals and bishops, who, faithful to his cause, or rather to his principles, had attended him to Salerno. He spoke to them of the events of his past life, and, while he disclaimed any right to glory in anything which he had done, he acknowledged the satisfaction which he derived from the thought that his course had been guided by principle, by a zeal for the right, and by an abhorrence of evil. His auditors, plunged in sincere sorrow, expressed to him their melancholy anticipations of the fate of the Church when deprived of his guiding hand. 'But I,' said he, with eyes and hands upraised to heaven, 'am mounting thitherward; and with supplications the most fervent will I commend your cause to the goodness of the Almighty.'

"Being solicited to express his opinion with respect to the choice of a successor, he mentioned the names of Desiderius, Abbot of Monte Cassino;[147] of Otho, Bishop of Ostia;[148] and of

[316]

---

[147] *Desiderius, Abbot of Montecassino*: eventually succeeded Gregory VII as Victor III in 1086 but died the following year; he was beatified in 1887.

Hugo, Bishop of Lyons;[149] suggesting, as a reason for giving priority to the former of the three, his presence at the moment in Italy.

"Three days before his death, on the question being brought before him of absolving the persons whom he had excommunicated, he replied, 'With the exception of Henry, styled by his followers the king; of Guibert, the usurping claimant of the Roman See; and of whose[150] who, by advice or assistance, favour their evil and ungodly views, I absolve and bless all men who unfeignedly believe me to possess this power, as the representative of St. Peter and St. Paul.' And then, addressing those around him for some time, in the language of warning, he thus impressively concluded: 'In the name of the Almighty God, and by the power of His holy Apostles St. Peter and St. Paul, I adjure you, recognize no one as my successor in the Roman See, who shall not have been duly elected and canonically ordained by Apostolic authority.'

"On the 25th of May, 1085, he peacefully closed his earthly career; just rallying strength, amid the exhaustion of his powers, to utter, with his departing breath, the words, 'I have loved justice and hated iniquity; and therefore I die in exile.'

[317]   "'In exile!' said a prelate who stood by his bed, ... in exile thou canst not die! Vicar of Christ and His Apostles, thou hast received the nations for thine inheritance, and the uttermost parts of the earth for thy possession.'"[151]—Vol. ii., pp. 322, 324.

Gregory thought he had failed: so it is; often a cause seems to decline as its champion grows in years, and to die in his death; but this is to judge hastily; others are destined

---

[148] *Otho, bishop of Ostia*: He became Pope Urban II (1088-1099) and is best known for calling the 'First' Crusade in 1096. He was beatified in 1881.

[149] *Hugo, bishop of Lyons*: Archbishop 1081-1106. He was excommunicated for his criticism of Victor III but returned to favour under Urban II.

[150] *whose*: evidently a mistake for 'those'

[151] *"thou hast received the earth for thine inheritance ... "*: Psalm 8:2.

to complete what he began. No man is given to see his work through. "Man goeth forth unto his work and to his labour until the evening,"[152] but the evening falls before it is done. There was One alone who began and finished and died.

April, 1841.

NOTE ON ESSAY XIII[1]

A SHORT memoir of Mr. Bowden, prefixed, under date of St. Bede's Day (May 27), 1845, to a posthumous publication, his "Thoughts on the Work of the Six Days of Creation,"[2] may be fitly appended to the foregoing Essay, as a record of one whom to have known is to have loved and to hold in perpetual remembrance.

After stating that the small volume in question "was the occupation and solace of the last illness of its author," and, both from its subject and the character of its composition, a suitable memorial of a mind "at once active and serene, deeply interested in the histories both of nature and of man, apprehensive of the Divine Hand in all he found in them, and contemplating with an unclouded faith the tokens they exhibit, and Divine Love and Wisdom," it proceeds to say:

"He was born in London on February 21, 1798; went to Harrow School in 1812; entered as a commoner at Trinity College, Oxford, in Lent term, 1817; and, after obtaining mathematical honours in Michaelmas Term, 1820, proceeded in due course to the degrees of B.A. and M.A.

"In the autumn of 1826 he received the appointment of Commissioner of Stamps, which he resigned in 1840. For some years he was a member of the Geological Society of London. In June, 1828, he married.

---

[1] *XIII*: incorrectly numbered XI in some editions.
[2] *"Thoughts on the Work of the Six Days of Creation"*: (1845) edited by Newman who wrote the biographical note which he now quotes. Bowden had died that year.

"In 1833, and following years, he engaged zealously in the revival which took place of the ecclesiastical principles of the seventeenth century, and was one of the earliest [319] assistants and supports of a friend[3] who at that time commenced the series called the *Tracts for the Times*. That most intimate friendship, which, begun with the first months of his residence at Oxford, showed itself also in the contributions to the *Lyra Apostolica*, which bear the signature of *a*, and in several Articles which he wrote in the *British Critic* between the years 1836 and 1841.

"The Articles referred to, are those upon the 'Rise of the Papal Power,' in July, 1836; on 'Gothic Architecture,' in April, 1837; on the 'British Association,' in January, 1839; and on 'The Church in the Mediterranean,' in July, 1841.

"In the spring of 1839, he had the first attack of the malady which ultimately proved fatal. On his apparent recovery in the autumn, he went abroad with his family for the winter, which he passed at Malta. On his return in the course of the ensuing spring, he put to press his 'Life and Pontificate of Gregory VII.,' which had been written in previous years, during his intervals of leisure from official duties.

"His complaint returned in the summer of 1843; throughout a long illness, the gifts of clearness and equability of mind, and of a gentle, cheerful, composed spirit, with which he had ever been blessed, were mercifully increased to him. He died in the early morning of Sunday, September 15, 1844, in undoubting communion with the Church of Andrewes and Laud. He was buried at Fulham,

---

[3] *a friend*: Newman

which had been the home of his childhood and youth. He lives still here, the light and comfort of many hearts, who ask no happier, holier end than his."

----

[320]   The foregoing account of Mr. Bowden's History of Gregory VII. calls for no remark here, except as relates to the subject of the forged Decretals. As public attention has lately been drawn to them, I think it well to make the following extract concerning them, from the "Critique on Mr. Ffoulke's Letter, by H. I. D. Ryder, of the Oratory."[4]

1.

The pseudo-decretals, A.D. 859, "were but indications of a current that had long been setting steadily in one direction. What claims did they really put forward on the Pope's behalf, that had not been made before? Two points in particular have been marked as innovations: 1. The reservation, independently of appeal, of all the criminal causes of all bishops to the Holy See. 2. The assertion of the nullity of any synod, convened without the authority of the Holy See.

"1. As to the first, within the western Patriarchate, at least, it was no new claim; see Pope Xystus III., [A.D. 432-440,][5] Ep. 10, who reserves all such causes to himself or to his vicar, Anastasius of Thessalonica. For the reservation of

----

[4] *Critique of Mr Ffoulkes's Letter, by H.I.D.Ryder of the Oratory*: This defended the good faith of the popes against the charge of dishonestly accepting the false decretals. Cf. Letter of Newman to Canon Walker 11 July 1869, *LD* XXIV, p.286.
[5] *St. Xystus III*: Pope Sixtus III. Proculus the new bishop of Constantinople tried to detach the papal vicariate in Illyricum, but Xystus ordered the bishops to recognise Anastasius, the bishop of Thessalonica, as his vicar.

the causes of Metropolitans, see Greg. Magn. Ep. ad *Episcopos Sardiniæ*, and St. Leo I., Ep. 84.

"As regards the Oriental Bishops, there was a prescriptive reservation to the Pope of the criminal causes of Patriarchs and Exarchs, as being autocephalous: see the Epistle of Julius [A.D. 337-352] *ad Euseb.*; also the Epistle of the Council of Ephesus [A.D. 481], which speaks of the reservation of the Pope of the cause of John of Antioch.[6] Again, as to the criminal causes of common Bishops, Pope Julius[7] in the same Epistle, although he is speaking particularly of the case of Alexandria, insinuates that it is fitting that these causes also should come before him; and Gelasius [A.D. 492-496], *Ep. ad Orient*, speaks of an ancient custom to this effect. [321]

"For the reservation of the 'causæ majores'[8] to the Vicar of the Holy See, see Xystus III., *Ep.* 8 *ad Syn. Thessalonic.* and Innocent I. [A.D. 402-417], *Ep. ad Victric.* Boniface I. [A.D. 418-422], *Ep.* 15, insists upon the invariable custom in the Eastern Church of submitting their 'magna negotia'[9] to the Pope ...

"2. As to the second, so far as it establishes the nullity of a diocesan or provincial synod unsupported by the authority of the Pope, it is undoubtedly an innovation. But it is certain, says Blascus[10] (*Comment. in Pseud-Isid.*, ch. 9), that the popes never applied it, even within their own

---

[6] *John of Antioch*: bishop 429-449.

[7] *Pope Julius I*: (337-352) He founded S. Maria in Trastevere and welcomed St Athanasius on his way back to Alexandria in 346.

[8] *'causæ majores'*: important causes

[9] *'magna negotia'*: great business

[10] *Blascus*: Karl Blascus, historian, who produced *De Collectione Canonorum Isidori Mercatoris,* Naples, 1760.

patriarchate, to any synod but such as pretended to be general, or to deal with the reserved causes of bishops. No writer, says the same authority, before the twelfth century applies this prohibition to synods generally; and the Roman correctors of Gratian,[11] *Adnot. ad Can.* 4, *Hist.* 17, limit it expressly to General Synods.

"3. Two other points have been sometimes regarded as novelties: the extension of the right of appeal to clerics generally, and the anticipation of judgment by an appeal to Rome, instead of appealing from the sentence, when pronounced. As regards the former, Dr. Döllinger[12] remarks, (Church Hist., vol. iii., § 7,) that the appeal of simple priests to Rome was by no means uncommon, previous to the pseudo-decretals. As regards the latter, it is sufficient to observe that Hincmar, in his controversy with Nicholas I. concerning Rothad, Bishop of Soissons,[13] whom he had deposed, justifies himself solely on the ground that Rothad had withdrawn the appeal, by which he had at first attempted to bar the proceedings of his judges. I think after this we may very contentedly acquiesce in Ballerini's[14] moderate and judicial summing-up, when he says, in his Essay on the Canons, part iii., cap. 6, § 3, that, when these decretals appeared, they represented a discipline, which was

[322]

---

[11] *Gratian*: Camaldolese monk of Bologna and founder of the science of Canon Law. Of particular note is his *Concordium Discordantium Canonum* (1140), a collection of Papal and Conciliar decrees to that date.

[12] *Dr. Döllinger*: Johann Joseph Ignaz von Döllinger (1799-1890), Bavarian church historian and an admirer of Newman; he translated Newman's *Lectures on the Present Position of Catholics in England* (1851) into German. He defended a liberal form of Catholicism and was a critic of Papal infallibility; after refusing to submit to the decision of the Council he was excommunicated in 1871 and later identified with the Church of the Old Catholics.

[13] *Rothad, Bishop of Soissons*: (d. 869) In the conflict with Hincmar he was disposed as bishop in 862/3 but was restored by the pope in 865.

[14] *Ballerini*: Pietro Ballerini (1698-1769), Italian canonist.

already forming, particularly in those parts where they had their birth.

"This judgment of Ballerini's is so amply borne out by two non-Catholic writers of different nationalities and different schools of thought, but like one another, at least, in their learning and their candour, that I cannot forbear quoting them. The first is Neander[15] (Church History, vol. vi., p. 7, ed. Bohn). He says, 'He, the pseudo-Isidore,[16] was at all events but the organ of a tendency of the religious and ecclesiastical spirit which prevailed with the great masses of the men amongst whom he lived. He had no idea of introducing a new code; but only of presenting, in a connected form, the principles which must be recognized by every one as correct, and on which depended the well-being of the Church ... In truth, even what had been said by Leo the Great [A.D. 440-461] concerning the Pope's primacy over the whole Church, involves the principle of all that is to be found in the decretals; though Leo could not bring into effect, in his own age, those outlines of the ideal of a papacy which floated before his mind.'

"The second is Mr. Bowden, who speaks thus in the Introduction to his Life of Gregory VII., p. 56: 'The immediate effect of the forgery was rather to sanction and consolidate relations already existing between the different orders of the Christian hierarchy, than to introduce new ones; and, though the work, having once been received, undoubtedly did much towards handing down in its

---

[15] *Neander*: August Neander (1789–1850), German church historian.

[16] *pseudo-Isidore*: apocryphal letters claimed to be by various early popes, incorporated into a 9th century collection of canons published between 847 and 852 under the name Isidore Mercator; the identity of Isidore is unknown, but he is thought to have been French.

completeness the system of Papal monarchy to subsequent ages, it derived its own weight at the epoch of its origin, from the tendency which already existed in that system to perfect and extend itself.'

"Even Dean Milman, in spite of a decided anti-papal bias, is obliged to admit (Latin Christ., vol. ii., p. 307) that it cannot be proved that the pseudo-decretals contain anything absolutely new, anything that had not been said before.

"If ... the Papal Monarchy be a usurpation, and destructive of that economy which Christ meant should reign throughout His Church, at least it is undeniable that the Church from the beginning bore and fostered the germ within her. To the Bishop of Rome all may appeal, and from him none. He is the judge of all, whom none may judge. Every corner of the vineyard is open to him, who is its guardian, whenever the faith or peace of the Church is in danger. No canon avails without his sanction; and it is for him to interpret the canons according to the exigencies of time and circumstance. What the ancient Church does not claim for the Pope, she allows him to claim for himself. Restrictive laws seem to have been made for others, not for him. Patriarchs, the most ancient and the most august, are keenly criticized and sharply rebuked, if they speak proud things, or interfere with even the humblest of their neighbours; the Bishop of Rome alone, it seems, cannot exalt himself above his rightful place, or intrude where he is not due. If he is rebuked, it is by heretics like the Eusebians,[17] whom he detects and punishes; or if a Saint

---

[17] *Eusebians*: followers of Eusebius of Nicomedia (d.341), Archbishop of Constantinoples, friend of Arius. Although he signed the Nicene Creed, he did so only reluctantly and subsequently promoted Arius's views. Eusebians were therefore essentially Arian in their beliefs.

says a sharp word, the Church lets it fall to the ground, as if it knew not what he said ... "

Here I interrupt the course of Mr. Ryder's argument to refer to my own Essay on the Development of Christian Doctrine, in which I have been led to enumerate such testimonies in behalf of the authority of the Holy See, and the Roman Church, as occur in the first three centuries, and do not fall within the range of his survey of the history. "Faint they may be one by one," I say, "but at least they are various, and are drawn from many times and countries, and thereby serve to illustrate each other, and form a body of proof." For instance, to St. Clement,[18] one of the first successors of St. Peter, the Corinthians have recourse in their domestic dissensions, and he, in the name of his Church, writes to them a letter of exhortation and advice; while St. Ignatius,[19] his contemporary, who gives his counsels freely to various churches of Asia, utters not one word of admonition in writing to the Roman Church, and calls it "the church which has the first seat" in its place. Again St. Polycarp of Smyrna,[20] in the next generation, betakes himself to the Bishop of Rome on the question of Easter; the heretic Marcion,[21] excommunicated in Pontus, goes off to Rome; and we read of Soter,[22] as observing the custom of his church, when he sent alms to the churches of the empire, and as "affectionately exhorting those who

[324]

---

[18] *St. Clement*: See note on p.[25].

[19] *St. Ignatius*: See note on p.[23].

[20] *St. Polycarp of Smyrna*: (69-156), bishop and martyr.

[21] *Marcion*: of Pontus (d.160), a Gnostic who held that the God of the Old Testament was a different being from the God of the New Testament and also rejected the Incarnation; he was excommunicated by Pope Pius I in 144.

[22] *Soter*: Pope St. Soter (reigned 166-74) sent alms to the church in Corinth in 168.

came to Rome," in the words of Eusebius,[23] "as a father his children." To Rome the Montanists[24] came from Phrygia to gain the countenance of its bishop; and Praxeas,[25] also, in order to expose them; Pope Victor[26] pronounces the Asian churches excommunicate, and Irenæus, in his interposition, questions, not his right but the charity of his act. The same Saint speaks of Rome as the church in which the churches from every side centre, and as being pre-eminently the "principal" church. He says it was founded by St. Peter and St. Paul, and he prefers its tradition to that of other churches;[27] Tertullian,[28] too, says that the Apostles poured out into it their whole doctrine; and, after he was a Montanist, acknowledges, while he complains, that the Pope acted as a Pontifex Maximus and Bishop of bishops.[29] Pope Dionysius entertains the accusation brought by Alexandrian priests against their Bishop in a matter of doctrine; and forthwith asks of him an explanation, which the latter grants without any protest. Cyprian speaks of Rome as "the See of Peter and the principal church;" and, when he and Firmilian withstood Pope Stephen who maintained the validity of heretical baptism, the Pope carries his point against the churches of Africa, Egypt, and Asia Minor. Basilides, deposed in Spain, betakes himself to Pope Stephen.

[325]

---

[23] *Eusebius*: (c.260-c.339), bishop of Cæsarea, church historian; the quotation is from his *Ecclesiastical History*, Book 23, 9-10.

[24] *Montanists*: See above note on p.184. The Montanists followed a different date for Easter from the rest of the church.

[25] *Praxeas*: 2nd-3rd century priest from Asia Minor; he opposed Montanism. His teaching on the Trinity was unorthodox.

[26] *Pope Victor*: Victor I, Pope 189-198.

[27] *Irenæus, in his interposition ... to that of other churches*: cf. *Advesus Haereses* 3, 3, 2.

[28] *Tertullian*: (160-225) layman apologist for Christianity, author of numerous works.

[29] *he complains, that the Pope acted ...* : in his *De pudicitia* 1,6.

Fortunatus and Felix, deposed by Cyprian, have recourse to Pope Cornelius. So much in the first three centuries.

In the fourth, Pope Julius [A.D. 337-351], as we learn from Athanasius, remonstrates with the Arian party for "proceeding on their own authority," "for what we have received from the blessed Apostle Peter, that I signify to you." "Julius wrote back," says Socrates,[30] "that they acted against the canons, because they had not called him to a Council, the ecclesiastical canon commanding that the Churches ought not to make canons beside the judgment of the Bishop of Rome." Sozomen[31] says, "It was a sacerdotal law, to declare invalid whatever was transacted beside the judgment of the Bishop of the Romans." The Arians themselves, whom the Pope was withstanding, were forced to confess that Rome was "the school of the Apostles, and the Metropolis of orthodoxy from the beginning." Pope Damasus[32] [A.D. 366-386] calls the Eastern bishops his "sons": "In that your charity pays the due reverence to the Apostolic See," he says, "ye profit most yourselves, most honoured sons;" and he speaks of himself as "placed in the See of that holy Church, in which the holy Apostle taught how becomingly to direct the helm to which we have succeeded." "I speak," says St. Jerome[33] to the same Pope, [326] "with the successor of the Fisherman and the disciple of the Cross. I, following no one as my chief but Christ, am associated in communion with thy blessedness, that is, with

---

[30] *Socrates*: (380-450), historian who continued the *Ecclesiastical History* of Eusebius.

[31] *Sozomen*: Salmaninius Hermias Sozomenus (early 5th century), church historian who also wrote an *Ecclesiastical History*.

[32] *Pope Damasus*: The quotation is from his *Decree*, n.16.

[33] *St. Jerome*: See note on p.[41]. The quotation is from his *Letter* 14.

the See of Peter. Whoso gathers not with thee, scatters." St. Basil entreats the same Pope to send persons to settle the troubles of Asia Minor; "we are asking nothing new," he says, "for we know from tradition of our fathers, and from writings preserved among us, that Dionysius," [35] a Pope of the third century, "sent letters of visitation to our church of Cæsarea, and of consolation, with ransomers of our brethren from captivity."[34]

Pope Siricius[36] [A.D. 386-398] says: "We bear the burden of all who are laden,—yea, rather the blessed Apostle Peter beareth them in us, who, as we trust, in all things protects and defends us, the heirs of his government." "Diligently and congruously do ye consult the *arcana* of Apostolical dignity," says Pope Innocent[37] [A.D. 402-417] to the African Bishops, "the dignity of him on whom, besides those things which are without, falls the care of all the churches, following the form of the ancient rule, which you know, as well as I, has been preserved always by the whole world." And Pope Celestine[38] to the Bishops of Illyria [A.D. 422-432], "About all men we especially have anxiety, we, on whom, in the holy Apostle Peter, Christ conferred the necessity of making all men our concern, when He gave him the keys of opening and shutting."[39] Mr. Ryder continues:—

---

[35] *Dionysius*: Pope St. Dionysius (reigned 260-8); his letters are mentioned in Eusebius' *Ecclesiastical History*, 4, 23.

[35] *"... our brethren from captivity"*: The quotation is from *Letter* 70.

[36] *Pope Siricius*: The quotation is from his decretal addressed to Himerius, bishop of Tarragona in 385.

[37] *Pope Innocent*: The quotation is from his letter of January 417 about Pelagianism.

[38] *Pope Celestine*: The quotation is from a letter urging the bishops of Illyria in 431 to observe the canons and respect the position of the Bishop of Thessalonica who was the papal representative in Church matters.

[39] Vid. "Development of Doctrine" [ed. 1878, pp. 157, &c.]. [N]

"Boniface I.[40] (an. 422) Ep. xiv. 'To the Bishops of Thessaly,' *ap. Coust. Ep. Rom. Pont.* p. 1037. 'The institution of the Universal Church began in the honour granted to St. Peter, in whom the supremacy (*regimen et summa*) was established. As religion prospered, from him as from its source, ecclesiastical discipline flowed throughout all the churches. Nor do the canons of Nicæa testify otherwise; inasmuch as they do not venture to add aught to him, seeing that nothing could be given above his deserts, and knowing that all things had been given him by the words of Christ. It is certain, then, that this See stands, in relation to the churches spread throughout the world, as the head to its members; from whom, if any divide himself, he becomes an outcast from the religion of Christ, since he is external to its organization.' And Ep. xv., *l. c.,* p. 1042: 'None ever raised his hand against that apostolic height whose judgment it is not lawful to retract; none has shown himself a rebel towards it, unless he would bring judgment upon himself.' [327]

"Xystus III. (an. 435) to the Synod of Thessalonica, *l. c.,* p. 1263: 'Let the Metropolitans of each province enjoy the rank which is their due, saving the privilege of him (the Papal Vicar) whom the most honourable might honour. Let them have the right of ordaining in their provinces, but let no one venture to ordain without his knowledge and goodwill, whom, in all cases of ordination (*i.e.* of bishops) we would have consulted.'

"Gelasius[41] (*circa an.* 480) to Faustus (Labbe, tom. v., p. 297): 'The canons have decided that no one whatever shall

---

[40] *Boniface I*: reigned 418-422
[41] *Gelasius*: Pope St. Gelasius I, reigned 492-496

appeal from this See; and so provide that it shall judge the whole Church, and itself be judged of none ... Timothy of Alexandria, Peter of Antioch, Peter, Paul, John, not one, but many, bearing the episcopal name, by the authority of this Apostolic See alone, were cast down ... Therefore we are in no fear lest the Apostolic judgment be reversed, to which the voice of Christ, tradition, and the canons, have given the decision of controversy throughout the whole Church.'

[328]

2.

"The second count ... takes the form of a reflection upon the honesty of the Holy See. But if there is a point in the whole subject, upon which there is a consensus of writers, Protestant and Catholic, it is precisely this, that the Pope had nothing to do with the forgery of the pseudo-decretals; and moreover that they were not forged in his interest. They were forged in Gaul, not in Rome; and their immediate object was to relieve the bishops and the inferior clergy from the tyranny of the Metropolitans, who were but too frequently the tools of the secular power ... When they exalt the Pope, it is only to pull themselves out of the mire; and it has been observed (see Blascus, *l. c.*, c. 10, *seq.*), that these decretals, where the interests of the episcopate are not at stake, do not concern themselves to uphold even the well-established privileges of the Holy See, and in some cases (whether wittingly or not is uncertain) actually contravene them ... '

"But ... 'if the Pope [St. Nicholas I.] be not the coiner, he is at least the conscious utterer of this false coin; he had duplicates of all the genuine letters of his predecessors in his portfolio; and, if he did not actually discover that these were forgeries, it was because he felt they were, and would not look.' … This assumption is simply false. On the contrary, I maintain that the fact of the duplicate of a papal letter not being found in the Roman archives, not only did not prove it spurious, but in very many instances could not create any fair presumption against it. It is true that the Popes, like other bishops, were in the way of laying up by their archives copies of the letters they wrote, and of the more important letters which they received. We have frequent references and appeals, in the letters to and from the Holy See, to the contents of the Roman archives; but it is impossible not to be struck with the short periods of time which these appeals cover. I think I am right in saying, that, with one exception, they do not extend beyond a century, and that most fall far short of it. I know of only one exception, and that was when, in 531, Theodore of Thessalonica produced from his archives Papal letters from Damasus downwards, a space of about 150 years, all extant and all genuine, and asked Boniface II. to verify them from the Roman scrinia.[42] Curiously enough, we do not know how far the Roman scrinia stood the trial, for the document (see Labbe,[43] tom. v., p. 843) is imperfect.

[329]

"1. Mabillon[44] (*de re Diplom. Supp.* p. 5), enumerates the many dangers that beset the ancient archives. They were, moreover, peculiarly liable both to be neglected, and tampered with, owing to the fact that the *notarii* and

---

[42] *scrinia*: literally, buckets or coffers in which papers were stored; this became the term for the archives of the Roman imperial chancery, the term being taken over for the papal archives.

[43] *Labbe*: Philippe Labbe (1607-67), French Jesuit, historian and philologist.

[44] *Mabillon*: Jean Mabillon (1632-1707), Benedictine monk and historian; his *De re diplomatica* (1681) investigated ancient and mediaeval manuscripts and assessed their authenticity.

scriniarii,[45] who were alone capable of reading, transcribing, and classifying the manuscripts, were a small, and consequently irresponsible class. This was so much felt to be the case, but we find that, from time to time, *custodes*[46] were appointed to watch over the honesty of the *notarii*, and keep them to their duty. The irresponsibility of the *notarii* was, of course, in direct ratio to the want of culture of their time and country; thus, in Italy, we may presume they had things very much their own way during the latter half of the fifth and throughout the seventh and eighth centuries. So deplorable was the state of knowledge in Italy, and particularly in Rome, in the seventh century, owing to the repeated wars of barbarians that had swept over the face of the country, that we find Pope Agatho [A.D. 678-682], in his letter to the Emperor Constantine, thus excusing the rudeness of his legates Labbe, tom. vii., p. 655: "Among us, planted as we are in the midst of the Gentiles, and winning our daily bread most precariously by bodily toil, how should literary knowledge in its fulness be found, more than that we preserve, in simplicity of heart and undoubtingly, what has been canonically defined by our holy predecessors in the Apostolical See, and by the five Holy Councils, of the faith delivered to us by our fathers?" And again, in his Synodical Letter to the same Emperor, *loc. cit.*, p. 707: 'As regards secular knowledge, I think there are not any in our times, who may boast of having reached its summit; since, in our land, the wrath of contrary nations rages, fighting, overrunning, and ravaging; and ... the ancient revenue of the Church has gradually, under diverse misfortunes, melted away. But our faith remains our one support, with which to

[330]

---

[45] notarii *and* scriniarii: secretaries and archivists
[46] *custodies*: guardians, supervisors

live is our glory, and for which to die is our eternal recompense.'

"Under such circumstances, nothing is more natural than that the Roman archives should have sustained vast and frequent losses, and we are not surprised when Baronius[47] (tom. v., an. 381, xxxi) points out to us that the Roman archives had evidently suffered a loss between the times of Damasus and Gregory I. [A.D. 366 and 590]. He quotes St. Gregory, lib. vi., Ep. 15 (ed. Ben. lib. vii., Ep. 34) to the effect that the Roman Church knew nothing of the condemnation of the Eudoxians,[48] except from doubtful or corrupt sources, and remarks that, seeing that several of the ancient Fathers speak of Eudoxius as accused and convicted of frightful heresy, St. Gregory's words clearly show, 'jacturam passa esse Romana archivia.'[49] I may observe that the letter of Liberius[50] to Constantius (see *Coustant.*,[51] p. 423,) speaks of Eudoxius as having refused to condemn Arius, and being therefore excommunicate; and this letter must have been originally in the Roman archives.   [331]

In this same letter Liberius testifies that he has got the letter of Alexander of Alexandria[52] to Pope Silvester,[53]

---

[47] *Baronius*: See note on p.[53].

[48] *Eudoxians*: followers of Eudoxia of Antioch (d.370) who defended Arius.

[49] *'jacturam passa esse Romana archivia'*: 'the Roman archives suffered damage'

[50] *Liberius*: See note on p.[59].

[51] *Coustant*: Pierrre Coustant (1654-1721), monk of the Benedictine Congregationn of Saint-Maur and patristic scholar. The reference is to his collection of papal letters, *Epistolae Romanorum Pontificum et quae ad eos scriptae sunt a S. Clemente I usque ad Innocentium III, quotquot reperiri potuerunt* (1721).

[52] *Alexander of Alexandria*: St. Alexander I (d.326/8), Patriarch of Alexandria; he opposed Arianism and was the mentor of St. Athanasius.

[53] *Pope Silvester*: St. Silvester I (d.335); he approved the decrees of the Council of Nicæa.

concerning the Arian controversy, 'manent literæ;'[54] and
Coustant remarks that, of course, there were numbers of
letters to and from Silvester on the same subject, though
none have come down to us.

"In the eighth century, St. Boniface of Mayence,[55] Ep.
15, tells Nothelm of Canterbury[56] that, as regarded the
famous letter of St. Gregory to Augustine, the Roman
scriniarii had looked in the archives of the Roman Church,
and could not find it.

"In 743, the Germans rested their right to marry 'in
quartâ generatione,'[57] upon an indult of Pope Gregory II.,
which could not be discovered in the Roman archives; but
Pope Zachary[58] did not on that account reject it as spurious
... 'Although we cannot find the document, we do not
hesitate to believe it genuine' (see Blascus, *l. c.*, cap. iv.)

"We have only to look through Coustant's volume, to
see that numbers of the Papal letters do not come from the
Roman archives, but from those of other Sees, particularly
Vercellæ, and the famous Gallic Sees of Arles and Vienne.
And the editor of the 'Bullarium Romanum, Rome 1739,'[59]
in his preface, after noticing the losses which the Roman
archives had sustained, particularly in Papal letters, from
Leo I. to Innocent III. [A.D. 440 to 1198], observes, that
numbers of these autographs, 'of which no longer any

---

[54] *'manent literæ'*: 'the written word remains', i.e. as evidence
[55] *Boniface of Mayence*: (c.675-754); born in Devon, he became a missionary on
Germany and was appointed Archbishop of Mainz where he was martyred; known
as the Apostle of the Germans.
[56] *Nothelm of Canterbury*: (d.739), Archbishop of Canterbury; he supplied Bede
with copies of papal letters.
[57] *'in quartâ generatione,'*: i.e. between first cousins, prohibited by the law of
consaguninity.
[58] *Pope Zachary*: (679-752)
[59] *Bullarium Romanum, Rome 1739*: the collection of papal bulls from Leo the
Great to Benedict XIV, published by Girolamo Mainardi from 1733 to 1762.

mention or trace remains in the Roman archives,' have been found intact in the archives of other cathedral towns and monasteries.

"It has been said, that the fact that so many of the pseudo-decretals profess to be the letters of Popes of the times of persecution, should have awaked the Pope's suspicions. But it must be remembered, first, that there is great reason for supposing that St. Nicholas never saw more than certain portions of these decretals, with which he shows an acquaintance, although he nowhere formally quotes them; secondly, that it is well known that the Popes, in the times of persecution, did write, and write frequently,—witness the genuine fragments of their writings in Eusebius, Hilary, and elsewhere. Moreover, the Fathers testify an acquaintance with other documents which are wholly lost. St. Augustine, for instance, Ep. 43 (olim 162) n. 16, shows that he knew, *in extenso*, the decree of Pope Melchiades [A.D. 310-314] condemning Donatus; and St. Jerome speaks of the four letters written by St. Cornelius [A.D. 250-252] to Fabius,[60] as extant in his time.

"There was nothing, then, in these relics of the times of persecution, in that age, to awaken suspicion; whilst there was much to attract devotion. Men naturally welcomed their discovery with the same devotion, and certainly with no greater surprise, than they did the kindred discovery of the martyrs' bodies. St. Nicholas, in his letter to the Bishop of Gaul (Labbe, tom. x., p. 282), shows what idea was uppermost in his mind, when he refers to those decrees, of which he had seen something, and heard more, as the

[332]

---

[60] *Fabius*: Bishop of Antioch 253-256

decrees of those 'quorum videmus Deo auctore Sanctam Ecclesiam aut roseo cruore floridam, aut rorifluis sudoribus et salubribus eloquiis adornatam.'[61]

"Again, it must be remembered that the Holy See received these decretals from the Gallic Church, upon whose learning it had been taught to depend in its controversies with the civil power and Greek heresy.

[333] "We find a remarkable instance of this dependence recorded by Paschasius Radbert, in his Life of Wala (ap. Mabillon Oct. S. Ord. Ben., sæc. iv., part i., p. 511).[62] He relates that he and Wala (an. 833) showed Gregory IV.[63]— then in France, engaged in the difficult and dangerous task of reconciling the king and his sons,—'sundry documents, confirmed by the authority of the holy Fathers and his own predecessors, against which none might deny that he had the power (forsooth God's, the blessed Apostle Peter's, and his own,) to go and send unto all nations for the faith of Christ the peace of the Churches, the preaching of the Gospel, and the assertion of the truth; and that in him resided the supreme authority and living powers of blessed Peter; in virtue of which he might judge all, and himself be judged of none. Which documents he graciously received, and was exceedingly comforted.'

"Some writers have thought that in this they discovered evidence of the pseudo-decretals; but the idea is very generally abandoned. One strong argument against it

---

[61] *'quorum videmus Deo auctore ... '* : 'of those who we see by God's authority either make Holy Church flower with their rosy blood, or adorn her by their nourishing words.'

[62] *Paschasius Radbert*: Saint Paschaius Radbert (785-865), abbot and theologian. Wala was a former abbot of his monastery.

[63] *Gregory IV*: reigned 827-844; his letter to the bishops of Gaul upheld the right of appeal to Rome by Bishop Aldric of Le Mans who had been ousted from his see.

appears to me to be the fact, that Agobard,[64] who belonged to the same party as Wala and Radbert, in his letter to the king,[65] which exactly coincides in time with his friends' mission to Gregory, and in which he has the same object in view with them, viz., the exaltation of papal prerogative, grounds his argument exclusively on genuine documents. However this may be, the whole story is a curious illustration of the influence of the French Church upon the Holy See.

"But, not only did the Pope receive these documents from the French Bishops, but they themselves furnished him with what he might well regard as a crucial test of their genuineness. For, even when Hincmar, in his controversy with St. Nicholas, does his utmost to disprove their cogency as law, he never so much as suggests a doubt of their [334] genuineness. It is true that, in his subsequent controversy with Adrian II., Hincmar uses rather different language; but even then he hints at nothing worse than that they have been garbled and interpolated by his own nephew and others, to serve their private ends.

"In the letter to the Bishops of Gaul, quoted above, the Pope clearly seems to indicate other sources of authentic decretals besides the archives; when, in meeting Hincmar's attempt to restrict the legal cogency of decretals to those contained in the Codex of Adrian, he says, 'God forbid that we should not embrace the decretals, which the Roman Church, 'penes se in suis archivis et *vetustis rite*

---

[64] *Agobard*: St. Agobard of Lyon (c.779-840), Archbishop of Lyon.
[65] *the king*: Louis the Pious (778-840)

monumentis recondita venerantur.'[66] The 'vetusta monumenta' no doubt included all such well-authorized collections as the pseudo-Isidorian professed to be.

2. "Besides the fact of the frequent losses which the Roman archives had sustained, rendering their contents at any given time an unsafe criterion of genuineness, it was exceedingly difficult to make out what they did contain. For, as I have observed, only a very small class, the *scriniarii*, were competent to engage in such a search. These were put upon their oath that they had produced all that they could find regarding the cause in hand, as we read in the Acts of the Sixth Council. And, for these experts, the search was doubtless exceedingly difficult, when covering any considerable length of time, and when documents were wanted, that had not been previously arranged for controversial purposes. Often, indeed, it could have been little else than a wild hunt among boxes of manuscripts in various stages of decay, when the subject of any successful discovery might well be described as 'Deo revelante reperta'[67] (see Nicholas' Letter to Herard, Labbe, tom. x., p. 298).

[335]

"Ballerini (St. Leo, tom. i., p. 511), after remarking upon the number of St. Leo's letters that were lost, thus accounts for these and other losses: 'After the general collections of the Canons and Papal letters, originally compiled by private persons for private use, had got so generally into circulation that the Popes themselves took their predecessors' letters oftener from these private collections than from the Apostolic *scrinia*, it came about that the autographs of these

---

[66] *'penes se in suis archivis ... '*: 'which they revere hidden away both in the archives in their possession, and in their ancient religious monuments.'

[67] *'Deo revelante reperta'*: 'God's revelation discovered'

same letters, which were in the Apostolic *scrinia*, gradually falling into neglect, as time went on, perished.'

"This, then, is St. Nicholas' position. He is presented with portions of documents, for we have no proof that they were more, which accurately represent the ecclesiastical spirit of the day, a recommendation, rather than a difficulty, in an uncritical age. Their genuineness is attested by the Church of Gaul, a church incomparably more learned than his own; and attested, moreover, even against that church's interests. The genuineness of these documents was in no sense upon its trial; it was undisputed. The presumption was strongly in favour of the genuineness of documents, containing doctrine so orthodox and so apposite; if any heresy had cropped up in them, then, indeed, it would have been another matter. But more than this, the Pope, even if a doubt of these had crossed his mind, which is in the highest degree impossible, had not, in the Roman archives, any satisfactory test of their genuineness."

XIV[1]

PRIVATE JUDGMENT[2]

THERE is this obvious, undeniable difficulty in the attempt to form a theory of Private Judgment, in the choice of a religion, that Private Judgment leads different minds in such different directions. If, indeed, there be no religious truth, or at least no sufficient means of arriving at it, then the difficulty vanishes: for where there is nothing to find, there can be no rules for seeking, and contradiction in the result is but a *reductio ad absurdum*[3] of the attempt. But such a conclusion is intolerable to those who search, else they would not search; and therefore on them the obligation lies to explain, if they can, how it comes to pass, that Private Judgment is a duty, and an advantage, and a success, considering it leads the way not only to their own faith, whatever that may be, but to opinions which are diametrically opposite to it; considering it not only leads them right, but leads others wrong, landing them as it may

---

[1] *XIV*: incorrectly numbered XIII in some editions.
[2] The original essay in the *British Critic* was a review of eight different publications. Newman omits many references to them in the version included in *Essays Critical and Historical*; see the Textual Appendix.
[3] reductio ad absurdum: See note on p.[115].

be in the Church of Rome, or in the Wesleyan Connexion,[4] or in the Society of Friends.[5]

Are exercises of mind, which end so diversely, one and all pleasing to the Divine Author of faith; or rather must they not contain some inherent, or some incidental defect, since they manifest such divergence? Must private judgment in all cases be a good *per se*; or is it a good under circumstances, and with limitations? Or is it a good, only when it is not an evil? Or is it a good and evil at once, a good involving an evil? Or is it an absolute and simple evil? Questions of this sort rise in the mind on contemplating a principle which leads to more than the thirty-two points of the compass, and, in consequence, whatever we may here be able to do, in the way of giving plain rules for its exercise, be it greater or less, will be so much gain.

1.

Now the first remark which occurs is an obvious one, and, we suppose, will be suffered to pass without much opposition, that whatever be the intrinsic merits of Private Judgment, yet, if it at all exerts itself in the direction of proselytism and conversion, a certain *onus probandi*[6] lies upon it, and it must show cause why it should be tolerated, and not rather treated as a breach of the peace, and silenced *instanter*[7] as a mere disturber of the existing constitution of things. Of course it may be safely exercised in defending what is established; and we are far indeed from saying that

---

[4] *Wesleyan Connexion:* at the heart of the Methodist tradition was the idea of a non-episcopal Church with ministers (often itinerant) attached or 'connected' to particular circuits and sharing a common practice and discipline.

[5] *Society of Friends*: Quakers; see note on p.[114].

[6] *onus probandi*: burden of proof

[7] *instanter*: without delay

it is never to advance in the direction of change or revolution, else the Gospel itself could never have been introduced; but we consider that serious religious changes have a *primâ facie*[8] case against them; they have something to get over, and have to prove their admissibility, before it can reasonably be allowed; and their agents may be called upon to suffer, in order to prove their earnestness, and to pay the penalty of the trouble they are causing. Considering the special countenance given in Scripture to quiet, unanimity, and contentedness, and the warnings directed against disorder, insubordination, changeableness, discord, and division; considering the emphatic words of the

[338] Apostle, laid down by him as a general principle, and illustrated in detail, "Let every man abide in the same calling wherein he was called;"[9] considering, in a word, that change is really the characteristic of error, and unalterableness the attribute of truth, of holiness, of Almighty God Himself, we consider that when Private Judgment moves in the direction of innovation, it may well be regarded at first with suspicion and treated with severity. Nay, we confess even a satisfaction, when a penalty is attached to the expression of new doctrines, or to a change of communion. We repeat it, if any men have strong feelings, they should pay for them; if they think it a duty to unsettle things established, they should show their earnestness by being willing to suffer. We shall be the last to complain of this kind of persecution, even though directed against what we consider the cause of truth. Such disadvantages do no harm to that cause in the event, but they bring home to a man's mind his own responsibility;

---

[8] *primâ facie*: at first sight
[9] *"Let every man abide ... "*: 1 Corinthians 7:20

they are a memento to him of a great moral law, and warn him that his private judgment, if not a duty, is a sin.

An act of private judgment is, in its very idea, an act of individual responsibility; this is a consideration which will come with especial force on a conscientious mind, when it is to have so fearful an issue as a change of religion. A religious man will say to himself, "If I am in error at present, I am in error by a disposition of Providence, which has placed me where I am; if I change into an error, this is my own act. It is much less fearful to be born at disadvantage, than to place myself at disadvantage."

And if the voice of men in general is to weigh at all in a matter of this kind, it does but corroborate these instinctive feelings. A convert is undeniably in favour with no party; he [339] is looked at with distrust, contempt, and aversion by all. His former friends think him a good riddance, and his new friends are cold and strange; and as to the impartial public, their very first impulse is to impute the change to some eccentricity of character, or fickleness of mind, or tender attachment, or private interest. Their utmost praise is the reluctant confession that "doubtless he is very sincere." Churchmen and Dissenters, men of Rome and men of the Kirk,[10] are equally subject to this remark. Not on extraordinary occasions only, but as a matter of course, whenever the news of a conversion to Romanism, or to Irvingism,[11] or to the Plymouth sect,[12] or to Unitarianism,[13] is

---

[10] *the Kirk*: the Church of Scotland, which is Presbyterian.
[11] *Irvingism*: Edward Irving (1792-1834), a Scottish minister, helped to found the 'Catholic Apostolic Church' in 1832 which was popularly referred to by this name.
[12] *the Plymouth Sect*: also sometimes called the Plymouth Brethren; it was established by J. N Darby (17800-1882) at Plymouth in 1830. It has no organized ministry but breaks bread each Sunday as a symbol of Christian union. Members of the 'Exclusive Brethren' are discouraged from social or business contacts with

brought to us, we say, one and all of us, "No wonder, such a one has lived so long abroad;" or, "he is of such a very imaginative turn;" or, "he is so excitable and odd;" or, "what could he do? all his family turned;" or, "it was a re-action in consequence of an injudicious education;" or, "trade makes men cold," or "a little learning makes them shallow in their religion." If, then, the common voice of mankind goes for anything, must we not consider it to be the *rule* that men change their religion, not on reason, but for some extra-rational feeling or motive? else, the world would not so speak.

Now, for ourselves, we are not quarrelling with this testimony,—we are willing to resign ourselves to it; but we think there are parties whom it concerns much to ponder it. Surely it is a strong, and, as they ought to feel, an alarming proof, that, for all the haranguing and protesting which goes on in Exeter and other halls,[14] this great people is not such a conscientious supporter of the sacred right of Private Judgment as a good Protestant would desire. Why should we go out of our way, one and all of us, to impute personal motives in explanation of the conversion of every individual convert, as he comes before us, if there were in us, the public, an adhesion to that absolute, and universal, and unalienable principle, as its titles are set forth in heraldic style, high and broad, sacred and awful, the right, and the duty, and the possibility of Private Judgment? Why should

[340]

non-members. Newman's elder brother Francis (1895-1897) 'was very influenced by the Founder' (Ian Ker, *John Henry Newman*, p.106).

[13] *Unitarianism*: stresses the unity of God as opposed to belief in the Trinity.

[14] *in Exeter and other halls*: Exeter Hall on the Strand, which opened in 1831, was used for meetings of the Protestant Association and the Protestant Reformation Society. Newman satirised such meetings in an article in *The British Critic* in 1838 reviewing *Random Recollections of Exeter Hall in 1834-1837 By one of the Protestant Party*.

we confess it in the general, yet promptly and pointedly deny it in every particular, if our hearts retained more than the "magni nominis umbra,"[15] when we preached up the Protestant principle? Is it not sheer wantonness and cruelty in Baptist, Independent, Irvingite,[16] Wesleyan, Establishment-man, Jumper,[17] and Mormonite,[18] to delight in trampling on and crushing these manifestations of their own pure and precious charter, instead of dutifully and reverently exalting, at Bethel, or at Dan,[19] each instance of it, as it occurs, to the gaze of its professing votaries? If a staunch Protestant's daughter turns Roman, and betakes herself to a convent, why does he not exult in the occurrence? Why does he not give a public breakfast, or hold a meeting, or erect a memorial, or write a pamphlet in honour of her, and of the great undying principle she has so gloriously vindicated? Why is he in this base, disloyal style muttering about priests, and Jesuits, and the horrors of nunneries, in solution of the phenomenon, when he has the fair and ample form of Private Judgment rising before his eyes, and pleading with him, and bidding him impute good motives, not bad, and in very charity ascribe to the influence of a high and holy principle, to a right and a duty of every member of the family of man, what his poor human instincts are fain to set down as a folly or a sin. All this would lead us to suspect that the doctrine of private judgment, in its simplicity, purity, and integrity,—private

[15] *"magni nominis umbra"*: "the shadow of a great name"
[16] *Irvingite*: See note on p.[126].
[17] *Jumper*: name given to Welsh Calvinist Methodists who used to 'leap for joy' at their meetings.
[18] *Mormonite*: or Mormon, a member of the Church of Jesus Christ of Latter Day Saints, founded by Joseph Smith (1804-44) in Manchester, New York, in 1830.
[19] *at Bethel, or at Dan*: Jeroboam I set up idols at Dan and Bethel, cf. 1 Kings 12:28ff.

[341]   judgment, all private judgment, and nothing but private judgment,—is held by very few persons indeed; and that the great mass of the population are either stark unbelievers in it, or deplorably dark about it; and that even the minority who are in a manner faithful to it, have glossed and corrupted the true sense of it by a miserably faulty reading, and hold, not the right of private judgment, but the private right of judgment; in other words, their own private right, and no one's else. To us it seems as clear as day, that they consider that they themselves, indeed, individually can and do act on reason, and on nothing but reason; that they have the gift of advancing, without bias or unsteadiness, throughout their search, from premiss to conclusion, from text to doctrine; that they have sought aright, and no one else, who does not agree with them; that they alone have found out the art of putting the salt upon the bird's tail,[20] and have rescued themselves from being the slaves of circumstance and the creatures of impulse. It is undeniable, then, if the popular feeling is to be our guide, that, high and mighty as the principle of private judgment is in religious inquiries, as we most fully grant it is, still it bears some similarity to Saul's armour which David rejected,[21] or to edged tools which have a bad trick of chopping at our fingers, when we are but simply and innocently meaning them to make a dash forward at truth.

Any tolerably serious man will feel this in his own case more vividly than in that of any one else. Who can know ever so little of himself without suspecting all kinds of

---

[20] *putting the salt upon the bird's tail*: i.e. capturing something by means of the advice given humorously, e.g. to children, that this is how to capture birds; it does not, of course, work.

[21] *Saul's armour which David rejected*: Cf. 1 Samuel 17:39

imperfect and wrong motives in everything he attempts? And then there is the bias of education and of habit; and, added to the difficulties thence resulting, those which arise from weakness of the reasoning faculty, ignorance or imperfect knowledge of the original languages of Scripture, [342] and again, of history and antiquity. These things being considered, we lay it down as a truth, about which, we think, few ought to doubt, that Divine aid alone can carry any one safely and successfully through an inquiry after religious truth. That there are certain very broad contrasts between one religion and another, in which no one would be at fault what to think and what to choose, is very certain; but the problem proposed to private judgment, at this day, is of a rather more complicated nature. Taking things as they are, we all seem to be in Solomon's case, when he said, "I am but a little child; I know not how to go out or come in; and Thy servant is in the midst of a great people, that cannot be numbered nor counted for multitude. Give, therefore, Thy servant an understanding heart, that I may discern between good and bad."[22] It is useless, surely, attempting to inquire or judge, unless a Divine command enjoin the work upon us, and a Divine promise sustain us through it. Supposing, indeed, such a command and promise be given, then, of course, there is no difficulty in the matter. Whatever be our personal infirmities, He whom we serve can overrule or supersede them. An act of duty must always be right; and will be accepted, whatever be its success, because done in obedience to His will. And He can bless the most unpromising circumstances; He can even lead us forward by means of our mistakes; He can turn our mistakes

---

[22] *"I am but a little child... "*: 1 Kings 3:7

into a revelation; He can convert us, if He will, through the very obstinacy, or self-will, or superstition, which mixes itself up with our better feelings, and defiles, yet is sanctified by our sincerity. And much more can He shed upon our path supernatural light, if He so will, and give us an insight into the meaning of Scripture, and a hold of the sense of Antiquity, to which our own unaided powers never could have attained.

[343]

All this is certain; He continually leads us forward in the midst of darkness; and we live, not by bread only, but by His Word converting the hard rock or salt sea into nourishment. The simple question is, *has* He, in this particular case, commanded, has He promised? and how far? If He has, and as far as He has, all is easy; if He has not, all is, we will not say impossible, but what is worse, undutiful or presumptuous. Our business is to ask with St. Paul, when arrested in the midst of his frenzy, "Lord, what wilt Thou have me to do?"[23] This is the simple question. He can bless our present state; He can bless our change; *which* is it His will to bless? If Wesleyan or Independent has come over to us apart from this spirit, we do not much pride ourselves in our convert. If he joins us because he thinks he has a right to judge for himself, or because forms are of no consequence, or merely because sectarianism has its errors and inconveniences, or because an established Church is an efficacious means of spreading religion, he plainly thinks that the choice of a communion is not a more serious matter than the choice of a neighbourhood or of an insurance office. In like manner, if members of our communion have left it for Rome, because of the *æsthetic* beauty of the latter,

---

[23] *"Lord, what wilt Thou have me to do?"*: Acts 9:6

and the grandeur of its pretensions, we are grieved, but, good luck to them, we can spare them. And if Roman Catholics join us or our "Dissenting brethren," because their own Church is behind the age, insists on Aristotelic dogmas,[24] and interferes with liberty of thought, such a conversion is no triumph over popery, but over St. Peter and St. Paul. Our only safety lies in obedience; our only comfort in keeping it in view.

If this be so, we have arrived at the following conclusion: that it is our duty to betake ourselves to Scripture, and to observe how far the private search of a religion is there sanctioned, and under what circumstances. This then is the next point which comes under consideration. [344]

2.

Now the first and most ordinary kind of Private Judgment, if it deserves the name, which is recognized in Scripture, is that in which we engage without conscious or deliberate purpose. While Lydia heard St. Paul preach, her heart was opened.[25] She had it not in mind to exercise any supposed sacred right, she was not setting about the choice of a religion, but she was drawn on to accept the Gospel by a moral persuasion. "To him that hath more shall be given,"[26] not in the way of judging or choosing, but by an inward development met by external disclosures. Lydia's instance is the type of a multitude of cases, differing very much from each other, some divinely ordered, others merely human, some which would commonly be called cases of

[24] *Aristotelic dogmas*: e.g. transubstantiation, which uses the terminology of 'substance' and 'accidence' originally found in Aristotle.
[25] *While Lydia heard St Paul preach ...* : Acts 16:14. Lydia, a seller of purple dye at Philippi, was the first European to be baptised.
[26] *"To him that hath more shall be given"*: Matthew 13:12

private judgment, and others which certainly would not, but all agreeing in this, that the judgment exercised is not recognized and realized by the party exercising it, as the subject-matter of command, promise, duty, privilege, or anything else. It is but the spontaneous stirring of the affections within, or the passive acceptance of what is offered from without. St. Paul baptized Lydia's household also; it would seem then that he baptized servants or slaves, who had very little power of judging between a true religion and a false; shall we say that they, like their mistress, accepted the Gospel on private judgment or not? Did the thousands baptized in national conversions exercise their private judgment or not? Do children when taught their catechism? Most persons will reply in the negative; yet it will be difficult to separate their case in principle from what Lydia's may have been, that is, the case of religious persons who are advancing forward into the truth, how they know not. Neither the one class nor the other have undertaken to inquire and judge, or have set about being converted, or have got their reasons all before them and together, to discharge at an enemy or passer-by on fit occasions. The difference between these two classes is in the state of their hearts; the one party consist of unformed minds, or senseless and dead, or minds under temporary excitement, who are brought over by external or accidental influences, without any real sympathy for the Religion, which is taught them *in order* that they may *learn* sympathy with it, and who, as time goes on, fall away again if they are not happy enough to become embued with it; and in the other party there is already a sympathy between the external Word and the heart within. The one are proselytized by force, authority, or their mere feelings, the others through their

[345]

410

habitual and abiding frame of mind and cast of opinion. But neither can be said, in the ordinary sense of the word, to inquire, reason, and decide about religion. And yet in a great number of these cases,—certainly where the persons in question are come to years of discretion and show themselves consistent in their religious profession afterwards,—they would be commonly set forth by Protestant minds as instances of the due exercise of the right of private judgment.

Such are the greater number perhaps of converts at this day, in whatever direction their conversion lies; and their so-called exercise of private judgment is neither right nor [346] wrong in itself, it is a spontaneous act which they do not think about; if it is anything, it is but a means of bringing out their moral characteristics one way or the other. Often, as in the case of very illiterate and unreflecting persons, it proves nothing either way; but in those who are not so, it is right or wrong, as their hearts are right or wrong; it is an exercise not of reason but of heart. Take for instance, the case of a servant in a family; she is baptized and educated in the Church of England, and is religiously disposed; she goes into Scotland and conforms to the Kirk, to which her master and mistress belong. She is of course responsible for what she does, but no one would say that she had formed any purpose, or taken any deliberate step. In course of time, when perhaps taxed with the change, she would say in her defence that outward forms matter not, and that there are good men in Scotland as well as in England; but this is an afterthought. Again, a careless person, nominally a churchman, falls among serious-minded dissenters, and they reclaim him from vice or irreligion; on this he joins their communion, and as time goes on boasts perhaps of his right of private judgment. At the time itself, however, no process of inquiry took place within him at all; his heart was "opened," whether for good or for bad, whether by good influences or by good and bad mixed. He was not conscious of convincing reasons, but he took what came to hand, he embraced what was offered, he felt and he acted. Again, a man is brought up among Unitarians, or in the frigid and worldly school which got a footing in the Church during last century, and has been accustomed to view religion as a matter of reason and form, of obligation, to the exclusion of affectionateness and devotion. He falls among persons of [347] what is called an Evangelical cast, and finds his heart interested, and great objects set before it. Such a man falls in with the sentiments he finds, rather than adopts them. He follows the leadings of his heart, perhaps of Divine grace, but certainly not any course of inquiry and proof. There is nothing of argument, discussion, or choice in the process of his conversion. He has no systems to choose between, and no grounds to scrutinize.

Now, in all such cases, the sort of private judgment exercised is right or wrong, not as private judgment, but according to its circumstances. It is either the attraction of a Divine Influence, such as the mind cannot master; or it is a suggestion of reason, which the mind has yet to analyze, before it can bring it to the test of logic. If it is the former, it is above a private judgment, popularly so called; if the latter, it is not yet so much as one.

A second class of conversions on private judgment consists of those which take place upon the sight or the strong testimony of miracles. Such was the instance of

Rahab,[27] of Naaman,[28] if he may be called a convert, and of
Nebuchadnezzar;[29] of the blind man in John ix.,[30] of St. Paul,
of Cornelius,[31] of Sergius Paulus,[32] and many others. Here
again the act of judgment is of a very peculiar character. It
is not exactly an unconscious act, but yet it is hardly an act
of judgment. Our belief in external sensible facts cannot
properly be called an act of private judgment; yet since
Protestants, we suppose, would say that the blind man or
Sergius Paulus were converted on private judgment, let it
even so be called, though it is of a very particular kind.
Again, conviction after a miracle also implies the latent
belief that such acts are signs of the Divine Presence, a
belief which may be as generally recognized and
maintained, and is as little a peculiar or private feeling as
the impression on the senses of the miracle itself. And this [348]
leads to the mention of a further instance of the sort of
private judgments to which men are invited in Scripture,
viz., the exercise of the moral sense. Our Creator has
stamped certain great truths upon our minds, and there they
remain in spite of the fall. St. Paul appeals to one of these at
Lystra, calling on the worshippers of idols to turn from
these vanities unto the Living God;[33] and at Athens, "not to
think that the Godhead is like unto gold, or silver, or stone
graven by art and man's device," but to worship "God who
made the world, and all things therein." [34] In the same tone
he reminds the Thessalonians of their having "turned to God

---

[27] *Rahab*: Cf. Joshua 2:2; 6:17
[28] *Naaman*: Cf. 2 Kings 5:1ff.
[29] *Nebuchadnezzar*: Cf. Daniel 3:28ff.
[30] *the blind man in John ix*: Cf. John 9:1-12
[31] *Cornelius*: Cf. Acts 10:17-46
[32] *Sergius Paulus*: a proconsul in Cyprus converted in Acts 13: 17
[33] *St Paul appeals to one of these at Lystra ...* : Cf. Acts 14:15
[34] *"not to think the Godhead is like unto gold ... "*: Acts 17:29

from idols to serve the Living and True God."[35] In like manner doubtless other great principles also of religion and morals are rooted in the mind so deeply, that their denial by any Religion would be a justification of our quitting or rejecting it. If a pagan found his ecclesiastical polity essentially founded on lying and cheating, or his ritual essentially impure, or his moral code essentially unjust or cruel, we conceive this would be a sufficient reason for his renouncing it for one which was free from these hateful characteristics. Such again is the kind of private judgment exercised, when maxims or principles, generally admitted by bodies of men, are acted upon by individuals who have been ever taught them, as a matter of course, without questioning them; for instance, if a member of the English Church, who had always been taught that preaching is the great ordinance of the Gospel, to the disparagement of the Sacraments, thereupon placed himself under the ministry of a powerful Wesleyan preacher; or if, from the common belief that nothing is essential but what is on the surface of Scripture, he forthwith attached himself to the Baptists, Independents, or Unitarians. Such men indeed often take their line in consequence of some inward liking for the religious system they adopt; but we are speaking of their proceeding as far as it professes to be an act of judgment.

[349]

A third class of private judgments recorded in Scripture, are those which are exercised at one and the same time by a great number; if it be not a contradiction to call such judgments private. Yet here again we suppose staunch Protestants would maintain that the three thousand at Pentecost, and the five thousand after the miracle on the

---

[35] *"turned to God from idols ... "*: 1 Thessalonians 1:9

lame man, and the "great company of the priests," which shortly followed,[36] did avail themselves, and do afford specimens, of the sacred right in question; therefore let it be ruled so. Such, then, is the case of national conversions to which we have already alluded. Again, if the Lutheran Church of Germany with its many theologians, or our neighbour the Kirk,—General Assembly, Men of Strathbogie, Dr. Chalmers, and all,[37]—came to a unanimous or quasi-unanimous resolve to submit to the Archbishop of Canterbury as their patriarch, this doubtless would be an exercise of private judgment perfectly defensible on Scripture precedents.

Now, before proceeding, let us observe, that as yet nothing has been found in Scripture to justify the cases of private judgment which are exemplified in the popular religious biographies of the day. These generally contain instances of conversions made on the judgment, definite, deliberate, independent, isolated, of the parties converted. The converts in these stories had not seen miracles, nor had they developed their own existing principles or beliefs, nor had they changed their religion in company with others, nor had they received new truths, they knew not how. Let us then turn to Scripture a second time, to see whether we can gain thence any clearer sanction of Private Judgment as now exercised among us, than our search into Scripture has hitherto furnished.

[350]

---

[36] *the three thousand at Pentecost ...* : Cf. Acts 2:1-41; 3:1-4:4; 6:7

[37] *General Assembly, Men of Strathbogie, Dr. Chalmers, and all*: The General Assembly suspended seven men from Strathbogie for proceeding with an induction in Marnoch without permission in 1841. Dr Thomas Chalmers (1780-1847) led the Disruption in 1843 which was the founding of the Free Church. Cf. *The Strathbogie Case,* Simon MacGregor 1841.

3.

There certainly is another method of conversion upon private judgment described in Scripture, which is much more to our purpose, viz., by means of the study of Scripture itself. Thus our Lord says to the Jews, "Search the Scriptures;"[38] and the treasurer of Candace was reading the book of Isaiah when St. Philip met him,[39] and the men of Berea are said to be "more noble than those of Thessalonica, in that they received the word with all readiness of mind, and searched the Scriptures daily, whether those things were so." And it is added, "therefore many of them believed."[40] Here at length, it will be said, is a precedent for such acts of private judgment as are most frequently recommended and instanced in religious tales; and indeed these texts commonly are understood to make it certain beyond dispute, that individuals ordinarily may find out the doctrines of the Gospel for themselves from the private study of Scripture. A little consideration, however, will convince us that even these are precedents for something else; that they sanction, not an inquiry about Gospel doctrine, but about the Gospel teacher; not what has God revealed, but whom has He commissioned? And this is a very different thing.

The context of the passage in which our Lord speaks of searching the Scriptures, shows plainly that their office is that of leading, not to a knowledge of the Gospel, but of Himself, its Author and Teacher. "Whom He hath sent," He says, "Him ye believe not. Search the Scriptures, for in them ye think ye have eternal life, and they are they which

---

[38] *"Search the Scriptures"*: John 5:39
[39] *the treasurer of Candace was reading* ... : Acts 8:27-39
[40] *"more noble than those of Thessalonica* ... *"*: Acts 17:11-12

testify of Me."[41] He adds, that they "will not come unto Him, [351] that they may have life,"[42] and that "He is come in His Father's name, and they receive Him not."[43] And again, "Had ye believed Moses, ye would have believed Me, for he *wrote of Me*."[44] It is plain that in this passage our Lord does not send His hearers to the Old Testament to gain thence the knowledge of the doctrines of the Gospel by means of their private judgment, but to gain tests or notes by which to find out and receive Him who was the teacher of those doctrines; and, though the treasurer of Candace appears in the narrative to be contemplating our Lord in prophecy, not as the teacher but the object of the Christian faith, yet still in confessing that he could not "understand" what he was reading, "unless some man should guide him," he lays down the principle broadly, which we desire here to maintain, that the private study of Scripture is not intended ordinarily as the means of gaining a knowledge of the Gospel. In like manner St. Peter, on the day of Pentecost, refers to the book of Joel, by way of proving thence, not the Christian doctrine, but the divine promise that new teachers were to be sent in due season, and the fact that it was fulfilled in himself and his brethren. "This is that," he says, "which was spoken by the prophet Joel, I will pour out My Spirit upon all flesh, and *your sons and your daughters shall prophesy*."[45]

While, then, the conversions recorded in Scripture are brought about in a very marked way through a teacher, and *not* by means of private judgment, so again, if an appeal *is*

---

[41] *"Him ye believe not. ... "*: John 5:39

[42] *"will not come unto Him, ... "*: Cf. John 5:40

[43] *"He is come in His Father's name, ... "*: Cf. John 5:43

[44] *"Had ye believed Moses, ... "*: John 5:46.

[45] *"This is that," he says, "which was spoken by the prophet Joel... "*: Acts 2:16

made to private judgment, this is done in order to settle who the teacher is, and what are his notes or tokens, rather than to substantiate this or that religious opinion or practice. And if such instances bear upon our conduct at this day, as it is [352] natural to think they do, then of course the practical question before us is, *who* is the teacher now, from whose mouth we are to seek the law, and *what are his notes*?

Now, in remarkable coincidence with this view, we find in both Testaments that teachers are promised under the dispensation of the Gospel, so that they, who like the noble Bereans, search the Scriptures daily, will be at little loss *whither* their private judgment should lead them in order to gain the knowledge of the truth. In the book of Isaiah we have the following express promises: "Though the Lord give you the bread of adversity, and the waters of affliction, yet shall not thy teachers be removed into a corner any more, but *thine eyes shall see thy teachers*, and thine ears *shall hear a voice behind thee*, saying, This is the way," etc. Several tests follow descriptive of the condition of things or the circumstances in which these teachers are to be found. First, the absence of idolatry: "Ye shall defile also the covering of thy graven images of silver, and the ornaments of thy molten images of gold;" and next, the multitude of fellow-believers: "Then shall He give the *rain of thy seed*, that thou shalt sow the ground withal; in that day shall thy cattle feed *in large pastures*."[46] Elsewhere the appointed teacher is noted as speaking with authority and judicially: as "Every tongue that shall rise against thee in judgment thou shalt condemn."[47] And here again the promises or tests of extent and perpetuity appear: "Thou shalt break forth on the

---

[46] *"Though the Lord give you bread of adversity, ... "*: Isaiah 30:20-23
[47] *"Every tongue that shall rise against thee ... "*: Isaiah 54:17

418

right hand and on the left, and thy seed shall inherit the Gentiles;"[48] and "My kindness shall not depart from them, neither shall the covenant of My peace be removed."[49] Elsewhere holiness is mentioned: "It shall be called, The way of holiness, the unclean shall not pass over it."[50] One more promise shall be cited: "My Spirit that is upon thee, and My words which I have put in thy mouth, shall not depart out of thy mouth, nor out of the mouth of thy seed ... from henceforth and for ever."[51] [353]

In the New Testament we have the same promises stated far more concisely indeed, but, what is much more apposite than a longer description, with the addition of the *name* of our promised teacher: "The *Church* of the living God," says St. Paul, "*the pillar and ground of the truth*."[52] The simple question then for Private Judgment to exercise itself upon is, what and where is the Church?

Now let it be observed how exactly this view of the province of Private Judgment, where it is allowable, as being the discovery not of doctrine, but of the teacher of doctrine, harmonizes both with the nature of Religion and the state of human society as we find it. Religion is for practice, and that immediate. Now it is much easier to form a correct and rapid judgment of persons than of books or of doctrines. Every one, even a child, has an impression about new faces; few persons have any real view about new propositions. There is something in the sight of persons or of bodies of men, which speaks to us for approval or disapprobation with a distinctness to which pen and ink are

---

[48] *"Thou shalt break forth on the right hand ... "*: Isaiah 54:3

[49] *"My kindness shall not depart from them ... "*: Isaiah 54:10

[50] *"It shall be called, The way of holiness ... "*: Isaiah 35:8

[51] *"My Spirit that is upon thee ... "*: Isaiah 59:21

[52] *"The Church of the living God," says St. Paul, ... *: 1 Timothy 3:15

unequal. This is just the kind of evidence which is needed for use, in cases in which private judgment is divinely intended to be the means of our conversion. The multitude have neither the time, the patience, nor the clearness and exactness of thought, for processes of investigation and deduction. Reason is slow and abstract, cold and speculative; but man is a being of feeling and action; he is not resolvable into a *dictum de omni et nullo*,[53] or a series of hypotheticals, or a critical diatribe, or an algebraical [354] equation. And this obvious fact does, as far as it goes, make it probable that, if we are providentially obliged to exercise our private judgment, the point towards which we have to direct it, is the teacher rather than the doctrine.

In corroboration, it may be observed, that Scripture seems always to imply the presence of teachers as the appointed ordinance by which men learn the truth; and is principally engaged in giving cautions against false teachers, and tests for ascertaining the true. Thus our Lord bids us "beware of false prophets,"[54] not of false books; and look to their fruits. And He says elsewhere that "the sheep know His voice," and that "they know not the voice of strangers."[55] And He predicts false Christs and false prophets, who are to be nearly successful against even the elect. He does not give us tests of false doctrines, but of certain visible peculiarities or notes applicable to persons or parties. "If they shall say, Behold, he is in the desert, go not forth; behold, he is in the secret chamber, believe it not."[56]

---

[53] dictum de omni et nullo: the maxim of all and none (a concept in Aristotelian logic)
[54] *"beware of false prophets"*: Matthew 7:15
[55] *"the sheep know His voice", and that "they know not the voice of strangers"*: John 10:4-5
[56] *"If they shall say, Behold, he is in the desert ... "*: Matthew 24:26

St. Paul insists on tokens of a similar kind: "Mark them which cause divisions, and avoid them;"[57] "is Christ divided?"[58] "beware of dogs, beware of evil-workers;"[59] "be followers together of me, and mark them which walk so, as ye have us for an ensample."[60] Thus the New Testament equally with the Old, as far as it speaks of private examination into teaching professedly from heaven, makes the teacher the subject of that inquiry, and not the thing taught; it bids us ask for his credentials, and avoid him if he is unholy, or idolatrous, or schismatical, or if he comes in his own name, or if he claims no authority, or is the growth of a particular spot or of particular circumstances.

If there are passages which at first sight seem to interfere with this statement, they admit of an easy explanation. [355] Either they will be found to appeal to those instinctive feelings of our nature already spoken of which supersede argument and proof in the judgments we form of persons or bodies; as in St. Paul's reference to the idolatry of Athenian worship, or to the extreme moral corruption of heathenism generally. Or, again, the criterion of doctrine which they propose to the private judgment of the individual turns upon the question of its novelty or previous reception. When St. Paul would describe a false gospel, he calls it *another* gospel "than that ye have received;"[61] and St. John bids us "try the spirits,"[62] gives us as the test of truth and error the "confessing that Jesus Christ is come in the flesh,"[63] and

---

[57] *"Mark them which cause divisions, and avoid them"*: Romans 16:17

[58] *"is Christ divided?"*: 1 Corinthians 1:13

[59] *"beware of dogs, beware of evil-workers"*: Philippians 3:2

[60] *"be followers together of me, ..."*: Philippians 3:17

[61] *"than that ye have received"*: Galatians 1:9

[62] *"try the spirits"*: 1 John 4:1-2

[63] *"confessing that Jesus Christ is come in the flesh,"*: 1 John 4:2

warns us against receiving into our houses any one who "brings not this doctrine."[64] We conceive then that on the whole the notion of gaining religious truth for ourselves by our private examination, whether by reading or thinking, whether by studying Scripture or other books, has no broad sanction in Scripture, is neither impressed upon us by its general tone, nor enjoined in any of its commands. The great question which it puts before us for the exercise of private judgment is,—Who is God's prophet, and where? Who is to be considered the voice of the Holy Catholic and Apostolic Church?

4.

Having carried our train of thought as far as this, it is time for us to proceed to the thesis in which it will be found to issue, viz., that, on the principles that have been laid down, Dissenters ought to abandon their own communion, but that members of the English Church ought not to abandon theirs. Such a position has often been treated as a paradox and inconsistency; yet we hope to be able to recommend it favourably to the reader.

[356]

Now that seceders, sectarians, independent thinkers, and the like, by whatever name they call themselves, whether "Wesleyans," "Dissenters," "professors of the national religion," "well-wishers of the Church," or even "Churchmen," are in grievous error, in their mode of exercising their private judgment, is plain as soon as stated, viz., because they do not use it in looking out for a teacher at all. They who think they have, in consequence of their inquiries, found the teacher of truth, may be wrong in the result they have arrived at; but those who despise the notion

---

[64] *"brings not this doctrine"*: 2 John 1:10

of a teacher altogether, are already wrong before they begin them. They do not start with their private judgment in that one special direction which Scripture allows or requires. Scripture speaks of a certain pillar or ground of truth,[65] as set up to the world, and describes it by certain characteristics; dissenting teachers and bodies, so far from professing to be themselves this authority, or to contain among them this authority, assert there is no such authority to be found anywhere. When then we deny that they are the Church in our meaning of the word, they ought to take no offence at it, for we are not denying them anything to which they lay claim; we are but denying them what they already put away from themselves as much as we can. They must not act like the dog in the fable, (if it be not too light a comparison,) who would neither use the manger himself, nor relinquish it to others:[66] let them not grudge to others a manifest scriptural privilege which they disown themselves. Is an ordinance of Scripture to be fulfilled nowhere, because it is not fulfilled in them? By the Church we mean what Scripture means, "the pillar and ground of the truth;" a [357] power out of whose mouth the Word and the Spirit are never to fail, and whom whoso refuses to hear becomes thereupon to all his brethren a heathen man and a publican. Let the parties in question accept the Scripture definition, or else not assume the Scripture name; or, rather, let them seek elsewhere what they are conscious is not among themselves. We hear much of Bible Christians, Bible Religion, Bible preaching; it would be well if we heard a little of the Bible Church also; we venture to say, that Dissenting Churches

---

[65] *pillar or ground of truth*: Cf. 1 Timothy 3:15
[66] *the dog in the fable* ... : The fable is found in ancient Greek literature; since the 15th century it has been included among Aesop's fables.

would vanish thereupon at once, for, since it is their fundamental principle that they are not a pillar or ground of truth, but voluntary societies, without authority and without gifts, the Bible Church they cannot be. If the serious persons who are in dissent would really imitate the simple-minded Ethiopian, or the noble Bereans, let them ask themselves, "Of whom speaketh" the Apostle, or the Prophet, such great things?—Where is the "pillar and ground"?—Who is it that is appointed to lead us to Christ?—Where are those teachers which were never to be removed into a corner any more, but which were ever to be before our eyes and in our ears? Whoever is right, or whoever is wrong, they cannot be right, who profess not to have found, not to look out for, not to believe in, that Ordinance to which Apostles and prophets give their testimony. So much then for the Protestant side of the thesis.

One half of it then is easily disposed of; but now we come to the other side of it, the Roman, which certainly has its intricacies. It is not difficult to know how we should act towards a religious body which does not even profess to come to us in the name of the Lord, or to be a pillar and ground of the truth; but what shall we say when more than [358] one society, or school, or party, lay claim to be the heaven-sent teacher, and are rivals one to the other, as are the Churches of England and Rome at this day? How shall we discriminate between them? Which are we to follow? Are tests given us for that purpose? Now if tests are given us, we must use them; but if not, and so far as not, we must conclude that Providence foresaw that the difference between them would never be so great as to require of us to leave the one for the other.

However, it is certain that much is said in Scripture about rival teachers, and that at least some of these rivals are so opposed to each other, that tests are given us, in order to our shunning the one party, and accepting the other. In such cases, the one teacher is represented to be the minister of God, and the other the child and organ of evil. The one comes in God's name, the other professes to come simply in his own name. Such a contrast is presented to us in the conflict between Moses and the magicians of Egypt;[67] all is light on the one side, all darkness on the other. Or again, in the trial between Elijah and the prophets of Baal.[68] There is no doubt, in such a case, that it would be our imperative duty at once to leave the teaching of Satan, and betake ourselves to the Law and the Prophets. And it will be observed that, to assist inquirers in doing so the representatives of Almighty God have been enabled, in their contest with the enemy, to work miracles, as Moses was, for instance, and Elijah, in order to make it clear which way the true teaching lay.

But now will any one say that the contrast between the English and the Roman, or again, the Greek, Churches, is of this nature?—is any of the three a "*monstrum nullâ virtute redemptum*"?[69] Moreover, the magicians and the priests of Baal "came in their own name;"[70] is that the case with the [359] Church, English, Roman or Greek? Is it not certain, even at first sight, that each of these branches has many high gifts and much grace in her communion? And, at any rate, as regards our controversy with Rome, if her champions would

---

[67] *the conflict between Moses and the magicians of Egypt*: Cf. Exodus 7-8

[68] *the trial between Elijah and the prophets of Baal*: Cf. 1 Kings 18:20-40

[69] *monstrum nulla virtute redemptum*: monster with no redeeming feature

[70] *"came in their own name"*: Cf. John 5: 43

maintain that the Church of England is the false prophet, and she the true one, then let her work miracles, as Moses did in the presence of the magicians, in order to our conviction.

Probably, however, it will be admitted that the contrast between England and Rome is not of that nature; for the English Church confessedly does not come in her own name, nor can she reasonably be compared to the Egyptian magicians or the prophets of Baal; is there any other type in Scripture into which the difference between her and the Church of Rome can be resolved? We shall be referred, perhaps, to the case of the false prophets of Israel and Judah, who professed to come in the name of the Lord, yet did not preach the truth, and had no part or inheritance with God's prophets. This parallel is not happier than the former, for a test was given to distinguish between them, which does not decide between the Church of Rome and ourselves. This test is the divine accomplishment of the prophet's message, or the divine blessing upon his teaching, or the eventual success of his work, as it may be variously stated; a test under which neither Church, Roman or Anglican, will fail, and neither is eminently the foremost. Each Church has had to endure trial, each has overcome it; each has triumphed over enemies, each has had continued signs of the divine favour upon it. The passages in Scripture to which we refer are such as the following.—Moses, for instance, has laid it down in the Book of Deuteronomy, that, [360] "when a prophet speaketh in the name of the Lord, if the thing follow not, nor come to pass, that is the thing which the Lord hath *not* spoken, but the prophet hath spoken it presumptuously."[71] To the same effect, in the Book of Ezekiel, the denunciation against the false prophet is, "Lo! *when the wall is fallen*, shall it not be said unto you, *where* is the daubing wherewith ye have daubed it?"[72] And Gamaliel's advice to "refrain from these men, and let them alone, for if this counsel or this work be of men, it will come to nought,"[73] may be taken as an illustration of the same rule of judgment. Hence Roman Catholics themselves are accustomed to consider, that eventual failure is the sure destiny of heresy and schism; what then will they say to us? the English Church has remained in its present state three hundred years, and at the end of the time is stronger than at the beginning. This does not look like an heretical or schismatical Church. However, when she does fall to pieces, then, it may be admitted, her children *will* have a reason for deserting her; till then, she has no symptom of being akin to the false prophets who professed the Lord's name, and deceived the simple and unlearned; she has no symptom of being a traitor to the *faith*.

However, there is a third type of rival teaching mentioned in Scripture, under which the dissension between Rome and England may be considered to fall, and which it may be well to notice.[74] Let it be observed, then, that even in the Apostles' age very grave outward differences seem to have existed between Christian teachers, that is, the organs of the one Church, and yet those differences were not, in

---

[71] *"when a prophet speaketh in the name of the Lord, ... "*: Deuteronomy 18:22

[72] *"Lo!* when the wall is fallen, ... "*: Ezechiel 13:12

[73] *"refrain from these men, and let them alone ... "*: Acts 5:38

[74] In the original essay, the Anglican Newman adds here: 'though whether its application to present circumstances will serve those who, with the characters real and fictitious in our heading, leave the Anglican for the rival communion, in justification of their procedure, is not so clear.' See the Textual Appendix.

consequence, any call upon inquirers and beholders to quit one teacher and betake themselves to another. The state of the Corinthian Christians will exemplify what we mean:

Paul, Cephas, and Apollos,[75] were all friends together, yet parties were formed round each separately, which disagreed with each other, and made the Apostles themselves seem in disagreement. Is not this, at least in great measure, the state of the Churches of England and Rome? Are they not one in faith, so far forth as they are viewed in their essential apostolical character? are they not in discord, so far as their respective children and disciples have overlaid them with errors of their own individual minds? It was a great fault, doubtless, that the followers of St. Paul should have divided from the followers of St. Peter, but would it have mended matters, had any individuals among them gone over to St. Peter? was that the fitting remedy for the evil? Was not the remedy that of their putting aside partisanship altogether, and regarding St. Paul "not after the flesh,"[76] but simply as "the minister by whom they believed,"[77] the visible representative of the undivided Christ, the one Catholic Church? And, in like manner, surely if party feelings and interests have separated us from the members of the Roman communion, this does not prove that our Church itself is divided from theirs, any more than that St. Paul was divided from St. Peter, nor is it our duty to leave our place and join them;—nothing would be gained by so unnecessary a step;—but our duty is, remaining where we are, to recognize in our own Church, not an establishment, not a party, not a mere Protestant denomination, but the Holy

---

[75] *Paul, Cephas, and Apollo*: Cf. 1 Cor 1:12

[76] *"not after the flesh"*: Romans 8:1

[77] *"the minister by whom they believed"*: 1 Corinthians 4:15

Church Catholic which the traditions of men have partially obscured,—to rid it of these traditions, to try to soften bitterness and animosity of feeling, and to repress party spirit and promote peace as much as in us lies. Moreover, let it be observed, that St. Paul was evidently superior in gifts to Apollos, yet this did not justify Christians attaching themselves to the former rather than the latter; for, as the Apostle says, they both were but ministers of one and the same Lord,[78] and nothing more. Comparison, then, is not allowed us between teacher and teacher, where each has on the whole the notes of a divine mission; so that even could the Church of Rome be proved superior to our own (which we put merely as a hypothesis, and for argument's sake), this would as little warrant our attaching ourselves to it instead of our own Church, as there was warrant for one of the converts of Apollos to call himself by the name of Paul. Further, let it be observed, that the Apostle reproves those who attached themselves to St. Peter equally with the Paulines or with the disciples of Apollos; is it possible he could have done so, were St. Peter the head and essence of the Church in a sense in which St. Paul was not? And, again, there was an occasion when not only their followers were at variance, but the Apostles themselves; we refer to the dissimulation of St. Peter at Antioch, and the resistance of St. Paul to it: was this a reason why St. Peter's disciples should go over to St. Paul, or rather why they should correct their dissimulation?[79]

[362]

We are surely bound to prosecute this search after the promised Teacher of truth entirely as a practical matter, with reference to our duty and nothing else. The simple

---

[78] *ministers of one and the same Lord*: Cf. 1 Corinthians 3:5

[79] [In answer to this whole argument, *vid. supr.*, p.103 and vol. I p.185.] [N]

question which we have to ask ourselves is, Has the English Church *sufficiently* upon her the signs of an Apostle? is she the divinely-appointed teacher to *us*? If so, we need not go further; we have no reason to break through the divine rule of "being content with such things as we have;"[80] we have no warrant to compare our own prophet with the prophet given to others. Nor can we: tests are not given us for the purpose. We may believe that our own Church has certain imperfections; the Church of Rome certain corruptions: such a belief has no tendency to lead us to any determinate judgment as to which of the two on the whole is the better, or to induce or warrant us to leave the one communion for the other.

[363]

5.

One point remains, however, which is so often felt as a difficulty by members of our Church that we are tempted to say a few words upon it in conclusion, and to try to show what is the true practical mode of meeting it. And this perhaps will give us an opportunity of expressing our general meaning in a more definite and intelligible form.

It cannot be denied, then, that a very plausible ground of attack may be taken up against the Church of England, from the circumstance that she is separated from the rest of Christendom; and just such a ground as it would be allowable for private judgment to rest and act upon, supposing its office to be what we have described it to be. "As to the particular doctrines of Anglicanism, (it may be urged,) Scripture may, if so be, supply private judgment with little grounds for quarrelling with them; but what can be said to explain away the Note of forfeiture, which

---

[80] *"being content with such things as we have"*: Cf. Hebrews 13:5

attaches to us in consequence of our isolated state? We are, in fact (it may be objected) cut off from the whole of the Christian world; nay, far from denying that excommunication, in a certain sense we glory in it, and that under a notion, that we are so very pure that it must soil our fingers to touch any other Church whatever upon the earth, in north, east, or south. How is this reconcilable with St. Paul's clear announcement that there is but one body as well [364] as one spirit? or with our Lord's, that 'by this shall *all men know*,' as by a Note obvious to the intelligence even of the illiterate and unreasoning, 'that ye are My disciples, if ye have love one to another'?[81] or again, with His prayer that His disciples might all be one, 'that the world may know that *Thou hast sent Me*, and hast *loved them* as Thou hast loved Me'?[82] Visible unity, then, would seem to be both the main evidence for Christianity, and the sign of our own participation in its benefits; whereas we English despise the Greeks and hate the Romans, turn our backs on the Scotch Episcopalians, and do but smile distantly upon our American cousins. We throw ourselves into the arms of the State, and in that close embrace forget that the Church was meant to be Catholic; or we call ourselves *the* Catholics, and the mere Church of England *our* Catholic Church; as if, forsooth, by thus confining it all to ourselves, we did not *ipso facto* forfeit all claim to be considered Catholic at all."

What increases the force of this argument is, that St. Augustine seems, at least at first sight, virtually to urge it against us in his controversy with the Donatists,[83] whom he

---

[81] *"by this shall all men know ... if ye have love one to another"*: John 13:35

[82] *"that the world may know that Thou hast sent Me, and hast loved them as Thou hast loved Me"*: John 17:23

[83] *Donatists*: See note on p.[34].

represents as condemned, simply because separate from the "orbis terrarum," and styles the point in question "quæstio facillima," and calls on individual Donatists to decide it by their private judgment.[84]

[365]   Now this is an objection which we must honestly say is deeply felt by many people, and not inconsiderable ones; and the more it is openly avowed to be a difficulty the better; for then there is the chance of its being acknowledged, and in the course of time obviated, as far as may be, by those who have the power. Flagrant evils cure themselves by being flagrant; and we are sanguine that the time is come when so great an evil, as this is, cannot stand its ground against the good feeling and common sense of religious persons. It is the very strength of Romanism against us; and, unless the proper persons take it into their very serious consideration, they may look for certain to undergo the loss, as time goes on, of some whom they would least like to be lost to our Church. If private judgment can be exercised on any point, it is on a matter of

---

[84] Ego cùm audio quenquam bono ingenio præditum, doctrinisque liberalibus eruditum, quamquam non ibi salus animæ constituta sit, tamen in quæstione facillimâ sentire aliud quàm veritas postulat, quo magis miror, eò magis exardesco nosse hominem et cum eo colloqui; vel si id non possim, saltem litteris quæ longissimè volant [to the nineteenth century?] attingere mentem ejus atque ab eo vicissim attingi desidero. Sicut te esse audio talem virum, et ab Ecclesiâ Catholicâ, quæ sicut Sancto Spiritu pronunciata est, toto orbe diffunditur, discerptum doleo atque seclusum.—Ep. 87, vid. cp. 61. [N] 'I know that it is not on the possession of good talents and a liberal education that the salvation of the soul depends; but when I hear of any one who is thus endowed holding a different view from that which truth imperatively insists upon on a point which admits of very easy examination, the more I wonder at such a man, the more I burn with desire to make his acquaintance, and to converse with him; or if that be impossible, I long to bring his mind and mine into contact by exchanging letters, which wing their flight even between places far apart. As I have heard that you are such a man as I have spoken of, I grieve that you should be severed and shut out from the Catholic Church, which is spread abroad throughout the whole world, as was foretold by the Holy Spirit.'

the senses; now our eyes and our ears are filled with the abuse poured out by members of our Church on her sister Churches in foreign lands. It is not that their corrupt practices are gravely and tenderly pointed out, as may be done by men who feel themselves also to be sinful and ignorant, and know that they have their own great imperfections, which their brethren abroad have not,—but we are apt not to acknowledge them as brethren at all; we treat them in an arrogant John Bull[85] way, as mere Frenchmen, or Spaniards, or Austrians, not as Christians. We act as if we could do without brethren; as if our having brethren all over the world were not the very tenure on which we are Christians at all; as if we did not cease to be Christians, if at any time we ceased to have brethren. Or again, when our thoughts turn to the East, instead of recollecting that there are sister Churches there, we leave it to the Russians to take care of the Greeks, and to the French [366] to take care of the Romans, and we content ourselves with erecting a Protestant Church at Jerusalem,[86] or with helping the Jews to rebuild their temple there, or with becoming the august protectors of Nestorians, Monophysites, and all the heretics we can hear of, or with forming a league with the Mussulman against Greeks and Romans together. Can any one doubt that the British power is not considered a Church power by any country whatever into which it comes? and if so, is it possible that the English Church, which is so closely connected with that power, can be said in any true sense to exert a Catholic influence, or to deserve the Catholic name?

---

[85] *John Bull*: the figure of a typical Briton, with an attitude of truculent patriotism
[86] *erecting a Protestant Church at Jerusalem*: There was a project of the British and Prussian governments in 1841 to set up a Protestant bishop in Jerusalem who would alternately be an Anglican and a Lutheran; see the Editor's Introduction, p.xliv.

How can any Church be called Catholic, which does not act beyond its own territory? and when did the rulers of the English Church ever move one step beyond the precincts, or without the leave, of the imperial power?

> "pudet hæc opprobia nobis
> Et dici potuisse, et non potuisse refelli."[87]

There is indeed no denying them; and if certain persons are annoyed at the confession, as if we were thereby putting weapons into our enemies' hands, let them be annoyed more by the fact, and let them alter the fact, and, they may take our word for it, the confession will cease of itself. The world does not feel the fact the less for its not being confessed; it *is* felt deeply by many, and is doing incalculable mischief to our cause, and is likely to hurt it more and more. In a word, this isolation is doing as much as any one thing can do to unchurch us, and it and our awakened claims to be Catholic and Apostolic cannot long stand together. This then is the main difficulty which serious people feel in accepting the English Church as the promised prophet of truth, and we are far indeed from undervaluing it, as the above remarks show.]

[367]   But now taking the objection in a simply practical view, which is the only view in which it ought to concern or perplex any one, we consider that it can have legitimately no effect whatever in leading us from England to Rome. We do not say no legitimate tendency in itself to move us, but no legitimate influence with serious men, who wish to know how their duty lies. For this reason—because if the note of schism on the one hand lies against England, an antagonist

---

[87] *"pudet haec opprobia nobis / Et dici potuisse, et non potuisse refelli."*: 'I am not ashamed that these reproaches can be cast upon us, and that they cannot be repelled.' (Ovid *Metamorphoses* 1, 758).

disgrace lies upon Rome, the Note of idolatry. Let us not be mistaken here: we are neither accusing Rome of being idolatrous nor ourselves of being schismatical, we think neither charge tenable; but still the Roman Church practises what looks so very like idolatry, and the English glories in what looks so very like schism, that, without deciding what is the duty of a Roman Catholic towards the Church of England in her present state, we do seriously think that members of the English Church have a providential direction given them, how to comport themselves towards the Church of Rome, while she is what she is. We are discussing the subject, not of decisive proofs, but of probable indications and of presumptive notes of the divine will. Few men have time to scrutinize accurately; all men may have general impressions, and the general impressions of conscientious men are true ones. Providence has graciously met their need, and provided for them those very means of knowledge which they can use and turn to account. He has cast around the institutions and powers existing in the world marks of truth or falsehood, or, more properly, elements of attraction and repulsion, and notices for pursuit and avoidance, sufficient to determine the course of those who in the conduct of life desire to approve themselves to Him. Now, whether or no what we see in the Church of Rome be sufficient to warrant a religious person   [368] to leave her (a question, we repeat, about which we have no need here to concern ourselves), we certainly think it sufficient to deter him from joining her; and, whatever be the perplexity and distress of his position in a communion so isolated as the English, we do not think he would mend the matter by placing himself in a communion so superstitious as the Roman; especially considering, agreeably to a remark we have already made, that even if he be schismatical at present, he is so by the act of Providence, whereas he would be entering into superstition by his own. Thus an Anglo-Catholic is kept at a distance from Rome, if not by our own excellences, at least by her errors.

That this is the state of the Church of Rome, is, alas! not fairly disputable. Dr. Wiseman[88] has lately attempted to dispute it; but if we may judge from the present state of the controversy, facts are too clear for him. It has lately been broadly put forward, as all know, that, whatever may be said in defence of the *authoritative documents* of the faith of Rome, this imputation lies against her *authorities*, that they have countenanced and established doctrines and practices from which a Christian mind, not educated in them, shrinks; and that in the number of these a worship of the creature which to most men will seem to be a quasi-idolatry is not the least prominent.[89] Dr. Wiseman, for whom we entertain most respectful feelings personally, and to whom we impute nothing but what is straightforward and candid, has written two pamphlets[90] on the subject, towards which we should be very sorry to deal unfairly; but he certainly seems to us in [369] the former of them to deny the fact of these alleged additions in the formal profession of his Church, and then, in the second, to turn right round and maintain them. What account is to be given of self-contradiction such as this, but the fact, that he would deny the additions, if he could, and

---

[88] *Dr. Wiseman*: Nicholas Wiseman (1802-65), at this date Vicar Apostolic of the Central District and President of Oscott College. Newman had met him in Rome during his trip to Italy in 1833.

[89] [This is an exaggeration; I have reconsidered the whole subject in my essay on "Development of Doctrine" in 1845; and in my letter to Dr. Pusey in 1866.] [N]

[90] *two pamphlets*: The first was *A Letter respectfully addressed to the Rec. J. H. Newman, upon some Passages in his Letter to the Rev. Dr. Jelf* (London, 1841). The second was *Remarks on a Letter from the Rev. W. Palmer* (London, 1841).

defends them, because he can't? And that dilemma is no common one; for, as if to show that what he holds in excess of our creed is in excess also of primitive usage, he has in his defence been forced upon citations from the writings of the Fathers, the chief of which, as Mr. Palmer[91] has shown, are spurious; thus setting before us vividly what he looks for in Antiquity, but what he cannot find there. However, it is not our intention to enter into a controversy which is in Mr. Palmer's hands; nor need we do more than refer the reader to the various melancholy evidences, which that learned, though over-severe writer, and Dr. Pusey,[92] and Mr. Ward[93] adduce, in proof of the existence of this Note of dishonour in a sister or mother, towards whom we feel so tenderly and reverently, and whom nothing but some such urgent reason in conscience could make us withstand so resolutely.

So much has been said on this point lately, as to increase our unwillingness to insist upon a subject in itself very ungrateful; but a reference to it is unavoidable, if we would adequately show what is the legitimate use and duty of private judgment, in dealing with those notes of truth and

---

[91] *Mr. Palmer*: William Palmer (1803-88). See *Essays Critical and Historical* Vol.I (Gracewing, 2019), Editor's Introduction pp.xxxii ff, 180 ff. Newman is referring here to his *A Letter to N. Wiseman, D.D. (calling himself Bishop of Melipotamus): containing remarks on his letter to Mr. Newman* (Oxford, 1841).

[92] *Dr. Pusey*: Edward Bouverie Pusey (1800-82), Anglican divine and fellow member of the Oxford Movement, whose members were often termed Puseyites. Newman is referring to his *The Articles treated on in Tract 90 reconsidered and their Interpretation vindicated, in a Letter to the Rev. R. W. Jelf, D.D., Canon of Christ Church* (Oxford, 1841).

[93] *Mr. Ward*: William George Ward (1812-82), Anglican divine and fellow member of the Oxford Movement. In 1845 he became a Catholic and taught for many years at the seminary of St Edmund's, Ware, despite being a layman. Newman is referring to his *A few more Words in Support of No. 90 of the Tracts for the Times* (Oxford, 1841).

error, by which Providence recommends to us or disowns the prophets that come in His name.[94]

What imparts an especial keenness to the grief which the teaching in question causes in minds kindly disposed towards the Church of Rome, is, that not only are we expressly told in Scripture that the Almighty will not give His glory to another, but it is predicted as His especial grace upon the Christian Church, "the idols He shall utterly abolish;"[95] so that, if Anglicans are almost unchurched by the Protestantism which has mixed itself up with their ecclesiastical proceedings, Romanists also are almost unchurched by their superstitions. Again and again in the Prophets is this promise given, "From all your filthiness and from all your idols will I cleanse you;"[96] "Neither shall they defile themselves any more with their idols;"[97] "Ephraim shall say, What have I to do any more with idols?"[98] "I will cut off the names of the idols out of the land."[99] And the warning in the New is as strong as the promise in the Old: "Little children, keep yourselves from idols;"[100] "Let no man beguile you of your reward in a voluntary humility and worshipping of Angels;"[101] and the Angel's answer, to

[370]

---

[94] *So much has been said ... :* In his original 1841 article Newman went on at this point to quote at length from Ward's, Palmer's and Pusey's criticisms of Catholic devotional writings and practices, particularly about the Blessed Virgin Mary; see the Textual Appendix. It is not surprising that Newman decided to omit all this in his revised 1871 text of this Essay since by now he had dealt exhaustively with the subject in his *A Letter addressed to Rev. E. B. Pusey, D.D., on occasion of his Eirenicon of 1864* (London, 1866).
[95] *"the idols He shall utterly abolish":* Isaiah 2:18
[96] *"from all your filthiness ... ":* Ezechiel 36:25
[97] *"neither shall they defile themselves ... ":* Ezechiel 37:23
[98] *"Ephraim shall say ... ":* Hosea 14:18
[99] *"I will cut off the names ... ":* Zechariah 13:12
[100] *"Little children, keep yourselves from idols":* 1 John 5:21
[101] *"Let no man beguile you ... ":* Colossians 2:18

whom St. John fell down in worship, was "See thou do it not, *for* I am thy fellow-servant; worship God."[102] [103]

It is then a Note of the Christian Church, as decisive as any, that she is not idolatrous; and any semblance of idolatrous worship in the Church of Rome as plainly dissuades a man of Catholic feelings from her communion, as the taint of a Protestant or schismatical spirit in our communion may tempt him to depart from us. This is the Via Media which we would maintain; and thus without judging Rome on the one hand, or acquiescing in our own state on the other, we may use what we see, as a providential intimation to *us*, not to quit what is bad for what may be worse, but to learn resignation to what we inherit, nor seek to escape into a happier state by suicide.

6.

And in such a state of things, certain though it be that St. Austin invites individual Donatists to the Church, on the simple ground that the larger body must be the true one, he is not, he cannot be, a guide of *our* conduct here.[104] The Fathers are our teachers, but not our confessors or casuists; they are the prophets of great truths, not the spiritual directors of individuals. How can they possibly be such, considering the subject-matter of conduct? Who shall say that a point of practice which is right in one man, is right

[371]

---

[102] *"See thou do it not, ... "*: Revelation 22:9

[103] This passage proves, on the one hand, that such worship as St. John offered is wrong; on the other, that it does not unchurch, unless we can fancy St. John guilty of mortal sin. [N]

[104] *St. Austin ... the larger body must be the true one*: In an article on Donatism in the *Dublin Review* in July 1839 Wiseman had quoted St. Augustine's dictum 'securus judicat orbis terrarum' (the whole world judges justly); see the Editor's Introduction, pp.iv-v. It is interesting that here in 1841 Newman is trying to convince himself that the dictum does not apply to Anglicans now.

even in his next-door neighbour? Do not the Fathers differ from each other in matters of teaching and action, yet what fair persons ever imputed inconsistency to them in consequence? St. Augustine bids us stay in persecution, yet St. Dionysius[105] takes to flight; St. Cyprian[106] at one time flees, at another time stays. One bishop adorns churches with paintings, another tears down a pictured veil; one demolishes the heathen temples, another consecrates them to the true God. St. Augustine at one time speaks against the use of force in proselytizing, at another time he speaks for it.[107] The Church at one time comes into General Council at the summons of the Emperor; at another time she takes the initiative. St. Cyprian re-baptizes heretics; St. Stephen[108] accepts their baptism. The early ages administer, the later deny, the Holy Eucharist to children.[109] Who shall say that in such practical matters, and especially in points of casuistry, points of the when, and the where, and the by whom, and the how, words written in the fourth century are to be the rule of the nineteenth?

We have not St. Austin to consult; we cannot go to him with his works in our hand, and ask him whether they are to

---

[105] *St. Dionysius*: See note on p.[45].

[106] *St. Cyprian*: See note on p.[25]. He went into hiding during the Decian persecution. However, when the Emperor Valerian began another persecution, Cyprian refused to sacrifice to the pagan gods and was executed.

[107] *St. Augustine speaks ...* : In *Letter 23*, Augustine opposed the use of force to eradicate heresy: 'I do not propose to compel men to embrace the communion of any party'. But he later changed his mind and used the text 'Whomsoever you shall find, compel them to come in' (Luke 14:23) to justify the use of force against the Donatists (cf. *Letter 93, To Vincentius*).

[108] *St. Stephen*: See note on p.[31]. His view that baptism by heretics was valid, against St. Cyprian's view that it was not, became the established view in the church.

[109] [All these are merely points of discipline or conduct; but whether there is a visible Church, and whether it is visibly one, is a question which as it is answered affirmatively or negatively changes the essential idea and the entire structure of Christianity.] [N]

be taken to the letter under our altered circumstances? We cannot explain to him that, as far as the appearance of things go, there are, besides our own, at least two Churches, one Greek, the other Roman; and that they are both marked by a certain peculiarity which does not appear in his own times, or in his own writings, and which much resembles what Scripture condemns as idolatry. Nor can we remind him, that the Donatists had a Note of disqualification upon them, which of itself would be sufficient to negative their claims to Catholicity, in that they refused the name of Catholic to the rest of Christendom; and moreover, in their bitter hatred and fanatical cruelty towards the rival communion in Africa. Moreover, St. Austin himself waives the question of the innocence or guilt of Cæcilian,[110] on the ground that the *orbis terrarum* could not be expected to have accurate knowledge of the facts of the case;[111] and, if contemporary judgments might be deceived in regard to the merits of the African Succession, yet, without blame, much more may it be maintained, without any want of reverence to so great a saint, that private letters which he wrote fourteen hundred years ago, do not take into consideration the present circumstances of Anglo-Catholics. Are we sure, that had he known them, they would not have led to an additional chapter in his Retractions? And again, if ignorance would have been an excuse, in his judgment, for the Catholic world's passing over the crime of the Traditors, had Cæcilian and his party been such, much more, in so nice a question as the Roman claim to the *orbis terrarum* at this day, in opposition to England and Greece, may we fairly consider that he who condemned the Donatists only in the

[372]

---

[110] *Cæcilian*: See note on p.[46].
[111] Epp. 93, 144. [N]

case of "quæstio facillima," would excuse us, even if mistaken, from the notorious difficulties which lie in the way of a true judgment. Nor, moreover, would he, who so constantly sends us to Scripture for the Notes of the Church Catholic, condemn us for shunning communions, which had been so little sensitive of the charge made against them of idolatry. But even let us suppose him, after full cognizance of our case, to give judgment against us; even then we shall have the verdict of St. Chrysostom,[112] St. Basil,[113] and others virtually in our favour, supporters and canonizers as they were of Meletius,[114] Bishop of Antioch, who in St. Augustine's own day lived and died out of the communion of Rome and Alexandria.[115]

We do not think then that St. Austin's teaching can be taken as a direction to us to quit our Church on account of its incidental Protestantism, unsatisfactory as it is to have such a Note lying against us. And it is pleasant to believe, that there are symptoms at this time of our improvement; and we only wish we could see as much hope of a return to a healthier state in Rome, as is at present visible in our own communion. There is among us a growing feeling, that to be a mere Establishment is unworthy of the Catholic Church; and that to be shut out from the rest of Christendom is not a subject of boasting. We seem to have embraced the idea of the desirableness of being on a good understanding with the Greek and Eastern Churches; and we are aiming at sending

[373]

---

[112] *St. Chrysostom*: See note on p.[62].

[113] *St. Basil*: See note on p.[60].

[114] *Meletius*: See note on p.[62]. The Anglican Newman uses Meletius as an analogue for the Tractarian Anglican claim of being orthodox even if in schism from the wider church.

[115] [As has been said above, this statement is too absolute; at least, Athanasius was reconciled to Meletius.] [N]

out bishops to distant places, where they must come in contact with foreign communions; and though the extreme vagueness, indecision, and confusion, in which our theological and ecclesiastical notions at present lie, will be almost sure to involve us in certain mistakes and extravagances, yet it would be unthankful to "despise the day of small things,"[116] and not to recognize in these movements a hopeful stirring of hearts, and a religious yearning after something better than we have. But not to dwell unduly on these public manifestations of a Catholic tendency, we should all recollect that a restoration of intercommunion with other Churches is, in a certain sense, in the power of individuals. Every one who desires unity, who prays for it, who endeavours to further it, who witnesses for it, who behaves Christianly towards the members of Churches alienated from us, who is at amity with them, (saving his duty to his own communion and to the truth itself,) who tries to edify them, while he edifies himself and his own people, may surely be considered, as far as he himself is concerned, as breaking down the middle wall of division,[117] and renewing the ancient bonds of unity and concord by the power of charity. Charity can do all things for us; charity is at once a spirit of zeal and of peace; by charity we shall faithfully protest against what our private judgment warrants us in condemning in others; and by charity we have it in our own hands, let all men oppose us, to restore in our own circle the intercommunion of the Churches.

[374]

There is only one quarter from which a cloud can come over us, and darken and bewilder our course. If, *nefas*

---

[116] *"despise the day of small things,"*: Zechariah 4:10.

[117] *breaking down the middle wall of division*: Cf. Ephesians 2:14

dictu,[118] our Church is by any formal acts rendered schismatical, while Greek and Roman idolatry remains not of the Church, but in it merely, denounced by Councils, though admitted by authorities of the day,—if our own communion were to own itself Protestant, while foreign communions disclaimed the superstition of which they are too tolerant,—if the profession of Ancient Truth were to be persecuted in our Church, and its teaching forbidden,—then doubtless, for a season, Catholic minds among us would be unable to see their way.

July, 1841.

---

[118] nefas dictu: 'offensive to say', i.e. such a thing is too horrible or offensive even to be said

XV[1]

JOHN DAVISON

THE author on whose character and writings we are now proposing to remark, Mr. Davison, may be considered as an instance of the operation of a mysterious law which is often witnessed in the course of history. It is surely mysterious, considering what the world is, how it needs improvement, and moreover that this life is the appropriate time for action, or, what is emphatically called in Scripture, *work*,[2] that they who seem gifted for the definite purpose of influencing and edifying their brethren, should be allowed to do so much less than might be expected. For instance, no one certainly, it must be admitted, can pretend to measure the effect produced by as much as Mr. Davison has been appointed to say and to do; still, left to ourselves, we are apt to grudge that the powers of such a mind as his have not had full range in his age and country, and that a promise of such high benefits, should, owing to circumstances beyond man's control, have been but partially accomplished. Here is one of the most original thinkers of his day, deep, serious, reverential, various, suffered to end his course, as it may be

---

[1] *XV*: incorrectly numbered XIV in some editions
[2] *called in Scripture* work: e.g. "do the work of an evangelist, make full proof of thy ministry" 2 Timothy 4: 5.

[376] called, prematurely;[3] absorbed moreover during the greater part of it in employments which, though sacred in their nature and honoured by a special blessing, and zealously fulfilled by him, yet apparently might have been left to those who had not his particular endowments; and, as the consequence of those employments, stinted in his apprehension and possession of dogmatic knowledge, so that what he has written is rather true in principle and admirable in sentiment, than complete in system. Here is a man of the cast of Hooker[4] and Butler,[5] fitted to be a doctor of the Church, yet confined pretty much to the contemplation of the first principles of Christian doctrine, and allowed but once or twice to give utterance to the truths on which he lived, and to manifest the flame which burned unceasingly within him.

Of course in such cases we may rest quite secure that all is ordered according to the most perfect wisdom, though we do not understand it. But what deserves notice in the case before us is, that the bent and temper of Mr. Davison's own mind did but concur in and carry out this external disposition of things, which we have been noticing, as if within and without one Agent was present, or as if his inner man was instinctively resigning itself to his outward destination. At the time of his death, the common report was that he had ordered all his manuscripts to be destroyed; and in the Preface to the present collection it is pointedly observed that "nothing hitherto unpublished appears in it."

---

[3] *end his course ... prematurely*: Davison died at the age of 57, having suffered ill-health for much of his life.
[4] *Hooker*: Richard Hooker (1554-1600), Anglican divine and theologian who wrote *Of the Lawes of Ecclesiastical Politie* (1594-97) and influenced the Caroline divines.
[5] *Butler*: See note on p.[45].

We also learn from the Preface that the same feeling has operated to the maintenance of an almost absolute silence about the author's history. It professes to give "the few brief notes of his life, which those who are entrusted with his Remains[6] feel to be all that they are permitted here to set down. A Memoir greatly more detailed, and so far more satisfactory, might very easily have been compiled. But in this, and in many like particulars, the wishes of those who survive have given way to their decided conviction of what his would have been."—P. iii.

[377]

Moreover, if we may continue our remarks on this subject, it would appear as if there were something even in the outward bearing and demeanour of this revered person, which answered the same purpose of concealing from the gaze of the world what he was. We do not write as being his friends or acquaintance; he was of a generation before us; we do not write as if in apology or explanation; but we write as thinking him a man of a great mind, and as feeling, we cannot deny, some curiosity and pleasure in contemplating an instance, the more interesting because not uncommon, of the secrecy and solitude in which great minds move, as if, like our Lord's forerunner,[7] they would not force themselves on the world, but were bidding it, if it thought worth while, to "go out into the wilderness"[8] after them. In the Preface to these Remains, it is observed of their author, that "perhaps his whole character might be cast in a mould of severer goodness than this age could easily endure,"—p. v.,

---

[6] *his Remains*: *Remains and Occasional Publications* (1840) which this article was reviewing.

[7] *our Lord's forerunner*: St. John the Baptist

[8] *"go out into the wilderness"*: Matthew 11:7

reminding us of the plaintive distich, "Few were the admirers of Thucydides, son of Olorus."[9] "They that wear soft clothing are in kings' houses."[10] We can conceive such an one, epicurean or academic, refined, fastidious, accomplished, indolent, spending an aimless life amid society and literary leisure, falling in with the subject of these remarks, and shrinking from the reality of mind which he could not appreciate, and disgusted with the staidness or abruptness which he could.

[378]   The confessions of such a man of the world, small in the midst of his endowments and advantages, have lately got abroad. "I saw D. the other day in town," he says: "it is quite astonishing that with such an understanding and such acquirements, his manners should be entirely *odious and detestable*. How you could live with him without hating him, I do not understand. Clever as he is, there must be some great defect in his mind, or he would try to make himself a little more sufferable."—*Letters*, p. 58. Of course such a judgment can give pain to no friend of the subject of it. Probably Lord Dudley[11] was very offensive in his own way, and found his match. Of course he would have no perception that this was the case; and feeling that he had been struck by something very hard, would consider, not that he had himself impinged, but that he had been assailed. Certainly men of reverential and religious tempers are apt to

---

[9] *"Few were the admirers of Thucydides, son of Olorus."*: Thucydides (c.400-c.460 BC) was an Athenian general and author of the *History of the Peloponnesian War*. This distich (verse) refers to his literary style which commentators criticised as obscure. In the 1842 *British Critic* article, Newman gives it in the original Greek: παῦροι δ' ἀγάσαντο Θουκυδίδην ὀλόρου (see the Textual Appendix); it is found in the *Anthologia Palatina*, a collection of Greek poems and epigrams.

[10] *"They that wear soft clothing are in king's houses"*: Matthew 11:8

[11] *Lord Dudley*: William Ward (1750-1823) who became 3rd Viscount Dudley and Ward in 1788. His wealth stemmed from his estates and the coal found in them. He is said to have offered to pay off the National Debt himself.

hide themselves from those who are not worthy of them; nay, it must be confessed too, they often put on a very rough jacket for their special benefit. The above record then on the part of a man, whom with all his estimable points few persons will take as an authority, is not one which deserves dwelling on for its own sake; yet it may be taken, not without profit, as a specimen of the judgments, so often found in history, so often at this day, which the world forms of those who are endeavouring to live within the veil, and to view things as He views them who sees all things as they really are. Men of cultivated minds consider great divines or great philosophers merely in an intellectual point of view, and think they have a right to be admitted at once to their familiarity, when they meet them. They have no objection to exclusiveness, when talent and education, or again when wealth and station, are made the tickets of admission; but they are very much disgusted, when they find the exclusiveness conducted on quite another principle, when [379] the brotherhood of mind or the talisman of good society avails them nothing, and when they find themselves without, not within, the privileged circle. Till this "odious" and "insufferable" reserve is introduced, they will bear with a great deal in the way of difference, singularity, or, as they call it, even error of opinion. A man, for instance, to take what principally meets our view at this time, may go a great way in Catholic opinions, and will be allowed to say and do what would be considered monstrous in another, if he does but conform himself to the existing state of things, adopt the tone of the world, take his place in the social body, and become an integral member, and a breathing and living portion, and a contented servant, of things which perish. But if he will not put an establishment or a philosophy in the place of the Church, if he will not do homage to talent as such, or wealth as such, or official eminence as such, then he is out of joint with the age, and not only his words, but his look and his air, are like a pail of cold water thrown over every man of the world whom he meets.[12] Thus, to instance the phenomenon in an extreme case, Hume[13], as is well known, said he never fell in with a religious man who was not melancholy.

The writer of the Preface to these Remains makes one remark about Mr. Davison, which serves with much appositeness to illustrate what we have been saying:

"He always showed himself particularly anxious to favour and befriend all kinds of moral worth, as distinct from mere ability. His pupils knew him to be especially on his guard against the idolizing of intellectual talent or successful study. *He saw nothing admirable in it, except as guided by an energetic sense of duty.*"

This seems written at Lord Dudley by anticipation: the writer proceeds;

[380]   "The following extract of a letter is inserted as expressive of this feeling: 'I am cast upon this place' (Colstersworth)[14] 'by the division of my journey between York and London. It is a great spot, for it has Newton[15] on the right, and Sanderson[16] on the left. My mind turns most to Boothby Pagnel. Newton I can only

---

[12] *A man, for instance* ... : Newman is writing indirectly about himself in this passage.

[13] *Hume*: David Hume (1711-76), Scottish philosopher and historian.

[14] *Colstersworth*: Colsterworth, a village in Lincolnshire.

[15] *Newton*: Isaac Newton (1642-1727), the celebrated scientist, born at Woolsthorpe Manor at Colsterworth.

[16] *Sanderson*: Robert Sanderson (1587–1663), Anglican Divine, Rector of Boothby Pagnel, not far from Colsterworth. He was a supporter of Charles I and was imprisoned during the Commonwealth but at the Restoration became Bishop of Lincoln. He published a number of theological and scholarly works.

admire. Sanderson is nearer to imitation, though still far above it. What a delight it is to dwell upon the memory of such a man! much more would it be to be able to live like him.'"—P. v.

In like manner the following noble passage occurs in his note upon his Sermon on Education:[17]

"Our civilization itself, what is it but a speculative or a mechanical phantom, except as it gives larger scope to the exercise of virtue, private, social, or religious? We might as well be in the woods, where our forefathers were, as in the midst of looms and engines, pictures and libraries, or in the midst of the enjoyments of pleasure or accommodation which these things produce, unless we lift our views to a point of moral elevation above them, and are intent on some better object which the conscience can approve, as the proper aim and business of the responsible creatures of God."—P. 250.

2.

We have got into our subject without such introductory formalities as are usual and befitting; and now it is too late to do more than notice our irregularity. And, since the "qualis ab incepto"[18] is always more respectable than inconsistency, we hope to be allowed, as we have begun, so to proceed, not without something of arrangement in our own minds, but with not a very perceptible one, and with frequent digressions as they occur, and at last perhaps without any plan or order at all. It will be recollected that we have been speaking of that economy of reserve and secresy, to which our author seems to have been inclined, as other similar minds; and now we will point out another of

---

[17] *Sermon on Education*: preached at St Hilda's, South Shields, on 11 September 1825 (*Remains*, pp. 225-254).
[18] *"quails ab incepto"*: the same as from the beginning

[381] its secondary causes, or, as they may be called, its phenomena. We mean the difficulty he seems to have had in expressing himself, and the consequent effort which, not only composition, but even conversation, or we may say speech, cost him, and the effect of this difficulty visible in his writings.

It would be great presumption, except in one who knew such a person well, to attempt to analyze the causes in his particular case for this peculiarity, and the manner in which it operated; and we have no sort of intention of incurring it. Yet, viewing him not in himself, but, as it were, in the abstract, as an historical portrait offered for our contemplation, it may be not without its use to set down, not what actually were the causes, but some of what might be its causes, and what are the causes of this characteristic in similar instances. We suppose it then to be undeniable, that there are persons, whose minds are full of thought even to bursting, in whom it is pent up in a strange way, and in whom, when it at last forces itself out in language, it does so with the suddenness, brevity, completeness, and effectiveness (if the comparison be allowed) of a steam-boiler. The more fully formed is the image of truth in the mind, the greater task is it to find door or window for it to escape by; and, when it makes egress, perhaps it comes head-foremost. Again, minds which vividly realize conclusions, often are irritated at the necessity of drawing out premises; or they are inadequate to the task; or they are impatient of many words; or they are at a loss where to begin; or they despair of conveying their meaning to others; or they find a relief to their feelings in some sudden and strong outbreak. When, under such circumstances, there is a habit of self-government, and a watchful control of feeling and language, there will often be an abruptness of speech in consequence; or an unseasonable silence; or an uneasy [382] patience, an unaccountable constraint, a composure without repose; or a variable jerking manner, as if a man were riding his horse with a tight rein. Or sometimes, to recur to our former figure, he will let off the steam in the shape of humour. Or when the mind feels its own separation from others, its strangeness, its isolation, a distance of demeanour in general society is the consequence, which apparently argues a want of frankness and cordiality, or a recklessness, which may be set down to arrogance and pride. All these mental states are destructive of ease of deportment; to which must be added what is sometimes called *consciousness*, the painful perception of the presence of self, quite distinct from self-importance and self-conceit, though looking like them to undiscriminating eyes.

Mr. Davison's style is an illustration of what we have been saying. We consider its characteristic to lie in the force and vividness of its separate expressions, phrases, or sentences; and, though there is always a danger of generalizing beyond our data, we are tempted to pronounce that he is more happy in his words and clauses than in his conduct of an argument. His style, viewed in its general tenor and substance, is but one of those imperfect manifestations of the inner man, which are characteristic of him. He does not *compose* well; there is a want of vigour and skilfulness in putting his arguments and views out of hand; he is circuitous and unready in the management of his matter, and inelegant in his grammatical constructions. And where this is the case, that very force and richness in the lesser portions of the composition, which we would specially ascribe to Mr. Davison, does but increase of course the appearance of elaborateness, we may even add of heaviness, in it, viewed as a whole. They act as weights upon it, not as supports. It may be added that, in consequence of what may be called his unreadiness, he promises more than he fulfils, and gives us the appearance of a mere dwelling on the style more than on the argument, and of selecting his words and phrases more for the sake of embellishment than of illustration. Nor is it any disparagement of him to say, that in his case his words do sometimes go beyond what they convey, though this at first sight may sound like a paradox; for in truth, he had deeper thoughts than he could well bring to light; so that his language is rather the index of his mind than of his sense, of the objects which possessed him than of the subject-matter which he treated. And again, we may bear to say that his style is laboured in its details; for what is this but to allow that he is so engrossed with realities which are close at hand, and feels it so difficult to shake off their impression, that he is but a second-rate artist in bringing out those broad lights and effects, and in taking those general views, which are so clear and so persuasive in the literature of the day, because they are so superficial? We will add, that his apparent negligence in composition is sometimes so great, as almost to look like intention. What, for instance, if it be worth noticing, can be more inartificial and ungraceful, than the following commencement, literally the first sentence, of a Sermon delivered, if we mistake not, at an anniversary meeting of some very high persons?

"In the following discourse I propose, first, to consider these words of the Apostle, as they encourage to active usefulness in life; next to speak of the value and advantage of societies instituted for the furtherance of objects of public utility; and lastly, to advert to some of the peculiar objects which come under the care of your ancient incorporated Society."—*Remains*, p. 205.

And these three separate heads, when entered upon, [384] prove to be so distinct from each other, so entire in themselves, that we are presented rather with three half-finished sermons, preached one after another, than with the *bonâ fide* treatment of one subject, such as we might fairly anticipate on such an occasion. But we shall have more to say about this Sermon by-and-by, in a different connexion.

3.

We have been speaking of Mr. Davison's style, as unattractive in its general course, yet as happy in its separate portions, as being a sort of type of that economy of reserve which an unseen hand wrapped round him. Of its excellence indeed, in its separate portions, it is impossible to speak too highly; the energy of his mind discharges itself concisely and forcibly on the matter in hand, with the flashing power of artillery directed against a fortress; at other times with the calm clear light of some sudden rent in a dark sky. His brilliant sententiousness, the beauty of his images, the terseness and truth and freshness of his expressions, their graphic distinctness,—in a word, his remarkable originality, an originality more remarkable in style even than in matter, give a charm to his discussion which amply compensates for whatever is wanting in its *set*, in the vigour and ease of its movements, or the knitting and suppleness of its joints. The mere man of letters will desiderate purity and harmony of language; but Mr.

Davison is *sui similis*[19] beyond any other religious writer of his day, and, though it is very difficult to analyze what it consists in, there is a certain definite character, one and the same, which all persons will recognize, running through his sayings, his conversation, and his writings, which belongs [385] to no one else. If any writer has reason to have his name turned into a grammatical root, surely as Cicero is the author of Ciceronian Latin, so we may be permitted without offence to call Mr. Davison's style Davisonian. It was probably in allusion to this peculiarity that a French refugee, resident in Oxford in his day, used to say of his language that it was like Minerva, issuing armed *cap-à-pie*[20] from Jupiter's head. No better illustration can be given of it than the short dialogue about truth and accuracy, which for a different purpose is recorded in the Preface. It is an instance of a remark, grave and sensible indeed in itself, but striking especially from the manner in which it is conveyed.

> "'D. That is rather a minute accuracy. But I have a respect for all accuracy, for all accuracy is of the *noble family of truth.*' *Answ.*, 'And is to be respected accordingly.' D. 'Even to her *most menial servant.*'"—P. 10.

Accordingly, few persons seem to have left more of their sayings in the memory of their friends than Mr. Davison; and that quite as much from their being *like* their author, and reminding them of one they loved and admired, as because of their intrinsic value. Some of them are in their circumstances of a lighter character. A college servant used to tell a story how, when Mr. Davison in his younger years was pro-proctor, he chased an undergraduate all the way

---

[19] sui similis: like himself, uniquely characteristic

[20] *armed cap-à-pie*: i.e. armed from head to foot; cf. *Hamlet*, Act I, scene ii.

from Magdalen Bridge to the Star Hotel, where he caught him; by which time the narrator, who was his "bull-dog,"[21] was, to use a familiar word, completely winded. Mr. Davison, however, was as even in his breathing and sedate in his deportment as before the race begun, and thereupon spoke his first and last words to his captive, "Sir, it has not availed." One day a pupil burst into his dressing-room full of hope and joy to tell him that the report was, that he had got the Newdigate;[22] he replied with mock gravity, "Do you come here, Mr. Rickards, to occupy me with rumours?" On another occasion he interrupted a rambling reasoner in a low tone, "Stop, stop, you reason uncomfortably." We hope these instances, which of course only occur at random out of an indefinite number of similar ones, are not beneath the purpose for which we select them, nor are inconsistent with the reverent feelings which we entertain and wish to express towards the subject of them; but they seem to us to have their value, as serving to depict a mind under control, relieving itself briefly and strongly, not without a dash of humour in the expression, by way of discharging itself the more safely.

[386]

But it is hardly fair to the reader, to say nothing of the claims of our author himself, to record the mere colloquial effusions of a great mind. In order to form a judgment of the vividness, felicity, and graceful festivity of Mr. Davison's language, we extract the following *locus classicus*,[23] as it

---

[21] *"bull-dog"*: Name given to the private police force of the University of Oxford. In 2003 they were reconstituted as 'Proctors' Officers'.

[22] *the Newdigate*: A prestigious prize established in 1806 in memory of Sir Roger Newdigate, awarded to the Oxford student who produced the best composition in English verse. This is read aloud at the honorary degrees ceremony, Encænia.

[23] *locus classicus*: classical passage or source

may be called, from his review of Edgeworth's Professional Education.[24] He has told us in a previous page that "in a series of Essays Mr. Edgeworth has traced different plans of education, calculated for the wants of the several professions. His plans begin at a very early period, and undertake to regulate the habits, studies, and sometimes the amusements of the boy, in almost every particular, with a view to his civil employment in future life. The advantage to be secured by this concentration of his tastes and studies is the enabling him to fulfil his station well, and enlarge his attainments, as applicable to it."—P. 422. This theory was supremely distasteful to Mr. Davison, and he thus comments on it:—

[387]

"Instead of making well-educated men, the object of his system is to make pleading and prescribing machines. So far does he carry the subdivision of his relative aims, that the knowledge of the first and plainest truths of religion, is made to belong to a particular profession. The little uncassocked clergyman, of six years old, is to be made acquainted with the being of a God, in a proper philosophical way. But his lay-brothers have no such regular instruction provided for them. It is no part of their business. They must recollect that they are not designed for the Church, and follow their proper profane studies. Who knows but that they may live to hear their brother in the pulpit, and get some religion from him there?

"The lawyer is to have his appropriate management as soon as he begins to speak. A nurse of good accent is to be procured for him, to modulate his first babbling to the right tone of the bar. He is to prattle for a fee. He is afterwards to be encouraged to a little ill-bred disputatiousness for the same worthy purpose. Mr.

---

[24] *his review of Edgeworth's Professional Education*: originally published in the *Quarterly Review*, October 1811 (*Remains*, pp. 405-456). Richard Lovell Edgeworth (1744-1817) was an Anglo-Irish politician and writer.

Edgeworth quotes a trite passage of Roman history to show that the Romans bestowed much care upon the elocution of their children, and repeats over again the tale of Cornelia and the Gracchi. The Romans thought it a grace in their children to speak their own language well. So thinks every one. The peculiarity of Mr. Edgeworth's mind consists in making it exclusively a lawyer's accomplishment.

"The physician that is to be, as soon as he can wield a spade, is to have his garden in imitation of the great Sir Charles Linnæus, and vex the ground with his botanical arrangements. The culture of opium and rhubarb will be his first step to the prescription of them.

"The infant soldier is to be made a hero as soon as possible. Indeed no time is to be lost with him, for Mr. Edgeworth recommends that he be accustomed to the presence of domestic animals without terror, 'and be taken to the exhibitions of wild beasts, that he may be familiarized to their forms and cries.' His nurse too must be chosen for her aptitude to the duties of rearing a great captain. When the defender of his country is grown up to be a boy, his sports should be of the military cast. Without making too much parade, he should begin to work upon some fortification in the corner of a shrubbery. He must be trained also to a sense of honour, and abhor the disgrace of corporal punishment as a soldier ought.

"Such is the grand scheme of partition to be made among the professional aspirants according to their destinations of future life. Religion, a good elocution, gardening and other amusements, a manly constitution of body and mind, and a tenderness of honour, we have always thought to be good for boys as sensitive rational beings capable of instruction, health, and pleasure. To make cunning sport for them, and defraud them of the natural right of amusing themselves in their own way, does not agree with our feelings of kindness for them. It sophisticates them in the very point where they should be most free and natural. But to delegate

[388]

459

the moral qualities, such as a just impression of religion and a right sense of honour, to a station or title, or a piece of cloth, or to make the slightest difference in these respects, is to confound the essence of morality, and run deliberately insane upon a spurious conceited wisdom."—P. 452-454.

4.

We have already alluded to Mr. Davison's images: they are severe, yet graceful; just and natural, yet poetical. They are sometimes introduced into the gravest discussion, yet without any detriment to its keeping. For instance, Mr. Edgeworth, as we have seen, is for settling every one's profession in his cradle, which he considers, to use his own words, "in a family where there are more sons than one, would prevent all injurious competition. As all the brothers would early know that they were to pursue different modes of life, there could never be any crossing interests or jealousy of particular talents, *though there might and ought to be among them an emulation of general excellence.*" Mr. Davison observes upon the hint thrown out in the last words:

"A more unlikely method of inspiring emulation, or leaving any scope for it, we can hardly conceive, than a complete separation, at an early age, of every feeling and pursuit among them. It is like setting horses on their speed against each other, by running them on different grounds that they may not jostle."—P. 418.

In a later part of the same paper he observes:

[389] "To make the connexion of them (the liberal studies) with the immediate technical business of any profession apparent, is no part of our manner of arguing. If they cherish and invigorate the mental powers, it is enough. When the tide flows strong in the

main sea we shall never doubt but it will, in due time, fill every channel, creek, and harbour."—P. 444.

In his review of the charges of the Edinburgh Review against Oxford[25] and the controversy which they occasioned, he speaks of the fallacy of making the University examinations in the last century the measure of what was taught in Oxford, when "everything of importance, in the way of examination, and by far the greatest part in the way of instruction, was done," whether rightly or wrongly, "within the walls of each particular college, and could be seen only there." This takes him to the image contained in the last extract for a fresh illustration:

"When the reviewer is disposed to propagate the belief that either the subjects or the state of learning in the place were to be judged of by those open examinations, mere relics of form, he proceeds upon what we know to be a most gross historical mistake; and a person might as well record the rise of the tide by measures taken on a shore which the sea had abandoned."—P. 463.

Presently he pursues the subject thus:

[The Review] "enters upon a train of reflections which suppose all along the existence of some forms or statutes at Oxford at this day in force, to 'chain down the mind and check inquiry.' Acquitting the critic of unfairness, we cannot so easily acquit him of palpable false reasoning about forms and statutes. These things may be of very little efficacy, to do either good or harm. If the public mind is not conformable to them, they are

---

[25] *his review of the charges of the Edinburgh Review against Oxford*: His 'Review of Replies to the Calumnies of the Edinburgh Review against Oxford' first appeared in the *Quarterly Review* of August 1810. The controversy chiefly focussed on Oxford's alleged scientific and mathematical backwardness.

virtually abolished while they subsist. So it was in Oxford, according to the author's statement, that 'the new doctrines were received and taught' in the face of the old exercises: that is, the genius of the place was not so feeble but that it could carry a few links of the old chain about it, after it had sprung into liberty."— P. 371.

[390]   These illustrations are sufficient for the purpose which has led us to cite them; but there are others of a different kind, introduced as if rather for his own refreshment and recreation in the midst of a dry discussion, than for the sake of the subject. Sometimes they have a character of grave humour; sometimes they are almost eccentric. The Edinburgh Reviewer had been labouring to show that what he considered in a former publication to be *beyond* the elements of mathematics might be included *within* those elements, by the time at which he was then writing. Mr. Davison uses a figure quite his own on the occasion;—not to confute a quibble, but to vent his disdain of it:

"The idea of a floating boundary, which is included in that criterion, is rather exceptional; but, granting it, still we cannot suppose that science has made such a flight during the last six years, active as it has been, that conic sections, which Professor Playfair[26] in 1804 ranked beyond the elements, should now be considered as only 'elementary.' Does the boundary of the elements advance so rapidly? Let the empire abroad be extended in all quarters; but we do not wish, upon every new conquest, to have the *pomœria*[27] put in motion."—P. 369.

---

[26] *Professor Playfair*: John Playfair (1748–1819), Church of Scotland minister and Professor of Natural Philosophy at Edinburgh University.
[27] pomœria: the bounds or limits of a city

In his Considerations on the Poor Laws,[28] a matter-of-fact subject, *if any other*, in the midst of a grave paragraph, he suddenly breaks out into the vivid and energetic image contained in the following extract; which is almost as startling, where it occurs, as if in the middle of a college lecture he had attempted to fulfil it in his own person:

"At the same time, projects of amendment have no right to be very sanguine in the extent of their aims. For the particular interests of the country, which are the most nearly affected by the constitution of our poor laws, are by no means beholden to those laws for all the injury or benefit of which they are capable. We must not suppose, therefore, that, if those interests were set as completely at ease, as the most satisfactory removal of all that is objectional in those laws could set them, they would immediately pass at once into a state of extraordinary high order, vigour, and perfection, *like so many smooth spheres, spinning on their axes, in free space, along the national ecliptic*. This is no more than a truism, resulting from the complexity of all such affairs; and I mention it," etc., etc.—P. 569. [391]

This extraordinary *capriccio*[29] has brought to our minds a reminiscence of Bishop Butler, which, we believe, is a tradition at Stanhope,[30] and may, for what we know, have before this got into print, viz., that he was a very hard rider. Cannot we trace something of a common cause in these two similar minds, grave, contemplative, reserved, profound, manifesting itself in the violent exercise of the one, and the sallies of wit in conversation or in writing of the other?

---

[28] *Considerations on the Poor Laws*: Published in 1817 and reprinted in *Remains*, pp.499-608.

[29] capriccio: a caprice, a sudden fantasy

[30] *Bishop Butler ... at Stanhope*: Joseph Butler (1692–1752), Anglican divine and eminent theologian, much quoted by Newman. He was Rector of Stanhope, County Durham, before being appointed Bishop of Bristol and then of Durham.

If the reader is tired of these specimens, it is because we have no business to transplant them out of their proper soil, into, as it were, a nursery garden, where they lose their meaning; yet, at the risk of this damage, we are tempted to give one more, and it shall be the image of a tree, and that growing out of the rock of that same dry Essay on the Poor Laws. He is contrasting the national debt with the then poor law system:

"It is quite possible for a very opulent country to be most seriously shaken, and disturbed by obstructions and embarrassments in the balance of a sum, or the making up of a debt, which may be absolutely insignificant in comparison of its whole opulence. It makes a vast difference, whereabout in the sum of its public affairs, that difficulty of balance or debt may happen to rest. If it affects the first sources of supply, if it cramps and disorganizes the system of the labour of the country, by converting labourers into mere spenders and consumers, the real detriment produced by it is infinitely greater than it would be if there be a defalcation from its means to the same nominal extent in any other part of its system. ... A nation would better afford to owe its stockholders five times the amount. It eats, in fact, like a canker, at the root of our resources, for the labour of the kingdom, with its myriads of working hands, is that fibrous root, which extracts for us the first element of our growth and sap of circulation. If this root of labour makes its way, and can strike its last fibres freely, the timber will thrive in its strength of trunk, and pride of branch and foliage; if it does not, the finest suns and rains overhead will not be able to make the plant grow. It is commonly said of the palm tree, that no weight laid upon its head can kill it. I have not heard whether naturalists have made the other experiment upon that indestructible species, but I should suppose that a much smaller force would be sufficient to do it a serious mischief at the root."—Pp. 566, 567.

[392]

5.

We have above remarked on the inequality of excellence between the course of Mr. Davison's composition and his separate sentences and phrases. Some of the above extracts may seem to disprove this distinction, and, as has already been remarked, it is true that he is at one time far more successful than at another. He sometimes writes without effort, and at another he is like an Atlas with the world on his shoulders. We supposed at first that this was owing to increasing expertness in composition, and that his last writings were his more vigorous and well compacted: but this is by no means the case. His review of Mr. Edgeworth's Professional Education, the best sustained and most self-possessed, is also one of the earliest of his writings. His Inquiry into the Origin of Sacrifice,[31] not to say his Lectures on Prophecy,[32] which, eloquent as they are, can neither of them be called easy compositions, were published thirteen or fourteen years later. In truth, it is very plain that the *subject* was the cause of the difference; and so we think it will be found respecting him generally, that according as he [393] approaches religious topics, his power of sustaining an argument flags, and his course becomes impeded; but as soon as he has no overshadowing awe to subdue him, he is able again to write with vigour and grace. Hence his occasional Sermons, though very valuable in point of

[31] *Inquiry into the Origin of Sacrifice*: Originally published in April 1825 as *An Inquiry into the Origin and Intent of Primitive Sacrifice, and the Scripture Evidence Respecting It. With Observation on the Opinions of Spencer, Bishop Warburton, Archbishop Magee and Other Writers on the Same Subject. And Some Reflections on the Unitarian Controversy.* Reprinted in *Remains* (pp. 1-176). Newman was reading the *Inquiry* on 12 October 1825 (*LD* I, p.262).

[32] *Lectures on Prophecy*: These were not included in *Remains* but had been published separately in 1824 as *Discourses on Prophecy* and were based on his Warburtonian Lectures. Newman read the *Discourses* in April 1825 (see diary entry for 22 April 1825 in *LD* I, p.228).

matter, are some of his least satisfactory specimens of style. Again, his Essay on Baptismal Regeneration,[33] which appeared as a Review, begins at a distance from its subject, and with an elasticity of step, which is just the quality we generally desiderate in him; but he loses it page by page as he gradually comes to walk amid sacred truths and solemn arguments. We shall quote the opening, as a rare specimen of what may be called *momentum* in style; it has all the weight of Johnson, with a lighter, more springy tread:

... "We wish openly to disavow the officious service of labouring for an accommodation of opinion, between persons who may have their reasons for avoiding all approaches to it. Because, first, we cannot pretend to the authority which ought to go along with the assumption of such an office; and next, not being willing to concede any part of our own belief, we will adopt no principle of accommodation between others, except the firm and temperate statement of our own opinions, which could be conciliatory only just so far as the grounds of them are convincing; and lastly, we are well aware that nothing is less welcome to persons strongly engaged in a debate than the neutrality of a peace-maker, who is likely with many to provoke the anger he would disarm, by his suspected censure of it. And therefore, as we have no special call, in our pages, to this offensive and ungracious moderation, we request that we may not incur the prejudice and evil report of it with any description of men ...

"Controversy, when it is carried on in the sound and manly spirit of investigation, is so favourable to the advancement or the more firm establishment of our knowledge, that we shall never presume to check or decry it. While it is so conducted, religion is

---

[33] *Essay on Baptismal Regeneration*: Originally published as 'Remarks on Baptismal Regeneration' in the *Quarterly Review* in July 1816 (*Remains*, pp. 277-346).

only more securely rooted by its friendly violence. Indolent and implicit knowledge is roused by it to a more honest discipline; and error flies before it. If some degree of animation, inspired perhaps [394] more by the ardour of conflict in discussion than by the exact unprejudiced concern for the subject, should insinuate itself, we still should regard that accident as a venial one, which may render the advocates on either side more alert, and quicken their research without perverting their principles of judgment. The more severe and jealous accuracy, which we must be contented often to take from personal feelings, may in the end produce that best of all results, a more certain and a better reasoned apprehension of the truth. In this light our infirmities may serve us better than our duties. They may give us a vigour of research, which those more tardy motives might fail to supply; for we never hail the progress of truth so much as when we hope ourselves to share her triumph." ...—P. 280.

Such is the vigour and exactness of his gait when his mind is at ease; but in proportion as it becomes anxious, serious, or abstracted, and

"Ajax strives some rock's vast weight to throw,
The line too labours and the words move slow."[34]

6.

An intimate friend of Mr. Davison's, Mr. Keble,[35] was once asked what he considered to be Mr. Davison's habitual and ruling idea. It was at the time when his Visitation Sermon,[36] preached at St. Helen's, Worcester, which is reprinted among his "Remains," had just made its appearance. Mr. Keble took it up and turned to the page in it

---

[34] *"Ajax strives ... move slow."*: Alexander Pope, *An Essay on Criticism*, lines 27-28.
[35] *Mr. Keble*: See Essay XV.
[36] *Visitation Sermon*: preached at St Helen's, Worcester on 20 May 1823 (*Remains*, pp. 255-276).

in which the following sentence occurs, and put his finger upon the words which we have printed in italics:

"A clergyman's virtue ... consists not in singularities. All Christian excellence is in great and substantial duties; in the doctrines of faith cordially embraced and applied; in the love of God; in charity to man; in temperance, in integrity, in humility; in the control of the appetites and desires; in prayer and other exercises of piety; *in the fixed love and admiration of heavenly things.*"—P. 269.

[395] We should say that Mr. Davison's writings abundantly confirm this testimony,—if we understand it to ascribe to him, as we consider was meant as his special characteristic, an awful contemplation of the *providential dealings of God with man.* This is the occupation in which he is engaged through his greater works, and to which we find him drawn even amid subjects of secular interest. His Discourses on Prophecy and Inquiry into the Origin of Sacrifice are but simple exercises of this habit of mind, and it manifests itself again and again in the occasional Sermons and Essays of which the Volume of his Remains mainly consists. It is remarkable, there is very little dogmatic teaching in his writings, as in the case of Bishop Butler's; vast as is the store of holy meditations which the articles of the faith provide, and essential as they are to all Christian life, yet these were not the characteristic subjects of either the Bishop or Mr. Davison. But they each seem to have been absorbed in the vision of the Scheme of Religion Natural and Revealed, of the divine judgments, the divine ways, the divine works; and at this great sight, the latter, not to speak of Butler, seems to have been unable to go forward, and, somewhat after the pattern of the man greatly beloved, to

have "set his face towards the ground, and" as regards the great objects of faith themselves, to have "become dumb."[37]

In the Sermon just now quoted, he enumerates the parts of Christian knowledge, with a selection, and a relative prominence, remarkably illustrative of this characteristic of his mind:

"And here, if I did not hasten to a conclusion, I might enter upon an inviting subject, in descanting upon the excellence and intrinsic pleasure of Christian knowledge, with its kindred pursuits, whatever they may be. The mystery of our Redemption; the dispensations of God; the economy of His all-wise governing [396] Providence; the life, death, doctrines, and mercies of the Holy Jesus, our Saviour; our own moral nature; our duties; the prospects of our future immortal state; the history of the Church of Christ in its brighter and its darker periods; the fortunes of its propagation; with the lives of its pastors, sages, and martyrs; these are subjects for which other literature can furnish no equivalent in dignity of character, and which, if cultivated, will yield to none in point of interest to our feelings. No good reason, therefore, can be assigned why our taste should be directed, by preference, to other studies, even if motives of duty did not intervene to decide our choice."—P. 275.

In like manner his Assize Sermon[38] on the text, "For rulers are not a terror," etc.,[39] begins by reminding us that "our own nature and the scene of life around us" are "equally the subject of Divine Revelation, and the improvement of the one" is "designed by every light thrown

---

[37] *"set his face towards ... become dumb."*: Daniel 10:15; the prophet's reaction when God speaks to him.

[38] *Assize Sermon*: preached at St Mary's, Oxford during the Lent Assize on 6 March 1817 *(Remains*, pp. 177-202).

[39] *"For rulers are not a terror," etc.*: Romans 13:3.

upon the constitution of the other" (p. 179); and proceeds in a similar strain; speaking presently of our being able "to perceive the agency of a divine appointment in the affairs of men, deterring and restraining crime, supporting its first efforts of virtue, and providing for a system of improvement and discipline among men, by the very frame of society itself, by sanctions temporal as well as eternal, the terror of the first being only a present, sensible anticipation of the other" (p. 190). In his Sermon at Deptford he finds his favourite subject on the sea, and breaks out into a meditation, which we are prompted by its beauty to transfer to our pages:

"Its [this earth] intercepting seas were meant to provoke his enterprise; its divided climates and countries to diversify his enjoyments and his arts for obtaining them. The dispersion of his kind was thus counteracted by the bonds of a mutual communication. The works of God were to be seen and known in the great waters. And how rich and various in its stores is this [397] world made, to create the desire, invigorate the faculties, and reward the labour of that master being, who has received for a time the delegated possession of it. Sea and land yield him their increase. Productions are removed to a distance to be recommended by their cost and peril of acquisition. The whole society of the species consolidated by the intervention of a mutual want, and the variety of a partial privation; and many wholesome qualities of morals and understanding, with the general circulation of arts and knowledge growing out of the meaner pursuits, which are secured in their activity by the progressive demands of our mere physical nature. The worse is here made to serve the better part; for that some may eat the fruit or wear the clothing of foreign lands, what labour and skill to be laid out in the attempt, and how richly freighted does the vessel return, in experience, in discovery, in information, in the value of hardships patiently endured, and of dangers bravely encountered. And this commerce of the world is daily becoming an object which the wise and good man may contemplate with the greater pleasure, as he sees it purged of one evil which an inveterate avarice had long been permitted to reckon among its acquired possessions."—Pp. 216, 217.

To this "fixed love and admiration" of the providences of Almighty Wisdom we trace many of the characteristics of Mr. Davison's writings. One is that embarrassment and constraint to which we have already referred, and which is analogous to what a subordinate feels every day when told to do a thing in the presence of superiors. If we consider how awkward a young teacher or a schoolmaster feels when bid to catechise when his instructor or employer is by, or the anxiety and distrust of self with which a well-conducted child undergoes an examination, we shall have some insight perhaps into the diffidence and fear with which Mr. Davison touches on sacred subjects. Again, it seems to have led him to elaborate embellishment of style, from the feeling with which devout persons spend time, thought, and substance on the decoration of churches. There is often an evident prolonged dwelling on the subject on which he is speaking, [398] or the low tones of a yearning affection, or a beating of heart, or a glow of delight, or an importunate exhibition, or a simple earnest statement, which show what is going on within him. Of course it is very difficult to show this in isolated passages detached from the context, and chosen by the arbitrary feeling and taste of individual critics, yet we will attempt, even at this risk, to convey what we mean to the reader, leaving it to him, when he has once entered into our view, to find more apposite passages for himself, and not doubting that he will enter into it.

Sometimes, as in the following extract, his deep thoughts make him eloquent, not constrained; but the principle is the same:

"Sacred religious knowledge," he says, in a Sermon from the Note to which we made our opening extract, "if it feed not the flame of a holy and obedient life, is vain and unprofitable like the rest. For what is knowledge? Evil spirits have it, and in great perfection. Bad men may have it. But the soul, actuated by its knowledge to obedience, and governed by this divine principle of the love of God, this it is which is the glory of saints, and which peoples heaven, and turns the schools of education into nurseries of God's Church, and does His work in the world, and makes the world and His Church to be the nurseries of His eternal kingdom."—P. 236.

Again, the following passage brings to remembrance that calm, tender, eager, wistful, unearthly tone, which is characteristic of a very different author of a very different age—St. Cyprian:[40]

"The devout apprehension of God is better than the unhallowed speculation of His works ... All other knowledge, if unaccompanied with this, or not ministering to it, is but a learned ignorance, a stir and curiosity after shadows and trifles. For God, and our duty, and our last end, and the doctrines of salvation and [399] humility which illuminate the Christian faith, are the greatest things that we can know, and the highest objects upon which we can exercise our understanding."—P. 234.

In the sentences with which he concludes his Origin of Sacrifice, we find the same contemplative spirit, the same

[40] *St. Cyprian:* See note on p.[25].

affectionate reverence for the saints of other days, the same solemn waiting for the future, which have appeared in some former extracts:

"Of the first generations of men, and of their faith and piety, a brief memorial is all that remains. We might wish to see further into the lives and notions of the progenitors of our race, but the wish is denied to us; and our researches in that line must rest where the only authentic record terminates our view. But this memorial of the Old World, brief as it is, is not insufficient to the ends of a Christian contemplation. 'Abel was a righteous man, and God testified of his gifts;' [41] and 'Enoch walked with God, and God took him;'[42] and 'Noah was a just man, and perfect in his generations.'[43] These are the great relics of piety and virtue, spared to us out of the ruins of time and the deluge. They are monuments which perpetuate the names of those servants of God from the beginning of things, and occupy the annals of His Church beyond the flood with an imperishable inscription to their memory. We do not look back into the distant antediluvian scene as to a dreary void. We find there the instances of their approved faith and obedience, and therein a bond and a motive to our sympathy of communion with them.

"If their information, in the method of their redemption and ours, was less, whilst they remained upon earth, than was given to some later ages, perhaps by this time the defects of it have been supplied, and its measure made complete. But if not opened to them already, the full revelation of that mystery, we know, is only delayed. It is only deferred till the time arrives which shall symmetrize all irregularities of faith and knowledge; when the Church of God of every age shall be but 'one general assembly,' and 'the spirits of just men made perfect,' being gathered to the

---

[41] *'Abel ... testified of his gifts'* : Cf. Hebrews 11:4

[42] *'Enoch ... God took him'*: Cf. Genesis 5:24

[43] *Noah .. perfect in his generations*: Genesis 6:9

holy Jesus, 'the mediator of the new covenant,'[44] shall receive the completion of whatever has been wanting in their faith, by a direct illumination from the Fountain of Light."—Pp. 162, 163.

[400] To make one more extract, in illustration of the point under review:—who will not discern in the following passage that same devout sedulous earnestness to offer his best eloquence to the divine honour, which is so well understood in regard to the obligations and dedications of pious opulence?

"The doctrine of the Gospel had been revealed, and not revealed. It was dark with the excess of the mystery, till it shone in the person of the Saviour; in Him was seen 'the fulness of grace and truth.'[45] For then was come the time when the plan of grace and redemption was to be revealed by being accomplished, and the doctrines of it to be made explicit objects of faith. These doctrines were no more to be wrapped in figure, nor taught by the tongue of prophecy, which spoke the secrets of heaven to earthly ears, and represented things which the eye had not yet seen. They were things too precious to lie buried any longer, like gold in the Indian mines, to ripen against a distant day; or to shine darkly, as jewels at the bottom of the great deep, the abyss of God's counsels. They were brought forth in their lustre, and planted, where they now are seen, on the forehead of the evangelical revelation. Thus we receive the completion of type and of prophecy, and the luminous crown of Christian faith."—Pp. 156, 157.

7.

The reverence which Mr. Davison's writings show toward sacred subjects, they also pay in free and ungrudging measure to the institutions and the persons whereby he had learned his knowledge of them. We do not augur much

[44] *'one general assembly ... the new covenant'* : Hebrews 12:23-24
[45] *'the fulness of grace and truth'*: Cf. John 1:14

good of any one who does not in the first instance throw himself into the system under which he has been born, accept the voices of the teachers, divines, and pastors, by which he is providentially surrounded, as the voice of heaven, and identify their pattern and their faith with the holy doctrine which they have been the instruments of conveying to him. Of course, such implicit confidence cannot last in all cases, as time goes on, for there is but one [401] truth, whatever it is, whereas there are "many kinds of voices in the world;"[46] and it is not to be anticipated that all minds everywhere, as they grow morally and intellectually, will just happen felicitously to concur in the respective systems in which they find themselves.[47] And, moreover, as regards the multitude of sects, there cannot, from the nature of the case, be any loyal attachment to them on the part of their individual members, seeing they do not call for it, or provide any object for its exercise. So far from it, their very principle commonly is, that every one is as able to judge as another, that every one should follow his own judgment, and that they are narrow-minded and superstitious who do not. However, as regards the members of any Christian community of long standing, with ranks and offices, with a succession of divines, and with a traditionary body of doctrine, that is, any community which *asks* for their allegiance and trust, that heart and mind must be in a very unsound state which does not from the first, without formal deliberation, but spontaneously and generously, accord it. Certainly with such a temper Mr. Davison would appear to

---

[46] *"many kinds of voices in the world;"* : 1 Corinthians 14:10

[47] *Of course, such implicit confidence* ... : An indirect reference to Newman's own situation at the time he is writing.

have no sort of sympathy, which is the more remarkable, for he is just such a person as, from his peculiar manner of writing and speaking, a superficial observer might have set down as a man of what is called "original mind;" that is, one who despises all who have gone before him, and employs himself in framing new truths expressly for the benefit of the nineteenth century. On the contrary, we suppose scarcely a writer can be produced, who in the same compass (that is to say, in the Volume containing his miscellaneous publications and Remains, a thick one, but still only one, and of which two hundred pages are on [402] politics, economy, and law,) has introduced, in one way or other, a respectful mention or eulogy of so many of our writers, and that of different schools. Never certainly was an author further removed from "setting up for himself" than the subject of these remarks. He speaks of Hooker's[48] as "a great judgment, with which I reckon it almost a pledge of the truth of any opinion to agree"—(p. 111); "of the incomparable Bishop Taylor," "the high authority of his mind and reason, which is as great as any can be," and "his freedom of strength of thought," and "his immortal work, the 'Ductor Dubitantium'" (p. 30);[49] presently of "the services of Hooker's great and capacious mind, the eloquent wisdom of Taylor, and the patient and laborious learning of the excellent Hammond"[50] (p. 96); of his "affection to the memory, and respect to the orthodox learning, of

---

[48] *Hooker*: See above p.[376].

[49] *Ductor Dubitantium*: *Ductor Dubitantium or The Rule of Conscience in all her general Measures serving as a great instrument for the determination of Cases of conscience* (London 1660) by the philosopher and Church of Ireland bishop Jeremy Taylor (1613-67).

[50] *Hammond*: Henry Hammond (1605-1660), Anglican divine, Archdeacon of Chichester from 1643. He compiled *A Paraphrase and Annotations upon all the Books of the New Testament* (1653).

Hammond," *ibid.*; again, of Sanderson,[51] in language which has already been quoted; of Bacon,[52] as "an author whom it is much safer to take as an authority than to attempt to copy" (p. 441); of "our own virtuous and learned Bishop Bull,[53] whose mind was much nurtured in the sentiments of the primitive Church" (p. 260); of Tillotson,[54] as one of "our best divines" (p. 345); of Burke,[55] as "our immortal statesman, whose eloquence is inferior only to his more admirable wisdom" (p. 442).

This characteristic in Mr. Davison will go far to account for certain opinions or avowals which we find in his writings, and in which it is very obvious that we ourselves, for instance, should be unable to follow him. He put himself, as it were, into the hands of the authors he respected. A friend of his and ours was once asked, "Why Mr. Davison did not attempt the interpretation of the Apocalypse?" he answered, that Mr. Davison had expressed to him that overwhelming sense of Mede's[56] powers, which [403] made it seem quite presumptuous in him to attempt it after him. And accordingly, in his Discourse upon the "Prediction of the great Apostasy," we find him speaking of the system contained in the Apocalypse as having given "scope to the exercise of Mede's capacious understanding." Probably we owe to Mede, not only what he did not write in way of

---

[51] *Sanderson*: See above p.[380].

[52] *Bacon*: Francis Bacon (1561-1626), Viscount St. Albans, philosopher and essayist. His *Novum Organum* (1620) summarises his ideas.

[53] *Bishop Bull*: George Bull (1634-1710). Bishop of St David's and author of *Defensio Fidei Nicaenae* (1685).

[54] *Tillotson*: John Tillotson (1630-1694), Archbishop of Canterbury (1691-94).

[55] *Burke*: Edmund Burke (1729-97), Member of Parliament and conservative political philosopher; best known for his *Reflections on the Revolution in France*.

[56] *Mede*: Joseph Mede (1586-1639), biblical scholar; author of *Clavis Apocalyptica* (1627).

comment on the Apocalypse, but in a measure what he did write; though doubtless we owe it to the provisions of the Warburton Lecture[57] that he committed himself to the theory to which we allude, viz., that the prophecies concerning Antichrist have been fulfilled in the Church of Rome. That is, he was bound by the very foundation which gave occasion to his Discourses to take this side of the controversy; and the following passage, with which he introduces his contribution to it, is sufficient to suggest how much he may have been unconsciously biassed by his deference to the authority which exacted it of him:

"As the distinguished prelate, the founder of this Lecture, had it in view, as one object of his institution, to enforce a special reference to those parts of prophecy which will fall within my present discourse, by bringing them under your notice I shall comply with that his particular design, and at the same time prosecute the inquiry into the use and inspiration of the Scripture oracles, which I have wished to follow in a settled course and order, and with a more extended view. As to this one subject of prophecy, on which his mind was intent, he has not only prescribed it to others, but he has cultivated it himself, and that with so much strength of reason and eloquence of discussion, in one of those learned and argumentative discourses which he delivered in this place, that the author has in a manner surpassed the founder, by anticipating, in this argument at least, with so much skill and success, the purpose of his institution."— *Prophecy, Discourse X.*

It will be observed that the author here says that it was "*one object*" of Warburton to secure lectures against the Church of Rome, whereas the words of the endowment, we believe, speak of Lectures "to prove the truth of revealed

[404]

---

[57] *Warburton Lecture*: See above Essay XI, p.[130].

religion in general, and of the Christian in particular, from the completion of the prophecies of the Old and New Testament, which relate to the Christian Church, *and especially* to the apostasy of papal Rome." We believe we are correct in saying, that in the great controversy between the Roman and Anglican divines in the reign of Charles II. and James II., the topic of Antichrist was never brought forward; its revival is due to Bishops Newton,[58] Warburton, and Hurd,[59] men of not very serious or spiritual minds, in the middle of the following century.

There is another eminent person for whom he has a great respect, and to whose memory we should be unjust, if we did not mention the fact,—Bishop Jewel.[60] Parties impeached ought always to have every possible advantage given them, and, if testimonies to character can possibly avail in what is a question of fact, Bishop Jewel certainly should have the benefit of a witness so very different in mind and temper from himself. And we have another reason for citing Mr. Davison's testimonial; it is drawn up in such very choice and significant language, that, even were we disposed to be unfair, we should not have the heart to pass over what is as pregnant in meaning as beautiful in expression:

"Had all the serious and learned divines of our Church to give their voice in favour of the one man whom they would hold forth as the greatest light of the Reformation,—as the person whose mind had most fully comprehended and laboured upon the whole compass of reformed truth, and whose writings do still preserve

---

[58] *Newton*: See above Essay XI, p.122ff.

[59] *Hurd*: See note on p.[126].

[60] *Bishop Jewel*: See note on p.[51].

John Davison,

the most highly sanctioned memorial of it,—we know not whether they would name any other than him, who, having received from the great fathers of the Reformation the office of unfolding, complete in all its parts, that truth which they with their faithful voices had proclaimed among us, first reduced and recorded our whole national creed with its illustration and evidence, Bishop Jewel. He, with a more leisurely survey of the bearing of every doctrine than could be taken even by the leading reformers themselves, who, in the first effort and agony of their work, with rude and noble simplicity, threw down the fabric of error, and hewed the granite from the quarry, and brought it for the building, he, coming in the close of their labours, executed and perfected all that they had prepared or done, as much as any one man can be said to have done it. To the theological inquirer he is a master-builder of the system of our doctrine. His formal and deliberate judgment, therefore, is of the greatest value."—Pp. 300, 301.

Presently he adds, that Jewel's Defence of his Apology "may be reckoned perhaps the most accurately digested system of reformed doctrine, as far as it goes, the most scrupulously and deliberately worded, which our Church produced in its debate with the Church of Rome."—P. 312.

What makes this testimony of the greater value is, that Mr. Davison, in spite of his reverent and admiring temper, is not indiscriminate in his praise. He has his antipathies and dislikes; and it will serve to give some further notions of his theological system, on which we have imperceptibly fallen, to state who are the objects of them. This will be pretty evident by two or three clauses or expressions from his various works. Lightfoot,[61] he says, "is one of the last writers to deserve our confidence, either for his perspicuity

[61] *Lightfoot*: John Lightfoot (1602-75), Anglican divine and biblical scholar, expert in Hebrew; a prolific author, he is best remembered for his multi-volume *Horæ Hebraicæ et Talmudicæ*.

[405]

as a scholar, or his justness of thinking as a divine" (p. 60); though he owns him (p. 62) as a "really learned and good man." Speaking of Bochart,[62] he says, "Here is a person, a prodigy of learning," yet "setting the example of" a "licentious theology" (p. 144). He speaks of "the rash positions of Clopperburch,[63] Heidegger,[64] and Witzius"[65] (p. 96); and of certain "superficial ideas of Witzius," whom he calls a "foreign divine." He speaks of some arguments of Carpzov[66] and Leidekker,[67] as "planè inepta et futilia"[68] (p. 111, note); is disrespectful towards Buddeus[69] (p. 128); considers certain representations of Warburton as "most unsatisfactory or erroneous" (p. 151), and observes that that writer "had no dislike of bold ingenuity, not free from paradox" (p. 152). Although he speaks respectfully of the continental Reformers, he says, "We do not require any foreign aid, either to ascertain or uphold our own belief" (p. 317), and refuses "to accept them as arbiters or witnesses in our own doctrine" (p. 318). He speaks of Beccaria,[70]

[406]

---

[62] *Bochart*: Samuel Bochart (1599-1667), French Protestant biblical scholar; best known for his *Hierozoicon sive bipartitum opus de animalibus sacrae scripturae* (1663) on animals in the Bible.

[63] *Clopperburch*: Johann Clopperburch (1592-1652) Dutch Calvinist theologian.

[64] *Heidegger*: Johann Heinrich Heidegger (1633-98) Swiss Calvinist theologian; not to be confused with Martin Heidegger, his more famous twentieth century philosopher namesake.

[65] *Witzius*: Hermann Witsius or Wits (1636–1708), Dutch Calvinist theologian.

[66] *Carpzov*: Johann Gottlob Carpzov (1679-1767) German Old Testament scholar, Professor of Oriental Languages at Leipzig (1719-1730).

[67] *Leidekker*: Melchior Leidekker (1642-1721), Dutch Calvinistic theologian and Professor at Utrecht, best known for his historical/archaeological treatise, *De Republica Hebraeoarum* (1704).

[68] *planè inepta et futilia*: plainly inept and useless things

[69] *Buddeus*: Johann Franz Buddeus (1667-1729), German Lutheran theologian and Professor of Moral Philosophy at Halle.

[70] *Beccaria*: Cesa Benesana-Beccaria (1738-94), Marquis of Gualdrasco and Villareggio, philosopher and critic of capital punishment.

Voltaire, and the Empress Catherine[71] as "all foreigners," and adds, "perhaps there is a vulgar taste in many of our speculators at home to admire the wisdom of other countries, as we do their fashions" (p. 486).

Considering the hereditary and habitual opinions of his day, it is not wonderful that he does not look upon the Fathers as the spokesmen and witnesses of a far more pure and religious age than our own; yet it is remarkable, still, how different his tone is concerning them from that of most of his contemporaries. Speaking of an opinion on the Origin of Sacrifice in "modern theology," which contradicted theirs, he says:

"This, at the best, is a cheerless and unsatisfactory state of the controversy. For, although the Fathers of the Church are neither to be reckoned infallible, nor free from serious error, yet it is a mortification to our charity, in our communion with them, to find that any important opinion which they have taught shall be deemed to be at variance with the foundations of our faith. One would wish to think there might be piety and safety in their error; although, if we have been blessed in later times with some superior light, there can be no reason for us to retain their mistakes, but only to spare their honour and memory. But when the primitive Fathers took their impression from the Scripture history, concerning the first appointment of Sacrifice, I believe that they derived it by reading, in this instance, with a candour and ingenuousness of mind, which we should do well to imitate."—P. 128.

[407]

The writer of the Preface informs us that Mr. Davison, after he had completed his Origin of Sacrifice, entertained

---

[71] *Voltaire and the Empress Catherine*: François-Marie Arouet (1694-1778), best known by his *nom de plume* Voltaire, was a philosopher and writer of the French Enlightenment. He was an ardent admirer and correspondent of the Empress Catherine the Great of Russia (1729-96).

an intention of editing a selection from the writings of the early Church, with a view, as he expressed it, of "introducing the study of the Fathers a little, and blending old and new divinity together."—P. x. He also observes, with reference to the additional notes which he now publishes of Mr. Davison's upon that work, that "many of them are references to the Fathers, to the study of whose works he found himself drawn more and more in the later years of his theological reading."—P. xiii.

8.

It has been suggested above, that Mr. Davison is rather a teacher of *principles* than of *doctrines*. This might be illustrated at some length from his separate publications; the Essay on Baptismal Regeneration is of course doctrinal, but, with this exception, nearly every one of them, as it comes, has its own philosophical principle or view which it undertakes to maintain. Thus, in the Essay on Sacrifice, we are taught with great force of reasoning the acceptableness of "will worship," or spontaneous piety, the real obligation and character of Natural Religion, and the mistake of "asking a revelation for every duty of religion," which, he adds, "has been actively employed in the Christian Church, to its misfortune and disturbance, ever since the Reformation," and "has been the master-engine of the Puritan system."—P. 95. In his Assize Sermon he considers "this principle laid down by the Apostle, that lawful power for the administration of justice is not less than the minister of God."—P. 183. In his Sermon before the Corporation of [408] the Trinity House,[72] he lays down the maxim, that "the union of religion with all our graver concerns is in a manner the main, I had almost said the only, work of our lives here." "And," he proceeds, "to point out the consistency of the one with the other, and the strict relation they bear to each other, may be useful to their joint interests. It is a vain faith and piety which does not penetrate the concerns of life."—P. 210. In his National School Sermon (which embraces most important subjects, and in which he was the first distinctly and boldly to lay down positions, at the time almost paradoxes, but now happily taken for granted among religious people), he says that "education will never produce virtue by precepts repeated and truths inculcated," that "the power of reading, or the use of it, makes no man either wise or virtuous,"[73] and that "no mechanism as yet has invented the wheel to make a nation brave, united, or happy." In his review of Mr. Edgeworth's work, he insists that "the professional character is not the only one which a person engaged in a profession has to support" (p. 424), and "that certain studies improve the judgment and others do not" (p. 434). In his remarks on our criminal law, he discusses the true principles of punishment, capital punishment, the expedience of discretionary power, and the like. And his Dialogue between a Christian and a Reformer lays down the duty of religious fear, as of the essence of all true religion.

---

[72] *Corporation of Trinity House*: the body that provides buoys and lighthouses around the coast, licensed by Henry VIII in 1514

[73] *"the power of reading ... "*: This was a key part of Newman's own educational philosophy, as argued in the *Tamworth Reading Room* articles which he had written the previous year (1841) and would develop fully in his Dublin university lectures of 1852 later republished in *The Idea of a University.*

Doctrines are the limits or issues of principles, and if the principles be religious, they do legitimately and naturally lead to revealed doctrines, where such revelation is made. It was Mr. Davison's unhappiness to live at a time when Christian doctrine was under a partial eclipse, and hence his [409] principles are far more Catholic, or, we will rather say, positive and defined, than his dogmatic statements. His principles and their definiteness are his own; his doctrines, or rather their indistinctness, is the peculiarity of his age. Thus, to take one instance, in his Assize Sermon some excellent remarks occur on the necessity which exists, that the principles of morals and religion should be externally recommended to the individual, as a memento and protection to him, by public positive institutions; and he says, and truly, that the law of the land fulfils this office; but still, it is observable, he keeps a profound silence about the Institution, directly divine, which has been far more highly honoured and favoured than any national law, and which is the true realization of the principle under review.

What a most serious witness is it against an age, when so deep and reverential a writer, giving utterance to its meditations in the heart of the most religious University in the world, does not recognize the Church Catholic as an authoritative instrument of teaching, warning, impressing, fortifying the minds of a Christian people; but speaks as he does, of the human law as "their most certain instruction," as their earliest guardian, as furnishing them at least "with *some* stock of ideas for duty," as "their plainest rule of action;" nay, as if the Mother of Saints were dead or banished, a thing of past times or other countries, actually applies to the law of the land language which *she* had introduced, figures of which *she* exemplified the reality, and speaks of the law as "laying crime *under the interdict* and infamy of a public condemnation"!

Men cannot at their will change the state of things; it would have been unreal in Mr. Davison to have spoken otherwise. Had he said that the law was *not* the most authoritative teacher in the country, but that the Church had the higher authority and the more urgent influence, he would have said the thing that was not. Had he enlarged on the prerogatives of the Church, he would have been set down as a theorist or a papist for his pains. He was quite bold enough in publishing his Remarks on Education; and we know an instance of a young clergyman, not very long afterwards,—one of the many who are indebted to his writings,—preaching a Sermon for some schools near London, in which he innocently ventured to repeat some of the sentiments of Mr. Davison's own discourse, and encountering thereupon the extreme surprise and disgust of his principal hearers, who hardly would speak to him when they met in vestry to count the collection, and who pronounced his composition to be "truly a charity sermon, for it required great charity to sit it out." This was, at that day, the award of opinions which now are taken as first principles within the Church, which circulate as free as air, and which the stars of the season go about spouting, with great satisfaction, at all meetings, and in any episcopal chapel, secure of the risk of any *ism* whatever being affixed to their names in consequence. But, if such was the strangeness of opposing Campbell the poet[74] and my Lord

[410]

---

[74] *Campbell*: Thomas Campbell (1777-1844), Scottish poet.

Brougham[75] in the year 1827, how great would have been the extravagance, the wildness, the inanity, in 1817, of speaking, in the pulpit of St. Mary's, of the Rule and the Majesty and the Jurisdiction and the Sanctions of Holy Church? We know the fate of St. Paul at Areopagus,[76] and without forgetting the venerated names of Van Mildert[77] and others, then in authority, we suspect they would have been as quite alive as others, though more indulgent, to so unseasonable and abrupt an exhibition of the pearls of the Gospel.

9. [411]

There is another quality akin to reverence in Mr. Davison, which makes it unsafe to accept his words in their very letter; and that is his extreme courteousness and consideration towards those for or to whom he is writing. He adopts somewhat of the tone of St. Paul on the occasion just referred to, or before Festus and Agrippa,[78] and takes their part or their side as much as ever he can, sometimes, perhaps, a little too much. It should be recollected, for instance, that the panegyric on the Law of the land to which we have referred, was preached before the Judges; one is only tempted to regret that he had not sometimes the Church herself to preach before, as well as the Queen's representatives. The same tendency is conspicuous in his

---

[75] *Lord Brougham*: Henry Brougham (1778-1868), 1st Baron Brougham and Vaux, prominent Liberal statesman; Newman critiqued his utilitarian and secular educational philosophy in *The Tamworth Reading Room* and *The Idea of a University*.

[76] *St. Paul at Areopagus*: Cf. Acts 17:19ff. Paul was scorned by the Athenian philosophers when he preached about the Resurrection.

[77] *Van Mildert*: William Van Mildert (1765–1836), Anglican divine, Bishop of Durham; one of the founders of Durham University; known for his forthright expression of his views.

[78] *before Festus and Agrippa*: Cf. Acts 25:8; 26:2ff.

praise of Warburton, in the passage from his Warburtonian Lectures above quoted; a very different view of that bold writer being given us in his Origin of Sacrifice. On such occasions we could even suspect our revered author of indulging in a little amiable rhetoric. Surely it is not unnatural to suppose that the extreme *goût*[79] with which he sets about the production of Jewel's evidence, arises from the circumstance of its telling so completely on the side of the high Church.

One other instance shall be given of this peculiarity of Mr. Davison's manner; and, since it is very tame to carry a critique to an end without some spice of criticism, we shall take the opportunity of raising a small quarrel with him upon it, even were it only to show that we have views of our own, and then we shall take our leave of him and his writings.

[412] Mr. Davison, then, in his Sermon at Deptford, is led to praise Societies for public objects generally, and that of the Trinity House in particular. We cannot of course quarrel with such a judgment, because, as any one will admit, there is, to say the least, a great deal of truth in it. But what we think ungracious and hard is, that, by way of heightening his eulogy, the author contrasts the Societies of this day with a certain Institution of times past, as if the latter just did *not* contemplate, and did *not* do, what present Societies both contemplate and do; whereas it both contemplated and it did what existing Societies, even if they all contemplate, certainly often fail to do, and fully exemplified all those benefits which Mr. Davison justly attributes to the principle of combination itself,—we mean the Monastic Rule. Let our

---

[79] goût: taste

complaint be clearly apprehended; Mr. Davison does not merely contrast Monastic with Protestant and other Societies of this day, as if, whereas they both had the same general end, the former failed in what the latter succeeded in effecting; but, what seems to us paradoxical, he denies that the monastic principle *is* gregarious, co-operative, industrious, practical, and productive. This seems to be contrary to well-known historical fact. His words are these:

"[The Gospel] is full and positive in requisitions applying to the distributive welfare of society; insomuch that it may be reckoned *one of the most evident perversions* of religious doctrine, which in an age of darkness exalted the *secluded exercise of a monastic virtue* as the perfection of a Christian spirit. Read but the discourses of our Saviour, or His parables, or read a page of His apostles, and you will see they all imply, that the persons to whom they are addressed are engaged in the active and mixed duties; and were they not so engaged, that those discourses and writings might in great measure have been spared. The matter contained in them would have nothing to attach upon; it would be addressed to beings not in the state which the instruction supposes, and would be instructing them in sentiments and offices which their actual occupation did not need."—Pp. 206, 207.

Now it is difficult to do justice to the various thoughts to [413] which this representation gives rise. First of all, is it not a violence to history to speak of "monastic virtue" as "secluded," in the sense here intended, viz., as not "engaged in the active and mixed duties"? Would our author say that a *family* was secluded from social relations and occupations? would he speak of "the secluded exercise of a *domestic* virtue"? for what is a monastery but a family? and in what sense is it secluded, in which the greater part of the world is not secluded already? How was a nun more secluded from active duties in her cloister, who had her duties found for her, than most single women of small means and few acquaintances, who have no duties at all, are secluded now? The difference is, that the one may walk about as she will, may speak to whom she will, may dress as she will, may read what she will, may visit about if she will, and may do nothing if she will; and does the exercise of "the active and mixed duties" so depend upon this liberty, that not to have this liberty is to be cut off from that exercise altogether? Would our author go the length of saying that it is a duty for every young woman to marry, lest she should incur the "perversion" of a dark age?

Supposing a monastic life were nothing else than seclusion in the cloister, would it in consequence have no trials and duties? Is there not trial, duty, self-denial, of many kinds in a family? Is it not as difficult, as it is "good and joyful, for brethren to dwell together in unity"?[80] Is there not much exercise of temper, much call on a placable, unselfish, patient, forbearing, cheerful disposition, much occasion for self-control in word and in deed, in family life? How is it then to the purpose, true though it be, as Mr. Davison says, that "meekness, forgiveness of injuries, humility, preference of each other in honour, would have no room to be practised, if every man, as he is a Christian, were to be shut up in solitude in a sphere of his own"? It is true that "the meek and chastened spirit, which is the sum of these duties, could neither be tried nor acquired, were the collision and intercourse of other men's feelings and interests so studiously avoided, as that we should have nothing to

[414]

---

[80] *"good and joyful, for brethren to dwell together in unity"*: Psalm 133:1

conceal, nothing to forgive, nothing to forbear" (p. 207); but what a pretty sort of a monk is he who has a will of his own, and is *not* meek, *not* self-abasing, *not* forgiving? *Obedience* is one of the three special characteristics of the monastic life, as its professed instance in our Great Exemplar is that of his "going down to Nazareth and being *subject* to his parents;"[81] had He no opportunity of meekness and humility till He was thirty, and began to preach?

We have said this as contemplating a monastic life in its essence, and when viewed at the least advantage. But commonly it has been united or rather devoted to employments, directly productive of the graces specified; or, again, of a directly beneficial and useful nature. Mr. Davison says that—"the whole of the active part of a Christian charity manifestly derives its very being from a participation in the concerns of our fellow-creatures. Bountifulness, beneficence, personal kindness, personal service, are only so many other modes of expression for a manner of living with others, and living for them. They are wholly relative in their feeling and their practice; and the same divine authority which enjoins them, places us in that busy and peopled world which gives them their proximate motive and their opportunity of action. In short, the very love of our neighbour, which is the second great commandment, must fall to the ground, unless we keep a [415] station of intercourse with him, and make him the better for our existence; and even the first commandment, the love of God, is made to have its evidence and its perfect work in the fulfilment of the second."—P. 207.

---

[81] *"going down to Nazareth and being subject to his parents"*: Cf. Luke 2:51

John Davison,

Most accurate and important sentiments surely; but in order to show how a monastic life is not destructive, but rather is the great fulfilment of both the first and the second commandment of the law, it is only necessary to take up any work such as Alban Butler's[82], in which a hundred instances will be found of active and self-denying charity, in men and women bound by the monastic vows. The service of hospitals is one out of various religious objects and active labours with which the religious life has ever been connected. Schools, whether for high or low, are another; orphan-houses are another; literary or theological pursuits another. Again, from the first the monastic bodies have been an instrument in the hands of Providence for the maintenance of orthodoxy; the sons of St. Antony[83] were the champions and the refuge of St. Athanasius.[84] All the great Fathers and Bishops of the Church were monks; yet who was more busy in the crowd of men than Chrysostom?[85] who has been so influential in theology as Augustine?[86] who such revivers of religion as Gregory[87] and Basil?[88] who is more fruitful in practical lessons than Pope Gregory?[89] who so large and so minute and exact in thought as St. Thomas?[90] Even in those times when monastic bodies seemed to do least, and when the sloth and corruption of some brought

---

[82] *Alban Butler:* (1710–73), English Catholic priest; his life's work was *The Lives of the Fathers, Martyrs and Other Principal Saints* (4 volumes, 1756-59).

[83] *St. Antony:* (c.251-356), Abbot. He lived a solitary ascetic life in the desert where others also drawn to the eremitical life gathered round him. His monks were subsequently zealous upholders of orthodoxy against Arianism.

[84] *St. Athanasius:* See note on p.[52].

[85] *Chrysostom:* See note on p.[62].

[86] *Augustine:* See note on p.[21].

[87] *Gregory:* presumably St. Gregory Nazianzen. See note on p.[42].

[88] *Basil:* See note on p.[60].

[89] *Pope Gregory:* See note on p.[37].

[90] *St. Thomas:* Aquinas (1225-74), Dominican friar and Doctor of the Church, the great mediaeval theologian and philosopher.

disgrace upon all, they were, as we all know, the preservers of ancient literature; and let any one reflect what the state of our historical and doctrinal knowledge would be now, were it not for those whom we are tempted to accuse as "fruges consumere nati."[91] And as regards the other sex, so far from [416] making women idle and profitless, it is the only institution which hitherto has been able to give dignity, and, as it were, rank to female celibacy, and to secure an honourable and useful application of it. How great a number of women in this Protestant land spend their lives in doing nothing! how much labour, to use secular language, is lost to the community! what numbers are led to throw themselves and their happiness away on husbands unworthy of them, because, when they would fain not be useless in their day, marriage is the only path open to their ambition!

Mr. Davison speaks forcibly and well of the divine wisdom of the Gospel in "reducing the matter of duty to some *plain specific exercise*, some *direct and substantial* instance of application" (p. 209); now is not this one special object of the monastic rule, to give a definite penance to those who would repent, definite duties to those who would grow in love, definite safeguards to those who are under temptation, definite objects to those who have high but vague aspirations? Again, he says, that "when that object is really a good and praiseworthy one," Societies for the furtherance of objects of public utility are like *main works and fortresses* in the map of life against the evils and deficiencies which lie around it" (p. 211); but why are the

---

[91] *"fruges consumere nati."*: "born to consume the fruits of the earth", Horace, Epistles 1, II, 31.

learned Benedictines, or the Order of the Trinity[92] for the redemption of captives, to be exempted from this eulogy? We can enter into, though we disown, the opinion or prejudice that the monastic rule does more harm than good, nay, is to be condemned as pure evil; but we do not know what is meant by the statement, as an historical fact, that it has been destructive of the action and influence of man on man. If retirement and secresy are incompatible with [417] usefulness, what becomes of the remarks on Mr. Davison's own history with which we commenced? Was his life at Oriel College a more public one than that of St. Jerome at Bethlehem,[93] or St. Anselm at Bec?[94] Again, it is in Societies for public objects, says our author, "that the better feelings of our kind, being trained and brought forward, look abroad for *connection and co-operation*; that men *attract one another to a common cause*; and their union becomes *safe* and *useful* under the auspices of *responsible personal character*, and with the sanction of an *acknowledged public confidence*" (p. 211). And in a passage already quoted, "Such institutions give a *fixed point* and *a tone*, as well as a system, to the purpose which they adopt." But it would be as tedious, as it is, we think, a needless work, to show in all its details, that the wise and philosophical remarks he has made upon the principle of combination for public objects, do in a special and singular way find their fulfilment and

---

[92] *Order of the Trinity*: Order of the Most Holy Trinity and of the Captives, or Trinitarians, founded by St John de Matha at the end of twelfth century. One of its original aims was the ransom of Christian captives held by Muslims.

[93] *St. Jerome*: See note on p.[41].

[94] *St. Anselm*: (c.1033-1109) Benedictine monk at the abbey of Bec and later Archbishop of Canterbury; a philosopher and theologian, he was the author of many works, the most celebrated of which is his *Cur Deus Homo* on the Incarnation.

exemplification in that holy and ancient discipline which he opens them by disparaging.

But there is one sentiment of his which surprises us more than any other, viz., that monachism is inconsistent with our Lord's precepts, which literally have no subjects, no drift, if it is to be allowed. Now let us take the monastic rule, not as practised by those who lived in community, but even as carried out into its extreme by hermits, anchorites, fathers of the desert, and the like: are there no commands, as, for instance, concerning poverty and humility, which, taken in their first and obvious meaning, such a life literally and strikingly fulfils? We are not at all saying or dreaming, of course not, that all our Lord's precepts must be taken in the letter, yet it is better to observe them in the letter, than not to observe them at all. Now it is pretty clear that society, as at present constituted, does not keep the commands in question either in letter or spirit; also it seems to us clear, that whether a literal observance of them be necessary or not, monastic institutions do, of all others, most accurately and comprehensively fulfil the *code* of Gospel commandments, whether those which the present age does not fulfil, or those which it does. Indeed there cannot be a doubt who they are, and where they are to be found, who give us instances of obedience to the precept of "not resisting evil;"[95] of "turning the cheek to the smiter;" of "selling that we have and giving alms;"[96] "of selling all that we have," in order to be "perfect;"[97] of having our "loins

[418]

---

[95] *"not resisting evil" … "turning the cheek to the smiter"*: Matthew 5:39
[96] *"selling that we have and giving alms"*: Luke 12:33
[97] *in order to be "perfect"*: Matthew 19:21

girded about and lights burning;"[98] of "watching and praying always;"[99] of "taking no thought for the morrow;"[100] of "taking up the cross daily;"[101] and a number of other particulars which might be mentioned. And if, as we have already been urging, monastic bodies are on the other hand far from neglecting those social duties which Mr. Davison truly says have so essential a portion and so exalted a place in Christian obedience, then it will follow that they fulfil more of our Lord's precepts than any other set of men, and instead of being "one of the most violent perversions of religious doctrines," they are the nearest approach to the perfection of a Christian spirit.

Nor is even the eremitical rule itself, nor surely (much less) are associations for the main purpose of prayer and intercession, incapable of justification or excuse. Mr. Davison excepts all associations which are for the good of the community; and considering that Christianity has made the offering of praise and prayer its especial "Liturgy," or public service, it is surely a want of faith to deny that those above all men may be benefactors to their brethren, who [419] spend their lives in devotional exercises. Moreover, it should be recollected that there is no one, to speak in general terms, but is the better for occasional retreats from the world; and the more active and useful is a man's life, the greater is his need of them. But the occasional retirement of the many requires the livelong retirement of the few, and an establishment of recluses is but the sanctuary of the uncloistered. To be shut out from the world is their very

---

[98] *"loins girded about and lights burning"*: Luke 12:35
[99] *"watching and praying always"*: Luke 21:36
[100] *"taking no thought for the morrow"*: Matthew 6:34
[101] *"taking up the cross daily"*: Luke 9:23

duty to the world; to be in leisure is their business; and as well might we call a schoolmaster inactive, or a private circle anti-social, as an institution which devotes itself to repentance, intercession, and giving of thanks, for the benefit of seculars,—as a propitiation in the sight of heaven, and a witness and warning before men,—as the home of the helpless, and the refuge of the downcast,—as a common mould of character, and a bond of mutual love, and a principle of united worship to all, because it is successively the school and confessional of each.

And, lastly, if objectors point to the well-known history of St. Simeon Stylites[102] as an instance of that "secluded exercise of a monastic virtue in an age of darkness," to which Mr. Davison must be referring, we remind such persons that Theodoret,[103] an author for whom he entertained a special respect, informs us, on his own knowledge, that this mystical religionist converted, by means of his pillar, "many myriads" of pagans, which is good work for any man's lifetime, and more than they are likely to do by their own rational religion, one and all of them together.

On the whole, then, we look upon the sentiment of Mr. Davison, on which we have been thus freely commenting, as only another instance, in addition to those which we have mentioned, in which a great mind was unconsciously swayed by deference to the opinions among which he lived, [420] and which, for what we know, could not have been rejected by him, in his particular place and time, without some

---

[102] *St Simon Stylites*: or Simeon Stylites (c.390-459), the first of the pillar (*stulos*) ascetics at Telanissos, between Antioch and Aleppo. The pillar on which he lived was progressively raised from ten to sixty-seven feet.
[103] *Theodoret*: (393-457), monk and later Bishop of Cyrrhus; author of many works, including a Life of St. Simeon Stylites who has his contemporary.

portion of irreverence, love of paradox, or self-confidence, most foreign to his character. There are ten thousand questions, whether of fact or of opinion, on which every one of us must be content to remain without any view of his own, and must take the current notions of his day, unless he would incur the certainty of being unreal and the risk of being untrue. Mr. Davison probably as little thought of analyzing the popular sentiments of which he was the spokesman, as of looking out for "death in the pot" at his meals, or suspecting arsenic in his candles. It is the trial and mystery of our position in this age and country, that a religious mind is continually set at variance with itself, that its deference to what is without contradicts its suggestions from within, and that it cannot follow what it presages without rebelling against what it has received.

April, 1842.

XVI[1]

JOHN KEBLE

1.

IN venturing some remarks on the poems just now published at Oxford under the title of the Lyra Innocentium, it is far from our intention to adopt the tone of controversialists, or even of critics. The name of their author would hinder us from so doing. That they are really Mr. Keble's,[2] we make no question, though we are not told so in the title-page. There are few of them which do not bear clear marks of their relationship to those in the Christian Year[3] and the Lyra Apostolica,[4] which are so familiar to our memories and our hearts; and, that (unlike the Lyra Apostolica,) they have all one and the same parentage, is evident, on the principle that *exceptio probat regulam*,[5] from the circumstance that one of them, and one only, is ascribed, in a note appended to it, to another person. One or two there are which are somewhat different from the

---

[1] *XVI*: incorrectly numbered XV in some editions
[2] *Mr Keble*: John Keble (1792-1866), churchman, Professor of Poetry at Oxford and founding father of the Oxford Movement.
[3] *Christian Year*: a highly popular book of poems for Sundays and feast days, first published in 1827.
[4] *Lyra Apostolica*: a further volume of poetry published in 1836.
[5] *exceptio probat regulam*: the exception proves the rule

rest in style; and there are metres introduced which do not occur in the Christian Year; the matter too is not so condensed, nor the thoughts so recondite; but such varieties are found in the separate works of every author,—time, place, age, frame of mind, subject, circumstances, giving to [422] each its distinctive character. The Christian Year was published in 1827; the Lyra Apostolica (as far as it is Mr. Keble's) is the Christian Year of 1833; the Lyra Innocentium is the Christian Year of 1846. The circumstances of 1827 and 1846 differ from each other more than the character of the two Volumes which belong to those respective dates.

We have not the analytical powers which would warrant us to attempt a critical estimate of the poems contained in the Volume before us; and we have not quite the heartless officiousness to view them in a controversial aspect. If they have a special characteristic, it is that they are not controversial, in this respect differing from other poems which other writers of his school have given to the world, and he at other times. Whether we look into the Lyra Apostolica, or into the Cathedral and Baptistery, loyalty to the Anglican Church is here or there enforced or insinuated by attacks on the See of Rome and the Catholic Church; some few traces of this peculiarity are found even in the Christian Year. But the Lyra Innocentium preserves an emphatic silence on the subject of other Churches. It will teach the happy children who are submitted to its influence, at least by implication, that there is no contrariety, no separation between the different portions of Christendom; that Christianity is everywhere the same, the religion of peace and truth, with one and the same great daily rite, one and the same profession of faith. Catholics, at least, are not called upon to find fault with such a representation.

Nor do we find in this Volume any strong language against those who have recently left the Anglican Church, as is the manner with the periodicals and pamphlets which express the sentiments of the party with which the author's name is connected. That he seriously disapproves of their step, is evident even from the fact that he does not take it himself; for such a step is either a duty or a sin; nay, he distinctly records his feeling on the subject; at the same time he records it without bitterness, violence, or injustice towards the persons concerned. In his introductory stanzas "To all friendly readers," he desires their prayers [423]

> "that he
> A true and timely word may frame
>   For weary hearts that long to see
> Their way in our dim twilight-hour:
>   His lips so purged with penance-fire,
> That he may guide them, in Christ's power,
>   Along the path of their desire;
>
> "And with no faint and erring voice
>   May to the wanderer whisper, 'Stay:
> God chooses for thee: seal His choice,
>   Nor from thy Mother's shadow stray.'"

It will be observed that he here recognizes himself distinctly as "guiding" others, and that "with no faint nor erring voice." And in another place he seems to compare those who "mistrust their elders" and leave the Anglican Church, to St. Thomas, who would himself see, before he believed the Resurrection; a kind comparison, because St.

Thomas was an Apostle notwithstanding, but still of a very decided meaning. The poem is on the general subject of wilfulness and "worldly wisdom," in refusing to "see with others' eyes;" it ends thus:

> Alas that man his breath should lose
> In wayward, doubting race,
> Nor his still home in shelter choose
> *Where Thou hast set his place.*"—P. 109.

[424]

2.

Would that others had confined themselves to this—we will not say kind and gentle, but—*equitable* tone in their reproofs! we speak not of one person or another, but of the generality of those who have felt it a duty to animadvert on recent converts to the Catholic Church. We are not here crying for mercy, but asking justice, demanding common English fairness; we have a right to expect, but we do not find, that considerate, compassionate, comprehensive judgment upon their conduct, which, instead of fixing on particular isolated points in it, views it as a whole,—uses the good, which is its general character, to hide its incidental faults, makes one part explain another, what is strong here excuse what is weak there, and evident sincerity of intention atone for infirmity of performance;—which has a regard to circumstances, to the trial of an almost necessary excitement, to the necessity of acting beyond criticism, yet without precedent, and of reaching a certain object when all paths to it have respectively their own difficulties. We are not apologizing for their great and momentous decision itself, but for the peculiarities which have accompanied its execution; if to do as much as this be considered after all asking for mercy, not for equity, it is only such mercy, to say the least, as the parties censuring, as well as the parties censured, will require themselves on a day to come. In the well-known words of the poet—

> "In the course of justice, none of us
> Should see salvation; we do pray for mercy;
> And that same prayer doth teach us all to render
> The deeds of mercy." [6]

And we on our parts will show to these our good friends so much consideration, as to allow that at least they do not [425] pass their censures wantonly. We do not hold them justified in those censures, but we are able to enter into the reasons why they pass them. Such censures are necessary for their own position. When men of education, of good abilities, of blameless lives, make great sacrifices, give up their place in society, their friends, and their means of living, in order to join another communion, it is a strong argument, as far as any single argument is strong, for that communion's claim on the dutiful regard of Christians generally. And in the instances before us, the argument told with particular cogency on those persons, and they were not few, who were united to the converts by ties of friendship, kindred, or gratitude. It was impossible that such persons should not be moved by the example thus held out to them; and, this being the case, there was no saying how far its influence might spread. In consequence it became very necessary for those who had no doubts or difficulties to show to all who wavered or might waver, that there was something faulty in the mode in which the seceding parties had severally

---

[6] *"In the course of justice ... The deeds of mercy"*: Shakespeare, *The Merchant of Venice*, IV, I.

detached themselves from their original communion,—some fault such as to invalidate the testimony of each, and to destroy its logical and rhetorical force. It was a great point to be in a condition to say, that there was not any one of them who might not have acted better than he did; and, whereas by the fact of seceding they had shown no pity towards the Church of England, its doctors, or its living divines and prelates, there was no special call for any delicacy in dealing with them, and no reason against imputing motives to them or using personalities about them, freely and without scruple. If motives could not be plausibly conjectured, faulty tendencies at least were discoverable in their several characters; or hypothetical failings were assignable, as restlessness, or flightiness, such as would, if existing, account for their conduct by what Gibbon calls "human causes;"[7] or, if everything else failed, words might be cast at them, and they might be accused of "rationalism." Nay, since no man living is perfect, and such critical junctures bring out an individual mind, such as it is, into full play, develop its qualities and faculties, and magnify for the time, as by a lens, even its minutest peculiarities, and represent its faintest shades and colours, we may readily grant that never was there a case of conversion, except under the influence of extraordinary inspiration, which might not have proceeded more holily, more wisely, more religiously than it did—never a case which did not present an opportunity of criticism, to those who had the heart, or felt it a necessity, or thought it a duty, to criticise.

[426]

---

[7] *what Gibbon calls "human causes;"*: Gibbon, *History of the Decline and Fall of the Roman Empire*, Vol.I, Ch.XV, Part V: "As it is my intention to remark only such human causes as were permitted to second the influence of revelation … " Gibbon notoriously excluded any divine agency in his account of the early history of Christianity.

Such is the condition of all of us in this world. "Posuisti iniquitates nostras in conspectu tuo, sæculum nostrum in illuminatione vultus tui."[8] Good friends, you have not far to seek; *habetis confitentem reum*;[9] he pleads guilty; he has given up a fellowship or a living, or he has forfeited an inheritance, or ruined the prospects or present provision of wife and children, or damaged his reputation for judgment or discernment; he has cheerfully made himself a scoff, submitted himself as a prey to the newspapers, has made himself strange to his brethren; and besides and amid all this, it is true, he has said a strong word he had better not have said—or uttered a sarcasm—his successive disclosures have not severely kept time with the growth of the misgivings,—he has spoken to those with whom he should have been reserved, and has been silent where he should have spoken; at times he has not known where he stood, and perhaps promised what he could not perform. Of his sacrifices he thinks and says nothing; what he does know [427] and does painfully think of, is in substance just that which you so rhetorically urge against him, yes, and before you urge it. His self-scrutiny has preceded your dissection of him. What you proclaim to the world, he confesses without grudging, viz., that he has but acted *secundum captum suum*,[10] according to what he is, not as an Angel, but as a man. In the process of his conversion he has had to struggle with uncertainty of mind, with the duties of an actual

---

[8] *"Posuisti iniquitates nostras in conspectu tuo, saeculum nostrum in illuminatio vultus tui. "*: "Thou hast set our iniquities before thee, our secret sins in the light of thy countenance." Psalm 90:8

[9] habetis confitentem reum: a legal maxim meaning 'we have a confessing defendant'

[10] secundum captum suum: 'according to his capacity to comprehend'

position, with misgivings of its untenableness, with the perplexity of fulfilling many duties and of reconciling conflicting ones. He is not perfect; no one is perfect; not they who accuse him; he could retaliate upon them; he could gratuitously suggest reasons for their retaining their stations, as they can suggest reasons for his relinquishing his own; it is easy to impute motives; but it would be unworthy of him to do so. He leaves his critics to that Judgment to which he himself appeals. May they who have spoken or written harshly of recent converts to the Catholic Church, receive at the Great Day more lenient measure than they have in this case given!

3.

Returning to the Volume which has led to these remarks, we find the author's silence concerning the matters of the day still more emphatic than we have as yet described it. Not only is he entirely uncontroversial, as beseemed one who writes of "Christian Children, their ways and their privileges,"[11] but he abstains almost entirely from any allusion whatever to the existing state and prospects of the English Church. In this respect he is singularly in contrast with himself in the Christian Year, which, though written [428] for the personal edification of private Christians, abounds in sentiments about ecclesiastical matters, as they stood at the date of its composition. Those sentiments wear the character of forebodings, and those forebodings seem from the event and the present position of affairs to be almost prophetic. He wrote and published in a time of peace and plenty for his

---

[11] *"Christian Children, their ways and their privileges,"*: The full title of Keble's volume is *Lyra Innocentia: Thoughts on Christian Children, Their Ways and Their Privileges.*

Church, when Lord Liverpool's[12] government was in power, when Church patronage was dispensed more respectably than perhaps it ever had been, and when Church Reform had not showed itself even on paper. In those palmy days of the Establishment, our author discerned, that neither in doctrine nor in ethical standard was it even as much as it might have been according to its own principles, and as it had actually been from time to time in the persons of certain of its members. He thought he perceived in it, not merely corruption of life, but failure of faith, and judgment in the horizon. He described the world, which once attended our Lord in triumph into Jerusalem, as now

> "Thronging round to gaze
> On the dread vision of the latter days,
> Constrained to own Thee, but in heart
> Prepared to take Barabbas' part;
> 'Hosanna' now, tomorrow 'Crucify,'
> The changeful burden still of their rude lawless cry."

And then he asked:

> "But what are heaven's alarms to hearts that cower
> In wilful slumber, deepening every hour,
> That draw their curtains closer round,
> The nearer swells the trumpet's sound?"

He speaks of the "watchman true," as

> "Waiting to see what God will do,
> As o'er the Church the gathering twilight falls;"

and

---

[12] *Lord Liverpool*: Robert Banks Jenkinson (1770-1828), politician who became Lord Liverpool in 1809 and served as Prime Minister 1812-1827.

[429]

> "Contented in his darkling round,
> If only he be faithful found,
> When from the east the eternal morning moves."

He addresses the clergy in general in a similar strain

> "Think not of rest; though dreams be sweet,
> Start up, and ply your heavenward feet; …
> Till, when the shadows thickest fall,
> Ye hear your Master's midnight call."

And elsewhere,—

> "Is this a time for moonlight dreams
> Of love and home by mazy streams ...
> While souls are wandering far and wide,
> And curses swarm on every side?
> No—rather steel thy melting heart
> To act the martyr's steadfast part,
> To watch with firm, unshrinking eye,
> Thy darling visions as they die,
> Till all bright hopes and hues of day
> Have faded into twilight grey ... "

At another time, speaking of the English Church more directly, after commencing with "Stately thy walls and holy are thy prayers," he continues—

> "O mother dear,
> Wilt thou forgive thy son one boding sigh?
> Forgive, if round thy towers he walk in fear,
> And tell thy jewels o'er with jealous eye?"

And then he proceeds to apply to his Church Ezekiel's fearful Vision in the Temple. Elsewhere he speaks of

> "God's new Israel, sunk as low,
> Yet flourishing to sight as fair,
> As Sion in her height of pride."

And, to make one additional extract, speaking of Aaron's
sin in the matter of the golden calf, he asks,—

[430]

> "For what shall heal when holy water banes?
>> Or who may guide
>> O'er desert plains
> Thy loved yet sinful people wandering wide
>> If Aaron's heart unshrinking mould
>> An idol form of earthly gold? ...

And he intercedes for those

> "That nearest to Thine altar lie,
> Yet least of holy things descry."

4.

Such plaintive notes, "quales populeâ Philomela sub
umbra,"[13] have by this time altogether left the Poet's Lyre:
as far as we have observed, not a sound remains of them in
the present Volume. What is the meaning of this? is it that
singing-birds are silent when a storm is at hand, and that the
evil in his Church is too awful and imminent for verse?
Actual England is too sad to look upon. The Poet seems to
turn away from the sight; else, in his own words, would it
"bruise too sore his tender heart;" and he takes refuge in the
contemplation of that blessed time of life, in which alone
the Church is what God intended it, what Christ made it, the
time of infancy and childhood. He strikes the Lyra
Innocentium. He hangs over the first springs of divine
grace, and fills his water-pots with joy "ex fontibus

---

[13] *"quales populeâ Philomela sub umbra"*: The full passage is 'Qualis populea
moerens Philomela sub umbra Amissos queritur foetus ...' from Virgil, *Georgics*
IV: 'Just as the nightingale, mourning under the poplar's shade laments her stolen
chicks ...'

Salvatoris,"[14] before heresy, schism, ambition, worldliness, and cowardice have troubled the still depths. He would fain have the morning last till evening; he confesses it:

> "O sweet morning-dream, I pray,
>   Pass not with the matin-hour:
> Charm me:—heart and tongue allay,
>   Thoughts of gloom and eyes that lower.
> From the Fountain to the Shrine,
> Bear me on, thou trance divine;
> Faint not, fade not on my view,
> Till I wake and find thee true."—P. 11.

[431]

Thus he would live and die in a "trance" or "dream;" a dream, as he confesses it to be, since souls fall from their first innocence, as time goes on. And yet we cordially thank him for his "dream;" that is, we thank him for choosing a subject for his verse in which Catholics and he are at one,— a subject such, that Catholics can claim and use his poems as expressing their own mind, not merely imposing a higher and fuller sense on them, but taking them in that very sense in which he speaks. Whatever differences Catholics may have with Mr. Keble, they have none in the main doctrine and fact on which his Volume is written. If there be one point from which they are able to look with satisfaction on this bewildered land, it is as regards the state of its baptized infants. Those infants are, in their estimation, as good Catholics as themselves, or better. The Catholic Church is the very "Church of their baptism;" and the "Mother of their new birth;" they were baptized into nothing short of that Church: too soon indeed they pass into the hands of others, who detach them from their true Mother; but in their first

---

[14] *"ex fontibus Salvatoris"*: "from the wells of salvation", Isaiah 12: 3.

years, till they come to years of discretion, and commit acts which separate them from her, they are as fully and absolutely the children of the Catholic Church as if they were baptized by Catholics. They have Angels to guard them, and saints to intercede for them; they are lovely and pleasant in their lives, and blessed in their deaths. Thus the death of children in this Protestant country is attended by a consolation unspeakable; the dreadful controversy about the two communions does not touch them; they are recognized as innocents on all hands, and they have been taken away [432] from the evil to come. Bright, precious thought, though dimmed of late years with a shade of sadness, from the negligence and ignorance with which the sacred rite of baptism has been so often administered!

Well would it be for all men, could they always live the life they lived as infants, possessed of the privileges, not the responsibilities of regeneration. Our author, as we have said, especially feels it at the present time; and, leaving the Anglican Church to go on as it will, and to deny truth as it will, he hides from himself all that is national, local, schismatical, existing,—he withdraws his pleading eye and his warning voice from a generation which scorns him,—he leaves bishops and clergy, cathedral chapters and ecclesiastical judges, town mobs and country squires, to the tender mercies of history, in order to enjoy a blameless Donatism, to live in a church of children, to gaze on their looks and gestures, to encourage them in good, and to guard them from harm and sin.

Thus, in some beautiful stanzas he compares a child sleeping in his cradle, first to the infant Moses in his ark of bulrushes, then to our Lord Himself asleep in the vessel:

"Storms may rush in, and crimes and woes
　　Deform the quiet bower;
They may not mar the deep repose
　　Of that immortal flower.
Though only broken hearts be found,
　　To watch his cradle by,
No blight is on his slumbers sound,
　　No touch of harmful eye.

"So gently slumbered on the wave
　　The new-born seer of old,
Ordained the chosen tribes to save,
　　Nor dreamed how darkly rolled
The waters by his rushy brake,
　　Perchance even now defiled
With infants' blood for Israel's sake,
　　Blood of some priestly child.

＊　　　＊　　　＊

"Hail, chosen Type and Image true
　　Of Jesus on the sea!
In slumber, and in glory too,
　　Shadowed of old by thee.
Save that in calmness thou didst sleep,
　　The summer stream beside,
He on a wider, wilder deep,
　　Where boding night-winds sighed."—Pp. 33-34.

He inquires whether regenerate infants do not see their Saviour, and by their sudden transport on waking is reminded of the unborn Baptist at the Visitation:

"Oft as in sun-bright dawn
The infant lifts his eye, joying to find
　　The dusky veil of sleep undrawn,
And to the East gives welcome kind,

Or in the morning air
Waves high his little arm,
As though he read, engraven there,
His fontal name, Christ's saving charm.

*　　　*　　　*

"Still in love's steady gaze,
In joy's unbidden cry,
That holy Mother's glad amaze,
That infant's worship we descry."—P. 43.

To this intimate approach to the Saviour of all,
vouchsafed to children, he is led to attribute, in another
poem, the sort of understanding which exists between them
and the brute creation.

"Thou makest me jealous, infant dear, [434]
Why wilt thou waste thy precious smiles,
Thy beckonings blithe, and joyous wiles.
On bird or insect gliding near?
Why court the deaf and blind?
What is this wondrous sympathy,
That draws thee so, heart, ear, and eye,
Towards the inferior kind?

"We tempt thee much to look and sing—
Thy mimic notes are rather drawn
From feathered playmates on the lawn—
The quivering moth, or bee's soft wing,
Brushing the window pane,
Will reach thee in thy dreamy trance,
When nurse's skill for one bright glance
Hath toiled an hour in vain."—Pp. 49, 50.

Then he speaks of the "baying bloodhound" and the
"watch-dog stern," the "war-horse," nay, the "tiger's

whelp," "wild elephant and mountain bull," as well as "bounding lamb or lonely bird," as being in league with children, and thus is led on to his conclusion:

> "Ah, you have been in Jesus' arms,
> The holy fount hath you imbued
> With His all-healing kindly blood;
> And somewhat of His pastoral charms,
> And care for His lost sheep,
> Ye there have learned: in ordered tones
> Gently to soothe the lesser ones,
> And watch their noonday sleep."

In another poem he traces to the same intimacy with the Unseen the power of children over the wicked:

> "A little child's soft sleeping face
> The murderer's knife ere now hath stayed:
> The adulterer's eye, so foul and base,
> Is of a little child afraid.
> They cannot choose but fear,
> Since in that sign they feel God and good Angels near."

[435]   He continues:

> "Heaven in the depth and height is seen;
> On high among the stars, and low
> In deep clear waters: all between
> Is earth, and tastes of earth: even so
> The Almighty One draws near
> To strongest seraphs there, the weakest infants here."

And thus he accounts for cherubs being represented in churches under the form of infants:

> "O well and wisely wrought of old,
> Nor without guide be sure, who first
> Did cherub forms as infants mould,

> And lift them where the full deep burst
>   Of awful harmony
> Might need them most, to waft it onward to the sky;
>
> "Where best they may, in watch and ward,
>   Around the enthroned Saviour stand,
> May quell with sad and stern regard
>   Unruly eye and wavering hand,
>   May read the blessed dole
> Of saving knowledge round from many a holy scroll."
>
> Pp. 268-271.

While the above extracts sufficiently show Mr. Keble's deep reverence towards the state of infants, they do not always connect the holiness of that state with the rite of baptism. On the latter point, however, he is very earnest; and, if we might theorize on the subject, we should fancy that he was not quite pleased with the Platonic tone, as it may be called, of much of the poetry of the day, which extols indeed the divine blessedness of infancy, but in so unguarded or ignorant a manner as to forget the source of it, as if this divinity belonged to children in their own nature and original state, and not as new-made by baptism. There is a studious accuracy of the author on this point.

5. [436]

But now we come to notice a second peculiarity in these poems, which immediately follows from their main topic being such as we have described it to be. If the author is to sing of regenerate infants and their sinless blessedness, and is to view them in such lights as thence belong to them, to what is he necessarily brought back at once, but to the thought of our Lord in the first years of His earthly existence, when He was yet a little one in the arms and at the breast of His Blessed Mother? Hence the Virgin and Child is the special vision, as it may be called, which this truly evangelical poet has before him throughout his "Thoughts in Verse on Christian Children;" like "that holy painter" and evangelist, whom he himself speaks of,

> "Who with pen and pencil true
> Christ's own awful mother drew."—P. 98.

He even introduces the thought of her, where there are neither children to suggest it, nor Scripture texts to declare it. He observes that, at the first Whitsuntide, "all estates, all tribes of earth" were collected; "only sweet infancy seemed silent in the adoring earth." "Mothers and maidens" were there, "widows from Galilee," "Levites," and "elders sage." He continues:

> "But nought we read of that sweet age
> Which in His strong embrace He took,
> And sealed it safe, by word and look,
> From earth's foul dews, and withering airs of hell:
> The Pentecostal chant no infant warblings swell."—
>
> P. 343.

And he goes out of his way, as follows, to supply the imagined deficiency:

> "Nay, but *She* worships here,
> Whom still the Church in memory sees,
> (O thought to mothers dear!)
> Before her babe on bended knees,
> Or rapt with fond adoring eye,
> In her sweet nursing ministry.
> How in Christ's anthem fails the children's part,
> While Mary bears Him throned in her maternal heart?"

[437]

516

"that Mother undefiled," "Christ's awful Mother," "Mother of God;" "the spotless Mother, first of creatures." And Christ is "the dread Son of Mary," "Mary's child," "the awful Child on Mary's knee." Perhaps the author's most beautiful lines on this subject are those addressed to a child who had lost her mother, in which he applies to the child the words spoken by our Lord on the cross to St. John. He says that, though she has lost her natural mother, yet surely she now has the blessing of the Virgin's patronage, to whom she had already, on the birth of a younger sister, shown her devotion.

> "Thy vision (whoso chides, may blame
>   The instinctive reachings of the altar flame,)
>   Shows thee above, in yon ethereal air,
>   A holier Mother, rapt in more prevailing prayer.
>
> "Tis *she* to whom thy heart took flight
>   Of old in joyous hour,
>   When first a precious sister-spright
>   Came to thy nursery bower.
>   And thou with earnest tone didst say,
>   Mother, let Mary be her name, I pray,
>   For dearly do I love to think upon
>   That gracious Mother-Maid, nursing her Holy One."
>   P. 153.

The deep and tender devotion which this language discovers is no novelty with our author. No reader of the Christian Year can forget his "Ave Maria! Thou whose name *All but* adoring love may claim;" and we may even say that, judging from these poems, his devotional feeling has but become more decided, and has more firmly based itself in his reason, as life has advanced. Shall we observe,

[440] there is one thing we "desiderate" in this volume?—to use Mr. Froude's[15] word on a similar occasion. We do not discover one "Ave Maria" throughout it, though he has used that invocation in the above passage of the Christian Year. We cannot doubt it has been upon his lips; why, then, is it excluded from his book? Perhaps he feared to give scandal, or to cause distress or excitement, in the use of a form of words not sanctioned by his Church; the case was different at the date of the Christian Year, when it would pass for mere poetry. Moreover, in two of the passages above quoted the author studiously speaks of Mary as "bending to adore the Babe," and before her Babe "on bended knees." No Catholic can quarrel with such an image, which indeed is represented in some of the paintings of the great masters; but as introduced into these passages it is surely out of place, as if intended to give satisfaction to Protestants,—as more adapted for polemics than for devotional poetry, and savouring much of the evangelical school, which never allows the mention of one doctrine of religion without a recapitulation of all the rest, as if in our prayers and praises we must ever have an eye to controversy.

6.

Such a Volume as this is a clear evidence that what is sometimes called "the movement" in the Anglican Church is not at an end. We do not say that it is spreading,—or that it will obtain permanent footing in the communion in which it has originated,—or that it will or will not lead to a

---

[15] *Mr. Froude*: Hurrell Froude (1803-36), Anglican divine and Fellow of Oriel College; a leading figure in the early Oxford Movement and Newman's close friend. Newman edited his posthumous *Remains* which shocked his contemporaries with Froude's criticism of the Protestant Reformers and sympathy for the pre-Reformation Catholic Church.

reaction, and eventually protestantize—or again weaken—a religious body, to which, under favourable circumstances, it might have brought strength. We are not prophets; we do but profess to draw conclusions; and the above conclusion respecting "the movement" which these poems have [441] suggested, seems a very safe one. Nor can we venture on predicting the destiny of individuals who are connected with that movement; for them the gravest anxieties will naturally be felt by sensitive friends, lest they should be resisting a call, and risking their election.[16] Cases may be expected which will pierce to the heart those among ourselves who have to deal with them, or are led to witness them. We only mean to say, that more has still to come of the opinions, which have lately found such acceptance in the Church of England, because they are still alive within its pale. Our author has doubtless published the poems before us with the intention of calling people's minds off external and dangerous subjects and present perplexities, of leading them back to the memory of the years when they were young, innocent, and happy, and thus of persuading them calmly to repose under the shadow of the tree beneath which they were born.[17] He has published them at a critical time, and much will be expected of them by his friends. Much certainly came of the Christian Year: it was the most soothing, tranquillizing, subduing work of the day; if poems can be found to enliven in dejection, and to comfort in anxiety; to cool the over-sanguine, to refresh the weary, and

---

[16] *election*: salvation; Newman is implying that consciously rejecting the duty of conversion to Catholicism may be a mortal sin. He is trying to put pressure on Keble and others to follow him into the Catholic Church, but Keble remained an Anglican until his death.

[17] *repose under the tree* ... : i.e. remain Anglicans.

to awe the worldly; to instil resignation into the impatient, and calmness into the fearful and agitated—they are these.

> "Tale tuum carmen nobis, divine poeta,
> Quale, sopor fessis in gramine: quale per æstum
> Dulcis aquæ saliente sitim restinguere rivo."[18]

[442] Or like the Shepherd's pipe, in the Oriental Vision, of which we are told, that "the sound was exceedingly sweet, and wrought into a variety of tunes that were inexpressibly melodious and altogether different from anything I had ever heard. They put me in mind of those heavenly airs that are played to the departing souls of good men upon their first arrival in paradise, to wear out the impressions of the last agonies, and qualify them for the pleasures of that happy place. I drew near with that reverence which is due to a superior nature; and as my heart was entirely subdued by the captivating strains I had heard, I fell down at his feet and wept."[19]

Such was the gift of the author of the Christian Year, and he used it in attaching the minds of the rising generation to the Church of his predecessors, Ken[20] and Herbert.[21] He did that for the Church of England which none but a poet could do: he made it poetical. It is sometimes asked whether poets are not more commonly found external to the Church than among her children; and it would not surprise us to find the question answered in the affirmative. Poetry is the refuge of

---

[18] *Tale tuum carmen nobis* ... : From Virgil's Fifth *Eclogue* (45-47): 'So is thy song to me, poet divine,/As slumber on the grass to weary limbs,/Or to slake thirst from some sweet-bubbling rill/In summer's heat.'

[19] *... fell at his feet and wept."*: From Joseph Addison's (1672-1719) *The Vision of Mirza*.

[20] *Ken*: Thomas Ken (1637–1711), nonjuring bishop of Bath and Wells and hymn writer.

[21] *Herbert*: George Herbert (1593–1633), Anglican clergyman and poet.

those who have not the Catholic Church to flee to and repose upon, for the Church herself is the most sacred and august of poets. Poetry, as Mr. Keble lays it down in his University Lectures on the subject,[22] is a method of relieving the over-burdened mind; it is a channel through which emotion finds expression, and that a safe, regulated expression. Now what is the Catholic Church, viewed in her human aspect, but a discipline of the affections and passions? What are her ordinances and practices but the regulated expression of keen, or deep, or turbid feeling, and thus a "cleansing," as Aristotle would word it,[23] of the sick soul? She is the poet of her children; full of music to soothe the sad and control the wayward,—wonderful in story for the imagination of the romantic; rich in symbol and imagery, so that gentle and delicate feelings, which will not bear words, may in silence intimate their presence or [443] commune with themselves. Her very being is poetry; every psalm, every petition, every collect, every versicle, the cross, the mitre, the thurible, is a fulfilment of some dream of childhood, or aspiration of youth. Such poets as are born under her shadow, she takes into her service; she sets them to write hymns, or to compose chants, or to embellish shrines, or to determine ceremonies, or to marshal processions; nay, she can even make schoolmen of them, as she made St. Thomas,[24] till logic becomes poetical. Now the

---

[22] *his University Lectures on the subject*: Keble's lectures delivered during his time as Professor of Poetry (1832–41) were published (in Latin) in 1844 and dedicated to his hero, the poet William Wordsworth.

[23] *"cleansing" as Aristotle would word it*: Aristotle said that in tragedy the verse effects a 'purgation' of the emotions of pity and fear, cf. *Poetics*, Part I.

[24] *St Thomas*: St Thomas Aquinas (1225-74) wrote some well-known hymns, such as the 'Pange lingua' for the Feast of Corpus Christi.

John Keble,

author of the Christian Year found the Anglican system all
but destitute of this divine element, which is an essential
property of Catholicism;—a ritual dashed upon the ground,
trodden on, and broken piece-meal;—prayers, clipped,
pieced, torn, shuffled about at pleasure, until the meaning of
the composition perished, and offices which had been
poetry were no longer even good prose;—antiphons, hymns,
benedictions, invocations, shovelled away;—Scripture
lessons turned into chapters;[25]—heaviness, feebleness,
unwieldiness, where the Catholic rites had had the lightness
and airiness of a spirit;—vestments chucked off, lights
quenched, jewels stolen, the pomp and circumstances of
worship annihilated; a dreariness which could be felt, and
which seemed the token of an incipient Socinianism,[26]
forcing itself upon the eye, the ear, the nostrils of the
worshipper; a smell of dust and damp, not of incense; a
sound of ministers preaching Catholic prayers, and parish
clerks droning out Catholic canticles; the royal arms for the
crucifix; huge ugly boxes of wood, sacred to preachers,
frowning on the congregation in the place of the mysterious
altar;[27] and long cathedral aisles unused, railed off, like the
tombs (as they were,)[28] of what had been and was not; and
for orthodoxy, a frigid, unelastic, inconsistent, dull, helpless

[25] *prayers, clipped, pieced, torn* ... : Newman is referring to how the services of
Matins and Evensong in the Anglican *Book of Common Prayer* had been created
by Cranmer out of elements of the Catholic Divine Office.
[26] *Socinianism*: denial of the divinity of Christ; it is interesting that Newman sees
this heresy as underlying Protestant liturgical practice.
[27] *... in the place of the mysterious altar*: In Anglican churches of the time,
including the University Church of St. Mary the Virgin in Oxford where Newman
had been Vicar, the pulpit was placed in the centre of the church, blocking the
view of the Communion table.
[28] *the tombs (as they were,)*: The aisles of the mediaeval cathedrals frequently
contain the tombs of bishops and other notables, often in chantry chapels in which
Mass was said for their souls, a practice abolished at the Reformation.

dogmatic, which could give no just account of itself, yet [444]
was intolerant of all teaching which contained a doctrine
more or a doctrine less, and resented every attempt to give it
a meaning,—such was the religion of which this gifted
author was,—not the judge and denouncer, (a deep spirit of
reverence hindered it,)—but the renovator, as far as it has
been renovated. Clear as was his perception of the
degeneracy of his times, he attributed nothing of it to his
Church, over which he threw the poetry of his own mind
and the memory of better days.

His happy magic made the Anglican Church seem what
Catholicism was and is. The established system found to its
surprise that it had been all its life talking not prose, but
poetry.

> "Miraturque novas frondes et non sua poma."[29]

Beneficed clergymen used to go to rest as usual on
Christmas Eve, and leave to ringers, or sometimes to
carollers, the observance which was paid, not without
creature comforts, to the sacred night; but now they
suddenly found themselves, to their great surprise, to be
"wakeful shepherds;" and "still as the day came round," "in
music and in light," the new-born Saviour "dawned upon
their prayer."[30] Anglican bishops had not only lost the habit
of blessing, but had sometimes been startled and vexed
when asked to do so; but now they were told of their

---

[29] *Miraturque novas frondes et non sua poma.*: 'The trunk of the tree was marked
with his own name'. Virgil, *Georgics*, Book 2, 1.82.
[30] *"wakeful shepherds" ... "dawned upon their prayer"*: from 'Christmas Day',
The Christian Year; Newman has slightly altered some of the quotations to fit his
sentence, or he may be quoting from memory.

"gracious arm stretched out to bless;"[31] moreover, what they had never dreamed when they were gazetted or did homage,[32] they were taught that each of them was "an Apostle true, a crowned and robed seer."[33] The parish church had been shut up, except for vestry meetings[34] and occasional services, all days of the year but Sundays, and one or two other sacred days; but church-goers were now [445] assured that "Martyrs and Saints" "dawned on their way,"[35] that the absolution in the Common Prayer Book was "the Golden Key each morn and eve;"[36] and informed moreover, at a time too when the Real Presence was all but utterly forgotten or denied, of "the dear feast of Jesus dying, upon that altar ever lying, while Angels prostrate fall."[37] They learned, besides, that what their pastors had spoken of, and churchwardens had used at vestry meetings, as a mere table, was "the dread altar;"[38] and that "holy lamps were blazing;"[39]

---

[31] *"gracious arms stretched out to bless"*: from 'Sunday next before Advent', *The Christian Year*.

[32] *gazetted or did homage*: The appointments of Anglican bishops were announced in the official *Gazette*, along with other government appointments. A new bishop did homage to the Sovereign on his appointment.

[33] *"an Apostle true ... robed seer"*: from 'Commune Pontificium', CLXI, *Lyra Apostolica* (1836).

[34] *vestry meetings*: meetings of parishioners to elect parish officials for the coming year

[35] *"saints and martyrs" .. "dawned on their way"*: a slight misquotation of "Martyrs and saints—each glorious day/Dawning in order on our way—/Remind us ...", 'Sunday next before Advent', *The Christian Year*.

[36] *"The Golden key each morn and eve"*: 'Forgiveness, XV. The Three Absolutions', *Lyra Apostolica*.

[37] *"The dear feast of Jesus ... while Angles prostrate fall."*: 'Sunday next before Advent', *The Christian Year*. Newman has omitted a line; the full quotation is "the dear feast of JESUS dying,/Upon that altar ever lying,/Where souls with sacred hunger sighing/Are called to sit and eat, while angels prostrate fall".

[38] *"the dread altar"*: 'Forgiveness, XV. The Three Absolutions', *Lyra Apostolica*.

[39] *"holy lamps were blazing"*: 'Lighting of Lamps. LX.', *Lyra Apostolica*. Newman has slightly misquoted; the original line is: "The holy Lamps have blazed".

"perfumed embers quivering bright,"[40] with "stoled priests ministering at them,"[41] while the "floor was by knees of sinners worn."[42]

Such doctrine coming from one who had such claims on his readers from the weight of his name, the depth of his devotional and ethical tone, and the special gift of consolation, of which his poems themselves were the evidence, wrought a great work in the Establishment. The Catholic Church speaks for itself, the Anglican needs external assistance; his poems became a sort of comment upon its formularies and ordinances, and almost elevated them into the dignity of a religious system. It kindled hearts towards his Church; it gave a something for the gentle and forlorn to cling to; and it raised up advocates for it among those, who otherwise, if God and their good Angel had suffered it, might have wandered away into some sort of philosophy, and acknowledged no Church at all. Such was the influence of his Christian Year; and doubtless his friends hail his Lyra Innocentium, as being likely to do a similar work in a more critical time. And it is to be expected that for a while something of a similar effect may follow its publication. That so revered, so loved a name as the author's, a name known by Oxford men for thirty years and more,—that one who has been "a hermit spirit"[43] unlike the world all his days, who even in his youth caused the eyes of   [446]

---

[40] *"perfumed embers quivering bright"*: *ibid.*

[41] *"stoled priests ministering at them"*: a misquotation for "the stoled Priest in sight", *ibid.*

[42] *"floor was by knees of sinners worn"*: *ibid.*

[43] *"hermit spirit"*: perhaps a reference to 'Fire. CLI, Elijah and the Messengers of Ahaziah', *Lyra Apostolica*: 'One hermit, strong in fast and prayer,/Shall gird his sackcloth on, and scare/Whate'er the vain earth boasts:/And thunder-stricken chiefs return/To tell their Lord how dire the Church's lightnings burn.'

younger men to turn keenly towards him, if he was pointed out to them in public schools or college garden, who by the mere first touch of his hand has made them feel pierced through, so that they could have sunk into the earth for shame, and who, when removed from his loved University, was still an unseen silent influence moving hearts at his will,—that a "whisper" from such a man, "with no faint and erring voice,"[44] will for the time retain certain persons in the English Church, who otherwise, to say the least, would have contemplated a return to that true Mother whose baptism they bear, the one sole Ark of salvation, of this we make no question at all. But there is another point, of which we entertain just as little doubt, or rather are a great deal more confident,—that as far as the Volume has influence, that influence will, on the long run, tell in favour of the Catholic Church; and will do what the author does not, nay, from his position, alas! cannot, may not contemplate,—will in God's good time bring in a blessed harvest into the granaries of Christ. And being sure of this, much as the immediate effects of its publication may pain the hearts of those who are sighing and praying for the souls of others, we can bear to wait, we can afford to be patient, and awfully to watch the slow march of the divine providences towards this poor country.

7.

Take the Volume; consider its doctrine; consider, too, that it seldom insists upon the English Church as a definite and substantive body, but seems almost to view the infant's breast as *the* true visible Church, the only doctor and saint

---

[44] *"with no faint and erring voice"*: perhaps a misquotation of "On me, that am but voice, fading and weak,/A wither'd leaf inscribed with heaven's decree,/And blown where haply some in fear may learn." 'Jeremiah. CXXIII., *Lyra Apostolica.*

in the land; and then imagine what will be the direction and
course of thought in those children, who grow up under the [447]
teaching which it imparts. It tells them, for instance, that in
the very act and moment of baptism the soul is
regenerated,[45] and, ordinarily, is regenerated in no other
way; that each soul has an Angel for its guardian;[46] that,
whereas Christ works His miracles of mercy now as at the
beginning, St. Mary is an instrument in them as in the
marriage of Cana, and also the Apostles;[47] that the Saints are
rightly called gods;[48] that "the Infinite" is present in the
"unbloody rite;"[49] that the Eucharistic sacrifice is offered up
daily all over the world, and that the sun never sets upon it;[50]
that the Church has ever spread in that shadow of St. Peter,[51]
which in the beginning wrought miracles, and that it shall
never grow less; and that it is "duteous"[52] to pray for the
dead as well as the living, a position with which he opens
the first stanza in his Volume. Now in what sense is this a
Church-of-England training? How can a child ever learn
from it sympathy with and attachment to that communion,
as he grows up? How is such teaching dutiful towards it?

[45] *"baptism .. the soul is regenerated!*: Cf. 'Holy Baptism. 3. New Creation,. *Lyra Innocentium*, pp.4-7.

[46] *an Angel for its guardian*: cf. 'Early Encouragements. 2. Samuel's Prayer', *ibid.*, p.80.

[47] *St. Mary is an instrument ... the Apostles*: cf. 'Holy Places and Things. 10. Church Rites', *ibid.*, p.275.

[48] *the Saints are rightly called gods*: ibid.

[49] *"the Infinite" ... "unbloody rite"*: '17. Continual Services. (For the Sunday Before Advent)', *ibid.*, p.304.

[50] *the Eucharistic sacrifice is offered up ...*: cf. ibid, p.308: 'No waste so dark and lone,/But to the hour of sacrifice/Comes daily in its turn'.

[51] *the Church has ever spread in that shadow of St. Peter*: Cf. '8. Relics and Memorials', *Lyra Innocentium*, p.267, 'from Godhead made Man/The virtue goes out, the whole world to bless,/O'er lands parched and weary that shadow began/To spread from Saint Peter, and ne'er shall grow less.'

[52] *"duteous"*: 'To All Friendly Readers', *Lyra Innocentium*, p.v.

The Ethiopian, on reading the prophet Isaiah, inquired, "Of whom speaketh the prophet this?"[53] and so the boy, the youth, the man, as he looks wider and further into the world, as he is gradually thrown upon his own thoughts, will surely ask with louder and louder voice where this teaching is to be found? whence it comes? which of the living English bishops or departed divines, and how many, which of the Anglican formularies, what part of the Prayer Book, which of the Articles, what obsolete canon, or what ecclesiastical judge, sanctions its doctrines; and how far literal tangible facts bear out its statements?—and next whether there are not existing bishops elsewhere, and divines, and decrees, and usages, which do bear it out fully, and offer him what [448] he is seeking; whether, in short, the author's comment is sanctioned by his text; or belongs to some other text not his? There is but one Church which has firmly, precisely, consistently, continually held and acted upon these doctrines of the Lyra Innocentium; and, if holding them to be token of the true Church, one and only one Church is true.

It must be recollected, too, that these doctrines are part of a system; they lead to other doctrines; they gradually and imperceptibly draw the mind into the reception of others, whether it will or no. At this very moment souls are being led into the Catholic Church on the most various and independent impulses, and from the most opposite directions. True it is, that such persons as have been taught from childhood certain principles are able without prejudice to them to admit other doctrines which are their direct contradictories, and which in themselves tend inevitably to

---

[53] *"Of whom speaketh the prophet this?"*: Acts 8:34

their destruction. Anglicans of forty years' standing may admit that St. Peter is the foundation of the Church, yet feel no misgivings in consequence that the Church of England is external to Catholic communion; but the Lyra Innocentium is not addressed to grown men, but to children, whose hearts and heads have yet to be formed, and who, if "trained up" (as they will be) "in the way they should go," are not likely in the end to "depart from it."[54] Is it not, indeed, by this time abundantly clear, that, as children of the Evangelical school of the last age have so often become Latitudinarians,[55] so the young generation whose pious and serious parents are now teaching them to cross themselves, to fast or abstain, to reverence celibacy, and to say the Ave Mary, should they grow up as serious and pious as their instructors, will end in being converts to the Catholic Church?

Well would it be, if the really honest holders of Anglo-Catholic principles could be made to see this; it would be the removal of a veil from their eyes; they would at once perceive that they ought to be plain Catholics. Some of them, indeed, may hitherto have had thoughts of leavening the whole English Church with their doctrine; they may have described that Church as what it ought to be and was not, in the hope thereby of tending to make it what it ought to be; and now, though they see or suspect their own tendency to be towards Rome, they may put this suspicion aside, and remain where they are, in the confidence that, if they are but patient, they shall ultimately succeed in bringing over their whole communion to their own views. But such a confidence has not been the feeling of the author

[449]

---

[54] *"trained up" ... "depart from it."*: Proverbs 22:6
[55] *Latitudinarians*: theological liberals, rationalists

of the Christian Year, if we may judge from his writings. His imagination, creative as it is, has been under the control of too sober a judgment, as we cannot but surmise, to acquiesce in the notion that the English Church is the natural seat of Catholicism; that you have but to preach the truth, and the heart of her members will recognize in that truth their own real sentiments, and claim their lost inheritance; that Erastianism[56] in high places will ever become a mere matter of history; that ecclesiastical courts, university authorities, mobs and vestries, will ever lose their keen scent for detecting popery, and their intense satisfaction in persecuting it. He seems to resign himself and his friends, as if it were no "strange thing," to the prospect of unkind, unnatural treatment *for ever*, from her whom the word of prophecy has depicted as the mother of her children. He has some beautiful lines on a child's clinging to its mother's gown who appears the while to disregard it, with a reference to the miracle wrought upon the issue of blood: and it is impossible not to see that he is [450] all the while drawing himself and the English Church in a parable.

> "She did but touch with finger weak
> The border of His sacred vest,
> Nor did he turn, nor glance, nor speak,
> Yet found she health and rest.
>
> "Well may the Word sink deep in me
> For I full many a fearful hour,
> Fast clinging, Mother dear, to thee,
> Have felt love's guardian power.
>
> "When looks were strange on every side,

---

[56] *Erastianism*: See note on p.[45].

> *When, gazing round, I only saw*
> *Far-reaching ways unknown and wide,*
>   I could but nearer draw:

"I could but nearer draw, and hold
    Thy garment's border as I might,
This while I felt, my heart was bold,
    My step was free and light.

"Thou haply on my path the while
    Didst seem unheeding me to fare,
Scarce now and then, by word or smile,
    Owning a playmate there.

"What matter? well I know my place
    Deep in my Mother's inmost heart;
I feared but, in my childish race,
    I from her robe might part."—P. 147.

We are ourselves reminded of a different image. We have somewhere seen some lines by Darwin,[57] in which a mother is described as killed by a chance ball in a battle; her children are found clinging to her in the persuasion that she is asleep;—when she is discovered by those who know better, the poor babes say in surprise, "Why do you weep, mamma will soon awake?" None other but that miraculous Voice, which used the same words over Jairus' daughter[58], can wake the dead.

8. [451]

There is one other issue, to which we have not yet drawn attention, to which Anglo-Catholic writers may reduce the

[57] *Darwin*: Erasmus Darwin (1731-1802), a physician and writer; grandfather of Charles Darwin. His poems include the 'Death of Eliza at the Battle of Minden', which Newman refers to here.

[58] *the same words over Jairus' daughter*: Cf. Luke 8:52

inquiring mind;—they may throw it, by a reaction, into rationalism. When the opening heart and eager intellect find themselves led on by their teachers, as if by the hand, to the See of St. Peter, and then all of a sudden, without good reason assigned, are stopped in their course, bid stand still in some half position, on the middle of a steep, or in the depth of a forest, the natural reflection which such a command excites is, "This is a mockery; I have come here for nothing; if I do not go on, I must go back." Of course such a feeling, though the natural, will not, and ought not to be, the first feeling of the young. Reverent minds will at first rest on the word of their teachers by the instinct of their natures, and will either receive them without examination, or accept on faith what does not approve itself to their reason. But as time proceeds, and the intellect becomes more manly, and has a greater hold of the subjects of thought and the relations of those subjects to each other, it will at length come to feel that it must form its own judgment on the questions which perplex it, unless the authority, to which it has hitherto submitted, claims to be infallible. To an infallible authority it will submit; but since no teacher of the Anglican Church, no, nor that Church itself, claims to have the power of absolutely determining the truth in religious matters, the moment must arrive when the young inquirer feels it right to have an opinion of his own, and then it is that a peremptory prohibition of his advancing onward, without sufficient reason assigned for it, [452] will act as a violent temptation to recede. A forlorn feeling comes over the mind, as if after all there was nothing real in orthodoxy—as if it were a matter of words, about which nothing is known, nothing can be proved—as if one opinion were as good as another. The whole Roman faith it thinks it could receive; but a half-and-half system, which both does and does not appeal to reason—which argues as far as it thinks argument tells in its favour, and denounces argument when it tells the other way—flies to authority, puts forward great names, and talks in a vague way of "reverence," "submission," "the Church of our baptism," "restlessness," and the like, neither commands its faith nor wins its love. O that we could be sure about our author, that however he might think it his duty to treat the gentle and unlearned who depend on him, at least when men of independent minds, young or old, come to him in doubt—men of the world, or rising men of active minds, whose characters are yet undetermined, (we are speaking in entire ignorance whether he has knowledge of such cases,) what a blessing it would be to be able to think that, instead of placing an obstacle in the path of such, he felt himself at liberty to say to them as much as this: "Stay with us, if you do not risk your Christian faith and hope by staying; but, little as I can countenance your departure to the Church of Rome, better do so than become a rationalist." This surely is not asking a very great deal.

As to the author personally, we cannot help cherishing one special trust, which we hope is not too sacred to put into words. If there be one writer in the Anglican Church who has discovered a deep, tender, loyal devotion to the Blessed Mary, it is the author of the Christian Year. The image of the Virgin and Child seems to be the one vision upon which both his heart and intellect have been formed; and those [453] who knew Oxford twenty or thirty years ago, say that, while other college rooms were ornamented with pictures of Napoleon on horseback, or Apollo and the Graces, or Heads of Houses lounging in their easy chairs, there was one man, a young and rising one, in whose rooms, instead of these, might be seen the Madonna di Sisto[59] or Domenichino's St. John[60]—fit augury of him who was in the event to do so much for the revival of Catholicism. We will never give up the hope, the humble belief, that that sweet and gracious Lady will not forget her servant, but will recompense him, in royal wise, seven-fold, bringing him and his at length into the Church of the One Saviour, and into the communion of herself and all Saints whom He has redeemed.

June, 1846.

---

[59] *the Madonna di Sisto*: the Sistine Madonna by Raphael, commissioned by Pope Julius II for the church of San Sisto in Piacanenza.
[60] *Domenichino's St. John*: Saint John the Evangelist by Domenico Zampieri (1581-1641), known as Domenichino ('little Domenico').

POSTSCRIPT

I HERE subjoin, what had quite gone out of my mind, Mr. Palmer's disavowal of some of the opinions which I ascribed to him in my review of his Treatise on the Church *(vid.* above, Essay iv.)[1] His remarks upon it are to be found among the "Notices of Books" in the *British Critic* for April 1839, and have accidentally met my eye since the publication of these volumes. Neither at the time did they lead me, nor do they lead me now, to change the judgment which I formed of the direct drift of his teaching; but in fairness he ought to have the benefit of them. They run as follows:—

"I have not anywhere maintained that the whole Catholic Church 'does even at this day preach everywhere one and the same doctrine, except *in very minor and secondary points,* or except as popular errors interfere with it,' *British Critic"* [*supr.,* vol. i., p. 169]. "A reference to what I have above stated, p. 567,will show that I am not on *principle* bound to sustain this position; nor do I practically admit it, because, in my opinion, several of the errors and abuses of the Roman Church are of a very important nature, and very detrimental to Christian piety, though they be not, strictly speaking, contrary to the articles of faith.

---

[1] *Essay iv:* in Volume I.

Postscript

"I know not what part of my work had led to the notion that I hold 'that the faith of the Church admits of addition,' and that 'any doctrine which has once been generally received must be apostolic, or in other words that the majority cannot be wrong'" [*supr.*, vol. i., p. 176], "I have expressly argued against the latter position, vol. ii, p. 136, etc. As to the former, I have distinctly stated that the articles of our faith were but once revealed and admit of no addition, vol. i., p. 89. Perhaps it may be supposed that, in admitting that, before the universal Church has decided some question of controversy, different opinions may be held without heresy, while I hold, that, after the judgment of the Church, there should be no more diversity, I may seem to admit the articles of faith to be capable of addition. This was not my intention; I only mean, that, in the heat of controversy when different opinions are supported by men of learning, it may for a time be doubtful what the revealed truth is, and therefore persons may for a time not receive that truth, may even hold what is contrary to it; and yet, until the authority of the universal Church has decided the question, and left them without excuse, they may be free from the guilt of formal heresy. I only speak here of controversies which the Church had not decided in former ages; or in which the testimony of tradition as well as Scripture is disputed."

November, 1871.

[455]

INDEX [1]

Aaron's rod, i. 326; ii. 26, 233 golden calf, 429.

Abbot, Jacob, i. 30; his *Corner Stone*, 72; introduces himself to Dr. Newman, 100.

Acacius of Constantinople, i. 164.

Adelbert, Archbishop of Bremen, ii. 255.

Æschylus, the action of his plays always simple and inartificial, i. 2, his *Agamemnon*, 5.

Agatho, Pope, his Letter to the Emperor Constantine, ii. 329.

Ainsworth, Henry, his *Arrow against Idolatry*, ii. 166.

Ambrose, St., his opposition to the Empress Justina, i. 116; Confession ascribed to, 201; on dialectics, ii. 42.

Ancona, seizure of by the French, i. 130.

Andrewes, i. 400; ii. 45, 59.

Anglo-AmericanChurch, the, i. 308.

Antichrist, the Protestant idea of, ii. 112.

Antigone, i. 3.

Apollinarianism, i. 200.

Apostle's Creed, the, ii. 6.

Arianism, i. 239.

Aristotle, his Poetics, i. 1; his treatment of dramatic composition, 7; fragmentary character of his work, 8; his definition of poetry, 9;

on pity, 106; condemned by the early Fathers, ii. 42.

Arius, cross examined by the Fathers at Nicæa, i. 278.

Armida, garden of, i. 310.

Arnold, Dr., ii. 113.

Athanasian Creed, *need* of, in these dangerous times, i. 87; its protest against Apollinarianism, 200; antithetical structure of, 205.

Athanasius, i. 203; quoted, 205, 214; bears witness to the genuineness of the Ignatian Epistles, 245; quoted, ii. 52.

Augustine, St., i. 164; his theology, 286; motto from, ii. 21; on Unity, 35, 40, 41; against the Donatists, 364.

Avenir, the, i. 127-128.

Bacchus, worship of, i. 6.

Bacon, Lord, on poetry, i. 9; ii. 402.

Baillie, Joanna, her *Chough and Crow*, i. 17.

Barrow, his Discourse on the Unity of the Church, ii. 21; quoted, 159.

Basil, St., ii. 60, 326.

Bastwick, quoted, ii. 163.

Baxter, Richard, a gibe of his answered, ii. 173.

Becket, ii. 58.

Bede, i. 309.

---

[1] The Index covers both Volumes. The page numbers refer to the 1885 edition.

Index

[459]

541

[460]

[461]

[462]

Index

[463]

545

FINIS.

APPENDIX: TEXTUAL VARIANTS

The following list contains variants in the 1871 text (except for the Notes added at the end of each essay) from the original articles published 1840-46. Where words in the '1871 text' column have nothing equivalent in the '1840-46 texts' column, they are additions to the earlier text; and where words in the '1840-46 texts' column have nothing equivalent in the '1871 text' column, they were omitted from the later text. Trivial variations in capitalising, punctuation and spelling have been ignored, as have insignificant verbal variations which do not affect Newman's meaning.

page	1871 text	1840-46 texts
1	**IX.** **CATHOLICITY OF THE** **ANGLICAN CHURCH**	ART. III – *An Apology for the Doctrine of Apostolical Succession, with an Appendix on the English Orders.* By the Hon. And Rev. A. P. Perceval. 12mo. Rivingtons. 1839.
1	In his recent work on the Apostolic Succession and the English Orders, Mr. Perceval has done us a service which was very much needed, and had never been attempted.	The principal value and interest of this compact work will be found to lie in its Appendix, which takes up more than half the whole volume.
1	but no one but he has had the opportunity, and been at the pains, of exhibiting to the general reader the evidence of the fact of the Succession in the English Church.	but no one but he has had the opportunity, and been at the pains of doing, what nevertheless has been for a long time called for, of exhibiting to the general reader the evidence of the *fact* of the Succession in the English Church. The body of the work, written with Mr Perceval's usual terseness and perspicuity, treats successively of Congregationalism, Presbyterianism and Episcopacy, and brings together in a short compass the chief arguments which occur in the controversy, and the chief objections, with their answers. The Appendix, for which we especially thank the author, contains a number of documents and tables illustrative of some of the most important points in the history of the spiritual descent of our existing bishops and clergy from the Apostles. He begins by enumerating six objections which the Roman Catholics have urged against our succession, as passing through Archbishop Parker

and his colleagues; - first, the Nag's Head story, viz. that at a tavern, so named, Scorcy, a single bishop, placed a Bible on the heads of the candidates and said, "Take thou authority to preach the word of God sincerely." Next, that our form of consecration since the time of Edward VI has been essentially defective; thirdly, that at least the form of ordaining Presbyters was and is defective, and therefore that candidates for the Episcopate, so ordained, were, on that ground, disqualified; fourthly, that the consecrators of Archbishop Parker were not themselves validly consecrated; fifthly, that the English ordinations are made in schism, as made in opposition to the bishop of Rome; lastly, that some of Archbishop Parker's consecrators were married men. Against the last two objections, in which Anglicans dispute the point of doctrine or principle, and concede the fact alleged, documents are out of place; Mr Perceval therefore dispatches the one with the 13th canon of the Council of Ephesus, and the other with 1 Cor. ix. 5, references which he considers decisive in the respective subjects in debate. The four first, however, admit of historical illustration on the matter of fact, which Roman writers dispute and we maintain; accordingly Mr Perceval has undertaken to lay before us some chief portions of the evidence in our favour, and presents us with the records of Parker's consecration as contained in the registers at Lambeth and in the library of Corpus Christi College, Cambridge; and with the offices for consecration and ordination, according to the Antenicene, Eastern, Ancient Western, Coptic, and Queen Elizabeth's ritual.

Appendix: Textual Variants

2	for four steps

for four successions

4   This is the point, which deserves, as we think, to be attentively considered...

Mr Perceval includes this argument, we suppose, under his fifth objection; else he does not notice it. It deserves, however, to be attentively considered...

5-6   *Rom.*—On the contrary, you, as a body, oppose and denounce us, as a body, in all possible ways; and we too oppose and denounce you. Let us look at facts, and not speak by book. And you are small, we are large; therefore we, not you, are the Church.

Rom. - Yes, you, as a body, oppose and denounce us, as a body, in all possible ways; and we too oppose and denounce you. Let us look at facts and not speak by book. There is no peace between us, but in God's Church there is peace.

6   *Angl.*—If we two cannot be at peace, the worse for you; for your teaching is corrupt, and ours is pure.

Rom.—No, we preach the whole gospel, and you halve it.

Angl.—Our teaching is the true, because it is the primitive; yours is not true, because it is novel.

Rom.—Our teaching is the true, for it is everywhere the same; yours has no warrant, for it is but local and private.

Angl.—We go by Antiquity; that is, by the Apostles. Ancient consent is our standard of faith.

Rom.—We go by Catholicity. Universal consent is our standard of faith.

Angl.—You are cut off from the old Fathers.

Rom.—And you are cut off from the present living Church.

Angl. – If so, the worse for you. If we cannot both be true, look to yourselves; you are excluded, for you are corrupt, and we a primitive and pure Church. However, we would fain be kinder to you and you are to yourselves.

Rom. – How do you determine that you are pure and we corrupt?

Angl. – We are pure because we are primitive. You are corrupt because you are novel. We go by antiquity; whatever was held everywhere in the first ages, must have come from the Apostles. Ancient consent is our standard of faith.

Rom. – Who is to judge of antiquity? The works of the Fathers are large. It is one difficulty to read them; another to find out the points in which they agree; another, those in which they differ; another, to settle what number of them are virtually equal to all; and whether and how far silence has an affirmative or negative force; and whether and when individual Fathers speak from their own minds or are spokesmen of the whole; and what doctrines were implicit before they took explicit shape; and what is conjectural and what dogmatic statement. To refer then to antiquity is like referring to Scripture; if any doctrine may be made plausible by Scripture, still more so from the Fathers.

Angl. – I join issue here. Certainly there are points on which the evidence of antiquity is doubtful. Those we are willing to leave as open questions. But there are a large number on which its witness is distinct, strong, unanimous. If this is not felt by the generality of those who read the Fathers, we will cease to appeal to them. We are advocating no eclecticism; we refer to a standard which does not need interpreter. We wish to go by the common sense of the world. If the world gives it against us, we submit. There *are* truths too plain to doubt about; no one doubts that Voltaire's writings are of an infidel cast; that Luther insisted on justification by faith; or that the Jacobites held the divine right of kings. There are limits to the possibility of doubting about what men hold, as well as about what they do. We maintain that the world will in the main agree as to the unanimous opinions of the Fathers. Their opinions so determined are the rule of our faith. Nay, I will make yourself the judge. Can you deny that your Church enforces many doctrines and usages unsanctioned by the Fathers.

Rom. – I grant it so far as this, that such points were implicitly held by the Fathers, not in set terms.

Angl. – There has been but one creed from the beginning. It was received, preached, transmitted by the Fathers. What they held is the faith; what is more than they held is an addition to the faith. What they practised is the discipline of Christ; what is more than they practised is at best unnecessary and may be erroneous.

Appendix: Textual Variants

Rom. – Then does the Creed itself contain additions to the faith. The words "of one substance" were inserted in it against the Arians; "whose kingdom shall have no end," against the Marcellus; "He descended into hell," and perhaps "for us and for our salvation" against the Apollinarians. Tell me then, what age of the Church do you mean by antiquity? what point of time – what year – do you consider the standard for all subsequent times? and when you have settled this, then determine how it was that the year before held less and the year after more, and why we again may not in turn hold more also.

Angl. – These statements you speak of were added, either as explanations of existing articles, or as truths universally and openly received at the time, parts of that one system of which the existing creed was the outline, and inserted from circumstances.

Rom. – The case is the same with those of our articles which you reject. Thus in begging the saints' prayers and praying for the faithful departed, we do but interpret and fulfil the article in the Creed which recognizes the communion of saints. We realize what you only profess. In like manner the doctrine of purgatory is as much a development of "the forgiveness of sins," as is the doctrine of baptism. The Nicene Creed explains the Apostles' by the words "*one baptism* for the remission of sins;" and the Creed of Pope Pius explains is still more fully by teaching that there is a *purgatory* for the remission of certain sins.

Angl. – There is a plain difference between developments such as yours, even supposing they may be so considered, which really change and supersede the elementary

551

symbol from which they are deduced, and such as serve merely to ascertain and fix its meaning in its separate articles. Your existing creed is not formed on the type of the Apostles'. A change from chrysalis to moth may in one sense be called a development; but no one would say that the latter state existed at the time of the former. Your creed exists in the ancient Church no otherwise than Christianity existed in Judaism. At best it is but under the ancient creed. Do you mean to say the religion of Jew and Christian is the same?

Rom. – We conceive that the doctrine of purgatory was ever in the Church; and was authenticated and made an article of faith when occasion required.

Angl. – I join issue on the fact.

Rom. – That is, on the fact what is in the Fathers; - who shall arbitrate between us? As I said just now, and you denied, the Fathers need an interpreter. We, the greater part of Christendom, see in them what you do not see.

Angl. – Your Church makes you see in one way; you cannot help yourselves.

Rom. – What has the Church ever been, considered as a teacher, but a vast number of individuals agreeing together? How does it supersede the witness of many that it has been one and the same? and should not the unanimity of competent judges bind the assent of those who are not?

Angl. – The many have agreed together in one at this time or that, from one adventitious cause; and what they have once settled, cannot be altered in after times. the Church, *when* corrupt, has *committed* herself to corruptions.

Rom. – This is your theory; we have an opposite theory, which is as good as yours. You say the many went wrong because they were corrupt; we say they could not but go right, because they were promised infallibility. But now observe the contrast between your system and ours, how simple ours, how perplexed yours. You move on two foundations, we on one; you hold by the primitive Creed *and* the Church; you count it a duty to keep to the Creed and to keep to the Church, making no due provision for the case of a discordance between them, yet maintaining that very case to have happened. We have but one rule, to follow the Church; for in following the body, we are sure to be adhering to the faith. That society which we are to *join* is the teacher of what we are to *believe*. Accordingly in our view heresy and schism are never disjoined. You, on the contrary, almost assert that we are heretics, and almost grant that you are schismatics; yet maintain withal we are both one Church, and both have one faith.

Angl. – Your theory is simple, but how is it proved?

Rom. – By Scripture and antiquity, which make it clear that our theory of infallibility is true, and yours of corruption false. It is foretold that the Church should be infallible; it is nowhere foretold she should err.

Ang. – Here I use your own arguments; - who is to interpret the passages you bring from either?

Rom. – And I meet with yours; - yourselves. You shall interpret them against us, if you can. Isaiah as *[sic]* certainly foretold that the Church should be one, ecumenical, and infallible, as the Fathers recognize her as such in word and deed. The Prophet declares that truth shall be easy to find, and that all shall be taught it, and that its teachers shall be never hidden, and that all shall agree, and that the Church shall teach, and that the Holy Spirit shall guide her, and that the divine Word shall never depart out of her mouth. And the Fathers apply this simple and practical rule in all controversies of faith and morals: "Follow the Church and you cannot go wrong."

Angl. – Say what you will, you never will persuade me that images are not forbidden in Scripture and unknown in antiquity, though in use among you; that the worship of angels which you practise is not discountenanced in Scripture; that antiquity honoured St Mary as you honour her; or that your doctrine of pardon was known to St Cyprian or St Basil.

Rom. – Scripture explains for you this difficulty. It is said expressly "I have yet many things to say unto you, but ye cannot bear them now. Howbeit, when He, the Spirit of truth is come, He shall guide you into all truth." If "I am with *you* always" applies not only to the Apostles but to the Church after them, so does the other promise. If we deny the continuance of the Holy Spirit's office after the Apostles' age, why not of His presence also?

Now let the warfare stop, and let us take a review of what has been said, and how each party stands now it would seem that in the above discussion each disputant has a strong point; our strong point is the argument from primitiveness, that of the Romanists is the argument from universality. It is a fact, however it is to be accounted for, that Rome has added to the Creed, and it is a fact, however we justify ourselves, that we are estranged from the great body of Christians over the world; and each of these facts is at first sight a grave

Appendix: Textual Variants

		difficulty in the respective systems to which they belong.
8	comprises Christ	contains Christ
9	the words of the Apostle, about preaching any other Gospel besides that which has been received.	the awful words, "Though we, or an angel from heaven, preach any other Gospel unto you, than that you have received, let him be accursed."
9	the body of Christians	the great body of Christians
10	On the one hand, Anglo-Catholics say, "Even though we were in schism, as we are not, such separation would not be disadvantageous, when faith is in danger;" and Roman Catholics say, "Even though we had innovated, as we have not, such innovation is not in error, when the Church is the author of it."	On the one hand, Anglo-Catholics say, "Even though we were in schism, which we are not in, this is not a disadvantage, when faith is in danger" and the "Catholic" says 'Even though we had innovated, which we have not, this is not error, when the Church is the author of it"
11	that which we allege against him, want of primitiveness in doctrine, while the logical force of his fact is such as plausibly to throw discredit upon our contrary fact.	that which we allege against him, want of primitiveness, while the significancy of his fact is such as plausibly to throw discredit upon our contrary fact.
11	by the very fact, unquestionable as it is, that	by the aforesaid unquestionable fact that
13	or that St. John has written a Gospel, on the one hand later, on the other more dogmatic	or that St. John has written a Gospel as later, so also more dogmatic
15	that age not having these portions of Christian truth, (as Romanists allege,)	and these ages not having these portions of Christian truth, (as Romanists say,)
17	ignores or denies the Scripture promises	sacrifices the Scripture promises
17	It denies the Church of Rome to be a Church	It denies that the Church of Rome *exists*
18	but is intended, instead of following any one of them exclusively, rather	but, instead of following any one of them, is intended rather as a

555

	as a statement of the general view	statement of the general view
18	its separate portions need not be united together	its portions need not otherwise have been united together
18	They are like a number of colonies sent out from a mother country, or as the tribes or nations which spring from a common parent	They are like a number of colonies sent out from a mother country.
18	Each Church is independent of all the rest, except indeed so far as the civil power unites any number of them together.	Each Church is independent of all the rest, and is to act on the principle of what may be called Episcopal independency, except indeed so far as the civil power unites any number of them together.
20	If indeed the Church is essentially one and one only organized body in every age and country	If the Church is essentially one organized body in every age' (p55).
22	autonomy	αὐτονομία
23	and are our Lord's Council	or a council to Christ
26	Logos	Λόγος
28	This will enable us to understand	This leads us to understand
28	As soon as we comprehend that	Directly we comprehend that
29	his object in it being	the object in it being
30	"…Let those only	"…Let them only
30	This relation to Africa also decides his meaning	The circumstance is decisive of his meaning, also
32	and the *sine qua non* sanction	and the sanction
32	and as though schism were separation from this one whole body, and from this or that bishop only as far as he was the organ or representative of all bishops, that is, of the Bishop of Rome	and schism therefore were separation from this one whole body, and from this or that bishop only as far as he was the organ or representative of all bishops, or of the Bishop of Rome'

Appendix: Textual Variants

38	in the opinion of those who use them	in the opinion of the writers
43	*omnibus numeris*	*totis numeris*
45	Here again we will avail ourselves of the labours of the learned Launoy, though Augustine's judgment	We have already alluded to this deference of St Austin to the Universal Church as amply discussed by the learned Launoy, whose labours we here shall make use of, so far as quoting one or two passages, though Augustine's judgment
47	As soon as it is granted that active intercourse is not *absolutely necessary* as a note of the Church, an opening is made for adducing *other* circumstances which may serve to be an evidence of that, which such intercourse would evidence, if it existed.	Directly it is granted that active intercourse is not *absolutely necessary* as a note of the Church, leave is given for adducing *other* circumstances which may serve to evidence what intercourse would evidence, if it existed.
50	unless Roman divines are content to create a territory for themselves by merely mapping it	and if Roman divines would not have to create a territory by mapping it
64	was delivered by him on its fifth return.	was delivered by him on the fifth.
71	so rife, so widely spread,	so rife, so general,
110	I think it is Mr. Alexander Knox who says or suggests that, if so great a gift be given, it must have a rite. I add, if it has a rite, it must have a *custos* of the rite.	I think it is Mr. Alexander Knox who says or suggests that, if so great a gift be given, it must have a *custos.*
112	But at least there is a great presumption that where evidently our Lord has not provided a rigid rule of baptism, He has not provided a valid ordination.	I think there is a great presumption then, that where our Lord has not made a rigid rule of Baptism, he has not left a valid Ordination.
112	**X.** **THE PROTESTANT IDEA OF THE ANTICHRIST**	Art. V.- *Discourses on the Prophecies relating to Antichrist in the Writings of Daniel and St. Paul, preached before the University of Dublin, at the Donnellan Lecture, 1838.* By James Henthorn Todd,

B.D., M.R.I.A., Fellow of Trinity College, and Treasurer of St. Patrick's Cathedral, Dublin. London: Rivingtons. 1840.

112 The Discourses which Dr. Todd has recently given to the world, are, perhaps, the first attempt for a long course of years in this part of Christendom to fix a dispassionate attention and a scientific interpretation upon the momentous "Prophecies relating to Antichrist in the writings of Daniel and St. Paul."

Dr. Todd's Discourses are, perhaps, the first attempt for a long course of years in this part of Christendom to fix a dispassionate attention and a scientific interpretation on the momentous Prophecies which he specifies in his title-page.

115 And another serious question is this,

And a still further serious reflection is this,

118-19 and the notes that stand at the end of his Lectures,

and the notes A, C, and D, which stand at the end of his Lectures,

128 "...The superiority of the Pope over the Creator *has been boldly and unblushingly maintained* by pontiffs, theologians, canonists and councils."

"...The superiority of the Pope over the Creator has been boldly and unblushingly maintained by pontiffs, theologians, canonists and councils."

3.
Now it may readily be granted...

One other misrepresentation we will notice in addition, and on a collateral point, rather than others which might be taken in the interpretation of prophecy, for variety's sake. We mean the calumny which was published against St Eligius, and which a periodical exposed some years since. First Mosheim, and after him Robertson, Jortim, and White in his Bampton Lectures, all refer to a certain sermon of this saint, who was Bishop of Noyon in the seventh century. This sermon they bring in proof of the doctrinal corruptions of that period; to show, in Robertson's words, that "the Christian religion had degenerated into an illiberal superstition;" and that, "instead of aspiring to sanctity and virtue," the barbarous converts to the Gospel "imagined that they satisfied every obligation of duty by a scrupulous observance of *external ceremonies*." "Religion," he adds, "according to their conception of it, comprehends *nothing else*." Then he appeals to the sermons of St Eloy, or Eligius, in confirmation; and, copying Mosheim, represents him as saying that "he is a good Christian" who frequents church, makes offerings and pays tithes, lives chastely before festivals, uses the Creed and Lord's Prayer, implores the patronage of saints, and can say at the day of judgement, "Give to me, Lord, for I have given to Thee." On this Maclaine, translator of Mosheim, whom Robertson quotes approvingly, says, "We see here a large and ample description of a good Christian, in which *there is not the least mention* of the love of God, resignation to his will, obedience to his laws, or of justice, benevolence, and charity towards men." In like manner Jortin says, "As to true religion, here is *the sum and substance of it*, as it is drawn up by Eligius, one of the principal saints of that age." White, too, observes that "no representation can convey stronger ideas of the melancholy state of religion in the seventh century than" this same description. Now will it be believed that the above clauses, which are set down by these writers as the *substance* of St Eligius's description, are but a few scattered bits of a long series of details which make up his picture of a Christian; that he distinctly denounces thieving, false witness, lying, adultery, hatred, revenge, discord; and exhorts to loving all men as oneself, praying for enemies, and making peace?

"He who will be a true Christian," he continues, "must needs keep these commandments; because *if he does not keep them, he deceives himself.* He therefore is a good Christian who puts faith in no charms or diabolical inventions, but *places all his hope in Christ alone*; who receives strangers with joy, even as if it were Christ himself; who, according to his means, giving alms to the poor; who has not a false balance or deceitful weights. He who is such a one is without doubt a true Christians, and Christ dwelleth in him, who hath said, 'I and the Father will come and make our abode with him,' &c."

These are portions of a sermon which four distinguished writers exhibit as a specimen of formality and superstition.

Now it may readily be granted...

129	who can hope to overcome it?	who can hope to escape it?
130	or even men of deep intellects	or even deep men
133	whose words we quote from a periodical, in which we find them	who, however, is too little of a gentleman to be mentioned by name
144	"...whom he regarded as the special objects of his care." – *Ibid., p.230.*	"...whom he regarded as the special objects of his care. He had a very wide correspondence on religious subjects; and composed several books full of piety and devotion, but of course not altogether free from the superstitions of his age and communion. His compassion was so excited by the unhappy condition of a poor deaf and dumb man, that he received him into his own family, taught him by signs, and instructed him in religion. He founded a new order of nuns, in which few bodily austerities were practiced, and no great burdens of religious observances were imposed, his object being to render it suitable even for the sickly and weak."

Appendix: Textual Variants

144	In 1619, while he was in Paris, he preached	"In 1619 he accompanied the Cardinal of Savoy to Paris to demand the sister of Lewis XIII. in marriage for the prince of Piedmont. While he was in Paris, he preached
144	"On one occasion," says Mr. Palmer, "seeing	On one occasion seeing
144	that moment."	that moment." p.230-23
148	mere exclusion of Romanists	exclusion from them
148	on his coming over to it	on his conversion now
149	"...either a vine figs?" What then is there in Antichrist that we can admire or take interest in?	"...either a vine figs?"
150	But all this is to give up the point in dispute, for either the Popes come up to full stature of Antichrist, or we must look for Antichrist elsewhere.	But all this is to give up the point in dispute; but either it grants that the Pope is not the Lawless One whose touch is perdition, it withal explains away Scripture and destroys the specific announcement therein contained of certain temptations which are in God's providence destined to come upon us. It is to make no use of the prophecies and yet to keep others from using them. And this is one chief charge which we bring against the doctrine in question, that it is unjust both to the Word of God and to His Church. It makes the prophetical announcements much less, and the Roman corruptions much more than they are; it is founded in a combined process of exaggeration and dilution, and succeeds in becoming uncharitable towards man at the expense of making free with what is divine.
150	So much on the calumny itself; but it may be objected that the mere fact that	We are writing no orderly dissertation, but setting down such thoughts as have struck us, and

might strike others, on the general aspect of the subject. Let us then proceed to the consideration of an objection on which the mind may naturally fall back after the remarks which have been last suggested, which we know has before now been felt by inquirers, and which will open the way to some further illustrations of the subject. It may strike a person then that the mere fact that

152 and act conformably to their function in the history of Christianity.

and act conformably to their function in the Gospel system.

166 for *filthy lucre's* sake," (Oh, Dr Newton!)

for *filthy lucre's* sake,' (!)

185 which relate to Antichrist, but which cannot by any sober mind be applied to the ecclesiastical events or persons of the past ages of Christianity.

which relate to the enemy of the Church.
We do not gather from his volume whether it is his intention to proceed to those still more awful prophecies, to which we have been especially alluding in the last several pages, but we earnestly hope that he will give us the like benefit of his clearness, accuracy, and learning in the Apocalypse which we have received from him as regards the prophetic announcements which preceded it.

186 **XI.**
MILMAN'S VIEW OF CHRISTIANITY

ART. III. – *The History of Christianity, from the Birth of Christ to the Abolition of Paganism in the Roman Empire*. By the Rev. H. H. Milman. Three volumes. Murray. 1840.

186 The "History of Christianity" which Mr. Milman has lately given to the world, is a work of very considerable ability,

This is a work of very considerable ability,

190 "...In the honesty of his purpose he will seek his excuse for all imperfection or deficiency in the execution of his scheme." – p.47.

"...In the honesty of his purpose he will seek his excuse for all imperfection or deficiency in the execution of his scheme. Nor is he

562

aware that he enters on ground pre-occupied by any writers of established authority, at least in our own country, where the history of Christianity has usually assumed the form of a history of the Church, more or less controversial, and confined itself to annals of internal feuds and divisions in the Christian community, and the variations in doctrine and discipline, rather than to its political and social influence. Our attention, on the other hand, will be chiefly directed to its *effects on the social and even political condition* of man, as it extended throughout the Roman world, and at length entered into the administration of government and of law; the gradual manner in which it absorbed and incorporated into the religious commonwealth the successive masses of population, which, after having overthrown the temporal polity of Rome, were subdued to the religion of the conquered people; the separation of the human race into the distinct castes of the clergy and laity; the former at first an aristocracy, afterwards a despotic monarchy; as Europe sank back into barbarism, the imaginative state of the human mind, the formation of a *new poetic faith*, a mythology, and a complete system of symbolic worship; the interworking of Christianity with barbarism, till they slowly grew into a kind of semi-barbarous heroic period, that of Christian chivalry; the gradual expansion of the system, with the expansion of the human mind, and the *slow, perhaps not yet complete, certainly not general, development of a rational and intellectual religion.* Throughout his work the author will equally, or his disposition inclines, even more diligently labour to show the *good* as well as

Appendix: Textual Variants

the evil of such phasis of Christianity; since it is his opinion, that, at every period, much more is to be attributed to the circumstances of the age, to the collective operation of certain principles which grew out of the events of the time, then to the intentional or accidental influence of any individual or class of men. Christianity, in short, may exist in a certain form in a nation of savages as well as in a nation of philosophers, yet its specific character will almost entirely depend upon the character of the people who are its votaries. It must be considered, therefore, in constant connection with that character: it will darken with the darkness and brighten with the light of each succeeding century; in an uncongenial time it will recede so far from its genuine and essential nature as scarcely to retain any sign of its divine original: it will advance with the advancement of human nature, and keep up the moral to the utmost height of the intellectual culture of man." – pp. 47-50.

194	irreconcilable with the letter of the sacred text	irreconcilabe with the sacred text
194-195	Thus the great characteristic of Revelation is addition, substitution.	The great characteristic of Revelation is addition, not substitution.
197	but, anyhow, it is to be feared that too many persons will unfairly run away from his book with the notion that to ignore the Almighty in ecclesiastical history is really to deny Him.	but it is to be feared that too many persons will unfairly run away with this notion that it is *immediately involved* in it.
202	Thus Christianity certainly is superior to Budhism.	
204	object and only object is to show	very object is to *connect*

Appendix: Textual Variants

	how like Christianity is to heathenism?	Christianity with the heathen religions?'
207	to be fundamental in that doctrine, and primary in that object.	to be the fundamental and essential doctrines of revealed religion.
208	the recognitions or discoveries of Greek tragedy	άναγνωρισεις
216	These are some of the enunciations of doctrine, true or false, peremptorily advanced by Mr. Milman	These are some of Mr Milman's articles of profession
218	will concur, and which others again, with greater reason, will consider partly true, and partly false: - now let us see what comes of it, as Mr. Milman uses it.	will concur: now let us see what comes of it.
220	that God will never do anything which to philosophers is difficult to receive, and that the Blessed Virgin is more likely to have been mistaken than unbelievers to be irrational.	that God will never do what philosophers will not believe; and that St Mary was incorrect rather than unbelievers inexcusable. And so again of Kepler's notion, that the star seen by the Magi was a conjunction between Jupiter and Saturn he says, "For my own part, I cannot understand why the words of St. Matthew, relating to such a subject, are to be so rigidly interpreted; the same latitude of expression may be allowed on astronomical subjects, as necessarily must be in the Old Testament. The vagueness and uncertainty, possibly the scientific inaccuracy, seem to me the inevitable consequence of the manner in which such circumstances must have been preserved, as handed down, and subsequently reduced to writing *by simple persons, awe-struck under such extraordinary events.*" – p.111, note. Such a philosophy might seem to invalidate the former or evidential

Appendix: Textual Variants

class of miracles also, which may possibly in like manner have come to us on the testimony of "simple and awe-struck persons," but Mr. Milman observes, that what he has been suggesting "*of course* does not apply to facts which must have been either historical events or direct fictions, such as the resurrection of Jesus. The re-appearance of an actual and well-known bodily form, *cannot* be refined into one of those airy and unsubstantial appearances which may be presented to, or may exist solely through, the imaginative faculty. I would strictly *maintain* this important distinction." – p.131.

Whether or not it is an "important distinction," it certainly is very important to be "strictly maintained," – if it can. To proceed however: - Mr. Milman's rule seems to be this, to doubt all miracles which Almighty God has not displayed to a great many, or subjected to exact scrutiny; for instance, which He only *declares*. Accordingly, Mr. Milman very consistently says of the pool of Bethesda, that it "was *supposed* to possess properties for healing diseases. At certain periods there was a strong commotion in the waters, which probably bubbled up from some chemical cause connected with their medicinal effects. *Popular belief*, or *rather perhaps popular language*, attributed this agitation of the surface to the descent of an angel." – vol. i. p. 215.

On the other hand, the Evangelist says expressly, "an angel *went down* at a certain season into the pool." Mr. Milman adds in a note, that "the verse relating to the angel is rejected as spurious by many critics, and is wanting in some manuscripts." *That* is a fair argument against it: if the verse

Appendix: Textual Variants

cannot be supported on external evidence, let it be rejected; but let it not be kept, and explained away on a theory.

221 This does not seem to be any great achievement.*

> * Mr. Milman says of the pool of Bethesda, that it "was *supposed* to possess remarkable properties for healing diseases. At certain periods there was a strong commotion in the waters, which probably bubbled up from some chemical cause connected with their medicinal effects. *Popular belief*, or *rather perhaps popular language*, attributed this agitation of the surface to the descent of an Angel."—Vol. i., p. 215. On the other hand, the Evangelist says expressly, "an Angel *went down* at a certain season into the pool." Mr. Milman adds in a note, that "the verse relating to the Angel is rejected as spurious by many critics, and is wanting in some manuscripts." *That* is a fair argument against it: if the verse cannot be supported on external evidence, let it be rejected; but let it not be kept, and explained away on a theory.

228 This, we suppose, is to show that he need not have a verdict of *felo de se* recorded against him.

229 he would be sure to say we were unfair

we should be sure not to satisfy him

233 without gradual enlargement

without gradual accretion

240 However, there *are* two doctrines

It is remarkable that there are two doctrines

240 This is remarkable.

241 Instances, however, such as these, deserving as they are of notice,

Exceptions, however, such as these, deserving as they are of notice, scarcely do more than illustrate the rule to which they are exceptions. We repeat, then, in perfect sincerity and much anxiety, our inquiry,— What tenet of Christianity will escape proscription, if the principle is once admitted, that a sufficient account is given of an opinion, and a sufficient ground for making light of it, as soon as it is historically referred to some human origin?

cannot be supposed to have any practical weight with men who once thoroughly adopt the External Theory, which we have been all along illustrating. We repeat, it may be inquired, in perfect sincerity and much anxiety, what tenet of Christianity will escape pro-scription, if the principle is once admitted, that a sufficient account is given of an opinion, as soon as it is historically referred to some human origin?'

244-245	Christianity did not even bring the immortality of the soul to light; where then, after all, and what is Christianity?	

245   and then, as if by way of make-up

and then, as if by way of bribe (so to speak), or make-up

245   "On a *wide* and *comprehensive* survey of the whole history of Christianity,..."

"The singular felicity, the skill and dexterity, if we may so speak, with which Christianity at first wound its way through these conflicting elements, combining what was pure and lofty in each, in some instances unavoidably speaking their language, and simplifying, har-monizing and modifying each to its own peculiar system, increases our admiration of its unrivalled wisdom, its deep insight into the universal nature of man, and its pre-acquaintance, as it were, with the countless diversities of human character prevailing at the time of its propagation. But, *unless* the same profound wisdom had watched over its inviolable preservation, which presided over its origin; *unless* it had been constantly administered with the same superiority to the common passions and interests and speculative curiosity of man, a reaction of the several systems over which it prevailed was inevitable. On a *wide* and *comprehensive* survey of the whole history of Christianity,...."

245 ...it sprang from the "insidious principle of Gnosticism."

...it sprang from the "insidious principle of Gnosticism."

In the following passage also Mr Milman asserts and maintains our *principle* to the full, though he arbitrarily limits the *period of its operation.* It seems, according to him, that at the very time of the Apostles, or rather during a certain portion of their time, or in certain of their writings, there was vouchsafed to man from above, an instinctive discernment of the truth, accurate, discriminating, eclectic, plastic, definitive, which was not granted either in Jewish times before, or in Christian afterwards. Daniel's account of angels is mythic, because (if so be) it is like Zoroaster's; St Cyprian's celibacy is a corruption, because (if so be) it is like the Oriental; nay, our Lord can "condescend," and St Peter's preaching be "encumbered" with Judaism, and St John's Apocalypse countenance a "doting fable," but still *"Christianity,"* in spite of this, with "singular felicity wound its way amid conflicting elements." Such has been Mr Milman's doctrine in the foregoing extracts; the following, which is concerning St John's Gospel, throws fresh light upon its perplexities.

"In Ephesus, according to universal tradition, survived the last of the Apostles, and here the last of the Gospels – some have supposed the latest writings of the New Testament – appeared *in the midst of this struggle with the foreign elements of conflicting systems.* This Gospel was written, we conceive, not against any peculiar sect or individual, but to *arrest* the spirit of Orientalism, which was working into the essence of

Christianity, destroying its beautiful simplicity, and threatening altogether to change both its design and its effects upon mankind. In some points it *necessarily* spoke the language, which was common alike, though not precisely with the same meaning, to the Platonism of the West, and the Theogonism of the East; but its sense was different and peculiar. It kept the moral and religious, if not altogether distinct from the physical notions, yet clearly and invariably predominant. While it *appropriated* the well known and almost universal term, the Logos, or word of God, to the divine author of Christianity, and even *adopted* some of the imagery from the hypothesis of conflicting light and darkness; yet it altogether rejected all the wild cosmological speculations on the formation of the world; it was silent on that elementary distinction of the Eastern creed, the separation of matter from the ethereal mind. The union of the soul with the Deity, though in the writings of John it takes *something of a mystic tone*, is not the pantheistic absorption into the parent Deity; it is an union by the aspiration of the pious heart, the conjunction by pure and holy love with the Deity, who, to the extatic moral affection of the adorer, is himself pure love. It insists not on abstraction from matter, but from sin, from hatred, from all fierce and corrupting passions; its new life is active as well as meditative; a social principle, which incorporates together all pure and holy men, and conjoins them with their federal head, Christ, the image and representative of the God of Love; it is no principle of isolation in solitary and rapturous meditation; it is a moral, not an imaginative purity." – vol. ii. pp. 103-4.

Who will deny that all this is,

Appendix: Textual Variants

argumentatively considered, very feeble? Does Mr Milman really think, that no broader basis will be required to maintain his peculiar position? It seems that, for a certain particular time, limits when and reasons why unassigned, "Christianity" is *incorruptible*, nay, *purifies* every thing it takes hold of; but afterwards, just as Judaism before it, it is on the contrary *corruptible*, and is *actually corrupted* by every thing it comes near. Such a view, of course, is not impossible, but it is not self-evident. Let us have the proof of it. We have seen Mr Milman excepting against St Peter's, nay, our Lord's language: do not certain writers of the day carry their exceptions further still? nay, does not Mr Milman himself seem in some parts of his work to give up the inspiration of Scripture? Where then, and what *is*, "Christianity"?

246-247 And now, in bringing our remarks on this able work to an end, we must confess the mixed feeling with which we have made them. We have felt it to be an imperative duty to take that view of Mr. Milman's volumes which first presents itself to a Churchman. It is also their prominent aspect, and such as is likely to arrest the attention of the general reader, as well as of those whose habit of mind it is to associate the visible world with the invisible. The second aspect in which we should regard them, is as being a serviceable collection, or commonplace-book, of the worst which can be said by a candid enemy against the theory of Catholicism. The third remark we make upon them, and we make it with great sincerity and much pleasure, only wishing it could come first instead of third, is in their praise as a work of unusual learning and thought,

And now, in bringing our remarks to an end, we can assure the Christian student, in spite of them, that if he is tolerably well grounded in Church principles, he will find little to harm him, and much to instruct him, amid much to distress him, in these volumes. They bring together a great deal of useful information in a very compact form, and may be put to good service, at least as a common-place book of the worst which a candid enemy can say against Catholicism. His sketches …

containing a large mass of information, valuable to the students of ecclesiastical history. The author's method has its good side as well as its bad. He treats Catholic persons, proceedings, and events, in a large and tolerant spirit. His sketches ...

248 On their controversial principles his reasonings and conclusions are irresistible.

On their principles he is irresistible.

249 **XII.**
REFORMATION OF THE ELEVENTH CENTURY

ART II.-*The Life and Pontificate of Gregory the Seventh*. By John William Bowden, M.A. 2 vols. London: Rivingtons. 1840.

250 Every department of theology

Every department of divinity

253-54 for the life of Hildebrand, known in history as Pope Gregory VII., which he has lately given to the world. No one can write without opinions: we are far from saying that Mr. Bowden has not his own, and that of a very decided character; but what we principally thank him for is his narrative of facts; he has drawn out

for a work like that which is now before us. No one can write without opinions: we are far from saying that Mr. Bowden has not his own, and that very decidedly; but he has drawn out

255 (A.D. 887)

255-56 Adelbert, Archbishop of Bremen, though himself a man of pure life and austere practice in an age of general dissoluteness, conceived a plan, by means of the imperial influence which he enjoyed, of making Hamburg the seat of his power, and establishing a sort of papacy in the North. With this purpose in view, he was tempted to grasp at every method of increasing his revenues, and disgraced his rule by a wide-spread system of corruption and plunder. Associating himself with a profligate favourite of the Emperor, he despoiled without shame the lands and revenues of the less powerful religious communities,

In Lombardy, the Archbishop Guido in the eleventh century was said to have invariably demanded a price for the favour of admission into holy orders; his clergy were in their own way as deeply involved in the guilt of simony as himself, till their very flocks learned to treat them with open manifestations of contempt, reviled them in the house of God itself, and hooted them along the streets. When Hildebrand went as legate into France, he first brought to confession an archbishop who had contrived to bribe to silence the principal evidences against him of simony; and upon his deposition, no less and put up to sale every office, civil or ecclesiastical, which fell to his disposal. On an archbishop in France, who had contrived to bribe to silence the principal evidences against him of simony, at length being brought to confess his guilt and being deposed, no less than forty-five bishops and twenty-seven other dignitaries or governors of churches came forward to confess the criminal mode by which they had obtained their benefices, and retired from stations which they had no valid right to retain. In Lombardy, the Archbishop Guido in the eleventh century was said to have invariably demanded a price for the favour of admission into holy orders; his clergy were in their own way as deeply involved in the guilt of simony as himself, till their very flocks learned to treat them with open manifestations of contempt, reviled them in the house of God itself, and hooted them along the streets. In the times of St. Romuald, who died in 1027, the practice of emperors selling bishoprics, bishops their preferments, and laymen their benefices, was so recognized and ordinary, that when the saint had spoken even to religious persons of simony as a sin, he seemed to them to inculcate over-strained and fanciful notions.

than forty-five bishops and twenty-seven other dignitaries or governors of churches came forward to confess the guilty mode by which they had obtained their benefice*, and retired from stations which they had no valid claim to retain. Even two centuries earlier than this, when, as appears on the face of the facts, the corruption was not so general, a council of Paris had complained that many of the clergy were so occupied in the pursuit of gain and other worldly avocations, that they suffered many infants to die without baptism. A council of Aix-la-Chapelle of the same date prohibits extortion and intemperance in bishops, and protests against their non-residence. A synod of Pavia a little later prohibits the clergy the practice of sumptuous banquets and the use of dogs and hawks. Hincmar judged it expedient to issue a decree against the pawning by the clergy of the vestments and the communion plate. In the times of St. Romuald, who died in 1027, the practice of emperors selling bishoprics, bishops their preferments, and laymen their benefices, was so recognized and ordinary, that when the saint had spoken even to religious persons of simony as a sin, he seemed to them to inculcate overstrained and fanciful notions. Adelbert Archbishop of Bremen, himself a man of pure life and austere practices in an age of general dissoluteness, conceived a plan, by means of the imperial influence which he enjoyed, of making Hamburgh the seat of his power and establishing a sort of papacy in the North. With this purpose in view he was tempted to grasp at every method of increasing his revenues, and disgraced his rule by a wide spread system of corruption and plunder. Associating himself with a profligate favourite of the Emperor, he despoiled without shame the lands and revenues of the less powerful religious communities, and put up to sale every office, civil or ecclesiastical, which fell to his disposal. If such were the practices of men who were stricter than their brethren, what was to be expected of the multitude of ecclesiastics, who were involved in sensuality, or at least in carnal indulgence and sloth?

256-
57

Even two centuries earlier than this, when, as appears on the face of the facts, the corruption was not so general, a Council of Paris had complained that many of the clergy were so occupied in the pursuit of gain and other worldly avocations that they suffered many infants to die without baptism. A Council of Aix-la-Chapelle of the same date prohibits extortion and intemperance in bishops, and protests against their non-residence. A Synod of Pavia a little later prohibits the clergy the practice of sumptuous banquets and the use of dogs and hawks. Hincmar judged it expedient to issue a decree against the pawning by the clergy of the vestments and the communion plate. In 829, the prelates assembled in council at Paris found it necessary to urge Louis the Debonair to use all his influence in extirpating simony, "this heresy so detestable, this pest so hateful to God," from the Church. The Synod of Meaux, in 845, renewed the warning. And Leo IV., in or about 847, denounced it in an epistle to the Bishops of Britanny as a crime condemned by many Councils. The nobles secured the ordination of their younger sons or relatives for the sole purpose of qualifying them for the acceptance of lucrative benefices; giving them, while they did so, the same military training and secular habits with the rest of the family. Others procured admission to the priesthood for dependants whom they intended to retain in subordinate stations in their household. "Such," says Agobard, Archbishop of Lyons, "is the disgrace of our times, that there is scarcely one to be found who aspires to any degree of honour or temporal distinction who has not his domestic priest; and this, not that he may obey him, but that he may command his obedience alike in things lawful and things unlawful; in things human and things divine; so that these chaplains are constantly to be found serving the tables, mixing the strained wine, leading out the dogs, managing the ladies' horses, or looking after the lands."

260   and fornication."

2.

Had we lived in such deplorable times as have been above described,...

and fornication."

The external causes of this woeful corruption were, as we have already noticed, two; secular abundance and secular destitution. Never was instanced more forcibly the meaning of the divine petition, "Give me neither riches nor poverty." As regards the Roman see, its humiliations were the result of secular violence. If, as was not an uncommon idea in the middle ages, Antichrist was, according to the word of prophecy, to seat himself by force in the high throne of the Apostle, to the overthrow of its rightful occupant, surely we may well recognize in the mock-popes and anti-popes of that period the types of the fulfilment. The imperial power, begun in Charlemagne, becoming extinct, Rome became the prey of the lawless and licentious nobles of the neighbouring Carapagna. The pontifical elections were brought completely under their control, and it was by their creatures, violently introduced, that the holy see was subjected to the defilements which we have been describing. In France and Germany, on the other hand, the corruption was far more the direct sin of the Church, which had become secularized by the power and wealth with which the system of Charlemagne had burdened it; and thus, the continuance of that system led to the same results in the north which its extinction occasioned in the south. But on this subject let us hear Mr. Bowden:

"The Church in the transalpine dominions of Charlemagne, bore a character materially modified by the rudeness of her semi-barbarous members; and the efforts of that monarch, exerted toward her refinement, promoted at the same time her secularization. His own idea of her nature and essence seems to have been influenced by the impressions natural to a temporal and military monarch. The pope, as we have seen, he treated in several acts of government as his official adviser or chancellor; and his bishops, whom he endowed with ample territories, became his barons,—his counsellors and ministers at home, and the governors of his provinces abroad. Their positions in the new bishoprics partook, indeed, in some measure of the military character, as it was to them that the sovereign looked to repress the rebellions of his recently acquired subjects, as well as to resist the incursions of barbarous hordes from the wastes beyond the limits of his territory. And even those prelates, who had been fixed in stations apparently less likely to bring them into immediate contact with military operations, became, soon after the great monarch's death, of necessity involved in the general movement, military as well as civil, which ensued from the interminable feuds of his degenerate descendants. The spiritual dignitaries, therefore, of the whole Carlovingian empire were placed in a false and unecclesiastical position: and this circumstance, viewed in connection with the general rudeness of their age, and with the gross views and habits natural to nations just reclaimed, and that in the mass from idolatry, will in great measure enable us to understand the deplorable account given of the Western Church in the ninth century by the writers of the time."

"This diversion, so to call it, of the episcopate from its original destination, brought about, as a matter of course, the introduction into the episcopal body of persons by no means qualified for sacerdotal pre-eminence. In theory, the right of election to vacant bishoprics was recognized by Charlemagne and his descendants as existing, according to ancient and canonical practice, in the clergy and people of the diocese. But the founder of the Carlovingian dynasty was on several occasions induced, either by peculiar circumstances, or by the ambition and intrigues of those about him, to exercise a more than merely influential or confirmatory authority on such occasions Whatever, indeed, might have been thought of the Christian liberty of the Church in the selection of her spiritual pastors, the sovereign had unquestionably a plausible right to dictate in the nomination of those to whom he was to look for the maintenance of order, the administration of justice, and the collection of revenue, in the different districts of his empire. The transfer of elective power from the hands' of the Church herself to those of the temporal sovereign, may be regarded as a natural and necessary accompaniment to the process of her internal secularization."—vol. i. p. 42—46.

Mr. Bowden's able sketch is too long to quote entire, but we must gratify ourselves with another portion of it on the same subject:

"No sooner, indeed, had the munificence of Charlemagne rendered offices in the Church objects of eager desire to the worldly and the covetous, than the crime which, from the unhappy man who first attempted to purchase the gifts of the Holy Spirit, has received the appellation of simony, began to spread through the western empire to a fearful extent; and it became customary to purchase with gold, as well admittance into every rank of the sacred ministry, as the pastoral mission implied in the appointment to stations of ecclesiastical superintendence and responsibility. As early as 829, the prelates assembled in council at Paris found it necessary to urge Louis the Debonair to use all his influence in extirpating 'this heresy so detestable, this pest so hateful to God,' from the Roman Church. The synod of Meaux, in 845, renewed the warning. And Leo IV., in or about 847, denounced it in an epistle to the Bishops of Britanny as a crime condemned by many councils. But it was difficult to impress the enormity of the practice upon an age which had become accustomed to see not only ecclesiastical offices, but holy orders themselves, bestowed on grounds the most frivolous or unworthy. The nobles, in those times, continually procured the ordination of their younger sons or relatives, for the sole purpose of qualifying them for the acceptance of lucrative benefices; giving them, while they did so, the same military training and secular habits with the rest of the family. Others procured the admission to the priesthood of dependants whom they intended to retain in subordinate stations in their household, 'Such,' says the high-principled Agobard, Archbishop of Lyons in the time of Louis the Debonair, 'is the disgrace of our times, a disgrace to be deplored with the whole fountain of our tears, that there is scarcely one to be found who aspires to any degree of honour or temporal distinction who has not his domestic priest; and this, not that be may obey him, but that he may command his obedience alike in things lawful and things unlawful; in things human and things divine; so that these chaplains are constantly to be found serving the tables, mixing the strained wine, leading out the dogs, managing the ladies' horses, or looking after the lands.' And because it was of course impossible, however they might have heard it, to obtain, for stations so degrading, respectable members of the sacerdotal body; 'for what good clergyman,' continues the indignant prelate just quoted, 'could bear to defile his character and life with men like these?' they selected, without the slightest reference either to knowledge or principle, those whom they thought likely to perform most satisfactorily the various domestic offices above enumerated, and then called on Agobard himself, or his brother prelates, to admit, as a matter of course, the 'clerklings,' as they contemptuously styled them, to holy orders; a request with which the regulations of the empire, though no human enactments could in truth be binding in such a matter, compelled the insulted bishops to comply."— VOL. i. p. 48.

579

Had we lived in such deplorable times as have been above described,...

262 He held a Council of his bishops in 1047; in it he passed a decree that "Whosoever should make any office or station in the Church a subject of purchase or sale, should suffer deprivation and be visited with excommunication;" at the same time, with regard to his own future conduct, he solemnly pledged himself as follows:—"As God has freely of His mere mercy bestowed upon me the crown of the empire, so will I give freely and without price all things that pertain unto His religion." This was his first act; but he was aware that the work of reform, to be thoroughly executed, must proceed from Rome, as the centre of the ecclesiastical commonwealth, and he determined, upon those imperial precedents and feudal principles which Charlemagne had introduced, himself to appoint a Pope, who should be the instrument of his general reformation.

He thus dealt with the bishops of his own country:—

"Summoning around him, during the summer of 1047, the prelates of his country, he thus spoke:—'It is with sorrow that I address you, ye that stand in Christ's stead over the Church which He purchased with His blood. For, as it was out of the free grace of God the Father, that He was given unto us, and born of the Blessed Virgin, so did he enjoin His Apostles, "Freely ye have been received, freely give." But ye, corrupted by avarice, are under a curse, because ye give and take in barter for the holy treasures which ye dispense: and even my father, for whose soul I am most anxious, was in his lifetime too much led away by this accursed covetousness. He, among you, who feels himself sullied by this sin, should— according to the letter of the canon—should be forthwith deprived of the ecclesiastical office,—whatever it be,—which he may hold. For this—this is the fearful sin,—sin which brings down judicial calamities upon our suffering people: this it is which Heaven scourges among us by famine, by epidemic diseases, and by the sword."

"The prelates around him, too generally conscious of a participation in the guilt which he denounced, shrunk within themselves; and, aware as well of his determination of character, as of his plenitude of power, trembled for the issue. Great therefore was their relief, however overpowering their shame, when, in answer to their acknowledgment of guilt, and supplication for clemency, the monarch thus continued:—'Go hence, employ that well which you have ill obtained; and forget not, in your prayers, to implore mercy for the soul of my father, as of one involved in like criminality with yourselves.' He then dismissed them, demanding, previously to their departure, their assent to a decree, which enacted that no office or station in the Church should thenceforth be made the subject of purchase or sale, and that whosoever should attempt the practice of such nefarious traffic, should be deprived of any office which he might have attained, and be visited with the anathema of the Church. While, with regard to his own future conduct, the emperor, in the presence of the council, solemnly pledged himself as follows:—'As God has freely, of his mere mercy, bestowed upon me the crown of the empire, so will I give freely and without price all things that pertain unto His religion.'"—Vol. i. pp. 131, 132.

But he was aware that the work of reform, to be thoroughly executed, must proceed from Rome, as the centre of the ecclesiastical commonwealth, and he determined, upon those imperial precedents and feudal principles which Charlemagne had introduced, himself to appoint a Pope, who should be the instrument of his general reformation.

276	His "hours of sleep," says Mr. Bowden, "were systematically abridged by his devotions…"	"The personal habits of Leo, while he thus actively laboured in the cause of reformation, were of the most ascetic nature; his life formed a consistent course of abstinence and self-denial; and the hours of sleep were systematically abridged by his devotion…"
277-	This was the commencement of their	"Encouraged by the glowing

78   connexion with southern Italy; but it was not for ever of so edifying a character. They returned in the capacity of soldiers in the pay of its petty princes, and, with the duties, they practised the vices and excesses of their profession.

description given by their friends of the sunny clime which they had visited, and of the opportunities, there offered, of enterprise and honour, swarms of northern warriors crossed the Alps: they were readily, and honourably welcomed by Guaimar and other princes of southern Italy; and engaged, under one banner or another, in most of the intestine quarrels which at that period distracted the country."

278-79   Hildebrand's intimate friend

his intimate friend

281   He considered the failure of his arms to be a sign of divine displeasure that he had taken them up. He gave himself over to acts of penance. Though his health was declining, a carpet on the bare earth was his ordinary couch, a stone his pillow, and a hair shirt his garment.

"His ardent temperament," says Mr. Bowden, "had encouraged him too confidently to anticipate a blessing on his exertions; and the same disposition now led him to trace the displeasure of heaven in his calamity. While at Benevento, he employed all his hours, except those engaged in negociation or other necessary business, in religious meditation, in prayer, and in exercises of ascetic devotion. Though his health was declining, a carpet on the bare earth was his ordinary couch, a stone his pillow, and a hair shirt his garment next the skin."

281   He speaks of him "as a man of sincere and deep devotion, of extraordinary talents, and of a monastic austerity; of too ardent a temperament to be uniformly judicious in his proceedings;" while "his faith was of a description which led him to receive, without question, a host of legends of the most absurd description."

"Damiani was a man of sincere and deep devotion, of extraordinary talents, and of a monastic austerity. He was of too ardent a temperament to be uniformly judicious in his proceedings; and his faith was of a description which led him to receive, without question, a host of legends of the most absurd description. But there shone forth in him a singleness and purity of character, which, in connexion with his abilities, procured him the universal respect and admiration of his contemporaries. And though, in pushing to the extreme the notions of the age, he must be admitted to have played no unimportant part in forwarding the progress of doctrinal corruptions, yet his name—when the nature of his position is fairly taken into the account—can scarcely be thought undeserving of the veneration of posterity. His exaltation, in this instance, was resisted by him with all his might. He feared to be drawn from the unremitting austerities of his retirement; and it was not until he was threatened by Stephen and his council with excommunication, that he consented to change the life of seclusion and self-denial which he lived, for the activity and notoriety of a more responsible situation."— vol. i. pp. 189, 190.

282   After a time, he was sent to Milan

After this he was sent to Milan

282   Another point on which reform was demanded was their assertion that they had a right to marry, by virtue of a privilege granted them by the same Saint. In this business he was associated with Anselm da Badagio, Bishop of Lucca, afterwards Pope Alexander II.

They asserted also their right to marriage, which was another point on which reform was demanded, on ground of a privilege granted them by the same saint. In this business he was associated with Anselm da Badagio, Bishop of Lucca, afterwards Pope Alexander II. The person named Ariald in the course of the extract was a deacon of Milan, who had headed the reforming party.

285   5.
But it is time to return to Hildebrand himself, in whom all the interest of his times centres. A decree

Another personage who must not be passed without notice is the Empress Agnes, the wife of Henry III., the reforming emperor, and the mother of the prince of the same name, with whom, as we shall hereafter see, Hildebrand, as Pope, came into collision. Her husband dying young, she was appointed regent to her young son, and was led, from the political circumstances in which she found herself, to place herself in opposition to the papal party, who had elected Alexander II. *[sic]* Pope, without waiting for the emperor's concurrence, on the plea of his being a minor. Agnes in consequence had, by means of a German council, appointed in his place Cadalous, Bishop of Parma, who, coming to Rome, posted himself in St. Angelo, which belonged to a family of the name of Cencius, and for some years harassed the Pope in possession. Afterwards she underwent severe affliction; her son was stolen from her, and put into the hands of persons who corrupted him. The consequence is related in the following passage:—

"The Empress Agnes, when bereft of her son, had entertained, as we have seen, in the first moments of her anguish, the thought of devoting herself to a life of religious seclusion. Though she had been subsequently recalled to the court, and to her son's society, under the auspices of Adelbert, it was not to resume the commanding part which she had formerly played there, but to be treated with empty honours, while she beheld the unhappy youth guided, in courses which she deprecated, by counsellors whom she had no power to control. She continued, therefore, a mourner; and her sorrows strengthened and confirmed the devotional tendency of her mind. Earthly expectations fading before her, she learned to lean more steadfastly on hopes from above. Her friend and adviser, the Bishop of Augsburg, having died, she listened with pleasure to the ghostly counsels conveyed to her in the epistles addressed to her by Peter Damiani. Under this training, she learned to view the course of her late policy with altered eyes, and to mourn over the part which she had taken in the election of Cadalous, as over a grievous sin. And, after Adelbert's overthrow had once more put her son into the hands of those who had originally stolen him from her, she resolved on abandoning alike the name of earthly dignity, and the country in which that dignity had been enjoyed; and on spending the remainder of her days in repentance and devotion, at the threshold of St. Peter. Wonderful, according to Damiani, and edifying, was the spectacle of her entrance into the apostolic city. She rode, not on a stately palfrey, but on a short and sorry steed, scarcely exceeding the size of an ass: the robe had been changed for the veil, the purple for the sackcloth; and the hand which had wielded the sceptre, was worn by the constant use of the Psalter. Arrived in Rome, she humbled herself before the pontiff, whose title she had disputed; she sought and received his absolution; and then devoted herself to religious seclusion, in the convent of St. Petronilla, in the papal city."—vol. i. pp. 256, 257.

In these extracts much has incidentally been shown of the nature of the struggle which was in progress, and the results to which it was approximating. The most important of these was that above referred to in the history of Agnes. A decree

286 The attempt was vain; the uproar continued, and it was not until the cardinal presbyter, Hugo Candidus, coming forward, declared Hildebrand to be the unanimous choice of the cardinals, that the multitude suffered their cries to subside.

"'Brethren,' said the cardinal, 'ye know, and, as it appears, ye acknowledge, that, from the time of our Holy Father Leo, Hildebrand, our archdeacon, has proved himself a man of discretion and probity; that he has exalted the dignity of our Roman Church, and rescued our Roman city from imminent dangers. We can find no man more fitting to be entrusted with the future defence of our church or state; and we, the cardinal bishops, do, with one voice, elect Hildebrand to be henceforth your spiritual pastor and our own.'"

288   Mr. Bowden tells us, that his election, at the moment un-questionably unexpected by himself, seems to have overwhelmed for a while even his intrepid spirit. In letters written from his couch, he speaks of it in terms of terror, using the language of the Psalms, "I am come into deep waters where the floods overflow me," imploring the intercessions of his friends in his behalf, and expressing a hope that their prayers, though they had not sufficed to prevent his being called to that post of danger, might nevertheless avail to defend him when placed there.

"The event of his election, unexpected as, at the moment, it unquestionably was, seems to have overwhelmed for a while even his intrepid spirit. In letters written from the couch on which, exhausted in mind and body, he passed the following day, he speaks of it in terms of terror, and, using the poetical language of the Psalms, exclaims, 'I am come into deep waters, where the floods overflow me. I am weary of my crying: my throat is dried. Fearfulness and trembling are come upon me, and horror hath overwhelmed me.' And he concludes by anxiously imploring the intercessions of his friends with heaven in his behalf; expressing a hope that their prayers, though they had not sufficed to prevent his being called to that post of danger, might yet avail to defend him when placed there."

"The greatness, and,—in the actual state of the world,—the daring nature, of the desires which animated him, and those with whom he had for some time been acting, now stood, perhaps, more fully displayed before him than ever, at the moment in which he felt himself irrevocably pledged to be the leading instrument in their fulfilment. His election called him to occupy the foremost post in the great conflict of principle then pending; a conflict, on his part, against long-rooted customs, against long established authority; a conflict against the wishes, the prejudices, and even, in some respects, the affections natural to mankind; a conflict in which to fail was ruin and disgrace; from which to retire would be a sinful abandonment of duty. An irresistible necessity, as it would appear to him, suddenly brought him close to those gigantic events,—those fearful moments of crisis, which he had till then been permitted to contemplate through the mists of a comparatively dim and distant futurity; and his spirit may well have shrunk, for a moment, from more nearly and more directly contemplating them."—vol. i. p. 318, 519.

288   Well he might: we shall confine ourselves to two of the projects which he conceived and carried out,—the chief but not the only acts of his pontificate, and amply sufficient in themselves to exemplify the force of will and fortitude of spirit, which has made his name so memorable in Church history. The first was no less than the obliging the clergy either to separate from their wives or resign their preferments. The second was the abasement of the temporal below the spiritual power. And first of his enforcement of clerical celibacy:—

But now what was it which he thus contemplated as his destined trial? The first that shall be mentioned was no less than this: the obliging the clergy and their wives to separate, or to retire from their preferments, on the ground that clerical marriage was against the rule of the Church. Now this subject requires some explanation.

293   Such were Gregory's proceedings, and such his success with the high prelacy; but he had a new and formidable and, we must add, unjustifiable weapon in his arsenal

But Gregory had a new and formidable and, we must add, unjustifiable weapon in his arsenal

296   says Mr Bowden

305   We wish we had room to continue this exciting scene, which ends in a majestic address of Gregory to the Council, and the enthusiastic acclamations of the prelates assembled in answer to it.

We wish we had room to continue this most exciting scene, which ends in a majestic address of Gregory to the council; however, we cannot refrain from giving the close of this speech, and the termination of the meeting.

"'Now, therefore, brethren,' he concluded, 'it behoves us to draw forth the avenging sword. Now must we smite the enemy of God and of His Church, that the bruised head, now haughtily erect against the foundation of the faith, and of all the Churches, may recoil; that, according to the sentence pronounced against him in the first days of his pride, upon his belly he may go and eat the dust. "Fear not," saith the Lord, "little flock; for it is your Father's good pleasure to give you the kingdom." It is enough that ye have borne thus long with the adversary. Ye have warned him sufficiently and well. Now let him be made to feel that his conscience has been seared.'

"Here he paused, and appeared to wait the opinion of the prelates around him. But his suspense was not of long duration; the assembly, arising as one man, seemed eager to support him by the testimony of their unanimous approval. They called on him to wield, without delay, the high powers with which he was invested, and to pronounce the sentence of the Church against the blasphemer, the despoiler, the tyrant, the apostate. 'Pronounce,' they cried, 'the doom, by which he may himself be crushed, and from which others, for ages to come, may take warning. Draw forth the sword!—inflict judgment!—let the righteous rejoice when he seeth the vengeance,—let him wash his footsteps in the blood of the ungodly.'"—vol. ii. pp. 104, 105.

306   ...and had treated the Pope as one of their subjects, just as a naturalist of this day in despair ranks a whale among the mammalia.

On the present occasion, Mr. Bowden considers it a cause of thankfulness...

...and had treated the Pope as one of their subjects, just as a naturalist of this day in despair ranks a whale among the mammalia

"The Christian doctrine, that the Almighty Head of the Church 'ruleth over all the kingdoms of the earth, and giveth them to whomsoever be will,' was confounded with the idea that His imagined sole vicar and

Appendix: Textual Variants

representative below was invested with, what the language of the times entitled, a paramount lordship or suzerainty over the individual thrones of Christendom. Standing in the place of St. Peter, his successor was regarded as though clothed with an authority, similar in nature to that of kings, though exceeding theirs in extent; as occupying, in relation to them, a position analogous to that which they occupied in reference to their feudatory nobles; the great truth of the Church's substantive and, in her own province, supreme authority, being thus borne witness to, though in connexion with the then generally prevalent error, which represented her as forming a certain definite member, a component necessary department of the system of feudal society."—vol. i. pp. 330, 331.

On the present occasion, Mr. Bowden considers it a cause of thankfulness…

310	further service."—Vol. ii., pp. 161-164. Thus it was that Henry and the imperial family at last reached the plains of Lombardy.	further service. The party were, however, able to proceed with their journey; and henry arrived, without further obstacle, in the plains of Lombardy". —Vol. ii., pp. 161-164.
310-11	9. In Italy the report was at once	When the penitent arrived in Italy, it was at once
311	Matilda goes by the name of the Great Countess.	While he was on his way thither, we must take the opportunity of commemorating Matilda, called the Great Countess.
336	**XIII.** **PRIVATE JUDGMENT.**	Art. III. – 1. *Autobiography of Thomas Platter, a Schoolmaster of the XVIth Century. Translated from the German.* Wertheim. London. 1839. 2. *Reasons for becoming a Roman Catholic. Addressed to the Society*

of Friends. By F.Lucas, Esq., of the Middle Temple, Barrister at Law. Booker and Dolman. London. 1839.

3. *A Letter to the Hon. and Rev. George Spencer, on his Sermon preached at Manchester.* By the Rev. G. B. Sandford, M.A., Parker. Oxford. 1840.

4. *Geraldine, a Tale of Conscience.* By E. C. A. Vol. iii. Dolman. 1839.

5. *A Few Words in Support of No. 90 of the Tracts for the Times.* Parker. Oxford.

6. *A few more Words in Support of No. 90 of the Tracts for the Times.* By the Rev. W. G. Ward, M.A., Fellow of Balliol College. Parker. Oxford.

7. *Letters 1, 2, 3, 4, 5, to N. Wiseman, D.D.; containing Remarks on his Letter to Mr. Newman, &c.* By the Rev. W. Palmer, M.A. Parker. Oxford.

8. *The Articles treated on in Tract 90 reconsidered and their Interpretation vindicated, in a Letter to the Rev. R. W. Jelf, D.D., Canon of Christ Church.* By the Rev. E. B. Pusey, D.D. Parker. Oxford.

336-37

THERE is this obvious, undeniable difficulty in the attempt to form a theory of Private Judgment, in the choice of a religion, that Private Judgment leads different minds in such different directions. If, indeed, there be no religious truth, or at least no sufficient means of arriving at it, then the difficulty vanishes: for where there is nothing to find, there can be no rules for seeking, and contradiction in the result is but a *reductio ad absurdum* of the attempt. But such a conclusion is intolerable to those who search, else they would not search; and therefore on them the obligation lies to explain, if they can, how it comes to pass, that Private Judgment is a duty, and an advantage, and a success,

Geraldine has been already introduced to our readers as a convert to the Church of Rome, as real as the heroine of a tale can be; or more real, if, as report goes, she be in some respects the shadow of the authoress. Mr. Lucas is a convert in good earnest every inch of him, and writes to recommend the Protestant world in general, and the Society of Friends in particular, to follow his example. Mr. Spencer, it is scarcely necessary to say, is another; and his sermon preached at Manchester contains, according to Mr. Sandford, an account of the motives which occasioned his change. Thomas Platter is the example of a convert in the opposite direction, and of

590

Appendix: Textual Variants

considering it leads the way not only to their own faith, whatever that may be, but to opinions which are diametrically opposite to it; considering it not only leads them right, but leads others wrong, landing them as it may be in the Church of Rome, or in the Wesleyan Connexion, or in the Society of Friends.

Are exercises of mind, which end so diversely, one and all pleasing to the Divine Author of faith; or rather must they not contain some inherent, or some incidental defect, since they manifest such divergence? Must private judgment in all cases be a good *per se*; or is it a good {337} under circumstances, and with limitations? Or is it a good, only when it is not an evil? Or is it a good and evil at once, a good involving an evil? Or is it an absolute and simple evil? Questions of this sort rise in the mind on contemplating a principle which leads to more than the thirty-two points of the compass, and, in consequence, whatever we may here be able to do, in the way of giving plain rules for its exercise, be it greater or less, will be so much gain.

somewhat more than 300 years' standing. Here then we have four instances of conversion; one to Protestantism, and three to Rome, differing in most points from one another; but all of them illustrating the operation of private judgment in matters of faith.

We propose to use them as an occasion for one or two remarks on the subject of private judgment, if it is possible that readers are to be found of a patience equal to the toleration of a subject so exhausted and so hopeless; and we have added some of the pamphlets which the Oxford controversy has produced, in the belief that they furnish suitable illustrations of a point which must be introduced rather prominently in the course of our discussion. Of the pamphlets which have appeared on this occasion, the first in importance, and, we will add, in beauty of composition, is, as might have been anticipated, Dr. Pusey's, which it would be a great injustice to attempt to characterise or sum up in a few words, but which, we will venture to say, no fair person will be able to read without extreme interest and profit. Mr. Ward's two pamphlets are able and manly assertions of the right possessed by subscribers to the Thirty-nine Articles of holding anti-Protestant opinions, supported by a great deal of acute remark, and recommended by a most Christian and charitable tone. Mr. Palmer's are very learned and serviceable compositions, as what is not which he writes? About their tone, which has pained us, we will say a severe thing—that they are very unlike his gentle and amiable self, or rather, they are like a most amiable man thinking it a duty to be unamiable. However, we are pleased to add, that in the fifth letter he has thrown off this artificial dress, and appears in his natural character. So much for controversialists; now to return to our four converts.

Of these, Geraldine is a young lady, who professes to examine fathers and divines for herself. She admires the appearances of life in the (so called) Evangelical body, but thinks cheaply of their intellect; she much respects the opposite section in the Church, but does not sympathise in its ethical temper. She considers the former deficient in consistency of view, the latter in consistency of practice; the former shallow, the latter cold and formal; and she betakes herself to Rome, with the hope of gaining light and heat together. Such is the history of the conversion of Geraldine.

Mr. Lucas, an educated and able man, originally a disciple of Quakerism, to use his own term, considers it to be "the most spiritual" of all the sects, and that "the Anglican Protestants," on the other hand, are possessed of "solemn liturgies and devout services;" but then Anglicanism is the "gigantic skeleton" of what once had life, and the Friends again have "cast away the shell, and seek only for the kernel." He too, somewhat like Geraldine, recognises in the Church of Rome both the body and the soul—forms, which are withal divine, "the spiritual essence" of religion "everywhere indissolubly married by divine ordinance to the outward symbol." Here are the reasons which wrought Mr. Lucas's conversion.

Mr. Spencer, a gentleman of noble birth, high character, much earnestness, a clergyman of our Church, and a chaplain to the present Bishop of London, is converted on four reasons, as they are stated in Mr. Sandford's well reasoned and excellent tempered

Letter; first, because the English Church is Protestant, and no branch of the Catholic Church; next, because our clergy are not Well informed in regard to the doctrines which they themselves hold ; thirdly, because it is safer to belong to a communion which is not condemned by its opponents, than to one which is; lastly and principally, because whereas the Church of Christ is one, and cannot but be one, there are among Protestants very numerous divisions. Such are the reasons which Mr. Spencer's private judgment has created or adopted for leaving the English Church for the Roman.

Master Thomas Platter, a Swiss schoolmaster of the sixteenth century, of energetic mind, and eventually of some learning, exercised his private judgment in a far different way, and at afar earlier age. His first essay was when he was five years and a half old, on occasion of his being put to school with his uncle, Mr. Anthony, a priest and a very passionate man. In consequence of the ill treatment he received from the hands of this personage, he had often occasion, he tells us, to "scream like a goat, that had the knife sticking into it," and in the event he made up his mind to go on his travels with a relation, who was on his way to the German schools, in the capacity of his servant or fag. The engagement between them was, that Thomas was to beg as they went, and Paul, the student, was to support him out of his earnings. They first came to Breslaw, and then they migrated to Munich, where they fell in "with a soap-boiler of the name of Schrall, who was a Master of Arts at Vienna, but an enemy to the clerical state." Thomas was now in the way to gain light, and that way widened upon him, and grew broader and broader after he had run away from his kinsman and master, and begged and schooled on his own account at Zurich and elsewhere. He had been born on Shrove Tuesday, just as people were going to mass, and in consequence a persuasion prevailed, that he was destined to be a priest; but the life he had been leading for years, though nominally in the pursuit of knowledge, had issued in a knowledge rather of the world than of books. At eighteen he had not mastered his Latin grammar. Once when he came to his mother, after an absence of five years, in which he had travelled far and wide,—but let us use his own words,—

"The first word she said to me was, 'Has the devil carried you hither once more?' I answered, 'the devil has not carried me, but my feet; however, I will not long be a burden to you.' Then she said, 'You are not a burden to me; but it grieves me that you go strolling backwards and forwards in this manner, and, without doubt, learn nothing at all. If you learned to work, as your late father also did, that would be better; you will never be a priest.' So I remained with her two or three days." —p.44.

After this he went again to Zurich, and put himself under Myconius, who, "without doubt, was already acquainted with the pure doctrine," says he, "but was *obliged* notwithstanding to go to church at Frauenmiinster with his scholars, to sing the vespers, matins, and masses, and to direct the singing." Platter participated in his master's illumination, till at last we read of the following grand burst of private judgment, which, little as we wish to be thought patrons of idolatry, seems to us almost as bad. "At the time that I was custos, I often had no wood for the heating of the school. One morning Zuinglius was to preach before day at Frauenmiinster, and as they were ringing the bell for service, and there was no wood for heating the school, I thought in my simplicity, 'You have no wood, and there are so many idols in the church!' As no one was there, I went into the church to the nearest altar, seized a wooden St. John, hurried with him into the school into the oven, and said to him, 'Johnny, now bend yourself, you must go into the oven, even though you represent a St. John.' When he began to burn, there were nasty great blisters from the oil paint. I thought 'Now hold still; if you stir, which, however, you will not do, I will shut to the door of the oven, and you dare not come out, unless the evil one fetches you.' In the meantime the wife of Myconius came, who wished to go to church to the sermon, and said, 'God give you a good day, my son; have you heated the oven?' I closed the oven door, and said 'Yes, mother, I am quite ready.' I would not, however, tell it to her; for if it had been known, it would at that time have cost me my life. In the schools, Myconius said, 'Custos, you have had famous wood to-day.' I thought, 'St. John deserves the most praise.' When we were to sing the mass, two priests were quarrelling together, and one said to the other, 'You Lutheran knave, you have robbed me of a St. John.' This they continued a good while. Myconius did not know what the matter was; but St. John was never found again. Of course I never told it to any one till several years after, when Myconius was preacher at Basle; then I told it to him, and he wondered very much, and remembered well how the priests had quarrelled together.

Although it appeared to me then that Popery was a mere mummery, *yet I still had it in my mind to become a priest,* and to do the duties of my office faithfully, and deck out my altar smartly. For of real piety I understood at that time nothing; all rested merely on outward ceremonies."—pp. 48—50.

Next he got acquainted with Zuingle, and considers that he grew more serious in consequence; how his seriousness showed itself, the following extract is evidence:

"At that time six of us went home to St. Gall; and as we came on a Saturday to Glyss, we heard that the priests were singing vespers. After vespers, one came and asked, 'Whence do you come?' I, as the boldest, replied 'from Zurich.' Then the priest said, 'What have you done in that heretic city?' I became angry, and said, 'Why heretic city?' The priest replied, 'Therefore, because they have put away the mass, and removed the pictures from the churches.' Thereupon I said, 'That is not so, for they still celebrate mass there; they have also pictures: why are they then heretics?' 'For this reason,' be replied, 'because they do not consider the Pope as the head of the Christian Church, and do not call upon the saints.' I went on, 'Why is the Pope the head of the Christian Church?' He said, 'Therefore because St. Peter was Pope at Rome, and has given the popedom there to his successors." I said, 'St. Peter has very likely never been to Rome;' pulled my New Testament out of the bag, and showed him how (in the epistle to the Romans,) the Apostle salutes so many, and yet never mentions St. Peter, who, according to his assertion, was the most eminent among the Christians of that place.'

Thereupon he said, 'How could that be true then, that Christ met St. Peter outside the city of Rome, and he asked him where he was going to? whereupon Christ answered, to Rome, to allow myself to be crucified.' I asked, 'Where have you read this story?' He said, 'I often heard it from my grandmother.' Thereupon I answered, 'So then I perceive that your grandmother is your Bible. And why should one call upon the saints?' Answer: 'Therefore because it is written, God is wonderful in all his works.' Then I stooped down, broke off a little plant, and said, if one were to collect all men together, they would not be able to make a plant like this.' Then he became angry, and our conversation ended."—pp. 52—54.

Such is the history of the private judgment of Master Platter; very different, certainly, from that exhibited in the person of Geraldine or Mr. Lucas, yet equally private judgment with theirs. Are exercises of mind, which end so diversely, one and all pleasing to the Divine Author of faith; or rather must they not contain some inherent, or some incidental defect, if they manifest such divergence? Must private judgment in all cases be a good *per force;* or is it a good under circumstances, and with limitations? Or is it a good when it is not an evil? Or is it a good and evil at once, a good involving an evil? Or is it an absolute and simple evil? Questions of this sort rise in the mind on contemplating a principle which leads to Rome as well as to Zurich or Geneva; and, in consequence, whatever we may now be able to do, in the way of giving plain rules for its exercise, be it greater or less, will be so much gain.

349-50 Now, before proceeding, let us observe, that as yet nothing has been found in Scripture to justify the cases of private judgment which are exemplified in the popular religious biographies of the day. These generally contain instances of conversions made on the judgment, definite, deliberate, independent, isolated, of the parties converted. The converts in these stories had not seen miracles, nor had they developed their own existing principles or beliefs, nor had they changed their religion in company with others, nor had they received new truths, they knew not how. Let us then turn to Scripture a second time, to see whether we can gain thence any clearer sanction of Private Judgment as now exercised among us, than our search into Scripture has hitherto furnished.

Now, before proceeding, let us observe, that as yet nothing has been found in Scripture to justify the cases of private judgment which are exemplified in the books which lie before us. These are instances of a conversion, made on the judgment, definite, deliberate, isolated, of the persons converted. Geraldine does not profess to have seen miracles, nor Mr. Spencer to have been seduced on to Rome by received Protestant principles, or by accredited maxims of the see of London; nor Mr. Lucas to have been converted unconsciously without the possibility of any deliberate inquiry at all. Thomas Platter seems to have the most to say for himself; for at least he followed a multitude in renouncing the Catholic religion for Zuinglianism, whether such conduct was like that of the 3000 in the book of Acts or no. Let us then turn to Scripture a second time, to see whether we can gain thence any clearer sanction of private judgment as now exercised among us, than our search into it has hitherto furnished us.

350 Here at length, it will be said, is a precedent for such acts of private judgment as are most frequently recommended and instanced in religious tales; and indeed these texts commonly are understood to make it certain beyond dispute, that individuals ordinarily may find out the doctrines of the Gospel for themselves from the private study of Scripture.

Here at length, it will be said, is a precedent for such acts of private judgment as those of Geraldine or Thomas Platter; and indeed these texts commonly are so understood; as if they made it certain beyond dispute that individuals ordinarily may find out the doctrine of the Gospel for themselves from the private study of Scripture.

350 The context of the passage in which our Lord speaks of searching the Scriptures, shows plainly that their office is that of leading, not to a knowledge of the Gospel, but of

The connection in which our Lord speaks of searching the Scriptures, shows beyond dispute that they were calculated to lead his hearers, not to a knowledge of the Gospel,

Himself, its Author and Teacher.

but of Him its author and teacher.

355

4.

Having carried our train of thought as far as this, it is time for us to proceed to the thesis in which it will be found to issue, viz., that, on the principles that have been laid down, Dissenters ought to abandon their own communion, but that members of the English Church ought not to abandon theirs.

Having proceeded in our train of thought as far as this, it is time for us to lay before the reader the thesis which the examples of conversion with which we began suggest, viz., that, on the principles that have been laid down, Dissenters ought to abandon their own communion, but that members of the English Church ought not to abandon theirs.

357

So much then for the Protestant side of the thesis.

So much for Thomas Platter.

357

One half of it then is easily disposed of, but now we come to the other side of it, the Roman, which certainly has its intricacies.

One half, then, of our thesis is easily disposed of; but now we come to the other moiety, to which Geraldine and her companions invite us, and which certainly has its intricacies.

360

what then will they say to us?

what then will Geraldine say to this?

360

However, there is a third type of rival teaching mentioned in Scripture, under which the dissension between Rome and England may be considered to fall, and which it may be well to notice.

However, there is a third type of rival teaching mentioned in Scripture - though not as between truth and falsehood, or faith and heresy, – under which the dissension between Rome and England may be considered to fall, though whether its application to present circumstances will serve those who, with the characters real and fictitious in our heading, leave the Anglican for the rival communion, in justification of their procedure, is not so clear.

369

…by which Providence recommends to us or disowns the prophets that come in His name.

…by which Providence recommends to us or disowns the prophets that come in His name.
Mr. Ward, in the former of his able pamphlets, lays down a *distinctive* difference between the ancient honours paid to St. Mary and the modern; the modern Roman

599

opinion being "that the blessed Virgin is appointed by our Lord the *sole necessary channel* through which his grace shall flow to his Church; so that in fact," as he proceeds to observe, "addresses to her are more *immediate* applications for a supply of grace than to our Lord himself;" and then he refers, in a note, to certain extracts, which Ussher gives from St Bernardine, and which run as follows in translation:

"From the time wherein the Virgin-mother did conceive in her womb the Word of God, she had obtained such a kind of jurisdiction, so to speak, or authority, in all the temporal procession of the Holy Ghost, that no creature hath obtained any grace or virtue from God, but according to the dispensation of his holy mother. Because she is the mother of the Son of God, who doth produce the Holy Ghost; therefore all the gifts, virtues, and graces of the Holy Ghost are by her hands administered to whom she pleaseth, when she pleaseth, how she pleaseth, and as much as she pleaseth." *Bernardin. Senens. Serm. lxi. artic. i. cap. 8.* "She hath singularly obtained of God this office from eternity, as herself doth testify, Proverbs, viii. 23: *I was ordained from everlasting*, namely, a dispenser of celestial graces." *Id. ibid. artic. iii. cap. 3.* "As by the neck the vital spirits do descend from the head into the body, so by the Virgin the vital graces are transmitted from Christ, the head, into his mystical body; the fullness of grace being in him as in the head, from whence the influence cometh, and in her as in the neck, through which it is transfused." *Id. ibid. num. 2.* "Take away the patronage of the Virgin, you stop, as it were, the sinner's breath, that he is not able to live any longer." *Viegas. ibid. sect. ii. num. 6.* "As many creatures do serve the glorious Virgin Mary, as serve the Trinity; namely, all creatures, whatsoever degree they hold among the things created, whether they be spiritual as angels, or rational as men, or corporeal as the heavenly bodies or the elements; and all things that are in heaven and in earth, whether they be the damned or the blessed; all which being brought under the government of God, are subject likewise unto the glorious Virgin: forasmuch as he who is the Son of God and of the blessed Virgin, being willing as it were to equal in some sort his mother's sovereignty unto the sovereignty of his Father, even he who was God did serve his mother upon earth. Whence (Luke, xi. 51) it is written of the Virgin and glorious Joseph, *He was subject unto them;* that, as this proposition is true, all things are subject to the command of the Virgin, even God himself." *Id. ibid. cap. 6.*

Mr. Palmer again thus addresses Dr. Wiseman:

"You will not deny the authority of the litany of the blessed Virgin printed at the end of the Roman Catechism compiled by Cardinal Bellarmine, and to the repetition of which indulgences were attached by Sixtus V., Benedict XIII., and Pius VII. At the conclusion of this is the following prayer.

"'We fly to *thy protection*, Holy Mother of God, *despise not our prayers* in our necessities, but *deliver us* at all times *from all evils*, glorious and blessed Virgin.' The holy psalmist placed his trust in God. 'The Lord will be a refuge for the oppressed, a refuge in times of trouble.' (Ps. ix. 9.) He consoled the afflicted of Israel by the hope that the Lord 'will regard the prayer of the destitute, and not despise their prayer.' (Ps. cii. 17.) Our Lord Himself taught us to pray to our Heavenly Father to 'deliver us from all evil.' And yet, in spite of all this, the popes grant indulgences for the repetition of prayers which express the very same sort of confidence in the Virgin as the Scriptures teach us to feel towards God.

"I will here mention another prayer to the Virgin, to the repetition of which Pius VI. in 1786 granted indulgences. It is as follows: 'Condescend to permit me to praise thee, sacred Virgin. *Grant me strength against thine enemies.* Blessed be God in his saints.' The 'Stabat Mater,' which has indulgences annexed to its repetition by Innocent XI., is full of similar petitions. But I will not dwell further on this branch on subject.

"You wish for some proofs from your 'best writers,' or any of them, that the Virgin Mary is presented instead of the Trinity, and that she is the dispenser of mercy. You will readily admit the eminent learning and piety of Cardinal Bona. Hear then the following prayer extracted from his writings.

"'Oh most sweet Virgin Mary, Mother of God and our Lord Jesus Christ, *refuge of sinners* and *mother of mercy*, I commit myself this day and evermore to thy peculiar *protection* with most humble devotion. Place me near unto thee, and *protect me from all my enemies visible and invisible. Say unto my soul*, I am thy Salvation. Direct me thy servant in all my ways and actions. Console me in all my griefs and afflictions. Defend and preserve me from all evils and dangers. Turn thy face unto me when the end of my life shall come; and may *thy consolation*, in that tremendous hour, rejoice my spirit.

Thou canst do all that thou wilt in Heaven and earth, nor can any resist thy will, for thou obtainest from the Almighty whatever thou seekest. Hear therefore and receive my prayers, and despise me not when I confide in thy mercy. Behold *I fall down and worship* in thee *thy Son*, and I implore thy suffrages to obtain that my sins may be blotted out, to reconcile the heart of thy Son to my heart, that He may possess me, and make a man according unto His heart.'"

Again, shortly after

"Pius VII. by his Rescript of September 21st, 1802, granted a year's indulgence, applicable to the dead, to every Catholic priest, who should recite the following prayer.

"'O holy Joseph, guardian and father of virgins, to whose faithful care Christ Jesus, who was innocence itself, and Mary, Virgin of virgins, was committed, I beseech and pray thee by both these dear pledges *Jesus and Mary, to preserve me from all uncleanness* and *make* me ever most chastely to serve Jesus and Mary, with an undefiled mind, a pure heart, and a chaste body. Amen. (Te per hoc utrumque charissimum pignus Jesum et Mariam obsecro et obtestor, ut me ab omni immunditiâ præservatum, mente incontaminatâ, puro corde, et casto corpore Jesu et Mariæ semper facias castissimè famulari. Amen.)' Bouvier, p. 265.

"In this prayer Joseph is addressed as a *Deity* – a being who has the power of bestowing divine grace, and of enabling Christians to serve God. The Son of God is made a sort of *Mediator* between Joseph and his worshippers; and, in fine, the service of Christians is supposed to be divided between Jesus and Mary! And yet this is a prayer sanctioned by the biggest authority in your Church, and unscrupulously published in your most approved practical Treatises on Indulgences."

And again:

"His loving patroness, our blessed Lady, rewarded his zeal in the cause of charity and devotion by appearing to him in the sight of an immense crowd of people collected in the church of Foggia, to listen to a discourse upon his *favourite subject*, the intercession and patronage of Mary. From her countenance a ray of light, like that of the sun, was reflected upon the face of *her devout servant*, which was seen by all the people, who cried out a miracle! a miracle! and *recommended themselves with great fervour and many tears to the Mother of God*; and many women of abandoned life were seized with such intense sorrow, that they mounted upon a platform in the church, and began to discipline themselves and cry aloud for mercy; and then leaving the church, retired to the house of penitents in that city. Alphonsus, in his judicial attestation, deposed, that during the sermon, he, together with the assembled audience, saw the countenance of the blessed Virgin resembling that of a girl of fourteen or fifteen years of age, who turned from side to side, as was witnessed by every one present.

Whilst he was preaching on the patronage of the blessed Virgin, and exciting his hearers to recur with confidence to her in all their wants, he suddenly exclaimed, 'O, you are too cold, *in praying to our blessed Lady! I will pray to her for you.*' He knelt down in the attitude of prayer, with his eyes raised to heaven, and was seen by all present lifted more than a foot from the ground, and *turned towards a statue of the blessed Virgin* near the pulpit. The countenance of our Lady (the statue!) darted forth beams of light, which shone upon the face of the ecstatic Alphonsus. This spectacle lasted about five or six minutes, during which the people cried out, '*Mercy, mercy! a miracle, a miracle!*' and every one burst into a flood of tears. But the saint rising up exclaimed in a loud voice, 'Be glad, *for the blessed Virgin has granted your prayer.*'"

In like manner Dr. Pusey quotes as follows, from Archbishop Ussher.

"In the crowns composed by Bonaventure, this is one of the orizons that is prescribed to be said: 'O, Empress, and our most kind Lady! by the authority of a mother, command thy most beloved Son, our Lord Jesus Christ, that he would vouchsafe to lift up our minds from the love of earthly unto heavenly desires;' which is suitable to that versicle, which we read in the 35th psalm of this Lady's psalter; 'Incline the countenance of God upon us, - compel him to have mercy upon sinners,' the harshness whereof our Romanists have a little qualified in some of their editions, reading thus:- ;Incline the countenance of thy Son upon us, - compel Him, by thy prayers, to have mercy upon us sinners.' The psalms of this psalter do all of them begin as David's do, but with this main difference, that where the Prophet, in the one, aimeth at the advancement of the honour of our Lord, the friar, in the other, applieth all to the magnifying of the power and goodness of our Lady. so in the first psalm: 'Blessed is the man (quoth Bonaventure) that loveth thy name, O Virgin Mary! thy grace shall comfort his soul;' and in the others following: 'Lady, how are they multiplied that trouble me? With thy tempest shalt thou persecute and scatter them. Lady, suffer me not to be rebuked in the fury of God, nor to be judged in His wrath. My Lady, in thee have I put my trust: deliver me from my enemies, O Lady. In our Lady have I put my trust, for the sweetness of the mercy of her name. How long wilt thou forget me, O Lady, and not deliver me in the day of tribulation? Preserve me, O Lady; for in thee have I put my trust: and impart unto me the drops of thy grace. I will love thee, O Lady of heaven and earth, and I will call upon thy name among the nations.' 'The heavens declare thy glory; and the fragrance of thine ointment is spread among the nations.' 'Hear us, Lady, in the day of trouble; and turn thy merciful face unto our prayers. Unto thee, O Lady, have I lifted up my soul: in the judgment of God, by thy prayers, I shall not be ashamed. Judge me, Lady, for I have departed from my innocency; but because I will trust in thee, I shall not be weakened. In thee, O Lady, have I put my trust, let me never be confounded; in thy favour receive me. Blessed are they whose hearts do love thee, O Virgin Mary; their sins by thee shall mercifully be washed away. Lady, judge those that hurt me; and rise up against them, and plead my cause. Waiting have I waited for thy grace; and thou hast done unto me according to the multitude of the mercy of thy name. Lady, thou art our refuge in all our necessities; and the powerful strength treading down the enemy. Have mercy upon me, O Lady, who art called the mother of mercy, and according to the bowels of thy mercies cleanse me from all mine iniquities. Save me, Lady, by thy name, and deliver me from mine unrighteousness. Have mercy upon me, O Lady, have mercy upon me: because my heart is prepared to search out thy will, and in the shadow of thy wings will I rest. Let Mary arise, and let her enemies be scattered: let them all be trodden down under her feet. In thee, O Lady, have I put my trust, let me never be put to confusion: deliver me in thy mercy, and cause me to escape."

After this and other extracts from divines and devotional writers of past times, Dr. Pusey continues thus –

"It would probably be a first impression on reading these extracts from Archbishop Ussher, that he had with much learning brought together a mass of objectionable language, which it might be hoped was now done away; that all these were the exaggerations of individual minds, and that it was not fair to charge them as teaching now received in the Roman Church. This was my own hope; I reprinted them in illustration of the article, but certainly, little thinking of reputing them to Rome at the present day. The contrary, however, of all this sadly the case. The same extracts which Archbishop Ussher adduced as illustrating the difference between 'the Romish doctrine of the invocation of saints,' and ancient addresses to them, are, in 'the Glories of Mary, Mother of God, by Saint Alphonsus Ligouri, and carefully revised by a Catholic Priest,' (third edit. Dublin, 1837,) adduced as authoritative teaching. The subjects of the early chapters, which they are adduced to establish, are 'how great should be our confidence in Mary, Queen of Mercy' (#1), 'as our Mother' (#2), 'the great love borne us by Mary our Mother' (#3), that 'Mary is *the* refuge of repentant sinners,' and so (#4), 'our life, since she obtains us the pardon of our sins' (c. 2, #1), 'because she obtains us perseverance' (#2), the *necessity* of Mary's intercession in order to

607

obtain salvation' (c. 5), &c. The sayings of Bernardine of Siena, Albertus M. Bonaventure, &c. are alleged as authorities. It is still alleged as a true saying, 'All is subject to Mary's empire, even God' (p. 138, see Abp. Ussher, above, p. 196). 'It is not of course to be supposed that no mention should be made of her Son, or from time to time that her intercession is available through her Son, or that Jesus is our Redeemer, Mary our advocate' (p. 88). 'Jesus is my only hope, and after Him, you, O Virgin Mary' (p. 90). One could not imagine anything written by a Christian in entire forgetfulness of his Lord; but these are but scanty; the main object of the work is (as it professes) 'the glories of Mary,' and these are so set forth, as for the most part to end in her, to place her where a Catholic would expect mention of his Lord. Thus at the hour of death, it is said, May I invoke you during life, and die when calling on 'Mary, my Mother, my blessed amiable Mother' (p. 38). To whom again could it be thought that such language as the following is addressed?

"'If you grant me your aid, what can I fear? during life and at my death, your name and remembrance shall be the delight of my soul (p. 74). I desire to consecrate myself more particularly to your service, dispose of me according to your good pleasure; direct me; I abandon myself wholly to your conduct; never more let me be guided by myself; chastise me, if I disobey you; your correction will be sweet and agreeable' (Ps. cxli. 5). 'I am then no longer mine, *I am all yours'* (p. 30). 'My sins render me unworthy of approaching you. I should expect nothing but chastisement from your hands. I place in you *all my confidence,* and

Appendix: Textual Variants

provided I may be happy enough to die before your image, I shall fiormly hope to join in Heaven that innumerable multitude who have been saved by your intercession' (pp. 53, 54). 'How dare a sinner, unworthy as I, appear before you? I am the last of sinners; I have offended the divine Majesty more than any other; since I cannot recall the past, help me to amend the present' (p. 57). 'O consolation of the afflicted! have pity upon me; remorse of conscience gnaws me; my best actions are but imperfectly performed; hell awaits to carry off my soul; divine justice must be satisfied; what then shall become of me? what shall be my eternal lot?' (p. 83). 'He who is protected by you cannot be lost; heaven and earth confess it. Hence though all creatures forget me, though the whole world abandon me, provided you forsake me not, I should think myself secure' (p. 90). 'I cannot abandon myself to despair; because you are my refuge, and your clemency is unbounded' (p. 135). 'All power has been given unto you in heaven and in earth; nothing is impossible to you, for you can give hope to the desponding' (p. 138)."

Once more; after noticing the painful assertion in a popular and authoritative work, called the "Treatise on the Scapular," that St. Mary possesses a "participated omnipotency," Dr. Pusey observes,

"Yet this has been said yet more strongly in 'the Glories of Mary,' that she not only 'partakes His omnipotence,' but that He has 'resigned it to her.'

"'Now the King of Heaven, whose bounty is infinite, desiring nothing so ardently as to confer His favours on us, in order to increase our confidence in Him, has given us his Mother for our mother, and in her hands resigned (if we may say so)

609

his omnipotence in the sphere of grace that we might place in her the hope of our salvation, and all the hope necessary to attain it' (p. 85).

"And this power they are fond of representing as belonging to her, not as the creature of whom our Lord deigned to take His nature, but (as before in Archbishop Ussher, p. 195, 196, 198, 199, 202) derived from her own merit towards her Son, as the result of a debt which He owed her. They are painfully fond of placing her in the same relation as the Father.

"'Mary owes her Son an infinite gratitude for choosing her for His mother, but it is not less true to say that Jesus Christ has contracted a species of obligation towards her for the human existence He received from her, and in recompense for this benefit, he honours her by hearing her prayers' (Ib. p. 26, 27).

"'Mary has not spared her own Son, her own soul, for the salvation of many.' (p. 36). If to evince the love of God the Father for man it is said that 'He delivered up His own Son for them;' may we not use the same terms to express the love of Mary? 'Yes,' says St. Bonaventure, 'Mary has so loved us, that she has given us her only Son.' 'She gave him us,' says F. Nieremberg, 'when in virtue of her jurisdiction over Him as Mother, she permitted Him to deliver Himself up to the Jews.' 'She gave him for us – she hath given this well-beloved Son; she sacrificed for us a Son, who was infinitely dearer to her than herself.' 'If our salvation was then so near his heart' (pp. 41-43). 'This Divine Saviour whom she has given to the world' (p. 131). Richard of St. Lawrence beautifully explains this passage (Prov. xxx. 11) in reference to the Holy Virgin. 'The heart of the man of God who trusts in Mary, he shall not want spoils,' 'for she has snatched from hell its prey, to enrich with spoils our Lord Jesus Christ.'

"'In taking flesh in your caste womb, a God has been pleased to become your debtor, in order to place afterwards at your disposal all the treasures of His unbounded mercy' (p. 144), 'as it was revealed to St. Bridget, Jesus has obliged Himself to grant all the desires and requests of His blessed Mother, not willing to refuse her anything in heaven, since she has refused Him nothing on earth' (pp. 139, 139).

"St. Germanus says to Mary, 'You – O Holy Virgin, have over God the authority of a mother, and hence you obtain a pardon for the most obdurate sinners.'

"So that at last, it seems nothing strange, that she should be introduced as upbraiding an apostate. 'Thou hast renounced *me* and my Son' (p. 136); or that she should be addressed by a penitent, 'I have by my impurity sinned against God and against *thee*' (p. 80); or with the attribute of Divinity, 'O, sweet in *communicating* thyself to those that love you, to those that seek you' (p. 193)."

XIV.
JOHN DAVISON.

Art. IV. - *Remains and Occasional Publications of the late Rev. John Davison, B.D. formerly Fellow of Oriel College, Oxford, Author of Discourses on Prophecy.* Rivingtons. 1841.

375 THE author on whose character and writings we are now proposing to remark, Mr. Davison, may be considered as an instance of the operation of a mysterious law which is often witnessed in the course of history.

THE author of the miscellaneous compositions which are now at length collected together in the volume of which we have above given the title, may be considered as an instance of the operation of a mysterious law which is so often witnessed in the course of human affairs.

377   as if, like our Lord's forerunner, they would not force themselves on the world, but were bidding it, if it thought worth while, to "go out into the wilderness" after them. In the Preface to these Remains, it is observed of their author, that "perhaps his whole character might be cast in a mould of severer goodness than this age could easily endure,"—p. v., reminding us of the plaintive distich, "Few were the admirers of Thucydides, son of Olorus."

as if they were calling on the world, if it thought it worth while, to "go out into the wilderness" after them. In the Preface to these Remains, it is observed of their author, that "perhaps his whole character might be cast in a mould of severer goodness than this age could easily endure,"—p. v. According to the plaintive though unprosodiacal verses παῦροι δ᾽ ἀγάσαντο Θουκυδίδην ὀλόρου.

378   Of course such a judgment can give no friend of the subject to it.

Of course such a judgment can give no friend of the subject to it. There is something almost ludicrous, when we consider that probably the truth of the matter was that Mr. Davison did not choose to be "hail fellow well met" with such a sort of person, or to show off and play the accomplished man of the world.

378   nay, it must be confessed too, they often put on a very rough jacket for their special benefit.

nay, it must be confessed too, they often put on over them a very rough jacket for the special benefit of such persons.

378   whom with all his estimable points few persons will take as an authority,

whom with all his estimable points few persons will *respect,*

380-81   We mean the difficulty he seems to have had in expressing himself, and the consequent effort which, not only composition, but even conversation, or we may say speech, cost him, and the effect of this difficulty visible in his writings.

We mean the difficulty he seems to have had in expressing himself, the consequent effort which, not only composition, but even conversation, or we may say speech cost him, and the effect of this visible in his writings.

381   to attempt to analyse the cause in his particular case for this peculiarity

to attempt to analyse the reasons in his particular case for this peculiarity

381   an historical portrait offered for our

an historical portrait, it may be not

contemplation, it may be not without its use to set down, not what actually were the causes, but some of what might be its causes, and what are the causes of this characteristic in similar instances.

without its use to set down, not what *were* the reasons, but some of what might be, and what are the reasons of it in similar instances.

381   We suppose it then to be undeniable

We suppose then that it is undeniable

382   All these mental states

All these feelings

382   Mr. Davison's style is an illustration of what we have been saying. We consider its characteristic to lie in the force and vividness of its separate expressions, phrases, or sentences; and, though there is always a danger of generalizing beyond our data, we are tempted to pronounce that he is more happy in his words and clauses than in his conduct of an argument.

It will show most plainly that we are not speaking of Mr. Davison personally in these remarks, to draw attention to the gravity and deliberateness which mark all his writings, and in particular to the great patience and exactness with which he draws out principles or doctrines in their elementary state; as in his first lecture on Prophecy, where he carefully analyses some of the first elements of Christian Evidence, while, by apologizing for the minuteness of his discussion, he betrays his own feeling that it was tiresome. "To men," he observes, "already satisfied of the truth and the importance of the Gospel, few things are less acceptable, than to be recalled from the career of their past conviction, to take up again the original proofs of their faith, and resume the principles of an inquiry which they have had happily answered in the effect of a well persuaded reason, and a regulated life. To such persons the debate with Scepticism is a tedious and worn-out speculation; their life has outrun the question; they enjoy what we are asking them to believe." – p. 19, 2d edit.
We consider the characteristic of Mr. Davison's style to lie in the force and vividness of its separate expressions, phrases, or sentences; and, though there is always a danger of generalizing beyond our

Appendix: Textual Variants

		data, we are tempted to pronounce that he is more happy in his words and clauses than in his conduct of an argument.
382-83	does but increase of course the appearance of elaborateness, we may even add of heaviness, in it, viewed as a whole	do but increase of course the appearance of elaborateness, we may even add of heaviness in it, as a whole
383	It may be added that, in consequence of what may be called his unreadiness, he promises more than he fulfils,	It may be added, that he may be accused of promising more than he fulfils,
383	and in taking those general views, which are so clear and so persuasive in the literature of the day, because they are so superficial?	and in taking those general views, which writers of the day are so successful in accomplishing, at the cost of being sketchy and superficial?
383	literally the first sentence	literally the first sentences
384	3. We have been speaking of Mr. Davison's style, as unattractive in its general course, yet as happy in its separate portions, as being a sort of type of that economy of reserve which an unseen hand wrapped round him. Of its excellence indeed, in its separate portions, it is impossible to speak too highly; the energy of his mind discharges itself concisely and forcibly on the matter in hand, with the flashing power of artillery directed against a fortress; at other times with the calm clear light of some sudden rent in a dark sky. His brilliant sententiousness, the beauty of his images, the terseness and truth and freshness of his expressions, their graphic distinctness,—in a word, his remarkable originality.	We have been speaking of Mr. Davison's unattractiveness in general style, yet felicity in its separate portions, as being a sort of type of that economy of reserve which an unseen hand wrapped round him. Of his talent indeed in the latter it is impossible to speak too highly; the energy of his mind discharges itself calmly, concisely and forcibly on the matter in hand with the power of artillery directed against a fortress. The beauty of his images, the terseness and truth and freshness of his expressions, in a word their remarkable originality
385	their intrinsic value.	their extrinsic value.

614

386   This theory was supremely distasteful to Mr. Davison, and he thus comments on it:-

Presently he illustrates it as follows, from Mr. Edgeworth, in the passage to which we call attention.

388   Is to confound the essence of morality, and run deliberately insane upon a spurious conceited wisdom." – P. 452-454.

Is to confound the essence of morality, and run deliberately insane upon a spurious conceited wisdom." – P. 452-454.

4.

We have already alluded to Mr. Davison's images: they are severe, yet graceful; just and natural, yet poetical.

We suggest the following extract from the author's Observations on the Criminal Law, to all examiners for fellowships and scholarships as a good passage for translation into Latin.

"In different stages of society there will be a succession of new crimes to exercise the vigilance of the law; and the general habits and state of the times cannot vary faster than the vices produced or fostered by them. In a ruder age the violent crimes will prevail; in a more civilized one, the meaner. We rather believe, however, that in a rude age there is much violence and baseness joined together; as none are more addicted to theft and sordid cunning than savages; but atrocities throw the humbler vices into the shade, and cause them to be less felt in their own age, and less known in another. Commerce itself, however, is the fruitful mother of the crimes of theft in all their varieties: not more from the habits it bestows than the opportunity it affords to that offence. It pours in wealth in a shape the most convenient for plunder. The rural opulence of our forefathers was not completely safe; still, their oaken tables and their wheat ricks could not be carried off without some trouble, and men were honest because property was immoveable. But when commerce has collected together the enjoyments of life, and given to more men the taste then the means of them, dishonesty is whetted by all it sees, and by the ease of invading it. We need not wonder at the activity of theft when we look at the accumulated riches of a metropolis, crowded with shops and houses overflowing with loosely guarded plenty; shops where trade thrives so well that the owner cannot attend to his customers and the thief at the same time; and houses where the display of wealth is more a fashion than the economy of it. In Newgate biography, perhaps, examples might be found of a man's setting out perfectly honest at the one end of Cheapside and becoming fit for prison before he reached the other. The circulating force which keeps property continually afloat, and ready to fly at a touch, places it equally in the way of traffic and of pillage.to be ready to be sold, it must be ready to be stolen. To protect all this plenty, and especially in all its less divisions, the law is called upon to exert its power. The small proprietor, indeed, could hardly be called the owner of what he enjoys but for the strong hand of the law. His inventories and title-deeds would be nothing without the statute book." – pp. 496-498.

We have already alluded to Mr. Davison's images; they are severe, yet graceful; just and natural, yet poetical.

394 for we never hail the progress of truth so much as when we hope ourselves to share her triumph."...- p.280

for we never hail the progress of truth so much as when we hope ourselves to share her triumph.

"The tendency which controversy has, however, at the same time, to overstep these limits, and at once destroy charity and perplex the truth, is a topic which we do not mean now to enlarge upon. Without adverting to so great an evil, it must be confessed, that while even the more moderate warfare lasts, the truth itself is not unfrequently a sufferer:- we do not mean from the mistakes or injudiciousness of the parties, which is too palpable a thing to be noticed, but from the temper of the public mind, as affected by the existing controversy. The direction of thought, at such a moment, is all turned towards the field of warfare, and not to the valuable interest to be decided upon it. It is intent upon the proceedings of the debate more than the doctrine at issue. It becomes controversial by habit, a temper most adverse to the love and improvement of that very treasure of doctrine, for the sake of which all are so hotly engaged; as no ground is less cultivated than that which is the scene of present and active hostilities. Nor is it uncommon to see many, who, having ranged themselves on the one side or the other, with a very imperfect knowledge of the reasons and merits of the case, make up in feeling what they want in information, and studiously aggravate the state of suspicion and unfriendliness in order to meet the need of being zealous opponents in a public and important cause." – p. 280-282.

395	seems to have been unable to go forward, and, somewhat after the pattern of the man greatly beloved, to have "set his face towards the ground, and" as regards the great objects of faith themselves, to have "become dumb."	seems, somewhat after the pattern of the man greatly beloved, to have "set his face towards the ground, and become dumb."
395	In the Sermon just now quoted, he enumerates the parts of Christian knowledge, with a selection, and a	We find, for instance, in the sermon from which a quotation has just been made, an enumeration of the

	relative prominence, remarkably illustrative of this characteristic of his mind:	parts of Christian knowledge, which, both in the selection made, and the relative prominence given them, is remarkably illustrative of the turn of his mind.
396	(p. 179)	(p. 180)
396	(p. 190)	(p. 189)
396	[this earth]	[this world's]
398	which show what is going on with him.	which show how it is with him within.
401	that every one should follow his own judgment, and that they are narrow-minded and superstitious who do not. However, as regards the members of any Christian community of long standing,	that every one should follow his own judgment, and that he is narrow-minded and superstitious if he does not. However, in any orderly Christian community, established, of long standing,
401-02	who in the same compass (that is to say, in the Volume containing his miscellaneous publications and Remains, a thick one, but still only one, and of which two hundred pages are on politics, economy, and law,) has introduced, in one way or other, a respectful mention or eulogy of so many of our writers, and that of different schools.	who in the same compass, we will say in the volume before us, a thick one, but still only one, and of which two hundred pages are on politics, economy, and law, has introduced, in one way or other, a respectful mention or eulogy of so many of our writers, and that of different schools.
403	That is, he was bound by the very foundation	Indeed, he was bound by the very Lecture
404	Parties impeached ought always to have every possible advantage given them, and, if testimonies to character can possibly avail in what is a question of fact, Bishop Jewel certainly should have the benefit of a witness so very different in mind and temper from himself. And we have another reason for citing Mr. Davison's testimonial; it is drawn up in such very choice and significant language, that, even were we	We should recommend the passage to the special notice of the excellent and universally esteemed divine who is reported to have in preparation the works of that celebrated man, were we not sure he was already well acquainted with it; and we should do so from a feeling that parties impeached ought always to have every possible advantage given them, and from an entire readiness that, if testimonies

disposed to be unfair, we should not have the heart to pass over what is as pregnant in meaning as beautiful in expression:

to character are found to avail in what is a question of fact, Bishop Jewel should have the benefit of a witness so very different in mind and temper from himself. And we have another reason; for Mr. Davison's testimonial is drawn up in such very choice and significant language, that, even were we disposed to be unfair, we should not have the heart to pass over what is as pregnant in meaning as beautiful in expression:

407   The writer of the Preface informs us that Mr. Davison, after he had completed his Origin of Sacrifice, entertained an intention of editing a selection from the writings of the early Church,

The writer of the Preface informs us that, after he had completed his Origin of Sacrifice, he entertained an intention of editing a selection from the writings of the early Church,

407   8.
It has been suggested above

It has been implied above

409   Thus, to take one instance, in his Assize Sermon some excellent remarks occur on the necessity which exists, that the principles of morals and religion should be externally recommended to the individual, as a memento and protection to him, by public positive institutions; and he says, and truly, that the law of the land fulfils this office; but still, it is observable, he keeps a profound silence about the Institution, directly divine, which has been far more highly honoured and favoured than any national law, and which is the true realization of the principle under review.

    What a most serious witness is it against an age, when so deep and reverential a writer, giving utterance to its meditations in the heart of the most religious University in the world,

Thus, to take one case in point, in his Assize Sermon some excellent remarks occur on the necessity of the principles of morals and religion being externally recommended to the individual, as a sort of memento and protection to him, by public positive institutions, and he says, and truly, that the law of the land fulfils this office; but still it is observable, he keeps a profound silence about that Institution, directly divine, which has been indefinitely more highly honoured and favoured than any national law, and which is the true realization of the principle under review.

"If," he justly argues, "we make the whole of this world in its affairs a contrivance of man, and see nothing in it beyond its combinations, &c. ... But...more rational is it to regard Him as working unseen by things visible, the instruments of His providence. The moral discipline of the social law claims at least to be derived from Him. The apostle has so represented it. Its fitness, its necessity, to the state of man, is the internal evidence that he has represented it truly... Those who may think themselves individually so far raised by the advantageous care of education, or the inestimable privilege of religion, as to be independent of the restraints of human jurisdiction, for their integrity of principle, should be reminded of two things, which may not always reach them, in the elevation of their moral security. First, that *the most universal, the most certain instruction*, which falls to the lot of their humble fellow creatures, when they come to years of moral competence, is that which results from the known institutions of the law of the country in which they live. This is their education and theory. It is the *obvious practical address* to their understanding and conscience. *It meets them at their entrance into life*, and *prepares them* with some stock of ideas for duty. It is their *first* and *plainest* rule of action. That it should be their only one, no Christian could ever desire. Neither should he desire, that it should be weakened or taken away from them. Let none, therefore, disparage an order of things imparting to others a benefit which he himself perhaps may not stand in need of. But, secondly, who will presume to say how far the highest principles of duty in his own mind are independent of that *amelioration of society*, which is the acknowledged result of a wise and equitable system of judicature, laying crime under the interdict and infamy of a public condemnation; propagating through all orders a *deference to some known rule*; inducing peace, civilization, security of private life, culture of faculties and feelings, and even *preparing the way* for a more general and enlightened knowledge of *religion*." – p.191

That the law does all that this admirable passage attributes to it we shall be the last to deny: but what a most serious witness is it against an age, when so deep and reverential a mind, giving utterance to its meditations in the heart of the most religious University in the world,

409 but speaks as he does,	but speaks

411 the high Church.

the high Church. And we must plainly state our feeling that the following passage in his Review of the Oxford and Edinburgh Controversy is written under the generous bias which the defence of a friend would create. The eminent person, who had defended the University against the Northern Review, had been accused of writing with 2heat and asperity." Mr. Davison observes:-

One other instance shall be given of this peculiarity of Mr. Davison's manner; and, since it is very tame to carry a critique to an end without some spice of criticism, we shall take the opportunity of raising a small quarrel with him upon it, even were it only to show that we have views of our own, and then we shall take our leave of him and his writings.

"It is a bad symptom when a party is too patient under bold calumny before the world. Far from censuring some warmth of language in repelling an accusation, we should hardly believe a person had virtue enough to feel the infamy of the charge, or was in earnest about his character, who should preserve exactly the same courtesy and coolness in replying to his accuser, which we shall require of him in discussing a point of abstract criticism, and setting up one opinion against another. It is something wholly different from the credit of an opinion that is at stake. The courtesy of amicable hostilities is at an end, when personal reputation is deeply wounded; and we must think of another criterion whereby to judge of the propriety of controversial language in such a case as this. Coarseness, illiberality, and vulgar insult are in every case to be condemned; but there are offences for which our censure must fall, not upon the champion of the learned body, but upon his assailants." – pp. 404, 405.

One other instance shall be given of this peculiarity of Mr. Davison's manner; and, since it is very tame to carry a critique to an end without some spice of criticism, we shall take the opportunity of raising a small quarrel with him upon it, even were it only to show that we are *not* courteous, and then we shall take our leave of his volume.

412   truth in it. But what we think ungracious and hard is, that, by way of heightening his eulogy, the author contrasts the Societies of this day with a certain Institution of times past, as if the latter just did *not* contemplate, and did *not* do, what present Societies both contemplate and do; whereas it both contemplated and it did what existing Societies, even if they all contemplate, certainly often fail to do, and fully exemplified all those benefits which Mr. Davison justly attributes to the principle of combination itself,—we mean the Monastic Rule. Let our complaint be clearly apprehended; Mr. Davison does not merely contrast Monastic with Protestant and other Societies of this day, as if, whereas they both had the same general end, the former failed in what the latter succeeded in effecting; but, what seems to us paradoxical, he denies that the monastic principle *is* gregarious, co-operative, industrious, practical, and

truth in it. And we have a pleasure in availing ourselves of his expressive language:-

"The great number of institutions, confessedly of a religious, benevolent, or useful design in this country, may pass for one of its distinguishing excellences. They are the offspring of the improved mind of the country, fostered in the shade of security, and as they serve to invite to the profit of some serious purpose the social dispositions which might otherwise run to waste in a frivolous indulgence, with no rational designation upon it, nor leaving any benefit behind it, they contribute their share to the increase of the whole stock of public virtue, as well as of public service. For we should greatly err if we did not look at institutions and establishments, not merely as depositories of public utility, but also as nourishers of the virtue and personal qualifications productive.

that are to produce it. Private beneficence, indeed, has its duty always at hand, but there are interests and services of value to the community, which no single or separate efforts could either adequately arrange or accomplish. When, therefore, by the hallowed patriotism of such foundations, a well ordered system of any public utility has been set on foot, it enlists into its service the zeal of those who have the power and the will to think for their neighbourhood or their country, and turns their endeavours into a safe and judicious course, instead of leaving them to be lost in the desultory, uncombined, and ill-applied attempts of their own private suggestion. Such institutions give a fixed point and a tone, as well as a system, to the purpose which they adopt. They offer a place, therefore, where all who can may cast in their share towards it, to the greatest advantage. Nor is it unworthy of being mentioned, that they lend a fair opening to mutual esteem and good will; as men meet in them not like competitors for an interest, nor to divide the labour of a compulsory duty, but with the liberal heart of men pledged to each other in a free service, and learn to love their brethren and companions for their common work's sake...

"In that course of change, however, to which all human works are liable, it will happen sometime, that institutions of ancient utility lose this application to present use, or decline from that industry and vigour which they need to be supported; and remain them as monuments of a departed benefit, sacred even in its ashes. The substantial credit and efficacy of your institution, however, remain to this day unimpaired; and if I did not fear to offend by the indelicacy of praise, I ought, in following the general voice, to say more, and state that the administration of it is as highly maintained, as it is certain that its ends and purposes, instead of being passed away, are rather daily rising in their importance." – p. 212-214

These last sentences explain the meaning and drift of that eulogy upon Societies in general of which the whole extract forms but a part; not that we have any complaint against it in the abstract, (on the contrary we entirely concur in the sentiments it expresses,) whatever may be our opinion of certain existing associations, religious and irreligious, whether viewed in their constitution or in their practical working. But what we do think ungracious and hard is, that by way of heightening his eulogy, the author *contrasts* the societies of this day with a certain institution of times past, as if the latter just did *not* contemplate, and did *not* do, what present societies both contemplate and do; whereas it both contemplated and it did what existing societies, even if they all contemplate, certainly often fail to do, and fully exemplified all those benefits which Mr. Davison justly attributes to the principle of combination itself,—we mean the Monastic Rule. Let our complaint be clearly apprehended; Mr. Davison does not merely contrast Monastic with Protestant and other societies of this day, as if they both had the same general end, but the former failed in what the latter succeeded in effecting; but, what seems to us paradoxical, he denies that the monastic principle *is* gregarious, co-operative, industrious, practical, and productive.

414-
15

of the law, it is only necessary to take up any work such as Alban Butler's, in which a hundred instances will be found of active and self-denying charity, in men and women bound by the monastic vows. The service of hospitals is one out of various religious objects and active labours with which the religious life has ever been connected. Schools, whether for high or low, are another; orphan-houses are another; literary or theological pursuits another.

of the law, we are tempted to refer to the life of a Spanish saint, whom another Church commemorates on the very day on which we happen to be writing, and who was on the one hand the founder of the order of *Charity*, on the other, for his work's sake, received the name "John *of God*." He began, says Alban Butler, by hiring

"A house to harbour poor sick folks in, whom he served and provided for with an ardour, prudence, economy and vigilance that surprised the whole city. This was the foundation of the Order of Charity in 1540, which, by the benediction of heaven, has since been spread all over Christendom. John was occupied all day in serving his patients; in the night he went out to carry in new objects of charity, rather than to seek out provisions for them, for people of their own accord brought him in all necessaries for his little hospital. Indeed, the charity, patience and modesty of St. John, and his wonderful care and foresight, engaged to every one to admire and favour the institute. But his charity was not confined to his own hospital; he looked upon it as his own misfortune if the necessities of any distressed person in the whole country had remained unrelieved. He, therefore, made strict inquiry into the wants of the poor over the whole province, relieved many in their own houses, employed in a proper manner those who were able to work, and with wonderful sagacity laid himself out every way to comfort and assist the afflicted members of Christ. He was particularly active and vigilant in settling and providing for young maidens in distress, to prevent the danger to which they are often exposed of taking bad courses. He also reclaimed many who were already engaged in vice; for which purpose he sought out public sinners, and holding a crucifix in his hand, with many tears exhorted them to repentance. Though his life seemed to be taken up in continual action, he accompanied it with perpetual prayers and incredible corporal austerities. And his tears of devotion, his frequent raptures, and his eminent spirit of contemplation gave a lustre to his other virtues."

Perhaps it may be thought unfair to take the Order of Charity as a specimen of the ordinary course of monastic discipline, an order which commands the respect even of enlightened Protestants; yet it will be found that the service of hospitals is one out of various religious objects and active labours with which the religious life has ever been connected. Schools, for instance, whether for high or low, are another of these occupations; orphan-houses are another: literary or theological pursuits another.

415   as Augustine? who such revivers of religion as Gregory and Basil? who is more fruitful in practical lessons than Pope Gregory? who so large and so minute and exact in thought as St. Thomas?

as Augustine? To whom is our personal faith more indebted than to Athanasius? Who had greater sway in king's courts than Ambrose? Who is more fruitful in practical lessons than Pope Gregory?

416   We can enter into, though we disown, the opinion or prejudice that the monastic rule does more harm than good, nay, is to be condemned as pure evil; but we do not know what is meant by the statement, as an historical fact, that it has been destructive of the action and influence of man on man.

We can perfectly understand its being said, that the monastic rule may be perverted and may become mischievous; we can comprehend the state of mind under which it might be pronounced to do more harm than good, or might be condemned as pure evil; but we do not know what the language means when it is spoken of historically as *destructive* of our influence upon

Appendix: Textual Variants

our fellow creatures.

417	Was his life at Oriel College a more public one than that of St. Jerome at Bethlehem, or St. Anselm at Bec?	When we attempt to analyse the popular prejudice on the subject, it seems to result in a proposition of this kind:- that the only channel of doing good to others is, first, married life, secondly, going into society, for monarchism forbids at most nothing beyond; and, to repeat our words, how many among ourselves are so far constrained monks, without its principle of association or its high religious idea in compensation!
417-18	hermits, anchorites, fathers of the desert, and the like: are there no commands, as, for instance, concerning poverty and humility, which, taken in their first and obvious meaning, such a life literally and strikingly fulfils? We are not at all saying or dreaming, of course not, that all our Lord's precepts must be taken in the letter, yet it is better to observe them in the letter, than not to observe them at all. Now it is pretty clear that society, as at present constituted, does not keep the commands in question either in letter or spirit; also it seems to us clear, that whether a literal observance of them be necessary or not, monastic institutions do, of all others, most accurately and comprehensively fulfil the *code* of Gospel commandments, whether those which the present age does not fulfil, or those which it does. Indeed there cannot be a doubt who they are, and where they are to be found, who give us instances of obedience to the precept of "not resisting evil;" of "turning the cheek to the smiter;" of "selling that we have and giving alms;" "of selling all that we have," in order to be "perfect;" of having our "loins girded about and lights burning;" of "watching and praying	hermits, anchorites, fathers of the desert, and the like. Supposing then, for argument's sake, that they are violating plain commands of the Gospel, about which a word shall be added presently, yet are there no commands, as, for instance, concerning poverty and humility, which, taken in their first and obvious meaning, a life other than monastic plainly violates? We are not at all saying or dreaming, of course not, that persons who do not take our Lord's precepts in the letter are actually violating them, yet we think that if they do not care to keep them at least in the spirit instead, they certainly are. And while it is pretty clear that society, as at present constituted, does not keep the commands in question either in letter or spirit, it seems to us clear also, that whether a literal observance be necessary or not, monastic institutions do, of all others, most accurately and comprehensively fulfil the *code* of Gospel commandments, whether those which the present age does not fulfil, or those which it does. Indeed there cannot be a doubt *who* the instances are, and *where* we must look for them, of obedience to the precept of "not resisting evil;"

always;" of "taking no thought for the morrow;" of "taking up the cross daily;" and a number of other particulars which might be mentioned. And if, as we have already been urging, monastic bodies are on the other hand far from neglecting those social duties which Mr. Davison truly says have so essential a portion and so exalted a place in Christian obedience, then it will follow that they fulfil more of our Lord's precepts than any other set of men, and instead of being "one of the most violent perversions of religious doctrines," they are the nearest approach to the perfection of a Christian spirit.

of "turning the cheek to the smiter;" of "selling that we have and giving alms;" "of selling all that we have," in order to be "perfect;" of having our "loins girded about and lights burning;" of "watching and praying always;" of "taking no thought for the morrow;" of "taking up the cross daily;" and a number of other particulars which might be mentioned. And if, as we have already been urging, monastic bodies are on the other hand far from neglecting those *social* duties which Mr. Davison truly says have so essential a portion and so exalted a place in Christian obedience, then it will follow that they fulfil *more* than any other set of men, and instead of being "one of the most violent perversions of religious doctrines," they are the nearest approach to the perfection of a Christian spirit.

418 Nor is even the eremitical rule itself, nor surely (much less) are associations

Nor is even the eremitical rule itself, nor surely, much less, are associations

419 and the more active and useful is a man's life, the greater is his need of them.

and the more active and useful is his life, the greater is his need of them.

420 Mr. Davison probably as little thought of analyzing the popular sentiments of which he was the spokesman, as of looking out for "death in the pot" at his meals, or suspecting arsenic in his candles. It is the trial and mystery of our position in this age and country, that a religious mind is continually set at variance with itself, that its deference to what is without contradicts its suggestions from within, and that it cannot follow what it presages without rebelling against what it has received.

Mr. Davison probably as little thought of analyzing the sentiments to which we have called attention in these last pages, as of seeking "death in the pot" at his meals, or suspecting arsenic in his candles. It is the trial and mystery of our position in this age and country, that a religious mind is continually set at variance with itself, that its deference to what is without contradicts its suggestions from within, and that it cannot obey what is over it without rebelling against what was before it.

421 **XV.**

ART. VIII. – *Lyra Innocentium:*

Appendix: Textual Variants

JOHN KEBLE.

Thoughts in Verse on Christian Children, their Ways and their Privileges. Oxford, Parker, 1846.

421 | IN venturing some remarks on the poems just now published at Oxford under the title of the Lyra Innocentium, it is far from our intention to adopt the tone of controversialists, or even of critics. The name of their author would hinder us from so doing. That they are really Mr. Keble's, we make no question, though we are not told so in the title-page. | It is far from our intention to approach the work of so deservedly celebrated a writer as the author of the Christian Year, in a controversial, or even in a critical spirit. That the poems, which we have named at the head of this article, are really his, we make no question, though we are not told so in the title-page.

422 | We have not the analytical powers which would warrant us to attempt a critical estimate of the poems contained in the Volume before us; and we have not quite the heartless officiousness to view them in a controversial aspect. If they have a special characteristic, it is that they are not controversial, in this respect differing from other poems which other writers of his school have given to the world, and he at other times. Whether we look into the Lyra Apostolica, or into the Cathedral and Baptistery, | We have not the analytical powers which would warrant a critical survey of so gifted an intellect as has given birth to these poems; and we have not quite the heartless officiousness to view them in a controversial aspect. If they have a special characteristic, it is that they are not controversial, in this aspect differing from other poems of the same school. Whether we look into the Lyra Apostolica, or the Cathedral and Baptistery,

422 | But the Lyra Innocentium preserves | But the volume before us preserves

424 | which has a regard to circumstances, to the trial of an almost necessary excitement, to the necessity of acting beyond criticism, yet without precedent, and of reaching a certain object when all paths to it have respectively their own difficulties. | to the trial of an almost necessary excitement, the necessity of acting beyond exception, yet of acting without precedent, and of reaching a certain object when each assignable path has its difficulties.

424 | as the parties censuring, as well as the parties censured, will require themselves on a day to come. | as they, as well as the subjects of their censure, will require on a day to come.

425 | In consequence it became very necessary for those who had no doubts or difficulties to show to all | In consequence it became very necessary to show, with respect to the seceding parties, that there was

who wavered or might waver, that there was something faulty in the mode in which the seceding parties had severally detached themselves from their original communion,

something faulty in the mode in which they had severally detached themselves from their original communion

425 for any delicacy in dealing with them.

for delicacy in dealing with them.

425 and no reason against imputing motives to them or using personalities, freely and without scruple.

and no reason against imputing motives or using personalities.

428 private Christians, abounds in sentiments about ecclesiastical matters, as they stood at the date of its composition.

private persons, abounds in sentiments about ecclesiastical matters as existing at the date of its composition.

429 "Think not of rest; though dreams be sweet,
Start up, and ply your heavenward feet;...
Till, when the shadows thickest fall,
Ye hear your Master's midnight call.

"Think not of rest; though dreams be sweet,
Start up, and ply your heaven-ward feet;
Is not God's oath upon your head,
Ne'er to sink back on slothful bed –
Never again your loins untie,
Nor let your torches waste and die,
Till, when the shadows thickest fall,
Ye hear your Master's midnight call?

429 twilight grey ...

twilight grey.
Pray only that thine aching heart,
From visions vain content to part.
Strong for love's sake its woe to hide,
May cheerful wait the Cross beside,
Too happy if that dreadful day,
Thy life be given thee 'for a prey.'

429 height of pride.

height of pride,
With queens for handmaids at her side,
With kings for nursing fathers, throned high,
And compassed with the world's too tempting blazonry.

430	form of earthly gold? …	form of earthly gold?

Therefore on fearful dreams her [the Church's] inward sight
Is fain to dwell;
What lurid light
Shall the last darkness of the world dispel –
The Mediator, in His wrath,
Descending down the lightning's path.

He ends addressing the Divine Mediator, with a continued allusion to Moses in the Mount:

"But at Thy touch let veiled hearts awake,
That nearest to Thine altar lie,
Yet least of holy things descry.
Teacher of teachers! Priest of priests! from Thee
The sweet strong prayer
Must rise, to free
First Levi, then all Israel from the snare.
Thou art our Moses out of sight –
Speak for us, or we perish quite.

431	as times goes on. And yet we cordially thank him for his "dream;" that is, we thank him for choosing a subject for his verse	as time goes on; a dream, as we should add, because children in the Anglican Church, though commencing their course as Catholics, yet when they come to years of discretion fall into a schismatical state. Yet we cordially thank him for his "dream;" we thank him for choosing a subject for his verse
431	they are able to look	Catholics are able to look
431	The Catholic Church is the very	The Catholic Church is the very

Appendix: Textual Variants

"Church of their baptism;" and the "Mother of their new birth;" they were baptized into nothing short of that Church: too soon indeed they pass into the hands of others, who detach them from their true Mother; but in their first years, till they come to years of discretion, and commit acts which separate them from her, they are as fully and absolutely the children of the Catholic Church as if they were baptized by Catholics. They have Angels to guard them,

Church of their baptism; they were baptized into nothing short of that Church; whoever baptized them, baptized them into her and for her; she claims them as her property. There is but one baptism for the remission of sins, and she it is who administers it, wherever it is legitimately administered. Heretics and schismatics may be her instruments in this work, as perfectly as saints. She baptizes by means of the Anglican communion, which is not their real mother but a stranger. By the Catholic Church they are suckled; - alas, at length the time comes when they are weaned; and then they pass into the hands of one or other foster parent, who soon detaches them from their true mother. But in their first years, till they come to years of discretion, and commit acts which separate them from her, they are as fully and absolutely the children of the Catholic Church as if they were baptized in the Catholic communion. They have angels to guard them

431   this Protestant country

this poor country

433   priestly child.

priestly child.

*   *   *

"Hail, chosen Type and Image true
  Of   Jesus   on   the   sea!
In   slumber,   and   in   glory   too,
  Shadowed   of   old   by   thee.
Save that in calmness thou didst sleep,
  The   summer   stream   beside,
He   on   a   wider,   wilder   deep,
  Where   boding   night-winds
sighed."—Pp. 33-34.

"What recks he of his mother's tears –
  His sister's boding sigh?
The whispering reeds are all he hears,
  And Nile, soft weltering by,
Sings him to sleep; - but he will wake,
  And o'er the haughty flood
Wave his stern rod – and, lo! A lake,
  A restless sea of blood!

"Soon shall a mightier flood thy call
  And out-stretched rod obey;

To right and left the watery wall
  From Israel shrinks away.
Such honour wins the faith that gave
  Thee and thy sweetest boon
Of infant charms to the rude wave,
  In the third joyous moon.

"Hail, chosen Type and Image true
  Of   Jesus   on   the   sea!
In slumber, and in glory too,
  Shadowed of old by thee.
Save that in calmness thou didst sleep,
  The summer stream beside,
He on a wider, wilder deep,
  Where boding night-winds sighed.
"Sighed when at eve He laid Him down,
  But with a sound like flame
At midnight from the mountain's crown
  Upon his slumber's came.-
Lo! how they watch, till he awake,
  Around His rude low bed:
How wishful count the waves that break
  So near his sacred head!" – Pp. 32-34

433	As though he read, engraven there,
	  His fontal name, Christ's saving charm.
	          * * *
	"Still in love's steady gaze,
	  In joy's unbidden cry,
	That holy Mother's glad amaze,
	  That infant's worship we descry.—P. 43.
		As though he read, engraven there,
		  His fontal name, Christ's saving charm.
		Oft as in hope untold
		  The parent's eye pursues that eager look;
		Still in love's steady gaze,
		  In joy's unbidden cry,
		That holy Mother's glad amaze,
		  That infant's worship we descry.
		Still Mary's Child unseen
		  Comes breathing, in the heart just sealed His own,
		Prayers of high hope: what bliss they mean,
		  And where they soar, to Him is known." – P. 43.

633

Appendix: Textual Variants

434	And thus is led on to his conclusion:	The poem proceeds:
435	And thus he accounts for cherubs being represented in churches under the form of infants.	This leads him to an interpretation of the sculptured cherubs in churches, which will not be satisfactory to Iconoclasts.
435	While the above extracts sufficiently show Mr. Keble's deep reverence towards the state of infants, they do not always connect the holiness of that state with the rite of baptism.	'The above extracts rather show the view Mr Keble takes of the infants of the Church, than exemplify his earnestness in connecting their holy condition with the rite of baptism.
435	as if this divinity belonged to children in their own nature and original state, and not as new-made by baptism.	as if this divinity belonged to children as they are born into the world, and not as washed from original sin, and gifted with regeneration.
436	regenerate infants and their sinless blessedness	regenerate infants and children
436	to view them in such lights as thence belong to them	to view them in such lights as Scripture will furnish
438	if he had not been born.	he had not been born.

"Sure, as to blessed Mary come
The saints' and martyrs' host,
To own, with many a thankful strain,
The channel of undying bliss,
The bosom where the Lord hath lain,
The hand that held by His:

"Sure, as her form for evermore
The glory and the joy shall wear,
That robed her, bending to adore
The Babe her chaste womb bare."- p.67

| 440 | No Catholic can quarrel with such an | No Catholic can quarrel with such |

634

image, which indeed is represented in some of the paintings of the great masters; but as introduced into these passages it is surely out of place, as if intended to give satisfaction to Protestants,—as more adapted for polemics than for devotional poetry, and savouring much of the evangelical school, which never allows the mention of one doctrine of religion without a recapitulation of all the rest, as if in our prayers and praises we must ever have an eye to controversy.

an image, which indeed is represented in some of the paintings of the great masters; but, as introduced in these places, it is surely out of place – is introduced to give satisfaction, or to furnish a safeguard, to others – is more fitted for polemics than for devotional poetry, and savours much of the evangelical school, who never mention one doctrine of religion by itself, lest they should be supposed thereby to deny every other, not of the author of the Christian Year.

441 with the intention of calling people's minds off external and dangerous subjects and present perplexities,

with the intention of calling people's minds off external and dangerous subjects,

442 and thus a "cleansing"

and thus a κάαρσις

444 the observance which was paid, not without creature comforts, to the sacred night;

the sole duties which were performed towards the sacred time;

www.ingramcontent.com/pod-product-compliance
Lightning Source LLC
Chambersburg PA
CBHW060417100426

42812CB00030B/3215/J